W9-ABP-331

ART

in

LIFE

by

Jane Clapp

The Scarecrow Press, Inc.
New York   1959

L.C. Card No. 59-6544

Description and Directions for Use

This index is designed, by cumulating and augmenting the listings of art reproductions in indexes issued by LIFE, to provide immediate reference to reproductions of paintings and graphic arts in LIFE, from its first issue, November 23, 1936, through 1956.

In addition to pictorial art reproductions, this index also includes selective listing of photographs of architecture; sculpture; and decorative arts, such as ceramics, furniture, glassware, jewelry, and metal work. Also included are portraits of artists and of historic and literary personages--photographs, as well as representation in other media.

The listings were made from an examination of the issues of LIFE. A check of the indexes issued by LIFE, of the Readers' Guide, and of the Monro indexes of reproductions of paintings offered valuable aid in determining the form of listings and of subjects.

Artists, titles, and subjects are arranged in one alphabet, with cross references as necessary. Subject listings are suggestive, rather than comprehensive or complete. Pictures are in color, except where noted: bw (black and white).

Portraits depicting an artist, including self-portraits, are listed under the artist's name following his works, and are designated: port. When the works of an artist are listed in several media, as decorative arts, lithographs, and sculpture, as well as painting, the works are grouped alphabetically by medium, following paintings.

Sample Listings

Artist

Title

Subject

Homer, Winslow
   The gulf stream 2:26 Ja 11
   '37; 5:36 O 31 '38
The Gulf Stream. Homer 2:26
   Ja 11 '37; 5:36 O 31 '38
Seascapes
Homer. The gulf stream 2:
   26 Ja 11 '37; 5:36 O 31 '38

Explanation: Two reproductions in color of The gulf stream, a
picture painted by Winslow Homer will be found in LIFE in
   (1) volume 2, page 26, January 11, 1937 issue; and
   (2) volume 5, page 36, October 31, 1938 issue.

Key To Abbreviations

archt.   architect
Ag   August
Ap   April
bw   black and white
D   December
F   February
Ja   January
Je   June
Jy   July
Mr   March
My   May
N   November
O   October
photog.   photograph
port.   Portrait
S   September
*   Descriptive title, used when exact
              title not indicated

A

Aardvark
  Drawings from 7 diction-
    aries bw 30:125 F 12 '51
Abbeys See also names of spe-
    cific abbeys, as Mont St.
    Michel
  Finck. Recollections of an
    English abbey 39:113 S 12
    '55
  Hitler. Old abbey at Mes-
    sines, Belgium 1:43 N 30
    '36
  St. Lucien, France. Miseri-
    cords bw 37:79-80 S 27 '54
Abbott, George
  George Abbott. photogs bw
    7:80-5 O 23 '39
Abduction of the body of St. Mark.
    Tintoretto 23:51 Ag 4 '47
'Abud'L--Baha. photog bw 29:
    160 D 11 '50
Abe, Nobuye
  Artist and his work. photog
    32:100 Je 23 '52 port.
Abel, Karl Friedrich
  Gainsborough. Karl Friedrich
    Abel 4:27 Ja 24 '38
Abelard See Heloise and Abelard
Above the clouds walks the moon-
    light. montage bw Ernst
    34:25 My 25 '53
Abrahamson, Rod
  Artist and his work. photog
    bw 34:115 Jy 13 '53 port.
Abramovitz, Max, Architect
  U.S. embassy, Rio de Janeiro
    34:45 Je 22 '53
L'absinthe. bw Degas 11:85 D 1
    '41
The absinthe drinker. Picasso
    40:74 My 28 '56

Abstraction. Donati 37:161
    N 22 '54
Abu, Sumerian God, "Lord of
    Vegetation," and wife.
    statue 40:89 Je 4 '56
Acadians
  Removal of the Acadians
    from Nova Scotia, 1755
    bw 9:112 S 9 '40
Acasius, Saint
  St. Acasius. santo, wood
    carving bw 24:58 My 17 '48
Accordion Players See
    Musicians and Musical In-
    struments--Accordion
Accused of witchcraft. Volk
    13:78 N 23 '42
Ack-Ack guns in action. Orr
    12:40 Mr 2 '42
Ackermann, Emil
  Temperance poster. litho-
    graph 39:72-3 D 26 '55
Acoma, New Mexico
  San Esteban Rey Mission
    church, 1640 photog 8:74
    My 13 '40; 40:48 Ja 16 '56
  Stairway. photog 40:48 Ja
    16 '56
Acorn clock, Bristol, Conn.,
    1850. photog 39:62 Ag 29
    '55
Acorn house, prefabricated.
    photogs Koch 26:70-2 Ja
    24 '49
Acrobats See also Circus
  Cadmus. Gilding the acrobats
    2:47 Mr 29 '37
  Curry. The flying Cadonas
    1:31 N 23 '36
  Curry. The passing leap bw
    15:19 N 29 '43
  Greenbaum. Acrobat sculp-
    ture bw 4:62 Ap 25 '38

Gross. Acrobats 2 sculptures
30:66-7 Ja 8 '51
Hooft. Tumblers and pigeons
30:36-7 Ja 15 '51
Picasso. The family of sal-
timbanques 23:93 O 13 '47
bw 5:29 O 10 '38
Picasso. Two acrobats with
dog 8:57 Mr 4 '40 bw 6:83
My 22 '39
Riggs. Clown acrobats print
bw 3:47 S 13 '37
Riggs. Tumblers print bw
3:47 S 13 '47
Shahn. Acrobats 37:100 O 4
'54
Acropolis, Athens, 421 B.C.
photog bw 18:56 Ja 1 '45
Across the continent: "Westward
the course of empire takes
its way." Currier and Ives
print 9:34 D 30 '40
Actaeon See Mythological Themes
--Actaeon
Action in chains. sculpture bw
Maillol 8:108 Ap 15 '40
Actors and Acting See also
Theaters; names of actors
Mummers, Middle Ages.* bw
22:74 My 26 '47
Acuna, Luis Alberto
Masquerade bw 9:67 O 14 '40
Adam, Robert, furniture and in-
terior designer
Great Marble Hall, Kedleston,
England bw 23:136 S 8 '47
Osterley Park tapestry room,
England 23:71-4 Ag 25 '47
Syon House rooms, England
23: 72-3 Ag 25 '47
Robert Adam bw 23:70 Ag 25
'47 port.
Adam and Eve
Adam and Eve. mosaic, vesti-
bule dome, St. Mark's,
Venice 35:34 D 28 '53
Adam and Eve. misericord,
Worcester cathedral, Eng-
land bw 37:80 S 27 '54
Adam and Eve. illumination,
Codex Paulinus 34:77 F
23 '53
Black. God creating Adam
and Eve print bw 6:45 Ja
16 '39
Cowles. Dawn of the spirit
24:76 F 9 '48
Coxie. God and Adam tapes-
try 35:94 D 14 '53
Cranach, Lucas, the elder.
Eve with serpent 11:57 S 8
'41
Epstein. Adam sculpture bw
33:66 N 3 '52
Garden of Eden. stained
glass Chartre cathedral
22:73 Ap 7 '47
Lucas van Leyden. Adam and
Eve engravings bw 6:46
Ja 16 '39
Michelangelo. Creation of
Adam fresco 11:77 D 1 '41;
21:66-7 Jy 1 '46; 27:30-1
D 26 '49
Michelangelo. Creation of
Eve fresco 27:32-3 D 26
'49 bw 21:66-7 Jy 1 '46
Michelangelo. The temptation
and the expulsion fresco
bw 21:64 Jy 1 '46
Piero della Francesca.
Death of Adam 20:61 Ap
22 '46
Raphael. Creation of Eve
27:119 D 12 '49
Titcomb. Adam and Eve tex-
tile, 1760 38:120 Ap 18
'55
Van Eyck brothers. Adam
and Eve 26:64-5 Ap 18 '49
Adams, Abigail (Brooks)
King. Mrs. Charles Francis
Adams, 1829 41:75 Jy 2
'56
Adams, Abigail (Smith)
Blyth. Abigail Adams, 1763
41:70 Jy 2 '56
Mrs. John Adams. bw 16:48
Ja 17 '44
Adams, Brooks
Brooks Adams. bw 22:77 Je
23 '47

Adams, Cassily
  Custer's last fight bw 11:75
    D 8 '41 lithograph copy
    24:14 Je 21 '48
Adams, Charles Francis
  Charles Francis Adams. bw
    22:77 Jy 23 '47
  King. Charles Francis Adams,
    1829 41:74 Jy 2 '56
Adams, Mrs. Charles Francis
  See Adams, Abigail (Brooks)
Adams, Henry
  Henry Adams bw 22:77 Je 23
    '47
Adams, John
  Blyth. John Adams, 1763
    41:70 Jy 2 '56
  John Adams. 31:98 N 5 '51;
    39:64 Jy 4 '55 bw 9:8 Ag 5
    '40; 15:8 Jy 5 '43; 16:56 F
    7 '44; 22:77 Je 23 47: 30:
    102 Mr 12 '51
Adams, Mrs. John See Adams
  Abigail (Smith)
Adams, John Quincy
  Copley. John Quincy Adams,
    1795 41:72 Jy 2 '56
  Forestier. Treaty of Ghent
    41:72-3 Jy 2 '56
  Gilbert, J. John Quincy Adams,
    age 77 41:72 Jy 2 '56
  John Quincy Adams. 19:85 S 24
    '45 bw 10:26 Mr 3 '41; 11:
    91 S 8 '41; c1812 19:89 Ag
    27 '45; 22:77 Je 23 '47
    photog 7:20 N 20 '39
    sculpture, Boston Athenaeum
    bw 10:65 Mr 24 '41
  "King of Diamonds." playing
    card 38: Cover My 30 '55
Adams, Louisa Catherine (John-
    son) Mrs. John Quincy
    Adams, 1797, miniature,
    41:72 Jy 2 '56
Adams, Maude
  Maude Adams. photog bw 28:
    64 Ja 2 '50; age 64 3:48 O
    18 '37
  Maude Adams as Joan of Arc
    31:117 N 19 '51
Adams Samuel

Samuel Adams. bw 15:8 Jy
  5 '43; 29:37 Jy 3 '50
Adams, Wayman
  Gregor Piatigorsky 16:75
    Ap 24 '44
Adams House, Quincy, Mass.,
    18th century. photogs 41:
    70-5 Jy 2 '56 bw 22:76 Je
    23 '47
Addams, Charles, cartoonist
  Cartoons from "New Yorker."
    bw 13:98-9 D 7 '42
  House of horrors. cartoon on
    radio horror programs bw
    24:14-5 F 16 '48
Addie. Eakins 41:160 D 24 '56
Addison Gallery, Phillips Acad-
    emy, Andover, Mass.
  Collection of American art
    12:58-62 Je 15 '42
  Student exhibit from 25 Ameri-
    can art schools 25:98-101
    D 6 '48
Admont, Giant Bible of, page
    34:78, 82 F 23 '53
Adobe building. Eisenhower 28:
    151 Ap 17 '50
Adolescence. Etnier 6:27 F 13
    '39
Adolescence. bw Wood, G.
    14:58 Ja 18 '43
Adolescent girl. Kroll 24:69
    Je 28 '48
Adonis See Mythological
    Themes--Adonis
Adoration. Ford 17:36 D 25 '44
Adoration, after Botticelli. bw
    11:61 O 27 '41
Adoration for heroes. bw Carr
    9:59 Ag 12 '40
Adoration of Magi and Shep-
    herds See Jesus Christ--
    Adoration
Adoration of the Lamb. Van
    Eyck brothers 26:64-5
    Ap 18 '49
    bw 16:68 Ja 10 '44
Adultress brought before Christ.
    Giorgione; Piombo; Ti-
    tian 39: 169 O 24 '55

Advertising Figures See
    Figures--Holiday, Festival,
    and Advertising
"Aeneid," Virgil. illuminated
    manuscript, 5th century,
    Vatican 32:86 Ap 14 '52
Aerial fantasy. Schwartz 32:70
    Ja 14 '52
Aetna Life Insurance Company
    building, Hartford, Conn.
    bw 41:78 Ag 13 '56
Africa
    Lee, D. Paintings of the
        Arab world--Tangiers to
        Tunis 33:109-12 N 10 '52
    Martin, F. North Africa:
        World war in Algeria and
        Tunis 15:60-7 D 27 '43
After the bath. pastel Degas
    38:107 My 23 '55
After the heat of the day. Bowen,
    O. 23:84 N 17 '47
After the market, Mexico. Lee,
    D. 22:74-5 My 12 '47
After the show. Peirce, W. 12:
    74 Ap 20 '42
Afternoon. Wyeth, A. 24:106
    My 17 '48
Afternoon in the bar. Jackson,
    H. 41:74-6 Jy 9 '56
Afternoon refreshment. Sharon
    33:76 Jy 21 '52
Afternoon shift. Sellitti 10:58
    Je 16 '41
Afternoon tea party. print
    Cassatt 36:98 My 17 '54
Afterthoughts of Earth. bw
    Davies, A.B. 16:79 Ap
    24 '44
Agassiz, Jean Louis
    Jean Louis Agassiz. photog
        bw 25:100 N 22 '48
Agincourt, Battle of   bw 40:
    180-1 Ap 9 '56
Agnew, G. Harvey
    A day in port 23:98 N 10 '47
    G. Harvey Agnew photog bw
        23:101 N 10 '47 port.
The Agnew clinic. Eakins 16:
    75 My 15 '44

The agony in Gethsemane.
    Huber 39:28 D 26 '55
The agony in the garden. bw
    El Greco 29:92 Ap 24 '50
Agricultural Themes
    Benton. Cotton pickers 13:
        45 Ag 31 '42
    "Book of Hours" of the Duc de
        Berry. illuminations, 15th
        century 24:38-50 Ja 5 '48
    Corbino. Harvest festival
        4:28 Je 13 '38
    Cowles. The farmer and the
        raincloud 24:75 F 9 '48
    Currier and Ives print. A-
        merican farm scenes 9:
        28 D 30 '40
    Currier and Ives print.
        Autumn in New England:
        Cider making 9:29 D 30
        '40
    Curry. Line storm 1:30 N 23
        '36
        bw 15:19 N 29 '43
    Curry. Wisconsin landscape
        8:65 My 27 '40
    Dehn. Threshing in Minne-
        sota 11:42 Ag 11 '41
    Emett. Farming, Midwest
        cartoon 37:48-9 Jy 5 '54
    Flax-scutching, U.S. 19th
        century. 31:72-3 Jy 2 '51
    Glover. My harvest home,
        Tasmania bw 12:78 F 9 '42
    Gwathmey. Hoeing 16:78 Ap
        24 '44
    Harvesting. illumination,
        Flemish, 15th century
        22:80 My 26 '47
    Herdsmen leading cattle. *
        bas-relief, Egypt 41:109
        N 26 '56
    Hogue. Drouth-stricken ar-
        ea 2:60 Je 21 '37
    Hogue. Drouth survivors bw
        2:61 Je 21 '37
    Hogue. Dust bowl 2:60 Je 21
        '37
    Homer. Weaning the calf
        41:72-3 D 10 '53

Hurd. Old pioneers mural
10:46 Ja 27 '41
Hurd. Riverbank farm* 23:
78 Ag 18 '47
Jones, Joe. Dust storm 8:
66 My 27 '40
Jones, Joe. Harvest 13:46
Ag 31 '42; 21:77 N 25 '46
Kroll. The road from the
cove bw 16:79 Ap 24 '44
Lea. The nesters mural 10:
46 Ja 27 '41
Lee, D. Noon 3:46 S 20 '37;
21:74 N 25 '46
Limbourg brothers. Calen-
dar pages, "Book of Hours"
of the Duc de Berry illlumi-
nations 24:38-50 Ja 5 '48
Luce. Vegetable gardens.*
13:45 Ag 31 '42
Memling. June, calendar
page bw 18:42 Ja 1 '45
Millet, J. F. The gleaners
25: 96-7 N 22 '48
Millet, J. F. The man with a
hoe 9:46-7 Jy 29 '40
Moses. Sugaring off bw 25:
77 O 25 '48
Mount. Ringing the pig 18:
66 Je 25 '45
Pleissner. Stacking alfalfa
13:47 Ag 31 '42
Roberts. Shearing the rams
bw 12:79 F 9 '42
Rothstein. Dust bowl storm*
photog bw 28:83 Ja 2 '50
Sheets. Reaping winter
wheat, India 20:81 Ja 21
'46
Sheets. Returning from work,
India 20:81 Ja 21 '46
Sheets. Water for irrigation,
India bw 20:80 Ja 21 '46
Sowing and plowing, Bishop
Hill, Ill., c1850 31:72 Jy
2 '51
Van Gogh. Vegetable gardens,
Arles 27:83 O 10 '49
Wood, G. Dinner for
threshers 13:46-7 Ag 31
'42; 21:77 N 25 '46

Wood, G. Fall plowing bw
14:57 Ja 18 '43
Wood, G. Spring turning 2:
34-5 F 8 '57
Wood, G. Young corn bw
14:57 Ja 18 '43
Wyeth, N.C. Nightfall 20:
80 Je 17 '46
Wyeth, N.C. Portrait of a
farmer 16:78 Ap 24 '44
Wyeth, N.C. The spring
house 20:79 Je 17 '46
Young, M. Ploughing in the
Valley of the Great Salt
Lake painting, relief,
sculpture in round bw
10:76 F 17 '41
Ah, God--herrings, buoys, the
glittering sea. Albright,
I. 16:78 Ap 24 '44
Ahusuerus, king of the Persians
Rembrandt. Esther's feast
41:74 D 10 '56
Aiding a comrade. bw Reming-
ton 21:116 O 21 '46
Ain, Gregory, architect
Row houses, California bw
26:147 Ap 11 '49
Air fight over Portland. Eurich
26:46 F 28 '49
Air Transport Command (ATC)
route. 18:43-6 Ap 30 '45
Airhole. Marsh 6:26 Ja 9 '39
Airing in Central Park, c1860.
32:116-7 Ap 7 '52
Airplanes
Arai. Take-off from carrier
28:67 F 27 '50
Davis, F. Air raid on Ham-
burg 15:68-71 D 27 '43
Gross, A. Hurricane
fighter plane 26:60 Mr 21
'49
Hurd. 8th U.S. Army Air
Force: operation 15:58-
64 Jy 26 '43
Hurd. Return from Rouen
14:52-3 Je 21 '43 bw 14:
6 Je 28 '43
Lea. C-47 flies over the
Hump 35:56 N 2 '53

Leonardo da Vinci. Flying
    machine design drawing
    39:63 O 3 '55
McCoy. Air training in the
    army 14:50-1 My 24 '43
McCoy. Airplanes of the U.S.
    navy 9:71-4 O 28 '40
Nash. Dead Sea 26:46 F 28
    '49
Norris. Army planes in
    Hawaii 13:51 N 9 '42
Sample. Naval aviation--
    World War: planes, por-
    traits, scenes 14:36-41 Ja
    4 '43
Sample. PBM hauled to rest
    bw 14:6 Je 28 '43
U.S. combat planes, World
    War. photogs 17 major
    types and models; silhou-
    ettes of 28 planes bw 12:
    39-49 F 2 '42
Airport. Sterne, H. 31:51 Ag
    27 '51
Aitken, Robert Ingersoll
    World's great artists frieze
    bw 68 portraits, Gallery of
    Fine Arts, Columbus, Ohio
    4:36-7 Ja 3 '38
Aitken, Russell B.
    Futility of a well-ordered life
    ceramic bw 3:94 O 11 '37
    Russell Aitken photog bw
    3:94 O 11 '37 port.
Ajanta Caves, India
    Reclining Buddha sculpture
    bw 38:80 Mr 7 '55
Akhenaton, King of Egypt.
    sculpture bw 41:122 N 26
    '56
Alabama monument, Gettysburg
    bw 4:35 Je 27 '38
Alabaster
    Ashurnasirpal winged lion.
    sculpture, Mesopotamia,
    c850 B.C. bw 6:53 Mr 20
    '39
    Sarcophagus 37:34 Ag 2 '54
    Urn, Mausoleum of Aelii.
    Rome, 3rd century 28:75
    Mr 27 '50

Alain, D. A.
    "New Yorker" cover 21:72
    Jy 15 '46
Alajalov, Constantin
    "New Yorker" cover 21:70-2
    Jy 15 '46
    Examples of work bw 13:98-9
    D 7 '42 (Cartoons)
    Christmas tree bw 19:8 D 28
    '45 (Drawings)
    Cinderella bw 15:79-80 S 13
    '43 (Illustrations)
The Alamo, Texas. photog bw
    6:72 Ap 10 '39
Alba, Maria del Pilar, 13.
    Duchess of
    Goya. The Duchess of Alba
    4:44 My 16 '38 bw 26:86
    Mr 28 '49
Alba Madonna. Raphael 13:
    Cover D 28 '42
Albert II, King of Belgium
    Diamond equestrian figure of
    King Albert bw 7:59 Jy 3
    '39
Albert, Consort of Victoria,
    Queen of England
    Prince Albert. bw 23:71-2
    O 20 '47
Albright, Adam Emory
    The anglers, the artist's
    sons bw 16:64 Mr 27 '44
Albright, Ivan Le Lorraine
    Ah, God--herrings, buoys,
    the glittering sea 16:78
    Ap 24 '44
    And God created Man in his
    own image (George Wash-
    ington Stafford) 16:68 Mr.
    27 '44
    Heavy the oar to him who is
    tired, heavy the coat,
    heavy the sea 16:68 Mr
    27 '44
    Picture of Dorian Gray bw
    16:70-1 Mr 27 '44; 18:99-
    105 Mr 19 '45
    Portrait* 33:98 O 27 '52
    That which I should have done
    I did not do 16:68 Mr 27
    '44 bw 14:47 Mr 8 '43

Wherefore now ariseth the il-
lusion of the third dimen-
sion 16:66-7 Mr 27 '44
Woman 16:65 Mr 27 '44; 21:
78 N 25 '46
Bust 33:98 O 27 '52 (Sculpture)
Artist in his studio photog bw
16:63 Mr 27 '44 port.
Painting the picture of Dori-
an Gray. photog bw 44:
71 Mr 27 '44 port.
Self-portrait. bw 16:64 Mr
27 '44 port.
Albright, Malvin Marr (known
as Zsissly)
Girl in red 16:65 Mr 27 '44
Victoria 16:65 Mr 27 '44
Artist in his studio. photog
bw 16:63 Mr 27 '44 port.
Painting the picture of Dorian
Gray. photog bw 44:71
Mr 27 '44 port.
Self-portrait. bw 16:64 Mr
27 '44 port.
Album quilt. 11:62 S 22 '41
Albuquerque Indians rain dance.
cartoon Emett 37:51 Jy 5
'54
Alchemist's shop. drawing bw
Brueghel, Pieter, the
elder 22:84 Ap 7 '47
Alcoholism and Intoxication
See also Bars and Bar-
rooms
Ackermann. Temperance
poster lithograph 39: 72-3
D 26 '55
Currier and Ives print. The
drunkard's progress bw
20:66 My 27 '46
Hogarth. Gin lane bw 20:66
My 27 '46; 21:83 D 16 '46
Kirby. Prohibitionist* cari-
cature bw 20:67 My 27 '46
Li T'ang, attributed to. Man
on a water buffalo return-
ing intoxicated from a vil-
lage feast 12th century 15:
65 O 11 '43
Philipp, R. Derelicts 8:64
Ap 8 '40

Wickey. Saturday night
sculpture bw 12:53 F 23
'42
Alden, John
John Alden and Priscilla
Mullins out riding* bw
25:131 N 29 '48
John Alden house, Duxbury,
Mass., 1653 photog bw
11:87 S 8 '41
Millet, F.D. John and Pris-
cilla bw 11:85 S 8 '41
Aleutian Islands
Pleissner. Airmen in the
Aleutians 16:57-62 My
22 '44
Alexander, Harold
Field-Marshal Alexander 29:
94 O 23 '50
"Time" cover portrait 17:62
D 11 '44
Alexander, Shiela
Shiela Alexander. photog
bw 24:131 Mr 8 '48
Alexander I, Czar of Russia
Alexander I. bw 14:94 Mr
29 '43
Alexander II, Czar of Russia
Alexander Romanov. bw
19:89 Ag 27 '45
Alexander II miniature 38:60
Ja 31 '55
Coronation, 1856--series of
paintings 38:60-7 Ja 31
'55
Czar and family photog bw
14:95 Mr 29 '43
Alexander III, Czar of Russia
Czar and family photog bw
14:95 Mr 29 '43
Alexander the Great
Puget. Alexander and his
horse, Bucephalas, riding
over foes bw 39:86 N 14
'55
Alexandra, Consort of Edward
VII, King of England
Alexandra, photog bw 23:
72 O 20 '47
Edward VII and Alexandra
photog bw 23:74 N 17 '47

Alert one. bw Ruvolo 22:78 F
    17 '47
Alfieri, Vittorio
    Vittorio Alfieri. bw 15:108
    Ag 23 '43
Alfred the Great. statue, Win-
    chester, England bw 40:
    103 Mr 19 '56
Alger, John
    Red barns 16:46 Ja 3 '44
Alger, Joseph
    Joseph Alger, amateur artist
    at work photogs bw 21:8-
    10 Jy 29 '46
Algerian women. bw Delacroix
    38:130 Je 27 '55
    Picasso. Variations of Dela-
    croix's Algerian women
    38:130 Je 27 '55
The Alhambra, building and
    gardens. photogs 33:52
    Ag 18 '52
Alice, Consort of Louis IV of
    Hesse
    Alice. bw 23:72 O 20 '47
"Alice's adventure in Wonder-
    land, " book by Charles
    Dodgson
    Original manuscript, written
    and illustrated by Dodgson
    bw 20:100-1 Ap 15 '46
    Tenniel. Illustrations for
    "Alice" bw 29:22-3 N 27
    '50; 30:85-7 Je 18 '51
    True-life "Alice" photog bw
    6:27 Jy 11 '38
Alicia. bw Speicher 8:70 My 27
    '40
Alken, Henry Thomas (known as
    Ben Tally-o)
    Leading the field aquatint bw
    6:38 F 6 '39
Alkmena. sculpture bw Young,
    M 10:79 F 17 '41
Allebe, Auguste
    Jan Six VII bw 31:66 Jy 16 '51
Allegorical landscape showing
    New York university. Morse
    17: 62 D 18 '44
Allegorical and Symbolical
    Themes See also Biblical

and Christian Themes; Mytho-
logical Themes; Seasons;
Statue of Liberty
Albright, I. That which I
    should have done I did not
    do 16:68 Mr 27 '44 bw
    14:47 Mr 8 '46
Barnard. The struggle of the
    two natures in Man sculp-
    ture bw 6:57 Mr 20 '39
Benjamin Franklin. print
    1780 40:80 Ja 9 '56
Biddle. Society freed through
    Justice mural 2:34 Ja 4
    '37
Blake. The four Zoas 36:
    66 Ap 19 '54
Blake. The great red drag-
    on and the woman clothed
    with the sun bw 10:94 Je
    9 '41
Blume. The eternal city bw
    3:20 D 6 '37
Blume. The rock 26:108-9
    Ap 11 '49
Bosch. The garden of de-
    lights 27:75-82 N 14 '49
Brueghel, Pieter, the elder.
    Flemish proverbs 24:74-
    5 Mr 22 '48
Brueghel, Pieter, the elder.
    The triumph of Death 31:
    66-7 O 1 '51
Brumidi. Dome murals,
    U.S. Capitol, Washing-
    ton, D.C. 31:52-3 Jy 2 '51
Callahan. The search 35:86
    S 28 '53
Car of history, Statuary Hall,
    U.S. Capitol, Washington,
    D.C. 31:50 Jy 2 '51
Carreno. Birth of the Amer-
    ican nations bw 10:106
    Mr 17 '41
Catholics marching toward
    ruin. * Flemish, c 1550
    24:64 Je 14 '48
Columbia placing Victory
    wreath on bust of George
    Washington 31:69 Jy 2 '51

Courbet. The studio 26:62-
3 My 30 '49

Crawford. Armed freedom
(cast) bw 19:9 S 24 '45

Dali. Madonna of Port Lligat
29:48 D 18 '50

Delacroix. Liberty leading
the people 25:84 N 22 '48

Diego. Elements of recon-
struction 20:82 Mr 11 '46

Dore. The crusades bw 39:
40-1 D 26 '55

Epstein. Social consciousness bw 33:65 N 3 '52

The four humors, Middle
Ages. bw 22:84 Ap 7 '47

French. The angel of Death
and the sculptor sculpture
bw 6:57 Mr 20 '39

Freund. The reach 39:116 S
12 '55

George Washington and Benjamin Franklin. painted
textile, English, 1782 40:
82 Ja 9 '56

Greene. The burial 29:65
O 23 '50

Greuze. The broken eggs 5:
36 S 26 '38

Gropper. Civilization 8:71
My 27 '40

Grunewald. Isenheimer altarpiece 30:79 Mr 26 '51

Guardian of the Law. sculpture bw 30:104 Mr 12 '51

Guston. If this be not I 20:
92 My 27 '46

Hegh. Unto one of the least
of these 8:44 F 12 '40

Inness. Peace and plenty,
detail bw 19:82 S 10 '45

Koerner. Looking 24:78 My
10 '48

Koerner. Vanity Fair 24:78-
9 My 10 '48

Kroll. Triumph of Justice
mural 4:38 Ap 25 '38

Leutze. "Westward the
course of Empire" 36:76
Mr 8 '54

McCrady. Swing Low,
Sweet Chariot 3:39 O 18
'37

Milles. The wedding of the
Mississippi and the Mis-
souri, fountain 2: Cover,
26 F 22 '37 bw 8:110-2
Je 10 '40

Montenegro. The slaughter
wall 4:29 Mr 14 '38

Picasso. Guernica fresco
bw 3:64 Jy 26 '37

Pickins. Carnival 28:88 Mr
20 '50

Ryder. Death on a pale
horse 5:36 O 31 '38; 15:
67 S 20 '43

Saint-Gaudens. Grief sculpture bw 24:110 Mr 15 '48

Siqueiros. Sunrise of Mexico 20:60 Je 3 '46

Stanley. Muse of Music
sculpture bw 9:82 O 21
'40

Tchelitchew. Phenomena
bw 5:57 S 5 '38

Tintoretto. The allegory of
Vigilance 35:149 N 16 '53

Titian. Sacred and profane
love 23:52 Ag 4 '47 bw
16:65 Ja 10 '44

Uccello, School of. The triumph of Death bw 4:28 F
7 '38

Van Eyck brothers. Ghent
altarpiece 26:58-69 Ap
18 '49

Van Nierlandt. The Protestant triumph 24:58 Je 14
'48

Victory monument, Gettys-
burg. sculpture bw 4:36
Je 27 '38

Vos. The birth of a nation
bw 3:71 Ag 9 '37

West. Benjamin Franklin
and the lightning 40:81
Ja 9 '56

Yvon. The genius of America bw 33:44 S 29 '52

The allegory of Vigilance. Tin-
toretto 35:149 N 16 '53
The allegory of Virtue and Vice
(The choice of Hercules).
Veronese 3:38 D 27 '37
Allegri, Antonio See Correggio
Allen, Ethan
Ethan Allen. statue, Mont-
pelier, Vt. bw 3:42 Jy 19
'37
Allen, Frederick H.
Frederick H. Allen. photog
bw 26:75 Ja 31 '49
Alligators
Gold alligator. Pre-Colum-
bian 18:49 Je 4 '45
Allston, Washington
Elijah fed by the ravens (Eli-
jah in the desert) 19:84 S
10 '45
Brackett Washington Allston
bust bw 19:9 S 24 '45
port.
Almansa, walled city, Spain.
photog 33:53 Ag 18 '52
Alnwick castle, Northumber-
land, England. photog 40:
92 Mr 19 '56
Alphabet of odd animals. Baker,
M. 26:12-4 Mr 28 '49
Altars and Altarpieces
Altar of Heaven, Peiping.
photogs 20:71 Ap 29 '46
Confucian temple photog
bw 38:71, 76 Ap 4 '55
Basel altarpiece. gold re-
lief of Christ and saints
33:38-9 D 29 '52
Bernini. Altar, St. Peter's,
Rome photog bw 18:27
Ja 15 '45
Buddhist altar, San Francis-
co temple photog 25:76
S 20 '48
Buddhist altar with ancestor
tablets, Japan photog bw
3:41 Ag 30 '37
Confucian altar of Heaven
photog bw 38:71, 76 Ap
4 '55

Duccio. The annunciation
1:46 D 28 '36
Duccio. Resurrection of
Lazarus 1:46 D 28 '36
Fazzini. Altarpiece sculpture bw 32:70 Mr 10 '52
Golden Meru, cremation altar, Thailand photogs
bw 28:132, 138-41 Ap 17
'50
Grunewald. Isenheimer al-
tarpiece 30:74-85 Mr 26
'51
Holy Trinity. santero painting, Mission San Jose,
Laguna, N. Mex. photog
40:48-9 Ja 16 '56
Kifuku temple, Japan photog
32:99 Je 23 '52
Medici chapel altar 19:43 D
24 '45
Ossorio. Altar fresco, Ne-
gros Island Catholic
church, Philippines 30:
15 Ap 30 '51
St. Patrick's cathedral, New
York City photog 16:67
Ja 31 '44 bw 4:32 Mr 21
'38
St. Sophia Greek Orthodox
cathedral, Los Angeles
photog 33:54 N 3 '52
Van Eyck brothers. Ghent
altarpiece 26:58-69 Ap 18
'49
Voodoo altar, Port-au-
Prince photog bw 3:28
D 13 '37
"Altmark" (ship) German, 1940
Wilkinson. The navy's here*
24:66 My 17 '48
Alva Studios sculpture repro-
ductions bw 38:115-6 Ap
25 '55
Alzira, the artist's wife.
Peirce, W. 10:47 F 3 '41
Amateur Art See Art, Amateur
Amazons See Mythological
Themes--Amazons

The ambassadors. Holbein 24:
82 Mr 22 '48

Amel, Ambrose
Artist at work photog bw 10:
79 Mr 31 '41 port.

Amelung, John Frederick, A-
merican glassmaker
Saltholder 39:59 Jy 18 '55
Wine glass 39:58 Jy 18 '55

Amenemhet III, King of Egypt.
sculpture 29:107 N 27 '50;
41:108 N 26 '56

Amendola, R. F.
Kineglyph--sculpture for the
blind bw 21:102 N 11 '46

American Art See Art, American

American beauties. sculpture
bw Lentelli 6:Cover Mr 13
'39

American dream house. cartoon
Emett 37:43 Jy 5 '54

American farm scenes. Currier
and Ives print 9:28 D 30
'40

American Gothic. Wood, G. 14:
52-3 Ja 18 '43 bw 5:30 O
31 '38; 6:58 Mr 27 '39

American independence, 1776.
print bw 16:46 Ja 17 '44

American Indians See Indians--
North American; Art--Indian
(North American)

American parade. Steinberg 31:
52-3 Ag 27 '51

American Revolution See United
States--History--Revolution

The American school. Pratt
6:31 Je 19 '39

"American Turtle," first U.S.
submarine drawing bw 22:82
Ja 13 '47

The American way. Rockwell
18:45 Ja 1 '45

American winter scenes: Evening. Currier and Ives
print 9:27 D 30 '40

American winter sports: Trout
fishing in Chateaugay Lake.
Currier and Ives print 9:
27 D 30 '40

America's Arts and Skills See
Art, American

The America's Cup, silver
ewer, yachting trophy
photog bw 3:32 Ag 2 '37

Amethyst. bw Baroness de
Kuffner 21:101 Jy 1 '46

Amherst College mascot: Sabrina. statue bw 32:110
Je 30 '52

Amida, Lord of Light. Japanese screen, 13th century
34:99 Ap 20 '53

Amino, Leo
Hunter sculpture bw 37:162
N 22 '54
Artist at work photog 37:
162 N 22 '54 port.

Amitabha Buddha
China 8:31 Ja 8 '40
Kamakura, Japan sculpture
38:91 Mr 7 '55

Amon. statue, gold 41:115 N
26 '56

Ampulla. gold, English 2:38
Mr 15 '37

Anatomist. woodcut Baskin 37:
89 O 18 '54

Anatomy lesson of Professor
Tulp. Rembrandt 1:30 N
30 '36

And God created man in his own
image. Albright, I. 16:
68 Mr 27 '44

Andalusia. Greek revival,
Doric, house, 1830-35
photog 39:58-9 Ag 29 '55

Anderson, Donald
City at night 32:68-9 Ja 14
'52

Anderson, Edward O., architect
Mormon temple, Los
Angeles 39:115 D 26 '55

Anderson, Guy
Deposition of the miner 35:87
S 28 '53
Artist and his work photog 35:
87 S 28 '53 port.

Anderson, Karl
Man* 18:76 My 14 '45

Anderson, Marian
Halsman. Marian Anderson
photog bw 16:45 Mr 13 '44
Anderson, Maxwell
Maxwell Anderson. photog
bw 5:58 O 3 '38; 21:50 O
7 '46
Anderson, Ronald Lee
Still life bw 38:83 F 28 '55
Anderson, Sherwood
Sherwood Anderson carica-
ture bw 23:82 S 1 '47
"Winesburg, Ohio," locale
and characters photogs
bw 20:74-9 Je 10 '46
Andersonville. drawing bw,
1864 39:166 S 12 '55
Andirons, Silver. English,
George I bw 3:77 D 13 '37
Andre, John
Indians and soldiers in a tav-
ern* bw 35:92 S 28 '53
(Drawing)
River* bw 35:92 S 28 '53
Andre's hanging bw 29:54 Jy
3 '50 port.
Arnold and Andre meet. bw
29:54 Jy 3 '50 port.
Major John Andre. drawing
bw 35:91-2 S 28 '53 port.
Self-portrait. drawing bw
29:54 Jy 3 '50 port.
Andreef, Alexis, furniture de-
signer
Chair, parachute cord bw 34:
105-7 Mr 23 '53
Andreef photog bw 34:106-7
Mr 23 '53 port.
Andrew of Greece. photog bw
23:72 O 20 '47
Androcles See Mythological
Themes--Androcles
Anemones. Braque 26:83 My 2
'49
The angel and Jacob fighting.
Carena 3:27 D 20 '37
The angel of Death and the sculp-
tor. sculpture bw French
6:57 Mr 20 '39
An angel summons the shepherds.
Lu Hung Nien 11:43 D 22 '41

Angelica. Brackman 8:60 F 5
'40
Angelico, Fra (Giovanni da
Fiesole)
The annunciation 21:52 D 23
'46
At the sepulcher 21:61 D 23
'46
The betrayal 21:58 D 23 '46
Christ bearing the cross 21:
59 D 23 '46
The entombment 16:71 Ap 10
'44; 21:60 D 23 '46
The flight into Egypt 21:
Cover, 54 D 23 '46
The last judgment 21:56-7
D 23 '46
The nativity 21:53 D 23 '46
The raising of Lazarus 21:
55 D 23 '46
Angels See also Mary, Virgin--
Annunciation
Angel. mosaic, Early Chris-
tian 28:68 Mr 27 '50
Angel. stained glass, Chartre
cathedral, France 22:73
Ap 7 '47
Angel Gabriel. mosaic,
Santa Sophia, Istanbul 29:
58 D 28 '50
Barlach. Floating angel
sculpture 41:140 N 5 '56
Blake. The four Zoas 36:60-
4 Ap 19 '54
Breiner. Silent Night, Holy
Night 23:50-1 D 22 '47
Burlin. Fallen angel bw 26:
84 F 21 '49
Couturier. Angel Gabriel;
Angel Raphael stained
glass 28:74 Je 19 '50
Dali. Madonna of Port Lli-
gat 29:48 D 18 '50
Davis, G. R. We Three
Kings of Orient Are 23:52
D 22 '47
Dore. Lord smiting the first-
born of Egypt bw 4:48 Ap
18 '38
El Greco. The Holy Trinity
31:72 O 1 '51

El Greco. The Virgin with
Santa Ines and Santa Tecla
7:26 D 25 '39

Epstein. Lucifer sculpture
bw 33:66 N 3 '52

Ford. Baptism of Arnauld
17:35 D 25 '44

Ford. Guardian angel 10:71
Ap 14 '41; 17:42 D 25 '44

Gauguin. Peasants and angel
mural 28:93 My 1 '50

Giotto. Lives of Christ and
Mary, Arena church fres-
coes 25:Cover, 34-57 D
27 '48

Giotto. Eternal and angels
4:30 F 7 '38

Gozzoli. Journey of the
Magi fresco 19:Cover, 43-5
D 24 '45

Grunewald. Isenheimer altarpiece 30:84 Mr 26 '51

Kent. Angel woodcut bw 5:
9 D 12 '38

Leonardo da Vinci. Madonna
of the rocks 7:54 N 20 '39

Lippi, Fra Filippo. Madonna
and Child with two angels
29:108 S 11 '50

Lu Hung Nien. The annunciation 11:42 D 22 '41

Luini. Body of St. Catherine
borne by angels to Sinai
fresco bw 6:32 F 13 '39

Memling. Shrine of St. Ursala 34:82-5 Ap 6 '53

Michelangelo. Avenging angel drawing bw 27:26 D
26 '49

Raphael. Sistine Madonna
40:113 My 7 '56

Saint-Gaudens. General
Sherman, with angel of
Victory sculpture bw 24:
109 Mr 15 '48

Stark. Hark! the Herald Angels Sing 23:55 D 22 '47

Tintoretto. The last supper
39:26-7 D 26 '55

Tintoretto. Life of Christ
31:30-49 D 24 '51

Van Eyck, J. Archangel
Michael 40:109 My 7 '56

Van Eyck brothers. Ghent
altarpiece 26:58-69 Ap 18
'49

Van Nieulandt. The Protestant triumph 24:58 Je 14
'48

Angkor-Wat, temple of, Cambodia photog bw 5:37 Ag
1 '38

Anguissola, Sofonisba
Philip II, King of Spain 24:80
Mr 22 '48 bw 31:60 O 1 '51

Animal form I. sculpture bw
Caparn 32:78 Ja 7 '52

Animals See also names of animals, as Birds; Horses;
Lions

Audubon. Quadruped plates
from "Audubon's Ameri-
ca" 9:115 O 21 '40; 30:47-
9 Ja 29 '51

Baker. Alphabet of odd animals 26:12-4 Mr 28 '49

Bosch. Garden of Eden 27:
76 N 14 '49

Cranach. Cardinal Albrecht
as Saint Hieronymus 5:39
Jy 11 '38

Curry, Sanctuary 1:30 N 23
'36 bw 15:19 N 29 '43

Curry. Tornado over Kansas
1:29 N 23 '56; 21:73 N 25
'46

De Bry. Animals of India*
drawing bw 24:87 Mr 22
'48

Diego. Unexpected encounter
20:82 Mr 11 '46

Freund. Animals in winter
25:76-80 N 29 '48

Giacometti. Animals* sculpture bw 31:152 N 5 '51

Hicks. Peaceable kingdom
17: 72 O 16 '44

Hicks. Residence of David
Twining in 1787 9:76 D
9 '40

Rousseau, H. The waterfall
11:58 S 8 '41

Rudy. Animals sculpture bw
15:81-2 D 20 '43
Thurber. Animals drawings
bw 20:55 Ja 21 '46
Animals, Imaginary
Bayeux tapestry: griffins,
phoenixes, monsters bw
16:8-10 Je 26 '44
Bosch. Garden of delights
27:75-82 N 14 '49
Chi-Lin, one-horned beast,
in Reception of the Immor-
tals at the court of Hsi
Wang Mu 38:76-7 Ap 4 '55
Clews. Cat-woman sculpture
bw 31:123 O 15 '51
Clews. Gods, ogs, wogs
sculpture bw 31:119 O 15
'51
Dali. Soft construction with
boiled beans: Premonition
of civil war, 1936 31:27 D
20 '37 bw 19:64-5 S 24 '45
Denslow. Kalidahs 35:57-8 D
28 '53
Denslow. Winged monkeys
35:57-8 D 28 '53
Ernst. Monsters bw 32:61
Ja 21 '52
Freund. Basilisk 30:116-7
Ap 23 '51
Freund. Manticore 30:117
Ap 23 '51
Freund. Su 30:115 Ap 23 '51
Komainu. sculpture bw
Kyoto 18:91 F 19 '45
Lewicki. Callicantzari 39:64
D 19 '55
Makara. fish, Hinduism 38:
68 F 7 '55
The phoenix. sculpture bw
4:14 F 21 '38

Birds

Bird-man. wood carving
Easter Island bw 21:80 N 4
'46
Bird-woman. sculpture, Bangkok 31:32 D 31 '51
Escher. Man-bird drawing
bw 30:18 My 7 '51

Garuda. man-bird, Hinduism
38:69 F 7 '55
Garuda. religious float, Cambodia 40:212 Ap 9 '56

Centaurs

Centaurs, Elgin marbles,
sculpture bw 35:158-9 O 26
'53
Picasso. Centaurs drawing
bw 23:97 O 13 '47
Poussin. The triumph of Bacchus 7:53 O 9 '39

Dragons

Blake. The great red dragon
and the woman clothed with
sun bw 10:94 Je 9 '41
Ch'en Jung. Nine dragons detail 15:66-7 O 11 '43
Dragon head fountain, Fushimi
shrine. sculpture bw 18:
91 F 19 '45
Dragon parade figure. 38:81
Ap 4 '55
Dragon pillars, Ta-Cheng-
Tien temple bw 4:17 My 16
'38
Dragon screen, Peiping sculpture 20:74-5 Ap 29 '46
Dragon throne, Hall of Supreme Harmony, Forbid-
den City, Peiping 20:69 Ap
29 '46 bw 3:58 Ag 23 '37
Dragon wall, Peiping glazed
porcelain 3:55 Ag 23 '37
Dragons. wood carving bw,
Viking 40:97 Mr 19 '56
Imperial dragons, Peiping
sculpture bw 32:23 Je 30
'52
Lurcat. St. John's revelation
tapestry 28:76 Je 19 '50
Martorell. St. George killing
the dragon 33:91 O 27 '52
Raphael. St. George and the
dragon 33:37 D 29 '52

Gorgons

Freund. Gorgon 30:117 Ap 23
'51

Gorgon handle, bronze urn
   Greek, 6th century 37:86
   S 13 '54

Griffins
Freund. Griffin 30:116 Ap 23
   '51
Griffons, Persepolis sculpture
   35:156 N 23 '53
Revere. Griffin, symbol of
   England, 1884 cartoon bw
   38:56 My 30 '55
Tons. Gryphons tapestry 35:98-
   9 D 14 '53

Lions
Lion-dog in Reception of the
   Immortals at the court of
   Hsi Wang Mu 38:76-7 Ap 4
   '55
Winged lion, Ashurnasirpal
   sculpture bw, Mesopotamia,
   c850 B.C. 6:53 Mr 20 '39
Winged lion of Brazil sculp-
   ture bw 10:61 Ja 6 '41

Sea Horses
Cellini. Saltcellar goldwork,
   c1540 31:18-9 S 24 '51
Sea horses. gondola prow,
   Venice 40:75 Je 25 '56

Snakes
Ananta. many-headed serpent,
   Hinduism 38:68-9 F 7 '55
Feathered serpent sculpture
   bw, Toltec 28:62 Ja 9 '50
Winged serpent amulet, E-
   gypt, c1375 B.C. 24:81 Ja
   19 '48

Unicorns
Duncan. Unicorn bw 22:78 F
   17 '47
Freund. Unicorn 30:119 Ap
   23 '51
Thurber. Unicorn in the garden 24:84 Ap 19 '48
Unicorn hunt tapestry 22:70-
   2 My 26 '47

Yales
Freund. Yale 30:116 Ap 23
   '51
Yales, St. John's gateway,
   Cambridge, England bw
   15:97 S 20 '43
Animals howling for food.
   Tamayo 34:101 Mr 16 '53
Ankhaf, Prince of Egypt. bust,
   c2560 B.C. 41:106 N 26
   '56
Ann in white scarf. Kroll 5:30
   S 19 '38
Anna digs clams. Peirce, W.
   19:85 N 12 '45
"Anna Kerenina," illustrations.
   Reisman 8:46-9 F 5 '40
Anna turns painter. Peirce, W.
   19:85 N 12 '45
Annah the Javanese. Gauguin
   29:112 S 11 '50
Anne, Saint
Durer. Madonna and Child
   with St. Anne 5:40 Jy 11
   '38
Ribera. Holy family with St.
   St. Catherine 4:42 My 16
   '38
Anne of Cleves, Consort of Hen-
   ry VIII, King of England.
   bw 32:24 F 18 '52; 41:88
   O 29 '56
Anne in white. Bellows 20:74
   Mr 25 '46
Annigoni, Pietro
   Elizabeth II, Queen of Eng-
   land 38:93 My 30 '55
Annunication See Mary, Virgin--
   Annunciation
Anshen and Allen, architects
   Chapel of the Holy Cross,
   Arizona photog 41:105-6
   O 15 '56
   Contemporary house, San
   Francisco photogs, plan
   bw 31:127 S 10 '51
   Glass-walled pent house, San
   Francisco photogs 27:48-9
   S 5 '49
An answer to Yorktown. cartoons
   Emett 37:42-53 Jy 5 '54

Antaeus See Mythological
Themes--Antaeus
Ante meridian. bw Waugh, F.J.
2:57 Je 14 '37; 3:24 D 30 '37
Anteater. sculpture bw Clews
31:119 O 15 '51
Antelopes. paper cutouts
Mochi 34:18, 20 Mr 9 '53
Antelopes head dress. sculp-
ture bw, Bambara, Sudan
33:118 S 8 '52
Anthony, Saint
Grunewald. Isenheimer altar-
piece: Temptation; Visit
with St. Paul 30:76-85 Mr
26 '51
Hagenauer. St. Anthony stat-
ue 30:80-1 Mr 26 '51
Patiner and Massys. The temp-
tation of St. Anthony 31:
62-3 O 1 '51
St. Anthony tapestry, France,
1450 21:81 S 30 '46
"Anthony Adverse," illustrations.
Wilson, E. A. 18:57 Ap 23
'45
Anti-aircraft battery. Cole 28:
52 F 6 '50
Antietam Creek, Maryland, 1862.
13:62 Jy 6 '42
Antiope See Mythological
Themes--Antiope
Antiques See also Art; Ceramics;
Glassware; Furniture
Lick-Boner house, Winston-
Salem, N.C. photogs bw
37:167 O 25 '54
Tacchi. Antique furniture re-
productions 37:91-2 O 25
'54
Webb Museum of American
arts and crafts 35:46-53 Jy
6 '53
Antonella da Messina
The crucifixion 7:51 N 20 '39;
39:29 D 26 '55
St. Sebastian bw 40:104 F 20
'56
Antwerp
Festival in Antwerp, 16th
century. bw 4:52-3 My 23 '38

Apartment houses
Markelius. Kollectivhuset,
Stockholm photog bw 22:
34 My 26 '47
Mexico City apartments bw
21:98-9 F 24 '47
Sao Paulo apartment photog
bw 13:132 O 26 '42
Ape. sculpture bw Moselio 3:42
N 22 '37
Aphrodite See Mythological
Themes--Venus
Aphrodite of Melos. sculpture
bw 19:48 Jy 30 '45; 35:51
Ag 17 '53
Apolinere enameled. collage
Duchamp 32:103 Ap 28 '52
Apotheosis of Pope Martin V.
bw Luti 18:91 Mr 5 '45
Appel, Marianne
Juneau, Alaska 16:76 Ap 24
'44
Appian way. photog bw 17:95 S
4 '44
Apollo Belvedere. sculpture bw
5:46 D 25 '38
Approaching storm. Grosz 12:
76 Ap 20 '42
Apres le bain. Renoir 24:66
Mr 1 '48
Aqueducts
Claudian aqueduct. photog bw
16:13 Je 5 '44
Roman aqueduct, Smyrna.
photog bw 8:81 Ap 8 '40
Arai, Shori
Take-off from carrier 28:67
F 27 '50
Arango, Dorote See Villa,
Pancho
Arbor day. Wood, G. 14:56 Ja
18 '43
Arc de Triomphe, Paris. photog
8:63 Je 3 '40 bw 2:70 Je 14
'37; 17:25 S 11 '44; 23:163
N 17 '47
Arch of Constantine. photog bw
5:59 Jy 18 '38
Arch of Heaven, Peiping.
photogs 20:71 Ap 29 '46

Arch of Octavius, Rome. Bier-
stadt 33:91 S 15 '52
Arch of Titus, Rome, 81 A.D.
Arch of Titus photog bw 16:13
Je 5 '44; 17:95 S 4 '44
Healy. Arch of Titus, Rome
33:89 S 15 '52
Archduke Leopold in his gallery.
Teniers 27:62-3 O 24 '49
Archer, Edmund
Waiting for the departure 10:
68 My 26 '41
Arches
Arch, near Keranikos, Athens,
c300 B.C. photog bw 18:54
Ja 1 '45
Chinese arch, Imperial Plea-
sure Island photog 20:67 Ap
29 '46
Chinese arches, Peiping
photogs 20:70-1 Ap 29 '46
Churchill arch, Parliament,
London photog 31:120 O 8
'51
Mayan arch, Ball Court, Chi-
chen Itza photog 22:60 Je
30 '47
Parabolic arch building, Fair
Grounds, Raleigh, N.C.
photog 36:34-5 Ja 4 '54
Saarinen, Eero. Gateway to
the West, memorial arch,
St. Louis, Mo. bw 24:113
Mr 8 '48
Triumphal arch, Egypt, con-
temporary photog bw 3:18
Ag 23 '37
Washington Arch, New York
City photog bw 16:113 Je 5
'44; 29:71 Ag 14 '50
Architectural Orders See Corin-
thian; Doric; Ionic
Architecture See also types of
structures, as Castles;
Churches; Colleges; Domes;
Embassy Buildings; Hotels;
Office Buildings; Temples.
Also, names of architects,
as Goff, B.; Harrison, W.
K.; Jefferson, T.; Skid-
more, Owings and Merrill;

Stone, E.D.; Wright, F.L.
Also, names of structures,
as Andalusia; The White
House

America
Colonial architecture's herit-
age from the French 39:84-
5 N 28 '55
Colonial houses independence
built 38:61 My 30 '55
Greek revival architecture
39:64-5 Ag 29 '55
Italian models of New York
City structures bw 16:12-
4 Je 5 '44

Arabia
Ibn Saud's palaces: El Kharj;
Muraba bw 14:72-3, 77 My
31 '43
Yemen buildings bw 21:59 N
18 '46

Brazil
Modern public and office
buildings, apartments bw
13:132-4 O 26 '42
Niemeyer and Portinari.
National monument, Belo
Horizonte bw 27:76-7 Jy
4 '49

China
Peiping architecture: pagodas,
temples, palaces, arches
20:67-77 Ap 29 '46
Ta-Cheng-Tien, Palace of
the Most Perfect bw 4:17
My 16 '38

Egypt
Pyramids, temples and tombs
of ancient Egypt 24:74-85
Ja 19 '48

Mexico
Modern hotels, apartments,
public buildings, Mexico
City bw 21:98-9 F 24 '47

Russia
Churches, palaces, public
buildings 14:83-5, 88-90
Mr 29 '43

Tibet
Great assembly hall, Lama-
sery, Kumbum 24:76-7 F
16 '48
Architecture--Adobe
Southwest adobes--Taos;
Santa Fe 40:47, 49 Ja 16
'56
Architecture--Aluminum Struc-
ture Fuller. Round house,
suspended from mast bw 20:
73-4, 76 Ap 1 '46
Architecture--Baroque
Georgian and baroque man-
sions 24:75-82 Je 7 '48
Reid. Trygveson, Atlanta, Ga.
24:80 Je 7 '48
Russian church, Fili, 17th
century bw 14:83 Mr 29 '43
Architecture--Cantilever Struc-
ture. Wright. Heliolab 29:8-
10 D 11 '50
Architecture--Commercial
Buildings. Art shop, Bremen,
Germany bw 36:148 My 10
'54
Gruen, Victor, Associates.
Northland shopping center,
Detroit 37:81-3 Ag 30 '54
Architecture--Concrete Con-
struction. Harrison. Housing
project bungalow bw 27:
103-4 O 10 '49
Architecture--Details See also
Columns; Mural Paintings;
Sculpture
Buttresses, Ulm cathedral
35:41 D 28 '53
Ceiling decoration, Kenmore
mansion, Fredricksburg,
Va. 38:62 My 30 '55
Rosenthal. Facade 34:137
Ap 6 '53
Architecture--Domestic

England
English country houses 19:
97-107 O 29 '45; 41:154-61
N 5 '56
Wren. Chatsworth house bedroom, Devonshire bw 15:
106-7 N 15 '43

France
Chenonceaux, France, 15th
century 33:40 D 29 '52

Japan
House design adapted to U.S.
buildings 31:60-1 D 31 '51
Yoshimura. Japanese house,
Museum of Modern Art bw
37:71-2, 74 Ag 23 '54

Surrealist
Terry. The snail 1:24 D 14
'56

United States
Acorn house. Koch 26:70-2
Ja 24 '49
American Gothic 39:100-1 O
17 '55 bw 12:8-9, 11 My
11 '42
Balloon frame houses, Chi-
cago bw 39:89 N 28 '55
Balloon houses bw 26:12-4
My 8 '49
Basic expansible house.
sketches, plans Wills 21:
68-9 Ag 26 '46
Bay region modern 27:44-53
S 5 '49
Beach cottage, Malibu, Calif.
bw Raetze 26:148 Ap 11
'49
Best houses under $15,000,
mass-produced bw 31:
123-7 S 10 '51
Bird-cage house, Miami,
Fla. Polevitzky 28:63-5
Je 5 '50
Birthplaces of U.S. Presi-
dents bw 6:6-8 F 20 '39

Bulfinch curved housefronts,
  Boston bw 10:64 Mr 24 '41
California houses bw 26:146-
  8 Ap 11 '49
California "Mission" style
  40:56-7 Ja 16 '56
Cape Cod cottage. plan Wills
  21:71 Ag 26 '46
Center-kitchen house. Hunter
  41:34-6 D 24 '56
Cinder-block house. Waterval
  3:15 D 13 '37
Colonial farmhouse. plan
  Wills 21:73 Ag 26 '46
Country houses bw 9:76-87
  Jy 1 '40
Creole-style: La Prete, New
  Orleans bw 12:8-9, 11 Ap
  6 '42
Desert house. Loewy 22:113-
  7 Mr 24 '47
Desert house. bw Neutra 26:
  146-7 Ap 11 '48
Designer's house. bw Eames
  29:148-9 S 11 '50
Dream house. plan Burns
  20:83-6 My 6 '46
Dream house. bw Evans 3:13-
  4 D 13 '37
Dutch colonial house bw
  Dreisler 3:15 D 13 '37
Eight houses for 1940 plans
  bw 9:76-92 Jy 1 '40
Endless house. egg-shaped
  model and plan bw Kiesler
  32:82 My 26 '52
Executive mansions, 48 states
  bw 10:22-3 Ja 20 '41
Family house. bw plan Good-
  paster 36:75 Mr 29 '54
Family living house. Stonorov
  29:40-1, 43 Jy 10 '50
Fuller house: round, alumin-
  um, suspended from mast
  bw 20:73-4, 76 Ap 1 '46
Garrison house. Wills 21:73
  Ag 26 '46
Glass house, New Canaan,
  Conn. Johnson 27:94-6 S
  26 '49

Hillside house, Carmel,
  Calif. plan bw Konishofer
  32:131-2 Mr 17 '52
Hilltop home, La Jolla, Calif.
  bw Harris 19:114 O 22
  '45
Home planning ideas. 18:49-
  73 My 28 '45
Horizontal-style house,
  Springfield, Ill. Wright
  40:98 Mr 5 '56
Housewives ideas on housing
  drawings bw 40:66 Je 4
  '56
Hudson River bracketed:
  Tuscan villa, 1855 print
  39:99 O 17 '55
Hudson River houses:
  Bracketed, rustic-pointed,
  hexagonal, octagonal bw
  7:62-3 O 2 '39
Inverted-gable roof house,
  San Francisco. Harris
  27:50 S 5 '49
Italian baroque: Trygveson,
  Atlanta, Ga. Reid 24:80
  Je 7 '48
Lakeside home. bw Neutra
  26:148 Ap 11 '49
Levittown houses bw 26:74
  Ja 31 '49; 28:141 My 22
  '50
"LIFE" house for $2-3000
  income family bw 5:35 D
  12 '38
Log cabin, squared-oak logs
  39:78-9 N 28 '55
Minimum house. plan bw
  Clark 9:78-9 Jy 1 '40
Modern conservative house.
  plan bw Shreve, Lamb and
  Harmon 9:88-9 Jy 1 '40
Modern houses: suburban,
  minimum, country. blue-
  prints 22:77-91 Ap 28 '47
Modern "idea house." bw
  Walker Art Center, Min-
  neapolis 25:105-7 O 18
  '48
Modern post-war house plans
  18:49-73 My 28 '45

Modern town house, San Francisco. Dinwiddie, Hill and Joseph 27:44 S 5 '49
Neo-Greek style house. bw Barney and Wright 3:39 Ag 9 '37
New England Federal: Pierce house, Salem, Mass. McIntire 38:63 My 30 '55
New England houses bw 15:12-3, 15 D 6 '43
Plantation houses: Greek revival; Steamboat Gothic 32: 72-83 Je 9 '52
Ranchhouse, Montecito, Calif. May 40:58-9 Ja 16 '56
Ranchhouse: Las Flores, Oceanside, Calif. 40:58-9 Ja 16 '56
Round houses
Fuller. Round, aluminum house, suspended from mast bw 20:73-4, 76 Ap 1 '46
Goff. Round house plan, diagrams 30:70-5 Mr 19 '51
Row house, California. bw Ain 26:147 Ap 11 '49
Rustic-pointed Vassar house. bw Downing 7:63 O 2 '39
Salt-box house. plan Wills 21:72 Ag 26 '46
Shingle-style house, Bristol, R.I. McKim, Mead and White 40:98 Mr 5 '56
Six houses of U.S.A. built 1677 to 1851 18:52-7 My 7 '45
Space and saucer house. bw Goff 39:155-6 S 19 '55
Split-level house. plan Little 34:113-6 Je 15 '53
Sprayed concrete. plan Noyes 36:75-8 F 22 '54
Storage walls. diagrams 18: 64-71 Ja 22 '45
Swiss Gothic: Loch Aerie, West Chester, Pa. 39:98 O 17 '55

Texas houses bw 19:57-8 S 10 '45
Trade secrets house plan 34: 8-15 Ja 5 '53
Tudor-style Victorian house, Newport, R.I. Richardson 40:98 Mr 5 '56
Vanderbilt mansions 28:89-92 Ja 2 '50
Wright-style houses: Fallingwater, Bear Run, Pa; Taliesin West, Arizona bw 21:84, 94 Ag 12 '46
Architecture--Dormitories
Jeanneret. Swiss students' dormitory, University of Paris bw 22:35 My 26 '47
Architecture--Georgian
Georgian and baroque mansions, Atlanta, Ga. 24:75-82 Je 7 '48
Georgian house: Carter's Grove, Williamsburg, Va. 38:61-2 My 30 '55
Georgian house, Kittery, Me. bw 15:13 D 6 '43
Architecture--Glass Construction. Anshen and Allen. Glass-walled pent house 27:48-9 S 5 '49
Bridger and Paxton. Glass-walled, solar-heated office building bw 41:71 D 17 '56
Church--colored glass octagons inset in concrete blocks bw 36:150 My 10 '54
Harrison and Abramovitz. U.S. embassy, Rio de Janiero 34:45 Je 22 '53
Heinz Vinegar factory, Pittsburgh, Pa. 36:35 Ja 4 '54
Hentrich. Office building--glass encased stairwy bw 36:150 My 10 '54
Johnson. Glass house, New Canaan, Conn. 27:94-6 S 26 '49

Skidmore, Owings and Mer-
rill. Lever house, New
York City 32:44-5 Je 2 '52
Skidmore, Owings and Mer-
rill. Manufacturers Trust
Co., Fifth Avenue Office,
New York City 37:62 O 25
'54
United Biscuit Company, Mel-
rose Park, Ill. 36:34 Ja 4
'54
United Nations, New York City
photogs 30:62-3 Mr 26 '51
bw 33:Cover, 113-9 N 3 '52;
33:34 O 27 '52
Architecture--Gothic
Barry. Houses of Parliament,
London 24:49 Ap 26 '48 bw
16:81 My 22 '44
Carcassone, walled city,
France bw 22:66-7 My 26
'47
Mont-Saint-Michel 26:72 Je
13 '49 bw 22:67 Ap 7 '47
Notre Dame, Paris 8:60-1 Je
3 '40 bw 2:70 Je 14 '37
Princeton University Buildings
21:82-9 S 23 '46
Dining hall bw 2:55 Je 7 '37
Public buildings, churches in
Germany; Belgium bw 17:
85-8 O 9 '44
Reims cathedral bw 22:68 Ap
7 '47
Riverside church, New York
City bw 3:35-7 D 20 '37
Romantic decades--homes,
churches 39:98-101 O 17
'55
Salisbury cathedral, England
bw 8:84-5 Je 3 '40
San Francisco Gothic, c1900
bw 15:76 Jy 12 '43
Architecture--Greek
Acropolis, Athens bw 18:56
Ja 1 '45
Athena Victorious, temple,
Athens bw 18:56 Ja 1 '45
Erechtheum, Athens bw 18:
57-9 Ja 1 '45

Parthenon bw 35:152-62 O 26
'54; 36:44 Ja 11 '54
Stoa of King Attalus, Athens
bw 41:165-72 S 17 '56
Temple of Neptune bw 16:12
Je 5 '44
Temple of Olympian Zeus bw
18:58 Ja 1 '45
Architecture--Greek Revival
Andalusia, Doric 39:58-9 Ag
29 '55
Hermitage, Tennessee 18:52
My 7 '45 bw 13:65 Jy 6 '42
Homes and other buildings
39:58-67 Ag 29 '55
Louisiana plantation houses
32:72-83 Je 9 '52
Mansion, Atlanta, Ga. 24:82
Je 7 '48
Philadelphia buildings 39:64-
5 Ag 29 '55
Rattle and Snap, Corinthian
39:58-9 Ag 29 '55
White. Hyde Park, New York
28:89-92 Ja 2 '50 bw 6:61-
7 My 29 '39; 20:89-92 Ap
15 '46
Architecture--Heating and Venti-
lating
Bridger and Paxton. Solar-
heated office building, Al-
buerque, N. Mex. bw 41:
71 D 17 '56
Waterfilm roof as insulation
bw 20:81-3 Je 3 '46
Architecture--Indian (North A-
merican)
Adobe pueblo, Taos, N. Mex.,
c 1700 40:47 Ja 16 '56
Cliff house, Flagstaff, Ariz.
40:47 Ja 16 '56
San Ildefonso pueblo, N. Mex.
8:71 My 13 '40
Architecture--Industrial
Ferguson Company wall-less
factory, Corpus Christi,
Texas bw 28:10-2 Ja 9
'50
Fisher and Fisher. Ideal Cement Company, Boettcher,
Colo. 36:33 Ja 4 '54

Holabird, Root and Burgee.
Armour's pharmaceutical
center, Kankakee, Ill. 36:
31 Ja 4 '54
Parker Pen Factory, Janes-
ville, Wis. 36:33 Ja 4 '54
Skidmore, Owings and Merrill.
H. J. Heinz Vinegar factory,
Pittsburgh, Pa. 36:35 Ja 4
'54
Standard Oil Company of Indiana, Whiting, Ind. 36:36 Ja
4 '54
United Biscuit Company, Mel-
rose Park, Ill. 36:34 Ja 4
'54
Wright. Heliolab, S. C. John-
son and Son research lab-
oratory, Racine, Wis. 29:
8-10 D 11 '50
Architecture--Landscape See
Gardens; Landscape Garden-
ing; Parks
Architecture--Library
Garber and Associates. Cin-
cinnati public library, Ohio
bw 39:91 Mr 28 '55
Architecture--Mayan
Temples, public buildings 22:
100 F 24 '47; 22:51-67 Je
30 '47; 34:70-1 Ap 27 '53
Architecture--Moravian
Old Salem, Winston-Salem,
N.C. 37:166-7 O 25 '54
Architecture--Muhammadan
Baha'k temple, Chicago bw
29:159 D 11 '50
Blue mosque, Istanbul bw
8:82-3 Ap 8 '40
Cathedral, Cordova, Spain
38:75 My 9 '55
Dome of the Rock (Mosque of
Omar), Jerusalem 6:54 My
15 '39; 20:58 Ap 1 '46; 38:
78-9 My 9 '55 bw 31:61 D
D 24 '51
Marrakesh Villa 29:96-7 N
6 '50
Mecca 38:76 My 9 '55 bw 2:
62-3 Mr 15 '37

Moslem mosque, Seringapa-
tem, India bw 10:94 My 12
'41
Mosque of the Shah, Isfahan,
Iran 38:72 My 9 '55
Royal palace, Teheran bw 20:
35 Ap 8 '46
Architecture--Prefabricated
Acorn house. Koch 26:70-2
Ja 24 '49
Unistrut steel structure bw
38:69-70 My 9 '55
Architecture--Prehistoric
Stonehenge 40:78 My 19 '56
Architecture--Renaissance
Arena chapel 25:Cover, 34-
57 D 27 '48
Blenheim palace, England
24:32 Ap 19 '48
Brancacci chapel 39:22-3
D 26 '55
Compton Wynyates, Warwick-
shire, England bw 19:97
O 29 '45
Hatfield house, England 19:
106 O 29 '45; 41:156-7 N
5 '56
Medici-Riccardi palace bw
19:52 D 24 '45
St. Peter's, Rome bw 20:31-
3, 36-7 Mr 11 '46; 27:49
Ag 1 '49
Versaille, France air-views
8:64 Je 3 '40 bw 5:39 S 26
'38　Royal chapel 23:86
S 15 '47
Villa d' Este, Italy 28:78-9
My 8 '50
Wollaton Hall, England 10:
100 O 29 '45
Architecture--Revolving Con-
struction
Hotel, Atami, Japan--rotat-
ing top story bw 40:111 F
6 '56
Morse. Cullen and Foreman
office building, Grand
Junction, Colo. 38:133 F
7 '55

St. Benedict the Moor church,
Washington, D.C.--revolv-
ing altar bw 34:95-6 Mr 16
'53
Architecture--Roman
Arch of Constantine bw 5:59
Jy 18 '38
Arch of Titus bw 16:13 Je 5
'44; 17:95 S 4 '44
Claudian aqueduct bw 16:13
Je 5 '44
The Colosseum, Rome 27:44
Ag 1 '49 bw 17:95 S 4 '44
Landmarks in Provence,
France 35:76-85 Jy 13 '53
Pantheon, Rome bw 16:12
Je 5 '44
Port Nigra. Trier, Germany,
14 B.C. bw 17:85 O 9 '44
Roman aqueduct, Smyrna bw
8:81 Ap 8 '40
Roman bath, Bath, England
40:85 Mr 19 '56
Temple of Vesta, Rome bw
17:94 S 4 '44
Temples, arches, aqueducts,
towers bw 16:12-3 Je 5 '44
Architecture--Schools
Caudill, Rowlett, Scott and
Associates. Elementary
school plan, sketches bw
36:74-80 F 1 '54
Perkins and Will. Heathcote
elementary school, Scars-
dale, N.Y. bw 37:73 N 15
'54
Perkins and Will. Junior high
school plans, sketches bw
36:74-80 F 1 '54
Sakamota. Fujimi girls high
school, Tokyo bw 38:79-81
Mr 14 '55
Architecture--Spanish
Puebla cathedral, Puebla,
Mexico 6:33 Ja 23 '39
U.S. Southwest 40:48-50 Ja
16 '56
"Wave" architecture, Barce-
lona bw 2:40 F 22 '37
Architecture--Theaters and
Auditoriums

Coliseum, Spokane, Wash.
bw 38:71-3 Ja 10 '55
The Colosseum, Rome 27:44
Ag 1 '49 bw 17:95 S 4 '44
Corn palace, Mitchell, S.
Dak. 38:77 Ja 3 '55
Parabolic-arch fair building,
Raleigh, N.C. 36:34-5 Ja
4 '54
Architecture--Tudor
English country houses 41:
154-61 N 5 '56 bw 19:97,
102-3 O 29 '45
Architecture--Victorian
Age of gilded opulence 40:86-
8 Mr 5 '56
Gould mansion, New York
City bw 13:140-1 D 7 '42
Arcieri, Eugene
Brenda 16:46 Ja 3 '44
Arcimboldo, School of.
Summer (Reclining woman of
fruit and vegetables) bw
7:24 Ag 28 '39
Arden Gallery, New York City
Outdoor sculpture--then and
now, 1850-1941, exhibit
bw 10:118-21 Ap 21 '41
Ardizzone, Edward
Caricatures of British army
officers in Middle East bw
15:55-6 N 29 '43
Prelude to battle 26:60 Mr
21 '49
The arena. lithograph Oliviera
33:84 Jy 14 '52
Arena chapel, Padua
Giotto. Life of Christ and
Mary frescoes 25:Cover,
34-57 D 27 '48
Ares See Mythological Themes
--Mars
Arezzo, Italy
Piero della Francesca. Story
of the true cross, San
Francesco frescoes 20:60-
8 Ap 22 '46
Argentina
Campos. Argentina: pampas
and gaucho painting 4:34-5
Je 20 '38

Coast of Argentina, French
map, 1547 24:79 Mr 22 '48
(maps)
Ariadne See Mythological
Themes--Ariadne
Ariel. sculpture bw, Dome, Bank
of England, London 21:101
O 21 '46
Arizona, University of. Art gal-
lery collection of paintings
20:76-80 F 18 '46
"Ark Royal" (ship) English flag-
ship, 1588 bw 41:152 N 5
'56
L'Arlesienne. bw van Gogh 27:
82 O 10 '49
"Armed" (race horse). Reeves
24:101 Ap 12 '48
Armed freedom. sculpture, Cap-
itol Dome, Washington,
D.C. Crawford 16:56 Mr
20 '44; cast bw 19:9 S 24'45
Armida
Van Dyck, A. Rinaldo and
Armida 4:21 Ap 11 '38
Armor
Breastplate, French bw 40:
44 Ja 9 '56
Composite, mail and plate,
suit, 15th century 40:184
Ap 9 '56
Gold embossed helmet and
suit, Antwerp, c1565 bw
31:22 S 24 '51
Knight and horse armor, Ger-
man, 15th century 40:184-
5 Ap 9 '56
Medieval armor, Hearst col-
lection bw 5:49 N 28 '38
Plate, Gothic style 40:185 Ap
9 '56
Polish, 17th century 35:93 D
14 '53
Steel, Italy, 15th century bw
6:51 Mr 20 '39
Steel with velvet pantaloons,
England, c1590 bw 6:52 Mr
20 '39

Headcoverings
Basinets, great and visored

40:186-7 Ap 9 '56
Edwards Helmet for U.S.
Navy bw 13:82-3 Ag 10
'42
Gold engraved, Sumerian 40:
93 Je 4 '56
Jousting helm 40:187 Ap 9
'56
Ram's head crested bronze
helmet, Greek, 700 B.C.
29:23 D 25 '50
Roman's helmet bw 40:84 Mr
19 '56
Royal helmet, Anglian, 7th
century 31:83 Jy 16 '51
Sallett 40:186 Ap 9 '56

Shields
Anglian King's shield, 7th
century 31:85 Jy 16 '51
Turkish, 17th century 35:96
D 14 '53
Armory Show, New York City,
1913 Examples of painting,
sculpture 28:58-63 Ja 2
'50
Showroom bw 26:89 F 21 '49
Armour Laboratories, Kankakee,
Ill. Holabird, Root and Bur-
gee 36:31 Ja 4 '54
Arms, Coats of See Heraldry
Armstrong, Rolf
Toast of the town 18:46 Ja 1
'45
Army recruits (copy). Savitzki
14:45 Mr 29 '43
Arno, Peter
"Man in the shower" cartoons
bw 17:80-1 N 27 '44
"Peter Arno's Cartoon Re-
vue" cartoons bw 11:8-9,
11 O 13 '41
Arnold, Benedict
Peggy Shippen (Mrs. Bene-
dict Arnold) bw 29:54 Jy
3 '50
Arnold and Andre meet bw
29: 54 Jy 3 '50 port.
Benedict Arnold bw 35:92 S
28 '53 engraving bw 29:
54 Jy 3 '50 port.

Benedict Arnold's charge 29:
48-9 Jy 3 '50 port.
Arnold, Peggy (Shippen)
Arnold, B. Peggy Shippen (Mrs.
Benedict Arnold) bw 29:54
Jy 3 '50
Mrs. Benedict Arnold bw 35:
92 S 28 '53
Arnold, Mrs. Harry
Bellows. Mrs. Harry Arnold
41:162 D 24 '56
Arnold, Matthew
Matthew Arnold photog bw 22:
56 Mr 24 '47
Arnolfini, Giovanni
Van Eyck, J. Giovanni Arnol-
fini and his wife 33:36 D 29
'52
Arnould, Reynold
Camille Renault: portrait in
different styles bw 27:103-
4 N 7 '49
Around the campfire. Remington
13:75 S 14 '42
Arp, Jean
Vegetable symmetry 33:96 O
27 '52
Mili. Jean Arp, age 61 photog
27:91 D 12 '49 port.
Newman. Jean Arp photog
35:20 D 7 '53 port.
Arrangement in black and white
(Whistler's model, Maude
Franklin). Whistler 36:94
My 17 '54
Arrangement in flesh color and
black (Theodore Duret).
Whistler 36:95 My 17 '54
bw 6:54 Mr 20 '39
Arrangement in gray and black,
no. 1 (Mother). Whistler
5:29 O 31 '38
Arrest no. 2. Billings 4:27 Je
13 '38
Arrival of Joseph and Mary at
Bethlehem. Brueghel,
Pieter, the elder 37:Cover,
30-3 D 27 '54
Art   This heading includes
painting as well as general
art. See also Architecture;

Mural Painting; Prints;
Sculpture; and minor arts,
such as Bronzes; Carving;
Ceramics; Furniture;
Glassware; Jewelry;
Metalwork; Tapestry;
Textiles
Art, African
Belgian Congo paintings 34:
106-7 My 4 '53
Sculpture: portraits, masks,
household articles, fig-
ures bw 22:116-25 S 8 '52
Vatican holy year exhibit of
painting and sculpture bw
29:63, 66 S 4 '50
Art, Amateur See also names
of artists, as Churchill,
W.; Eisenhower, D.
"Art News" amateur compe-
tition painting 30:71-5 Ap
16 '51
Attica, Kansas, painters 39:
81-8 Ag 22 '55
Businessmen as artists bw
16:37 My 1 '44
Congressmen as artists bw
20: 12-3, 15 My 6 '46
Dentists as sculptors bw 29:
147 S 18 '50
Ithaca, New York, painters
26:68-70 Ap 4 '49
Lawyers as artists 24:72-3
Ap 5 '48
Medieval murals by teen-
agers 35:76 S 21 '53
Motion picture actors as artists bw 24:64 Mr 1 '48
Palmer portrait kits--num-
bered art 35:105-6 S 14
'53
Physicians as artists 23:98-9
N 10 '47
Prisoners as artists
Amano. Prison life in Si-
beria labor camp 29:
65-7 N 6 '50
Japanese prisoners. Life
in Sugamo Prison wood
blocks 34:10-1 F 16
'53

Prisoners as artists (cont.)
Watton. German prison
camp scenes sketches
bw 13:138-41 N 9 '42
Psychotics as artists 5:26-7
O 24 '38
Sculptures by amateurs 21:108
Jy 8 '46
Soldiers as artists--clay sculp-
ture bw 14:56, 58 Mr 1 '43
"Washington wives" as artists
bw 36:81-2 Je 21 '54
Wisconsin rural artists 10:76-
8 Mr 31 '41
Art, American
Addison Gallery American
paintings 12:58-63 Je 15 '42
American art, Golden Gate
International Exposition 6:
27-30 F 13 '39
American painting exhibit--
Colonial to present, Carne-
gie Institute 9:74-9 D 9 '40
American primitive artists
31:68-75 Jy 2 '51
American primitive portraits,
Garbisch collection, Na-
tional Gallery, Washington,
D.C. 39:95-6 Je 28 '54
America's arts and skills
   I.   Colonial period 38:108-
        31 Ap 18 '55
  II.   Revolutionary period
        38:56-69 My 30 '55
 III.   Age of homespun 39:54-
        65 Jy 18 '55
  IV.   Greek revival 39:58-67
        Ag 29 '55
   V.   Romantic decades 39:
        98-111 O 17 '55
  VI.   Fabulous frontier 39:
        74-87 N 28 '55
 VII.   Timeless southwest 40:
        46-59 Ja 16 '56
VIII.   Age of gilded opulence
        40:86-99 Mr 5 '56
  IX.   Beauty in tools of today
        40:96-114 My 21 '56
Art Students League of New York,
alumni photog 29:172-3 O 16
'50

Artists for Victory, Metropoli-
tan Museum exhibit 14:42-7
Mr 8 '43
California painters--8 con-
temporaries 11:72-6 O 27
'41
Colonial portraits 26:84-5 F
28 '49
Conservative vs modern Los
Angeles County Museum--
exhibit of local artists
bw 22:40 Je 16 '47
Metropolitan Museum--
first U.S. painting com-
petition 30:34-8 Ja 15
'51
Contemporary landscapes
23:67-70 Jy 14 '47
Downtown Gallery, New York
City, painters bw 32:87-8
Mr 17 '52
Expatriate painters 36:92-9
My 17 '54
Italy, 1830-70 and post-
World War II 33:88-96 S
15 '52
Paris, 1953 35:114-6 Jy
13 '53
Harvest paintings 13:44-8 Ag
31 '42
Highlights of 1938 art season
on 57th Street 4:24-9 Je
13 '38
History of American art--
Colonial to moderns of
West 5:27-38 O 31 '38
Hudson River School 19:82-6
S 10 '45
Life in America, 1616-1916,
Metropolitan Museum ex-
hibit 6:26-31 Je 19 '39
"LIFE's" defense paintings
by 7 major artists 11:60-
4 Jy 7 '41
"LIFE's" ten years of Ameri-
can painting: 25 paintings
reproduced in LIFE, 1936-
1946 21:72-80 N 25 '46
"LIFE's" war artists 11:60-
4 Jy 7 '41; 15:49-84 D 27
'43; 18:42-67 Ap 30 '45

Main trends in U.S. art since
1913 Armory Show, exhib-
it, Institute of Contempo-
rary Art, Boston 26:84-9 F
21 '49
Middle West art 34:143-55 My
18 '53
Modern U.S. art, University
of Nebraska exhibit 10:70-
5 Ap 14 '41
Mystic painters, Northwest
U.S. 35:84-9 S 28 '53
Negro prizewinners 21:62-5
Jy 22 '46
One hundred years of Ameri-
can taste, 1830-1930: popu-
lar paintings assembled by
Corcoran Gallery 27:56-62
Ag 29 '49
Opening of the West--paintings
of frontier life, pioneers,
Indians, miners 27:40-51
Jy 4 '49
Painting in the United States,
Carnegie Institute exhibit
1943: 16:75 Ap 24 '44
1955: 39:134-7 N 21 '55
Painting prizewinners of 1947-
48 season 24:103 Je 28 '48
Painting prizewinners major
U.S. shows 39:112-7 S 26
'55
Paintings by 19 U.S. painters
under 36 28:82-91 Mr 20
'50
Paintings: C. W. Peale to Demuth, Pennsylvania Acad-
emy of Fine Arts exhibit 38:
68-75 Mr 28 '55
Portrait painters, contemporary 10:46-8 F 3 '41 bw 41:
77-8 Ag 13 '56
Santa Fe artists 26:66-7 Mr
14 '49
Sixty American paintings,
Cranbrook Academy of Art
exhibit 8:64-71 My 27 '40
Tomorrow's masterpieces:
paintings of 250 contemporary artists sold in department stores 16:45-6 Ja 3 '44

U.S. Treasury Department
Section of Fine Arts.
Mural prizewinners: 10
commissions for public
buildings 10:42-6 Ja 27
'43
U.S Works Progress Ad-
ministration Children's
art 1:44 N 30 '36
Paintings sold in New York
City junk shop bw 16:
85 Ap 17 '44
Paintings started in Los
Angeles unit: General
MacArthur bw 13:51
Ag 17 '42
"Public Buildings," book
bw 8:61-7 Ap 1 '40
Webb Museum of American
arts and crafts 35:46-53
Jy 6 '53
Whitney Museum of American
art--outstanding paintings
12:73-5 Ap 20 '42
Art, Anglian
Sutton Hoo treasure: arms
and armor, jewelry,
drinking horn 7th century
31:82-5 Jy 16 '51
Art, Australian
Australian aboriginal paint-
ings 21:78 N 4 '46
Australian historical paint-
ings bw 12:78-9 F 9 '42
Art, British See Art, English
Art, Byzantine
Christ enthroned fresco bw
Spain, c1150 9:53 Jy 22
'40
Christ healing the blind
carved ivory c500 39:25
D 26 '55
Cross 6th century 33:130 O
20 '52
Early Christian mosaics;
frescoes bw Vatican Grot-
toes 28:65-78 Mr 27 '50
Head of Christ, Chora
church, Istanbul mosaic
29:54 D 25 '50

Art, Byzantine (cont.)
  Santa Sophia, Istanbul: archi-
    tecture, dome, mosaics
    29:54-61 D 25 '50
Art, Cambodian
  Cambodian jewelry, sculpture,
    architecture bw 5:35-9 Ag
    1 '38
Art, Canadian
  Historical scenes and portraits
    of Canada bw 9:112-5 S 9
    '40
Art, Children's
  Basile. Robinson Crusoe as
    a young man 1:44 N 30 '36
  Benevento. Circus parade
    1:44 N 30 '36
  Cooperative group-paintings
    33:83-5 S 29 '52
  Diagnostic aid to identify
    child's fears and frustra-
    tions 12:59-60 Je 8 '42
  French children's drawings
    for movie cartoon 36:62
    Je 14 '54
  Gifted children drawings of
    World War bw 9:45-6 Jy
    15 '40
  Hecht Company contest, Balti-
    more, Md. 37:75-6 D 20
    '54
  Japanese children's art 36:
    89-93 Mr 29 '54
  Kaptan. Paintings 32:85 My
    12 '52
  Liguore. Going to town 1:44
    N 30 '36
  Marsh. Fire, drawn at age
    7 bw 40:86 F 6 '56
  Novar. The butcher 1:44 N
    30 '36
  Shimada. Seated nude bw 28:
    104 Ja 23 '50
  Students of Augustus Peck 11:
    78-80 S 15 '41
  Wacker. Portraits bw 37:63-
    4 Ag 16 '54
  Young America paints, fourth
    annual exhibit of school
    children's art bw 6:46-7
    Ap 17 '39

Art, Chinese
  An album of Chinese paintings
    15:63-8 O 11 '43
  Buddhist scrolls and paint-
    ings 8:30-47 Ja 8 '40
  Cartoons by young Chinese
    artists 4:50-1 Ja 17 '38
  Festival on the Yellow River.
    Ch'ing Ming festival--33
    foot scroll 31:44-9 D 31
    '51
  Furniture, ceramics, scrolls,
    Philadelphia Museum of
    Art 31:72 S 3 '51
  Painting technique bw 4:65-6
    Mr 15 '43
  Paintings, religious figures
    38:64-81 Ap 4 '55
  Peiping architecture, sculp-
    ture, temple decoration
    20:67-77 Ap 29 '46
  Pettus collection of Chinese
    Christian art: Story of
    Christ 11:41-8 D 22 '41
  Woodcuts of Lu Hsun Acad-
    emy and others 18:57-60
    Ap 9 '45
Art, Collections See Galleries
  and Museums; Private Col-
  lections
Art, Dutch
  Great Dutch paintings in A-
    merica 5:30-5 Ag 29 '38
Art, Egyptian
  Alabaster sarcophagus 37:
    34 Ag 2 '54
  Arts: architecture, sculpture,
    painting, gold work--
    Nile Valley 24:74-85 Ja
    19 '48; 41:106-17 N 26 '56
  Egyptian taxpayers tomb
    painting bw 22:98 Mr 24
    '47
  Ivory whiphandle bw 1350 B.
    C. 6:52 Mr 20 '39
  Tomb of Ramesis VI murals
    c1100 B.C. 24:83 Ja 19
    '48
Art, English
  Britain's first navy 41:78-
    84 O 29 '56

British and French World War
paintings 9:57-9 Ag 12 '40
British war paintings, World
War 10:64-6 F 24 '41
Eighteenth century paintings
25:96-113 S 13 '48
Elizabethan England: portraits
and scenes 41:144-53 N 5
'56
England's greatest portraits
in America, 18th century
Huntington Library and Art
Gallery, San Marino, Calif.
4:23-9 Ja 24 '38
English landscape painting in
America, Huntington Li-
brary and Art Gallery, San
Marino, Calif. 5:42-4 S 12
'38
Kitchen sink school bw 40:163-
4 Ap 23 '56
Medieval England: portraits,
scenes 40:68-73 Ap 2 '40;
40:178-88 Ap 9 '40
Restoration England: portraits,
scenes 41:160-71 N 19 '56
Art, Eskimo
Carvings--stone, bone, ivory
bw 36:67-9 My 24 '54
Art, Etruscan
Etruscan art: bronzes, terra
cottas, gold work, ceramics,
sculpture, frescoes 40:58-
65 F 13 '56
Gold necklace, stone insets
c60 B.C. bw 9:94 D 9 '40
Art, Flemish
Great Flemish paintings in
America, 17th century 4:
20-4 Ap 11 '38
Art, French
British and French World War
paintings 9:57-9 Ag 12 '40
Eighteenth century paintings:
Watteau, Boucher, Fragon-
ard, Rigaud 23:79-86 S 15
'47
Eighteenth century paintings
in America 5:34-9 S 26 '38
French impressionists in A-
merica 5:24-9 O 10 '38

New French art--occupa-
tion and post-World War
17:72-6 N 13 '44
Parisian artists in New York
City 37:123-6 O 25 '54
Art, German
German World War art:
portraits of Cossack Di-
vision 28:67 F 20 '50
Germany's greatest painters
in America 5:38-40 Jy 11
'38
House of German Arts, Mu-
nich, fourth annual exhib-
it bw 9:96-7 S 23 '40
Post-World War artists of
Western Germany, the
New Berlin Group 36:143-
6 My 10 '54
Art, Greek
Corinth sculpture, art ob-
jects bw 5:50-3 Ag 15 '38
Dancing girls, Melos, c1340
B.C. terra cotta bw 23:
20 Jy 7 '47
Floor mosaic, Troy (Hissar-
lik), Turkey bw 13:102 N
16 '42
Greek figurine carvings, 5th
century B.C. bw 6:52 Mr
20 '39
Woman's head, Crete, c1500
B.C., fresco bw 23:21 Jy
7 '47
Art, Haitian
Contemporary primitive
paintings 23:58-61 S 1 '47
Four painters of Haiti 28:101
Mr 13 '50
Religious murals, Episcopal
cathedral, Port-au-Prince
33:64-5 D 22 '52
Art, Inca See Art, Pre-Colum-
bian
Art, Indian (American) See
also Art, Pre-Columbian
Altarpiece, Mission San Jose,
Laguna, N. Mex. 40:48-9
Ja 16 '56

Art, Indian (Amer.) (cont.)
  Santos: Death; Our Lady of
    Sorrows; Saint Acacius
    woodcarvings bw 24:57-8,
    60 My 17 '48
  Southwest Indians: blankets,
    baskets, jewelry, pottery
    40:54-5 Ja 16 '56
  Tlinglit Indians, Alaska.
    Carved cedar screen, c1825
    41:53 Jy 16 '56
Art, Indian (East Indian)
  Bridal painting 31:155 N 5 '51
  European man, 17th century
    24:82 My 22 '48
  Indian art: architecture, sculp-
    ture, carriages bw 9:69-73
    N 25 '40
  Indian art: Buddha and Buddh-
    ism 38:Cover, 80-9 Mr 7
    '55
  Rama-Lila pageant, giant ef-
    figies of Gods and Devils,
    New Delhi 30:90-5 F 12 '51
  Temples, parade floats of
    Jagannath bw 3:60-1 Ag 16
    '37
Art, Italian
  "Andrea Doria" (ship) murals
    34:58-9 Je 22 '53
  Contemporary Italian painters
    depict "Work" bw 29:14-6
    O 30 '50
  Fascist art prizewinning paint-
    ings bw 7:35-6 Ag 21 '39
  Italian renaissance masters
    in America 4:27-30 Mr 21
    '38
Art, Japanese
  Abstract art of Japan 32:98-
    101 Je 23 '52
  Early Christian relics bw 20:
    93-4 Mr 25 '46
  "The 47 Ronin" scenes by Ho-
    kusai; Hiroshige 15:53-6
    N 1 '43 bw 18:97 Ap 16 '45
  Ivory chessmen; mice bw 8:
    48 Ja 29 '40
  Japanese children's drawings
    36:89-93 Mr 29 '54

Japanese prisoners. Life in
    Sugamo Prison wood
    blocks 34:10-1 F 16 '53
  Japanese war artists. Pa-
    cific victories, 1941 28:
    65, 67-70 F 27 '50; 39:
    52 Ag 15 '55
  "Meriken Shinshi," illus-
    trated history of U.S.,
    1853 bw 25:6-8 Ag 2 '48
  Netsukes 37:15 Jy 2 '54
  Nusa, staff with inscribed
    streamers bw 18:94 F 19
    '45
  Paintings and sculpture from
    14 centuries 34:94-101 Ap
    20 '53
  Paintings of Perry's visit,
    1853 bw 19:55-6 S 17 '45
  Paintings, sculpture, archi-
    tecture, landscaping,
    masks 31:58-69 D 31 '51
Art, Latin American
  Sao Paulo exhibit of paintings
    and sculpture 36:78-84 My
    31 '54
Art, Medieval
  Medieval primitive paintings,
    Europe, 13th-15th centu-
    ries 4:28-30 F 7 '38
  Middle Ages: architecture,
    stained glass, manuscripts,
    sculpture, tapestry, prints
    22:67-85 Ap 7 '47; 22:65-
    83 My 26 '47
Art, Mesopotamian
  Ashurnasirpal winged lion
    sculpture bw 6:53 Mr 20
    '39
  Assyrian bas-reliefs bw 32:
    151 Ap 21 '52
  Assyrian taxpayers frieze bw
    22:98 Mr 24 '47
  Black obelisk of Shalmanesar,
    Babylon bw 24:147 Mr 15
    '48
  Hittite sphinx, Ankara sculp-
    ture bw 8:81 Ap 8 '40
  Royal standard of Ur, Sume-
    rian mosaic panels 40:90-
    1 Je 4 '56

Sumerian art: mosaics, gold-
work, sculpture 40:80-93
Je 4 '56
Wrestler vase, Sumerian bw
5:59 Ag 15 '38
Art, Mexican
Fifteen Mexican painters,
Valentine Gallery, New
York City 4:28-30 Mr 14
'38
Modern Mexican art--post-
revolution painters 20:58-
60 Je 3 '46
Art, Modern
Armory Show, 1913 28:58-63
Ja 2 '50
"LIFE's" roundtable discus-
sion: critics and connois-
seurs on modern art 25:56-
68 O 11 '48
Paintings of Stuart Davis and
other abstractionists in
U.S. 22:78-81 F 17 '47
Art, Moorish
The Alhambra, buildings and
gardens photogs 33:52 Ag
18 '52
Necklace, gold filigree and
cloisonne, c1340 bw 9:94
D 9 '40
Art, Negro
Negro prizewinners, U.S. 21:
62-5 Jy 22 '46
Art, Oriental
Religious sculpture and paint-
ings, Vatican holy year ex-
hibit bw 29:63, 66 S 4 '50
Art, Persian
Gold and enamel plate 33:43
D 29 '52
Gold jewelled dagger, 19th
century 33:43 D 29 '52
Kashan ceramic dish and jug,
12th century 20:92 Je 24
'46
Mulk. Mr. Churchill and his
friends overthrowing Hitler
and his 35:70 N 9 '53
Persepolis, 515 B.C. photogs
bw 35:155-8 N 23 '53

Persian art: bronzes, manuscript illuminations, ce-
ramics 20:90-2 Je 24 '46
Persian taxpayers bas-relief
bw 22:98 Mr 24 '47
Plate of Khosru II, carved
medallions on gold, 600
33:42 D 29 '52
Art, Polish
Polish art in Canada: tapestry, arms and armor,
vestments 35:92-9 D 14
'53
Art, Pre-Columbian
Andean art: paintings, ceramics, metal work, tex-
tiles, feather work 36:
100-5 Ap 12 '54
Aztec calendar drawing bw
6:29 Ja 23 '39
Aztec calendar stone bw 18:
41 Ja 1 '45
Bonampak mural, Mayan 27:
80-4 N 21 '49
Columbian gods and warrior
sculpture bw 5:58 Ag 15
'38
Feathered serpent, Toltec
sculpture bw 28:62 Ja 9
'50
Gold work--Mexico; Panama
33:130 O 20 '52
Inca art: gold work, textiles,
feather work bw 36:25-6
Ap 5 '54
Macchu Picchu ruins, Cuzco,
Peru 25:55 Ag 2 '48 bw
19:101-9 S 24 '45
Mayan art: architecture,
sculpture, ceramics,
painting 22:51-67 Je 30
'47
Mayan figure, Chichen Itza
22:Cover Je 30 '47
Olmec head sculpture bw
28:89 My 29 '50
Pre-Columbian art: mask,
pottery, gold work 18:49
Je 4 '45
Quetzalcoatl mosaic mask
bw 24:84 Mr 22 '48

Art, Pre-Columbian (cont)
  Temple of Quetzalcoatl, Teo-
    tihuacan, Toltec bw 4:57
    Ap 11'38; 22:100 F 24 '47
  Temple of the Inscriptions,
    Palenque, Mayan bw 34:70-
    1 Ap 27 '53
  Toltec idols, Tula sculpture
    bw 22:101 F 24 '47
Art, Russian
  Coronation of Alexander II,
    1856 series of paintings
    38:60-7 Ja 31 '55
  Davies' collection of Russian
    paintings 14:44-7 Mr 29
    '43
  Ice sculptures in Sokolniki
    Park, Moscow bw 6:7-8
    Ja 16 '39
  Russian posters of World War
    13:10-1, 13 Ag 24 '42
  Soviet paintings, Tretyakov
    Gallery, Moscow bw 38:
    147-8 My 16 '55
Art, South Seas
  Balinese animals and figures
    woodcarving bw 15:114-6
    O 25 '43
  Balinese sculpture and paint-
    ing 3:51 S 27 '37
  South Seas art: paintings,
    masks, headdresses, sculp-
    ture 21:76-83 N 4 '46
Art, Spanish
  Great Spanish paintings in
    America 4:40-4 My 16 '38
  The Prado, Madrid, cele-
    brated paintings 31:58-72
    O 1 '51
Art, Student
  Addison Gallery student ex-
    hibit from 25 American art
    schools 25:98-101 D 6 '48
  Art students' portraits of
    Gene Tierney, from photo-
    graph, age 3 28:129, 131
    Ap 17 '50
  Cape Cod art schools 23:64-7
    Jy 28 '47
  Carnegie Institute's 14th an-
    nual exhibit of high school

  art 10:56-9 Je 16 '41
Art, Sumerian See Art, Meso-
  potamian
Art, Tibetan
  Bodhisatva bw 38:92 Mr 7
    '55
  Kigu banner of Buddha as
    Messiah 6:25 Je 12 '39
  Lord Buddha's farewell,
    Persian-Chinese fresco
    6:26 Je 12 '39
Art, Toltec See Art, Pre-Co-
  lumbian
Art, Venetian
  Doge's palace, Senate cham-
    ber photog bw 23:50 Ag
    4 '47
  St. Mark's, with details of
    mosaics and sculpture
    35:28-35 D 28 '53
  Venetian art: paintings, prints,
    glassware 23:46, 50-61 Ag
    4 '47
Art, Western
  History of Western Cultures:
    paintings, sculpture,
    other arts, Renaissance
    to 1848 Mr 3 '47- N 22 '48
Art Cleaning and Restoration
  Botticelli. Three miracles of
    Zenobias bw 21:104-5 O
    28 '46
  Christ of the Depths, Porto-
    fino, Italy sculpture bw
    39:48 Ag 22 '55
  Fresco, Church, Viterbo,
    Italy bw 21:103 O 28 '46
  Goertschacher, Ecco Homo
    bw 9:108-9 D 2 '40
  Goya. Duchess of Alba bw
    26:86 Mr 28 '49
  Hooch. Garden scene bw 3:
    112 O 18 '37
  Jordaens. The king drinks
    bw 6:23 Ja 23 '39
  Kolbe. The large sitting wo-
    man sculpture bw 31:81 S
    24 '51
  Kuan Yin, Chinese, 12th cen-
    tury sculpture 41:73 S 3
    '56

Rembrandt. Night watch bw
21:106 O 28 '46
Tintoretto. Madonna and
Child bw 24:68 Ja 26 '48
Art Galleries and Museums
"Greek slave" exhibited in
New York, 1857 bw 19:8
S 24 '45; 27:56 Ag 29 49
Morse. Gallery of the Louvre
17:62 D 18 '44
Palazzo Colonna photog 27:53
Ag 1 '49
Stieglitz. Studio-Salon 291
photog bw 14:7 Ap 5 '43
Teniers. Archduke Leopold
in his gallery 27:62-3 O
24 '49
W. H. Vanderbilt Gallery,
New York bw 27:56 Ag 29
'49
Wright. Spiral design for
modern (Guggenheim) gal-
lery, New York bw 19:12-
5 O 8 '45
Additional listings of Art Gal-
leries and Museums will be found
under the name of the institution:
Addison Gallery; Arden Gal-
lery; Arizona, University of,
Art Gallery; Boston Museum
of Fine Arts; Brooklyn Museum; Carnegie Institute; Chicago Art Institute; Cincinnati
Art Museum; Clay Club; Cleveland Museum; Corcoran Gal-
lery; Cranbrook Academy of
Art; de Young Museum; De-
troit Institute of Arts; Dresden Gallery; Du Pont Museum;
Farnsworth Art Museum;
Frick Gallery; Galerie des
Beaux Arts; Graham Gallery;
Huntington Library and Art
Gallery; Institute of Contem-
porary Art; Kaiser Friedrich
Museum; Los Angeles County
Museum; Louvre; Metropoli-
tan Museum of Art; National
Gallery, Washington, D.C.;
National Museum, Stockholm;
Nelson Gallery of Art; North

Carolina Museum of Art;
Philadelphia Museum of Art;
Phillips Gallery; Prado;
Rhode Island School of De-
sign; St. Louis' City Art Mu-
seum; Syracuse Museum of
Fine Arts; Tate Gallery;
Toledo (Ohio) Art Museum;
Valentine Gallery; Vatican;
Virginia Museum of Fine
Arts; Webb Museum; Whitney
Museum; Widener Collection
"Art News" amateur competition
paintings 30:71-5 Ap 16 '51
Art Objects
Duchamp. Why not sneeze
(lumps of marble in cage)
32:103 Ap 28 '52
Object of destruction bw 34:
24 My 25 '53
Oppenheim. Fur-lined teacup
bw 1:24 D 14 '36
Ray, Man. Gift bw 34:25 My
25 '53
Wooden head bw 34:24 My
25 '53
Art on the beach bw 3:126 O 4
'37
Art Reproductions
Alva Studios, New York City
sculpture 38:115-6 Ap 25
'55
Art Students League of New
York. Famous alumni and
their work 29:172-3 O 16
'50
Arthur, Chester A.
Chester A. Arthur photog
bw 9:8 Ag 5 '40
Arthur, King of Britain
King Arthur relief bw Mo-
dena cathedral, 12th cen-
tury 40:93 Mr 19 '56
King Arthur tapestry Paris,
14th century 22:80-1 Ap
7 '47
Tintagel castle, Cornwall,
England, legendary birth-
place of King Arthur
photog 40:90-1 Mr 19 '56
bw 14:76 Je 14 '43

Arthur, Revington
 Monhegan Harbor, Maine 29:
 72 Ag 21 '50
Arthur, Timothy Shay
 "Ten Nights in a Barroom"
 (book), title page, scenes
 bw 32:63-4 Mr 17 '52
Artigas, Jose
 Jose Artigas statue bw Bo-
 gata, Columbia 29:74 O 9
 '50
Artillerymen in the desert.
 Berry 26:59 Mr 21 '49
Artis, William E.
 Draped head sculpture bw 21:
 63 Jy 22 '46
The artist and his studio.
 Vermeer 27:71 O 24 '49 bw
 5:30 Ag 29 '38; 16:63 Ja
 10 '44
Artists See also entries followed
 by port. under names of
 artists
 Aitken. World's great artists
 frieze bw 68 portraits 4:
 36-7 Ja 3 '38
 Prendergast. Young American artist 20:79 F 18 '46
Artists, Blind
 Blind sculptors and their
 work, San Francisco bw
 29:83 O 2 '50
 Cohen, blind artist, at work
 36:169-70 My 3 '54
Artists at Work See also entries
 followed by port. under
 names of artists
 Bohrod. Crowd of artists*
 25:66 Ag 23 '48
 Bouche. Mural assistant 6:
 28 F 13 '39
 Bread-and-butter jobs 36:89-
 92 Ja 25 '54
 Cartoonists at work bw 36:114
 Ap 26 '54
 Eakins, S. Thomas Eakins at
 work 16:72 My 15 '44
 Eakins, T. William Rush carving his allegorical figure
 of the Schuylkill River 16:
 73 My 15 '44 bw 5:29 O

31 '38
 Eau Claire, Wisconsin, artists bw 34:151 My 18 '53
 Hogfeldt. Painter and cherub
 model* 17:57 Jy 3 '44
 Koch. Children painting 29:
 Cover D 25 '50
 Ku Yuan. Yenan art academy
 woodcut bw 18:60 Ap 9 '45
 Peirce, W. Anna turns
 painter 19:85 N 12 '45
 Pratt. The American school
 6:31 Je 19 '39
 Renoir. Monet at Argenteuil
 32:93 My 19 '52
 St. Ives, Cornwall fishing
 village, artists photogs
 29:44-7 Ag 14 '50
 Vagnetti. Artists at work*
 bw 29:16 O 30 '50
 Vermeer. The artist in his
 studio 27:71 O 24 '49 bw
 5:30 Ag 29 '38; 16:63 Ja
 10 '44
The artist's brother. bw Rem-
 brandt 28:58 Ja 30 '50
The artist's daughters. Peale,
 Rembrandt 12:65 Mr 20
 '42
The artist's dream. Watteau
 5:37 S 26 '38
The artist's father. bw Rembrandt 28:58 Ja 30 '50
Artist's father listening to guitarist, Pagans. Degas 25:
 79 N 1 '48
"Artists for Victory," modern
 American painters and
 sculptors exhibit, Metropolitan Museum 14:42-7
 Mr 8 '43
The artist's wife. Clemens 18:
 76 My 14 '45
The artist's wife. bw Picasso
 16:79 Ap 24 '44
Artzybasheff, Boris
 Gods and goddesses of Hindu-
 ism 38:67-9 F 7 '55
 "Time" cover portraits 17:
 59-66 D 11 '44

Versions of Nazi swastika 13:
11 S 14 '42
War machines as human be-
ings gouache 11:10-3 N 3
'41
Christmas tree bw 19:9 D 24
'45 (drawing)
Machine tools 34:59-61 Ja 5
'53 (drawing)
Boris Artzybasheff photog bw
11:11 N 3 '41; 13:11 S 14
'42 port.
Arundel castle, England, 1433
photog bw 15:101 N 15 '43;
23:134-5 S 8 '47
As the Earth sings. sculpture bw
Swallow 14:42 Mr 8 '43
Asbury, Francis
Francis Asbury statue bw
Drew University, Madison,
N.J. 23:116 N 10 '47
Ascension Island scenes, World
War. Hurd 18:62-3 Ap 30 '45
Ascetic. woodcarving bw Steig
6:36 Ap 10 '39
Ashes are flowers. Ernst 32:58
Ja 21 '52
Ashlawn, Virginia. photog bw
Jefferson, archt. 14:70
Ap 12 '43
Ashurnasirpal II, King of Assyria
Ashurnasirpal bas-relief bw
Nimrud, Iraq 32:151 Ap 21
'52
Ashurnasirpal winged lion sculp-
ture bw Mesopotamia, c850
B.C. 6:53 Mr 20 '39
Asquith, Herbert Henry
Henry Asquith 24:53 Ap 26 '48
Assassination of President Lin-
coln. bw Currier and Ives
print 5:7 Jy 11 '38
Assassination of Umberto I,
King of Italy bw 20:28 Je
24 '46
Assumption See Mary, Virgin--
Assumption
Assy church, France
Decorations by France's lead-
ing artists: facade mo-
saics, stained glass, altar

tapestry 28:72-6 Je 19 '50
Astaire, Fred and Adele
Fred and Adele Astaire,
1915 photog bw 11:78 Ag
25 '41
The Astors of New York, 1870.
Rossi 25:92 O 18 '48
The astronomer. Martinez 20:
60 Je 3 '46
At high tide. Haines 12:39 Mr
2 '42
At la mie. Toulouse-Lautrec
28:99 My 15 '50
At Noank. Dirk 16:46 Ja 3 '44
At the blackboard. Rosenthal
15:66 N 22 '43
At the cafe. Toulouse-Lautrec
15:68 S 20 '43
At the loom. American primi-
tive, c1795 24:68 Mr 1 '48
At the Moulin Rouge. Bonnard
25:53 Jy 26 '48
At the Moulin Rouge. Toulouse-
Lautrec 28:98-9 My 15 '50
At the races. Degas 40:74-5
My 28 '56
At the sepulcher. Angelico 21:
61 D 23 '46
Ataturk, Mustapha Kemal
Ataturk equestrian statue bw
Ankara, Turkey 8:76 Ap
8 '40
Ates, Nejla
Manca. Nejla Ates sculpture
bw 38:129 Je 6 '55
Athena See Mythological Themes
--Athena
Athena Victorious, temple
Athens photog bw 18:56
Ja 1 '45
Athens, Georgia
Dodd. View of Athens 27:64-
5 S 26 '49
Athens, Greece
Parthenon frieze photog
bw 36:44 Ja 11 '54
Stoa of King Attalus, c150
B.C. photog bw 41:165-
72 S 17 '56

Athens, Greece (contined)
Temple and buildings of an-
cient Athens photogs bw
18:53-9 Ja 1 '45
Atherton, Gertrude
Gertrude Atherton photogs bw
21:95 N 11 '46
Athletes See Acrobats; Games
and Sports
Atkinson, Brooks
Newman. Brooks Atkinson
photog bw 35:18-9 D 17 '53
Atlanta, Georgia
Georgian and baroque man-
sions: Pine Ridge, Try-
geveson, others photogs
24:75-82 Je 7 '48
"Atlantic" (locomotive), Balti-
more and Ohio, 1832 25:
13 S 27 '48
Atlantic cable
Dudley. Awaiting the reply
6:30 Je 19 '39
Atlantic Ocean map, 1513. bw
Waldseemuller 18:61 My
21 '45
Atlantide. sculpture bw Mestro-
vic 22:135 Je 2 '47
Atlas. sculpture, Rockefeller
Center Lawrie 4:52 Je 27
'38
Atom-smasher 3:37 Ag 30 '37
Attack on an emigrant train.
Wimar 27:43 Jy 4 '49
Attack on Fort Moultrie 29:56-
7 Jy 3 '50
Attack on the supply wagon.
Remington 13:76 S 14 '42
Attacks on the Catholic church.
Flemish artist, c1550 24:
64-5 Je 14 '48
Atzerodt, George
George Atzerodt photog bw
4:46 F 14 '38
Aubusson, France
Lurcat tapestry factory 21:
80-4 S 30 '46
Rug photog bw 27:56-7 O 3
'49
Auden, William H.
Lynes. William Auden photog

bw 27:16 O 10 '49
Audubon, John James
Baltimore oriole 3:42 Jy 12
'37
Black squirrel 30:47 Ja 29
'51
Blue jay 3:39 Jy 12 '37
Canada lynx 9:115 O 21 '40
Carolina parakeets 7:60 N
27 '39
Collared peccary 30:48 Ja
29 '51
Cross fox 9:115 O 21 '40
Flying squirrels 9:115 O 21
'40
Golden eagle 3:40 Jy 12 '37
Mink 9:115 O 21 '40
Passenger-pigeons 7:60 N
27 '39
Quadruped plates from "Au-
dubon's America" 9:115
O 21 '40
Red fox 30:48 Ja 29 '51
Ruby-throated hummingbird
3:41 Jy 12 '37
Wild cat 30:49 Ja 29 '51
Wild turkey 5:28 O 31 '38
Wolverine 30:49 Ja 29 '51

Glassware
Audubon bird plates, Steuben
glass bw 23:19 N 10 '47
Artist; wife bw 3:38 Jy 12
'37 port.
John James Audubon bw 5:
28 O 31 '38 port.
Self-portrait 9:115 O 21 '40
bw 30:46 Ja 29 '51 port.
Auguste, Toussaint
Garden of Eden 21:101 Mr
13 '50
Augustine, Saint
Hagenauer. St. Augustine
statue Isenheimer altar-
piece 30:80 Mr 26 '51
St. Augustine bw 22:70 Ap
7 '47; 39:42 D 26 '55
Signorelli. Madonna and
Child with saints 35:154
N 16 '53

Augustus, first Roman emperor
 Augustus Caesar statue bw
  Greco-Roman 5:46 D 25
  '38
Augustus II, King of Poland
 King Augustus II bw 5:55
  Ag 29 '38
Aul, Hilda
 Ouch sculpture bw 10:59 Je
  16 '41
The aunts. Castellanos 4:30
  Mr 14 '38
Austin, Alice
 Alice Austin photogs bw 31:
  67 O 29 '51
Austin, Darrel
 Beast enchanted 19:82 O 1 '45
 Europa and the bull 19:81 O
  1 '45
 Girl with a wand 19:82 O 1 '45
 The legend 19:81 O 1 '45
 The sisters 19:81 O 1 '45
 Artist at work photog bw 19:
  80 O 1 '45 port.
Austin, Stephen A.
 Stephen A. Austin bw 6:73 Ap
  10 '39
Australia
 Historical paintings bw 12:78-
  9 F 9 '42
Automobiles
 Bohrod. Landscape near Chi-
  cago 2:24 F 1 '37
 Burchfield. Promenade bw
  6:82 My 22 '39
 Daugherty. The Model T
  decade mural 3:49 O 25 '37
 Melton collection of antique
  automobiles photogs bw
  13:8-11 Jy 27 '42
 Reinhardt. Flashy autos 32:
  90 Mr 24 '52
 Sterne. Flivver 31:54 Ag 27
  '51
 Warshaw. Wrecked automo-
  biles 28:84 Mr 20 '56
 Wood, G. Death on Ridge
  Road 14:55 Ja 18 '43
Autumn
 Corbino. Harvest festival 4:
  28 Je 13 '38

Harvesting. illuminated manu-
 script Flemish, 15th cen-
 tury 22:80 My 26 '47
Autumn at Salisbury Mills.
 Dehu 11:41 Ag 11 '41
Autumn garden party. Chiang
 Kai-Shek 33:6-7 O 13 '52
Autumn in New England: Cider
 making. Currier and Ives
 print 9:29 D 30 '40
Autumn light. Brackman 8:59
 F 5 '40
Autumn still life. Lane 16:45
 Ja 3 '44
Aux aguets (On watch). sculp-
 ture bw Creeft 24:95 Ap
 12 '48
Avaric pin, 7th century 33:130
 O 20 '52
The avenger. sculpture
 Barlach 41:136-7 N 5 '56
Aviators
 Hurd. U.S. airmen, World
 War tempera 14:67-73 F
 15 '43
Avignon pieta, c1465 35:57 Ag
 17 '53
Avila, walled city, Spain photogs
 bw 33:50-1 Ag 18 '52
Avilov, M. I.
 Communication troops 14:47
 Mr 29 '43
Avril, Jane
 Toulouse-Lautrec. Jane Av-
 ril billboard poster 28:92
 My 15 '50
Awaiting the reply. Dudley 6:
 30 Je 19 '39
Awakened Danae. Correggio
 41:105 O 22 '56
The awakening. Karfiol 10:73
 Ap 14 '41
The awakening of sex sculp-
 ture bw 11:145 O 13 '41
Aye-aye drawing bw 30:130 F
 12 '51
Aztec calendar
 Aztec calendar drawing bw
 6:29 Ja 23 '39
 Aztec calendar stone bw 18:
 41 Ja 1 '45

Azulejos. da Silva 29:104 D 11
    '50

B

BBC's nine o-clock news.
    Davis, F. 16:68 Ap 3 '44;
    31:77 O 29 '51
BBC's nine o-clock news.
    Thomas, B. 17:64-5 O 9
    '44
Babe. cartoons Roese 10:12-5
    Ap 21 '41
Babe, ox
    Paul Bunyan and his blue ox,
    Babe sculpture, colored
    concrete, Minnesota 18:
    58-9 F 5 '45
    Paul Bunyan and his great
    blue ox 11:85 D 15 '41
    Watrous. Paul Bunyan and
    his blue ox, Babe 25:58 N
    29 '48
Babirusa. sculpture bw Jonas
    12:89 Mr 23 '42
The baby twins.* bw Peirce 19:
    82 N 12 '45
Bacchante. Brook 5:30 S 19 '38
Bacchus See Mythological
    Themes--Bacchus
Bache collection of old masters,
    gift to the Metropolitan
    Museum 2:40-3 Je 28 '37
Bachellor, Irving
    Irving Bachellor photog bw
    11:91 S 8 '41
Back country. Simkhovitch 11:
    40 D 29 '41
Back from the forest, Tahiti.
    bw Gauguin 6:58 Mr 27 '39
Backstreet city. bw Johnson, F.
    32:91 Mr 17'52
Bacon, Henry, architect
    Lincoln memorial bw 20:
    Cover F 11 '46
Bacon, Peggy
    A desperate character bw 6:
    57 My 8 '39
    Great Caesar's ghost bw 6:
    58 My 8 '39
    Hecate's court bw 6:58 My
    8 '39

The optimist bw 6:57 My 8
    '39
Wanderlust 20:80 F 18 '46
A young New Yorker bw 6:
    57 My 8 '39
"Buttons" (book) bw 6:61 My
    8 '39 (illustrations)
Brook. Peggy Bacon and
    Metaphysics bw 6:57 My
    8 '39 port.
Peggy Bacon. in group
    photog 29:172-3 O 16 '50
    port.
Bacon, Roger
    Roger Bacon bw 22:77 Ap 7
    '47
Baden-Powell, Lord and Lady
    Lord and Lady Baden-Powell
    photog bw 32:110 Mr 24
    '52
Baha'i
    Major prophets of Baha bw
    29:160 D 11 '50
    Temple and leaders bw 29:
    159-60 D 11 '50
Bailed up. bw Roberts 12:79
    F 9 '42
Bailey, Liberty Hyde
    Liberty Hyde Bailey photogs
    bw 26:63-4 Ja 17 '49
Baizerman, Saul, sculptor
    Aphrodite bw 25:180 O 4 '48
    The miner bw 25:157 O 4 '48
    Night (Unknown soldier) 25:
    158 O 4 '48
    The suckling bw 25:157 O 4
    '48
    Saul Baizerman photogs bw
    25:157-8 O 4 '48 port.
Baker, Bryant
    George Washington in ma-
    sonic dress sculpture bw
    26:56 Mr 28 '49
Baker, Ernest Hamlin
    Economic activities in the
    days of the Naragansett
    planters mural Post of-
    fice, Wakefield, R.I.
    10:44 Ja 27 '41
    "Time" cover portraits 17:
    59-62, 64 D 11 '44

Baker, George
Sad Sack, cartoon in "Yank"
bw 15:118-9 N 15 '43; 19:
8-10 D 31 '45
Artist at work photog bw 19:
8 D 31 '45 port.
George Baker photog bw 15:
119 N 15 '43 port.
Baker, Mary
Alphabet of odd animals 26:
12-4 Mr 28 '49
Bal des Quatres Arts. Du Bois,
G. 26:68-9 Je 20 '49
Balchen, Bert
Lea. Bert Balchen drawing
bw 16:70 My 29 '44
Baldwin, Stanley
Stanley Baldwin 24:53 Ap 26
'48
Stanley Baldwin as Prime
Minister of England, 1936
28:88 Je 5 '50
Balfour, Arthur James
Arthur James Balfour 24:53
Ap 26 '48
Bali
Covarrubias. Drawings and
paintings of Bali 3:46-9
S 27 '37
Woodcarvings--animals and
figures bw 15:114-6 O 25
'43
Covarrubias. Bali picture
map 3:50 S 27 '37(map)
Balilla memorial statue bw
Rome 4:32 My 9 '38
Balinese festival. Covarrubias
3:49 S 27 '37
Balinese fisherman. Covarrubi-
as 3:48 S 27 '37
Balinese girl. Covarrubias 3:47
S 27 '37
Balinese opera. Covarrubias 3:
48 S 27 '37
Balinese war dance. Covarrubi-
as 3:48 S 27 '37
Ball for Grand Duke Alexis,
Brooklyn, 1871 bw 19:89
Ag 27 '45
Ball game, Dufy 30:65 Ja 22 '51

Ballet dancer. Cowles 24:78 F
9 '48
Ballet dancer. sculpture bw
Rudy 15:82 D 20 '43
Ballet girls on stage. Degas
11:59 S 8 '41
Ballet scenes and dancers.
Davis, G. R. 16:77-80
Mr 20 '44
Balloon ascension, Versailles,
1783 bw 23:76 S 15 '47
Balloon house supported by air.
photogs bw 26:121-4 My
9 '49
Balloon site. bw Knight 24:82
My 3 '48
Balloons
Balloon ride, Philadelphia,
c1850 bw 31:14-5 Ag 6 '51
Charles et Robert. Descente
de la machine aerostatique
40:77 Ja 9 '56
Civil war observation balloon
of Professor Thaddeus
Lowe photog bw 22:90 Ja
13 '47
Flying fortress, 1803 bw 9:9
S 30 '40
Gromaire. Balloons 33:96 O
27 '52
"Intrepid," observation bal-
loon, U.S. Civil war,
1862 photog bw 6:36 Je 5
'39
Lee. Catastrophe 3:45 S 20
'37
Napoleon's plan to attack
England, 1799-1805 bw 2:
57 Mr 29 '37; 9:8-9, 11
S 30 '40
Baltasar Carlos, Infante of
Spain
Velazquez. Don Baltasar
Carlos 31:71 O 1 '51
Velazquez. Don Baltasar
Carlos and his dwarf 4:43
My 16 '38
Baltimore oriole. Audubon 3:42
Jy 12 '37

Balzac, Honore de
  Honore de Balzac engraving
    bw 22:19 F 24 '47
  Rodin. Balzac sculptures bw
    38:20-2 My 9 '55
Bamburgh castle, Northumber-
  land, England photog 40:
  88-9 Mr 19 '56
Bananas
  Rosenthal. Girls and bananas
    15:68 N 22 '43
Bancroft, George
  George Bancroft photog bw
    10:26 Mr 3 '41
Band concert. Sample 3:44 N
  15 '37
Bandholtz, Harry Hill
  General Bandholtz statue bw
    Budapest 30:167 My 7 '51
Bangkok
  Architecture, spires, and
    temples photogs 31:30-5
    D 31 '51
  Wat Bovornives Monastery
    38:80 Mr 7 '55
Banjo clock
  Willard, A. Banjo clock,
    c1800 photog 39:64 Jy 18
    '55
  Willard, S. Banjo clock
    photog bw 6:52 Mr 20 '39
Bank of England
  Ariel, statue on dome bw
    21:101 O 21 '46
  Bank of England photog bw
    2:65 My 31 '37
  Bank's nun bw 21:100 O 21
    '46
  Gillray. Old lady of Thread-
    needle Street, 1797 bw 21:
    99 O 21 '46
Banks, James Francis
  Old Richmond 10:68 My 26 '41
Banquet. sculpture bw Smith,
  David 33:76 S 22 '52
Banquet aboard Perry's flagship,
  1853 bw 19:62 S 17 '45
Baptisms See also Jesus Christ
  --Baptism
  Curry. Baptism at Big
    Stranger Creek bw 15:18

N 29 '43
  Curry. Baptism in Kansas 12:74
    Ap 20 '42 bw 15:18 N 29 '43
Baptism of Arnauld. Ford 17:
  35 D 25 '44
Baptismal party. Steen 24:77
  Je 14 '48
Baptizing day. Hayden 21:65 Jy
  22 '46
Bar-X ranch, New Mexico.*
  Hurd 23:76-7 Ag 18 '47
Baradewal, Buddhist sanctuary
  photog bw 3:61 Ag 16 '37
Baranov, Alexander
  Alexander Baranov bw 19:90
    Ag 27 '45
Barbara, Saint
  Raphael. Sistine Madonna
    40:113 My 7 '56
  Santa Barbara santero
    painting, Mission San
    Jose, Laguna, N. Mex.
    40:48-9 Ja 16 '56
Barber, Samuel
  Samuel Barber, composer
    photog bw 40:142 My 21
    '56
Barber shop. Sample 3:43 N
  15 '37
Barberini
  La suppliante sculpture bw
    19:50 Jy 30 '45
Barcaldini castle, Scotland,
  15th century photog bw 8:
  44 Je 3 '40
Barcelona architecture and
  churches photogs bw 2:40-
  1 F 22 '37
Barclay, McClelland
  Artist at work photog bw 2:
  60 Mr 1 '37 port.
Bare willows and distant moun-
  tains. May Yuan 15:62 O
  11 '43
Bargaining for a horse. Mount
  18:65 Je 25 '45
Barlach, Ernst, sculptor
  The avenger 41:136-7 N 5
  '56
  The ecstatic one 41:138 N
  5 '56

Floating angel 41:140 N 5 '56
Laughing old woman 41:138 N
    5 '56
The reunion 41:137 N 5 '56
Sudden panic 41:138-9 N 5 '56
Ernst Barlach photog bw 41:
    137 N 5 '56 port.
Kollwitz. The artist in death
    drawing bw 41:140 N 5 '56
    port.
Barlow, Perry
    "New Yorker" covers 21:69 Jy
        15 '46
Barn dance. Kelly, H.O. 29:71
    Jy 17 '50
Barnard, George Grey
    The struggle of two natures in
        Man sculpture bw 6:57 Mr
        20 '39
Barnes, Albert C.
    Albert C. Barnes photog bw
        2:44 Ap 12 '37
Barnet, Will
    Will Barnet. in group photog
        29:172-3 O 16 '50 port.
Barns See Farmyards and Farm
    Buildings
Barovier, Angelo
    Venetian glass wedding cup,
        15th century 37:55 Ag 2 '54
Barr, Stringfellow
    Stringfellow Barr photog bw
        8:61 F 5 '40
Barrage. Groth 16:78 Je 12 '44
Barraud, Francis
    His master's voice, Victor Co.
        trademark bw 33:92 N 17
        '52
    Artist and his work photog bw
        33:92 N 17 '52 port.
Barringer, D. Moreau
    Drawings for netsuke bw 37:2-
        3 Jy 12 '54
Barrooms, Inns and Taverns
        See also Alcoholism and
        Intoxication
    Andre, J. Indians and soldiers
        in a tavern drawing bw 35:
        92 S 28 '53
    Benton. Frankie and Johnny
        mural 2:36-7 Mr 1 '37

Bohrod. Taverns at night 11:
    93 N 10 '41
Bouche. McSorley's bar 10:
    73 Ap 14 '41
Common room, Red Lion Inn,
    Delaware, 1820 photog 29:
    62-3 Jy 18 '55
Currier and Ives print. Even-
    tide--October: The village
    inn 9:32 D 30 '40
Davis, F. The Scribe Hotel
    barroom 19:50-1 Jy 16 '45
Degas. L'absinthe bw 11:85
    D 1 '41
Gem saloon, New York, c1850
    32:117 Ap 7 '52
Greenwood. Sea captains ca-
    rousing in Surinam, 1758
    26:84-5 F 28 '49
Hogarth. Scene in a tavern
    bw 35:31 S 14 '53
Hopper. Corner saloon 28:
    101 Ap 17 '50
Jackson, Harry Afternoon in
    the bar 41:74-6 Jy 9 '56
Mount. A barroom oracle re-
    lates 18:66 Je 25 '45
Mount. The breakdown 18:67
    Je 25 '45
Martin. Celebration 9:92 N
    11 '40
Paris cartoonist at "Le Vil-
    lage" bw 36:114 Ap 26 '54
Picasso. The absinthe drinker
    40:74 My 28 '56
Rouault. Couple in cabaret 34:
    59 F 2 '53
Saber. Bar patrons mural
    bw 27:16-7 D 5 '49
Sloan. McSorley's bar 7:46
    D 11 '39; 26:85 F 21 '49
Solid comfort lithograph 27:
    49 Jy 4 '49
Steen. The dancing couple 5:
    32 Ag 29 '38
Teniers. Interior of a public
    house 4:22 Ap 11 '38
Van Gogh. Night cafe 2:34
    F 15 '37; 27:85 O 10 '49

Barry, James, architect
  Houses of Parliament, London
    24:49 Ap 26 '48 bw 16:81
    My 22 '44
Barrymore, Ethel
  Ethel Barrymore, c1900
    photog bw 28:65 Ja 2 '50
  John and Ethel Barrymore
    photog bw 31:117 N 19 '51
Barrymore, John
  John and Ethel Barrymore
    photog bw 31:117 N 19 '51
Barthe, Richmond, sculptor
  Head bw 21:62 Jy 22 '46
  Katharine Cornell as Juliet
    bw 18:108 Ap 16 '45
Bartholdi, Frederic Auguste,
    sculptor
  Libert enlightening the world,
    Luxembourg Garden, Paris
    17:93 O 2 '44 bw 10:6 Je
    23 '41
  Statue of Liberty, New York
    Harbor 8:Cover Je 3 '40;
    16:Cover Je 26 '44; 23:48
    Je 7 '47; bw 6:Cover Je 5
    '39; 10:94-7 Je 2 '41
  Torch, Philadelphia Centenni-
    al Exposition, 1876 bw 6:
    35 Je 5 '39
Bartholomew, Saint
  El Greco. St. Bartholomew
    39:77 Ag 8 '55
  Rembrandt. St. Bartholomew
    25:59 O 11 '48
Bartlett, Josiah
  Josiah Bartlett bw 15:8 Jy 5
    '43
Barton, Clara
  Clara Barton bw 14:7 Ja 4 '43
Baruch, Bernard
  Bernard Baruch. "Time"
    cover 17:61 D 11 '44
Basaldella, Mirko
  The unknown political prisoner
    sculpture bw 34:40 Je 1 '53
Baseball See Games and Sports--
    Baseball
Basile, Alphonse
  Robinson Crusoe as a young
    man 1:44 N 30 '36

Basilica of Sacre-Coeur, Paris
  photog bw 17:92 O 2 '44
Basilica, Roman. ruin, Samaria,
    Palestine photog 20:52-3
    Ap 1 '46
Basilisk. Freund 30:116-7 Ap
    23 '51
Basinet. photog 30:186-7 Ap 9
    '56
Baskerville, Charles
  Mrs. E. M. Warburg 10:48
    F 3 '41
Basket and fruit. Blanch 7:26
    Ag 28 '39
Basket bouquet. Knaths 30:35
    Ja 15 '51
Basket of fruit. Hynckes 29:102
    D 11 '50
Baskin, Leonard
  Anatomist woodcut 37:89 O
    18 '54
Bastille, Paris
  Fall of the Bastille, July 14,
    1789 engraving bw 3:32 Jy
    5 '37
  Mob storming the Bastille bw
    31:78 Jy 30 '51
  Surrender of the Bastille
    print bw 3:32 Jy 5 '37
  Palloy. Map of the Bastille
    3:35 Jy 5 '37 (map)
Batchelor, Clarence D.
  Pre-and post-Pearl Harbor
    cartoons bw 11:8 D 22 '41
Bates, Edward
  Edward Bates photog bw 14:
    75 F 15 '43
Bates, Gladys
  Morning sculpture bw 14:42
    Mr 8 '43
Bath, order of 26:73 F 7 '49
Bathers and Bathing
  Bellows. Forty-two kids 20:
    80 Mr 25 '46
  Benton. Susanna and the
    elders bw 5:30 O 31 '38;
    6:40 F 20 '39; 6:70 Ap
    24 '39
  Bonnard. Cabinet de toilette
    25:56 Jy 26 '48

Bouguereau. Bathers bw 11:
54 S 8 '41

Brown. Bather sculpture bw
12:90 My 19 '41

Chabas. September morn
bw 2:53 My 24 '37; 21:90
D 23 46; 29:96 N 27 '50

Chavannes. Summer 15:66 S
20 '43

Courbet. Bather 41:108 O 22
'56

Cowles. Nova Scotia morning
24:77 F 9 '48

Cremonini. Bather* 38:72 Ja
17 '55

Degas. After the bath pastel
38:107 My 23 '55

Hirsch. Nine men 30:37 Ja 15
'51

Hogfeldt. Susanna and elders
17:57 Jy 3 '44

Ingres. Bather of Valpincon
41:Cover O 22 '56

Ingres. Turkish bath 10:73
Ap 28 '41; 41:107 O 22 '56

Kroll. The pool 24:68 Je 28
'48

Lee, D. The bath 10:73 Ap
14 '41

Lee, D. Woman bathing,
Mexico 22:76 My 12 '47

Maillol. Little bather standing sculpture bw 8:106 Ap
15 '40

Picasso. The bathers drawing
bw 23:94 O 13 '47

Rembrandt. Susanna and the
elders 24:79 Mr 22 '48

Rembrandt. Toilet of Bathsheba after the bath 1:33
N 30 '36 bw 12:44 Mr 9 '42

Rembrandt. A woman bathing
29:105 S 11 '50

Renoir. Apres le bain 24:66
Mr 1 '48

Renoir. Bather 41:109 O 22
'56

Renoir. Bathers. 7:53 N 20
'39

Renoir. Three bathers with
crab 3:47 Jy 5 '37

Rosenthal. Between two
screens 12:46 Mr 9 '42

Rosenthal. The source 15:67
N 22 '43

Tintoretto. Susanna and the
elders 27:69 O 24 '49

Titian. Diana and Actaeon
41:106-7 O 22 '56

Wilson. River scenes: Bathers
and cattle 5:43 S 12 '38

Wolford. Saturday night in
Harlem ceramics bw 9:
129 N 11 '40

Woman putting-up hair in rag
curlers bw 30:37 F 5 '51

Bathory, Stephen, King of Poland
Dictating peace in Russian
Pskov, 1582* bw 17:86
Ag 28 '44

Bathrooms
Bonnard. Cabinet de toilette
25:56 Jy 26 '48

Greek revival bathroom, New
York, 1845 print bw 39:
69 Ag 29 '55

Roman bath, England photog
40:85 Mr 19 '56

Baths of Caracalla, Rome bw
25:80 Ag 9 '48

Bathsheba
Rembrandt. Toilet of Bath-
sheba after the bath 1:33
N 30 '36 bw 12:44 Mr 9 '42

Bathtubs
Antique bath 40:93-4 F 27 '56

Hip bath with shower, England 1847 bw 25:79 Ag 9
'48

Hooded bath, Victorian, England, c1900 bw 25:82 Ag
9 '48

Outdoor shower, Germany,
19th century bw 25:79 Ag
9 '48

Steam-bed bath, U.S., 1814
bw 25:79 Ag 9 '48

Vapor bath, Russia, 18th
century bw 25:79 Ag 9 '48

Batons, Field Marshal's, presented to Duke of Wellington 26:72 F 7 '49

Bats
  Gold bat, Inca ornament 36:
    102 Ap 12 '54
Battle Axes See Weapons
Battle of Agincourt bw 40:180-1
  Ap 9 '56
Battle of Barbary, 1390 40:188
  Ap 9 '56
Battle of Barnet, 1471 bw 40:
  204 Ap 9 '56
Battle of Blenheim. mural
  Churchill, J. 35:81 N 23
  '53
Battle of Blenheim. tapestry
  Brussels 24:34-5 Ap 19 '48
Battle of Britain window, West-
  minster Abbey photog 26:
  58 F 7 '49
Battle of Buena Vista, Mexican
  War, 1847 drawing bw 22:
  110-1 Je 9 '47
Battle of Cape Vincent, 1797 24:
  67 My 10 '48
Battle of Chapultepec See Chapul-
  tepec
Battle of Crecy 40:188 Ap 9 '56
Battle of Germantown, 1777
  The Chew House 29:50 Jy 3
  '50
Battle of Hastings
  Bayeux tapestry bw 16:8-10
    Je 26 '44; 40:88-9 Mr 26
    '56
  French chronicle, 15th cen-
    tury 40:86 Mr 26 '56
Battle of Jena, 1806 bw 8:25 Ap
  22 '40
Battle of Jericho. illumination
  34:79 F 23 '53
Battle of Jutland, My 31, 1916.
  bw Howard 3:90 S 13 '37
Battle of Kolin, Seven Years'
  War bw 15:96 N 22 '43
Battle of Lake Erie. Garneray
  9:48 O 28 '40; 31:54 Jy 2
  '51
Battle of Lepanto, 1571. Vero-
  nese 23:58 Ag 4 '47
Battle of Lexington. stained glass
  bw Burnham 16:96 Ja 10 '44

Battle of Magenta, June 4, 1859
  bw 15:20 Ag 9 '43
Battle of Marathon bw 20:34 Ap
  8 '46
Battle of Milvian Bridge. fres-
  co bw Raphael 39:39 D 26
  '55
Battle of Mobile Bay, 1864.
  Davidson 9:49 O 28 '40
Battle of Monmouth
  Washington and Lee at the
    Battle of Monmouth bw 29:
    51 Jy 3 '50
Battle of Nicholson. Miyamoto
  28:70 F 27 '50
Battle of Princeton, 1776. Mer-
  cer 29:46 Jy 3 '50
Battle of Queenstown Heights
  bw 9:114 S 9 '40
Battle of Saratoga, 1853. Japa-
  nese artist bw 25:7 Ag 2
  '48
Battle of Scheveningen, 1654
  24:66 My 10 '48
Battle of Solferino, June 24,
  1859 bw 15:20 Ag 9 '43
Battle of the Lapiths. sculpture
  detail, Elgin Marbles bw
  35:158-9 O 26 '53
Battle of the Little Big Horn
  Adams, C. Custer's last
    fight bw 11:75 D 8 '41 lith-
    ograph copy 24:14 Je 21
    '48
  Battle of the Little Big Horn
    lithograph bw 24:13 Je
    21 '48
  Benton. Custer's last stand
    bw 24:14 Je 21 '48
  Eber. Custer's letzte Schlacht
    bw 24:13 Je 21 '48
  Elder. Custer's last fight bw
    24:12 Je 21 '48
  Fuchs. Custer's last charge
    bw 24:12 Je 21 '48
  General Custer's death strug-
    gle lithograph bw 24:13 Je
    21 '48
  Mulvaney. Custer's last rally
    bw 24:112 Je 21 '48

Battle of the Nile 24:67 My 10
    '48
Battle of the Saints 24:66 My 10
    '48
Battle of Trenton, 1776 print 29:
    47 Jy 3 '50
Battle scroll. Japanese 9:50 Jy
    22 '40
Battleship Warspite. Wilkinson
    24:66 My 17 '48
Battleship Wien. Hitler 7:53
    O 30 '39
Baum, L. Frank. "Wonderful
    Wizard of Oz," illustrated
    by Denslow 35:52-9 D 28 '53
Baum, Mark
    Top of a town bw 36:90 Ja 25
    '54
    Artist and his work photog
    bw 36:90 Ja 25 '54 port.
Baumeister, Willi, printmaker
    Artist and his work photog 36:
    144 My 10 '54
"Bay Psalm Book" photog bw 37:
    95 N 22 '54
Bay region modern, architec-
    ture 27:44-53 S 5 '49
Bayeux tapestry
    Etching of 40:88-9 Mr 26
    '56 photog bw 16:8-10 Je
    26 '44
Baylinson, Abraham S.
    Girl with mountain snow 16:
    46 Ja 3 '44
    Walkowitz bw 16:77 F 21 '44
Bayon temple, Angkor-Wat
    photog bw 5:38 Ag 1 '38
Bayou teche. Meeker, J. R. 28:
    78 Mr 6 '50
Bazaine, Jean
    King David; St. Cecelia; St.
    Gregory stained glass 28:74
    Je 19 '50
Bazerie's cylinder. drawing bw
    19:63 N 26 '45
Bazile, Castera
    Parade* 28:101 Mr 13 '50
Baziotes, William
    Cyclops 24:103 Je 28 '48
    The dwarf 25:63 O 11 '48 bw
    26:84 F 21 '49
William Baziotes photog bw
    30:34 Ja 15 '51 port.
Beach house. Dodd 27:64 S 26
    '49
Beach party. Miller, B. 11:73
    O 27 '41 bw 9:79 D 9 '40
Beach scenes
    Bellows. The big dory 29:71
    Ag 21 '50
    Bellows. The sand team 20:
    81 Mr 25 '46
    Bohrod. Chicago beach 25:
    62-3 Jy 26 '48
    Courbet. Cliffs at Etretat
    26:64 My 30 '49
    Dike. California holiday 11:
    75 O 27 '41
    Feininger, Lyonel. Dunes
    and breakwater 31:92-3 N
    12 '51
    Homer. The wreck 2:26 Ja
    11 '37
    Levi, J. Tarring nets 20:78
    F 18 '46
    Lie. Smuggler's cove 4:26
    Je 13 '38
    Moran, E. Embarkation of
    the pilgrims 24:68-9 Je
    14 '48
    Palmer. Summer pleasures
    4:26 Je 13 '38
    Rand. Seascape with figures
    39:114 S 12 '55
    Ryder. Smugglers' cove 30:
    91 F 26 '51
    Ryder. Shore scene 30:90 F
    26 '51
    Toulouse-Lautrec. The black
    countess 28:97 My 15 '50
    Van Gogh. Boats on the beach
    bw 27:82 O 10 '49
Beached. Levi, J. 10:73 Ap 14
    '41
Beal, Gifford
    Walkowitz bw 16:77 F 21 '44
    Gifford Beal. in group photog
    29:172-3 O 16 '50 port.
Beale, Joseph Boggs
    Betsy Ross bw 32:58 F 18
    '52

Beale, Joseph Boggs (cont.)
  Magic lantern slides, illus-
    trations bw 8:4-6 Ja 8 '40
  Joseph Beale photog bw 8:5
    Ja 8 '40 port.
A bear hunt. drawing bw Rubens
    6:58 Mr 27 '39
"The Bear Party," illustrations.
    Du Bois, W. 29:44-9 D
    25 '49
Bear with nude. ice sculpture bw
    Schwerzmann 6:6 Ja 16 '39
Beard, Charles A.
  Charles A. Beard photog bw
    4:16 F 21 '38; 16:Cover Ja
    17 '44; 16:53 F 28 '44
Beardon, Romare
  Factory workers 21:64 Jy 22
    '46
Beards
  Types and fashions in beards
    photogs bw 6:8-9, 11 Ap
    24 '39
Bears
  Bingham. Fur traders descend-
    ing the Missouri 28:76-7
    Mr 6 '50
  Bufano. Bear cubs sculpture
    bw 17:107 D 4 '44
  Grizzly bear with cubs sculp-
    ture bw 12:90 Mr 23 '42
  Shephard. Winnie-the-Pooh
    drawings bw 30:75-6 F 19
    '51; 40:117-8, 122 F 27
    '56
Bearsville Meadows. Ganso 5:
    26 Ag 29 '38
Beast enchanted. Austin 19:82
    O 1 '45
Beaton, Cecil
  American and English actors
    drawings 21:6-7, 9 Jy 22
    '46
  Elizabeth II, Queen of Eng-
    land 40:89 Ja 30 '56 photog.
  Gertrude Stein and Alice B.
    Toklas bw 4:49 Ja 2 '38
    photog.
  Cecil Beaton photog bw 4:46
    Ja 3 '38; 14:13 Ap 19 '43
    port.

Beatty, David F.
  Earl of Beatty sculpture bw
    Trafalgar Square 25:93
    N 15 '48
Beauchamp, Mary Ellen
  Mary Ellen Beauchamp photog
    bw 9:72 Jy 15 '40
Beaujolais, Madamoiselle de
  Nattier. Madamoiselle de
    Beaujolais 41:71 D 10 '56
Beauregard, Pierre
  General Beauregard photog
    bw 7:51 Ag 28 '39
Beauty shop. ceramics bw
    Reich 9:130 N 10 '40
Beauvais tapestry
  Boucher. La noble pastorale
    bw 4:28 Ja 24 '38
Beauvoir, Simone de
  Sartre and de Beauvoir
    photog bw 20:66 Je 17 '46
Bec de corbin (weapon) 40:187
    Ap 9 '56
Becker, Joseph
  First train of Central Pacific
    in Utah* 36:78 Mr 8 '54
Beckett, Thomas a, archbishop
  Burial of Thomas a Beckett
    40:98 Mr 26 '56
  Murder of Thomas a Beckett
    40:98 Mr 26 '56
The Beckford children. Romney
    4:27 Ja 24 '38
Beckmann, Max
  Carnival 21:79 N 25 '46
Bed wrench, wood, U.S. Coloni-
    al 38:119 Ap 18 '55
Beddoes, Ivor
  Burnt out Italian tanks 26:60
    Mr 21 '49
Bede, The Venerable
  Saint Bede bw 34:84 F 23 '53
Bedford, Duke of
  Hoppner. The Duke of Bed-
    ford bw 11:54 N 10 '41
Bedford, Francis, Duke of
  Duke of Bedford statue bw
    15:112 N 15 '43
Beds See Furniture--Beds

Beecham, Thomas
    Sir Thomas Beecham conduct-
        ing; portraits photogs bw
        18:76-7 Ja 29 '45
Beecher, Catherine
    Catherine Beecher bw 23:90
        O 27 '47
Beecher, Henry Ward
    Henry Ward Beecher wood-
        carving, c1850 31:73 Jy 2
        '51
    Henry Ward Beecher and
        Grover Cleveland cartoon
        bw 31:19 O 22 '51
The beef. bw Rembrandt 7:24 Ag
    28 '39
Beerbohm, Max, cartoonist
    G. B. Shaw caricature bw 23:
        89 N 17 '47
    H. G. Wells caricature bw
        23:88 N 17 '47
    Oscar Wilde lecturing in U.S.
        bw 5:34 D 5 '38; 33:126 S
        22 '52
    The rare and rather awful
        visits of Albert Edward...
        bw 23:75 N 17 '47
    Rudyard Kipling caricature
        bw 33:126 S 22 '52; 23:88
        N 17 '47
    W. B. Yeats caricature bw
        23:89 N 17 '47
    Winston Churchill, 1907 bw
        33:126 S 22 '52
    Max Beerbohm photog bw 15:
        102 S 20 '43; 33:125 S 22
        '52 port.
    Self-portrait caricature bw
        33:125 S 22 '52 port.
Bees
    Freund. Bees--anatomy; in
        hive; predators 33:62-7 Ag
        11 '52
Beethoven, Ludwig von
    Milles. Orpheus fountain,
        Stockholm bw 2:29 F 22 '37
La befana. Lewicki 39:64 D 19
    '55
Before the window. Cassatt 12:
    56 Ja 19 '42

Beheading of Ann Boleyn bw 24:
    61 Je 14 '48
Behrman, S. N.
    S. N. Behrman photog bw 21:
        50 O 7 '46
Belasco, David
    David Belasco photog bw 31:
        117 N 19 '51
Belaying pins, U.S.S. Constel-
    lation photog bw 9:54 O
    28 '40
Belcher, George
    British biddy from "Punch"
        4:48-9 Mr 7 '38
    Artist at work photog bw 4:
        48 Mr 7 '38 port.
Belfort, May
    Toulouse-Lautrec. May Bel-
        fort poster 28:93 My 15
        '50
Belgiojoso-Peressutti-Rogers,
    furniture design
    Chaise 34:72-3 Mr 2 '53
Belgium
    Flemish fascist emblem: cog,
        sword, plow bw 8:13 Je
        17 '40
Bell, Alexander Graham
    Tetrahedral kite photog bw
        10:79 My12 '41
Belle Grove, Greek revival
    house, 1857 photog 32:72-
    3 Je 9 '52
La belle jardiniere. bw Raphael
    19:50 Jy 30 '45
Bellevue. Bodmer 15:88 Ag 30
    '43
Bellecourt war memorial, 1914-
    1918 war dead photog bw
    3:22 Ag 20 '37
Bellini, Gentile
    The Corpus Christi proces-
        sion 23:54-5 Ag 4 '47
Bellini, Giovanni
    Leonardo Loredano, Doge of
        Venice 23:46 Ag 4 '47
    Flight into Egypt 16:70 Ap
        10 '44
    Madonna and Child 37:64 Ag
        9 '54 bw 24:67 Ja 26 '48

Bellini, Giovanni (cont.)
  St. Francis in ecstasy 3:34-
    5 D 27 '37; 16:64 Ap 10 '44
  The transfiguration 39:24-5
    D 26 '55
Bellotto, Bernardo
  Dresden market, c1750 40:
    104 My 7 '56
Bellows, George Wesley
  Anne in white 20:74 Mr 25 '46
  Aunt Eleanor, artist's
    mother and daughter, Jean*
    bw 16:79 Ap 24 '44
  The big dory 29:71 Ag 21 '50
  Blackwell's bridge 7:36 Jy 31
    '39
  The crucifixion 9:78 D 9 '40
  Dempsey and Firpo bw 6:58
    Mr 27 '39
  Elinor, Jean and Anna 11:77
    O 6 '41
  Emma and her children 11:77
    O 6 '41
  Floating ice 12:75 Ap 20 '42
  Forty-two kids 20:80 Mr 25
    '46
  Gramercy park 20:79 Mr 25
    '46
  Jean in pink dress bw 11:76
    O 6 '41
  Jean with a doll bw 11:76 O
    6 '41
  Jean with blue book and apple
    bw 11:76 O 6 '41
  Lady Jean 7:58 N 20 '39 bw
    11:76 O 6 '41
  Mrs. Harry Arnold 41:162 D
    24 '56
  Mrs. Katherine Rosen 20:82
    Mr 25 '46
  Mrs. T. in cream silk 20:79
    Mr 25 '46
  My mother 11:60 S 8 '41
  Outside the big tent 12:62 Je
    15 '42
  The sand team 20:81 Mr 25
    '46
  Stag at Sharkey's 5:38 O 31
    '38; 26:85 F 21 '49
  Two women 20:82 Mr 25 '46
  Waldo Peirce 20:82 Mr 25 '46

The white horse 20:81 Mr 25
  '46
The artist's daughter, Jean
  bw 20:78 Mr 25 '46 (draw-
  ing)
Study drawing of a dress bw
  20:78 Mr 25 '46 (drawing)
Nude study bw 20:78 Mr 25
  '46 (lithograph)
George Bellows photog bw
  20:75 Mr 25 '46 port.
Bellows, Jean
  Bellows, G. Jean in pink
    dress bw 11:76 O 6 '41
  Bellows, G. Jean with a doll
    bw 11:76 O 6 '41
  Bellows, G. Jean with blue
    book and apple bw 11:76
    O 6 '41
  Bellows, G. Lady Jean 7:58
    N 20 '39 bw 11:76 O 6 '41
  Carroll. Jean 11:78 O 6 '41
  Carroll. Jean in pink organ-
    dy 11:78 O 6 '41
  Jean Bellows photog bw 11:
    76 O 6 '41
  Speicher. Jean in blue 11:
    77 O 6 '41
  Speicher. Portrait of Jean
    Bellows 11:78 O 6 '41
Bells
  The Lutine bell, Lloyd's,
    London photog bw 8:96
    Je 3 '40
Belluschi, Pietro, architect
  U.S. minimum house plan,
    photogs 22:83-7 Ap 28
    '47
  Zion Lutheran church, Port-
    land, Oreg. photog bw
    30:16 Ap 30 '51
Below Black Head. Kent 29:71
  Ag 21 '50
Belt buckle, Eagle symbol,
  U.S. bw 17:56 S 4 '44
Belter, John, furniture de-
  signer Victorian furniture,
  parlor photog 39:102 O
  17 '55
Bemelmans, Ludwig
  "Madeline," his illustrated

book bw 7:6-7 S 4 '39
Ludwig Bemelmans photog bw
7:7 S 4 '39 port.
Bench in a park. Vuillard 37:76-
7 N 1 '54
Benchley, Robert
"Chips off the Old Benchley,"
illustrated by Williams
bw 27:24-9 O 10 '49
Robert Benchley photog bw
27:23 O 10 '49
Bend in the road. Cezanne 25:78-
9 N 1 '48; 40:76 My 28 '56
Benedetto, Angelo di
Calling the loa 8:35 Ja 1 '40
Lovers in the cornfield 21:
77 N 25 '46
Morning in Port-au-Prince
8:36 Ja 1 '40
Angelo di Benedetto photog
bw 8:34 Ja 1 '40 port.
Benedict, Saint
De Coux. St. Benedict bw 27:
144 O 17 '49
St. Benedict, American
Indian woodcarving 40:56
Ja 16 '56
Benedict the Moor, Saint
St. Benedict, statue, St.
Benedict the Moor church,
Washington, D.C. bw 34:
96 Mr 16 '53
Benet, Stephen Vincent
Stephen Vincent Benet photog
bw 16:48 Ja 31 '44
Benevento, Tiberio
Circus parade 1:44 N 30 '36
Benevento cathedral, Benevento,
Italy photog 17:58-9 Jy 24
'44
Benjamin, Judah P.
Judah P. Benjamin photog bw
7:50 Ag 28 '39
Bennett, James Gordon
James Gordon Bennett bw 7:
60 Ag 14 '39
Bennett, Peggy
Peggy Bennett photog bw 22:
82 Je 2 '47
Benoit, Rigaud
Queen of Africa 23:59 S 1 '47

Ben-Shmuel, Aaron
Job sculpture bw 14:42 Mr 8
'43
Benton, Thomas Hart
Cotton loading on the Missis-
sippi bw 6:70 Ap 24 '39
Cotton pickers 13:45 Ag 31
'42
Custer's last stand bw 24:14
Je 21 '48
Danger--Butterfly and spider
bw 6:70 Ap 24 '39
Figure organization bw 6:70
Ap 24 '39
Frankie and Johnny mural
detail 2:36 Mr 1 '37
Goin' home bw 5:9 D 12 '38
History of Missouri mural,
State House, Jefferson
City, Mo. 2:35-7 Mr 1 '37
Hollywood 5:74-5 D 12 '38
Huck Finn mural detail 2:
36 Mr 1 '37; 21:74 N 25 '46
The Jealous Lover of Lone
Green Valley 6:71 Ap 24
'39
Jesse James mural detail
bw 6:70 Ap 24 '39
The lost penny 7:26 Ag 28 '39
Moonlight on the Osage bw 6:
70 Ap 24 '39
Persephone bw 6:39 F 20 '39
Pussy cat and roses 6:71 Ap
24 '39
Susanna and the elders bw 5:
30 O 31 '38; 6:40 F 20 '39;
6:70 Ap 24 '39
T. P. and Jake 6:71 Ap 24
'39 bw 10:70 Ap 14 '41
Communists and fascists in
Michigan bw 3:22-5 Jy 26
'37 (drawing)
Artist at work; portraits;
family photogs bw 2:33-4
Mr 1 '37; 3:22 Jy 26 '37;
6:70 Ap 24 '39 port.
Thomas Hart Benton photog
bw 6:38 F 20 '39 port.
Berchtesgaden, Hitler's home
photogs 7:52, 57-8 O 30
'39

Bercot, Paul
St. Francis stained glass 28:
74 Je 19 '50
Berenson, Bernard
Bernard Berenson--portraits,
home, art collection
photogs bw 26:158-60 Ap
11 '49
Beresford, Frank E.
George V's bier* 28:70 My
29 '50
Artist at work photog bw 10:
64 F 24 '41 port.
Bergan (ship)
Royal bergan of navigator
kings of Portugal, c1500
photog bw 23:26-7 Ag 11 '47
Berger, Meyer
Newman. Meyer Berger photog
bw 35:18-9 D 7 '53
Berger, Samuel Alexander
Central Park in winter* 24:
72 Ap 5 '48
Bergh, Elis, glassware
Cut crystal vases bw 17:66
Ag 7 '44
Bergman, Ingrid
Brook. Ingrid Bergman 18:37
Ja 15 '45
Bering, Vitus
Discovery of the Bering
Strait* 1730 bw 9:58 Jy 1 '40
Berks, Robert
Louis Brandeis statue bw 41:
70 N 26 '56
Berlin, Irving
Berlin and Noel Coward photog
bw 15:36 D 6 '43
Irving Berlin--portraits,
family, associates photogs
bw 5:44-7 Ag 15 '38; 14:79-
80 Ap 5 '43
Bermuda
Davis, F. Bermuda in World
War 13:90-4 S 21 '42
Davis, F. Front Street, Ham-
ilton, Bermuda bw 14:6 Je
28 '43
Bernal, Antonio Arias
Anti-axis cartoons from "Hoy"
12:8-9, 11 F 9 '42

Bernard, Saint
St. Bernard bw 22:70 Ap 7 '47
St. Bernard bw Cistercian
monastery, Clairvaux,
France 22:75 Ap 7 '47
St. Bernard statue bw Pass
of St. Bernard 20:45 Mr
4 '46
Bernatschke, Rudolf
Erma 10:47 F 3 '41
Bernini, Giovanni Lorenzo
Altar, St. Peter's, Rome
photog bw 18:27 Ja 15 '45
Bernstein, Henry, playwright
Karsh. Henry Bernstein
photog bw 29:78 Ag 7 '50
Lynes. Henry Bernstein
photog bw 27:17 O 10 '49
Bernstein, Leonard, composer
Leonard Bernstein photog bw
40:142 My 21 '56
Berry, John
Artillerymen in desert 26:59
Mr 21 '49
Berti, Antonio
Barbara Hutton sculpture bw
4:23 Jy 18 '38
Bertoia, Harry
Paintings; chairs designed;
sculptures 34:72-5 Mr 2
'53
Screen, metal 37:62 O 25 '54
Artist; family; home photogs
bw 34:76 Mr 2 '53 port.
Besieged city. Diego 20:81 Mr
11 '46
"Best Friend of Charleston"
(locomotive), Southern
Railway, 1830 photog bw
25:12 S 27 '48
Bethlehem   See also Biblical
and Christian Themes
Thomas, B.   Little Town of
Bethlehem 23:46 D 22 '47
The betrayal. Angelico 21:58
D 23 '46
Between rounds. Eakins 16:76
My 15 '44
Between the virgin and the bride.
Duchamp 32:103 Ap 28 '52

Between two screens. Rosenthal
12:46 Mr 9 '42

Bevans, Michael H.
American snakes--most common species 28:49-52 My
29 '50

Bewick's swan on a pond. Scott
7:54 N 13 '39

Bibles See Manuscripts

Biblical and Religious Themes
See also biblical charac-
ters, as Adam and Eve;
Jesus Christ; Mary, Virgin;
and biblical scenes, as The
Last Judgment. Also, Gods
and Goddesses

Allston. Elijah fed by ravens
19:84 S 10 '45

Attacks on Catholic church,
Flemish, c1550 24:64 Je
14 '48

Blake. The four Zoas 36:60-
4 Ap 19 '54

Blake. The great red dragon
and the woman clothed with
sun bw 10:94 Je 9 '41

Blake. The wise and the foolish virgins bw 10:94 Je 9
'41

Bosch. The garden of delights
27:75-82 N 14 '52

Botticelli. Three miracles of
St. Zenobias bw 21:104 O
28 '46

Brueghel, Pieter, the elder.
Massacre of the innocents
37:36-7 D 27 '54

Brueghel, Pieter, the younger.
Massacre of the innocents
copy 24:65 Je 14 '48

Camp meeting* print 39:71 D
26 '55

Carena. The angel and Jacob
fighting 3:27 D 20 '37

Chagall. Isaiah during Babylonian captivity bw 38:97
Je 13 '55

Chagall. Song of David 33:99
O 6 '52

Christian martyrs torn by
lions, Colosseum, Rome
bw 39:38 D 26 '55

Christus. St. Elgius and St.
Godeberta 37:65 Ag 9 '54

Council of Trent bw 24:87 Je
14 '48

Curry. The prodigal son bw
15:18 N 29 '43

Dore. The brazen serpent bw
23:45 S 22 '47

Dore. Deliverance of St.
Peter bw 39:37 D 26 '55

Dore. The Lord smiting the
first born of Egypt* bw
4:48 Ap 18 '38

Dore. The Red Sea closing
on the Egyptians bw 4:48
Ap 18 '38

Dore. The shipwreck of St.
Paul bw 39:37 D 26 '55

Duccio. Resurrection of Lazarus 1:46 D 28 '36

El Greco. The opening of the
fifth seal 28:87 Ap 24 '50

El Greco. St. Martin and the
beggar 33:91 O 27 '52

Emblems of Christianity
Cross 20:60-8 Ap 22 '46;
38:57 F 7 '55
Key of St. Peter 32:85 Ap
14 '52

Ford. Portfolio of religious
paintings 17:33-44 D 25 '44

Ford. The star of Bethlehem
7:25 D 25 '39

French Huguenots attack
Catholic priests* bw 24:
60 Je 14 '48

Gozzoli. Journey of the Magi
19:Cover, 43-5 D 24 '45

Hayden. Baptizing day 21:65
Jy 22 '46

Herod orders Magi to find
newborn Christ relief,
Ulm cathedral, Germany
35:28 D 28 '53

Japanese artists. Early
Christian relics, 16th-
19th centuries bw 20:93-
4 Mr 25 '46

Judgment day sculpture bw
Abbey church, Vezelay,
France 22:78 Ap 7 '47

Biblical and Religious Themes
(cont).
  Mantegna. Judith and Holo-
    fernes 4:28 Mr 21 '38 bw
    26:160 Ap 11 '49
  Marcier. Blind leading the
    blind 36:83 My 31 '54
  Martin, J. Parting of the Red
    Sea* bw 38:98-9 Je 13 '55
  Martorell. St. George and
    the dragon 33:91 O 27 '52
  Masaccio. The tribute money
    fresco 39:22-3 D 26 '55
  Memling. Shrine of St. Ursa-
    la 34:81-6 Ap 6 '53
  Michelangelo. Sistine chapel
    frescoes:
    ceiling 21:62-9 Jy 1 '46
    ceiling and altar 27:25-49
    D 26 '49
  Mosaics, Santa Sophia, Istan-
    bul 29:54-61 D 25 '50
  Murillo. Esau selling his
    birthright 41:73 D 10 '53
  Murillo. St. Thomas of Villa-
    nueva dividing his clothing
    among beggar boys 4:42
    My 16 '38
  New Testament scenes, bronze
    doors, Benevento cathedral
    bw 17:58 Jy 24 '44
  Oriental artists. Biblical fig-
    ures and scenes bw 29:63,
    66 S 4 '50
  Piero della Francesca. Story
    of the true cross fresco
    20:60-8 Ap 22 '46
  Reinhardt. Resurrection bw
    32:88 Mr 24 '52
  Rembrandt. Esther's feast 41:
    74 D 10 '56
  Rembrandt. Sacrifice of Isaac
    etching bw 6:54 Ja 30 '39
  Rubens. Departure of Lot and
    his family from Sodom 4:
    24 Ap 11 '38
  St. Bartholomew day massa-
    cre, Paris, August 23,
    1572 bw 24:60 Je 14 '48
  Sample. Matthew 6:19 OR Lay
    not up for yourselves trea-

sures upon Earth 8:66 My
27 '40
  Schnorr. The Feast of Pass-
    over engraving bw 6:55 Ja
    30 '39
  Schnorr. Israelites in slav-
    ery* engraving bw 6:55 Ja
    30 '39
  Schnorr. Jacob's ladder bw
    6:55 Ja 30 '39
  Schnorr. Joseph interprets
    pharoah's dreams bw 6:55
    Ja 30 '39
  Schnorr. Potiphar's wife bw
    6:55 Ja 30 '39
  Shaker ceremony, New York,
    1873 bw 26:143 Mr 21 '49
  Steen. Worship of the golden
    calf 41:74 D 10 '56
  Tintoretto. Massacre of the
    innocents 31:34-5 D 24 '51
  Van Eyck, J. St. Francis
    receiving the stigmata 4:
    30 F 7 '38
  Van Eyck brothers. Adora-
    tion of the lamb bw 16:68
    Ja 10 '44
  Van Eyck brothers. The vir-
    gin martyrs 26:60-1 Ap
    18 '49
  Van Meergeren. Isaac bap-
    tizing Jacob (forged Ver-
    meer) bw 23:145 N 17 '47
  Van Nieulandt, Peace of West-
    phalia 24:58 Je 14 '48
  Woosung. Christian martyrs
    bw 29:63 S 4 '50
Bicycling See Games and
  Sports--Bicycling
Biddle, George
  My neighbor, Mr. Lounsber-
    ry bw 9:79 D 9 '40
  Society freed through Justice
    mural detail 2:34 Ja 4 '37
  Tenement mural detail 2:35
    Ja 4 '37
  General Dwight D. Eisen-
    hower bw 16:14 Ja 3 '44
    (drawing)
  Italian front, 1944: scenes,
    portraits bw 16:13-7 Ja

3 '44 (drawing)

Lt. General Mark Clark bw
16:14 Ja 3 '44 (drawing)

Major General Alfred M.
Gruenther bw 16:14 Ja 3
'44 (drawing)

Artist at work; portrait
photogs bw 2:32 Ja 4 '37
port.

Poor. George Biddle in mural, Tennessee Valley Au-
thority 2:36 Ja 4 '37 port.

Biddle, Thomas
Sully. Major Thomas Biddle
38:71 Mr 28 '55

Biddle, Nicholas
Sully. Nicholas Biddle 39:59
Ag 29 '55

Bieber, Bruce
Lea. Bruce Bieber, top
sergeant 11:64 Jy 7 '41

Bielenberg, Bob
Memories of New York ink
drawing 10:58 Je 16 '41

The bier. Stamos 28:87 Mr 20
'50

Bierstadt, Albert
Arch of Octavius, Rome 33:
91 S 15 '52

Mount Corcoran 27:59 Ag 29
'49

Thunderstorm in the Rockies
19:86 S 10 '45

Albert Bierstadt bw 19:82 S
10 '45 port.

The big dory. Bellows 29:71 Ag
21 '50

Big Four at Versailles: Orlando,
Lloyd George, Clemenceau,
Wilson, 1919 photog bw 15:
22 Ag 9 '43; 33:41 D 22 '52

Big turkey. Cowles 24:77 F 9
'48

Big Utopia. sculpture bw Gerny
21:101 Jy 8 '46

The big water. Waugh, F. J.
2:57 Je 14 '37 bw 3:24 D
20 '37

Big wheel locomotive. Feininger,
Lyonel 31:92-3 N 12 '51

Bigaud, Wilson

Chicken thief pursued by
policeman mural 33:64 D
22 '52

The game 23:60 S 1 '47

A voodoo rite 28:101 Mr 13
'50

Bigelow, William
William Bigelow bw 9:54 Jy
22 '40

Bilibrid Prison, Manila. Millman 19:67 O 8 '45

Bill, the artist's son. Peirce,
W. 18:75 My 14 '45

Bill of Rights. Castellon 30:96-
7 Mr 12 '51

Bill plays an old mandolin.
Peirce, W. 19:85 N 12 '45

Billiards See Games and Sports
--Billiards

Billiken drawing bw 25:11 N 8
'48

Billboard
Nalpas. New poster 39:117
S 12 '55

Billings, Henry
Arrest no. 2 4:27 Je 13 '38

The descent bw 8:70 My 27
'40

Mobile three dimensional
mural, Ford Building,
World's Fair, New York
6:42 Mr 13 '39

On the defensive 29:172-3 O
16 '50

U.S.S. North Carolina 11:60
Jy 7 '41 bw 14:7 Je 28 '43

Henry Billings photog bw
11:60 Jy 7 '41 port.

Henry Billings. in group
photog 29:172-3 O 16 '50
port.

Billings, Josh
Josh Billings bw 16:92 My 8
'44

Bill's poolroom. Jones, B. 10:
58 Je 16 '41

Billy. Sculpture bw Hardy 37:
123 O 11 '54

Billy the Kid See Bonney, William

Biltmore, North Carolina. Hunt,
    archt. 28:89-92 Ja 2 '50
Binet, Alfred
    Alfred Binet bw 2:60 Ap 19 '37
Binford, Julien
    The artist's wife, Elizabeth
        13:140 N 16 '42; 18:76 My
        14 '45
    The crap shooter 10:67 My 26
        '41
    New York Harbor in wartime
        17:55-60 N 20 '44
    The preaching deacon bw 13:
        140 N 16 '42
    The razor fight bw 13:140 N
        16 '42
    River Jordan mural bw 13:138-
        9 N 16 '42
    Artist and his work photog bw
        10:66 My 26 '41 port.
    Julien Binford photog bw 13:
        140 N 16 '42 port.
Bing, Rudolph
    Rudolph Bing photog bw 30:75
        F 12 '51
Bingham, George Caleb
    County election 7:42 S 11 '39
    Daniel Boone escorting a band
        of pioneers into the western
        country 6:28 Je 19 '39
    Fishing 38:72 Mr 28 '55
    Fur traders descending the
        Missouri (The trappers' re-
        turn) 28:76-7 Mr 6 '50
    Order no. 11 7:41 S 11 '39
    Raftsmen playing cards 7:41
        S 11 '39
    Shooting for the beef 6:28 Je
        19 '39
    Stump speaking 7:42 S 11 '39
    Verdict of the people 5:32 O
        31 '38; 16:54 Mr 13 '44;
        31:96 N 5 '51
    County election bw 7:43 S 11
        '39 (drawing)
    Mississippi River boatmen bw
        28:76 Mr 6 '50 (drawing)
    Raftsmen playing cards bw 7:
        40 S 11 '39 (drawing)
    Stump speaking bw 7:43 S 11
        '39 (drawing)

Self-portrait bw 7:40 S 11 '39
    port.
Birch, Reginald
    "Little Lord Fauntleroy,"
        illustrations bw 27:71 D
        5 '49
Birch, Thomas
    Constitution and Guerriere 9:
        47 O 28 '40
Birch, William
    State House, Philadelphia,
        1799 engraving 39:61 Jy
        4 '55
The birches. Peirce, W. 12:61
    Je 15 '42
Bird. fresco, Rome c3rd cen-
    tury 28:75 Mr 27 '50
Bird, Kenneth (Fougasse, pseu-
    donym) Careless talk costs
    lives poster bw 26:62-3
    Mr 7 '49
Bird basket. sculpture bw
    Moore, H. 22:78 Ja 20 '47
Bird in space. sculpture Bran-
    cusi 39:130 D 5 '55
Birds See also Animals, Imagi-
    nary; Audubon; names of
    birds, as Eagles
    Aztec stylized bird of prey
        with frog in beak gold
        work 18:49 Je 4 '45
    Burlingame. Gulls in flight
        sculpture bw 10:120 Ap
        21 '41
    Goya. Don Manuel Osorio de
        Zuniga 2:41 Je 28 '37
    Graves. Little known bird of
        the inner eye 35:88 S 28
        '53
    Graves. Preening sparrow
        35:88 S 28 '53
    Jacques. Upland game birds
        9:57-8 N 4 '40
    Junkin. First robin 10:67 My
        26 '41
    Peterson. American song
        and marsh birds 4:26 My
        23 '38
    Peterson. Bird courtship
        18:69-74 Je 4 '45

Birds (cont.)

Peterson. Birds 22:84-8 Je 2 '47

Peterson. Birds of prey 7:60-4 S 25 '39

Peterson. Shore and marsh birds 11:49-52 Ag 4 '41

Peterson. State birds 8:58-9, 61-2 Je 17 '40

Peterson. Winter birds 18:55-8 Ja 15 '45

Pilipili. Birds and bees 34: 106 My 4 '53

Pilipili and Ilunga. Frieze of birds, bugs, and foliage 34:106-7 My 4 '53

Quastler. Counterpoint woodcut 37:89 O 18 '54

Reinhardt. Strings and dead bird 32:90 Mr 24 '32

Svanberg. The vigilant heart lithograph 33:86 Jy 14 '52

Vulture emblem, Upper E-gypt, 4th dynasty photog bw 41:94 O 1 '56

White, J. Flamingo 22:84 Mr 10 '47

White, J. Frigate bird 22:84 Mr 10 '47

Wood, J. M. Britons as birds caricatures bw 24:16-8, Ap 12 '48

Birds and rocks, lithograph Zao Wou-ki 33:87 Jy 14 '52

Birds and wisteria. watercolor on silk bw Chang Shu-Chi 14:65-6 Mr 15 '43

Birds of paradise. Ward 31:103-5 Jy 16 '51

Birkenhead, First Earl of
Earl of Birkenhead 24:53 Ap 26 '48

Birkhoff, George D.
George D. Birkhoff photog bw 8:43 Mr 18 '40

Birley, Oswald
Winston Churchill, 1946 28: 62 F 27 '50

Birth, Thomas
Penn's tree, c1800 38:70-1 Mr 28 '55

The birth of a nation. sculpture bw Vos 3:71 Ag 9 '37

"The Birth of a Nation" is filmed byGriffith. Taubes 8:40-1 Ja 15 '40

The birth of Jesus. Lu Hung Nien 11:41 D 22 '41

Birth of the American nations. bw Carreno 10:106-7 Mr 17 '41

Birth of Venus. Botticelli 7:52 N 20 '39; 41:103 O 22 '56 bw 6:31 F 13 '39; 12:44 Mr 9 '42

Birthplace of Herbert Hoover. Wood, G. 14:55 Ja 18 '43

Bishop. woodcarving bw Swabia, Medieval 15:64 S 20 '43

Bishop, Eloise.
Head of boy sculpture bw 21: 62 My 22 '46

Bishop, Isabel
Walkowitz bw 16:77 F 21 '44

Bishop Hill, Ill.
Kraus. Portraits and scenes of communal settlers bw 16:10-2 Ja 31 '44

Bismark, Otto von
Bismark and Napoleon III bw 8:24 Ap 22 '40
Otto von Bismark bw 4:14 Mr 28 '38; 8:25 Ap 22 '40; 25:91 N 22 '48

"Bismark" (ship)
Brooks, J. Sinking of the Bismark 11:34-5 Ag 11 '41

Bison See also Buffaloes
Hardy. Bison sculpture bw 37:123 O 11 '54

Bitton, Isaac
Roberts, P. Isaac Bitton, boxer etching bw 6:42 F 6 '39

Black city. Congdon 30:109 Ap 30 '51

The black countess. Toulouse-Lautrec 28:97 My 15 '50

Black dancer. sculpture bw Wheelock 8:116 My 20 '40

Black Friday, 1869 cartoon bw 30:71 Je 11 '51

Black Hawk and son. Jarvis 36:
  73 Mr 8 '54
Black Hawk Stree, Chicago.
  Bohrod 8:68 My 27 '40
"Black Light" painting
  Radebaugh. Fluorescent paint-
    ings to be viewed by ultra-
    violet light 28:93 Mr 6 '50
Black prince ruby, gemstone 2:
  40 Mr 15 '37
Black squirrel. Audubon 30:47
  Ja 29 '51
Black stone of Islam, set in
  Kaaba photog bw 38:92 My
  9 '55
Black table. Matisse 31:115 N
  26 '51
Blackbucks. paper cutouts Mochi
  34:18-9 Mr 9 '53
The blacksmith shop. Johnson,
  E. 41:71 D 10 '56
Blacksmiths
  Goya. The forge 3:37 D 27 '37
  Currier and Ives print. The
    village blacksmith 9:28 D
    30 '40
Blackstone, William
  William Blackstone bw 25:113
    S 13 '48
  William Blackstone plaque,
    U.S. Congress bw 30:74 F
    5 '51
Blackwell's bridge. Bellows 7:
  36 Jy 31 '39
Blaeuw, Gulielmus
  World map, 1630 bw 13:58 Ag
    3 '42
Blaine, James G.
  Gillam. James Blain political
    cartoon bw 31:20 O 22 '51
  James G. Blaine photog bw
    14:7 My 31 '43
Blair, Montgomery
  Montgomery Blair photog bw
    14:75 F 15 '43
Blair, William
  Raeburn. Master William
    Blair 4:27 Ja 24 '38
Blake, William
  The great red dragon and the
    woman clothed with sun

watercolor bw 10:94 Je
  9 '41
The wise and foolish virgins
  watercolor bw 10:94 Je 9
  '41
God creating Adam bw 6:45
  Ja 16 '39 (engraving)
God creating Eve bw 6:45
  Ja 16 '39 (engraving)
God creating the world bw
  6:44 Ja 16 '39 (engraving)
"The Four Zoas"--Christ's
  crucifixion and resurrec-
  tion watercolors 36:60-4
  Ap 19 '54 (illustration)
"Sons of Innocence" title
  page bw 36:66 Ap 19 '54
  (illustration)
Death mask bw 36:68 Ap 19
  '54 port.
Artist's home photog bw 36:
  68 Ap 19 '54 port.
Self-portrait bw 36:66 Ap
  19 '54 port.
Blakelock, Ralph Albert
  Moonlight 23:101 S 8 '47
  Pipe dance bw 5:29 O 31 '38
  Ralph Blakelock photog bw
    5:29 O 31 '38 port.
Blanch, Arnold
  Basket and fruit 7:26 Ag 28 '39
  Lake resort 25:66 Ag 23 '48
  Arnold Blanch photog bw 6:
    26 F 13 '39; 11:40 Ag 11
    '41 port.
  Arnold Blanch. in group
    photog 29:172-3 O 16 '50
    port.
Blanche of Castile bw 22:84 My
  26 '47
Bland, "Silver Dick"
  Silver Dick Bland statue bw
    17:81 N 6 '44
Blanding, Sarah
  Clemens. Sarah Blanding of
    Vassar 23:91 O 27 '47
Blarenberghe, Louis van
  British surrender, Yorktown,
    October 19, 1781 29:58-9
    Jy 3 '50
Blenheim palace, England.
  Vanbrugh, archt photog 24:

32 Ap 19 '48

Blessings of peace. cartoon bw
Shepard 24:60 Ap 26 '48

Blind, Art for   See also Artists,
Blind
Amendola. Kineglyph--sculp-
ture for the blind bw 21:
102 N 11 '46

Blind beggar. bw Picasso 38:
128 Je 27 '55

Blind leading the blind. Marcier
36:83 My 31 '54

Blochman, Lawrence G.
Lawrence Blochman photog
bw 22:21 Mr 10 ' 47

Bloch collection of modern art
33:94-5 O 27 '52

Blondie. cartoon bw Young 13:
8-9, 11 Aug 17 '42

Bloom, Hyman
Painting 33:98 O 27 '52

Bloor, Ella Reeve ("Mother
Bloor") Mother Bloor
photog bw 3:27 Jy 26 '37

Blowing Bubbles See Games and
Sports--Bubble Blowing

The blue bench. Raczka 28:90
Mr 20 '50

The blue boy (Jonathan Buttall).
Gainsborough 4:26 Ja 24
'38

The blue chair. Grosz 7:26 Ag
28 '39

The blue clown. Kuhn 26:88 F 21
'49

Blue dump. tempera Wyeth, A.
24:104 My 17 '48

Blue-eyed shell. Ernest 32:58
Ja 21 '52

Blue hat. Comfort 10:47 F 3 '41

Blue horse. Jackson, Harry 41:
70 Jy 9 '56

Blue jay. Audubon 3:39 Jy 12 '37

Blue jays. Peterson 12:43-5 Je 1
'42

Blue mosque, Istanbul photogs
bw 8:82-3 Ap 8 '40

The blue necklace. Speicher 3:
27 D 20 '37

"Blueberries for Sal," illustrations. McCloskey bw 25:

69-71 D 27 '48

Blueprint of the future. Diego
28:81 Mr 11 '46

Blume, Peter
The eternal city bw 3:20
D 6 '37
Lilies 8:67 My 27 '40
The rock 26:108-9 Ap 11 '49
South of Scranton bw 16:79
Ap 24 '44

Blumenfeld, Erwin, photographer
Salon photographs bw 7:4-6
Jy 3 '39
The spirit of the chair photog
bw 24:14 My 10 '48

Blyth, Benjamin
Abigail Adams, 1763 41:70
Jy 2 '56
John Adams, 1763 41:70 Jy
2 '56

Blythe, David Gilmour
General Doubleday crossing
the Potomac, 1863 6:29
Je 19 '39
The Pittsburgh horse market
9:76 D 9 '40
Post office 40:125 Je 4 '56

Boabdil, King of Granada
Boabdil statue bw 17:63 O
30 '44

Boadicea, Queen of the Iceni
Queen Boadicea bw 14:6 Ja
4 '43; 22:98 Mr 24 '47

Boas, Franz
Epstein. Professor Franz
Boas sculpture bw 3:90
N 15 '37

Boat and sea. watercolor Marin
29:63 Jy 10 '50

Boating party. Cassatt 36:98
My 17 '54

Boating party at Chatou. Renoir
3:46 Jy 5 '37; 32:93 My
19 '52

Boats See Ships

Boats of Saintes-Maries. bw
Van Gogh 27:82 O 10 '49

Boccacci, Marcello
Laundress* bw 29:15 O 30
'50

Boccaccio, Giovanni
  Giovanni Boccaccio bw 22:78
    Mr 3 '47
Bock, Vera
  Christmas tree drawing bw
    19:9 D 24 '45
Bodhisatva Tibet bw 39:92 Mr 7
    '55
Bodiam castle, England, 14th
    century photog 40:91 Mr
    19 '56 bw 8:44 Je 3 '40;
    22:74 My 26 '47
Bodmer, Charles
  Bellevue 15:88 Ag 30 '43
  Camp of the Gros Ventres of
    the prairies 15:88 Ag 30
    '43
  Encampment of the travelers
    15:88 Ag 30 '43
  Interior of an Indian hut, Man-
    dan tribe* 27:45 Jy 4 '49
  Missouri river 15:87 Ag 30
    '43
  White castels on the upper
    Missouri 15:87 Ag 30 '43
  Pehriska-Ruhpa, war chief of
    the Minnetaree tribe, Da-
    kota 27:41 Jy 4 '49 (litho-
    graph)
Boggs, Franklin
  Flying harrows 28:83 Mr 20
    '50
The bohemian. Hals 35:60 Ag 17
    '53 bw 9:6 S 30 '40
Bohrod, Aaron
  Black Hawk Street, Chicago
    8:68 My 27 '40
  Chicago beach 25:62-3 Jy 26
    '48
  Clinton in winter mural,
    Post Office, Clinton, Ill.
    10:45 Ja 27 '41
  Crowd of artists* 25:66 Ag
    23 '48
  England in World War 18:47-
    55 Ap 30 '45
  Evening in Roscommon 11:94
    N 10 '41
  Idle hour park 11:62 Jy 7 '41
    bw 14:6 Je 28 '43
  Landscape near Chicago 2:24

F 1 '37
Merrillan night 11:94 N 10
    '41
Omaha Beach: battle, ruins,
    dead 17:53-6 O 30 '44
Paddington Station, London
    31:78 O 29 '51
Rainy night 11:93 N 10 '41
Reflections on a shop window
    14:44 Mr 8 '43; 21:77 N
    25 '46
Rendova: the landing in New
    Georgia 15:72-7 D 27 '43
Ruined German village* 35:
    94 N 16 '53
Saluting in Grosvenor Square*
    31:78 O 29 '51
Sanctuary, church, Berdorf,
    Luxemburg 35:67 N 2 '53
Taverns at night 11:93 N 10
    '41
War in France: Normandy
    sketchbook bw 17:8-10 Ag
    28 '44 (drawing)
Aaron Bohrod photog bw 2:32
    F 1 '37; 11:60 Jy 7 '41;
    15:12 O 25 '43; 15:84 D
    27 '43 port.
Artist at work; home photog
    11:92 N 10 '41 bw 18:
    Cover Ap 30 '45 port.
Self-portrait bw 15:12 O 25
    '43 port.
Boit children. Sargent 36:96-7
    My 17 '54
Boleyn, Anne
  Anne Boleyn 41:Cover, 88 O
    29 '56 bw 3:34 O 18 '37
  Beheading of Ann Boleyn bw
    24:61 Je 14 '48
Boltraffio, Giovanni Antonio
  Portrait of a youth (Girolamo
    Casio) bw 24:67 Ja 26 '48
Bombardment of Fort Sumter
    bw 39:182 S 12 '55
Bombardment of Island No. 10.
    Currier and Ives print
    21:72 S 2 '46
Bombardment of Tripoli, 1804.
    Corne 9:47 O 28 '40

Bomberg, Manuel
Manuel Bomberg photog bw
9:65 O 7 '40 port.
Bonampak murals, Mayan 27:
80-4 N 21 '49
Bonaparte, Mme Lucien
Ingre. Mme Lucien Bonaparte
drawing 34:91 My 11 '53
Bonaparte, Napoleon See Na-
poleon I, Emperor of the
French
Bonawit, G. Owen
Life of Christ stained glass
6:31 Ap 3 '39
Bond, John R., interior design
Bond and Mary Miller. Con-
temporary Southern house
38:117 F 21 '55
Bone, Muirhead
The Alhambra, Court of Lions
1:44 D 7 '36
Bread-buyers, Astorga,
Spain 1:43 D 7 '36
Bridge, Ronda, Spain 1:42
D 7 '36
Cudillero, Spain 1:43 D 7 '36
"Lucerna" in dry dock 26:57
Mr 21 '49
The miracle of Dunkerque--
arrival at Dover bw 10:64
F 24 '41
Peasants, Caceres, Spain
1:43 D 7 '36
Whitehall--Thoroughfare of
empire pastel 24:60 My
10 '48
Church, Arevalo, Spain bw
1:45 D 7 '36 (drawing)
Life lines bw 10:64 F 24 '41
(drawing)
Gothic cathedral, Leon, Spain
bw 1:45 D 7 '36 (etching)
Bongo, African
Mochi. African bongo paper
cutout 34:19 Mr 9 '53
Bonheur, Rosa
The horse fair 6:55 Mr 20 '39
Bonhomme Richard and Serapis
(ships) 29:55 Jy 3 '50
Bonnard, Pierre
At the Moulin Rouge 25:53

Jy 26 '48
Cabinet de toilette 25:56 Jy
26 '48
Fish 17:75 N 13 '44
Golden hair 25:54 Jy 26 '48
The open window 38:107 My
23 '55
Portrait of a woman 25:54
Jy 26 '48
The Riviera 25:54-5 Jy 26
'48
Artist at work; portrait;
photog bw 17:74 N 13 '44;
25:52 Jy 26 '48 port.
Bonney, William H. (Billy the
Kid)
Associates; locale photogs
bw 11:67-9 Ag 4 '41
William Bonney photogs bw
11:66 Ag 4 '41
Bony, Paul
St. Peter stained glass,
France 28:74-5 Je 19 '50
Book Binding
"The Four Gospels," manu-
script cover, gold and
jewelled St. Gall, Switzer-
land, 9th century 18:57
Ap 2 '45
"Book of Hours" 15th century.
Arming of Henry V, King of
England 40:178 Ap 9 '56
"Book of Hours" (Tres Riches
Heures) of the Duc de
Berry
Calendar paintings--Limbourg
brothers; Colombe 24:38-
50 Ja 5 '48
Books and Printing see also
Illuminations; Illustra-
tions; Literary Land-
marks and Locale; Manu-
scripts; names of authors
Bay Psalm Book photog bw
37:95 N 22 '54
Constance Missal, oldest
typographical book (?)
photog 36:80-1 Mr 1 '54
Early printed calendars.
German, French, English
bw 18:42-3 Ja 1 '45

Books and Printing (cont.)
  Laning. Gutenberg printing
    Bible bw 33:92 O 20 '52
  Laning. History of printing
    mural, New York Public
    Library 9:65-6 S 30 '40
  Newton (A. Edward) collec-
    tion of rare books and
    manuscripts photogs bw 10:
    86-8 Je 9 '41
Bookstalls, Paris. Davis, G. R.
  19:49 Jy 16 '45
Bookstores
  Thomas Davies London book-
    store, 1763 bw 29:94 D 4
    '50
Boone, Daniel
  Bingham. Daniel Boone es-
    corting a band of pioneers
    into the western country
    6:28 Je 19 '39
  Lockwood, Daniel Boone's
    arrival in Kentucky 10:46
    Ja 27 '41
Booner, Arnold
  Jan Six II bw 31:66 Jy 16 '51
  Jan Six III bw 31:66 Jy 16 '51
Booth, Edwin Thomas
  Booth as Hamlet 31:116 N 19
    '51
  Edwin Booth photog bw 7:50
    Ag 28 '39
Booth, Evangeline
  Evangeline Booth photogs bw
    29:72-3 Jy 31 '50
Booth, John Wilkes
  Currier and Ives print. As-
    sassination of President
    Lincoln* bw 5:7 Jy 11 '38
  John Wilkes Booth photog bw
    4:44 F 18 '38; 5:5 Jy 11
    '38
Booth (Ralph H.) collection of
  Renaissance paintings given
  to National Gallery, Wash-
  ington, D.C. 24:66-7 Ja 26
  '48
Boquet. Roualt 34:61 F 2 '53
Boquet and stove. Kuniyoshi 28:
  86 F 21 '49
Borden, Lizzie

Lizzie Borden bw 25:60 Ag 2
  '48
Bores, Francisco
  Seated woman 17:76 N 13 '44
  Artist at work photog bw 17:
    74 N 13 '44 port.
Borgatta, Isabel Case, sculptor
  Expectation bw 37:101 D 6
    '54
  First born bw 37:102 D 6 '54
  Sleeping bw 37:102 D 6 '54
  Tender mother bw 37:102 D
    6 '54
Borglum, Gutzon, sculptor
  Abraham Lincoln bw 18:
    Cover Je 18 '45
  George Washington bw 11:103
    O 6 '41
  John W. Mackey statue bw
    12:110 My 11 '42
  Mount Rushmore national
    memorial, Black Hills,
    S. Dak. Washington, Jef-
    ferson, Lincoln photog 4:
    26 Je 27 '38 bw 3:104 O
    4 '37 completed with fourth
    unit: T. Roosevelt photog
    bw 7:19 Jy 17 '39
  Sacco-Vanzetti memorial
    plaque bw 3:24 S 6 '37
Bornet, John
  Niagara Falls, 1855 lithograph
    26:77 Je 6 '49
Boru, Sorcha, ceramicist
  Dancer bw 9:130 N 11 '40
  Sentimental letter bw 9:130
    N 11 '40
Bosa, Louis
  Family reunion mural 30:
    154-5 Mr 19 '51
Bosch, Hieronymus
  The betrayal 6:38 My 29 '39
  Creation of the world 27:75
    N 14 '49
  The crowning with thorns
    31:69 O 1 '51
  Garden of delights triptych
    27:75-82 N 14 '49
  Garden of Eden (Garden of
    Paradise) 11:56 S 8 '41;
    27:76 N 14 '49

Hell, triptych detail 27:77,
78-9, 82 N 14 '49
The heretical owl 27:80 N
14 '49
Mountain of heresy, triptych
detail 27:81 N 14 '49
Self-portrait bw 27:75 N 14
'49 port.
Boschi, Egidio, paintings on pin-
heads bw 30:146-7 Je 11
'51
Artist at work photog bw 30:
146-8 Je 11 '51 port.
Boston
Old Feather store, 1820-5
13:81 N 23 '42
View of Boston, 1730-40 13:
81 N 23 '42
Boston Harbor--Long and Cen-
tral wharves, 1832. Sal-
mon 6:29 Je 19 '39
Boston Massacre. engraving
Revere 20:39 Jy 3 '50
Boston Museum of Fine Arts.
Treasures from collection;
patrons 9:50-4 Jy 22 '40
Boston Tea Party, 1774 print bw
22:99 Mr 24 '47
Boswell, James
Reynolds. James Boswell bw
29:97 D 4 '50
Rowlandson. Johnson and Bos-
well caricature bw 29:93
D 4 '50
Bothwell, James Hepburn
Earl of Bothwell bw 24:67 Je
14 '48
Botticelli, Sandro
Adoration of the Magi 13:44-
5 D 28 '42
Amerigo Vespucci bw 37:106
O 11 '54
Birth of Venus 7:52 N 20 '39;
41:103 O 22 '56 bw 6:31 F
13 '39; 12:44 Mr 9 '42
Portrait of a young man 4:30
Mr 21 '38
St. Sebastian bw 19:24 D 31
'45
Three miracles of St. Zeno-
bias bw 21:104 O 28 '46

Sandro Botticelli bw 4:26 Mr
21 '38 port.
Bottles and Flasks
Amber whisky flask, eagle
design, U.S., c1850 17:
59 S 4 '44
Benjamin Franklin flask, U.S.
40:82 Ja 9 '56
Columbia blown flask, U.S.
39:58-9 Jy 18 '55
Ludlow bottle, U.S. 39:58-9
Jy 18 '55
Ohio "grandfather" flask 39:
58 Jy 18 '55
Ohio three-mold decanter
39:59 Jy 18 '55
Stiegel. "Daisy-diamond"
blown flask 39:58-9 Jy 18
'55
Swedish glass decanter bw
17:65-8 Ag 7 '44
Venetian misty glass bottle,
18th century 37:54 Ag 2
'54
Bouche, Louis
Broad Street Station, Phila-
delphia 11:49 Ag 18 '41
The Eads bridge over the
Mississippi 11:50 Ag 18 '41
Long Island sound 8:68 My
27 '40
McSorley's bar 10:73 Ap 14
'41
Mural assistant 6:28 F 13 '39
Patriotic still life 11:49 Ag
18 '41
Ten cents a ride (ferry) 14:
45 Mr 8 '43
Train through the night 11:
50 Ag 18 '41
Artist at work; wife photogs
bw 11:48 Ag 18 '41 port.
Louis Bouche. in group
photog 29:172-3 O 16 '50
port.
Boucher, François
Cupid and three graces bw
29:81 N 27 '50
Girl resting 41:104-5 O 22
'56

Boucher, François (cont.)
  Jupiter in the guise of Diane,
    and Callisto 5:36 S 26 '38
  Love disarmed bw 12:44 Mr
    9 '42
  Madame de Pompadour 23:81
    S 15 '47 bw 5:39 S 26 '38
  Panels, Pompadour room bw
    3:30 D 27 '37
  The toilet of Venus 23:85 S 15
    '47 bw 16:68 Ja 10 '44; 33:
    2 D 29 '52
  Nude 40:70 My 28 '56 (draw-
    ing)
  La noble pastorale bw Beau-
    vais 4:28 Ja 24 '38 (tapes-
    try)
  François Boucher bw 5:34 S
    26 '38 port.
Bouguereau, Adolphe
  Bathers bw 11:54 S 8 '41
Bouncing baby. sculpture bw
    Chaim 30:65 Ja 8 '51
Bound slave. sculpture bw Mi-
    chelangelo 27:99 D 5 '49
Bourges cathedral. Three a-
    postles stained glass 22:
    72-3 Ap 7 '47
Bourke-White, Margaret, pho-
    tographer Selected pictures
    from 25 years of work bw
    38:16-7 My 16 '55
  U.S. Capitol dome photog bw
    3:Cover N 29 '37
  Margaret Bourke-White photog
    bw 38:16-7 My 16 '55 port.
Boussac, Marcel
  Karsh. Marcel Boussac
    photog bw 37:133 O 4 '54
Bouts, Aelbrecht
  The annunication 1:45 D 28
    '36
Bowen, Nathaniel
  Morse. The Reverend Nathan-
    iel Bowen 17:60 D 18 '44
Bowen, Owen
  After the heat of the day 23:
    84 N 17 '47
Bowerman's Nose, rock forma-
    tion Devonshire, England
    photog bw 5:45 S 12 '38

The Bowery. Marsh 40:84 F 6
  '56
Bowles, Paul
  Paul Bowles photog bw 28:35
    Ja 30 '50
Bowling See Games and
  Sports--Bowling
Bowls
  African carved bowl, Baluba
    bw 33:120 S 8 '52
  American Indian bowls: A-
    coma; Hopi; Mimbres;
    Santa Domingo 40:55 Ja
    16 '56
  Italian basin, Middle Ages
    22:79 My 26 '47
  Melanesian bowl 21:81 N 4
    '46
  Neolithic Eridu bowl 40:81
    Ap 16 '56
  Ohio flat bowl 39:58 Jy 18 '55
  Sandwich pressed glass bowl
    39:58 Jy 18 '55
  Swedish glass bowl bw 17:65-
    8 Ag 7 '44
  Tiffany glass 40:92-3 Mr 5
    '56
  Waugh. Compass bowl en-
    graved glass bw 7:32 S
    18 '39
  Waugh. Merry-go-round
    bowl, Steuben glass bw
    23:18 N 10 '47
  Waugh. Zodiac bowl engraved
    glass bw 7:32 S 18 '39
Bowman, Isaiah
  Isaiah Bowman photog bw 19:
    118 O 22 '45
Bows See Weapons--Bows
Boxeadores. sculpture bw
    Yrurtia 8:17 Ja 29 '40
Boxer Rebellion bw 6:11 Ja 2
  '39
Boxes
  Bronze boudoir box, Etrus-
    can 4th century B.C. 40:
    64 F 13 '56
  Carved wooden strong box,
    Massachusetts, 1650 38:
    127 Ap 18 '55

Papered bandbox, U.S.,
c1830 bw 39:69 Ag 29 '55
Toleware box, U.S. 39:56 Jy
18 '55
Boxing See Games and Sports--
Boxing
Boy. bust bw Brancusi 39:135 D
5 '55
Boy. sculpture bw Kruger 39:189
N 14 '55
Boy blowing bubbles. Manet 29:
89 N 27 '50
Boy from the plains. Hurd 7:26
Jy 24 '39
Boy scout calendar. Rockwell
18:45 Ja 1 '45
Boy with mask. sculpture bw
Carlton 5:70 D 5 '38
Boy with rabbit. bw Raeburn 14:
111 Ja 25 '43
Boy with squirrel. bw Copley
5:28 O 31 '38
Boy with toys. bw Siporin 27:56
D 26 '49
Boyd, James
"Drums," illustrated by Wy-
eth, N.C. 20:81 Je 17 '46
Boyd, William S.
Fall morning 23:98 N 10 '47
William S. Boyd photog bw
23:101 N 10 '47 port.
Boyer, Adelbert
Pinhead painting and sculp-
ture bw 20:14-6 Mr 25 '46
Boyle, Ferdinand
Ulysses Grant bw 6:31 Je 19
'39
Boylston, Nicholas
Copley. Nicholas Boylston 9:
52 Jy 22 '40
Boys sleeping. Rosenthal 10:73
Ap 14 '41
Bracelets See Jewelry
Brackett, Edward
Washington Allston sculpture
bw 19:9 S 24 '45
Brackman, Robert
Angelica 8:60 F 5 '40
Autumn light 8:59 F 5 '40
Composition in life and still
life 5:29 S 19 '38

Francis Weld 8:60 F 5 '40
Still life with mask 8:60 F
5 '40
Artist and work; teaching
photogs bw 8:58 F 5 '40
port.
Bradford, Francis Scott
Mosaics, chapel, England
35:38 Ag 24 '53
Bradford, Gamaliel
Gamaliel Bradford photog
bw 11:91 S 8 '41
Bradford, William
Coat of arms bw 19:57 N 26
'45
William Bradford in Prayer
at sailing of Mayflower
bw 25:132 N 29 '48
Bradley, Lewis Rice
Lewis Bradley photog bw 26:
107 Ap 18 '49
Bradley, Omar
General Omar Bradley,
"Time" Cover portrait
17:61 D 11 '44
Brady, Matthew, photographer
Abraham Lincoln photogs bw
1860, 1864, 1865 38:23 F
14 '55
Abraham Lincoln, 1861
photog bw 12:52 Ja 5 '42
Abraham Lincoln, February
9, 1864 photog bw 14:75
F 15 '43
U.S. Supreme Court justices
photog bw 3:28 N 29 '37
Elliott. Matthew Brady
photog bw 6:31 Je 19 '39
port.
Matthew Brady photog bw
33:21 N 10 '52 port.
Bragg, Aston
Jackson, the American deer
6:40 F 6 '39
Brancacci chapel
Masaccio. The tribute money
fresco 39:22-3 D 26 '55
Brancusi, Constantin, sculptor
Bird in space bronze 39:
136 D 5 '55

Brancusi, Constantin (cont.)
  Boy bust bw 39:135 D 5 '55
  Bust, in Armory Show bw 26:
      89 F 21 '49
  The chief bw 24:95 Ap 12 '48
  Head bw 2:51 Ap 5 '37
  Head of Prometheus bw 39:
      135 D 5 '55
  The kiss bw 28:63 Ja 2 '50
  Mlle Pogany bronze 39:130
      D 5 '55
  Primitive figure bw 39:135
      D 5 '55
  Artist's studio; protraits
      photogs bw 39:130-9 D 5
      '55 port.
  Constantin Brancusi, c1912
      photog bw 28:62 Ja 2'50
      port.
Brandies, Louis
  Berks. Louis Brandeis statue
      bw 41:70 N 26 '56
  Louis Brandeis photog bw 23:
      118 N 4 '46
  Poor. Louis Brandeis in The
      Gold Case 2:36 Ja 4 '37
Brandenburg Gate, Berlin, 1945
    photog bw 19:21 Jy 23 '45
Brandt, Rex
  Purse seiner 11:76 O 27 '41
Brant, Isabella
  Rubens. The artist and his
      first wife 7:56 N 20 '39
  Rubens. Isabella Brant 24:
      63 My 3 '48
Brant, Joseph (Thayendenega)
  Humphreys. "Jack of Clubs,"
      playing card 38:Cover My
      30 '55
Braque, Georges
  Anemones 26:83 My 2 '49
  Billiard table 33:94 O 27 '52
  Collage: newspapers and wall-
      paper bw 26:82 My 2 '49
  Compote dish, bottle and man-
      dolin 26:85 My 2 '49
  L'Estaque bw 26:82 My 2 '49
  Guitarist bw 26:82 My 2 '49
  Pitcher and basket of fruit 26:
      83 My 2 '49
  The round table 38:109 My

  23 '55
  Still life bw 26:82 My 2 '49
  Still life: grapes and bananas
      33:95 O 27 '52
  Still life: Le Jour 26:84 My
      2 '39
  Still life with grapes 38:109
      My 23 '55
  Still life with pink back-
      ground 26:84 My 2 '49
  Studio* 33:93 O 27 '52
  Sugar bowl with fruit 26:83
      My 2 '49
  Sun flowers 26:86 My 2 '49
  The waltz 4:44 My 2 '38
  Woman with basket of fruit
      26:84 My 2 '49
  Woman with mandolin bw
      25:75 O 11 '48
  The yellow cloth bw 3:24
      D 20 '37
  The artist's mother, 1904
      bw 26:82 My 2 '49 (draw-
      ing)
  Palotte bw 3:113 Ap 26 '54
      (drawing)
  Artist at work photog 26:80
      My 2 '49 port.
  Gallatin. Georges Braque in
      his studio photog bw 4:
      45 My 2 '38 port.
  Georges Braque, ages 4 to
      33 photogs bw 26:81 My
      2 '49 port.
  Karsh. Georges Braque,
      age 68 photog bw 29:73
      Ag 7 '50 port.
Bratby, John
  Jean and still life in front of
      window bw 40:168 Ap 23
      '56
  Artist at work photog bw 40:
      164 Ap 23 '56 port.
Bratt, Clara
  Figure* sculpture bw 2:27
      Ap 19 '37
Brauner, Victor
  Kabyline in movement 1:26
      D 14 '36

Bravo, Nicolas
  Bravo pardoning soldiers*
    mural bw Palacio Nacional,
    Mexico City 18:31 Mr 19
    '45
Braxton, Carter
  Carter Braxton bw 15:8 Jy 5
    '43
The brazen serpent. bw Dore
    23:45 S 22 '47
Brazil
  Emblem: winged lion of Bra-
    zil sculpture bw 10:61 Ja
    6 '41
  Marsh. Brazil scenes--World
    War 18:64-5 Ap 30 '45
  Martins da Silveira. Proces-
    sion 36:82-3 My 31 '54
  Public and office buildings;
    apartments photogs bw 13:
    132-4 O 26 '42
  Brazil, French map, 1547 24:
    79 Mr 22 '48 (map)
Bread buyers, Spain. Bone 1:43
    D 7 '36
The breakdown. Mount 18:67 Je
    25 '45
The Breakers. Hunt, archt 31:
    46-9 Jy 23 '51
Breaking home ties. Hovenden
    9:76 D 9 '40; 27:60 Ag 29
    '49
Breast plates See also Armor
  Inca gold breastplate 36:102-
    3 Ap 12 '54
Breckinridge, John
  John Breckinridge photog bw
    9:8 Ag 5 '40
Breger, Dave
  G.I. Joe cartoon bw 15:12-4
    Jy 12 '43
Breinin, Raymond
  Silent Night, Holy Night 23:
    50-1 D 22 '47
Brenda. Arcieri 16:46 Ja 3 '44
Brenet, Albert
  Refugees* 9:58 Ag 12 '40
Brent in Strangford lough. Scott
    7:53 N 13 '39
Breteche, Monsieur de la
  Fragonard. M. de la Breteche

bw 3:43 N 29 '37
Breuer, Bessie (Mrs Henry
    Varnum Poor)
  Poor. March sun 12:61 Je
    15 '42
Breuer, Marcel
  Marcel Breuer photog bw
    10:96 My 5 '41
Brewster, William
  Coat of arms bw 19:57 N 26
    '45
  William Brewster in Signing
    of Mayflower Compact bw
    25: 130 N 29 '48
Bri, G. See Brinkmann, Ger-
    hard
Brice, Fanny
  Decker. Fanny Brice as
    Mona Lisa bw 4:34 Ap 18
    '38
Bridal painting, India 31:155
    N 5 '51
The bride stripped bare by her
    own bachelors, even.
    Duchamp 32:103 Ap 28
    '52
Bridger, Frank H.
  Bridger and Paxton. Office
    building, Albuquerque, N.
    Mex.--glass-wall solar
    heating unit bw 41:71 D
    17 '56
Bridges
  Bellows. Blackwell's bridge
    7:36 Jy 31 '39
  Bone. Bridge, Ronda, Spain
    1:42 D 7 '36
  Bouche. The Eads bridge
    over the Mississippi 11:
    50 Ag 18 '41
  Camel-back bridge, Summer
    palace, Peiping photog
    bw 3:58 Ag 23 '37
  Cezanne. The little bridge
    32:82 F 25 '52
  Chamberlain. Golden gate
    bridge 23:98 N 10 '47
  Corot. The bridge at Mantes
    29:90 N 27 '50
  Covered bridge, Vermont
    photog bw 3:40 Jy 19 '37

Bridges (cont.)
  Delaware memorial bridge
    photog bw 40:100-1 My 21
    '56
  Dufy. Brooklyn bridge 30:64-5
    Ja 22 '51
  Hiroshige. Enkyo bridge 31:
    67 D 31 '51
  Hopper. Manhattan bridge loop
    28:102-3 Ap 17 '50
  Kingman. Junk sailing under
    Brooklyn bridge* bw 30:
    100 My 14 '51
  Moore, C. H. The old bridge
    19:84 S 10 '45
  Pleissner. Remagen bridge*
    35:94 N 16 '53
  Renoir. The Pont Neuf 32:
    92 My 19 '52
  Sterne. Construction 31:54 Ag
    27 '51
  Thomas, B. Summer bw 10:
    53 Je 23 '41
  Vanbrugh bridge photog 24:
    32 Ap 19 '48
  Van Gogh. Bridge at Arles 2:
    34 F 15 '37
  Whistler. Old Battersea bridge
    12:62 Je 15 '42
  Whistler. Old Battersea bridge
    (Symphony in Brown and
    Silver) 36:94-5 My 17 '54
Brinkmann, Gerhard (G. Bri,
    pseudonym)
  Ellis island scenes bw 6:60-1
    Mr 13 '39
Brisbane, Arthur
  Arthur Brisbane photog bw 31:
    26 Ag 27 '51
British batteries, Crimean War
    bw 11:15 D 15 '41
British burn U.S. Capitol, 1814
    bw 12:97 My 25 '42
"British Character." cartoons
    bw Laidler 5:58-9 D 19 '38
British lion. sculpture
    Hardiman 2:43 Ja 25 '37
Brittany
  Gauguin. The swineherd,
    Brittany 21:62 Jy 29 '46
Brittany landscape. Gauguin

21:62 Jy 29 '46
Britten, Benjamin
  Benjamin Britten photog bw
    21:46 Ag 26 '46
Broad Street station, Philadel-
    phia. club car mural
    Bouche 11:49 Ag 18 '41
Brockhurst, Gerald
  Duchess of Windsor 28:110
    Je 12 '50
  Francis MacNamara, poet
    10:48 F 3 '41
Brockman, Ann
  Nude 5:30 S 19 '38
Brodie, Howard
  The last days of Guadalcanal
    cartoons bw 18:15 My 7
    '45
Brodovitch, Alexey, furniture
    designer
  Chair, knockdown wood-cord
    bw 28:98 My 8 '50
The broken eggs. Greuze 5:36
    S 26 '38
Broken-wreath hooked rug 8:45
    Ja 29 '40
Bromfield, Louis
  Louis Bromfield photogs bw
    25:111 O 11 '48
Bronco buster. Remington 13:
    73 S 14 '42
Bronco buster. sculpture bw
    Remington 11:54 N 10 '41;
    13:72 S 14 '42
Bronte, Emily
  Bronte, P. Emily Bronte bw
    6:39 Ap 3 '39
Bronte, Patrick Branwell
  The Bronte sisters bw 15:
    95 N 29 '43
  Emily Bronte bw 6:39 Ap 3
    '39
The Bronte sisters (Anne, Char-
    lotte, Emily).
  Bronte, P. The Bronte sis-
    ter bw 15:95 N 29 '43
  Home; mementoes; literary
    locale bw 15:95-9 N 29
    '43
Bronze doors, scenes from
    New Testament, Bene-

vento cathedral, Italy bw
17:58 Jy 24 '44

Bronzes

Graves. Han Bronze 35:88 S
28 '53

Egyptian--Cat, goddess U-
basti, 6th century, B.C.
bw 5:16 Ag 29 '38; 13:92
N 9 '42

Etruscan--Boudoir box, 4th
century B.C. 40:64 F 13
'56
Candalabra 40:63 F 13 '56
Goddess 40:63 F 13 '56
Perfume box, 8th century
B.C. 40:61 F 13 '56
Sea god, relief, c500 B.C.
40:59 F 13 '56
Warrior, 450 B.C. 40:62-
3 F 13 '56

German--Water vessel, 14th
century 37:63 Ag 9 '54

Greek--Demeter, 4th century
35:41 D 21 '53
Hercules, 500 B.C. bw 6:
52 Mr 20 '39
Ram's head crested hel-
met, 700 B.C. 29:23 D
25 '50
Two-piece mirror bw 6:53
Mr 20 '39
Urn, 6th century 37:86-8
S 13 '54

Italian--Vittoria. Nude negro,
Venice, c1600 bw 6:53 Mr
20 '39

Japanese--Miroku, c666 30:
72 My 28 '51

Persian--Ewer, 8th century
20:92 Je 24 '46
Ornaments and charms,
c1000 B.C. bw 20:90
Je 24 '46

Sumerian--Sargon of Akkad,
head, 24th century B.C.
bw 40:95 Je 4 '56

Victorian--Nymph lamp, U.S.
40:86 Mr 5 '56

Bronzino, Agnolo
Wife of Cosimo de' Medici bw
6:32 F 13 '39

Brooches See Jewelry--
Brooches and Pins

Brook, Alexander
Bacchante 5:30 S 19 '38
Bette Davis 17:73 N 20 '44
Georgia jungle 10:52 Ja 13
'41; 21:74 N 25 '46 bw
16:79 Ap 24 '44
Ingrid Bergman 18:37 Ja 15
'45
Katharine Hepburn 8:46 Ja
22 '40
Merle Oberon as George
Sand 18:69 F 5 '45
Pasture at Elk 10:52 Ja 13
'41
Peggy Bacon and Metaphys-
ics bw 6:57 My 8 '39
Sentimental ideas bw 8:69
My 27 '40
Summer wind 10:51 Ja 13 '41
Walkowitz bw 16:79 F 21 '44
Artist and wife; at work
photogs bw 10:50 Ja 13
'41 port.
Alexander Brook. in group
photog 29:172-3 O 16 '50
port.

Brook willow. Thomas, T. 10:
51 Je 23 '41

Brooklyn bridge. Dufy 30:64-5
Ja 22 '51

Brooklyn Museum. Sculptors
guild exhibit bw 5:4-7 N
7 '38

Brooks, James
James Brooks photog bw
30:34 Ja 15 '51 port.

Brooks, Joe
Sinking of the Bismark 11:
34-5 Ag 11 '41

Brooks, Theodore, architect
Brooks and Coddington. St.
Stephen's Episcopal
church, Columbus, Ohio
39:116-7 D 26 '55

Brown, Everett, interior designer
West Coast oriental house
38: 120-1 F 21 '55

Brown, George L.
  Castello Dell 'ovo 33:91 S 15
    '52
Brown, J. F.
  Indian maidens ghost, Niagara
    Falls 26:80 Je 6 '49
  Sacrifice of Indian maiden, *
    Niagara Falls 26:80 Je 6 ' 49
Brown, John
  Curry. John Brown bw 15:20
    N 29 '43
  Curry. John Brown mural
    study 7:35 D 25 '39
  John Brown bw 39:174 S 12 '55
  Pippin. John Brown goes to
    his hanging 21:64 Jy 22 '46
Brown, Joseph, sculptor
  Bather bw 12:90 My 19 '41
  Fighter bw 26:114 Je 20 ' 49
  Hammerlock bw 12:90 My 19
    '41
  The hunter bw 12:90 My 19 '41
  Joe Burk bw 12:90 My 19 '41
  Lou Pyle bw 12:90 My 19 '41
  Right uppercut bw 12:90 My
    19 '41
Brown, Mandeville Elihu Dering
  Buffalo hunter lithograph bw
    39:20 D 12 '55
Brown, Margaret Wise
  "Little Fun Family, " illus-
    trated by Williams, G. 21:
    59-61 D 2 '46
  Margaret Brown photog bw 21:
    59 D 2 '46
Brown, Margery
  School children drawings bw
    37:16-7 S 20 '54
Brown, Mather
  Jefferson as minister to
    France 14:64 Ap 12 '43
Brown, William
  Football paintings from photo-
    graphs 41:14-5 O 8 '56
  William Brown photog 41:15
    O 8 '56 port.
Browne, Aldis B., II
  Coast Guard's ice patrol water-
    colors 8:30-1 Ja 1 '40
Browne, Hablot Knight (Phiz,
  pseudonym)

"Nicholas Nickleby" illustra-
  tions bw 23:2-3 D 22 '47
Brownell, Charles De Wolf
  The charter oak, Hartford
    13:82 N 23 '42
Brownell, Kady
  Kady Brownell bw 14:8 Ja 4
    '43
Browning, Robert
  Robert Browning photog bw
    27:20 N 7 '49
Brownscombe, Jennie
  The first American Thanks-
    giving 13:77 N 23 '42
Bruce, Robert
  Robert Bruce statue, Stirling
    castle, Scotland 40:88 Mr
    19 '56
Bruce Family
  Shields of arms, 13th century
    22:69 My 26 '47
Brueghel, Pieter, the elder
  Adoration of the Magi 37:34-5,
    38-9 D 27 '54
  Arrival of Joseph and Mary
    at Bethlehem 37:Cover,
    30-3 D 27 '54
  Children's games (Children
    at play) 29:30-1 D 25 '50
    bw 31:94 Ag 20 '51
  Flemish proverbs (Proverbs
    of the Netherlands) 24:74-
    5 Mr 22 '48
  Massacre of the innocents,
    with details 37:36-7 D 27
    '54
  The triumph of Death 31:66-
    7 O 1 '51
  The wedding dance (Open-air
    wedding dance) 4:22 Ap
    11 '38 bw 35:31 S 14 '53
  Alchemist's shop bw 22:84
    Ap 7 '47 (drawing)
Brueghel, Pieter, the younger
  The groom 7:56 O 9 '39
  Massacre of the innocents
    copy 24:65 Je 14 '48
Bruges
  Gothic architecture: town
    hall; canal; grand palace
    photogs bw 17:86 O 9 '44

Halles building photog 33:62
S 15 '52
Brumidi, Constantin
Ceiling, corridor paintings,
Senate, Washington, D.C.
31:56 Jy 2 '51
Fresco, Dome, U.S. Capitol,
Washington, D.C. 31:52-3
Jy 2 '51
Brundage, Avery
Avery Brundage photog bw 24:
115 Je 14 '48
Brussel-Smith, Bernard
Hunting incidents wood engrav-
ings 39:190-201 N 14 '55
Bruyn, Bartel, the younger
Family group, 16th century
7:34 Jy 31 '39
Bryan, William Jennings
Kemble. William Jennings
Bryan political cartoon bw
31:20 O 22 '51
William Jennings Bryan bw
6:31 Je 19 '39 photog bw
2:28 My 31 '37; 14:7 My
31 '43; 28:80 Ja 2 '50
Three strikes and... political
cartoon, 1908 40:72 Ja 30
'56
Bryant, William Cullen
William Cullen Bryant photog
bw 7:51 Ag 28 '39; 11:91
S 8 '41
Bubble blower. bw Chardin 6:58
Mr 27 '39
Bucephalas
Puget. Alexander on his
horse, Bucephalas, riding
over foes bw 39:86 N 14 '55
Buchanan, James
James Buchanan 19:86 S 24
'45 bw 10:26 Mr 3 '41
Buck, Pearl
Pearl Buck photog bw 14:53
My 10 '43
Buddha and Buddhism See also
names of Buddhist divini-
ties, as Kuan Yin
Amida, lord of light, Japa-
nese screen, 13th century
34:99 Ap 20 '53

Amitabha Buddha
China 8:31 Ja 8 '40
Kamakura, Japan sculp-
ture 38:91 Mr 7 '55
Bodhisatva, Tibet bw 38:92
Mr 7 '55
Buddha, festival figure, Cey-
lon bw 40:28 Je 11 '56
Buddha, Kigu banner, Tibet
6:25 Je 12 '39
Buddha sculpture bw 24:120
F 23 '48; 29:160 D 11 '50;
Angkor 5:39 Ag 1 '38
Temple of 500 Gods 3:55
Ag 23 '37
Statues 31:37 D 17 '51; In-
ner Mongolia 7:50-1 Jy
10 '39; Kumbum, Tibet
24:79 F 16 '48; Shwe
Dagon Pagoda, Rangoon
26:65 My 9 '49
Buddha and two attendants
sculpture bw 13:92 N 9 '42
Buddha riding Kanthaka,
festival figure, Ceylon bw
40:27 Je 11 '56
Buddhas sculpture, Lama
Temple, Peiping 20:69 Ap
29 '46
Buddhist altar, San Francis-
co temple photog 25:76 S
20 '48
Buddhist altar with ancestor
tablets, Japan photog bw
3:41 Ag 30 '37
Buddhist scrolls and paintings,
China 8:30-47 Ja 8 '40
Buddhist temple, Kumbum,
Tibet bw 24:80 F 16 '48
Cave of Buddhas, Petchburi
photog 31:32-3 D 31 '51
Compassionate Buddha of
the future sculpture bw,
China, 400 9:50 Jy 22 '40
Darbha Malli-Putra, Buddhist
saint 15:66 O 11 '43
Emerald Buddha temple,
Bangkok photog 31:32 D
31 '51
The golden Buddha, Gyantze
temple, Tibet 6:26 Je

Buddha (cont.)
12 '39
Golden Buddha, Marble
temple, Bangkok sculp-
ture 31:35 D 31 '51
Golden Buddha, Shwe Dagon
Pagoda, Rangoon sculp-
ture 38:Cover Mr 7 '55
Golden Buddha, Wat Bovor-
nives monastery, Bangkok
sculpture 38:80 Mr 7 '55
The golden tower, shrine,
Tibet photog 6:26 Je 12 '39
Guardian image, Buddhist
temple, Peiping 38:65 Ap
4 '55
Jade Buddha, Peiping sculp-
ture 20:68 Ap 29 '46
Life of Buddha and disciples
8:30-7 Ja 8 '40
Lord Buddha' farewell* fres-
co, Persian-Chinese 6:26
Je 12 '39
Milles. Buddha of the sea
sculpture bw 2:32 F 22 '37
Miroku, sculpture, Japan,
c666 30:72 My 28 '51
Prayer wheels photogs bw 8:
35 Ja 8 '40; 24:80 F 16 '48
Reclining Buddha, Ajanta
caves sculpture bw 38:80
Mr 7 '55
Schwerzmann. Buddha ice
sculpture bw 6:6 Ja 16 '39
T'ien-T'ai trinity, T'ang
dynasty, 9th century 15:64
O 11 '43
Tsong-Kha-Pa, founder of
Yellow Hat order, Tibet
8:34 Ja 8 '40
The wheel of Life, China 8:
32-3 Ja 8 '40
Wheel of the Law, Buddhist
emblem 38:57 F 7 '55; 38:
81 Mr 7 '55
Yakushi sculpture, Japan, 8th
century 34:95 Ap 20 '53
Budway, Patrick
Hilltop barns 10:58 Je 16 '41
Buechner, Frederick
Frederick Buechner photog

bw 28:35 Ja 30 '50
Bufano, Beniamino, sculptor
Animals: bear, cat, mouse,
rabbit bw 17:106-7 D 4 '44
Bear bw 9:82 O 21 '40
Sun Yat-Sen bw 3:62 N 29 '37
Artist at work photog bw 9:
82 O 21 '40 port.
Bufano, Remo, sculptor
Puppets, giant papier mache
figures: witch, alchemist,
voodoo doctor, scientist
bw 6:6-8 My 1 '39
Remo Bufano photog bw 6:6-
7 My 1 '39 port.
Buffalo Bill See Cody, William
Buffaloes
Bison, Cro-Magnon cave
painting, Montignac,
France 22:67 F 24 '47
Bison, paleolithic cave paint-
ing, Spain 39:86 D 12 '55
Bison, paleolithic stone carv-
ing 39:86 N 7 '55
Bodmer. Missouri river 15:
87 Ag 30 '43
Brown, M.E.D. Buffalo
hunter lithograph bw 39:
20 D 12 '55
The buffalo hunter, c1830-40
39:111 N 21 '55
Hardy. Bison sculpture bw
37:124 O 11 '54
Li T'ang, attributed to
Man on a water buffalo re-
turning intoxicated from
a village feast, 12th
century 15:65 O 11 '43
Buffet, Bernard
Still lifes bw 38:78, 80 Mr 21
'55
War landscape* bw 38:77 Mr
21 '55
Bernard Buffet photog bw
38:77-80 Mr 21 '55 port.
Self-portrait bw 38:80 Mr
21 '55 port.
Building, manuscript illumination, Flemish, 15th cen-
tury 22:79 My 26 '47

The building of the Trojan horse.
  Tiepolo 9:48 Jy 29 '40
Buildings
  Cezanne. Gardanne 32:86 F
    22 '52
  Churchill. Reflections at St.
    Jean 20:46 Ja 7 '46
  Diego. The portentious city
    20:81 Mr 11 '46
  Dodd. Savannah 27:64 S 26 '49
  Dufy. Manhattan 30:66 Ja 22
    '51
  Guy. Ghost town hotel 16:46
    Ja 3 '44
  Hopper. The city 20:80 F 18
    '46
  Hopper. Early Sunday morning
    27:62 Ag 29 '49
  Hopper. Seven A.M. 28:101
    Ap 17 '50
  Lucioni. Red buildings in sun-
    light 3:48 Jy 19 '37
  Sheeler. Shaker buildings 5:43
    Ag 8 '38
  Sloan. Pigeons 7:46 D 11 '39
  Stuempfig. Industrial town*
    25:99 S 20 '48
  Stuempfig. Manayunk 25:64
    O 11 '48
  Utrillo. Hotel du Tertre 28:
    92-3 Ja 16 '50
  Utrillo. Sacre-Coeur et Rue
    Saint-Rustique 28:93 Ja 16
    '50
  Van Gogh. The cafe at night
    27:85 O 10 '49
Bulfinch, Charles, architect
  Curved housefonts, Boston bw
    10:64 Mr 24 '41
Bullet Mold, U.S., Colonial peri-
    od photog 38:60 My 30 '55
Bullfighting See Games and
  Sports--Bullfighting
Bulman, Orville
  Orville Bulman photog bw 34:
    154 My 18 '53 port.
Bullmoose in the bullrushes, 1912,
  T. Roosevelt in political
  cartoon 40:72 Ja 30 '56
Bulls See Cattle; Mythological
  Themes--Europa

Bulls eye Venetian glass 37:56 Ag
  2 '54
Bulls eye window pane, U.S. 39:
  58 Jy 18 '55
Bunker Hill. engraving Romans
  29:41 Jy 3 '50
Bunker Hill monument photog bw
  18:67 Ja 15 '45
Bunn, William
  City of St. Paul, steamboat
    9:72 O 14 '40
  Mississippi steamboat* 9:71
    O 14 '40
  Northern Bell, steamboat 9:72
    O 14 '40
  Artist at work photog bw 9:70
    O 14 '40
Buntline, Ned
  Ned Buntline photog bw 16:110
    Ap 10 '44; 22:68 Ap 28 '47
Bunyan, Paul
  Paul Bunyan festival figure bw,
    Chicago Railroad Fair 27:
    104-6 Jy 11 '49
  Paul Bunyan and his blue ox,
    Babe sculpture, colored
    concrete, Minnesota 18:58-
    9 F 5 '45
  Paul Bunyan and his great blue
    ox 11:85 D 15 '41
  Watrous. Paul Bunyan and his
    blue ox, Babe 25:58 N 29
    '48
Burchfield, Charles Ephraim
  Christmas morning bw 1:29
    D 28 '36
  Evening bw 8:69 My 27 '40
  House of mystery 1:25 D 28
    '36
  In memoriam 1:27 D 28 '36
  November evening 26:86-7 F
    21 '49
  Over the dam 1:28 D 28 '36
  Promenade bw 6:82 My 22 '39
  Pussy willows 1:28 D 28 '36
  Road and rain 1:26 D 28 '36
  Six o'clock 1:26 D 28 '36
  Skunk cabbage bw 1:24 D 28
    '36
  Wire fence in snow 1:27 D
    28 '36

Burchfield, C. E. (cont.)
  Charles Burchfield photog bw
    1:24, 29 D 28 '36 port.
Burden, William, Jr.
  Ridin' high 25:99 D 6 '48
  Artist at work photog bw 25:
    98 D 6 '48 port.
Burgess, Gelett
  Goop drawing bw 31:37 O 1 '51
  Gelett Burgess photog bw 11:
    91 S 8 '41; 31:37 O 1 '51
    port.
Burgess, Thornton
  Thornton Burgess; wife; home
    photogs bw 17:99-102 Ag 28
    '44
Burgis, William
  New York City, 1717 drawing
    bw 38:112-3 Ap 18 '55
Burgoyne, John
  Hudson. General John Burgoyne
    bw 28:56 Mr 6 '50
  John Burgoyne bw 29:53 Jy 3
    '50
The burial. Greene 29:65 O 23 '50
The burial. Wdowiszewski 3:25 D
  20 '37
Burial of burlesque. bw Waugh, C.
  5:56 N 28 '38
The burial of Count Orgaz. El
  Greco 28:94 Ap 24 '50
Burial of Thomas a Beckett, il-
  lumination, "Historia An-
  glorum," 13th century 40:
  98 Mr 26 '56
Burk, Joe
  Brown. Joe Burk sculpture bw
    12:90 My 19 '41
Burke, Edmund
  Edmund Burke bw 25:12 S 13
    '48
Burke, Major
  Major Burke photog bw 22:69
    Ap 28 '47
Burlin, Paul
  Fallen angel bw 26:84 F 21 '49
Burlingame, Sheila
  Gulls in flight sculpture bw
    10:120 Ap 21 '41
Burliuk, David
  Newman. David Burliuk photog

bw 20:11 F 4 '46 port.
Burmudez
  Musicians* 36:80-1 My 31 '54
Burnett, Frances Hodgson
  "Little Lord Fauntleroy,"
    illustrations by Birch, R.
    bw 27:71 D 5 '49
  Frances Hodgson Burnett
    photog bw 27:74 D 5 '49
Burney, Frances (?)
  Finishing school, England,
    18th century 25:104 S 13 '48
Burnham, Daniel, architect
  Flatiron building, New York
    City, 1902 photog 40:99 Mr
    5 '56
Burnham, Wilbur Herbert
  Battle of Lexington stained
    glass bw 16:96 Ja 10 '44
  Religious law stained glass
    6:32 Ap 3 '39
  Artist at work photog bw 6:30
    Ap 3 '39 port.
Burning of Bishops Latimer and
  Ridley* woodcut bw 41:107
  O 29 '56
Burning of John Huss, 1415 bw
  24:29 Mr 8 '48; 27:59 Ag
  1 '49
Burns, Fritz V., architect
  "Dream house," Los Angeles
    plan, photogs 20:83-6 My
    6 '46
Burns Robert
  Bobbie Burns statue bw Dum-
    fries, Scotland 26:80 Ja 3
    '49
Burns, Robert
  Troop movements 13:31 Jy 6
    '42
Burnt out Italian tanks. Beddoes
  26:60 Mr 21 '49
Burr, Aaron
  Aaron Burr bw 9:8 Ag 5 '40;
    23:68 Jy 7 '47; 1804, 6:31
    Je 19 '39
  Hamilton-Burr duel bw 14:62
    Ap 12 '43
  Riggs. Hamilton-Burr duel
    23:69 Jy 7 '47

Burro and foal. sculpture bw
    Young, M. 10:79 F 17 '41
The bush. Duchamp 32:103 Ap
    28 '52
Bush, Gladys Lewis
    May West sculpture bw 1:33
    D 7 '36
Bushman, William T.
    William T. Bushman photog bw
    24:127 Mr 8 '48
Businessmen as artists: Busi-
    nessman's Art Institute,
    Los Angeles photogs bw 16:
    37 My 1 '44
A busy day. advertising poster,
    c1900 Humphrey 28:40 Ja 2 '50
Butchers and butchershops
    Cremonini. Skinned oxen 38:
    72 Ja 17 '55
    Novar. The butcher 1:44 N
    30 '36
    Rembrandt. The beef bw 7:24
    Ag 28 '39
Butler, Nicholas Murray
    Dr. Butler; wife; home photogs
    8:108-10 Je 3 '40
Butler, Reg
    The unknown political prisoner
    sculpture bw 34:39 Je 1 '53
Buttall, Jonathan
    Gainsborough. The blue boy
    4:26 Ja 24 '38
Butter mold, eagle symbol, U.S.,
    c1784 photog bw 17:56 S 4
    '44
Butter paddle, U.S., Colonial
    photog 38:119 Ap 18 '55
Butterfish, treebark painting,
    North Australia 21:78 N 4
    '46
Butterflies. Thomas, B. 21:65-8
    Ag 12 '46
By the sea. Rosenthal 15:68 N 22
    '43
By the seashore. Renoir 3:46 Jy
    5 '37
Byers, Abrahamm
    Abraham Lincoln, age 49
    photogs bw 24:111 F 9 '48
Byzantine Art See Art, Byzan-
    tine

Byzantine church, Black Sea
    photog bw 3:56-7 My 3 '37

C

Ca d'Oro, Venetian Palazzo, 15th
    century 33:40 D 29 '52
Cabinet, Chinese-style. bw
    Chippendale 23:75 Ag 25 '47
Cabinet, U.S.
    Garfield's cabinet bw 23:45 Ag
    25 '47
Cabinet de toilette. Bonnard 25:
    56 Jy 26 '48
Cabinet work
    Study of Duke of Urbino, 15th
    century photogs bw 18:12-4
    My 21 '45
Cabins
    Flax-scutching, U.S., 18th
    century 31:72-3 Jy 2 '51
    Log cabin, Russia photog 14:
    89 Mr 29 '43
    Phillips. Two story cabin,
    New Salem, Ill., 1835 36:
    80 F 15 '54
Cabot, John
    John Cabot bw 24:93 Mr 22 '48
Cabrini, Frances Xavier
    Mother Cabrini photogs bw 3:
    61-2 N 8 '37
Cacoa plant* bw 24:83 Mr 22 '48
The Cacos of Leconte. Obin 23:
    61 S 1 '47
Cadena, Luis
    George Washington 9:67 S 2
    '40
Cadmus, Paul
    Coney Island 2:45 Mr 29 '37
    The fleet's in bw 2:44 Mr 29
    '37
    George Platt Lynes 10:48 F 3
    '41
    Gilding the acrobats 2:47 Mr
    29 '37
    Main street mural 2:45 Mr 29
    '37 detail 21:47 N 25 '46
    Playground 29:172-3 O 16 '50
    Puerto de Andraitx 2:46 Mr
    29 '37
    Sailors and floosies bw 9:68
    O 14 '40

Cadmus, Paul (cont.)
  Sloth, detail from Seven deadly
    ins bw 28:24 Ja 23 '50
  Y. M. C. A. locker room 2:46-7
    Mr 29 '37
  Portrait of three ladies bw
    draw at age 4 2:44 Mr 29 '37
    (drawing)
  Paul Cadmus photog bw 2:44 Mr
    29 '37 in group photog 29:
    172-3 O 16 '50 port.
  Self-portrait bw 15:13 O 25
    '43 port.
Cadwallader, Brooke, textile de-
  igner
  Silk scarves 21:123 S 16 '46
Caesar, Julius
  Julius Caesar bust bw 13:104
    O 5 '42; 24:120 F 23 '48
Caesarion
  Cleopatra and her son Caesari-
    on, intaglio bw 41:126 N 26
    '56
Cafes and Restaurants
  Bonnard. At the Moulin Rouge
    25:53 Jy 26 '48
  Coffeehouse, England, 18th
    century 25:104 S 13 '48
  Congden. Florian's cafe, Ven-
    ice 30:108 Ap 30 '51
  Davis, G. R. Chez Suzy 19:
    47 Jy 16 '45
  Gatto. Jungle cafe 25:72 N 8
    '48
  Hopper. Chop suey 28:102 Ap
    17 '50
  Hopper. Tables for ladies 2:
    45 My 3 '37
  Larance. Cafe scene 20:77 F
    18 '46
  Picasso. Moulin de la Galette
    8:57 Mr 4 '40
  Roualt. Couple in cabaret 34:
    59 F 2 '53
  Toulouse-Lautrec. At the cafe
    15:68 S 20 '43
  Toulouse-Lautrec. At the
    Moulin Rouge 28:98-9 My
    15 '50
  Toulouse-Lautrec. The dance
    at Moulin Rouge 28:99 My

    15 '50
  Utrillo. Moulin de la Galette 28:
    94 Ja 16 '50
  Van Gogh. Night cafe 2:34 F 15
    '37; 27:85 O 10 '49
Caffieri, Jean Jacques
  Benjamin Franklin bust (copy)
    40:82 Ja 9 '56
Cagli, Corrado
  Corrado Cagli photog bw 5:72
    D 12 '38 port.
Cain and Abel
  Lucas van Leyden. Cain slay-
    ing Abel* engraving bw 6:
    46 Ja 16 '39
  Van Coxie. Cain and Abel
    tapestry 35:95 D 14 '53
Calais gate. Hogarth 21:81 D 16
    '46
Calculating, Middle Ages bw 22:
    82 My 26 '47
Calder, Alexander, sculptor
    Cosmos bw 88 Ag 25 '52
  International mobile bw 26:112
    Je 20 '49
  Mobile 33:84-5 Ag 25 '52
  Mobile 34:72-3 Mr 2 '53
  Mobiles--6 sculptures bw 17:
    12-3 O 2 '44
  The monocle bw 24:95 Ap 12
    '48
  Nuclea, theater design, Paris
    33:86 Ag 25 '52
  Singer (Josephine Baker) bw
    33:88 Ag 25 '52
  Stabiles and mobiles 33:86 Ag
    25 '52
  Alexander Calder. in group
    photog 26:112 Je 20 '49 port.
  Artist at work photog 33:83, 86
    Ag 25 '52 bw 6:85 My 22 '39;
    17:14 O 2 '44 port.
  Newman. Alexander Calder
    photog bw 20:12 F 4 '46 port.
Caldwell, Erskine
  Erskine Caldwell and wife
    photogs bw 19:134-7 O 1
    '45
Calendars and Calendar Art
  Aztec calendar
    Aztec calendar drawing

bw 6:29 Ja 23 '39
  Aztec calendar stone bw 18:
    41 Ja 1 '45
  "Book of Hours" of the Duc de
    Berry 24:38-50 Ja 5 '48
  Calendar-almanac, Germany
    bw 18:43 Ja 1 '45
  French revolutionary calendar
    bw 18:43 Ja 1 '45
  Evolution of calendar art:
    sculptured Roman and Az-
    tec calendars to contempo-
    rary 18:41-6 Ja 1 '45
  Glockenden. Manuscript calen-
    dar, 1527 bw 18:42 Ja 1 '45
  Memling. June, c1478 bw 18:
    42 Ja 1 '45
  Moran, Earl. Calendar girls
    18:46 Ja 1 '45 bw 9:4 D 30
    '40
  Petty. Petty girls 6:34-5 Je
    26 '39
  Roman calendar, first centu-
    ries A.D. sculpture bw 18:
    41 Ja 1 '45
  U.S. calendar art, 1887 to
    present bw 9:4-6 D 30 '40
Calf-bearer sculpture bw Greek,
    c450 B.C. 23:22 Jy 7 '47
Calhoun, John C.
  John C. Calhoun bw 6:31 Je
    19 '39; 9:8 Ag 5 '40
California
  Chadwick. Placer mining in
    California 6:29 Je 19 '39;
    27:48 Jy 4 '49
  Nahl. Sunday morning in the
    mines 27:49 Jy 4 '49
  Solid comfort lithograph 27:
    49 Jy 4 '49
  Wheel shop, Hangtown, Cali-
    fornia, c1850 31:74 Jy 2 '51;
    39:104 O 17 '55
California holiday. Dike 11:75 O
    27 '41
California painters 11:72-6 O 27
    '41
California sculptors bw 9:79-82
    O 21 '40
Calisthenics. ceramics bw Klein
    9:131 N 11 '40

Calla lillies. O'Keefe 4:30 F 14
    '38
Callahan, Kenneth
  The search 35:86 S 28 '53
  Artist and his work photog
    35:87 S 28 '53 port.
Callender, John, architect
  Jackson and Callender.
    Hillside house plan, photogs
    bw 23:62-3 Jy 21 '47
Callery, Mary, sculptor
  Espaliered figure bw 33:143
    N 17 '52
  Reclining figure bw 26:114
    Je 20 '49
  Artist at work photog bw 33:
    143 N 17 '52 port.
Callicantzari. Lewicki 39:64 D
    19 '55
Callicrates, architect
  Athena Victorious temple,
    Athens photog bw 18:56 Ja
    1 '45
  Parthenon, Athens photogs bw
    35:152-62 O 26 '54; 36:44
    Ja 11 '54
The calling of apostles Peter and
    Andrew. Duccio 39:22 D
    26 '55
Calling the loa. Benedetto 8:35
    Ja 1 '40
Callister, Charles Warren, ar-
    chitect
  Christ Science church, Bel-
    vedere, Calif. 39:115 D
    26 '55
  Hall house, Marin County,
    Calif. 27:46-7 S 5 '49
Callisto See Mythological
    Themes--Callisto
The Calmady children (Nature).
    Lawrence, T. 6:55 Mr 20
    '39
Calotype
  Talbot. Outdoor group* bw 2:
    4 Mr 29 '37
Calvary See Jesus Christ--
    Crucifixion

Calvert, Charles
  Hesselius. Charles Calvert of
    Maryland 9:75 D 9 '40; 26:
    84 F 28 '49
Calvin, John
  John Calvin bw 39:43 D 26 '55
  John Calvin and colleagues
    statue bw, Geneva 24:59 Je
    14 '48
Camaro, Alexander
  Artist and his work photog 30:
    145 My 10 '54 port.
Cambridge university, England
    photogs bw 15:95-103 S 20
    '43
Camel-back bridge, Summer pal-
    ace, Peiping photog bw 3:
    58 Ag 23 '37
Camels
  Brueghel, Pieter, the elder.
    Adoration of the Magi, de-
    tail 37:34 D 27 '54
  Guardian figures, Ming dynas-
    ty, China bw 3:57 Ag 23 '37
  Milles. Sven Hedin, model,
    bw 2:32 F 22 '37
  Rosenthal, B. Camel 34:134
    Ap 6 '53
  Tons. Camels tapestry 35: 98-
    9 D 14 '53
Cameo, Roman, c60 B.C. bw 9:
    94 D 9 '40
Camp meeting* print 39:71 D 26
    '55
Camp of the Gros Ventres of the
    prairies. Bodmer 15:88
    Ag 30 '43
Campbell, Lily Bess
  Lily Bess Campbell photog
    bw 11:43 O 13 '41
Campbell, Mrs. Patrick
  Mrs. Patrick Campbell photog
    bw 33:64 O 6 '52
Campbell house, St. Louis, 1851
    18:55 My 7 '45
Campigli, Massimo
  The weavers 29:108 D 11 '50
  Workers* bw 29:14 O 30 '50
Camping in the wood. Currier
    and Ives print 9:33 D 30 '40
Campos, F. Molina

Argentina: paintings of
    pampas; gauchos 4:34-5 Je
    20 '38
  F. Molina Campos photog bw
    4:35 Je 20 '38 port.
Camus, Albert
  Karsh. Albert Camus photog
    bw 37:130-1 O 4 '54
Canada
  Historical scenes and portraits
    bw 9:112-5 S 9 '40
  Landing of Cartier in Canada,
    1534 24:78 Mr 22 '48
  Quebec Act, 1774 cartoon bw
    27:138 S 19 '49
  Canada, French map, 1534
    24:78 Mr 22 '48 (map)
The Canada lynx. Audubon 9:115
    O 21 '40
Canadians at Ypres. bw 9:116 S
    9 '40
Canaletto (Giovanni Antonio Ca-
    nale)
  The Thames 25:100-1 S 13 '48
Canby, Henry Seidel
  Henry Seidel Canby photog bw
    33:102 S 29 '52
Can-can girl. Clemens 24:66 Mr
    1 '48
Candalabra, bronze, Etruscan
    40:63 F 13 '56
Candela, Felix, architect
  Church of the Virgin of the mi-
    raculous medal, Mexico
    City photogs bw 40:138 My
    28 '56
"Candide" illustrations bw 23:88
    S 15 '47
Candle sconces, gilded classic
    design, U.S., 18th century
    17:58 S 4 '44
Candlesticks
  Dikirie, double candlestick
    photog bw 11:112 O 13 '41
  Socket candlestick, silver,
    James I bw 3:77 D 13 '37
  Trikirie, triple candlestick
    photog bw 11:112 O 13 '41
  Wistarberg candlestick 39:
    58-9 Jy 18 '55

El candy store. Lasker 28:84
    Mr 20 '50
Caniff, Milton, cartoonist
    Cartoons and sketches bw 10:
        34 Ja 6 '41
    Christmas tree bw 19:10 D
        24 '45
    Terry and the pirates; male
        call bw 14:10-2 Mr 1 '43
    Artist at work photog bw 10:
        34 Ja 6 '41; 15:14 O 25 '43
        port.
    Self-portrait cartoon bw 15:14
        O 25 '43 port.
Cannibals
    New world cannibals* engrav-
        ing bw, 16th century 41:
        181 N 12 '56
    Vespucci in Brazil drawing
        bw, 17th century 37:110 O
        11 '54
Canova, Antonio
    Napoleon sculpture 1:33 D 7
        '36
"Canterbury Gospels" manuscript
    bw 18:80 My 14 '45
"Canterbury Psalter" 34:40 F 23
    '53
"Canterbury Tales," illustration
    from Flemish manuscript,
    15th century bw 22:75 Ap
    7 '47
Caparn, Rhys
    Animal form I sculpture bw
        32:78 Ja 7 '52
Cape Cod afternoon. bw Hopper
    2:44 My 3 '37
Cape Cod cottage. Wills, archt.
    photog, plan 21:71 Ag 26
    '46
Capitol See United States
    Capitol Building
Capote, Truman
    Truman Capote photog bw 22:
        75 Je 2 '47
Capp, Al, cartoonist
    Autobiography in cartoons 20:
        59-62 Je 24 '46
    L'il Abner cartoon 32:Cover,
        100-1 Mr 31 '52
    Shmoo cartoon bw 25:46 S

20 '48
    Artist at work 20:58 Je 24 '46
        port.
Capricci
    Arcimboldo, School of. Sum-
        mer (Reclining figure of
        fruits and vegetables) bw
        7:24 Ag 28 '39
Capture of Fort Lee. watercolor
    Davies 29:45 Jy 3 '50
Capture of Fort Washington, 1776.
    watercolor Davies 29:45 Jy
    3 '50
Capture of Mexico City bw 21:46
    D 16 '46
Car of history sculpture, Statu-
    ary Hall, Capitol, Wash-
    ington, D.C. 31:50 Jy 2
    '51
Caracas, Venezuela
    Contemporary architecture
        37:126-7 S 13 '53
Caravaggio, Michelangelo.
    The musicians bw 32:47 Je 9
        '52
Carcassone, walled city, France,
    12th century photog bw 22:
    66-7 My 26 '47
Cardenas, Lazaro
    President Cardenas photogs
        bw 3:92-4 S 20 '37; 4:50,
        56 Ap 11 '38
Cardinals
    Cranach. Cardinal Albrecht
        as St. Hieronymus 5:39 Jy
        11 '38
    El Greco. Don Fernando Nino
        de Guevara, Cardinal 28:
        93 Ap 24 '50
    El Greco. St. Jerome as
        Cardinal 3:31 D 27 '37
    Manzu. Cardinal sculpture bw
        41:102 Ag 6 '56
    Titian. Antoine Perrenot de
        Granvella 7:55 O 9 '39
Cardozo, Benjamin
    Justice Cardozo photog bw
        16:52 F 14 '44; 23:118 N
        4 '46

Cards See also Games and
    Sports--Cards
  Catalonia playing cards: tra-
    ditional and loyalist bw 4:
    57 F 14 '38
  Contemporary artists' Christ-
    mas card designs, Ameri-
    can Artists Group bw 5:9
    D 12 '38
  Hall Brothers greeting cards
    for 29 "high spots of life"
    bw 10:10-3 My 5 '41
  Humphreys. Historical play-
    ing cards, U.S., 18th cen-
    tury 38:Cover My 30 '55
  Lewicki. First printing of
    Christmas cards, 1846 33:
    86 D 1 '52
  "LIFE's" art competition for
    men in armed services,
    prizewinners as Christmas
    cards bw 13:138-41 O 19
    '42
  Prizewinners in Hallmarks
    international contest for
    paintings on Christmas
    themes bw 27:55-7 D 26 '49
  Prizewinning designs of Hall-
    mark Christmas cards bw
    33:2-3 D 22 '52
  Victorian era Christmas
    cards, U.S. 5:6-7 D 12 '38
Careless talk costs lives.
    poster bw Bird 26:62-3 Mr
    7 '49
Carena, Felice
  The angel and Jacob fighting
    3:27 D 20 '37
The caress. sculpture bw Mal-
    darelli 22:140 Mr 24 '47
Caribbean area, French map,
    1547 24:79 Mr 22 '48
Caricature and Satire See also
    Cartoons; Social Comment
  Ardizzone. British army of-
    ficers in the Middle East
    bw 15:55-6 N 29 '43
  Beerbohm. G. B. Shaw bw 23:
    89 N 17 '47
  Beerbohm. H. G. Wells bw
    23:88 N 17 '47

  Beerbohm. Oscar Wilde lec-
    turing in U.S. bw 5:34 D
    5 '38; 33:126 S 22 '52
  Beerbohm. The rare and
    rather awful visits of Al-
    bert Edward...bw 23:75 N
    17 '47
  Beerbohm. Rudyard Kipling
    bw 33:126 S 22 '52; 23:88
    N 17 '47
  Beerbohm. W. B. Yeats bw
    23:89 N 17 '47
  Beerbohm. Winston Chruchill,
    1907 bw 33:126 S 22 '52
  Blythe. The Pittsburgh horse
    market 9:76 D 9 '40
  Daumier. Three lawyers (Les
    trois avocats) 38:108 My
    23 '55
  Dean. Satirical drawings bw
    13:150-3 N 23 '42
  Evergood. Art on the beach
    bw 3:126 O 4 '37
  Faulkner. Caricature bw 23:
    82 S 1 '47
  Ernest Hemingway bw 23:82 S
    1 '47
  Flagg. G. B. Shaw bw 41:104B
    Ag 6 '56
  Franklin Roosevelt as sphinx
    sculpture bw 11:21 Jy 14
    '41
  Gibson. Home for the holidays
    drawing bw 28:17 Ja 2 '50
  Gibson. The social push draw-
    ing bw 28:17 Ja 2 '50
  Gillray. Old lady of Thread-
    needle Street bw 21:99 O
    21 '46
  Greenwood. Sea captains ca-
    rousing in Surinam, 1758
    26:84-5 F 28 '49
  Gropper. The Senate 2:24 F 1
    '37
  Half-man, half-toad statue
    bw 35:39 Jy 27 '53
  Herford. "The yellow peril,"
    (W. R. Hearst) cartoon
    bw 31:27 Ag 27 '51
  Hirschfeld. Howard Lindsay
    and Robert Crouse bw 21:

116-7 N 11 '46

Hirschfeld. Motion picture
stars bw 36:20-1 My 17 '54

The hour of the hyena, (Mussolini), from "Punch" bw
26:55 F 14 '49

Kirby. Prohibitionist bw 20:
67 My 27 '46

Lambert. Harry Truman
sculpture bw 21:32 O 7 '46

Levine, String quartette 14:
43 Mr 8 '43; 26:86 F 21 '49

Lurcat. Nazi warfare tapestry 21:81 S 30 '46

Mason. Self-portrait bw 22:34
Ja 6 '47

Roualt. Mr. X 34:59 F 2 '53

Rowlandson. Johnson and Boswell bw 29:93 D 4 '50

Rowlandson. Quoits 25:102 S
13 '48

Thurber. "Fables for our
Time" bw 24:80 Ap 19 '48

Thurber. "The Last Flower"
bw 7:10-1 N 27 '39

Toulouse-Lautrec. Oscar
Wilde 28:97 My 15 '50

Wolverton. Political caricatures 22:14-6 My 5 '47

Wood, G. Adolescence 14:58
Ja 18 '43

Wood, G. American Gothic
14:52-3 Ja 18 '43 bw 5:30
O 31 '38; 6:58 Mr 27 '39

Wood, G. Daughters of revolution 14:53 Ja 18 '43; 21:
73 N 25 '46

Wood, J. M. Britons as birds
bw 24:16-8 Ap 12 '48

World War correspondents, in
"Yank" bw 18:12-4 Ja 8 '45

"Yellow kid," 1898 (W. R.
Hearst) bw 31:27 Ag 27 '51

Carlton, Guy
Guy Carlton bw 29:53 Jy 3 '50

Carlson, Richard
Richard Carlson photog bw
26:38 Ja 31 '49

Carlton, Brants, sculptor
Boy with mask bw 5:70 D 5 '38
Polynesian woman bw 5:70 D

5 '38

Carman, Bliss
Bliss Carman photog bw 16:96
My 8 '44

"Carmen"
Sketch of world premiere,
Paris, March 3, 1875 bw
16:70 My 8 '44

"Carmen Jones," four scenes.
Covarrubias 16:71-4 My 8
'44

Carnegie, Andrew
Andrew Carnegie cartoon bw
23:90 N 17 '47 photog bw
3:17 O 25 '37; 16:74 Ap 24
'44

Carnegie Institute, Pittsburgh
American painting exhibit:
survey from Colonial times
to present 9:74-9 D 9 '40

Carnegie international exhibition 3:24-8 D 20 '37; 5:
72-5 D 12 '38; 39:134-7 N
21 '55

Fourteenth annual exhibit of
high school art 10:56-9 Je
16 '41

Painting in the United States,
1943 16:75-9 Ap 24 '44

Carnivals See Holidays and Festivals

Carol. bw Withers 22:40 Je 16
'47

Caroler. Davis, G.R. 23:Cover
D 22 '47

Carolina parakeets. Audubon 7:
60 N 27 '39

Carousel. Davis, G.R. 22:96 Ap
21 '47

Carpaccio, Vittorio
St. Ursala legend, details 23:
56-7 Ag 4 '47

Venetian women (attributed
work)* 15th century 24:101
F 16 '48

Carpenko, Nikita, wood carver
Heads bw 32:12-3 F 11 '52
Mother and child bw 32:14 F
11 '52

Nikita Carpenko photog bw
32:12 F 11 '52 port.

Carpenter, John Alden
  John A. Carpenter photog bw
    11:91 S 8 '41
Carpenters
  Carpenters building a boat*
    bas-relief Egypt, fifth dy-
    nasty 41:108 N 26 '56
  Sheets. Village carpenter,
    India 20:82 Ja 21' 46
Carpets and Rugs
  Aubusson rug 27:56-7 O 3 '49
  Hanson. Genealogy rug,
    hooked rug 28:89 Ap 3 '50
  Hooked rugs, U.S. patterns:
    broken-wreath; roses and
    scroll; Hell on the border
    8:45-6 Ja 29 '40
  Mary, Consort of Edward VI,
    King of England. Needle-
    point rug, 1948 28:95 My
    8 '50
  Miro. Rug 33:93 O 27 '52
  Marquand rug, Persia, 16th
    century 31:68-9 S 3 '51
  Persian carpet bw 17:92 Jy
    17 '44
Carr, Henry M.
  Adoration for heroes bw 9:59
    Ag 12 '40
  A railway terminus 26:48-9
    Mr 7 '49
Carranza, Verustiano
  President Carranza photogs
    bw 4:53 Ap 11 '38
Carreno, Mario
  Birth of the American nations
    bw 10:106-7 Mr 17 '41
  Tropic of Cancer 36:80 My 31
    '54
  Young girl with a horse bw 10:
    107 Mr 17 '41
  Artist at work photog bw 10:
    107 Mr 17 '41 port.
Carriages See also Wagons and
  Carts
  Airing in Central Park, c1860
    32:116-7 Ap 7 '52
  Boston chaise, U.S., 1860
    photog 39:104 O 17 '55
  Concord coach, U.S., Wells
    Fargo overland stage photog

39:82 N 28 '55
Coronation coach, England
  photog bw 8:90 Je 3 '40
Currier and Ives print. Life
  in the country: The morn-
  ing ride 9:29 D 30 '40
Degas. Carriages at the races
  9:52 Jy 22 '40
Eakins. The Fairman Rogers
  four-in-hand 16:74 My 15
  '44
Gold and silver carriage,
  Baroda, India photog bw 9:
  70 N 25 '40
Lee, D. Twilight ride, Mon-
  terey, Mexico 22:78 My 12
  '47
Munnings. Procession to As-
  cot 28:120-1 My 22 '50
Phillips, A. F. Sawmill on
  the Saugamon River 36:79
  F 15 '54
Poussin. The triumph of
  Bacchus 7:53 O 9 '39
Roberts. Bailed up bw 12:79
  F 9 '42
Rockaway three-seater, U.S.,
  1860 photog 39:106 O 17
  '55
Royal coach of England photog
  bw 19:39 S 3 '45
Toulouse-Lautrec. The black
  countess 28:97 My 15 '50
Carroll, Anna Ella
  Anna Ella Carroll bw 25:101
  Jy 26 '48
Carroll, Charles
  Charles Carroll bw 15:8 Jy 5
  '43
Carroll, John
  Consuela bw 8:120 My 13 '40
  Draped figure bw 8:71 My 27
  '40
  The girl in red bw 8:120 My
  13 '40
  Jean 11:78 O 6 '41
  Jean in pink organdy 11:78
  O 6 '41
  Mrs. Ellsworth Ford bw 8:
  120 My 13 '40
  Mrs. Haass bw 8:121 My

13 '40

Sleeping bw 8:120 My 13 '40

White lace 7:36 Jy 31 '39; 21: 75 N 25 '46

John Carroll; wife photogs bw 8:118-9 My 13 '40 port.

Carroll, Lewis See Dodgson, Charles

Carter's Grove, Williamsburg, Va. photog. 38:61-2 My 30 '55

Cartier, Jacques

Jacques Cartier and Chief Hochelaga, 1535* bw 9:112 S 9 '40

Landing of Cartier in Canada, 1534 24:78 Mr 22 '48

Cartier-Bresson, Henri, photographer

Candid camera shots bw 22:14-6 Mr 3 '47

"The decisive moment," book of photogs bw 33:137-41 O 13 '52

Louvre exhibit of 25 years of his work bw 39:32-4 D 5 '55

William Faulkner bw 35:118 S 28 '53

Henri Cartier-Bresson photog bw 33:137 O 13 '52 port.

Cartoons See also Caricatures and Satire; Also, names of cartoonists, as Addams; Arno; Emett; Kelly, W.; Nast; Steig; Taylor, R.; Williams, G.; Young, A.

Dahl. Cartoons bw 21:14-6 D 9 '46

Dean. "It's a Long Way to Heaven" bw 19:14-6 D 10 '45

Faulkner. Dance, 1921 bw 35: 133 S 23 '53

Fox, F. Toonerville trolley, final cartoon bw 38:92 F 21 '55

Francois. "Tattooed sailor," book of cartoons bw 35:109 S 21 '53

Goldberg. Cartoons bw 17:76

N 27 '44

"Krokidil," Russian humor magazine cartoons of U.S. A. 27:145-6 D 12 '49

Marsh. Vaudeville teams bw 40:86 F 6 '56

Molnar. "Statues," book of cartoons bw 37:23 Ag 30 '54

Partch. Cartoons bw 17:75 N 27 '44

Price. "Who's in Charge Here," book of cartoons bw 16:12-4 F 7 '44

Rhode Island School of Design exhibit: 39 famous American cartoonists bw 8:71-4 Ap 22 '40

Russian bear and U.S. eagle bw 19:89 Ag 27 '45

Salazar. Kiki bw 34:14 Je 29 '53

Sir Winston Churchill bw 6: 28 Ja 9 '39

Two young giants (Russia and U.S.), 1873 bw 19:94 Ag 27 '45

Uncle Sam, evolution as symbol of U.S. bw 41:22-4 Jy 2 '56

Cartoons, political

Bullmoose in the bullrushes, 1912 (T. Roosevelt) 40:72 Ja 30 '56

Cavaliers and roundheads sicking dogs on each other* 41:195 N 12 '56

Le cow-boy (Mendes-France) bw 37:70 D 6 '54

General Ulysses S. Grant, 1880 40:70 Ja 30 '56

Grover Cleveland and Daniel Lamont, 1888 40:70-1 Ja 30 '56

Guareschi. Political cartoons 33:116 N 10 '52

Liberty threatens the old regime, 1848* "Punch" 25: 85 N 22 '48

Cartoons, political (cont.).
  Opposing third term, 1880;
    1912 bw "Puck" 8:10-1, 13
    Ap 22 '40
  Paying the exiseman bw 29:
    36 Jy 3 '50
  The Presidency: cartoons and
    caricatures of Presidents
    of U.S. bw 31:18-20 O 22
    '51
  Presidential campaign
    slanders, 19th century bw
    17:53-4, 60 O 2 '44
  Revere. Griffin, symbol of
    England, 1884 bw 38:56 My
    30 '55
  Revere. Snake, nine-seg-
    mented, symbol of U.S.
    colonies 38:56 My 30 '55
  Stamp Act repeal, 1766 bw 22:
    99 Mr 24 '47
  Three strikes and... (William
    Jennings Bryan), 1908 40:
    72 Ja 30'56
  U.S. political cartoons bw 37:
    14 Jy 5 '54
  U.S. political cartoons pre-
    sented to President Truman
    31:22-4 D 3 '51
  Wilhelm II, Kaiser of Germany.
    The yellow peril bw 6:11
    Ja 2 '39
Cartoons, War
  Anti-Nazi cartoons, British
    Ministry of Information bw
    9:10-3 O 14 '40
  Anti-Nazi cartoons, exiled
    German artist 12:10-2 Ap
    20 '42
  Baker. Sad sack bw 19:8-10
    D 31 '45
  Bernal. Anti-Nazi cartoons
    from "Hoy" 12:8-11 F 9
    '42
  Breger. G.I. Joe bw 15:12-4
    Jy 12 '43
  Chew. Caricatures and war
    cartoons bw 4:50-1 Ja 17
    '38
  French and German cartoons,
    World War, 1940 8:116-20

    Je 3 '40
  German cartoons, World War,
    1940 bw 8:51-4 Ap 8 '40
  Japan after Pearl Harbor,
    U.S. press cartoons bw
    11:6-8 D 22 '41
  Kukrynisky. Anti-Nazi war
    cartoons bw 14:4-7 Mr 29
    '43
  Low. Very well, alone bw 26:
    63 F 21 '49
  Mauldin. Up front bw 18:49-
    53 F 5 '45
  Napoleon's invasion of Eng-
    land, 1799-1805 bw 9:8-11
    S 30 '40
  "New Yorker" war album bw
    13:97-103 D 7 '42
  "Punch and the war," selected
    cartoons bw 11:61-3 Ag 25
    '41
  "Punch" cartoons bw 7:6-9 Jy
    10 '39
  Raemacker. War cartoons,
    1914-8 6:48-50 My 1 '39
  Robinson. British cartoons
    from "Sketch" bw 7:4-6 D
    25 '39
  Sansone. The wolf bw 17:6-8
    Jy 31 '44
  Sapajou. March of time bw
    28:65 F 27 '50
  Shepard, Blessings of peace
    bw 24:60 Ap 26 '48
  Steinberg. "Guitavir" line bw
    (inventions to end war) 8:
    14-7 My 27 '40
  "Yank," U.S. army weekly bw
    15:118-21 N 15 '43; 18:12-
    3 My 7 '45
Carts See Wagons and Carts
Caruso, Enrico
  Caruso with Helen Keller
    photog bw 4:20 F 28 '38
  Enrico Caruso photog bw 33:
    91 N 17 '52
Carver, George Washington
  George Washington Carver
    photogs bw 2:37-8 Mr 22
    '37
Carving See also Sculpture

Carving (cont.)

Melanesian wood and stone carvings 21:82 N 4 '46

Paleolithic bison 39:86 N 7 '55

Paleolithic reindeer horn carving bw 39:91 N 7 '55

Gems

Abraham Lincoln, head, black sapphire 34:99 F 9 '53

Albert II, King of Belgium, diamond equestrian figure bw 7:59 Jy 3 '39

Ivory

Chessmen, carved and painted bw 8:48 Ja 29 '40

Christ healing the blind, Byzantine, c500 39:25 D 26 '55

Comb, France, Middle Ages 22:80 My 26 '47

Dice, Egypt, c30 B.C. bw 6:53 Mr 20 '39

Female head, Paleolithic, France 39:83 D 12 '55

Mirror back, France, Middle Ages 22:79 My 26 '47

Netsuke, Japan bw 37:2-3 Jy 12 '54

Whiphandle, Egypt, 1350 B.C. bw 6:52 Mr 20 '39

Stone

Ceremonial fertility figure; statuettes, Paleolithic, France 39:76, 79 D 12 '55

Eskimo human and animal figures bw 36:67-70 My 24 '54

Horse, Paleolithic 39:85, 89 D 12 '55

Limestone coffin lid, Mayan, Palenque, c650 bw 34:71 Ap 27 '53

Mammoth, Magdalenian, 39:86 N 7 '55

Palette, Egypt, 3200 B.C. bw 24:74 Ja 19 '48

Prehistoric carvings, Southwell Minster, England 40:87-8 Mr 12 '56

Whalebone

Scrimshaw: corset stay, bodkin, pie crimpers, cane, clothespin, U.S., 1860 39:109 O 17 '55

Wood

Animals and figures, Bali bw 15:114-6 O 25 '43

Bellamy eagle figurehead, from frigate, "Lancaster" 38:Cover Ap 18 '55

Bird man, Easter Island bw 21:80 N 4 '46

Bishop, Swabia, Medieval bw 15:64 S 20 '43

Canoe, Micronesia, bw 21:79 N 4 '46

Carpenko. Heads bw 32:12-3 F 11 '52

Carpenko. Mother and child bw 32:14 F 11 '52

Cedar screen, Tlingit Indians, Alaska, c1825 41:53 Jy 16 '56

Cigar store Indian, U.S. 38:62 Ja 3 '55

Dish, South Seas bw 21:79 N 4 '46

Federal eagle, U.S. revolutionary emblem 35:48 Jy 6 '53; 38:63 Ja 3 '55 bw 17:56 S 4 '44

Fishing boat model, Egypt, 2000 B.C. bw 6:51 Mr 20 '39

Flight into Egypt, gilded, Flemish, 15th century bw 5:49 N 28 '38

Hepplewhite. Urn bw 23:75 Ag 25 '47

Henry Ward Beecher, U.S., c1850 31:73 Jy 2 '51

Horse, China, 4th century B.C 40:99 Ja 9 '56

King of the Bushongo, Africa, c1800 bw 33:123 S 8 '52

Kuan Yin, China, 12th century 41:73 S 3 '56

Carving (cont.) Wood
  Kuan Yin, the compassionate
    lord bw, China, 12th cen-
    tury 9:50 Jy 22 '40
  McIntire. Cornucopia 38:63
    My 30 '55
  McIntire. Federal eagle 38:
    63 My 30 '55
  McIntire. Fruit basket 38:
    63 My 30 '55
  Madonna and child, France,
    13th century 22:80 Ap 7
    '47
  Misericords bw 37:79-82 S
    27 '54
  Ornament, Viking bw 40:97
    Mr 19 '56
  Santos: Death, Our Lady of
    Sorrows; Saint Acacius
    bw 24:57-8, 60 My 17 '48
  Shrine of St. Ursala, Bruges,
    1489 34:81-6 Ap 6 '53
  Smiling figure, Bali bw 15:
    114 O 25 '43
  Strong box, Massachusetts,
    1650 38:127 Ap 18 '55
  Tax collector, Bali 15:116 O
    25 '43
  Taylor, W. B. Madonna bw
    9:55 Ag 12 '40
  Tolman. Double crucifix bw
    35:93 Jy 6 '53
  Washington on his white horse,
    U.S. 31:69 Jy 2 '51
Carey, Joyce
  Eisenstadt. Joyce Cary photog
    bw 32:100 Ja 14 '52
Caryatides
  Erechtheum, Athens photog
    bw 18:58-9 Ja 1 '45
Casals, Pablo
  Karsh. Pablo Casals photog
    bw 37:134-5 O 4 '54
Casanova, Francesco
  Jean Jacques Casanova bw
    35:48 Jy 27 '53
Casanova, Jean Jacques
  Casanova, F. Jean Jacques
    Casanova bw 35:48 Jy 27
    '53
  Jean Jacques Casanova, sketch

    bw 35:48 Jy 27 '53
  Mengs. Jean Jacques Casa-
    nova, 1767 bw 35:47 Jy 27
    '53
Casebier, Cecil
  Boy in Mexico 39:115 S 12 '55
Casey's famous wreck. bw Do-
    hanos 12:62 Ja 28 '42
Cash, Harold
  Standing nude, sculpture bw
    9:55 Ag 12 '44
Cashwan, Samuel
  Torso sculpture bw 24:95 Ap
    12 '48
Casilear, John
  Lake George* bw 5:28 O 31
    '38
Casimir the Great, 1333 bw 17:
    87 Ag 28 '44
Casio, Girolamo
  Boltraffio. Portrait of a youth
    24:67 Ja 26 '48
The Casos of Leconte. Obin 23:
    61 S 1 '47
Cass, Lewis
  Lewis Cass photog bw 14:6
    My 31 '43
Cassatt, Mary
  Before the window 12:56 Ja
    19 '42
  Boating party 36:98 My 17 '54
  In the box 36:98 My 17 '54
  Lady at the tea table (Mrs.
    Robert Riddle) 38:74 Mr
    28 '55
  Mother and child 12:56 Ja 19
    '42; 36:99 My 17 '54
  The toilet 12:55 Ja 19 '42
  Woman with a dog 40:67 Ja
    23 '56
  Young mother sewing 12:56
    Ja 19 '42
  Afternoon tea party 36:98 My
    17 '54 (prints)
  The coiffure 36:98 My 17 '54
    (prints)
  Degas. Portrait of Mary
    Cassatt bw 12:54 Ja 19
    '42 port.
  Mary Cassatt, age 68 photog
    bw 12:54 Ja 19 '42 port.

Self-portrait 41:162 D 24 '56
bw 12:54 Ja 19 '42; 36:92
My 17 '54 port.
Casson, Hugh
Eisenstadt. Sir Hugh Casson
photog bw 32:98 Ja 14 '52
Castelfranco Madonna. Giorgione
39:166 O 24 '55
Castellanos, Julio
The aunts 4:30 Mr 14 '38
Castello dell 'Ovo. Brown, G. L.
33:91 S 15 '52
Castello di Montalto, Pavese,
Italy--garden photog 28:76-
7 My 8 '50
Castellon, Frederico
Justinian's codification, Con-
stantinople, 527 A.D. 30:
90 Mr 12 '51
Frederico Castellon photog
bw 30:86 Mr 12 '51 port.
Castiglione, Baldassare
Baldassare Castiglione bw 23:
61 Ag 4 '47
El Castillo, Mayan, Chichen Itza
photog 22:60 Je 30 '47
Castle, Irene
Irene Castle, c1914 photog
bw 28:66 Ja 2 '50
Vernon and Irene Castle photog
bw 6:27 Mr 27 '39
Castle, Vernon
Vernon and Irene Castle photog
bw 6:27 Mr 27 '39
Castle rock, Edinburgh photog
bw 22:100-1 My 5 '47
Castles
Besieged castle, Middle Ages
bw 22:66 My 26 '47

Belgium
The Count of Flander's castle,
Ghent photog bw 22:Cover
My 26 '47
Steenockerzeel photog bw 2:
15 Mr 22 '37

Czechoslovakia
Lanyzamek castle photog bw
3:100 S 27 '37

Denmark
Elsinore photog bw 2:74 Je 28
'37
Kronberg, 1577 airview photog
bw 8:45 Je 3 '40

England
Agincourt in Battle of Agin-
court, 15th century chron-
icle 40:180-1 Ap 9 '56
Alnwick, Northumberland
photog 40:92 Mr 19 '56
Arundel, 1433 photog bw 15:
101 N 15 '43; 23:134-5 S
8 '47
Bamburgh, Northumberland
photog 40:88-9 Mr 19 '56
Bodiam, 1386 photog 40:91
Mr 19 '56 bw 8:44 Je 3 '40;
22:74 My 26 '47
Cockermouth photog bw 29:88
Jy 17 '50
Corfe, Dorsetshire photog
40:90 Mr 19 '56
Dover photog 26:54 F 21 '49
Ludlow, Shropshire photog
40:91 Mr 19 '56
Tintagel, Cornwall photog 40:
90-1 Mr 19 '56 bw 14:76 Je
14 '43
Walmer photog 26:53 F 21 '49
Windsor photogs 21:84-8 O 21
'46; 28:119 My 22 '50; 40:
86-7 Mr 19 '56

France
Duc de Berry's castles in
Tres riches heures de Duc
de Berry 24:39-50 Ja 5 '48
La Napoule, Canne photog bw
31:119 O 15 '51

Germany
Gutenfels, 12th century photog
bw 8:45 Je 3 '40
Marienburg photogs bw 19:116
N 19 '45
Rhine castles photogs bw 17:
78-9 D 4 '44
Vogelsdorf, Silesia photog
bw 15:94 N 22 '43

Castrogiovanni

Castles (cont.)
Holland
Castle de Haar photog bw 7:73
O 9 '39
Muiden photogs 28:122-3 Mr
6 '50
Muiderslot (Lock Castle),
c1200 photog bw 8:45 Je
3 '40

Ireland
Dromoland, County Clare bw
7:62 Jy 24 '39
Malahide photog bw 29:101 D
4 '50

Italy
Sant' Angelo, Rome photog bw
17:94 S 4 '44

Poland
Lancut photog bw 5:53 Ag 29
'38; 17:85 Ag 28 '44
Wawel photog bw 5:52 Ag 29
'38

Scotland
Barcaldine, 15th century
photog bw 8:44 Je 3 '40
Edinburgh photog 40:88 Mr 19
'56
Glamis photogs bw 3:67 Jy 19
'37; 22:95 My 5 '47
Kilchurn photog bw 29:90 Jy
17 '50

Spain
Almansa photog 33:53 Ag 18
'52
Marchenilla photog 33:53 Ag
18 '52

Wales
Harlech photog 40:90 Mr 19
'56
Castrogiovanni, N.
Pinocchio sculpture bw 40:128
Je 4 '56
Cat. sculpture bw Rudy 15:82
D 20 '43
Cat bronze, Egypt, 6th century

B.C bw 5:16 Ag 29 '38
Cat in snow. bw Sloan 5:29 O 31
'38
Catalans
Romantic painting, National
palace, Montjuich, Barce-
lona bw 2:41 F 22 '37
Catastrophe. Lee, D. 3:45 S 20
'37
Cathedral. Pollock 25:63 O 11
'48
Cathedral encampment, Leyte.
Sample 35:56 N 2 '53
Cathedral woods. Kantor 29:72-
3 Ag 21 '50
Cathedrals
Bellini. The Corpus Christi
procession 23:54-5 Ag 4
'47
Bone. Gothic cathedral, Spain
etching bw 1:45 D 7 '36
Congden. St. Mark's square
33:95 S 15 '52
Inness. St. Peter's basilica
33:90 S 15 '52
Monet. Rouen 5:26 O 10 '38
St Basil's, Moscow in Coro-
nation proclamation of Al-
exander II 38:60-1 Ja 31
'55
St. Basil's, Moscow. Mav-
rina 17:64-5 N 27 '44
Vidar. Consistory scenes, St.
Peter's, Rome bw 20:34-5
Mr 11 '46

Architecture & Decoration
(Photographs)

Austria
St. Stephan's, Vienna bw 21:
51 N 11 '46

England
Salisbury bw 8:84-5 Je 3 '40
Wells bw 16:75-80 Ja 24 '44

France
Notre Dame, Paris 8:60-1 Je
3 '40 bw 2:70 Je 14 '37

Christ story frieze bw 22:
  83 Ap 7 '47
Reims bw 22:68 Ap 7 '47

Germany
  Ulm, with details 35:28-31 D
    28 '53

Italy
  Modena, 12th century bw 40:
    93 Mr 19 '56
  St. Mark's, Venice, details
    of mosaics and sculpture
    35:28-35 D 28 '53
  St. Peter's, Rome bw 20:31-
    3, 36-7 Mr 11 '46; 27:49
    Ag 1 '49
    Bernini. Altar bw 18:27 Ja
    15 '45
    Early Christian and Roman
    mosaics, frescoes, and
    sculpture 28:65-78 Mr 27
    '50
  Siena bw 22:82-3 Mr 3 '47

Mexico
  Puebla 6:33, 36 Ja 23 '39

Russia
  Demetrius, Vladimir, Byzan-
    tine-Romanesque bw 14:84
    Mr 29 '43
  Ouspensky, Moscow 38:62-3
    Ja 31 '55
  Pskov, 1200 bw 14:93 Mr 29
    '43
  Riazan, 17th century bw 14:
    85 Mr 29 '43
  St. Basil, Moscow bw 2:54
    My 3 '37; 14:88-9 Mr 29
    '43; 22:118 Mr 10 '47

Spain
  Cordova cathedral 38:75 My 9
    '55
  Holy Family cathedral, Bar-
    celona 2:41 F 22 '37

Switzerland
  St. Pierre, Geneva bw 20:32
    Mr 18 '46

Turkey
  Santa Sophia, Istanbul: dome,
    mosaics 29:54-61 D 25 '50

United States
  St. Patrick's, New York City
    16:67 Ja 31 '44 bw altar
    4:32 Mr 21 '38; 14:75 F 1
    '43
  Santa Sophia Greek Orthodox,
    Los Angeles 33:54-5 N 3
    '52
Cather, Willa
  Willa Cather photog bw 17:14
    Ag 14 '44
  Willa Cather; family; literary
    locale photogs bw 30:113-
    4 Mr 19 '51
Catherine, Saint
  Luini. Body of St. Catherine
    borne by angels to Sinai
    fresco bw 6:32 F 13 '39
  Previtali. Madonna with St.
    John and St. Catherine 6:
    32 F 13 '39
  Ribera. Holy family with St.
    Catherine 4:42 My 16 '38
  Van Eyck, J. St. Catherine,
    altarpiece panel 40:109 My
    7 '56
Catherine of Aragon
  Catherine bw 41:88 O 29 '56
  Trial of Catherine of Aragon*
    bw 3:34 O 18 '37
Catherine of Braganza, Consort
    of Charles II, King of Eng-
    land 41:66 N 19 '56
Catherine II (the Great), Empress
    of Russia bw 14:94 Mr 29
    '43; 19:88 Ag 27 '45; 23:89
    S 15 '47 equestrian portrait
    14:7 Ja 4 '43
Catherine the Great's sapphire
    gemstone 32:68 Mr 17 '52
Cathey, Dan
  Lantz. Dan Cathey 10:47 F
    3 '41
Catlin, George
  Red Jacket, Seneca chief 36:
    72 Mr 8 '54

Catton, Bruce
  Bruce Catton photog bw 39:
    168 S 12 '55
Cat-woman. sculpture bw Clews
  31:123 O 15 '51
Cats
  Arcieri. Brenda 16:46 Ja 3
    '44
  Bacon. Paintings of cats; il-
    lustrations for "Buttons"
    bw 6:57-61 My 8 '39
  Benton. Pussy cat and roses
    6:71 Ap 24 '39
  Brook. Peggy Bacon and
    Metaphysics bw 6:57 My
    8 '39
  Bufano. Cats sculpture bw
    17:106-7 D 4 '44
  Christy. Timmie 20:94 Ap 22
    '46
  Goya. Don Manuel Osorio de
    Zuniga 2:41 Je 28 '37
  Jumping cat woodcarving bw
    Bali 15:114 O 25 '43
  Potter. "Tale of Tom Kitten,"
    illustrations bw 33:114 D 8
    '52
  Sloan. Backyards, Greenwich
    village bw 5:29 O 31 '38
  Weston. "Cats of Wildcat
    Hill" photogs bw 25:10-2 S
    6 '48
The Catskill mountains. Cole,
  T. 9:77 D 9 '40
Catskill Mountains
  Cropsey. View of Catskill
    house 19:84 S 10 '45
  Hudson River School 19:82-6
    S 10 '45
  Inman. Picnic in the Catskills
    27:57 Ag 29' 49
Cattle
  Boggs. Flying harrows 28:83
    Mr 20 '50
  Bull-headed pitcher, Etrus-
    can, 6th century B.C. 40:
    61 F 13 '56
  Bulls, Persepolis Throne
    Hall photogs bw 35:155 N 23
    '53
  Bull's head, gold and lapis

    lazuli, Ur 40:92-3 Je 4 '56
  Casilear. Lake George* bw
    5:28 O 31 '38
  Cow, incised on paleolithic
    pendant bw 39:91 N 7 '55
  Cow, Cro-Magnon cave paint-
    ing, Montignac, France
    22:66, 68 F 24 '47
  Curry. Sanctuary 1:30 N 23
    '36
  Hardy. Tall cow sculpture bw
    37:124 O 11 '54
  Havell. View of Sing Sing 19:
    85 S 10 '45
  Heifers sculptures bw Parthe-
    non 35:122 O 26 '53
  Horned bulls, Cro-Magnon
    cave painting, Montignac,
    France 22:66-8 F 24 '47
  Lea. Hazford Rupert LXXXI,
    prize Hereford bull 26:81
    Ap 25 '49
  Purple cow, illustration of
    Burgess' verse bw 31:37 O
    1 '51
  Wyeth, N.C. Summer night
    20:80 Je 17 '46
Cattle roundup. mural Fiene
  10:43 Ja 27 '41
Caudill, Rowlett, Scott and As-
  sociates, architects
  Junior high school plans,
    sketches bw 36:74-80 F 1
    '54
Cavalry charge on the southern
  plains. Remington 13:76
  S 14 '42
Cavalrymen crossing a river.
  mural French 10:44 Ja
  27 '41
Cave Paintings
  Bison, paleolithic, Spain 39:
    86 D 12 '55
  Cave of Buddhas, Petchburi
    photog 31:32-3 D 31 '51
  Cro-Magnon cave paintings,
    Montignac, France 22:64-
    8 F 24 '47
  Reclining Buddha, Ajanta
    caves bw 38:80 Mr 7 '55

Cavell, Edith
  Edith Cavell photog bw 7:77 S
    25 '39
  Edith Cavell portraits; mem-
    orial statue, London bw 7:
    76-7 S 11 '39
Cavernous impression. bw Preus-
    ser 32:91 Mr 17 '52
Caviar. sculpture bw Cherry 22:
    129 Je 16 '47
Cavour, Camillo Benso, Count
  Count Cavour photog bw 15:
    18 Ag 9 '43
Cecilia, Saint
  Bazaine. St. Cecelia stained
    glass 28:74 Je 19 '50
Celebrations See Holidays and
    Festivals
The celestial mother (Blessed
    Catherine Laboure). Ford
    17:40 D 25 '44
Cellini, Benvenuto, goldsmith
  Rospigliosi cup (attributed
    work) bw 6:53 Mr 20 '39;
    31:26 O 15 '51
  Saltcellar, c1540 31:18-9 S
    24 '51
Celtic art
  Jewelry bw 37:88 S 13 '54
  Pin 33:130 O 20 '52
Cello players See Musicians
  and Musical instruments--
  Cello
Cemeteries
  Burchfield. In memoriam 1:
    27 D 28 '36
  Burying plague victims, Lon-
    don, 1665 bw 41:173 N 19
    '56
  Herron. St. Louis cemetery
    20:80 F 18 '46
  Thomas. Moonlight 14:46
    Mr 8 '43
  St. John's churchyard, Rich-
    mond, Va. 6:28 Je 19 '39
Cenotaphs
  Sutton Hoo, Anglian, 7th cen-
    tury photogs 31:82-5 Jy
    16 '51
Censored and Rejected Art
  Chabas. September morn 21:

90 D 23 '46
Cousino. Virgin Mary sculp-
    ture bw Biarritz 31:163
    N 19 '51
Epstein. Lucifer sculpture bw
    33:66 N 3 '52
Gies. Crucifixion sculpture
    bw 3:72 Ag 18 '37
Grant. Bathers mural bw 18:
    34 Ap 2 '45
Lehmbruck. Kneeling woman
    sculpture bw 7:55 O 30 '39
Manet. Luncheon on the grass
    bw 12:44 Mr 9 '42
Niemeyer. Church of St. Fran-
    cis, Belo Horizonte, Bra-
    zil photog bw 25:76-7 Jy
    4 '49
Nude statues, Buenos Aires
    bw 11:144-7 O 13 '41
Portinari. St. Francis
    preaching to birds* mural
    bw 27:76 Jy 4 '49
Roemberg. Satan, bookjacket
    32:96 Ap 14 '52
Sculpture for 1939 Golden
    Gate Exposition, San Fran-
    cisco bw 4:14 F 21 '38
Zorach. Female figure, sym-
    bol of Texas bw 41:93 Jy
    23 '56
Centaurs See Animals, Imagin-
    ery--Centaurs
Center ring. print bw Riggs 3:
    46 S 13 '37
Central Pacific station, Sacra-
    mento, 1870. Hahn 39:83
    N 28 '55
Central Park lake. Gee 16:46 Ja
    3 '44
Central theater of red army,
    Moscow photog bw 14:85
    Mr 29 '43
Centurion's horse. Lebrun 30:
    35 Ja 15 '51
Ceramics
  Mask cups, 18th century 25:
    129 D 6 '48
  Taylor on goat bw 17:91 Jy
    17 '44

Ceramics, Chinese
  Sung vase 33:101 O 27 '52
  T'ang warrior; horse 33:101
    O 27 '52
  Tea caddy, American eagle,
    18th century 17:59 S 4 '44
  Teapot, American emblems
    and motto, 18th century
    17:58 S 4 '44
  Dancers, c500 B.C. 33:101 O
    27 '52
Ceramics, Egyptian
  Hippopotamus, lotus decora-
    tion, c1950 B.C. 6:53 Mr
    20 '39
  Isis holding son, Horus, blue
    faience 41:114 N 26 '56
  Pottery and stone dishes,
    Pharoah Aha's tomb, c1550
    B.C. bw 5:55 Ag 15 '38
Ceramics, English
  Landscape plates 26:71 F 7
    '49
  Staffordshire plates bw 5:47
    N 28 '38
Ceramics, French
  Chagall. Four plates 33:100
    O 6 '52
  Sevres ice bucket, 18th cen-
    tury bw 5:39 S 26 '38
Ceramics, German
  Beer mug, 14th century 22:
    80 My 26 '47
Ceramics, Greek
  Cup, cow's hoof shape, 500
    B.C. bw 6:52 Mr 20 '39
Ceramics, Indian (North Ameri-
  can) American Indian bowls
    and jars: Acoma; Hopi;
    Mimbres; Santa Clara; San-
    to Domingo; Socorro; Tewa;
    Zia; Zuni 40:55 Ja 16 '56
Ceramics, Italian
  Basin, Middle Ages 22:79 My
    26 '47
  Majolica 37:66-7 Ag 9 '54
  Puzzle cup--spilling liquid
    on drinker, 18th century
    25:129 D 6 '48
Ceramics, Mexican
  Blue pottery, Oaxaca 6:34

  Ja 23 '39
Ceramics, Persian
  Kashan dish; jug, 12th century
    20:92 Je 24 '46
Ceramics, Pre-Columbian
  Mayan ceramics 22:51-67 Je
    30 '47
  Inca figurine and llama jugs;
    trophy head 36:104 Ap 12
    '54
  Potter figures: dogs, humans
    18:49 Je 4 '45
Ceramics, Prehistoric
  Neolithic figurines; bowl;
    tray; pitcher; model sail
    boat 40:74-81 Ap 16 '56
Ceramics, United States
  Aitken. Futility of a well-
    ordered life bw 3:94 O 11 '37
  American tableware: Lenox,
    Vernon, Stangl 9:76-9 S
    9 '40
  America's best designed:
    Lenox, Steubenville 29:89
    D 25 '50
  Boru. Dancer bw 9:130 N 11
    '40
  Boru. Sentimental letter bw
    9:130 N 11 '40
  Ganine. Chess set bw 8:48-9
    Ja 29 '40
  Giant pots for flowers and
    trees 29:69 S 4 '50
  Greek revival vase, 1830 39:
    59 Ap 29 '55
  Jugs, Maine, 1667 38:126 Ap
    18 '55
  Kent. Dinner service 9:76-8
    S 9 '40
  Klein. Calisthenics bw 9:131
    N 11 '40
  Rawnsley. Pots that sing,
    oscillogram decorations
    bw 37:109-10 N 22 '54
  Reich. Beauty shop bw 9:
    130 N 10 '40
  Schreckengost. Samson and
    Delilah bw 9:129 N 11 '40
  Staffordshire plate, 15 stars
    and federal eagle, 1792
    17:59 S 4 '44

Syracuse Museum of Fine
Arts, 8th annual ceramics
exhibit bw 9:129-31 N 11
'40

Tracy. Jonah and the whale
bw 9:129 N 11 '40

Wolford. Saturday night in
Harlem bw 9:129 N 11 '40

Cerberus See Mythological
Themes--Cerberus

Ceres See Mytholþgical
Themes--Ceres

Cerf, Bennett

Bennett Cerf photogs bw 19:
63 O 3 '45

Ceschiatti, Alfredo

Three graces sculpture,
bronze 36:82 My 31 '54

Cezanne, Louis Auguste

Cezanne, P. Artist's father
2:46 Ap 12 '37 bw 32:88 F
25 '52

Cezanne, Marie Hortense (Fi-
quet) Cezanne, P. Madame
Cezanne 32:76 F 25 '52
bw 5:7 N 14 '38

Cezanne, Paul

Ambroise Vollard 32:81 F 25
'52

Artist's father 2:46 Ap 12 '37
bw 32:88 F 25 '52

The card players 2:47 Ap 12
'37; 32:84-5 F 25 '52

Classic goddess* mural bw,
1860 32:78 F 25 '52

Emil Zola bw 32:88F 25 '52

L'Estaque bw 26:82 My 2 '49

Farm at Jas de Bouffan 32:
83 F 25 '52

Flowers and oranges 32:79 F
25 '52

Gardanne 32:86 F 25 '52

House in the trees 37:66 Ag
9 '54

House of Emil Zola at Medan
2:47 Ap 12 '37

The little bridge 32:82 F 25
'52

Madame Cezanne 32:76 F 25
'52 bw 5:7 N 14 '38

Mont Sainte-Victoire 11:77 D

1 '41; 26:66 F 7 '49; 32:83
F 25 '52

Old woman with rosary 28:62
Ja 2 '50

Still life with apples 2:46 Ap
12 '37

The turn in the road (Bend in
the road) 25:78-9 N 1 '48;
40:76 My 28 '56

Victor Chocquet 32:80 F 25
'52

Nude bw 32:78 F 25 '52
(drawing)

Artist at work photog bw 26:
66 F 7 '49 port.

Cezanne and Pissarro photog
bw 32:92 F 25 '52 port.

Degas. The man and the
mannequin 29:88 N 27 '50
port.

Paul Cezanne photog bw 1904
28:62 Ja 2 '50 age 54 32:
77 F 25 '52 port.

Renoir. Paul Cezanne, 1880
32:93 My 19 '52 port.

Portrait of the artist before
his easel, c1885 (self-
portrait) 2:45 Ap 12 '37
port.

Self-portrait bw 32:77 F 25
'52 port.

Chabas, Paul

September Morn bw 2:53 My
24 '37; 21:90 D 23 '46;
28:96 N 27 '50

Paul Chabas photog bw 2:53
My 24 '37 port.

Chad, British symbol, World
War II bw 20:17 Mr 18 '46

Chadwick, W. F.

Placer mining in California
6:29 Je 19 '39; 27:48 Jy
4 '49

Chagall, Marc

Double portrait (The artist
and his wife) 22:59 My 5
'47

Homage to the Eiffel Tower
22:58 My 5 '47

The juggler 22:57 My 5 '47

The kiss 33:96 O 27 '52

Chagall, Marc (cont.)
  Rabbi of Vitebsk 22:58 My 5
    '47
  Rooster 27:89 D 12 '49
  Le soleil rouge 39:140 N 14
    '55
  Song of David 33:99 O 6 '52
  The trough 22:58 My 5 '47
  Four plates 33:100 O 6 '52
    (ceramics)
  Isaiah during Babylonian cap-
    tivity* bw 38:97 Je 13 '55
    (etching)
  Moses on Mount Sinai bw 38:
    97 Je 13 '55 (etching)
  Artist and his work; portrait
    photog 33:98-9 O 6 '52 port.
  Mili. Marc Chagall, age 62
    photog 27:89 D 12 '49 port.
  Newman. Marc Chagall
    photog bw 22:56 My 5 '47
    port.
  Self-portrait in Double portrait
    22:59 My 5 '47
Chairs See also Furniture--
  Chairs
  Abraham Lincoln's favorite
    rocking chair photog bw 11:
    111 N 10 '41
Chaise See Furniture--Chaises
Chalabi, Mohammed Yehia
  The visit 29:104 D 11 '50
Chaliapin, Boris
  Boris Chaliapin, "Time"
    cover portrait 17:61, 63 D
    11 '44
Chalices
  Diamond chalice of Pope Pius
    IX 32:84 Ap 14 '52
  Silver chalice, jewelled, gift
    of Czarina Alexandra to
    Rasputin 25:129 D 6 '48
  Zadok collection of chalices
    bw 32:77 Ja 14 '52
Challenging the Union vote sculp-
    ture bw Rogers 6:6 Mr 6
    '39
Chamberlain, Neville
  Neville Chamberlain 24:55 Ap
    26 '48
Chamberlain, Robert W.

Golden Gate bridge 23:98 N 10
    '47
  Robert Chamberlain photog bw
    23:101 N 10 '47 port.
Chamberlain, Samuel, photogra-
    pher New England houses bw
    15:12-5 D 6 '43
Chamberlain, Samuel E.
  "My Confession," illustrated
    journal of Mexican War
    I. 41:Cover, 68-82 Jy 23
      '56
    II. 41:52-9 Jy 30 '56
    III 41:64-72 Ag 6 '56
Chambers, Thomas
  Trapper 26:78 Je 6 '49
Chambor, Moura
  Nuns and children bw 37:123 O
    25 '54
  Moura Chambor photog bw 37:
    123 O 25 '54 port
Chamois. paper cutouts Mochi
    34:18 Mr 9 '53
Champin
  A new constitution, Paris,
    1848 25:89 N 22 '48
Champlain, Samuel de
  Champlain appointed governor
    of New France bw 9:112 S
    9 '40
Chandor, Douglas
  Eleanor Roosevelt, 1945 30:
    101 Je 18 '51
  Elizabeth II of England 35:83
    N 23 '53
  President Franklin Roosevelt
    26:82 Mr 14 '49
  Winston Churchill, in air com-
    modore's uniform 24:Cover
    124 Ap 19 '48
  Artist at work photog bw 26:83
    Mr 14 '49 port.
Chandos Family shield of arms
    22:69 My 26 '47
Chang Hsuan
  Ladies preparing newly woven
    silk 15:66-7 O 11 '43
Chang Shu-Chi
  Birds and wisteria watercolor
    on silk bw 14:65-6 Mr 15
    '43

Chapels
    Arena chapel, Padua: Giotto.
      Lives of Christ and Mary
      frescoes, 14th century 25:
      Cover, 34-57 D 27 '48
    Brancacci chapel, church of
      the Carmine, Florence:
      Masaccio. The tribute
      money fresco 39:22-3 D 26
      '55
    Dominican chapel, Vence,
      France: Matisse. architec-
      ture, glasswork, tile 31:
      108 N 26 '51
    Goff. University of Oklahoma
      chapel photogs bw 30:16-7
      Ap 30 '51
    Holyrood chapel photog bw
      24:67 Je 14 '48
    Medici-Riccardi chapel: Goz-
      zoli. Journey of the Magi
      fresco 19:Cover, 43-5 D
      24 '45
        Altar 19:43 D 24 '45
    Royal chapel, Versailles:
      Coypel. God the Father*
      ceiling painting 23:86 S 15
      '47
    San Francesco chapel, Arezzo:
      Piero della Francesca.
      Story of the true cross fres-
      co 20:60-8 Ap 22 '46
    Sistine chapel, Vatican: Michel-
      angelo. Ceiling and altar
      frescoes 21:62-9 Jy 1 '46;
      27:25-49 D 26 '49
    Windsor castle's St. George
      chapel: Dick. George V and
      Queen Mary, tomb effigy
      bw 36:44 F 8 '54
Chapin, Cornelia
    Frog sculpture bw 5:7 N 28 '38
Chapman, C. T.
    U.S.S. Maine 9:49 O 28 '40
Chapman, John Gadsby
    Davy Crockett bw 38:29
      Ap 25 '55
    Pines, Villa Barberini 33:92 S
      15 '52
Chappel, Alonzo
    Pocahontas saving Captain

    Smith* bw 31:154 D 3 '51
Chapultepec, Mexico City
    Battle of Ninos Heroes, 1847
      bw 22:47 Mr 17 '47
    Lee, D. Chapultepec park 22:
      76-7 My 12 '47
    Pena. Chapultepec park draw-
      ing bw 20:58 Je 3 '46
    Storming of Chapultepec castle,
      September 13, 1847 bw 4:
      52 Ap 11 '38; 22:122 Je 9
      '47
    Walker, J. Chapultepec 13:
      60-1 Jy 6 '42
Chardin, Jean Baptiste Simeon
    Bubble blowers bw 6:58 Mr
      27 '39
    Soap bubbles 5:37 S 26 '38
    Still life 38:125 My 2 '55; 40:
      72-3 My 28 '56
    Self-portrait bw 5:34 S 26 '38
      port.
Charge of the Light Brigade,
    Balaklava, 1854 bw 7:71 S
    25 '39; 13:71 N 16 '42
Charlemagne bw 22:70 Ap 7 '47
Charlemagne inspecting church
    construction bw, 15th cen-
    tury manuscript 22:69 Ap
    7 '47
Charles I, King of England
    Beheading of Charles I bw 22:
      98 Mr 24 '47; 41:204 N 12
      '56
    Charles I bw 41:182 N 12 '56
    King and Parliament drawing
      bw 41:186 N 12 '56
    Van Dyck. Charles I, King of
      England, accompanied by
      Duke of Epernou 41:189 N
      12 '56
Charles II, King of England
    Charles dancing at ball, The
      Hague, 1660 41:168-9 N 19
      '56
    Charles presented with pine-
      apple by gardener, John
      Rose* 41:169 N 19 '56
    Charles II wearing order of
      the garter* 41:165 N 19
      '56

Charles II (cont.)
  Coronation of Charles II,
    Westminster, 1661 bw 41:
    164 N 19 '56
  Mistresses of Charles II 41:
    166-7 N 19 '56
  A morning ride* 41:169 N 19
    '56
Charles IV, King of Luxemburg
    bw 24:28 Mr 8 '48
Charles V, Emperor of the Holy
    Roman Empire bw 24:61
    Je 14 '48
Charles V, King of Spain
    Titian. Charles V bw 31:60 O
    1 '51
Charles XIV, King of Sweden
    Westin. King Charles and
    family bw 33:92 D 1 '52
Charles Albert, King of Sardinia
    bw 20:28 Je 24 '46
Charles Albert of Piedmont bw
    15:19 Ag 9 '43
Charles et Robert
    Descente de la machine aero-
    statique 40:77 Ja 9 '56
Charles of Amboise
    de Conti. Charles of Amboise
    35:155 N 16 '53
Charles River. Dufy 30:65 Ja 22
    '51
Charleston, North Carolina
    Pittman. Charleston houses
    pastels 22:68-72 Ap 14 '47
Charlotte of Belgium, Consort of
    Maximilian, Emperor of
    Mexico, photog bw 4:52 Ap
    11 '38
Charon See Mythological
    Themes--Charon
Charpentier, Mme
    Renoir. Madame Charpentier
    and her children 3:47 Jy 5
    '37
The charter oak, Hartford.
    Brownell 13:82 N 23 '42
Charteris, Leslie
    Leslie Charteris photogs bw
    10:100-5 My 19 '41
Chartre cathedral
    Marin. Chartre cathedral

etching bw 29:62 Jy 10 '50
  Sculpture, Christ teaching 39:
    21 D 26 '55
  Stained glass 22:72-3 Ap 7 '47
Chartwell. bw Churchill 24:94
    Mr 15 '48
Chase, Philander
    Philander Chase bw 3:34 O 18
    '37
Chase, Salmon P.
    Salmon P. Chase photog bw 14:
    75 F 15 '43
Chase, Samuel
    Samuel Chase bw 15:8 Jy 5 '43
Chase, William Merritt
    James McNeill Whistler bw 5:
    29 O 31 '38; 6:54 Mr 20 '39
    Artist teaching photog bw 26:
    66 Je 20 '49 port.
Chateau-Thierry war memorial,
    1914-8 photog bw 3:23 Ag
    30 '37
Chatelet, Madame du
    Mme du Chatelet bw 23:78 S
    15 '47
Chaucer
    "Canterbury Tales," illustra-
    tion from Flemish manu-
    script, 15th century bw 22:
    75 Ap 7 '47
Chavannes, Pierre Puvis de See
    Puvis de Chavannes, Pierre
Chavez, Edward
    Convoy practice 13:32 Jy 6
    '42
Cheescake. Marsh 6:25 Ja 9 '39
Chekhov, Anton
    Chekhov, and wife photog bw
    40:136 Je 4 '56
Chelwood, Cecil, Lord of
    Lord Cecil of Chelwood photog
    bw 4:60 Ap 4 '38
Chen, Jack (Chen I-wan)
    Chinese-Japanes war, carica-
    tures; cartoons bw 4:50-1
    Ja 17 '38
Ch'en Hsu See Ch'en, Luke
Chen I-wan See Chen, Jack
Ch'en, Luke (Ch'en Hsu)
    The adoration of the Magi 11:
    44 D 22 '41

Artist at work photog bw 11:40
D 22 '41 port.
Ch'en Jung
Nine dragons, detail Sung dy-
nasty, 1244 15:66-7 O 11
'43
Chennault, Claire
Lea. Claire Chennault drawing
bw 16:72 My 29 '44
Chenonceaux, Chateau, France
15th century photog 33:40
D 29 '52
Cherry, Herman, sculptor
Caviar bw 22:139 Je 16 '47
Explosion bw 22:140 Je 16 '47
Rooster and chick bw 22:140 Je
16 '47
Silly fish bw 22:138-9 Je 16 '47
Herman Cherry photog bw 22:
138-9 Je 16 '47 port.
Cherubs
Boucher. The toilet of Venus
23:85 S 15 '47
El Greco. The virgin with
Santa Ines and Santa Tecla
7:26 D 25 '39
Raphael. Sistine Madonna 40:
113 My 7 '56
Rubens. The feast of Venus
27:66-7 O 24 '49
"Chesapeake" (ship)
American, 1812
Shannon capturing the Chesa-
peake 24:67 My 10 '48
Chess and Chessmen See Games
and Sports--Chess
Chester. sculpture bw Johnson,
S. 21:63 Jy 22 '46
Chesterfield, Philip Dormer
Stanhope, Earl of
Earl of Chesterfield bw 25:
112 S 13 '48
Chests See Furniture--Chests
Chew, Harriet
Trumbull. Harriet Chew
41:158 D 24 '56
The Chew house 29:50 Jy 3 '50
Cheyenne. sculpture bw Reming-
ton 13:72 S 14 '42
Chez Suzy. Davis, G. R. 19:47
Jy 16 '45

Chiang Kai-Shek, Mei-Ling (Soong)
Autumn garden party bw 33:6-
7 O 13 '52
Emerging from a gorge under
sail bw 33:8 O 13 '52
Enjoying snow scene bw 33:8
O 13 '52
Four occupations bw 33:6-7
O 13 '52
Looking up at distant Miao Kao
Terrace on the way home
from the Third Recluse
Pool bw 33:5 O 13 '52
Temple in the clouds bw 33:6
O 13 '52
Winter pines bw 33:7 O 13 '52
Artist at work photog bw 33:5
O 13 '52 port.
Chicago
Bohrod. Black Hawk Street,
Chicago 8:68 My 27 '40
Chicago, 1820 print 39:89 N
14 '55
Chicago, 1857 print 39:89 N
14 '55
Chicago Art Institute
Art students at work photog
bw 4:40-1 My 23 '38
Grant Wood retrospective ex-
hibit 14:52-8 Ja 18 '43
Old Masters and modern
French art from collection
11:55-60 S 8 '41
Private collector's art ear-
marked for Institute 33:90-
100 O 27 '52
View of the Institute photog bw
33:90 O 27 '52
Chicago beach. Bohrod 25:62-3
Jy 26 '48
Chichen Itza Mayan architecture
photog 22:60-1 Je 30 '47
Chickens
Chagall. Rooster 27:89 D 12
'49
Cherry. Rooster and chick
sculpture bw 22:140 Je 16
'47
Cockfighting, 1870 32:115 Ap
7 '52

Chickens (cont.)
  Cockfighting frieze bw, Bali-
    nese 3:51 S 27 '37
  Hountouaji. St. Peter and the
    cock bw 29:63 S 4 '50
  Jakuchu. Roosters scroll 31:
    66 D 31 '51
  Lamont, F. Gallic cock bw
    14:42 Mr 8 '43
  Leprince. Little farmer feed-
    ing chickens bw 3:43 N 29
    '37
  Picasso. Girl with cock bw 8:
    59 Mr 4 '40
  Plattner. Chickens 36:82 My
    31 '54
  Wood, G. Adolescence bw 14:
    58 Ja 18 '43
Chidester, Ann
  Ann Chidester photog bw 22:81
    Je 2 '47
The chief. sculpture bw Brancusi
  24:95 Ap 12 '48
Childhood memories of Christ-
  mas. drawing bw Dali 19:8
  D 24 '45
Children See also Family
  Groups; Holy Family; Mary,
  Virgin--Madonna and Child;
  Mother and Child
  Albright, A. E. Anglers bw
    16:64 Mr 27 '44
  Arabella and Winston Church-
    ill 24:35 Ap 19 '48
  Bellows. Anne in white 20:74
    Mr 25 '46
  Bellows. Jean in pink dress
    bw 11:76 O 6 '41
  Bellows. Jean with a doll bw
    11:76 O 6 '41
  Bellows. Jean with blue book
    and apple bw 11:76 O 6 '41
  Bellows. Lady Jean 7:58 N 20
    '39 bw 11:76 O 6 '41
  Benton. T. P. and Jake 6:71
    Ap 24 '39 bw 10:70 Ap 14
    '41
  Bishop. Head of boy sculpture
    bw 21:62 Jy 22 '46
  Boltraffio. Portrait of a youth
    bw 24:67 Ja 26 '48

Borgatta. Sleeping sculpture
  bw 37:102 D 6 '54
Brancusi. Boy sculpture bw
  39:135 D 5 '55
Brown. School children draw-
  ings bw 37:16-7 S 20 '54
Bruyn. Family group 7:34 Jy
  31 '39
Burden. Ridin' high 25:99 D
  6 '48
Carlton. Boy with mask sculp-
  ture bw 5:70 D 5 '38
Casebier. Boy in Mexico 39:
  115 S 12 '55
Child's head mosaic, Early
  Christian 28:68 Mr 27 '50
Copley. Boy with squirrel bw
  5:28 O 31 '38
Cox, G. Portrait of a boy 10:
  47 F 3 '41
Cranach, Lucas, the elder.
  A prince of Saxony 24:66
  Ja 26 '48
Cranach, Lucas, the elder.
  Princess of Saxony bw 24:
  67 Ja 26 '48
Davis, G. R. Caroler 23:
  Cover D 22 '47
Davis, G. R. Carousel 22:96
  Ap 21 '47
Davis, G. R. Companions bw
  18:44 Ja 1 '45
Davis, G. R. Deborah 14:45
  Ap 19 '43
Davis, G. R. Noel pastel 14:
  45 Ap 19 '43
Degas. Mademoiselle Hortense
  Valpincon 25:77 Ag 2 '48
De Peyster boy, 1730 26:85 F
  28 '49
Eisenhower. Grandson David
  28:151 Ap 17 '50
Epstein. Judith Margulies
  sculpture bw 33:66 N 3 '52
Etnier. Adolescence 6:27 F
  13 '39
Falter. Quality of mercy 26:
  101 F 21 '49
Ford. Guardian angel 17:42
  D 25 '44
Gainsborough. The blue boy

4:26 Ja 24 '38

Gainsborough. The cottage door 5:43 S 12 '38

Galvan. La vigornia 4:30 Mr 14 '38

Goya. Don Manuel Osorio de Zuniga 2:41 Je 28 '37

Greenaway. "A day in a child's life" drawings bw 18:87-8 Ap 9 '45

Greenaway. Illustrations of children from her books 23:87-92 D 1 '47

Greenham. Fancy dress 3:27 D 20'37

Greenough. Sears children Sculpture bw 37:41 O 25 '54

Guston. If this be not I 20:92 My 27 '46

Hals. Fisher girl bw 6:58 Mr 27 '39

Henri. Mary 12:60 Je 15 '42

Hesselius. Charles Calvert of Maryland 9:75 D 9 '40; 26:84 F 28 '49

Hine. Child worker in a cotton mill, 1908 photog bw 28:82 Ja 2 '50

Hurd. Boy from the plains 7: 26 Jy 24 '39

Jones. Portrait of sis 10:47 F 3 '41

Kidd. Young girl 29:71 O 9 '50

Koch. Children painting* 29: Cover D 25 '50

Kroll. Marie-Claude's birthday bw 10:70 Ap 14 '41

Kruger. Boy; Girl sculptures bw 39:187, 189 N 14 '55

Lasker. El candy store 28:84 Mr 20 '50

Lawrence, T. The Calmady children 6:55 Mr 20 '39

Lawrence, T. Pinkie (Sarah Moulton-Barrett) 4:25 Ja 24 '38

Le Clear, Thomas. Red Jacket's grandson 36:73 Mr 8 '54

Luks. The spielers 12:61 Je

15 '42

Manet. Boy blowing bubbles 29:89 N 27 '50

Manet. The Lange boy bw 6: 58 Mr 27 '39

Marcks. Girl reading Sculpture bw 28:71 F 6 '50

Mason children, c1670 38:111 Ap 18 '55

Matisse. Marguerite 31:111 N 26 '51

Michel. The yellow cage 20: 60 Je 3 '46

Modigliani. Portrait of a boy with red hair 40:72 My 28 '56

Mount. The truant gamblers 18:66 Je 25 '45

Murillo. Saint Thomas of Villanueva dividing his clothing among beggar boys 4:42 My 16 '38

Peirce, W. Anna digs clams 19:85 N 12 '45

Peirce, W. Anna turns painter 19:85 N 12 '45

Peirce, W. Bill plays an old mandolin 19:85 N 12 '45

Peirce, W. The birches 12: 61 Je 15 '42

Peirce, W. Mike fishes in Maine 19:85 N 12 '45

Peirce, W. The twins' concert 19:84 N 12 '45

Pierce, L. Stilts woodcuts 37:89 O 18 '54

Philipp. Brooke Hayward bw 8:62 Ap 8 '40

Prendergast. Young American artist 20:79 F 18 '46

Raeburn. Boy with rabbit bw 14:111 Ja 25 '43

Raeburn. Master William Blair 4:27 Ja 24 '38

Reinhardt. Mandrill and maidens 32:89 Mr 24 '52

Reinhardt. String and dead bird 32:90 Mr 24 '52

Renoir. Gabrielle and Jean 32:91 My 19 '52

Children (cont.)

Renoir. The Hunter 32:98 My 19 '52

Renoir. Jean sewing 32:94 My 19 '52

Renoir. Portrait of a child 25: 77 N 1 '48

Renoir. Two little circus girls 11:59 S 8 '41

Rockwell. The American way 18:45 Ja 1 '45

Rockwell. Boy scout calendar 18:45 Ja 1 '45

Romney. The Beckford children 4:27 Ja 24 '38

Rosenthal. At the blackboard 15:66 N 22 '43

Rosenthal. Corn foliage 22: 96 Ap 21 '47

Rosenthal. Sacred music 15: 66 N 22 '43

Rosenthal. Tops 15:65 N 22 '43

Saint-Gaudens. Homer, age 4 sculpture bw 24:112 Mr 15 '48

Salemme. Head of a little girl sculpture bw 7:36 Jy 17 '39

Sargent. Daughters of Edward Boit 36:96-7 My 17 '54

Sharon. May-day party 33:75 Jy 21 '52

Sharon. Playroom 33:75 Jy 21 '52

Shipbuilder's children, c1846 31:71 Jy 2 '51

Simkhovitch. Child* 18:75 My 14 '45

Simkhovitch. Jennifer 10:47 F 3 '41

Siporin. Boy with toys bw 27: 56 D 26 '49

Tamayo. Pretty little girl 34: 99 Mr 16 '53

Velazquez. Don Baltasar Carlos 31:71 O 1 '51

Velazquez. Infanta Margarita Theresa 27:72 O 24 '49

Velazquez. The maids of honor 7:57 N 20 '39; 31:61 O 1 '51

Verrochio. Child sculpture bw

bw 26:105 Mr 21 '49

Children's Art See Art, Children's

Children's crusade. bw Dore 16: 66 Ap 10 '44

Children's games. Brueghel, Pieter, the elder 29:30-1 D 25 '50 bw 31:94 Ag 20 '51

Chimney piece. furniture Chippendale bw 23:75 Ag 25 '47

China

De Bry. Chinese transportation* drawing bw 24:86 Mr 22 '48

Lea. Landscapes and portraits 17:63-6 Jy 10 '44

Lu Hsun Academy. Chinese scenes and portraits woodcuts 18:57-60 Ap 9 '45

Yang and Yin, cosmic force symbol 38:57 F 7 '55; 38: 69 Ap 4 '55; bw 24:131 F 23 '48

China (porcelain) See Ceramics

China patriot. Lea 17:63 Jy 10 '44

The Chinese swan. Stevens, E. 28:87 Mr 20 '50

Ch'ing Ming scroll, c1500 31:44 D 31 '51

Chippendale, Thomas, furniture and interior designer

Furniture: chairs, sofa, china cabinet, chimney piece bw 23:75 Ag 25 '47

Stairway, Pierce House, Salem, Mass. 38:62 My 30 '55

Chirico, Giorgio de

Faceless men* bw 19:64 S 24 '45

Maria Lani bw 19:16 D 3 '45

The sailors' barracks bw 1: 27 D 14 '36

Square* (declared forgery by artist; genuine by Court) bw 30:71 Mr 5 '51

Artist and wife photog bw 30: 71 Mr 5 '51 port.

Choate, Joseph

Joseph Choate photog bw 10:

27 Mr 3 '41

Chocolate grinder. drawing Duchamp 32:103 Ap 28 '52

Chocolate Pot

Winslow. Chocolate pot, silver, U.S., 1700 6:53 Mr 20 '39

Chocorua Mountain, New Hampshire. Hart 19:83 S 10 '45

Chocquet, Victor

Cezanne. Victor Chocquet 32: 80 F 25 '52

The choice of Hercules. Veronese 3:38 D 27 '37

Chop suey. Hopper 28:102 Ap 17 '50

Chopin, Frederic

Frederic Chopin photog bw 25: 99 N 22 '48

Frederic Chopin statue bw 17: 85 Ag 28 '44 statue bw, Poland 5:53 Ag 29 '38

Zamoyski. Chopin sculpture bw 26:98 F 14 '49

Chora church, Istanbul

Head of Christ mosaic, Byzantine 29:54 D 25 '50

Chou-Chi-Ch'ang

Darbha Malli-Putra, Buddhist saint 15:66 O 11 '43

Christ See Jesus Christ

Christian martyrs. bw Woosung 29:63 S 4 '50

Christian martyrs torn by lions, Colosseum, Rome bw 39: 38 D 26 '55

Christian nocturne. Roualt 34: 62 F 2 '53

Christmas

Nichols. Home for Christmas bw 5:9 D 12 '38

Sharon. Family reunion 33: 76 Jy 21 '52

Christmas Cards See Cards

"A Christmas Carol," illustrations bw Leech 25:78 D 27 '48

Christmas carols. Illustrations by famous artists 23:42-58 D 22 '47

Christmas customs and legends of many lands. Lewicki 19:

74-6 D 17 '45; 33:82-7 D 1 '52; 39:60-71 D 19 '55

Christmas morning. bw Burchfield 1:29 D 28 '36

Christmas trees. drawings bw Nine artists 19:8-10 D 24 '45

Christopher, Saint

Van Eyck brothers. St. Christopher 26:65, 67 Ap 18 '49

Christus, Petrus

St. Elgius and St. Godeberta 37:65 Ag 9 '54

Christy, Howard Chandler

"The Man in Lower Ten" illustrations bw 20:56 F 25 '46

The signing of the Constitution bw 8:26 Je 10 '40

Timmie bw 20:94 Ap 22 '46

Church, Frederick Edwin

The Hooker party migrates to Hartford, Connecticut, 1636 13:82 N 23 '42

Horseshoe Falls 26:78-9 Je 6 '49

Quest for freedom bw 24:70 Je 14 '48

Scene in the Catskills 19:84 S 10 '45

Churches See also Abbeys; Cathedrals; Missions; Temples; and names of specific churches, as Santa Sophia

Bohrod. Sanctuary 35:67 N 2 '53

Bone. Bread buyers, Spain 1: 43 D 7 '36

Bone. Church, Spain drawing bw 1:45 D 7 '36

Davidson. First meeting house of North Church, Salem, Mass. 13:80 N 23 '42

Dufy. Old church, Rockport, Mass. 30:63 Ja 22 '51

Feininger, Lyonel. The church 14:45 Mr 8 '43

Feininger, Lyonel. Church of Gelmeroda 31:96 N 12 '51

Churches (cont.)
  Ganso. The village church 2:
    34 F 1 '37
  Guardi. Santa Maria della
    Salute 35:152-3 N 16 '53
  Lee, D. Country wedding 14:
    45 Mr 8 '43
  Mavrina. Churches of Russia
    17:64-8 N 27 '44
  Pilgrim meeting house, 1683
    drawing bw 19:54 N 26 '45
  Robertson. Winter afternoon
    6:29 F 13 '39
  St. John churchyard, Rich-
    mond, Va. 6:28 Je 19 '39
    photog bw 11:104 N 10 '41
  Sample. Cathedral encamp-
    ment, Leyte 35:56 N 2 '53
  Shahn. Bronx church 37:97
    O 4 '54
  Siqueiros. The devil in church
    29:106 D 11 '50
  Thon. Venetian church 33:94
    S 15 '52
  Utrillo. The church of Saint-
    Severin 28:93 Ja 16 '50
  Wood, G. The midnight ride of
    Paul Revere 14:54 Ja 18 '43
  Zerbe. San Clemente church,
    Venice 33:96 S 15 '52

    Architecture & Decoration
       (Photographs)
Bolivia
  Spanish church, Laja 25:54 Ag
    2 '48

Brazil
  Niemeyer. St. Francis, Belo
    Horizonte bw 25:76-7 Jy 4
    '49

Canada
  St. Anne de Beaupre, Quebec
    bw 9:107 S 9 '40

Czechoslovakia
  Greek Catholic church, Uzho-
    rod bw 3:100 N 8 '37

England
  St. Giles church, Edinburgh
    bw 22:100 My 5 '47
  Southwell Minster 40:87-8 Mr
    12 '56
  Spence. Church, Coventry bw
    34:63-4 Mr 23 '53

France
  Assy Church, mosaics, stained
    glass, tapestry 28:72-6 Je
    19 '50
  Basilica of Sacre-Coeur,
    Paris bw 17:92 O 2 '44
  Gothic cathedrals, Middle
    Ages bw 22:67 Ap 7 '47
  Matisse. Dominican chapel,
    Vence 31:108 N 26 '51

Germany
  Kaiser Wilhelm memorial
    church, Berlin bw 36:121
    Ap 19 '54
  Pforzheim church bw 36:150
    My 10 '54
  Wittenberg church bw 24:62 Je
    14 '48

Guatemala
  Santa Tomas, Chichicasten-
    ango 22:67 Je 30 '47

Italy
  Carmine church, Florence
    39:22-3 D 26 '55
  Sant' Angelo in Formis, fres-
    coes, 11th century 17:62
    Jy 24 '44
  Santa Chiara, Naples, fres-
    coes, 14th, 18th centur-
    ies 17:60-2 Jy 24 '44

Mexico
  Church decoration, Aztec-
    Spanish motifs bw 28:62
    Ja 9 '50
  Virgin of the Miraculous
    Medal, Mexico City bw
    40:138 My 28 '56

Poland
  Holy Cross, Warsaw bw 26:
    18 My 30 '49

Russia
  Baroque church, Fili, 17th
    century 14:83 Mr 29 '43

United States
  Anshen and Allen. Chapel of
    the Holy Cross, Arizona
    41:105-6 O 15 '56
  Anderson, E.O. Mormon
    temple, Los Angeles 39:
    115 D 26 '55
  Baptist temple, Akron, Ohio
    bw 27:59-60 Jy 25 '49
  Belluschi. Zion Lutheran
    church, Portland, Oreg.
    bw 30:16 Ap 30 '51
  Blessed Sacrament church,
    Holyoke, Mass 35:88-9 Jy
    6 '53
  Brandeis university chapels,
    Boston bw 39:113 N 21 '55
  Brooks and Coddington. St.
    Stephen's Episcopal church,
    Columbus, Ohio 39:116-7
    D 26 '55
  Callister. Christ Scientist
    church, Belvedere, Calif.
    39:115 D 26 '55
  Ciampi. Corpus Christi Cath-
    olic church, San Francisco
    38:68-9 Ap 11 '55
  Goff. University of Oklahoma
    chapel bw 30:16-7 Ap 30
    '51
  Greek revival church, 1825,
    Talmadge, Ohio bw 17:
    Cover N 20 '44
  Maybeck. Christ Scientist
    church, Berkeley, Calif.
    bw 24:142 My 17 '48
  Mendelsohn. Synagogue, St.
    Louis bw 30:15 Ap 30 '51
  Modern church designs by
    U.S. architects 30:14-7
    Ap 30 '51
  Moravian church of Old Salem,
    Winston-Salem, N.C. bw

  37:166 O 25 '54
  Murphy and Mackey. Catholic
    church of the Resurrection,
    St. Louis 39:114 D 26 '55
  Puritan church, Groton, Mass.
    bw 13:Cover N 23 '42
  Raymond and Rado. Catholic
    church, Negros Island,
    Philippines 30:14-5 Ap 30
    '51
  Riverside church, New York
    City bw 3:35-7 D 20 '37;
    19:75 D 24 '45
  Saarinen, Eero. Massachu-
    setts Institute of Technol-
    ogy chapel 39:114-5 D 26
    '55
  Saarinen, Eliel and Eero.
    Christ Evangelical Luther-
    an church, Minneapolis
    bw 30:17 Ap 30 '51
  St. Benedict the Moor church
    bw 34:95-6 Mr 16 '53
  San Esteban Rey, Acoma, N.
    Mex. 8:74 My 13 '40; 40:
    48 Ja 16 '56
  Skidmore, Owings and Mer-
    rill, and Belluschi. Cen-
    tral Lutheran church,
    Eugene, Oreg. 39:112 D
    26 '55
  Tesuque church, N. Mex. 8:
    74 My 13 '40
  Wagoner. Presbyterian
    church, Vero Beach, Fla.
    39:116 D 26 '55
  Weber. Church, Cedar Hills,
    Oreg. 39:112-3 D 26 '55
  Wright. Unitarian church,
    Madison, Wis. bw 30:16-7
    Ap 30 '51
Churchgoing, York Springs,
    Pennsylvania, 18th century
    31:73 Jy 2 '51
Churchill, Arabella, 17th cen-
    tury
  Arabella and Winston Church-
    ill 24:35 Ap 19 '48
  Arabella Churchill 41:171 N
    19 '56

Churchill, John
  Mural, Marlborough Pavilion,
    Chartwell 35:81 N 23 '53
Churchill, Randolph
  Lord Randolph Churchill 28:
    73 F 27 '50
Churchill, Sylvester
  Sylvester Churchill 29:95 N
    13 '50
Churchill, Winston, 17th century
  Sir Winston Churchill 41:170
    N 19 '56
Churchill, Winston Leonard
    Spencer
  Chartwell bw 24:94 Mr 15 '48
  Goldfish pond 20:48 Ja 7 '46
  Lake Lugano, Italy 20:50 Ja
    7 '46
  Marrakesh 29:96 N 6 '50
  Mt. Sainte-Victoire 26:66 F
    7 '49
  Olive grove at La Dragoniere
    20:47 Ja 7 '46
  On the shores of Lake Como 20:
    45 Ja 7 '46
  Reflections at St. Jean 20:46
    Ja 7 '46
  Scene in Canne harbor 20:46
    Ja 7 '46
  Seascape* 20:50 Ja 7 '46
  Sorgue River* 26:65 F 7 '49
  Still life 20:49 Ja 7 '46
  Terrace at Chartwell* 20:48
    Ja 7 '46
  Villa on the Nivelle 20:47 Ja
    7 '46
  Artist at work bw 20:Cover,
    44 Ja 7 '46 port.
  Beerbohm. Winston Churchill,
    1907 bw 33:126 S 22 '52
    port.
  Birley. Winston Churchill,
    1946, House of Commons
    portrait 28:62 F 27 '50 port.
  Chandor. Winston Churchill in
    air commodore's uniform
    bw 24:Cover, 124 Ap 19 '48
    port.
  Lavery. Winston Churchill bw
    24:95 Mr 15 '48 port.
  Orpen. Winston Churchill bw

    24:94 Mr 15 '48 port.
  Portraits of Churchill family
    bw 24:94-5 Mr 15 '48 port.
  Searle. Churchill in Commons
    drawing 38:29 Ap 4 '55
  Sutherland. Sir Winston
    Churchill 37:30 D 13 '54
    port.
  Winston Churchill 24:34 Ap 19
    '54 photog 26:64-6 F 7 '49
    "Time" cover portrait 17:
    62 D 11 '44 port.
  Winston Churchil cartoons bw
    6:28 Ja 9 '39 port.
Churchill knight, 1644, memorial
  photog bw 9:92 N 18 '40
Churinga, paleolithic noisemaker
  photog 39:79 D 12 '55
Ciampi, Mario, architect
  Corpus Christi Catholic church
    San Francisco 38:68-9 Ap
    11 '55
Cicero, Marcus Tullius
  Cicero bw 22:79 Mr 3 '47
Cigar store figure sculpture 35:
  48-9 Jy 6 '53
Cigar store Indian wood carving
  38:62 Ja 3 '55
Cigaret premium cards, U.S.,
  c1900 28:42 Ja 2 '50
Cikovsky, Nicolai
  Walkowitz bw 16:79 F 21 '44
Cima, Giovanni Battista (known
    as Cima da Conegliano)
  Presentation of Mary 40:107
    My 7 '56
Cimabue (Cenni di Pepo)
  Madonna with angels 35:56 Ag
    17 '53
Cincinnati Art Museum
  International exhibit of colored
    lithographs 33:84-7 Jy 14
    '52
"Cinderella," illustrations. bw
  Alajalov 15:79-80 S 13 '43
The circuit rider print bw 39:
  78 D 26 '55
"Circular Staircase," illustra-
  tions bw Lester 20:56 F
  25 '46
Circus See also Acrobats; Clowns

Bellows. Outside the big tent
12:62 Je 15 '42
Benevento. Circus parade 1:
44 N 30 '36
Curry. Circus elephants 1:31
N 23 '36 bw 15:19 N 29 '43
Gatto. Circus bw 25:76 N 8
'48
Gergely. "Topsy Turvey
Circus" illustrations 11:85
D 15 '41
Marin. In the ring 29:64 Jy
10 '50
Marsh. Pip and Flip 40:80-1
F 6 '56
Peirce, W. After the show
12:74 Ap 20 '42
Priebe. Carnival interlude 23:
71 N 24 '47
Renoir. Two little circus
girls 11:59 S 8 '41
Riggs. Center ring print bw
3:46 S 13 '37
Riggs. Clown alley print bw
3:47 S 13 '37
Riggs. On stage four print bw
3:46 S 13 '37
Roualt. Circus dancer tapes-
try, Aubusson 21:84 S 30
'46
Toulouse-Lautrec In the cir-
cus--Fernando the ring-
master 11:59 S 8 '41
Cistercian monastery, Clairvaux,
France bw 22:75 Ap 7 '47
The city. Hopper 20:80 F 18 '46
The city. Leger 4:44 My 2 '38
City at night. Anderson, D. 32:
68-9 Ja 14 '52
City at night. Feininger, Lyonel
31:91 N 12 '51
City at night. Sterne 31:51 Ag 27
'51
The city dance. bw Renoir 28:
88 Ja 16 '50
The city from Greenwich Village.
Sloan 7:46 D 11 '39
City interior. Sheeler 5:43 Ag 8
'38
"City of St. Paul" (Mississippi
steamboat). Bunn 9:72 O

14 '40
City silhouette from a balcony at
headquarter, London Fire
Forces. Manwaring 12:40
Mr 2 '42
Civil War See Revolutions;
name of country, as Spain;
United States
Civilization. bw Gropper 8:71
My 27 '40
Claesz, Pieter
Lunch table bw 7:24 Ag 28 '39
"Clarissa, " by Samuel Richard-
son. illustrations bw 25:
109 S 13 '48
Clark, Abraham
Abraham Clark bw 15:8 Jy 5
'43
Clark, Allan, architect
Jacona, adobe, New Mexico
26:64-5 Mr 14 '49
Artist and his sculptures
photog 26:66 Mr 14 '49 port.
Clark, Cameron, architect
"Minimum" house, U.S. plan
bw 9:78-9 Jy 1 '40
Clark, George, interior designer
Northeast town house, U.S.
contemporary 38:116-7 F
21 '55
Clark, Mark
Biddle. Lt. General Mark
Clark drawing bw 16:14 Ja
3 '44
Lt. General Mark Clark,
"Time" cover portrait
17:60 D 11 '44
Clark, Mary Rebecca
Heade. Mary Rebecca Clark
41:161 D 24 '56
Clark, Walter van Tilburg
"Hook" (the hawk) illustra-
tions. Harzard bw 40:155-
60 Mr 19 '56
Clark, William, explorer
William Clark bust bw 13:70
O 12 '42
Claudel, Paul
Karsh. Paul Claudel photog
bw 37:131 O 4 '54

Claudian aqueduct, Italy photog
bw 16:13 Je 5 '44
Clausewitz, Karl von
Karl von Clausewitz bw 15:96
N 22 '43
Clay, Cassius
Cassius Clay bw 19:89 Ag 27
'45
Clay, Henry
Clevenger. Henry Clay bust
bw 19:9 S 24 '45
Henry and Mrs. Clay photog
bw 23:57 N 3 '47
Henry Clay 19:86 S 24 '45 bw
16:56 F 21 '44 photog bw
14:6 My 31 '43
The Clay Club, New York City
Sculptors and their work bw
21:101-5 Jy 8 '46
Cleaning Art Objects See Art
Cleaning and Restoration
Clear rivers and quiet seas boat,
marble, Summer palace,
Peiping 20:75 Ap 29 '46
Clemenceau, Georges
The Big Four at Versailles
photog bw 15:22 Ag 9 '43;
33:41 D 22 '52
Clemens, Paul
Ann Southern 24:65 Mr 1 '48
The artist's wife 18:76 My
14 '45
Can-can girl. 24:66 Mr 1 '48
Dorothy McGuire 21:57 S 2 '46
Katherine McBride of Bryn
Mawr 23:94 O 27 '47
Mildred McAfee Horton of
Wellesley 23:93 O 27 '47
Millicent Carey McIntosh of
Barnard 23:92 O 27 '47
Sarah Blanding of Vassar 23:
91 O 27 '47
South wind 8:67 My 27 '40; 21:
75 N 25 '46
Artist at work photog bw 41:
80 Ag 13 '56 port.
Clemens, Samuel
Samuel Clemens photog bw
28:80 Ja 2 '50
Samuel Clemens; family,
homes, scenes of books bw

16:89-92 My 8 '44
"Tom Sawyer" locale, Hanni-
bal, Mo. 9:90-1 Jy 15 '40
Cleopatra, Queen of Egypt
Cleopatra and her son,
Caesarion intaglio bw 41:
126 N 26 '56
Story. Cleopatra sculpture
bw 19:10 S 24 '45
"Clermont" Robert Fulton's
steamboat 39:67 Jy 18 '55
Clermont house photog bw 7:62
O 2 '39
Cleveland, Arthur
Wyeth, A. Arthur Cleveland
24:103 My 17 '48
Cleveland, Grover
Grover Cleveland political
cartoon 40:70-1 Ja 30 '56
with Henry Ward Beecher
bw 31:19 O 22 '51
Cleveland Museum, Cleveland,
Ohio
Art treasures of painting and
sculpture 15:64-8 S 20 '43
Clevenger, Shobal
Henry Clay sculpture bw 19:
9 S 24 '45
Clews, Henry, sculptor
Anteater bw 31:119 O 15 '51
Cat-woman bw 31:123 O 15
'51
Christ and the blind girl* 31:
120 O 15 '51
Gods, ogs, wogs bw 31:119
O 15 '51
Mayor of Mandeliew* bw 31:
120 O 15 '51
Sculptor's wife bw 31:120 O
15 '51
The thinker bw 31:119 O 15
'51
Henry Clews; family photogs
bw 31:119, 124 O 15 '51
port.
Cliff house, Pueblo, Flagstaff,
Ariz. photog 40:47 Ja 16
'56
Cliffs at Etretat. Courbet 26:64
My 30 '49

Clinton, George
George Clinton bw 9:8 Ag 5
'40
Clinton, Henry
Henry Clinton 29:53 Jy 3 '50
Clinton in winter. mural Bohrod
10:45 Ja 27 '41
Clive, Robert
Robert Clive bw 25:113 6 13
'48
Cloar, Carroll
Artist's family; biographical
scenes lithographs 24:79-
82 Ja 26 '48
Lull bw 32:88 Mr 17 '52
Carroll Cloar photog bw 32:
87 Mr 17 '52 port.
Group of myselves, self-por-
traits at 6 ages bw 24:79-
82 Ja 26 '48 port.
Clocks and Watches
Acorn clock, Bristol, Conn.,
1850 photog 39:62 Ag 29
'55
Dali. The persistence of
memory 1:25 D 14 '36 bw
19:64 S 24 '45
Eight-foot clock designed for
Henry VIII, 1540 photog 41:
91 O 29 '56
French clock, 18th century
photog bw 5:47 N 28 '38
George Washington clock,
Paris, 1780-1819 photog
17:58 S 4 '44
Rittenhouse. Grandfather
clock, Chinese Chippendale
case, Philadelphia, 1770
photog 39:64 Jy 18 '55
Sawin and Dyer. Lyre clock,
Boston, 1815 photog 17:58
S 4 '44
Sun clock, Laja, Bolivia
photog 25:54 Ag 2 '48
Willard, A. Banjo clock,
c1800 photog 39:64 Jy 18
'55
Willard, A. Shelf clock,
c1800 photog 39:64 Jy 18 '55
Willard, S. Banjo clock photog
bw 6:52 Mr 20 '39

Willard, S. Wall clock with
carved eagle, c1810 photog
17:58 S 4 '44
Cloisonne
Moorish necklace, gold fili-
gree, c1340 bw 9:94 D 9
'40
Cloudburst. Ernst 32:58 Ja 21
'52
Cloudburst. Hurd 23:77 Ag 18
'47
Clouds
Bellows. The big dory 29:71
Ag 21 '50
Bellows. The white horse 20:
81 Mr 25 '46
Burchfield. November even-
ing 26:86-7 F 21 '49
Cox. Wheat 25:86-7 Jy 12 '48
Cox. White clouds 16:78 Ap
24 '44
Curry. H mestead 7:36 D
25 '39
Ernst. Above the clouds walks
the moonlight 34:25 My 25
'53
Hartley. Storm clouds 32:85
Je 16 '52
Hurd. The dry river 7:25 Jy
24 '39
Lea. The empty places* 18:
43 Ap 30 '45
Lee, D. Hudson River excur-
sion 3:46 S 20 '37
Lucioni. Clouds over Equinox
3:48 Jy 19 '37
Magritte. The eye 1:25 D 14
'36 bw 19:64-5 S 24 '45
Ryder. Night and clouds 13:
96 N 9 '42
Taubes. Figures at the shore
12:46 Mr 9 '42
Taubes. Summer evening 8:
39 Ja 15 '40
Types and formation of
clouds photogs 6:28-32 My
8 '39
Varga. Road to Danbury 10:
72 Ap 14 '41
Wood, G. Spring in the country 14:56 Ja 18 '43

Clouds (cont.)
  Wyeth, N. C. Summer night 20:
    80 Je 17 '46
Clouds and shadows. Mathews, E.
  32:69 Ja 14 '52
Clouds over Equinox. Lucioni
  3:48 Jy 19 '37
Clouet, Jean
  Francis I, King of France
    35:50 Ag 17 '53
Clowns See also Circus
  Kuhn. The blue clown 26:88
    F 21 '49
  MacIver. Hobo clown (Emmett
    Kelly) 23:43 Jy 21 '47
  Patrix. Clown bw 20:64 Je 17
    '46
  Philipp, W. Clowns bw 24:160
    Mr 15 '48
  Riggs. Clown acrobats print
    bw 3:47 S 13 '37
  Riggs. Clown alley print bw
    3:47 S 13 '37
  Roualt. Three clowns 34:60
    F 2 '53
  Toulouse-Lautrec. Dancing
    clown drawing bw 28:96
    My 15 '50
Clymer, George
  George Clymer bw 15:8 Jy 5
    '43
Coale, Griffith Baily
  Hvalfjordur, Iceland bw 13:
    92-3 Jy 13 '42
  Newfoundland bw 13:90-1 Jy
    13 '42
  Payday, "Newfie" workmen
    bw 13:92-3 Jy 13 '42
  U.S. ships entering Reykjavik
    bw 13:90-1 Jy 13 '42
  North Atlantic patrol bw 12:
    39-43 Ja 19 '42 (drawings)
Coastal defense. bw Rowntree
  10:64 F 24 '41
Coats of Arms See Heraldry
Cobra
  Emblem of Lower Egypt, 4th
    dynasty photog bw 41:94
    O 1 '56
Cockermouth castle, England
  photog bw 29:88 Jy 17 '50

Cockfighting See Games and
  Sports--Cockfighting
Cocteau, Jean
  Maria Lani bw 19:14 D 3 '45
  Head bw 36:110 Ap 26 '54
    (drawing)
  Artist at work photog bw 3:35
    S 6 '37 port.
  Halsman. Jean Cocteau,
    surrealist portraits photogs
    bw 26:18-20 F 7 '49 port.
  Jean Cocteau, in uniform of
    French Academy, and
    other portraits photogs
    39:158-9 N 7 '55 port.
  Karsh. Jean Cocteau, age 61
    photog bw 39:76 Ag 7 '50
    port.
Coddington, Gilbert, architect
  Brooks and Coddington. St.
    Stephen's Episcopal
    church, Columbus, Ohio
    photogs 39:116-7 D 26 '55
Code of Hammurabi
  Cast bw 24:147 Mr 15 '48
  Stone replica bw 37:94 D 13
    '54
Codex Paulinus, page of 34:77,
  88 F 23 '53
Cody, William Frederick (Buffa-
  lo Bill)
  Buffalo Bill photog bw 22:68
    Ap 28 '47
  Buffalo Bill and Pawnee Bill
    photog bw 16:109 Ap 10 '44
  William Cody portraits,
    family, associates photogs
    bw 16:110-1 Ap 10 '44
Coffee grinder. drawing Duchamp
  32:103 Ap 28 '52
Coffee house, England, 18th cen-
  tury 25:104 S 13 '48
Coffee plant* bw 24:83 Mr 22 '48
Cohan, George M.
  The Four Cohans photog bw
    12:66 Je 15 '42
  George Cohan in "I'd Rather
    be Right" photog bw 3:27-
    9 O 25 '37
Cohen, David
  Artist and his work photog bw

35:114 Jy 13 '53 port.

Cohen, George
George Cohen, blind artist, at work photog bw 36:169-70 My 3 '54 port.

Cohn, Maralyn
La frutera sculpture bw 10:59 Je 16 '41

The coiffure. color print Cassatt 36:98 My 17 '54

Coins and Metals See also Emblems and Decorations
Eliasberg (Louis) coin collection--sample U.S. and foreign coins 34:114-6 Ap 27 '53

Medal, French hat ornament, 16th century 37:64 Ag 9 '54

Victory medal: Defeat of the Spanish Armada, Dutch bw 41:168 N 5 '56

Coke, Edward
Castellon. The law and the king 30:94 Mr 12 '51

Cole, Leslie
Antiaircraft battery 28:52 F 6 '50

Buzz bomb over Britain* 35:87 O 26 '53

"Matildas" (tanks) 28:73 F 20 '50

Cole, Thomas
The Catskill mountains 9:77 D 9 '40

Destruction of the empire 33:90 S 15 '52

Mountain sunrise 19:86 S 10 '45

Thomas Cole bw 19:82 S 10 '45 port.

Colescott, Warrington
Madison from the air 32:70 Ja 14 '52

Colet, Louise
Courbet. The amazon 26:61 My 30 '49

Colette (Sidonie Gabrielle Colette Gauthier-Villars de Jouvenal Goudeket)
Colette portraits, at work photogs bw 3:65 D 20 '37;

18:47 My 28 '45
Self-portrait drawing bw 37:83 Ag 16 '54

Colfax, Schuyler
Schuyler Colfax photog bw 9:8 Ag 5 '40; 14:76 F 15 '43

Collaborationist trial, Davis, F.
19:52-3 Jy 16 '45

Collaborationists' stores, Paris.
Davis, F. 19:52 Jy 16 '45

Collage
Braque. Collage: newspapers and wallpaper 26:82 My 2 '49

Duchamp. Apolinere enameled 32:103 Ap 28 '52

Ernst. Collage bw 25:163 N 8 '48

Marca-Relli. Seated man* 39:112 S 12 '55

Miro. Collage bw 25:163 N 8 '48

Stockman. Collage 15:10-2 S 6 '43

Vail. Collage 15:10-2 S 6 '43

Collared peccary. Audubon 30:48 Ja 29 '51

Colleges and Universities
Arkansas, University of, Fayetteville, art center photog 34:148 My 18 '53

Cambridge University, England photogs bw 15:95-103 S 20 '43

Jefferson. University of Virginia 2:48-9 Je 7 '37 bw 14:71 Ap 12 '43

Mexico, University of photogs 41:102-3 D 3 '56

Princeton University photogs Buildings 21:82-9 S 23 '46 Dining Hall bw 2:55 Je 7 '37

Saarinen, Eero. Massachusetts Institute of Technology auditorium, Cambridge Mass. photogs bw 38:79-81 Mr 14 '55

Weed and Manley. University of Miami photogs bw 25:72-3 D 27 '48

Colleges and Universities (cont.)
    Wren. College of William and
    Mary photog bw 14:66 Ap
    12 '43
Collier, John
    Lady Godiva bw 25:160 N 15
    '48
The colloquy. Priebe 23:69 N 24
    '47
Colloredo, Hieronymus
    Hieronymus, Colloredo, arch-
    bishop of Salzburg 40:117
    Ap 23 '56
Colman, Samuel
    Emigrant train 6:29 Je 19 '39
    Ships of the plains 39:74 N 28
    '55
Cologne cathedral photog bw 17:
    87 O 9 '44; 17:80 D 4 '44
    war ruin photog bw 18:37-8
    Mr 26 '45
Cologne radio station windows.
    stained glass Meistermann
    36:146 My 10 '54
Cologne Master
    Life of Christ 24:72-3 Mr 22
    '48
Cologne: The arrival of a packet
    boat. Turner 3:36 D 27 '37
Colombe, Jean
    "Book of Hours" of the Duc de
    Berry calender page illu-
    minations 24:38-50 Ja 5 '48
Colonel M' Cosmic. cartoons bw
    Jensen 12:28-9 My 11 '42
A colonial family. Zoffany 25:99
    S 13 '48
Colonna, Otto
    Pope Martin V (Otto Colonna)
    bw 27:52 Ag 1 '49
Colonna, Sciarra
    Sciarra Colonna threatening
    Pope Boniface VIII, 1303
    bw 27:52 Ag 1 '49
Colonna Palace See Palazzo
    Colonna
Color
    The science of color: spectrum;
    wave lengths, Munsell color
    tree, illusions, color wheel
    17:39-50 Jy 3 '44

Colorado Springs Fine Arts Cen-
    ter Artists at work photogs
    bw 9:65-7 O 7 '40
Colorprints
    Distributed by Living Ameri-
    can Art, Inc. 2:32-5 F 1
    '37
The Colosseum, Rome photog
    27:44 Ag 1 '49 bw 17:95 S
    4 '44
Colossi of Amen-Hotep III,
    c 1350 B.C. photog 41:116
    N 26 '56
Columbia blown flask, U.S. 39:
    58-9 Jy 18 '55
"Columbus" (ship)
    U.S.S. Columbus and Vin-
    cennes in Japan, 1846 9:48
    O 28 '40
Columbus, Christopher
    Christopher Columbus bw 37:
    102 O 11 '54
    Christopher Columbus, La
    Rabida monastery, Palos,
    Spain 39:121 O 10 '55
    Coat of arms 39:122 O 10 '55
    Columbus paying homage to
    Queen Isabella bw Japa-
    nese illustration, 1853 25:
    6 Ag 2 '48
    Davis, G. H. Columbus'
    "Santa Maria" 31:98-9 O
    15 '51
    Gatto. Columbus discovers
    America 25:72 N 8 '48
    Rogers. The watchers on the
    "Santa Maria" sculpture
    bw 6:8 Mr 6 '39
    Whitney. Christopher Colum-
    bus statue Palos, Spain 39:
    118 O 10 '55
Columns See also Corinthian,
    Doric, Ionic
    Column, Place Vendome,
    Paris photog 8:62 Je 3 '40
    bw 31:75 Jy 30 '51
    Columna Bellica, Palazzo
    Colonna, Rome photog bw
    18:91 Mr 5 '45

Dragon columns, Confucian temple photog bw 4:17 My 16 '38

Eleanor of Aquitane, head, bw French, 12th century 40: 107 Mr 26 '56

Henry II, King of England, head, bw French, 12th century 40:107 Mr 26 '56

U.S. Capitol: Tobacco flowers and leaves 39:64 Ag 29 '55

U.S. Senate vestibule: Corn ears and husks, 1809 39: 65 Ag 29 '55

Comfort, Barbara

Blue hat 10:47 F 3 '41

Coming home at night. bw Sedlacek 2:58 Ap 26 '37

The coming storm. Inness 12:59 Je 15 '42

Composition with figures. Takis 16:45 Ja 3 '44

Commander in armor. Van Dyck 40:107 My 7 '56

Commerce, Middle Ages bw 22: 82 My 26 '47

Commode, eliptical, Boston, c1880. Seymour 38:66-7 My 30 '55

Communication troops. Avilov 14:47 Mr 29 '43

Communism

Benton. Communists and fascists in Michigan sketches bw 3:22-5 Jy 26 '37

Nast. Communism and working people* cartoon bw, 1874 25:68 O 18 '48

Companions. bw Davis, G. R. 18:44 Ja 1 '45

Compass bowl. engraved glass bw Waugh 7:32 S 18 '39

Compassionate Buddha of the future, China, 400 sculpture bw 9:50 Jy 22 '40

Composite Animals See Animals --Imaginery

Composition. Mondrian 19:6-7 Jy 2 '45; 33:96 O 27 '52

Composition. sculpture bw Moore, H. 22:79 Ja 20 '47

Composition in life and still life. Brackman 5:29 S 19 '38

Composition in red and white. Mondrian 19:6 Jy 2 '45

Composition in white and blue. 3 paintings Mondrian 19:7 Jy 2 '45

Composition in white and red. Mondrian 19:6 Jy 2 '45

Compote dish, bottle and mandolin. Braque 26:85 My 2 '49

Compton Wynyates, English country house, Warwickshire 41:154-5 N 5 '56 bw 19:97 O 29 '45

Comstock, Anthony

Anthony Comstock photog bw 2:53 My 24 '37

The concert. Giorgione and Titian 39:168-9 O 24 '55

The concert. Ter Borch 24:80 Mr 22 '48

Concert champetre. Giorgione 23:52 Ag 4 '47; 39:170-1 O 24 '55

The concert singer. Eakins 16: 74 My 15 '44

Concerto in color. Lowinger 10: 58 Je 16 '41

Concha belt, American Indian 40:54 Ja 16 '56

Concord coach, U.S. frontier Wells Fargo overland stage photog 39:82 N 28 '55

Condition in New Hampshire. Duncan 28:86-7 Mr 20 '50

Conestoga Wagon See Wagons and Carts

Coney, John, silversmith

Communion cup, silver 38:116 Ap 18 '55

Inkstand, silver Boston, c1700 bw 6:52 Mr 20 '39

Tobacco box, silver Colonial 38:116 Ap 18 '55

Coney Island. Cadmus 2:45 Mr 29 '37

Coney Island. Melcarth 28:88 Mr 20 '50

Confidence. tapestry Picasso 21: 84 S 30 '46

Conflict. sculpture bw Zorach
     8:92-3 Ap 1 '40
Confucius and Confucianism
     Altar of Heaven, Confucian
          temple, Peiping photog bw
          38:71, 76 Ap 4 '55
     Confucius bw 38:72 Ap 4 '55
     Confucius teaching illustra-
          tion from "The Classic of
          Filial Piety," Confucian
          scripture 38:73 Ap 4 '55
     Tablet of Confucius, temple,
          Peiping 38:76 Ap 4 '55
     Ta-Cheng-Tien, "Palace of
          the Most Perfect" photog
          bw 4:17 My 16 '38
Congdon, William
     Black city 30:109 Ap 30 '51
     Florian's cafe, Venice 30:108
          Ap 30 '51
     St. Mark's square 33:95 S 15
          '52
     Venetian palace 30:108 Ap 30
          '51
     Artist at work; portraits
          photogs bw 30:108, 111 Ap
          30 '51
The Conress voting independence.
     Pine and Savage 40:78-9 Ja
     9 '56 bw 29:52 Jy 3 '50
Congress, U.S.
     Healy. Webster replying to
          Hayne, January 26-7, 1830
          16:54 F 21 '44
Congressmen as artists
     Artists and their work bw 20:
          12-5 My 6 '46
Connecticut
     Ford. Epiphany at Bethlehem,
          Connecticut 17:38-9 D 25
          '44
     Simkhovitch. Winter in Con-
          necticut 11:40 D 29 '41
Connick, Charles J.
     Rose window stained glass 6:
          31 Ap 3 '39
Conrad, 12th century German
     King. Conrad sculpture Ulm
          Cathedral 35:31 D 28 '51
Conrad, Joseph
     Davidson. Joseph Conrad

     sculpture. bw 32:34 Ja 14
          '52
Conrow, Wilfords
     Bruce Rogers 18:75 My 14 '45
Consangra, Pietro
     Pietro Consangra photog bw
          27:50 Ag 1 '49
Constable, John
     View on the Stour near Dedham
          5:44 S 12 '38
     John Constable bw 5:42 S 12
          '38 port.
Constable, Sarah
     Romney. Miss Constable 29:
          83 N 27 '50
Constance Missal, oldest typo-
          graphical book (?) photog
          36:80-1 Mr 1 '54
Constant, George
     Young girl with grapes bw 9:
          67 O 14 '40
Constantine, the Great, Emperor
          of Rome
     Constantine bw 22:70 Ap 7 '47
     Constantine in Virgin and
          Child, mosaic, Santa So-
          phia 29:56-7 D 25 '50
     Raphael. Battle of Milvian
          Bridge bw 39:39 D 26 '55
"Constellation" (ship)
     Constellation capturing L'In-
          surgente, 1799 bw 23:72 O
          27 '47
     U.S.S. Constellation, 1797
          9:49 O 28 '40 photogs bw 9:
          52-4 O 28 '40
"Constitution" (ship) (Old Iron-
          sides)
     Birch. Constitution and Guer-
          riere 9:47 O 28 '40
     Constitution firing on Guer-
          riere, 1812 lithograph 23:
          69 O 27 '47
     Pocock. Constitution and Java,
          1812 9:48 O 28 '40
     Surrender of Captain Dacres
          to Captain Hull aboard "Old
          Ironsides," 1812 bw 23:71
          O 27 '47
Constitution, U.S.
     Framers of the U.S. Consti-

tution, individual portraits
39:58-64 Jy 4 '55
Consuela. bw Carroll 8:120 My
13 '40
Construction
Fiene. Razing old New York
post office bw 8:69 My 27
'40
Laning, T. R. in Panama 6:
44-5 My 15 '39
Schnakenberg. Works of man
10:73 Ap 14 '41
Sterne. Construction 31:54
Ag 27 '51
Consummatum est. sculpture bw
Epstein 3:88 N 15 '37; 33:
68 N 3 '52
"The Contrast," play be Tyler,
scene from 31:111 N 19 '51
Convalescent. Koch 18:76 My 14
'45
Conventions
Political convention, Chicago,
1860 bw 14:9 My 31 '43
Republican convention, Phila-
delphia, 1872 bw 14:9 My
31 '43
Republican convention, Chi-
cago 1880 bw 14:9 My 31
'43
Convoy. Pears 28:73 F 20 '50
Convoy. Thon 20:97 Ap 29 '46
Convoy practice. Chavez 13:22
Jy 6 '42
Conway, Fred
Mother and child bw 27:55 D
26 '49; 30:79 Mr 5 '51
Oklahoma land rush mural
30:78-9 Mr 5 '51
Fred Conway photog bw 27:
55 D 26 '49; 30:79 Mr 5 '51
Conyngham, Elizabeth
Lawrence, T. Lady Elizabeth
Conyngham 6:38 My 29 '39
Cook, Frederick
Dr. Frederick Cook photogs
bw 41:86, 92 Ag 20 '56
Cook, Howard
Howard Cook photog 26:66 Mr
14 '49 port.
Cook, James

James Cook bw 25:113 S 13 '48
Cook, Robert, sculpture
Artist at work photog bw 33:
98 S 15 '52 port
Cook, Weda
Eakins. The concert singer
16:74 My 15 '44
Coolidge, Calvin
Calvin Coolidge photog bw 9:
9 Ag 5 '40
Coon, Zip
Zip Coon bw 11:74 Ag 25 '41
Cooney, John D.
Cosgrave. John D. Cooney 24:
19 Ja 19 '48
John D. Cooney photog bw 24:
19 Ja 19 '48
Cooper, Elizabeth (Fenimore)
Mrs. William Cooper 31:70-1
Jy 1 '51
Coots on the open sea. Ripley
29:127 D 4' 50
Copan, Honduras, ruins. Mayan
architecture photogs bw
22:52-7 Je 30 '47
Copernicus, Nikolaus
Copernicus bw 17:90 Ag 28
'44
Copland, Aaron
Aaron Copland photog bw 16:
58 Ap 24 '44; 40:145 My
21 '56
Copley, John Singleton
Boy with squirrel (Henry Pel-
ham) bw 5:28 O 31 '38
Epes Sargent bw 9:74 D 9 '40
John Quincy Adams 41:72 Jy
2 '56
Nathaniel Hurd 15:68 S 20 '43
Nicholas Boylston 9:52 Jy 22
'40
Paul Revere 38:57 My 30 '55
Sir William Pepperell and
his family 41:73 D 10 '56
Watson and the shark 9:76 D
9 '40
Copper figurine, painted, Ande-
an, c100 36:101 Ap 12 '54
Copper luster pitcher, Victori-
an, U.S. glassware 40:91
Mr 5 '56

Corbett, Mario, architect
Bay region modern hilltop
house, San Francisco pho-
togs 27:45, 52-3 S 5 '49
Mario Corbett photog 27:44
S 5 '49 port.
Corbett, Rachel
Artist at work photog bw 41:
80 Ag 13 '56 port.
Corbino, Jon
Fisherman 8:66 My 27 '40
Flood refugees 4:28 Je 13 '38
Harvest festival 4:28 Je 13 '38
Artist and his work photogs bw
4:29 Je 13 '38 port.
Corbusier, Le See Jeanneret,
Charles Edouard
Corcoran Gallery, Washington,
D.C Biennial prizewinners
and exhibits; buildings;
school 6:44-7 My 1 '39
One hundred years of Ameri-
can taste, 1830-1930: popu-
lar paintings assembled by
Corcoran Gallery 27:56-62
Ag 29 '49
Corcos, Lucille
Artist's home, summertime
37:91 Jy 12 '54
Artist's home, wintertime 37:
90 Jy 12 '54
Games in America 31:94-5 Ag
20 '51
Gilbert and Sullivan land 25:
86-7 O 11 '48
Lucille Corcos; family photog
bw 37:93 Jy 12 '54
Cordova cathedral, Spain photog
38:75 My 9 '55
Corfe castle, Dorsetshire, Eng-
land photog 40:90 Mr 19 '56
Corinthian Columns
Temple of Olympian Zeus,
Athens photog bw 18:58-9 Ja
1 '45
The corn dance. Laning 6:44 My
1 '39
Corn dance. Marin 29:64 Jy 10 '50
Corn foliage. Rosenthal 22:96
Ap 21 '47

Corne, Michele
Bombardment of Tripoli 9:47
O 28 '40
Cornelius, Aleta
'Long the Pennsy Line 28:90
Mr 20 '50
Cornell, Katharine
Barthe. Katharine Cornell as
Juliet bw 18:108 Ap 16 '45
Beaton. Katharine Cornell as
"Candida" drawing 21:6
Jy 22 '46
Speicher. Katharine Cornell
as "Candida" 8:47 Ap 29
'40 bw 10:70 Ap 14 '41
Corner grocery, Taos. Lockwood
6:30 F 13 '39
Corner saloon. Hopper 28:101
Ap 17 '50
Cornucopia. wood carving Mc-
Intire 38:63 My 30 '55
Cornwall Family shields of arms
22:69 My 26 '47
Cornwallis, Charles, Marquis of
General Cornwallis bw 4:60
Ap 4 '38; 29:53 Jy 3 '50
Cornwallis surrenders, 1781 bw
7:70 S 25 '39
Cornwell, Dean
"The Robe" (book) by Douglas
illustrations 23:91-4 D 8
'47
Dean Cornwell. in group
photog 29:172-3 O 16 '50
port.
Coronation of Alexander II, Czar
of Russias, 1856. Series
of paintings 38:60-7 Ja 31
'55
Coronation of Charles II, King of
England, Westminster,
1661 bw 14:164 N 19 '56
Coronation of St. Edward, the
confessor bw 2:45 Mr 15
'37
Coronation of the Virgin See
Mary, Virgin--Coronation
Coronation of Victor Emmanuel III, King of Italy bw 15:
22 Ag 9 '43

Corot, Jean Baptiste Camille
  The bridge at Mantes 29:90 N
    27 '50
  L'Italienne 24:65 Mr 1 '48
  Nude bw 40:168 Ap 9 '56
  View of Naples 25:96 N 22 '48
The Corpus Christi procession.
    Bellini 23:54-5 Ag 4 '47
Correggio, Antonio Allegri da
  Awakened Danae 41:105 O 22
    '56
  Leda and the swan bw 19:25 D
    31 '45
  Nativity, with details bw 40:
    101 F 20 '56
Cortes, Hernando
  Hernando Cortes bw 21:43 D
    16 '46
  Cortes capturing Mexico City,
    August 13, 1521 bw 4:52 Ap
    11 '38; 21:46 D 16 '46
  Riviera. Cortes conquest of
    Mexico mural details, Pal-
    ace of Cortes, Cuernevaca,
    Mexico 6:41 Ja 23 '39
Cortor, Eldzier
  Haitian couple 28:101 Mr 13
    '50
  Southern gate 21:63 Jy 22 '46
  The room number five 28:85
    Mr 20 '50
Coryn, Marjorie
  Marjorie Coryn photog bw 24:
    22 My 17 '48
Cosgrave, Esta
  The artist's husband bw 24:20
    Ja 19 '48
  Harold Rome and wife bw 24:
    18 Ja 19 '48
  Harry Shaw Newman bw 24:19
    Ja 19 '48
  John D. Cooney bw 24:19 Ja
    19 '48
  Mark van Doren bw 24:18 Ja
    19 '48
  Self-portrait bw 24:20 Ja 19
    '48 port.
Cosmos. sculpture bw Calder 33:
    88 Ag 25 '52
Cossa, Francesco del
  Portraits, Italian, 15th cen-

tury 37:63 Ag 9 '54
"Cossack" (ship) English, 1940
  Wilkinson. The Navy's here*
    24:66 My 17 '48
The cottage door. Gainsborough
    5:43 S 12 '38
Cotton, John
  Reverend John Cotton bw 13:
    74 N 23 '42
Cotton loading on the Mississippi
    bw Benton 6:70 Ap 24 '39
Cotton market in New Orleans.
    Degas 10:74 Ap 28 '41
Cotton pickers. Benton 13:45
    Ag 31 '42
Cottonwood trees. Tait 16:46 Ja
    3 '44
Coucy Family shields of arms
    22:69 My 26 '47
Council of Trent bw 24:87 Je 14
    '48
Counterpoint sculpture bw 40:
    128 Ap 30 '56
Counterpoint. woodcut Quastler
    37:89 O 18 '54
The country dance. bw Renoir
    28:88 Ja 16 '50
The country doctor. Ford 3:28
    D 20 '37
Country store, interior, reas-
    sembled at Webb Museum,
    Shelburne, Vt. photog 35:
    52-3 Jy 6 '53
Country tenement. Kallem 24:
    103 Je 28 '48
Country wedding. Lee, D. 14:
    45 Mr 8 '43
County election. Bingham 7:42 S
    11 '39 Drawings bw 7:43
    S 11 '39
County fair. Peirce, W. 3:34
    Ag 30 '37; 21:74 N 25 '46
Couple in cabaret. Roualt 34:59
    F 2 '53
Courbet, Gustave
  The amazon (Louise Colet)
    26:61 My 30 '49
  Bather 41:108 O 22 '56
  Cliffs at Etretat 26:64 My
    30 '49
  Landscape* 24:66 Mr 1 '48

Courbet, Gustave (cont.)
  Landscape with a mill near
    Ornans 26:64 My 30 '49
  The studio 26:62-3 My 30 '49
  Woman with parrot 6:56 Mr
    20 '39
  Self-portrait in The studio
    26:62-3 My 30 '49 port.
  Self-portraits in three paint-
    ings bw 26:60 My 30 '49
    port.
Court Room Scenes See also
  Lawyers and Judges
  Captain Dreyfus, second trial,
    1899 bw 13:77 N 16 '42
  Castellon. Freedom of the
    press (Trial of Peter Zen-
    ger) 30:95 Mr 12 '51
  Common pleas court, England,
    Middle Ages bw 22:81 My
    26 '47
  Davis, F. Collaborationist
    trial* 19:52-3 Jy 16 '45
  Du Bois, G. New evidence 26:
    68 Je 20 '49
  Marsh. Jelke trial bw 37:48
    Jy 26 '54
  Matteson. The trial of George
    Jacobs 13:78 N 23 '42
  Poor. Gold case 2:36 Ja 4 '37
  Royal Court (King's bench),
    England, Middle Ages bw
    22:81 My 26 '47
  Trial by combat bw 40:112 Mr
    26 '56
  Trial by jury, early English
    court bw 40:111 Mr 26 '56
  Trial of Catherine of Aragon*
    London, 1529 bw 3:34 O 18
    '37
  Trial of tax delinquents bas-
    relief, Egyptian, 6th dynas-
    ty 41:81 O 1 '56
  Witch trial, Salem, Mass.,
    1692 bw 27:76 S 26 '49
Cousino, Juan Luis
  Virgin Mary sculpture bw 31:
    163 N 19 '51
  Juan Luis Cousino photog bw
    31:163 N 19 '51
Couturier, Pierre

Angel Raphael stained glass
  28:74 Je 19 '50
Couturier, Robert
  Figures sculpture 29:101 D 11
    '50
Covarrubias, Miguel
  Balinese festival 3:49 S 27 '37
  Balinese fishermen 3:48 S 27
    '37
  Balinese girl 3:47 S 27 '37
  Balinese opera 3:48 S 27 '37
  Balinese war dance 3:48 S 27
    '37
  "Carmen Jones," four scenes
    16:71-4 My 8 '44
  Florida, picture map 20:52-3
    F 4 '46
  Trust Territory of the Pacific:
    Marshall, Caroline, Mari-
    anas, Islands, picture map
    26:96 Ap 25 '49
  Legong, Balinese dancer bw
    3:46 S 27 '37 (drawings)
  Miguel Covarrubias; wife
    photogs bw 3:46 S 27 '37
    port.
Coverdale, Miles
  Miles Coverdale bw 34:84 F
    23 '53
Covered Wagons See Wagons
  and Carts
Cow swishing. Tamayo 34:102
  Mr 16 '53
Coward, Noel
  Irving Berlin and Noel Coward
    photog bw 15:36 D 6 '43
  MacDonald. Noel Coward,
    1928 photog bw 14:12 Ja 11
    '43
Cowboys
  Campos. Paintings of gauchos
    4:34-5 Je 20 '38
  Le cow-boy (Mendes-France,
    Premier of France) car-
    toon bw 37:70 D 6 '54
  Remington. Around the camp-
    fire 13:75 S 14 '42
  Remington. Bronco buster 13:
    73 S 14 '42 sculpture bw
    11:54 N 10 '41; 13:72 S 14
    '42

Remington. Cowboy bw 5:29
   O 31 '38 sculpture bw 13:
   72 S 14 '42
Remington. Fired on 9:77 D
   9 '40
Russell. In without knocking
   39:86 N 14 '55
Young, M. Rolling his own
   sculpture bw 10:79 F 17 '41
Cowles, Russell
   Ballet dancer 24:78 F 9 '48
   Big turkey 24:77 F 9 '48
   The dawn of the spirit 24:76
      F 9 '48
   The farmer and the raincloud
      24:75 F 9 '48
   Fisherman's dream 24:77 F 9
      '48
   High water in winter 24:76
      F 9 '48
   Nova Scotia morning 24:77 F
      9 '48
   The parade 12:45 Mr 9 '42;
      21:75 N 25 '46
   Artist and his work photog bw
      24:74 F 9 '48 port.
   Russell Cowles. in group
      photog 29:172-3 O 16 '50
      port.
Cows See Cattle
Cox, Gardner
   Portrait of a boy 10:47 F 3 '41
   Artist at work photog bw 10:
      46 F 3 '41 port.
Cox, James M.
   James M. Cox photog bw 14:
      7 My 31 '43
Cox, Jan
   Head of a girl lithograph 33:
      86 Jy 14 '52
Cox, John Rogers
   Wheat 25:86-7 Jy 12 '48
   White cloud 16:78 Ap 24 '44
   Self-portrait 25:86 Jy 12 '48
      port.
Cox, Palmer
   Advertising poster, U.S.,
      c1900 28:41 Ja 2 '50
Coypel, Antoine
   God the Father* ceiling mural,
      Royal chapel, Versaille 23:

86 S 15 '47
Crabs
   Gold crab, Pre-Columbian 18:
      49 Je 4 '45
   Killer crabs drawing bw 24:
      86 Mr 22 '48
Crabtree, Lotta
   Lotta Crabtree photog bw 31:
      116 N 19 '51
Cradles
   Windsor cradle 38:65 My 30 '55
Craig, Tom
   Italy in World War 18:47-55
      Ap 30 '45
   Italy's war damage 19:73-6
      S 17 '45
   Rivals 11:74 O 27 '41
   Veterans from battle lines bw
      17:97 O 2 '44 (drawings)
Cranach, Lucas, the elder
   Cardinal Albrecht as St. Hier-
      onymus 5:39 Jy 11 '38
   Crucifixion 1:47 D 28 '36
   Eve with serpent 11:57 S 8 '41
   Henry the Pious 40:104 My 7
      '56
   The judgment of Paris 13:93
      N 9 '42
   Katherine, wife of Henry the
      Pious 40:105 My 7 '56
   Lucretia 24:78 Mr 22 '48
   Luther and his friends 24:63
      Je 14 '48
   A prince of Saxony 24:66 Ja
      26 '48
   Princess of Saxony 24:67 Ja
      26 '48
   Christ and the Pope* series
      bw 24:60-1 Je 14 '48 (wood-
      cuts)
   Lucas Cranach, the elder bw
      5:38 Jy 11 '38 port.
Cranborne Lodge, 17th century
   19: 99 O 29 '45
Cranbrook Academy of Art, De-
      troit
   Exhibit of sixty American
      paintings; invited exhibit
      8:64-71 My 27 '40
   Milles. Orpheus, copy, bw
      21:30 F 22 '37

Crane, Nathalia
   Nathalia Crane photog bw 11:
      91 S 8 '41
Cranes
   Crane, bronze, Peiping 20:74
      Ap 29 '46
   Marcks. Calling crane sculp-
      ture bw 28:71 F 6 '50
Cranes (machinony)
   Osver. Cranes 30:38 Ja 15 '51
The crap shooter. Binford 10:67
      My 26 '41
Cravath, Ruth, sculptor
   Ruth Cravath photog bw 9:62
      Ag 5 '40 port.
Craven, Henry
   Captain Anderson (Devil Anse)
      Hatfield bw 16:114 My 22
      '44
Crawford, Ralston
   Overseas highway 6:27 F 13 '39
Crawford, Thomas, sculptor
   Armed freedom, Capitol dome,
      Washington, D.C. 16:56 Mr
      20 '44 cast bw 19:9 S 24 '45
   The genius of mirth bw 19:9
      S 24 '45
Creamers See Sugars and
   Creamers
The Creation See also Adam
   and Eve
   Blake. God creating the world
      print bw 6:44 Ja 16 '39
   Bosch. Creation of the world
      27:75 N 14 '49
   Creation of the world mosaic,
      St. Mark's, Venice 35:34
      D 28 '53
   Michelangelo. Creation of the
      world fresco 21:62-9 Jy 1
      '46; 27:25-49 D 26 '49
The creation of Adam. fresco
      Michelangelo 11:77 D 1 '41;
      21:66-7 Jy 1 '46; 27:30-1
      D 26 '49
The creation of Eve. fresco
      Michelangelo 27:32-3 D 26
      '49 bw 21:66-7 Jy 1 '46
Creation of Eve. Raphael 27:119
      D 12 '49
Crecy, Battle of 40:188 Ap 9 '56
Creeft, Jose de

Aux aguets (On watch) sculp-
      ture bw 24:95 Ap 12 '48
Cremonini, Leonardo
   Bather* 38:72 Ja 17 '55
   Skinned oxen 38:72 Ja 17 '55
   Two rowers 38:72-3 Ja 17 '55
Cress, George
   Interior shadows 39:115 S 12
      '55
Crevecoeur, Hector St. John
   Hector Crevecoeur bw 16:49
      Ja 17 '44
Crimean War scenes bw 11:15 D
      15 '41
Crimson city. Zao Wou-Ki 36:
      102 F 22 '54
Crist, Richard
   Shanksville 16:45 Ja 3 '44
A critical moment. Poole 9:50
      O 28 '40
Crivelli, Carlo
   Madonna and Child 2:42 Je 28
      '37
Croce, Benedetto
   Benedetto Croce; family
      photogs bw 15:126-9 N 22
      '43
Croce, J. N. de la
   Mozart family, 1780 40:117
      Ap 23 '56
Crockett, David
   Chapman. Davy Crockett bw
      38:29 Ap 25 '55
Crocodiles
   Dodgson. Crocodile bw 16:12
      F 7 '44
   White. Crocodile 22:84 Mr
      10 '47
Crome, John ("Old Crome")
   The edge of the commons 5:
      43 S 12 '38
   John Crome bw 5:42 S 12 '38
      port.
Cromwell, Oliver
   Cromwell installed as Lord
      Proctor, 1657 bw 30:21
      Ja 8 '51
   Dissolution of Parliament by
      Cromwell, 1653* bw 41:
      162-3 N 19 '56
   Leutze. Cromwell and Mil-

ton 27:58 Ag 29 '49
Oliver Cromwell addressing
 Parliament bw 24:93 Je
 14 '48
Sir Oliver Cromwell bw 41:
 196 N 12 '56
Walker. Oliver Cromwell 41:
 160 N 19 '56
Cronbach, Robert
Flight, sculpture bw 37:160
 N 22 '54
Artist at work photog bw 37:
 160 N 22 '54 port.
Cronin, Archibald Joseph
A. J. Cronin; family; home
 photogs bw 5:35 N 28 '38;
 11:6 O 20 '41
Cropsey, Jasper S.
View of Catskill house 19:84
 S 10 '45
Croquet See Games and Sports
 --Croquet
Crosby, Bob, rodeo champion
Hurd. Bob Crosby 20:59 My
 13 '46
Cross, Louise
Opera singer* sculpture bw
 5:5 N 28 '38
Cross by the sea. O'Keefe 4:30
 F 14 '38
The cross fox. Audubon 9:115 O
 21 '40
Crossbows See Weapons--Bows
Crosses See also Jewelry
Iron cross, San Carlos Bor-
 romeo mission, Carmel,
 Calif. 40:56-7 S 12 '55
Ziegler. Plexiglass cross 39:
 116 D 26 '55
Crouching girl. sculpture bw
 Manzu 41:102-3 Ag 6 '56
Crouse, Russell
Hirschfeld. Lindsay and
 Crouse caricature bw 21:
 116 N 11 '46
Russell Crouse photog bw 21:
 120 N 11 '46
Crow. sculpture bw Kruger 39:
 189 N 14 '55
Crowd of artists. Bohrod 25:66
 Ag 23 '48

The crown of thorns. Roualt 39:
 28 D 26 '55
The crowning with thorns.
 Bosch 31:69 O 1 '51
Crowns
Crown of Iran photog 30:
 Cover Je 18 '51
Crown of Scotland, c1350
 photog bw 3:67 Jy 19 '37
Inca crown, gold with plumes
 photog 36:102-3 Ap 12 '54
Lombard crown, Italy photog
 bw 15:19 Ag 9 '43; 20:28
 Je 24 '46
Van Eyck brothers. Crown
 of the King of Kings, de-
 tail 26:68 Ap 18 '49
Holy crown of Hungary photog
 bw 29:61 Jy 3 '50
Royal crowns of England
 photogs 2:37, 40-1 Mr 15
 '37
St. Stephen's crown, Hungary
 photog bw 2:14 Mr 22 '37
Croziers
Gold crozier photog bw 12:68
 My 25 '42
Gold crozier of Archbishop
 of Canterbury photog bw
 18:79 My 14 '45
Crucifixion of Jesus Christ See
 Jesus Christ--Crucifixion
Cruikshank, George
Oliver asking for more, il-
 lustration bw, from "Oli-
 ver Twist" 25:78 D 27 '48
Crusaders disembarking at
 Damietta bw 16:67 Ap 10
 '44
Crusades
Dore. Children's crusade bw
 16:66 Ap 10 '44
Dore. The crusades bw 39:
 40-1 D 26 '55
Crystal
Carved quartz ewer; goblet,
 Vienna, c1800 25:129 D
 6 '48
Crystal palace, New York Fair,
 1853 bw 6:34 Mr 13 '39

Cudillero, Spain. Bone 1:43 D
    7 '36
Cugat, Xavier
    Caricatures of moving pic-
    ture scenes bw 13:70 N 9
    '42
Culberg collection of contempo-
    rary paintings 33:96-7 O
    27 '52
Cullinan diamond, gemstone 2:
    40-1 Mr 15 '37
Cumberland, Earl of
    Earl of Cumberland bw 41:144
    N 5 '56
Cundall, Charles
    Return of H.M.S. Exeter 10:
    65 F 24 '41
Cunne Shote, Cherokee chief.
    Parsons 36:75 Mr 8 '54
Cunningham, Andrew Browne
    Admiral Cunningham, "Time"
    cover portrait 17:63 D 11
    '44
Cupboard, English, 15th century
    22:79 My 26 '47
Cupid and Psyche. bw David 4:
    42 My 2 '38
Cupid and three graces bw 29:81
    N 27 '50
Cupids
    Boucher. Jupiter, in the guise
    of Diana, with Callisto 5:
    36 S 26 '38
    Boucher. Love disarmed bw
    12:44 Mr 9 '42
    Boucher. Toilet of Venus bw
    16:68 Ja 10 '44
    Van Dyck. Rinaldo and Ar-
    mida 4:21 Ap 11 '38
    Velazquez. Venus and Cupid
    (Venus at the mirror) 41:
    104 O 22 '56
Cups
    The America's cup, silver
    ewer, yachting trophy
    photog bw 3:32 Ag 2 '37
    Barovier. Wedding cup, deco-
    rated glass, Venice, 15th
    century 37:55 Ag 2 '54
    Cellini. Rospigliosi cup bw 6:
    53 Mr 20 '39; 31:26 O

    15 '51
    Coconut cup, silver, Eliza-
    bethan bw 3:77 D 13 '37
    Coney. Communion cup,
    silver, U.S. Colonial 38:
    116 Ap 18 '55
    Elizabethan covered cup,
    silver bw 3:77 D 13 '37
    Greek cup, cow's hoof, 500
    B.C. ceramics bw 6:52
    Mr 20 '39
    Hill and Sanderson. Dram cup,
    silver, U.S. Colonial 38:
    116-7 Ap 18 '55
    Italian cup, silver, 16th cen-
    tury 37:64 Ag 9 '54
    Mask cups, 18th century
    ceramics 25:129 D 6 '48
    Milky goblet, Venice, 15th
    century 37:55 Ag 2 '54
    Mumtaz Mahal's marriage
    cup, silver and enamel,
    France, 17th century 25:
    129 D 6 '48
    Puzzle cup, spilling liquid on
    drinker, Italy, 18th cen-
    tury 25:129 D 6 '48
    Two-handled silver cups and
    covers, James II, England
    bw 3:77 D 13 '37
    Winslow. Two-handled cups,
    silver, U.S. Colonial 38:
    117 Ap 18 '55
Curie, Eve
    Eve Curie photog bw 3:75-6
    N 22 '37
Curie, Irene
    Irene Curie photogs bw 3:75-
    6 N 22 '37
Curie, Marie
    Mme. Curie photogs bw 3:78
    N 22 '37 statue bw 5:53 Ag
    29'44; Warsaw 3:78 N 22
    '37
Curie, Marie and Pierre
    Marie and Pierre Curie and
    sons Jacques and Pierre
    photogs bw 15:122, 125
    D 13 '43
    Marie and Pierre Curie leav-
    ing for bicycle honeymoon

photog bw 3:76 N 22 '37
Currier Nathaniel
 Nathaniel Currier photog bw
  9:35 D 30 '40
Currier and Ives prints
 Abraham Lincoln: The Repub-
  lican party going to the
  right house 31:18 O 22 '51
 Across the continent: West-
  ward the course of empire
  takes its way 9:34 D 30 '40
 American farm scenes 9:28 D
  30 '40
 American soldier's return from
  Mexican War, 1847* bw 22:
  125 Je 9 '47
 American winter scenes: Even-
  ing 9:27 D 30 '40
 American winter sports:
  Trout fishing on Chateaugay
  Lake 9:27 D 30 '40
 Assassination of President
  Lincoln bw 5:7 Jy 11 '38
 Autumn in New England: Cider
  making 9:29 D 30 '40
 Bombardment of Island No.
  10 21:72 S 2 '46
 Camping in the woods 9:33 D
  30 '40
 De Soto's discovery of the
  Mississippi bw 21:70 S 24
  '46
 The drunkard's progress bw
  20:66-7 My 27 '46
 Eventide: October--The village
  inn 9:32 D 30 '40
 Farragut's victory at New Or-
  leans, April 18, 1862 21:
  73 S 2 '46
 The four seasons of life: child-
  hood, youth, middle age,
  old age 9:30-1 D 30 '40
 High water 21:73 S 2 '46
 Holiday in the country:
  troublesome flies 9:32 D
  30 '40
 Levee at New Orleans 21:71 S
  2 '46
 Life in the country: The morning ride 9:29 D 30 '40
 Loading cotton by moonlight

21:71 S 2 '46
 Low water in the Mississippi
  9:33 D 30 '40; 21:72 S 2
  '46
 Mississippi River: Discovery
  and other scenes 21:70-4 S
  2 '46
 New Orleans, c1850 bw 21:70
  S 2 '46
 A night on the Hudson: Through
  at daylight 9:34 D 30 '40
 Old Kentucky Home 41:60 S 3
  '56
 Peters collection of Currier
  and Ives prints 9:27-34 D
  30 '40
 Queen of the West vs Morning
  Star 21:74 S 2 '46
 Through the bayou by torch-
  light 21:74 S 2 '46
 The village blacksmith 9:28
  D 30 '40
 Winter farm scene bw 5:28 O
  31 '38
Curry, John Steuart
 Baptism at Big Stranger Creek
  bw 15:18 N 29 '43
 Baptism in Kansas 12:74 Ap
  20 '42 bw 15:18 N 29 '43
 Circus elephants 1:31 N 23
  '36 bw 15:19 N 29 '43
 Father and mother bw 1:29
  N 23 '36
 The flying Cadonas 1:31 N 23
  '36
 Hogs killing a rattlesnake bw
  15:19 N 29 '43 watercolor
  bw 15:18 N 29 '43
 Holy rollers bw 15:18 N 29
  '43
 Homestead 7:36 D 25 '39
 Hoover and the flood 8:58-9
  My 6 '40
 John Brown bw 15:20 N 29 '43
  mural study 7:35 D 25 '39
 Line storm 1:30 N 23 '36 bw
  15:19 N 29 '43
 Magazine illustrations and
  covers: "Country Gentle-
  man," "St. Nicholas,"
  "Wayside Tales" bw 15:

Curry, John Steuart (cont.)
  18 N 29 '43
  The Mississippi 13:96 N 9 '42
  Montmartre bw 15:18 N 29
    '43
  Oklahoma land rush 7:36 D 25
    '39 bw 15:19 N 29 '43
  The passing leap 15:19 N 29
    '43
  The prodigal son bw 15:18 N
    29 '43
  Sanctuary 1:30 N 23 '36 bw
    15:19 N 29 '43
  The tornado bw 15:19 N 29 '43
  Tornado over Kansas 1:29 N
    23 '36; 21:73 N 25 '46
  U.S. Supreme Court murals
    bw 1:28 N 23 '36
  Wisconsin landscape 8:65 My
    27 '40
  Wisconsin still life bw 15:20
    N 29 '43
  Artist at work photog bw 15:
    12 O 25 '43 port.
  Artist at work; wife; home
    photogs bw 7:34, 37 D 25
    '39 port.
  John Steuart Curry; photog bw
    1:28 N 23 '36; 4:24 Je 13
    '38 port.
  Self-portrait bw 15:12 O 25
    '43 port.
Curtin, John
  Prime Minister Curtin,
    "Time" cover portrait 17:
    63 D 11 '44
Curtis, Charles
  Charles Curtis photog bw 9:11
    Ag 5 '40
Curtis, Edward S.
  Sacred Navaho ritual photog
    bw 31:12 S 10 '51
Curtis, Nancy Hoyt
  Nancy Hoyt Curtis photog bw
    3:78 Jy 26 '37
Custer, George Armstrong See
    also Battle of the Little Big
    Horn
  General Custer photog bw 7:
    47 Ag 28 '39 equestrian por-
    trait, engraving after Brady

  photog bw 11:76 D 8 '41
  family; associates; burial
    bw 11:76 D 8 '41
Custer's last charge. bw Fuchs
  24:12 Je 21 '48
Custer's last fight. bw Adams
  11:75 D 8 '41 lithograph
  copy 24:14 Je 21 '48
Custer's last fight. bw Elder
  24:12 Je 21 '48
Custer's last rally. bw Mulvaney
  24:12 Je 21 '48
Custer's last stand bw 24:14 Je
  21 '48
Custer's letzte Schlacht. bw
  Eber 24:13 Je 21 '48
Custom house workers. mural
  Poor 2:36 Ja 4 '37
Cuvier, Baron
  Baron Cuvier, head bw 37:
    93 D 13 '54
Cuyp, Aelbert
  The travelers' halt 41:72-3
    D 10 '56
Cuzco, Peru ruins, Inca temples
  and forts photogs bw 19:
  101-9 S 24 '45
Cyclops. Baziotes 24:103 Je 28
  '48
Le cygne. sculpture bw Laurent
  10:64 Je 2 '41
Cypresses
  Gray. Cypresses 33:93 S 15
    '52
  Lee, D. Giant cypress tree,
    Oaxaca, Mexico 22:75 My
    12 '47
  Meeker. Bayou Teche 28:78
    Mr 6 '50
  Van Gogh. Cypress and flow-
    ering trees 40:72-3 My
    28 '56
  Van Gogh. The cypresses 27:
    86 O 10 '49
  Van Gogh. Road with cypres-
    ses 2:33 F 15 '37
Cyrus, the Great, King of Per-
  sia
    King Cyrus bw 20:34 Ap
      8 '46

Cytherea
    Watteau. Embarkation for
        Cytherea 23:84 S 15 '47
        bw 19:50 Jy 30 '45
                    D
Dadaism
    Paintings of dadaism bw 34:
        24-5 My 25 '53
Daddy in death. bw Turner 29:12
        Jy 10 '50
Daffodils
    Sharp. Spring night 16:45 Ja
        3 '44
Da Gama, Vasco
    Vasco da Gama, Portuguese
        manuscript, 17th century
        24:74 Mr 22 '48
Daggers See Weapons--Daggers
Daguerre, Louis
    Daguerre's studio, 1837;
        earliest daguerrotype bw
        2:4 Mr 29 '37
    Louis Daguerre, 1848 photog
        bw 2:5 Mr 29 '37
Dahl, Francis
    Cartoons bw 21:14-6 D 9 '46
    Francis Dahl photogs bw 21:
        14 D 9 '46 port.
D'Aiguirandes, Marquise
    Drouais. La marquise D'Ai-
        guirandes 15:66 S 20 '43
Dailey, Gardner A., architect
    Basic small-lot house photogs,
        plan bw 9:80-2 Jy 1 '40
Daily occurence in the Channel.
        Mullen 26:53 Mr 7 '49
"Daisy-diamond" blown flask.
        Stiegel 39:58-9 Jy 18 '55
Dalai Lama
    Tanchu, Dalai Lama 10:72
        Mr 24 '41
    Thunderbolt crest of the Dalai
        Lama photog bw 36:83 F
        22 '54
Dale (Chester) collection of
        French painting 5:25-9 O
        10 '38
Dali, Salvador
    Endless enigma bw 6:45 Ap
        17 '39
    The enigma of Hitler 6:44 Ap
        17 '39 bw 19:65 S 24 '45
    Leda Atomica bw 25:5 Ag 9 '48
    Madonna of Port Lligat 29:48
        D 18 '55
    Mrs. Harrison Williams bw
        19:66 S 24 '45
    The persistence of memory
        1:25 D 14 '36 bw 19:64 S
        24 '45
    The seven lively arts bw 18:
        4-6 Ja 1 '45
    Sleep 6:44 Ap 17 '39
    Soft construction with boiled
        beans: Premonition of
        civil war--1936 3:27 D 20
        '37 bw 19:64-5 S 24 '45
    Spain 25:64 O 11 '48
    Childhood memories of
        Christmas bw 19:8 D 24
        '45 (drawings)
    Engless enigma bw 6:45 Ap
        17 '39 (drawings)
    Train* bw 16:18 Mr 6 '44
        (drawings)
    Artist at work photog bw 18:
        6 Ja 1 '45 port.
    Halsman. Dali photog bw
        25:4-5 Ag 9 '48 port.
    Salvador Dali photog bw 1:24
        D 14 '36; 6:45 Ap 17 '39;
        6:85 My 22 '39; 19:63, 68
        S 24 '45; 29:49 D 18 '50
        port.
Dallas, George M.
    George Dallas bw 9:8 Ag 5
        '40
Dallas Museum of Fine Arts
    Exhibit of furniture and inter-
        iors by Knoll 34:72-3 Mr
        2 '53
Dalton, Peter
    Kneeling nude sculpture bw
        32:77 Ja 7 '52
Damrosch, Walter
    MacDonald. Walter Damrosch,
        1936 photog bw 14:13 Ja 11
        '43
Dana, Francis
    Francis Dana bw 19:88 Ag 27
        '45

Danae See Mythological
Themes--Danae
Dancers and Dancing
Ball for Grand Duke Alexis, *
Brooklyn, 1871 bw 19:89
Ag 27 '45
Blakelock. Pipe dance bw 5:
29 O 31 '38
Boru. Dancer ceramic bw 9:
130 N 11 '40
Brueghel, P., the elder. The
wedding dance 4:22 Ap 11
'38 bw 35:31 S 14 '53
Charles II of England dancing
at a ball, * The Hague,
1660 4:168-9 N 19 '56
Clemens. Can-can girl 24:66
Mr 1 '48
Covarrubias. Balinese opera
3:48 S 27 '37
Covarrubias. Balinese war
dance 3:48 S 27 '37
Covarrubias. Legong, Bali-
nese dancer bw 3:46 S 27
'37
Cowles. Ballet dancer 24:78
F 9 '48
Currier and Ives print. Levee
at New Orleans 21:71 S 2
'46
Currier and Ives print. Old
Kentucky Home 41:60 S 3
'56
Dancers, China, c500 B.C.
ceramics 33:101 O 27 '52
Dancing figures fresco, Early
Christian, c300 28:76 Mr
27 '50
Dancing girls, Egyptian bas-
relief 41:88, 90 O 1 '56
Dancing girls terra cottas,
bw Melos, c1340 B.C. 23:
20 Jy 7 '47
Dancing in Covent Garden
ballroom* 31:79 O 29 '51
Davis, G. R. Dancer, Hugh
Laing 16:78 Mr 20 '44
Davis, G. R. Giselle bw 22:
94 Ap 21 '47
Davis, G. R. Making up 16:77
Mr 20 '44

Davis, G. R. Petrouchka 16:
78 Mr 20 '44
Davis, G. R. Waiting for the
curtain 16:79 Mr 20 '44
Davis, G. R. Young man
from Ballet 16:78 Mr 20
'44
De Bry. Javanese dancers
bw 24:87 Mr 22 '48
Degas. Ballet girls on stage
11:59 S 8 '41
Degas. Dancer bronze sculpture bw 2:51 Ap 5 '37; 38:
115 Ap 25 '55
Degas. Dancer (4 figures)
wax sculpture 39:121-2 O
31 '55
Degas. Dancers* 5:28 O 10
'38
Degas. Dancers at the bar
38:107 My 23 '55
Degas. Dancers practicing
at the bar 6:56 Mr 20 '39
Degas. Dancing girl in her
dressing room bw 6:9 Ap
17 '39
Degas. Dancing girls at rest
bw 6:6 Ap 17 '39
Degas. The operatic star bw
6:7 Ap 17 '39
Degas. Waiting bw 6:7 Ap 17
'39
Du Bois, G. Bal des Quatres
Arts 26:68-9 Je 20 '49
Emett. Albuquerque Indians,
rain dance cartoon 37:51
Jy 5 '54
Ernst. The dancers asleep
32:58 Ja 21 '52
Ernst. Dancers walking west-
wards 32:59 Ja 21 '52
Eskimo dancer stone carv-
ing bw 36:69 My 24 '54
Farnsworth. The dancer 5:
30 S 19 '38
Gibson. The social push
drawing bw 28:17 Ja 2 '50
Hogarth. The dance (Masked
ball at Wanstead) 21:81 D
16 '46; 25:99 S 13 '48
Homer. West Point hop draw-

Kane. Harlem dancers sculpture bw 9:54 Ag 12 '40

Kane. Undersea ballet bas-relief bw 7:36-7 Jy 17 '39

Kelly, H. O. Barn dance 29:71 Jy 17 '50

Laning. The corn dance 6:44 My 1 '39

Lord and lady dancing, * Middle Ages bw 22:74 My 26 '47

Luks. The spielers 12:61 Je 15 '42

Maldarelli. Rumba dancer bw 22:138 Mr 24 '47

Manship. Dancer and gazelles sculpture bw 7:37 Jy 31 '39

Manzu. Dancers sculpture bw 41:101 Ag 6 '56

Marin. Corn dance 29:64 Jy 10 '50

Marini. Dancer sculpture bw 22:99 My 22 '50

Matisse. Dancer seated in an armchair 17:75 N 13 '44

Mazoff. Jitterbug sculpture bw 10:59 Je 16 '41

Milles. Two dancers sculpture bw 2:32 F 22 '37

Mount. The breakdown 18:67 Je 25 '45

Mount. Dance of the haymakers 18:67 Je 25 '45

Picabia. Dance at the spring 28:61 Ja 2 '50

Picasso. The three dancers 8:58 Mr 4 '40

Queen Elizabeth I and Earl of Leicester dancing a lavolta* 41:148 N 5 '56

Reinhart. Pas de deux 16:45 Ja 3 '44

Renoir. The city dance bw 28:88 Ja 16 '50

Renoir. The country dance bw 28:88 Ja 16 '50

Renoir. Dance at Bougival 3:45 Jy 5 '37

Rudy. Ballet dancer sculpture ing bw 6:2 Ja 2 '39

bw 15:82 D 20 '43

Russian ball, New York, 1863 bw 19:88 Ag 27 '45

Steen. The dancing couple 5:32 Ag 29 '38

Tamayo. Dancers 36:78 My 31 '54

Thorak. Dancer sculpture bw 9:96 S 23 '40

Toulouse-Lautrec. Couple at Moulin-Rouge drawing bw 28:96 My 15 '50

Toulouse-Lautrec. The dance at Moulin-Rouge 28:99 My 15 '50

Toulouse-Lautrec. Dancing clown drawing bw 28:96 My 15 '50

Toulouse-Lautrec. Jane Avril billboard poster 28:92 My15 '50

Wheelock. Black dancer sculpture bw 8:116 My 20 '40

Zorach. Spirit of the dance sculpture bw 8:92 Ap 1 '40

Danger--Butterfly and spider. bw Benton 6:70 Ap 24 '39

Daniel Boone escorting a band of pioneers into the western country. Bingham 6:28 Je 19 '39

Dannay, Frederic
Frederic Dannay photog bw 16:82 My 1 '44; 22:21 Mr 10 '47

Lee and Dannay (team writing under name of Ellery Queen) photog bw 15:70 N 22 '43

D'Annunzio, Gabriele (Gaetano Rapagnetta)
D'Annunzio photog bw 15:22 Ag 9 '43

Dante Alighieri
Dante bust bw 12:13 Je 8 '42 death mask bw 24:130 F 23 '48

Dore. Illustrations for Dante's "Inferno" bw 15:12-3 D 13 '43

Dante Alighieri (cont.)
Grosz. Illustrations for Dan-
te's "Inferno" bw 15:12-3
D 13 '43
"Daphnis and Chloe," illustra-
tions bw Maillol 8:108 Ap
15 '40
Darbha Malli-Putra, Buddhist
saint. Chou-Chi Ch'ang 15:
66 O 11 '43
D'Arista, Robert
Table with bottles and cheese
39:136-7 N 21 '55
Darius the Great rock sculpture
portraits bw, Behistun,
Iran 26:149 My 23 '49
Darnley, Henry Stuart
Lord Darnley bw 24:67 Je 14
'48
Darrow, Clarence
Davidson. Clarence Darrow
sculpture bw 32:34 Ja 14
'52
Darrow, Whitney, cartoonist
"You're sitting on my eye-
lashes," cartoon book bw
15:10-3 N 8 '43
Whitney Darrow. in group
photog 29:172-3 O 16 '50
port.
Dartmouth College winter carni-
val ice sculpture bw 6:8 Ja
16 '39
Darwin, Charles
Charles Darwin photog bw 15:
104 S 13 '43; 25:106 N 22
'48
D'Ascenzo, Nicola
Stained glass window, Mary-
land church 6:31 Ap 3 '39
Da Silva, Maria Vieira
Azulejos 29:104 D 11 '50
Daugherty, James
The iron horse mural 3:50 O
25 '37
The model T decade mural 3:
49 O 25 '37
Steamboat round the bend
mural 3:50 O 25 '37
Artist at work; wife photogs
bw 3:48 O 25 '37 port.

Daughters of revolution. Wood,
G. 14:53 Ja 18 '43; 21:73
N 25 '46
Daumier, Honore
Exit from theater 7:56 O 9 '39
Don Quixote 40:74-5 My 28
'56
Three lawyers (Les trois avo-
cats) 38:108 My 23 '55
Davenport, Fanny Lily Gipsy
Fanny Davenport photog bw
31:116 N 19 '51
Davey, Randall
Nude* 12:45 Mr 9 '42
Artist in his studio photog 26:
66 Mr 14 '49
David, King of Israel
Bazaine. King David stained
glass 28:74 Je 19 '50
Chagall. Song of David 33:99
O 6 '52
David, the psalm-maker,
First Bible of Charles the
Bold, manuscript 34:81 F
23 '53
Donatello. David sculpture bw
5:35 Ag 29 '38
King David sculpture bw, Ulm
cathedral 35:30 D 28 '53
Michelangelo. David sculp-
ture bw 26:104 Ja 24 '49
Verrochio. David sculpture
bw 6:32 F 13 '39
Vodicka. Song of David sculp-
ture bw 41:76 S 10 '56
David, Jacques Louis
Cupid and Psyche bw 4:42
My 2 '38
Madame Recamier 35:60 Ag
17 '53
Mlle Charlotte du Val D'Og-
nes 5:38 S 26 '38
Napoleon as first consul bw
16:68 Ja 10 '44
Jacque Louis David bw 5:34
S 26 '38 port.
Davidson, David
David Davidson photog bw
23:92 S 1 '47
Davidson, Julian O.
Battle of Mobile Bay, 1864

9:49 O 28 '40
Monitor and Merrimac, 1862
9:49 O 28 '40
Davidson, J. R., architect
Stothart home, Santa Monica,
Calif. photogs bw 19:110-
2 O 22 '45
Davidson, Jo, sculptor
Artist's mother bw 32:34 Ja
14 '52
Clarence Darrow bw 32:34
Ja 14 '52
Franklin Roosevelt bw 32:34
Ja 14 '52
Gertrude Stein bw 23:15 Ag
18 '47
Joseph Conrad bw 32:34 Ja 14
'52
Marshal Tito bw 32:34 Ja 14
'52
Torso bw 10:108 Mr 17 '41
Walt Whitman bw 26:112 Je
20 '49
Will Rogers bw 27:79 Jy 18
'49
Woodrow Wilson bw 32:34 Ja
14 '52; 41:103 D 17 '56
Artist in his studio photogs
bw 10:108 Mr 17 '41 port.
Jo Davidson. in group photog
bw 26:112 Je 20 '49
Self-portrait sculpture bw 32:
34 Ja 14 '52
Davidson, Thomas
First meeting house of North
Church, Salem, Mass 13:
80 N 23 '42
Davidson, Virginia
Female figure garden sculp-
ture bw 37:122 N 15 '54
Davies, Arthur B.
Afterthoughts of earth bw 16:
79 Ap 24 '44
Davies, Captain
Capture of Fort Lee, 1776
watercolor 29:45 Jy 3 '50
Capture of Fort Washington,
1776 watercolor 29:45 Jy
3 '50
Davies, Thomas
Thomas Davies' bookstore,

London, 1763 bw 29:94 D
4 '50
Davies (Joseph E.) collection of
Russian painting 14:44-7
Mr 29 '43
Davila, Enriqueta
Rivera. Enriqueta Davila 29:
109 D 11 '50
Davis, Alexander Jackson
Greek revival interior, 1845
watercolor 39:60-1 Ag 29
'55
Davis, Bette
Brook. Bette Davis 17:73 N
20 '44
Davis, Floyd
Air raid on Hamburg 15:68-
71 D 27 '43
BBC's nine o'clock news 16:
68 Ap 3 '44; 31:77 O 29
'51
Bermuda in World War 13:90-
4 S 21 '42
England at war: London and
other scenes 16:65-8 Ap
3 '44
Front Street, Hamilton, Ber-
muda bw 14:6 Je 28 '43
Paris, 1945: scenes and por-
traits since liberation 19:
50-2 Jy 16 '45
Safe convoy bw 14:6 Je 28 '43
Sailor and girl* 13:95 S 21
'42; 21:91 N 25 '46
The Scribe Hotel barroom 19:
50-1 Jy 16 '45
Softball game in Hyde Park, *
London 16:66-7 Ap 3 '44;
31:79 O 29 '51
Christmas tree bw 19:10 D
24 '45 (drawing)
Artist painting his wife photog
bw 16:64 Ap 3 '44 port.
Floyd Davis photog bw 13:90
S 21 '42; 14:8 Je 28 '43;
15:84 D 27 '43 port.
Davis, G. H.
Columbus' "Santa Maria" 31:
98-9 O 15 '51
G. H. Davis photog bw 31:
100 O 15 '51 port.

Davis, Gladys Rockmore
  Ballet dancers and scenes 16:
    77-80 Mr 20 '44
  Caroler 23:Cover D 22 '47
  Carousel 22:96 Ap 21 '47
  Companions bw 18:44 Ja 1
    '45
  Dancer, Hugh Laing 16:78
    Mr 20 '44
  Deborah, the artist's
    daughter 14:45 Ap 19 '43
  Flowers 14:46 Ap 19 '43
  Giselle bw 22:94 Ap 21 '47
  Luxembourg Gardens, Paris
    19:48 Jy 16 '45
  Making up 16:77 Mr 20 '44
  The music lesson 14:46 Ap
    19 '43
  Noel, the artist's son pastel
    14:45 Ap 19 '43
  The odalisque 14:45 Ap 19 '43
  Old woman* 18:75 My 14 '45
  Paris, 1945: scenes and por-
    traits since liberation 19:
    47-9, 54 Jy 16 '45
  Paris, street scene 35:88 O
    26 '53
  Petrouchka, ballet 16:78 Mr
    20 '44
  The pink skirt 6:30 F 13 '39
  Seated figure 14:46 Ap 19 '43;
    21:75 N 25 '46
  Waiting for the curtain 16:79
    Mr 20 '44
  We Three Kings of Orient
    Are 23:52 D 22 '47
  Young man from ballet 16:78
    Mr 20 '44
  Artist at work photog bw 14:
    44 Ap 19 '43 port.
Davis, Goode P.
  Wife of the artist 10:48 F 3
    '41
Davis, Jefferson
  Jefferson Davis statue bw 6:
    73 Ap 10 '39; Jackson,
    Miss. 2:45 Je 28 '37
  Jefferson and Mrs. Davis
    photog bw 23:55 N 3 '47
Davis, John W.
  John W. Davis photog bw 14:

    7 My 31 '43
Davis, Marshall
  Army life drawing bw 12:68-
    9 Ap 13 '42
Davis, Stuart
  Eggbeater no. 5 22:79 F 17
    '47
  For internal use only 22:81
    F 17 '47
  Hotel de France 22:80 F 17
    '47
  New York under gaslight 22:
    80 F 17 '47
  Place Pasdeloup 22:80 F 17
    '47
  Artist in his studio photog
    bw 22:78 F 17 '47 port.
  Stuart Davis. in group photog
    bw 32:87 Mr 17 '52 port.
Dawes, Charles
  Charles Dawes photog bw 9:9
    Ag 5 '40
The dawn of the spirit. Cowles
    24:76 F 9 '48
Day. sculpture bw Manship 4:
    15 Ja 31 '38
Day, Clarence
  Clarence Day; family photogs
    bw 7:45 N 27 '39
Day, Esther Worden
  The transfixed hour 10:68 My
    26 '41
Day, Robert
  "New Yorker" cover 21:71 Jy
    15 '46
A day in port. Agnew 23:98 N
    10 '47
Daybreak. Hinman 23:99 N 10
    '47
Dead head. Fulwider 6:30 F 13
    '39
Dead Jap. Vidar 19:70 O 8 '45
Dead sea. Nash 26:46 F 28 '49
Dead Sea Scrolls photogs bw
    34:95-6 Je 15 '53; 41:41
    Jy 23 '56
Dean, Abner, cartoonist
  "It's a long way to heaven"
    cartoon book bw 19:14-6
    D 10 '45
  "New Yorker" cover 21:70

Jy 15 '46

Satirical cartoons bw 13:150-3 N 23 '42

"What am I doing here" cartoon book 23:18-9 D 1 '47

Abner Dean photog bw 19:14 D 10 '45 port.

Death

Albright, I. That which I should have done I did not do 16:68 Mr 27 '44 bw 14:47 Mr 8 '46

Brueghel, P., the elder. The triumph of Death 31:66 O 1 '51

Death, santo wood carving bw 24:57 My 17 '48

McCrady. Swing Low, Sweet Chariot 3:39 O 18 '37

Milles. Fountain of faith sculpture bw 34:99-101 Mr 30 '53 plaster models bw 25:70-2 Ag 30 '48

Milles. Orpheus fountain, Stockholm sculpture bw 2:28-9 F 22 '37

Uccello, School of. The triumph of Death bw 4:28 F 7 '38

Death of Adam. Piero della Francesca 20:61 Ap 22 '46

Death of Dido. bw Rubens 16:65 Ja 10 '44

Death of Dillinger. Marsh 8:70 Mr 11 '40 bw 37:48 Jy 26 '54

Death of General Montgomery, Quebec. Trumbull 29:42-3 Jy 3 '50

The death of General Wolfe. West 5:31 O 31 '38; 25:106-7 S 13 '48 bw 7:70 S 25 '39; 9:112 S 9 '40

Death of Jane McCrea. Vanderlyn 29:49 Jy 3 '50

Death of St. Francis. fresco bw Giotto 16:68 Ap 10 '44

Death on a pale horse. Ryder 5:36 O 31 '38; 15:67 S 20 '43

Death on Ridge Road. Wood, G. 14:55 Ja 18 '43

De Berri, Duc

Duc de Berri in January calendar page from "Tres riches heures." Limbourg brothers 24:39 Ja 5 '48

Deborah. Davis, G. R. 14:45 Ap 19 '43

De Bry, Theodorus

Medieval travel scenes bw 24:86-7 Mr 22 '48 (drawings)

Deer hunt, after Le Moyne bw 22:85 Mr 10 '47 (engravings)

Drying meat, after Le Moyne bw 22:85 Mr 10 '47 (engravings)

Debs, Eugene Victor

Eugene Debs, Socialist Party poster bw 24:105 Ja 19 '48

"King Debs," 1894 caricature bw 33:33 D 8 '52

Decanters See Bottles and Flasks

De Carlo, Yvonne

Martin, F. Yvonne de Carlo in "Frontier Gal" 19:65 D 24 '45

De Castro, Joachim Machado (?) Zemayas 41:71 D 10 '56

Decker, Alice

Scrubwoman sculpture bw 5:5 N 28 '38

Decker, John

Fanny Brice as Mona Lisa bw 4:34 Ap 18 '38

Declaration of Independence

Signers of Declaration of Independence: 56 portraits and signatures bw 15:8-10 Jy 5 '43

Trumbull. Declaration of Independence 14:64 Ap 12 '43

De Conti, Bernardino

Charles of Amboise 35:155 N 16 '53

Decorations See Emblems and Decorations

De Coux, Janet
    St. Benedict sculpture bw 27:
        144 O 17 '49
Decoying broadbill. Pleissner
        21:64 O 7 '46
Decoys. Whedon 16:46 Ja 3 ' 44
De Creeft, Jose
    Maternity sculpture bw 14:
        42 Mr 8 '43
Deep south. Harrington 8:46 F
        12 '40
Deep vision. Pereira 34:73 Ja
        26 '53
Deer
    De Bry. Deer hunt, after Le
        Moyne engraving bw 22:
        85 Mr 10 '47
    Deer fresco Rome, 3rd cen-
        tury 28:75 Mr 27 '50
    Deer, Cro-Magnon cave
        painting, France 22:67 F
        24 '47
    Doe, paleolithic cave paint-
        ing, Spain 39:86 D 12 '55
    Rousseau. The waterfall 11:
        58 S 8 '41
    Zao Wou-Ki. Slim deer 36:
        104 F 22 '54
The defeat of Bobby Jones.
        Goodman, J. 7:33 S 4 '39
Deffaud, Madame du
    Mme du Deffaud bw 23:78 S
        15 '47
Defoe, Daniel
    "Robinson Crusoe" illustra-
        tions bw 25:109 S 13 '48
De Forest, David Curtis
    Morse. David Curtis De
        Forest 17:60 D 18 '44
De Forest, Julia Wooster
    Morse. Mrs. David Curtis
        De Forest 17:60 D 18 '44
De Gamundia, Johannes
    Calendar, Germany, 1479
        woodblock bw 18:42 Ja 1
        '45
Degas, Edgar
    L'absinthe bw 11:85 D 1 '41
    After the bath pastel 38:107
        My 23 '55
    Artist's father listening to

        guitarist, Pagans 25:79 N
        1 '48
    At the races 40:74-5 My 28
        '56
    Ballet girls on stage 11:59 S
        8 '41
    Carriages at the races 9:52
        Jy 22 '40
    Cotton market in New Orleans
        10:74 Ap 28 '41
    Dancers* 5:28 O 10 '38
    Dancers at the bar 38:107
        My 23 '55
    Dancers practicing at the bar
        6:56 Mr 20 '39
    Dancing girl in her dressing
        room bw 6:9 Ap 17 '39
    Dancing girls at rest bw 6:
        6 Ap 17 '39
    Mademoiselle Hortense Val-
        pincon 25:77 Ag 2 '48
    The man and the mannequin
        (Portrait of Paul Cez-
        anne) 29:88 N 27 '50
    The millinery shop 39:119 N
        7 '55
    The operatic star bw 6:7 Ap
        17 '39
    Portrait of Mary Cassatt bw
        12:54 Ja 19 '42
    Waiting bw 6:7 Ap 17 '39
    Dancer bronze sculpture bw
        2:51 Ap 5 '37; 38:115 Ap
        25 '55 (sculpture)
    Dancer (4 figures) wax sculp-
        ture 39:121-2 O 31 '55
        (sculpture)
    Jockey on race horse* wax
        sculpture 39:121 O 31 '55
        (sculpture)
    Edgar Degas photog bw 5:24
        O 10 '38 port.
De Grailly, Victor
    Maid of mist 26:79 Je 6 '49
De Grineau, Bryan
    British troops in France
        drawings bw 8:66-7 Ja
        22 '40
Dehn, Adolf Arthur, water-
        colorist
    Autumn at Salisbury Mills

11:41 Ag 11 '41
Farm in autumn 11:41 Ag 11
   '41
Ghost town 11:43 Ag 11 '41
Iron mines, Ironwood,
   Michigan* 34:78 Ja 5 '53
The Mojave Desert 11:44 Ag
   11 '41
Newburgh in winter 11:41 Ag
   11 '41
Sopris Peak 11:43 Ag 11 '41
South Dakota 11:42 Ag 11 '41
Sunset after rain 11:44 Ag 11
   '41
The three red houses 11:41
   Ag 11 '41
Threshing in Minnesota 11:
   42 Ag 11 '41
Tracks along the Hudson 11:
   41 Ag 11 '41
Winter over the Hudson 11:
   41 Ag 11 '41
Yosemite 11:44 Ag 11 '41
Adolf Dehn, at Colorado
   Springs Fine Arts Center
   photog bw 11:40 Ag 11 '41
   port.
Dejeuner sur l'Herbe. bw Manet
   12:44 Mr 9 '42
De Jong, Jacob
   Jan Six IV bw 31:66 Jy 16 '51
De Kerouaille, Louise
   Louise de Kerouaille 41:167
   N 19 '56
De Kooning, William
   Painting, 1948 25:62 O 11 '48
   Woman VI 39:134-5 N 21 '55
   Willem de Kooning photog
   bw 30:34 Ja 15 '51 port.
De Laszlo
   King Fuad I of Egypt bw 16:
   85 Ap 10 '44
De Lesseps, Ferdinand
   Ferdinand de Lesseps car-
   toon bw 31:85 O 22 '51
   Ferdinand de Lesseps and his
   family photog bw 31:85 O
   22 '51
Delacroix, Eugene
   Algerian women bw 38:130 Je
   27 '55

Christ on the Sea of Galilee
   39:23 D 26 '55
George Sand (Aurore Dupin)
   25:98 N 22 '48
Liberty leading the people 25:
   84 N 22 '48
Massacre at Scio 25:86 N 22
   '48
Nicolo Paganini, age 50 bw
   36:128 N 16 '53
Delaney, Beauford
   Artist and his work photog
   bw 5:54 O 3 '38 port.
Delaware Water Gap village.
   bw Eilshemius 7:51 N 6
   '39
A delicate compliment. print
   bw Leech 6:38 F 6 '39
Deliverance of St. Peter. bw
   Dore 39:37 D 26 '55
The Delphic sibyl. fresco
   Michelangelo 21:65 Jy 1
   '46
Delvaux, Paul
   The sirens 29:102-3 D 11
   '50; 33:97 O 27 '52
De Maistre, Joseph
   Joseph de Maistre bw 15:108
   Ag 23 '43
De Martelly, John Stockton
   Detroit skyline 34:80 Ja 5 '53
   Niagara Falls* 26:79 Je 6 '49
   No more mowing 13:48 Ag
   31 '42
   Tulip farm 25:68 Ag 23 '48
De Martini, Joseph
   In Squeaker Cove 29:72 Ag
   21 '50
   Lighthouse Point 23:69 Jy 14
   '47
Demeter See Mythological
   Themes--Ceres
Demetrius cathedral, Vladimir,
   Russia, Byzantine-Ro-
   manesque photog bw 14:84
   Mr 29 '43
Demidoff, Princess
   Sargent. Princess Demidoff
   7:36 Jy 31 '39

Demjanovich, Miriam Teresa
  Miriam Demjanovich bw 27:
    150 S 19 '49
Les demoiselles d'Avignon. Pi-
  casso 23:93 O 13 '47
Dempsey and Firpo. bw Bellows
    6:58 Mr 27 '39
Demuth, Charles
  My Egypt (grain elevator) 38:
    75 Mr 28 '55
Denis, Saint
  St. Denis walking with his
    head in his hands* bw 31:
    76 Jy 30 '51
Denslow, W. W.
  "The Wonderful Wizard of Oz"
    illustrations 35:52-9 D 28
    '53
Dennison, Miss
  Miss Dennison, American
    primitive, 1775 bw 36:95
    Je 28 '54
Dentists as sculptors bw 29:147
    S 18 '50
De Peyster boy, 1730 26:85 F
    28 '49
D'Epinay, Madame
  Mme D'Epinay bw 23:78 S 15
    '47
Departure. lithograph Picasso
    33:84 Jy 14 '52
Departure of Lot and his family
    from Sodom. Rubens 4:
    24 Ap 11 '38
Deposition See Jesus Christ--
    Deposition
Deposition of the miner. Ander-
    son, G. 35:87 S 28 '53
Derain, Andre
  Andre Derain photog bw 5:
    72 D 12 '38
Derain, Madame Andre
  Despiau. Mme Derain sculp-
    ture bw 38:110 My 23 '55
Derelicts. Philipp, R. 8:64
    Ap 8 '40
De Rougemont, Denis
  Denis de Rougemont photog
    bw 24:80 F 2 '48
Derujinsky, Gleb
  The rape of Europa sculp-

ture bw 6:36 Mr 13 '39
The descent. bw Billings 8:70
    My 27'40
Descente de la machine aero-
    statique. Charles et Rob-
    ert 40:77 Ja 9 '56
Desert windmill water tank.*
    Hurd 23:75 Ag 18 '47
Deserted house. Thomas 10:52
    Je 23 '41
Deserted house. Wyeth, A. 35:
    80-1 Jy 27 '53
Design See also area of appli-
    cation, as Furniture; In-
    terior Design
  Color relationships and pat-
    tern drawing 40:71 Mr
    26 '56
  House furnishings bw 37:83-
    6 Jy 26 '54
  Useful objects bw 27:120-1
    O 24 '49
Design, Industrial
  Dreyfuss. Perisphere and
    trylon, World's Fair,
    New York City plan,
    photogs bw 5:54-7 Ag 1
    '38 photog bw 4:11 Ja 31
    '38
  Loewy. Design of bottles,
    lamps, chairs, houses,
    automobiles 26:110-2 My
    2 '49
Design for a monument. bw Pi-
    casso 23:95 O 13 '47
Desk, "Bombe," Massachusetts,
    c1760 38:67 My 30 '55
De Soto, Ferdinand
  Currier and Ives print. De
    Soto's discovery of the
    Mississippi* bw 21:70 S
    2 '46
  Powell. De Soto's discovery
    of the Mississippi bw 24:
    88 Mr 22 '48
A desperate character. Bacon,
    P. 6:57 My 8 '39
Despero, Furtunato
  Workers* bw 29:15 O 30 '50
Despiau, Charles, sculptor
  Anne Lindbergh head bw 24:

95 Ap 12 '48
Head of Mme Derain 38:110
    My 23 '55
Maria Lani head bw 19:14 D
    3 '45
Desportes, Henriette
    Henriette Desportes bw 9:
    35 Jy 1 '40
Dessau, Paul
    Incendiaries* 26:50 F 28 '49
De Stael, Nicolas
    North 38:108 My23 '55
Destiny. lithograph bw von
    Physter 5:55 Ag 8 '38
Destroyer base. bw Lea 14:7
    Je 28 '43
Destruction of the empire. Cole,
    T. 33:90 S 15 '52
Detroit
    Emett. Detroit cartoon 37:
    45 Jy 5 '54
    Northland, shopping center.
    Gruen and associates
    photogs 37:81-3 Ag 20 '54
Detroit Institute of Arts
    Design exhibit: useful objects
    photogs bw 27:120-1 O 24
    '49
Detroit skyline. de Martelly 34:
    80 Ja 5 '53
Devil
    Beerbohm. George Bernard
    Shaw as the Devil carica-
    ture bw 23:89 N 17 '47
    Devil drawing bw, 11th cen-
    tury 24:78 F 2 '48
    Devil drawing bw, 13th cen-
    tury 24:78 F 2 '48
    Devil, as comic in mystery
    play drawing bw 24:79
    F 2 '48
    The Devil in Gounod's
    "Faust" bw 24:79 F 2 '48
    Devils in church vestments,
    anti-religious museum,
    Moscow stained glass bw
    11:121 O 13 '41
    Dore. Satan brooding, illus-
    tration for "Paradise Lost"
    bw 24:76 F 2 '48

Duccio. Temptation of Christ
    bw 4:28 F 7 '38
Epstein. Lucifer sculpture
    bw 33:66 N 3 '52
Grunewald. Temptation of
    St. Anthony 30:81 Mr 26
    '51
Hindu demon, with sword
    and snake sculpture bw 9:
    73 N 25 '40
Hindu festival figures 30:91-
    3 F 12 '51
Lady devil of free love re-
    jected* bw 24:85 F 2 '48
Luther throwing inkpot at
    the Devil* bw 24:84 F 2 '
    '48
Michelangelo. Satan, in
    The last judgment bw 24:
    78 F 2 '48
Mr. and Mrs. Devil sculp-
    ture bw 24:77 F 2 '48
Patiner and Massys. The
    temptation of St. Anthony
    31:62-3 O 1 '51
Siqueiros. The Devil in
    church 29:106 D 11 '50
Devil's aide. bw Kinigstein 32:
    88 Mr 17 '52
Devil's Island
    Scenes of former penal col-
    ony, French Guiana. Mi-
    chel 4:47-8 Ap 4 '38
Deutsch, Boris
    Figure bw 22:40 Je 16 '47
Devitt, Thomas
    Sargent. Sir Thomas Devitt
    23:81 N 17 '47
De Warenne Family shield of
    arms 22:69 My 26 '47
De Welden, Felix
    Flag raising, Mt. Suribachi,
    Iwo Jima, sculpture bw
    37:128-9 S 20 '54
Dewey, John
    John Dewey photog bw 2:66
    Ap 26 '37
Dewey, Thomas
    Wolverton. Thomas Dewey
    caricature bw 22:16 My
    5 '47

De Witt, C. H.
  "The Story of the Mississippi"
    illustrations 11:85 D 15
    '41
"Dewitt Clinton"(locomotive)
    New York Central, 1831
    photog bw 25:13 S 27 '48
DeYoung Museum, San Francis-
    co Exhibit of self-portraits
    of contemporary painters,
    illustrators and cartoon-
    ists bw 15:12-4 O 25 '43
Diagnostic art to identify chil-
    dren's fears and frustra-
    tions 12:59-60 Je 8 '42
Diamond, David
  David Diamond photog bw 16:
    62 Ap 24 '44
Diamond, Freda, furniture de-
    signer
  Artist and her work photog
    bw 36:69-70 Ap 5 '54 port.
Diamonds See also Gems
  Albert II, King of Belgium,
    equestrian figure bw 7:59
    Jy 3 '39
  Cullinan diamond photog 2:
    40-1 Mr 15 '37
Diana See Mythological
    Themes--Diana
Diaz, Porfirio
  Porfirio Diaz photog bw 4:
    53 Ap 11 '38
Di Benedetto, Angelo
  Corn field* 13:48 Ag 31 '42
Dice See Games and Sports--
    Dice
Dick, William Reid, sculptor
  Franklin Delano Roosevelt
    bw, Grosvenor Square,
    London 24:32-3 Ap 26 '48
    model bw 21:33 D 2 '46
  Mary, Consort of George V,
    King of England, tomb
    effigy, Windsor Castle bw
    36:44 F 8 '54
  Artist at work photog bw 21:
    33 D 2 '46 port.
Dick Tracy. cartoon bw Gould,
    C. 17:43-4 Ag 14 '44
Dickens, Charles

Aufray. Dickens at home bw
    25:76 D 27 '48
  Browne (Phiz). "Nicholas
    Nickleby" illustrations bw
    23:2-3 D 22 '47
  Charles Dickens; family;
    home 25:76-8 D 27 '48
  Cruikshank. Oliver asking
    for more, illustration
    from "Oliver Twist" bw
    25:78 D 27 '48
  Fildes. The empty chair
    (Dicken's study) drawing
    bw 25:84 D 27 '48
  Leech. "A Christmas Carol"
    illustrations bw 25:78 D
    27 '48
Dickie Dare. cartoon bw Waugh,
    C. 5:57 N 28 '38
Dickinson, Sidney
  Eugene Higgins 10:48 F 3 '41
  Sidney Dickinson. in group
    photog 29:172-3 O 16 '50
    port.
"Dictionary of the English lan-
    guage," April 15, 1755
  Samuel Johnson: portrait;
    glosses photogs bw 38:165-
    6 My 2 '55
Diderot, Denis
  Denis Diderot bw 23:89 S 15 '47
Dido See Mythological Themes
    --Dido
Didymion temple, ruin, Turkey
    photog bw 8:81 Ap 8 '40
Diego, Julio de
  Besieged city 20:81 Mr 11
    '46
  Blueprint of the future 20:81
    Mr 11 '46
  Elements of reconstruction
    20:82 Mr 11 '46
  The portentous city 20:81 Mr
    11 '46
  Unexpected encounter 20:82
    Mr 11 '46
  Artist at work photog bw 20:
    80 Mr 11 '46 port.
Dienes, Sari
  Tombstone rubbings, U.S. bw
    37:133-6 N 15 '54

Artist at work photogs bw 37:
133-4 N 15 '54 port.
Dietrick, William Henley, archi-
tect Fair grounds building,
Raleigh, N.C. 36:34-5 Ja
4 '54
Di Gioia, Frank
Fish market 20:78 F 18 '46
Dike, Phil
California holiday 11:75 O 27
'41
The park watercolor 16:45
Ja 3 '44
Dilbert. cartoon bw Osborn 14:
8-10 My 17 '43
Dillinger, John
Marsh. The death of Dillinger
8:70 Mr 11 '40 bw 37:48
Jy 26 '54
Di Maggio, Joe
Laning. Joe di Maggio tying
the record bw 11:64 N 10
'41
Dinasos, Flemish fascist em-
blem: cog, sword, plow bw
4: 38 Mr 14 '38; 8:13 Je
17 '40
Dining Rooms and Dining See
also Cafes and Restaurants
American family dinner. bw
Japanese illustration, 1853
25:7 Ag 2 '48
Banquet aboard Perry's flag-
ship, 1853 bw 19:62 S 17
'45
Greaves. The spaghetti eaters
bw 40:164 Ap 23 '56
Lee, D. Thanksgiving 3:44 S
20 '37
Lewicki. Christmas feast,
Tudor, England 33:87 D 1
'52
Manet. Luncheon on the grass
bw 12:44 Mr 9 '42
Middle class family banquet,
Egypt, Middle kingdom 41:
108-9 N 26 '56
Noble eating, bas-relief,
Egypt 41:90 O 1 '56
Renoir. Luncheon of the boat-
ing party 32:94 My 19 '52;

38:110 My 23 '55
Royal banquet, panel from
Royal Standard of Ur,
Sumerian mosaic 40:90-1
Je 4 '56
Sharon. Family reunion 33:76
Jy 21 '52
Van Gogh. The potatoe eaters
27:83 O 10 '49 bw 41:67
O 1 '56
Vuillard. The meal 37:77 N
1 '54
White, J. Indian meal* water-
color 22:82 Mr 10 '47
Wickey. Garbage man eating
his lunch bw 12:54 F 23
'42
Wood, G. Dinner for thresh-
ers 13:46-7 Ag 31 '42; 21:
77 N 25 '46
The dinky bird. bw Parrish 5:
29 O 31 '38
Dinosaurs
Triceratops, cement statue,
Dinosaur National Monu-
ment, S. Dak. bw 11:102
O 6 '41
Dinwiddie, Hill and Joseph,
architects
Modern town house, San
Francisco photog 27:44 S
5 '49
Diogenes in Benjamin Franklin
print, 1780 40:80 Ja 9 '56
Dionne quintuplets. Loomis 18:
45 Ja 1 '45
Dior, Christian
Christian Dior photog bw
24:84 Mr 1 '48
Karsh. Christian Dior photog
bw 37:132 O 4 '54
Dirk, Nathaniel
At Noank 16:46 Ja 3 '44
Discobolus. sculpture bw Myron
5:46 D 25 '38
The discovery. Remington 36:
77 Mr 8 '54
Disraeli, Benjamin
Benjamin Disraeli 24:71 My
24 '48

Disraeli, Benjamin (cont.)
Knighting of Disraeli, 1878 bw
13:76 N 16 '42
Dividers, brass, in Amerigo
Vespucci, woodcut, 16th
century 40:46 Ja 9 '56
Dix, Dorothea
Dorothea Dix bw 16:56 F 14
'44; 22:80 Ja 13 '47
Dix, Otto
Veronica's veil lithograph 33:
84 Jy 14 '52
Dixey, Henry F.
Henry E. Dixey, dancer
photog bw 11:74 Ag 25 '41
Dobrawa, Queen of Poland
Queen Dobrawa bw 17:86 Ag
28 '44
Dobson, Frank
The fount sculpture bw 25:103
S 27 '48
Dock Street Theater, Charleston
First U.S. theater restored
photogs bw 3:49-50 D 20 '37
Dr. Seuss See Geisel, Theodore
S.
Doctor's office. Soyer 4:27 Je 13
'38
Dodd, Lamar
Beach house 27:64 S 26 '49
Carnival 27:64 S 26 '49
Lumpkin Street 27:63 S 26 '49
Savannah 27:64 S 26 '49
View of Athens, Georgia 27:
64-5 S 26 '49
Artist and his work photog bw
27:62 S 26 '49 port.
Dodgson, Charles Lutwidge
(Lewis Carroll, pseudonym)
"Alice's Adventures in Wonder-
land" illustrated by Dodgson
bw 20:100-1 Ap 15 '46
original "Alice" photog bw
6:27 Jy 11 '38
Charles L. Dodgson photog bw
5:27 Jy 11 '38; 29:24 N 6 '50;
29:22-3 N 27 '50
Crocodile drawing bw, illustra-
tion from "Sylvie and
Bruno" 16:12 F 7 '44
Tenniel. "Alice's Adventures in

Wonderland" illustrations
bw 29:22 N 6 '50; 30:85-7
Je 18 '51
Dodo
Dodo drawing bw 30:131 F 12
'51
Savery. Dodo, 1599 sketch
from life bw 29:171 D 11 '50
Doenitz, Karl
Admiral Doenitz, "Time" cov-
er portrait 17:66 D 11 '44
Dog barking at the moon. Miro
4:44 My 2 '38
Doge's Palace, Venice. Senate
chamber photog bw 23:50
Ag 4 '47
Dogs
Benton. T.P. and Jake bw 10:
70 Ap 14 '41
Bingham. Shooting for the
beef 6:28 Je 19 '39
Brueghel, P., the elder,
Massacre of the innocents,
detail 37:34-5 D 27 '54
Brussel-Smith. Wood engrav-
ings of hunting incidents
39:190-201 N 14 '55
Cassatt. Woman with dog 40:
67 Ja 23 '56
Chinese stone dog bw 31:37 D
17 '51
Cranach. Henry the Pious,
1514 40:104 My 7 '56
Cranach. Katherine, wife of
Henry the Pious, 1514 40:
105 My 7 '56
Denslow. "The Wonderful
Wizard of Oz" illustrations
bw 35:53-9 D 28 '53
Dog, African devining statue
bw 33:119 S 8 '52
Dogs, Pre-Columbian ceram-
ics, Mexico 18:49 Je 4 '45
Hovenden. Breaking home ties
9:76 D 9 '40; 27:60 Ag 29 '49
Miro. Dog barking at the
moon 4:44 My 2 '38
Pekinese sculpture bw 18:91
F 19 '45
Picasso. Two acrobats with
dog 8:57 Mr 4 '40 bw 6:83

My 22 '39

Poker game bw 35:31 S 14 '53

Renoir. Mme Charpentier and
her children 3:47 Jy 5 '37

Rosenthal. Tops 15:65 N 22
'43

Rudy. Whippet sculpture bw
15:82 D 20 '43

Steen. The gallant offering 24:
78 Je 14 '48

Tamayo. Animals howling for
food 34:101 Mr 16 '53

Titian. Venus with organ
player 24:76 Mr 22 '48

Van Eyck. Giovanni Arnolfini
and wife 33:36 D 29 '52

Velazquez. The maids of honor
7:57 N 20 '39; 31:61 O 1 '51

Ylla. Portraits of dogs photogs
bw 23:Cover, 18-9 N 17 '47

Dohanos, Steven

Casey's famous wreck bw 12:
62 Ja 28 '42

Doisneau, Robert, photographer

Examples of work from Art
Institute of Chicago exhibit
bw 36:20-1 Je 7 '54

Dolan, J. J.

Murphy-Dolan crowd photog bw
11:68 Ag 4 '41

The doll. Greene 28:89 Mr 20 '50

Dolls and Puppets

Buffano. Giant papier-mache
Figures: witch, alchemist,
voodoo doctor, scientist
bw 6:6-8 My 1 '39

Comic strip dolls, U.S. bw
35:82-6 O 19 '53

Doll collection, Webb Museum,
Shelburne, Vt. 35:50 Jy 6
'53

Dolls from the first national
doll show: 1750 to present
5:38-41 Jy 18 '38

Dy-Dee dolls photogs bw 3:55
N 22 '37

Rag doll and doll houses
photogs bw 15:90-2 N 29 '43

Salzburg marionettes: Grimm
and Anderson fairy story
characters 33:Cover, 68-73

D 29 '52

Dolphins

Milles. Naiad and dolphins
sculpture bw 2:32 F 22 '37

Domenico Veneziano

The stigmatization of St.
Francis 1:48 D 28 '36 bw
16:68 Ap 10 '44

Domes See also United States
Capitol--Dome

Dome of the Rock, Jerusalem
(Mosque of Omar) photogs
6:54 My 15 '39; 20:58 Ap
1 '46; 38:78-9 My 9 '55 bw
31:61 D 24 '51

Fuller. Geodesic dome, Ford
Motor Company, River
Rouge photog bw 34:67-70
Je 8 '53

Jefferson. Monticello photog
bw 14:65 Ap 12 '43

Leonardo da Vinci. Basillica
models from sketches bw
7:16-8 Jy 17 '39

Michelangelo. Dome, St.
Peter's, Rome photog 20:
31-3, 36-7 Mr 11 '46; 27:
49 Ag 1 '49 bw 17:94 S 4
'44

Old court house, St. Louis
photog bw 13:75 O 12 '42

Onionate domes, Russian
churches and cathedrals
photogs bw 14:83-5 Mr 29
'43

Pantheon, Rome photog bw 16:
12 Je 5 '44

Puebla cathedral, Puebla,
Mexico photogs 6:33, 36 Ja
23 '39

Saarinen, Eero. Dome, Massachusetts Institute of Technology auditorium photog
bw 38:79-81 Mr 14 '55

St. Mark's, Venice photogs
35:28-35 D 28 '53

San Francisco city hall photog
bw 15:71 Jy 12 '43

Santa Sophia, Istanbul 29:54-
61 D 25 '50

"Don Giovanni," illustrations of
Mozart's opera. Vidar 22:
58-65 F 3 '47
Don Manuel Osorio de Zuniga.
Goya 2:41 Je 28 '37
Don Quixote
Daumier. Don Quixote 40:74-5
My 28 '56
Don Quixote, Gobelin tapestry,
c1714 21:82-3 S 30-46 bw
6:17 Je 19 '39
Don Quixote and Sancho Panza
sculpture bw, Madrid 31:
58 Ag 27 '51
Donatello, sculptor
David bw 5:35 Ag 29 '38
San Ludovici (Louis of Anjou)
gilded bronze statue, 13th
century 27:106-7 S 19 '49
Donati, Enrico
Abstraction 37:161 N 22 '54
Artist at work photog bw 37:
160 N 22 '54 port.
Donghi, Antonio
Worker rowing boat* bw 29:
115 O 30 '50
Donkeys
Bellini. Flight into Egypt 16:
70 Ap 10 '44
Brueghel, P., the elder.
Adoration of the Magi, de-
tail 37:33-4 D 27 '54
Shepard. Eeyore, illustration
for "Winnie-the-Pooh" bw
30:76 F 19 '51
Donovan, William Joseph
Bill Donovan, OSS chief photog
bw 19:119 N 19 '45
Donskoi, Dmitri
Dmitri Donskoi plaque portrait
bw 14:93 Mr 29 '43
Don't move there. We shall clear
you. print bw Leech 6:38
F 6 '39
Doolittle, Amos
Marching into Concord engrav-
ing 29:41 Jy 3 '50
On Lexington Green engraving
29:40 Jy 3 '50
Doolittle, James
Lea. Jimmy Doolittle drawing

bw 16:68 My 29 '44
Doorknocker, eagle symbol, U.S.,
c1784 bw 17:56 S 4 '44
Doors and Doorways See Gate-
ways and Doorways
Dore, Gustave
The brazen serpent bw 4:48 Ap
18 '38; 23:45 S 22 '47
Children's crusade bw 16:66
Ap 10 '44
Christ's entry into Jerusalem
bw 23:44 S 22 '47
The crusades bw 39:40-1 D 26
'55
De Custine's "Journey for Our
Time," humorous Russian
history illustrations bw 30:
108-13 Mr 5 '51
Deliverance of St. Peter bw
39:37 D 26 '55
Dante's "Inferno," illustra-
tions bw 15:12-3 D 13 '43
London slum, c1850 bw 4:52
My 23 '38
Lord smiting firstborn of
Egypt bw 4:48 Ap 18 '38
Red Sea closing on Egyptians*
bw 4:48 Ap 18 '38
Satan brooding, illustration
from Milton's "Paradise
Lost" bw 24:76 F 2 '48
The Scottish highlands 7:33 Jy
31 '39
Shipwreck of St. Paul bw 39:
37 D 26 '55
The birth of Christ bw 7:24
D 25 '39 (engravings)
The flood bw 6:47 Ja 16 '39
(engravings)
Moses receiving the Ten Com-
mandments* bw 4:48 Ap 18
'38; 6:53 F 20 '39 (engrav-
ings)
Gustave Dore photog bw 4:11
Ap 18 '38; 30:110 Mr 5 '51
port.
Doric Columns
Acropolis, Athens photog bw
18:56 Ja 1 '45
Propylaea, Acropolis gate-
way, Athens photog bw

18:56 Ja 1 '45

Dos Passos, John
John Dos Passos caricature bw
23:82 S 1 ' 47
John Dos Passos photog bw 17:
14 Ag 14 '44; 24:98 Ja 19
'48
Mr. and Mrs. Dos Passos
photog bw 27:33 Ag 22 '49

Dostoevsky, Feodor
Feodor Dostoevsky bw 14:95
Mr 29 '43

Double portrait (The artist and
his wife). Chagall 22:59 My
5 '47

Doubleday, Abner
Blythe. General Doubleday
crossing the Potomac, 1863
6:29 Je 19 '39

Doubleday, Mrs. Nelson
Koch. Mrs. Doubleday and
children 25:94 O 18 '48

Doughty, Thomas
Landscape and raft 19:84 S 10
'45

Douglas, Lloyd C.
Cornwell. Illustrations for "The
Robe" 23:91-4 D 8 '47
Lloyd Douglas photog bw 20:
109 My 27 '46

Douglas, Stephen A.
Stephen Douglas photog bw 14:
76 F 15 '43; 14:6 My 31 '43;
23:56 N 3 '47

Douglass, Frederick
Frederick Douglass bw 5:51 O
3 '38

Douw, Magdalena (Gansevoort,
Magdalena)
Girl with red shoes, American
primitive 38:115 Ap 18 '55

Dove, Leonard
"New Yorker" cover 21:69, 72
Jy 15 '46

Dove of the Holy Ghost, cathedral,
Moscow photog bw 11:110 O
13 '41

Dove of the Holy Spirit. stained
glass window Loire 38:66
Ap 11 '55

Dove shoot. watercolor Pleissner

21:65 O 7 ' 46

Dover Castle, England photog 26:
54 F 21 '49

Dow, Alden, architect
Contemporary homes: Lewis,
Pardee, and Ball houses;
office building; country
club photogs 3:50, 52 N 15
'37
Modern homes 24:88-92 Mr 15
'48
Architect and his home photog
24:88 Mr 15 '48 port.
Dow, archt. photog bw 3:52
N 15 '37 port.

Down on his luck. bw McCubbin
12:79 F 9 '42

Downe, Viscount
Gainesborough. Viscount
Downe bw 6:58 Mr 27 '39

Downing, Andrew Jackson, architect
"Rustic-pointed" Vassar house
photog bw 7:63 O 2 '39

The Downtown Gallery, New York
City
Artists and their work 31:87
Mr 17 '51

Doyle, Arthur Conan
Conan Doyle collection of
spirit photographs bw 7:8-9,
11 N 13 '39
Sherlock Holmes illustrations
bw 16:77, 79 My 1 '44
memorabilia; coat of arms
bw 16:82 My 1 '44
Sir Arthur Conan Doyle photog
bw 33:62 D 29 '52

Dozier, Otis
Texas jack rabbits* bw 5:30
O 31 '38

Dragons See Animals Imaginery
--Dragons

Drake, Francis
Drake's voyage, map, 1585
18:64 My 21 '45
Queen Elizabeth knighting
Drake bw 32:23 F 18 '52
Sir Francis Drake 41:81 O
29 '56 bw 24:88 Mr 22 '48;
41:65 N 5 '56

Drakenberg, Christian
    Christian Drakenberg print bw
      38:156 Ap 25 '55
Draped figure. bw Carroll 8:71 My
    27 '40
Draped head. sculpture bw Artis
    21:63 Jy 22 '46
Draper, Herbert
    Ulysses and the sirens 23:85 N
      17 '47
Drawer Handle, eagle symbol, U.
    S., c1784 bw 17:56 S 4 '44
Drawing of a girl. bw Maillol 2:
    50 Ja 4 '37
Drawings See also names of
    artists
    Aztec calendar bw 6:29 Ja 23
      '39
    Battle of Buena Vista, Mexican
      War, 1847 bw 22:110-1 Je
      9 '47
    Bellows. The artist's daughter,
      Jean bw 20:78 Mr 25 '46
    Bellows. Dress bw 20:78 Mr
      25 '46
    Bielenberg. Memories of New
      York 10:58 Je 16 '41
    Bingham. County elections bw
      7:43 S 11 '39
    Bingham. Mississippi river
      boatmen bw 28:76 Mr 6 '50
    Bingham. Raftsmen playing
      cards bw 7:40 S 11 '39
    Bingham. Stump speaking bw 7:
      43 S 11 '39
    Bone. Church, Spain bw 1:45
      D 7 '36
    Boucher. Nude 40:70 My 28 '56
    Braque. The artist's mother
      bw 26:82 My 2 '49
    Brueghel, P., the elder. Al-
      chemist's shop bw 22:84 Ap
      7 '47
    Burgis. New York City, 1717
      bw 38:112-4 Ap 18 '55
    Cezanne. Nude bw 32:78 F 25
      '52
    Children's drawings 37:75-6
      D 20 '54
    Colette. self-portrait bw 37:
      83 Ag 16 '54

Dali. Childhood memories of
    Christmas bw 19:8 D 24 '45
Dali. Endless enigma bw 6:45
    Ap 17 '39
Dali. Train* bw 16:18 Mr 6 '44
De Bry. Medieval travel scenes
    bw 24:86-7 Mr 22 '48
Duchamp. Chocolate grinder
    32:103 Ap 28 '52
Duchamp. Coffee grinder 32:
    103 Ap 28 '52
Dufy. Orchestra* bw 36:113 Ap
    26 '54
Eakins. Perspective drawings,
    study for painting bw 16:77
    My 15 '44
Escher. Self-portrait bw 30:
    19 My 7 '51
Execution of Mary Stuart,
    Queen of Scots, Fotheringay
    castle bw 41:150-51 N 5 '56
Gibson. Presentation to the
    King and Queen of England
    bw 23:88-9 N 17 '47
"Harper's Weekly" represen-
    tative illustrations 6:2-4 Ja
    2 '39
Homer. Confederate.pickets
    reconoitering* bw 5:29 O
    31 '38
Homer. West Point hop bw 6:
    2 Ja 2 '39
Ingre. Gown 34:86 My 11 '53
Ingre. Mme Lucien Bonaparte
    34:91, My 11 '53
Ingre. Nicolo Paganini, age
    37 bw 36:128 N 16 '53
Ingre. Slave 34:86 My 11 '53
Jan Six IX bw 31:66 Jy 16 '51
Kollwitz. Ernst Barlach in
    death bw 41:140 N 5 '56
Leonardo da Vinci. Anatomi-
    cal drawings bw 7:16 Jy 17
    '39
Leonardo da Vinci. Basillica
    bw 7:16-8 Jy 17 '39
Leonardo da Vinci. Flying
    machine 39:63 O 3 '55
Maillol. Drawing of a girl
    bw 2:50 Ja 4 '37
Marsh. Television backstage

37:47 Jy 26 '54

Matisse. Madonna and Child bw 36:113 Ap 26 '54

Michelangelo. Avenging angel bw 27:26 D 26 '49

Michelangelo. Figure bw 28:91 Je 26 '50

Middle Ages 22:69 Ap 7 '47

Middleton. Mathematical theory of straight-line drawings bw 8:43-4 Mr 18 '40

Nast. Confederate cavalry raiding Kentucky bw 6:3 Ja 2 '39

Picabia. Gertrude Stein bw 23:15 Ag 18 '47

Picasso. The bathers bw 23:94 O 13 '47

Picasso. Blind beggar bw 38:128 Je 27 '55

Picasso. Centaurs bw 23:97 O 13 '47

Savery. Dodo, sketch from life, 1599 bw 29:171 D 11 '50

Stretcher party bw unknown Marine artist 15:81 D 27 '43

Tchelitchew. Head in a state of rhythm 30:11 Ja 29 '51

Tchelitchew. Interior landscape with muscles 30:10 Ja 29 '51

Tchelitchew. Landscape with trachea 30:10 Ja 29 '51

Toulouse-Lautrec. Couple dancing at Moulin-Rouge bw 28:96 My 15 '50

Toulouse-Lautrec. Dancing clown bw 28:96 My 15 '50

Toulouse-Lautrec. Horses bw 36:110 Ap 26 '54

Toulouse-Lautrec. The jockey bw 28:96 My 15 '50

Utrillo. Place du Tertre, Montmartre bw 28:89 Ja 16 '50

Valadon. Artist's son bw 28:88 Ja 16 '50

Vespucci in Brazil, 17th century bw 37:110 O 11 '54

Whistler, R. Faces, revers-

ible drawing bw 22:22-3 Mr 31 '47

The dream. Rousseau 29:110-1 S 11 '50

Dream world. Wendell 25:101 D 6 '48

Dreiser, Theodore
Theodore Dreiser caricature bw 23:82 S 1 '47
Theodore Drieser photog bw 17:14 Ag 14 '44

Dreisler, Benjamin, architect
Dutch colonial house photog bw 3:15 D 13 '37

Dresden Gallery masterpieces of 16th century art 40:104-13 My 7 '56

Dresden Market, c1750. Bellotto 40:104 My 7 '56

Dressage, steps and tricks engravings, 18th century bw 21:53-5 O 14 '53

Drew, Daniel
Daniel Drew photog bw 30:68 Je 11 '51
Drew in his club* cartoon bw 30:71 Je 11 '51

Drew, John
John Drew photog bw 25:9 Ag 30 '48

Dreyfus, Alfred
Captain Dreyfus, second trial, 1899 bw 13:77 N 16 '42

Dreyfuss, Henry, industrial designer
Perisphere and trylon, World's Fair, New York City, photogs bw 4:11 Ja 31 '38
plan 5:54-7 Ag 1 '38

Driftwood. Homer 2:27 Ja 11 '37

Drinking Horns
Six-quart drinking horn, Anglian, 7th century photog bw 31:82 Jy 16 '51

Driving the golden spike, May 10, 1869. Hill 27:50-1 Jy 4 '49

Dromoland castle, County Clare, Ireland bw 7:62 Jy 24 '39

Drouais, François
  Madame du Barry 23:Cover S
    15 '47
  La marquise D'Aiguirandes
    15:66 S 20 '43
Drouth-stricken area. Hogue 2:
  60 Je 21 '37
Drouth survivors. bw Hogue 2:61
  Je 21 '37
Drowne, Shem
  Weather vane, copper Indian
    38:121 Ap 18 '55
Drugstore. Hopper 28:103 Ap 17
  '50
Drumlevitch, Seymour
  Trellis 39:116-7 S 12 '55
Drums See Musicians and Musi-
  cal Instruments--Drums
"Drums," illustrations. Wyeth,
  N.C. 20:81 Je 17 '46
The drunkard's progress. Cur-
  rier and Ives print bw 20:
  66-7 My 27 '46
Drunkeness of Noah. fresco bw
  Michelangelo 21:64 Jy 1 '46
The dry river. Hurd 7:25 Jy 24
  '39; 21:76 N 25 '46 bw 11:9
  N 17 '41
Drying meat. engraving bw De
  Bry, after Le Moyne 22:85
  Mr 10 '47
Du Barry, Jeanne
  Drouais. Madame du Barry 23:
    Cover S 15 '47
Du Bois, Guy Pene
  Bal des Quatres Arts 26:68-9
    Je 20 '49
  Carnival interlude 8:61 Ap 29
    '40
  Jeanne Eagels in "Rain" 26:67
    Je 20 '49
  The light in the mirror 26:68
    Je 20 '49
  New evidence 26:68 Je 20 '49
  Walkowitz bw 16:79 F 21 '44
  Yvonne, the artist's daughter
    10:47 F 3 '41
  Artist at work photog bw 26:66
    Je 20 '49 port.
  Guy Pene du Bois photogs bw
    8:58 Ap 29 '40 port.

Du Bois, Raoul Pene, theater de-
  signer
  Costumes for ballet, "Ghost
    Town" 8:63 Ap 29 '40
  Set for Aquacade 8:63 Ap 29
    '40
  Raoul Pene du Bois photog bw
    8:59 Ap 29 '40 port.
Du Bois, William Pene, illustra-
  tor
  "The Bear Party" 29:44-9 D
    25 '49
  "The Flying Locomotive" 11:
    86 D 15 '41
  "The Great Geppy" 8:60 Ap 29
    '40
  "Lion" 39:60-2 Jy 25 '55
  William Pene du Bois photog
    bw 8:59 Ap 29 '40 port.
Du Bois, Yvonne Pene
  East River 8:62 Ap 29 '40
  Wanamaker House 8:62 Ap 29
    '40
  Du Bois, G. Yvonne, the art-
    ist's daughter 10:47 F 3 '41
    port.
  Yvonne Pene du Bois photog
    bw 8:58 Ap 29 '40 port.
Dubuffet, Jean
  Firechief 33:96 O 27 '52
  The metro 33:96 O 27 '52
  Pink cow 33:96 O 27 '52
  Smoky black (Lili) 25:23 D 20
    '48
Duccio di Buoninsegna
  The calling of apostles Peter
    and Andrew 39:22 D 26 '55
  Christ and the Samaritan wo-
    man 1:46 D 28 '36
  Resurrection of Lazarus 1:46
    D 28 '36
  Temptation of Christ bw 4:28
    F 7 '38
Duchamp, Marcel
  Apolinere enameled collage
    32:103 Ap 28 '52
  Between the virgin and the
    bride 32:103 Ap 28 '52
  The bride stripped bare by
    her own bachelors, even
    32:103 Ap 28 '52

The bush 32:103 Ap 28 '52

Chess players 32:102 Ap 28 '52

Dr. Raymond Dumouchel 32: 102 Ap 28 '52

The king and queen surrounded by swift runners 32:103 Ap 28 '52

Mona Lisa with mustache 32: 102 Ap 28 '52

Nude descending a staircase 28:60 Ja 2 '50; 32:102 Ap 28 '52 bw 26:89 F 21 '49; 32:100 Ap 28 '52

Rioting at Austerlitz 32:103 Ap 28 '52

Rotator 32:102 Ap 28 '52

To be looked at with one eye, close to, for almost an hour bw 34:26 My 25 '53

To be stared at closely for almost an hour 32:103 Ap 28 '52

Chocolate grinder 32:103 Ap 28 '52 (drawings)

Coffee grinder 32:103 Ap 28 '52 (drawings)

Why not sneeze (Lumps of marble in a cage) 32:103 Ap 28 '52 (object d'art)

Duchamp descending stair photog bw 32:100 Ap 28 '52 port.

Marcel Duchamp photog bw 32: 111 Ap 28 '52; 34:26 My 25 '53; 1912, 28:60 Ja 2 '50 port.

Villon. Marcel Duchamp 32: 101 Ap 28 '52 port.

Ducks

Duck-shaped pitcher, Etruscan, c300 B.C. 40:60 F 13 '56

Jacques. Wild ducks 5:25-8 N 7 '38

Potter. Puddle ducks, illustration for "Tale of Tom Kitten" bw 33:114 D 8 '52

Scott. Mallards in sunshine 1: 41 D 21 '36

Scott. Mallards settling 1:43

D 21 '36

Scott. Tufted drakes diving 1: 42 D 21 '36

Young. Duck and shoat sculpture bw 10:79 F 17 '41

Dude ranch. cartoon bw Emett 37:50 Jy 5 '54

Dudley, Joseph

Governor Dudley bw 17:65 Jy 31 '44

Dudley, Robert

Awaiting the reply 6:30 Je 19 '39

Dufaut, Prefet

Church procession mural 33: 64-5 D 22 '52

Dufy, Raoul

Aphrodite 39:144 N 14 '55

Ball game 30:65 Ja 22 '51

Brooklyn bridge 30:64-5 Ja 22 '51

Charles River 30:65 Ja 22 '51

The great concert bw 34:136 Ap 13 '53

Manhattan 30:66 Ja 22 '51

New York harbor 30:66 Ja 22 '51

New York parade 30:64 Ja 22 '51

Old church, Rockport, Mass. 30:63 Ja 22 '51

Times Square 30:65 Ja 22 '51

Orchestra* bw 36:113 Ap 26 '54 (drawing)

Summer 21:84 S 30 '46 (tapestry)

Theater curtains for "Ring Around the Moon" 30:67 Ja 22 '51 (theater design)

Artist at work photogs bw 30: 62-3 Ja 22 '51 port.

Artist's studio photog bw 34: 135 Ap 13 '53 port.

Mili. Raoul Dufy, age 70 photog 27:89 D 12 '49 port.

Raoul Dufy photog bw 5:72 D 12 '38; 34:136 Ap 13 '53 port.

Duhamel, Georges

Georges Duhamel photog bw 3:65 D 20 '37

Dukes of England: portraits of the present 26 dukes photogs bw 15:100-3 N 15 '43

Dumas, Alexandre, pere
Alexandre Dumas photog bw 25:99 N 22 '48
Dumas and Adah Menken photog bw 31:116 N 19 '51

Dumaurier, Daphne
Daphne Dumaurier; family; English manor, setting for "Manderly" photogs bw 17: 122-5 S 11 '44

Du Mond, Frank Vincent
Frank Du Mond. in group photog 29:172-3 O 16 '50 port.

Dumouchel, Raymond
Duchamp. Dr. Raymond Dumouchel 32:102 Ap 28 '52

Dunbar, Paul
Paul Dunbar, poet bw 5:51 O 3 '38

Duncan, David, photographer
Photographs bw 29:16-7 Jy 24 '50
David Duncan photog bw 29:16 Jy 24 '50 port.

Duncan, Frank
Unicorn bw 22:78 F 17 '47
Condition in New Hampshire 28:86-7 Mr 20 '50

Duncan, Isadora
Steichen. Isadora Duncan in the Parthenon photog bw 28: 121 My 15 '50

Dunes and breakwater. Feininger, Lyonel 31:92-3 N 12 '51

Dunkirk beaches. Eurich 26:43 F 14 '49

Dunlap, William
"School for Scandal" scene, c1810 31:110-1 N 19 '51

Dunois Family shield of arms 22: 69 My 26 '47

Dunscombe, Frances
Gainsborough. The Honorable Frances Dunscombe 3:32 D 27 '37

Dupin, Aurore
Delacroix. George Sand

(Aurore Dupin) 25:98 N 22 '48

Duplessis, Joseph
Benjamin Franklin, 1778 40: 72 Ja 9 '56

Du Pont Museum collection of American arts and crafts, Winterthur, Delaware 38: 68-9 My 30 '55

Durand, Asher Brown
View of Rutland, Vermont 19: 85 S 10 '45
Asher Durand bw 19:82 S 10 '45 port.

Durand-Ruel, Paul
Renoir. Paul Durand-Ruel 32: 98 My 19 '52

Durante, Jimmy
Jimmy Durante, numbered portrait, Palmer portrait kit for children bw 35:105 S 14 '53

Durer, Albrecht
Hieronymus Holzschuher, 1526 bw 19:25 D 31 '45
Madonna and Child with St. Anne 5:40 Jy 11 '38
St. Jerome 34:76 F 23 '53 (etching)
Albrecht Durer bw 5:38 Jy 11 '38 port.
Self-portrait, age 26 31:68 O 1 '51 port.

Duret, Theodore
Whistler. Arrangement in flesh color and black (Theodore Duret) 36:95 My 17 '54 bw 6:54 Mr 20 '39

Durfee, Hazard
Fishermen's wharf 28:87 Mr 20 '50

Durga temple, Madras
Ghandi statue bw 24:29 Ap 5 '48

Durham, Earl of (John George Lambton)
Governor Durham of Canada bw 9:114 S 9 '40

Durst, David
Artist and his work 34:149 My 18 '53 port.

Dust bowl. Hogue 2:60 Je 21 '37
Dust storm. Jones, Joe 8:66 My
    27 '40
Dutch throne, Riddenzaal, The
    Hague photogs bw 3:100-1
    O 18 '37
Du Val d'Ognes, Charlotte David.
    Mlle Charlotte du Val d'Ognes
    5:38 S 26 '38
Duveen, Lord, of Millbank
    Lord Duveen of Millbank
    photog bw 2:40 Je 28 '37
The dwarf. Baziotes 25:63 O 11
    '48 bw 26:84 F 21 '49
Dwarf, tomb painting, Etruscan,
    2nd century B.C. 40:64 F
    13 '56
Dwarves
    Velazquez. Don Baltasar Car-
        los and his dwarf 4:43 My
        16 '38
    Velazquez. The maids of
        honor 7:57 N 20 '39; 31:61
        O 1 '51
Dyer, Mary
    Mary Dyer, c1659 bw 33:97 S
        29 '52
Dymaxion world: map drawn to
    show time scale and direc-
    tion, correct configuration.
    Fuller 14:41-55 Mr 1 '43
Dzerzhinzky, Felix
    Felix Dzerzhinzky photog bw
        31:115 O 29 '51

E
The Eads Bridge over the Mis-
    sissippi. mural Bouche 11:
    50 Ag 18 '41
Eagels, Jeanne
    Du Bois, F. Jeanne Eagels in
        "Rain" 26:67 Je 10 '49
Eagles see also Emblems and
    Decorations
    Audubon. Golden eagle 3:40 Jy
        12 '37
    Eagle wood carving 35:48 Jy 6
        '53
    Eagle and pines. Kano school,
        Japan, 17th century 31:66-
        7 D 31 '51

"Old Abe," mascot of 8th Wis-
    consin Regiment, U.S.
    Civil War bw 39:186 S 12
    '55
    Peterson. Bald eagles 21:51-4
        Jy 1 '46
Eakins, Thomas
    Addie (Mary Adeline Williams)
        41:160 D 24 '56
    The Agnew clinic 16:75 My 15
        '44
    Between rounds 16:76 My 15
        '44
    The cello player (Rudolph
        Henning) 16:75 My 15 '44
    The concert singer 16:74 My
        15 '44
    The Fairman Rogers four-in-
        hand 16:74 My 15 '44
    Henry A. Rowland 12:60 Je
        15 '42
    Max Schmitt in a single scull
        bw 5:33 O 31 '38; 16:72 My
        15 '44
    Mrs. William D. Frishmuth
        16:75 My 15 '44
    Professionals at rehearsal
        16:74 My 15 '44
    Shad fishing at Gloucester,
        New Jersey 16:73 My 15
        '44
    Swimming hole 38:72 Mr 28
        '55
    Turning the stake boat 15:68
        S 20 '43
    Walt Whitman, 1887 9:45 Jy
        29 '40 bw 6:31 Je 19 '39
    William Rush carving his alle-
        gorical figure of the Schuy-
        kill river 16:73 My 15 '44
        bw 5:29 O 31 '38
    Perspective drawing, study
        for sculling painting bw 16:
        77 My 15 '44 (drawing)
Eakins, S. Thomas Eakins at
    work bw 16:72 My 15 '44
    port.
Thomas Eakins photog bw 5:
    29 O 31 '38 port.
Eames, Charles, architect and
    designer

Eames, Charles (cont.)
  The designer's house photogs
    bw 29:148-9 S 11 '50 (archi-
    tecture)
  Armless "shell" chairs bw 28:
    98-9 My 8 '50 (furniture
    design)
  Furniture: chairs, tables bw
    25:118 N 15 '48 (furniture
    design)
  Molded plywood chair bw 29:
    152 S 11 '50 (furniture de-
    sign)
  Molded plywood resilient chair
    bw 20:49 My 20 '46 (furni-
    ture design)
  Cardboard construction toy bw
    29:151 S 11 '50 (toy design)
  Punch-out color cards 39:121
    O 17 '55 (toy design)
  Charles Eames photog bw 25:
    118 N 15 '48; 29:148-9 S 11
    '50 port.
Earl, Ralph
  Roger Sherman 38:64 My 30
    '55
Early Christian Art See also
    Art, Byzantine
  Christ blessing an apostle
    fresco bw, Rome, 4th cen-
    tury 40:148 Ap 23 '56
  Dancing figures fresco, c300
    28:76 Mr 27 '50
Early Sunday morning. Hopper
    27:62 Ag 29 '49
Earrings See Jewelry
East river. Du Bois, Y. 8:62
    Ap 29 '40
East River Drive. Weinstock 16:
    45 Ja 3 '44
Easter Eggs
  Russian jewelled easter eggs
    photogs 6:5 Ap 3 '39
Easter Island bird man wood
    carving bw 21:80 N 4 '46
Easter Island stone head bw 21:
    80 N 4 '46; 24:126 F 23 '48
Eastman, George
  George Eastman, 1879 photog
    bw 28:103 F 13 '50
Eaton, Myrwyn

Landscape with willows 16:45
    Ja 3 '44
Eau Claire, Wisconsin, amateur
    artists bw 34:151 My 18
    '53
Eber, Elk
  Custer's letzte Schlacht bw
    24:13 Je 21 '48
Ecce Home. bw Goerstchacher
    9:108-9 D 2 '40
Ecce Homo tapestry, Flemish,
    15th century bw 5:48 N 28
    '38
Economic activities in the days
    of the Naragansett planters.
    mural Baker 10:44 Ja 27
    '41
The ectatic one. sculpture
    Barlach 41:138 N 5 '56
The edge of the commons. Crome
    5:43 S 12 '38
Edinburgh castle, Scotland
    photog 40:88 Mr 19 '56
    bw 22:100-1 My 5 '47
Edison, Thomas Alva
  Brady. Thomas Alva Edison
    with phonograph, 1877
    photog bw 33:88 N 17 '52
  Thomas Edison photog bw 2:
    31 My 31 '37
Edmondson, William, sculptor
  Martha and Mary bw 3:79 N
    1 '37
  Mourning dove bw 3:79 N 1 '37
  William Edmondson photog bw
    3:79 N 1 '37 port.
Edward I, King of England
  Edward I, plaque, U.S.
    Capitol bw 30:74 F 5 '51
  Edward I accepts surrender
    of King John of Baliol,
    1296* bw 30:21 Ja 8 '51
  Parliament called by Edward
    I* bw 22:81 My 26 '47
Edward IV, King of England
  Edward IV bw 40:194 Ap 9
    '56
Edward VII, King of England
  Beerbohm. The rare and
    rather awful visits of
    Albert Edward...to

Windsor cartoon bw 23:75
N 17 '47

Edward VII photog bw 23:72 O
20 '47

Edward and wife, Alexandra
photog bw 23:74-7 N 17 '47

Edward VII reviewing troops,
1903* 23:82-3 N 17 '47

Fildes. Edward VII of England
35:82 N 23 '53

Edward, The Confessor
Coronation of St. Edward* bw
2:45 Mr 15 '37

Edward, the confessor, signa-
ture seal portrait bw 40:107
Mr 19 '56

Tomb of Edward, the confessor, Westminster photog bw
40:108 Mr 19 '56

Edwardian belle. sculpture bw,
Hudson Valley, 1890 10:121
Ap 21 '41

Edwards, Beaver, sculptor
Helmet designed for U.S.
Navy anti-aircraft gunners
bw 13:82-3 Ag 10 '42

Edward Beaver photog bw 13:
82-3 Ag 10 '42   port.

Eel spearing at Setauket. Mount
18:66 Je 25 '45

Eeyore, Donkey. illustration bw
Shepard 30:76 F 19 '51

Effingham, Charles
Lord Howard of Effingham 41:
81 O 29 '56

Egg plants. Gischia 17:76 N 13
'44

Eggbeater no. 5. Davis, S.
22:79 F 17 '47

Eggers, Otto, architect
Pope, Eggers, and Higgins.
Jefferson memorial, Wash-
ington, D.C. photog 23:49
Jy 7 '47 bw 14:Cover Ap 12
'43

Egypt See also Gods and
Goddesses
Dice, c30 B.C. bw 6:53 Mr 20
'39

Egyptian figure fresco 28:77
Mr 27 '50

Emblems of fourth dynasty:
Upper Egypt--vulture;
Lower Egypt--cobra bw 41:
94 O 1 '56

Pottery and stone dishes c1550
B.C. photogs bw 5:55 Ag
15 '38

Throne, contemporary photog
bw 3:18 Ag 23'37

Tomb art: fishing boat model
2000 B.C. bw 6:51 Mr 20
'39

Egyptian girl. Sargent 36:97 My
17 '54

Ehninger, John
Yankee peddler 6:29 Je 19 '39

Eichenberg, Fritz, wood engrav-
er
"Jane Eyre" illustrations bw
15:100-1 N 29 '43
"Wuthering Heights" illustrations bw 15:102-3 N 29 '43
Self-portrait wood engraving
bw 15:4 D 20 '43 port.

Eiffel Tower, Paris
Chagall. Homage to the Fiffel
Tower 22:58 My 5 '47
Eiffel Tower photogs 8:63 Je
3 '40

Eight bells. Homer 12:60 Je 15
'42

Eilshemius, Louis Michel
Delaware Water Gap village
7:51 N 6 '39
Seated figure bw 7:51 N 6 '39
Louis Eilshemius photog bw
7:50 N 6 '39 port.

Einstein, Albert
Albert Einstein photog bw 28:
23 Ja 9 '50
Epstein. Albert Einstein bust
bw 33:70 N 3 '52
Ljungdahl. Albert Einstein
photog 4:48 Ap 11 '38

Eisenhower, Dwight
Adobe building 28:151 Ap 17
'50
Bobby Jones 34:74 Mr 23 '53
Grandson David 28:151 Ap
17 '50

Eisenhower, Dwight (cont.)
Mamie Eisenhower, 1951 bw
33:155 O 13 '52
Mount Eisenhower bw 26:44 F
21 '49
Sun Valley scene 28:151 Ap 17
'50
Artist at work: painting Colo-
rado landscape 33:41 Ag 18
'52 port.
Biddle. General Dwight D.
Eisenhower drawing bw 16:
14 Ja 3 '44 port.
Dwight D. Eisenhower photog
34:74 Mr 23 '53 port.
Stephens, T. E. General of
the Army Dwight D. Eisen-
hower 29:92 N 6 '50 port.
"Time" cover portrait 17:83
D 11 '44 port.
Eisenhower, Mamie
Eisenhower, D. Mamie Eisen-
hower, 1951 bw 33:155 O 13
'52
Eisenstaedt, Alfred, photographer
Augustus John bw 32:10 Ja 14
'52
Oswald Veblen bw 24:15 My 10
'48
Portfolio of 18 distinguished
Britons bw 31:94-103 Ja 14
'52
Walter W. Stewart bw 24:15
My 10 '48
El Greco (Domenico Theotoco-
puli)
The agony in the garden bw
28:92 Ap 24 '50
The assumption of the Virgin
11:54 S 8 '41; 28:90 Ap 24
'50; 29:50 O 30 '50
The burial of Count Orgaz 28:
94 Ap 24 '50
Don Fernando Nino de Guevara,
cardinal and archbishop of
Seville 28:93 Ap 24 '50
The holy family 15:65 S 20 '43
The opening of the fifth seal
28:87 Ap 24 '50
The penitent Magdalene 7:55
O 9 '39 bw 6:58 Mr 27 '39

Portrait of a knight 31:70 O 1
'51
St. Bartholomew 39:77 Ag 8
'55
St. Jerome 37:64 Ag 9 '54
St. Jerome as a cardinal 3:31
D 27 '37
St. Jude bw 39:77 Ag 8 '55
St. Martin and the beggar 33:
91 O 27 '52
St. Paul bw 39:78 Ag 8 '55
St. Simon bw 39:77 Ag 8 '55
The trinity 31:72 O 1 '51
View and plan of Toledo 28:
88-9 Ap 24 '50
View of Toledo 4:41 My 16 '38
The Virgin with Santa Ines
and Santa Tecla 7:26 D 25
'39
El Greco bw 4:40 My 16 '38
port.
Manuel. Members of El Gre-
co's family bw 28:96 Ap 24
'50 port.
Self-portrait, age 68 bw 28:
86 Ap 24 '50 port.
El Kharj palace, Saudi Arabia
photog bw 14:77 My 31 '43
El Khazna, The Treasury,
ruined temple, Petra,
Trans-Jordan photog 27:67
O 31 '49
Elder, John
Custer's last fight bw 24:12
Ja 21 '48
Eleanor of Aquitaine, Consort of
Henry II, King of England
Eleanor of Aquitaine effigy
bw 22:73 My 26 '47
Eleanor of Aquitaine head,
capital, French, 12th cen-
tury bw 40:107 Mr 26 '56
Elections
Bingham. County election 7:
42 S 11 '39 drawings bw
7:43 S 11 '39
Bingham. Verdict of the
people 5:32 O 31 '38; 16:
54 Mr 13 '44; 31:96 N 5
'51
Election of Stanislaus II king

of Poland, 1764* bw 17:86
Ag 28 '44
Faulkner. Oregon settlers
voting mural 7:44 Ag 14 '39
Rogers. Challenging the union
vote sculpture bw 6:6 Mr 6
'39
Village election, China wood-
cut bw 18:60 Ap 9 '45
Women voting in New Jersey,
c1800* print bw 16:45 Ja
31 '44
Electric night. Tobey 35:85 S 28
'53
Electrification. mural, post office, Lenoir City, Tenn.
Martin, D.S. 10:44 Ja 27
'41
Elements of reconstruction. Di-
ego 20:82 Mr 11 '46
Elephants
Brueghel, P., the elder. Ele-
phants, detail from Adora-
tion of the Magi 37:34 D 27
'54
Curry. Circus elephants 1:31
N 23 '36 bw 15:19 N 29 '43
Ernst. The elephant Celebes
1:27 D 14 '36
The giraffe parade tapestry,
Flemish, c1525 24:76-7 Mr
22 '48
Wright. "How the Elephant got
its Trunk" sculpture bw 29:
122 Ag 28 '50
Eleventh Avenue flapper. sculp-
ture bw Wickey 12:54 F 23
'42
Elgin, Thomas Bruce, 7th earl of
Lord Elgin, preserver of the
Elgin marbles bw 35:160 O
26 '53
Elgin marbles bw 35:152-62 O 26
'53
Elgius, Saint
Christus. St. Elgius and St.
Bodeberta 37:65 Ag 9 '54
Elgstroem, Ossian
Eskimo myths and legends 20:
8-10 Ja 14 '46
Eliasberg (Louis) coin collection--

sample U.S. and foreign
coins 34:114-6 Ap 27 '53
Elijah fed by the ravens.
Allston 19:84 S 10 '45
Elinor, Jean and Anna. Bellows
11:77 O 6 '41
Elizabeth See Russell, Eliza-
beth Mary
Elizabeth, Saint
Leighton. St. Elizabeth 23:84
N 17 '47
Elizabeth, Consort of Franz
Joseph, Emperor of Aus-
tro-Hungary
Elizabeth bw 2:14 Mr 22 '37
Elizabeth, Consort of George
VI, King of England
Elizabeth photog bw 23:72 O
20 '47
Elizabeth I, Queen of England
Elizabeth 41:145 N 5 '56
The dying queen* Flemish 41:
172 N 5 '56
Elizabeth knighting Drake*
bw 32:23 F 18 '52
Queen and Parliament* engra-
ving bw 41:170 N 5 '56
Queen Elizabeth, standing on
map of England 24:81 Mr
22 '48
Queen Elizabeth and Earl of
Leicester dancing a lavol-
ta* 41:148 N 5 '56
Queen Elizabeth honoring a
wedding 41:148 N 5 '56
Young Elizabeth bw 32:23 F
18 '52
Elizabeth II, Queen of England
Annigoni. Elizabeth II, Queen
of England 38:93 My 30 '55
Beaton. Queen Elizabeth pho-
tog 40:89 Ja 30 '56
Chandor. Elizabeth II of Eng-
land 35:83 N 23 '53
Elizabeth II photog bw 23:72
O 20 '47
Ellery, William
William Ellery bw 15:8 Jy 5
'43
Elliott, C. L.
Mathew Brady bw 6:31 Je

Elliott, C. L. (cont.)
19 '39

Ellis, Dean
Fragments from yesterday
28:86 Mr 20 '50

Elman, Mischa
Mischa Elman, age 15 photog
bw 33:98 N 17 '52

"Eloise," illustrations. Knight
39:149 D 12 '55

Elphanta Caves, Bombay, India
Aspects of the god Shiva
sculpture 38:62 F 7 '55

Elsinore castle, Denmark photog
bw 2:74 Je 28 '37

Elting, Winston, architect
Scheiker and Elting. Suburban
house plan, photogs 22:78-
81 Ap 28 '47

Elves
Carnival and advertising figures 37:34 D 20 '54

Elwell, Fred
I dreamt St. Peter sat for his
portrait bw 22:40 My 19
'47

Elysian Fields
Benjamin Franklin crowns
Mirabeau print 40:80 Ja 9
'56
Watteau. The elysian fields
23:84 S 15 '47

Elysian Fields amusement park*
Hoboken, N.J. 32:117 Ap
7 '52

Embarkation for Cytherea.
Watteau 23:84 S 15 '47 bw
19:50 Jy 30 '45

Embarkation of the pilgrims
from Southampton, 1620.
Moran, Edward 13:75 N 23
'42 bw 24:68-9 Je 14 '48

Embassy Buildings, U.S.
Harrison and Abramovitz.
U.S. embassy, Rio de Ja-
niero photogs 34:45 Je 22
'53
Kerrigan, Edward and Leland
King. U.S. embassy,
Brussels photogs bw 34:
47 Ap 20 '53

Emblems and Decorations
See also Crowns; Flags;
Heraldry; Maces

Bath, order of 26:73 F 7 '49

Belgian Dinasos: fascist--cog,
sword, plow bw 4:38 Mr
14 '38

Brazil: winged lion sculpture
bw 10:61 Ja 6 '41

Buddhist wheel of life, China
8:32-3 Ja 8 '40

Buddhist wheel of the law 38:
57 F 7 '55; 38:81 Mr 7 '55

Chines cosmic forces: yang
and yin 38:57 F 7 '55; 38:
69 Ap 4 '55 bw 24:131 F
23 '48

Christian cross 38:57 F 7 '55
Pierro della Francesca.
Story of the true cross
fresco 20:60-8 Ap 22 '46

Christian key of St. Peter,
16th century 32:85 Ap 14
'52

Dalai Lama, Tibet: thunderbolt crest photog bw 36:83
F 22 '54

Egypt, fourth dynasty: Upper
Egypt--vulture; Lower
Egypt--cobra photog bw
41:94 O 1 '56

England: Royal emblems--
crowns, orb, ampulla, a-
nointing spoon, St. George's
spurs, coronation ring,
staff, sceptre, royal plate
photogs 2:37-42 Mr 15 '37

England: World War emblems
Chad bw 20:17 Mr 18 '46
"V" for victory, photogra-
phy contest bw 11:10-3
N 24 '41

Garter, order of 26:73 F 7
'49 Great George, dia-
mond and gold encrusted
26:72 F 7 '49; 35:74 N 23
'53

German nazi swastika, 1939
photog bw 9:68 Ag 19 '40

Golden fleece, order of 26:
73 F 7 '49

Hinduism: sacred word "OM"
38:57 F 7 '55

India: Star of India photog bw
16:62 Ja 24 '44

Islam: creed of the one God
38:57 F 7 '55

Italy Fasces: fascist symbol,
Mussolini's office, Rome
photog bw 2:57 Ap 5 '37

Judaism: Star of David 38:57
F 7 '55

New York World's Fair, 1939:
trylon and perisphere
photog bw 4:11 Ja 31 '38

"New Yorker" magazine: trade
mark--Irvin. Eustace Til-
ley 21:68 Jy 15 '46

Olympic games: sacred torch
of Greece, five linked rings
photog 41:150-1 N 26 '56

Poland: eagle bw 17:96 Ag 28:
44 eagles and horsemen,
grill, Cracow bw 17:84 Ag
28 '44

white eagles of Poland,
ironwork bw 5:54 Ag 29 '38

Poland nazi symbol: 14-cogged
wheel bw 8:13 Je 17 '40

Russia: double-headed eagle,
adopted 1472 by Ivan III 18:
50 Ja 29 '45

Scotland: clan tartans 22:103
My 5 '47

Spain Falangist: fascist--5
yoked arrows photog bw 3:
101 N 1 '37; 31:63 Ag 27 '51

Ties: old school ties, 32 English schools 8:73-4 Je 3 '40

Ukraine: official seal bw 21:
121 O 28 '46

United Nations bw 33:115 N 3
'52

Ur: Royal standard of Ur mosaic 40:90-1 Je 4 '56

Victor Company: trade mark--
Barraud. His master's
voice bw 33:92 N 17 '52

United States
Federal eagle woodcarving 31:
68 Jy 2 '51; 38:63 Ja 3 '55

Bellamy eagle figurehead,
from frigate, Lancaster
38:Cover Ap 18 '55

McIntire. American eagle
woodcarving 38:63 My
30 '55

Rush. American eagle woodcarving bw, 1838 5:27 O
31 '38

Great seal of the U.S.A.
Bald eagle bw 21:50 Jy 1 '46
Proposed designs, design
adopted 1782 drawings
bw 38:72 My 30 '55

Independence symbols
Eagle, pine tree, liberty
pole and cap in Colum-
bia 31:69 Jy 2 '51
Federal eagles and flag:
furniture, glassware
and ceramics, wood
carvings, wall paper,
c1784 17:56-60 S 4 '44
Revere. Nine-segment
snake, symbol of colo-
nies cartoon bw 38:56
My 30 '55

State birds
Peterson. Birds of 48
states 8:58-9, 61-2 Je
17 '40

State flags
Flags of 48 states 15:77-
82 D 6 '43

Uncle Sam
Cartoons showing evolution
of "Uncle Sam" bw 41:
22-3, 24 Jy 2 '56

Emblems of peace. Harnett 7:25
Ag 28 '39

The embrace. Nunes 36:81 My
31 '54

Embroidery See also Tapestry;
Textiles

Mary, Consort of George V,
King of England. Needle-
point rug, 1948 28:95 My
8 '50

Moore. Richardson memori-
al 39:63 Ag 29 '55

Embroidery (cont.)
  Strawberry Hill, home of
    Horace Walpole needlepoint
    bw 17:118 O 23 '44
Embry, Lloyd
  Artist at work photog bw 41:77
    Ag 13 '56 port.
The emerald coast. Feininger,
    Lux 31:94-5 N 12 '51
Emerging from a gorge under
    sail. bw Chiang Kai-Shek
    33:8 O 13 '52
Emerson, Ralph Waldo
  Emerson's home; memorabilia
    photog bw 9:94-5 O 14 '40
Emett, Rowland, cartoonist
  An answer to Yorktown, series
    of American scenes 37:
    Cover, 42-53 Jy 5 '54
  Preparation for coronation of
    Elizabeth II, of England
    34:92-4 Ap 27 '53
  "Punch," cartoons from bw 15:
    6-8 Ag 2 '43
Emigrant train. Colman 6:29 Je
    19 '39
Emigrant train. bw Ranney 27:40
    Jy 4 '49
Emma and her children. Bellows
    11:77 O 6 '41
Emmaus See Jesus Christ--
    Emmaus
Emmons, Alice P.
  Alice P. Emmons bw 38:83 F
    28 '55
Emmwood See Wood, John
    Musgrave
The empty chair (Dicken's study)
    drawing bw Fildes 25:84 D
    27 '48
Enamels
  Barovier. Decorated glass
    wedding cup, Venetian, 15th
    century 37:55 Ag 2 '54
  Italian gold and enamel cross,
    showing scenes of Christ's
    life c600 32:83 Ap 14 '52
  Mumtaz Mahal's marriage cup,
    Limoge silver and enamel,
    France, 17th century 25:129
    D 6 '48
  Moorish cloisonne necklace,
    gold filigree, c1340 bw 9:
    94 D 9 '40
  Persian gold and enamel plate
    33:43 D 29 '52
  Rospigliosi cup. bw Cellini 6:
    53 Mr 20 '39; 31:26 O 15
    '51
  Sacred reliquary, France,
    13th century bw 6:52 Mr 20
    '39
  Stiegel enamelled tumbler,
    U.S. 39:58 Jy 18 '55
  Tabernacle, jewelled and
    enamelled gold, 1403 33:32
    D 29 '52
  Venetian goblet, enamelled,
    c1475 bw 23:50 Ag 4 '47
  Zadok collection of chalices
    bw 32:77 Ja 14 '52
Encampment of the travellers.
    Bodmer 15:88 Ag 30 '43
End of the day. Sepeshy 20:80
    F 18 '46
Endecott, John
  John Endecott bw 13:74 N 23
    '42
Endless enigma. bw Dali 6:45 Ap
    17 '39 drawings bw 6:45 Ap
    17 '39
Endless house, egg shaped model
    and plan. bw Kiesler 32:
    82 My 26 '52
Enemy action. bw Hurd 14:7 Je
    28 '43
Enesco, Georges
  Karsh. Georges Enesco photog
    bw 37:135 O 4 '54
Engels, Friedrich
  Friedrich Engels photog bw
    25:64 O 18 '48
England
  Arming of Henry V, illumina-
    tion from "Book of Hours,"
    15th century 40:178 Ap 9
    '56
  Bohrod. England in World
    War 18:47-55 Ap 30 '45
  British Empire victories,
    1588-1915 bw 6:70-1 S
    25 '39

Churchill's "History of the English-Speaking Peoples," illustrated by paintings, prints, and other arts--excerpts v. 40 and 41: Mr 19, 26; Ap 2, 9; O 29; N 5, 12, 19

Country houses, 14th, 16th, 18th centuries 19:100-6 O 29 '45

Davis, F. England at war: London and other scenes 16:65-8 Ap 3 '44

Dukes of England: portraits of 26 present dukes photogs bw 15:100-3 N 15 '43

Emblems: Arms of England 22:69 My 26 '47

Emblems: Royal emblems -- crowns, orb, ampulla, anointing spoon, St. George's spurs, coronation ring, staff, sceptre, royal plate photogs 2:37-42 Mr 15 '37

Emblems: World War Chad bw 20:17 Mr 18 '46 "V" for victory, photography contest bw 11:10-3 N 24 '41

"Historia Anglorum," 13th century illuminations 40: 98 Mr 26 '56

Literary England--locale and landmarks photogs bw 14: 77-83 Je 14 '43

Old School ties, 32 schools 8: 73-4 Je 3 '40

Queens of England: portraits of 7 reigning queens bw 32: 22-4 F 18 '52

Salisbury. Royal family and nobility in Silver jubilee at St. Paul's 28:68-9 My 29 '50

Seven bishops imprisoned by James II, England* bw 41: 180 N 19 '56

Thomas. Wartime England 17: 57-66 O 9 '44

Wilkie. Knox harangues Mary, Queen of Scots 24:66 Je 14 '48

William and Mary driving out James II, England bw 41: 184 N 19 '56

Zoffany. Famous Englishmen of the 18th century in The tribune 25:104-5 S 13 '48

England's royal lion. sculpture Hardiman 2:Cover, 43 Ja 23 '37

Engravings See also Goldsmithing; Jewelry

Anna Seward bw 35:91 S 28 '53

Battles of American Revolution by contemporary artists 29:39-41 Jy 3 '50

Birch. State House, Philadelphia, 1799 39:61 Jy 4 '55

Blake. God creating Adam bw 6:45 Ja 16 '39

Blake. God creating Eve bw 6:45 Ja 16 '39

Blake. God creating the world bw 6:44 Ja 16 '39

De Bry. Deer hunt, after Le Moyne bw 22:85 Mr 10 '47

De Bry. Dring meat, after Le Moyne bw 22:85 My 10 '47

Doolittle. Marching into Concord 29:41 Jy 3 '50

Doolittle. On Lexington Green 29:40 Jy 3 '50

Dore. Birth of Christ bw 7: 24 D 25 '39

Dore. The flood bw 6:47 Ja 16 '39

Dore. Moses receiving the Ten Commandments* bw 4:48 Ap 18 '38; 6:53 F 20 '39

Dressage, steps and tricks, 18th century bw 21:53-5 O 14 '53

Fanny Kemble in "Romeo and Juliet" 31:110 N 19 '51

Feast of the Passover bw 6: 55 Ja 30 '39

Fourth of July, Philadelphia, 1876 bw 25:49 Jy 5 '49

Engravings (cont.)
 Glass blowers, New Jersey
  39:59 Jy 18 '55
 Honora Sneyd bw 35:91 S 28
  '53
 Lucas van Leyden. Adam and
  Eve bw 6:46 Ja 16 '39
 Lucas van Leyden. Cain and
  Abel bw 6:46 Ja 16 '39
 Lutherbaum, c1800 35:154 S
  21 '53
 Major John Andre 35:91 S 28
  '53
 Martin, J. Parting of the Red
  Sea* bw 38:98-9 Je 13 '55
 Momberger. Wooding up on
  the Mississippi 28:73 Mr 6
  '50
 Pelton, O. Poor Richard bw
  40:74-5 Ja 9 '56
 The people, 1887* bw 16:46 Ja
  17 '44
 Philadelphia, Market (High)
  Street 40:77 Ja 9 '56
 Revere. Boston Massacre,
  March 5, 1770 29:39 Jy 3
  '50
 Romans. Bunker Hill 29:41 Jy
  3 '50
 Samuel Johnson, portrait in
  "Dictionary," 1785, from
  Reynold's painting bw 38:
  166 My 2 '55
 Schnorr. Biblical illustrations
  bw 6:55 Ja 30 '39; 6:53 F
  20 '39
 Theater history, U.S. bw 31:
  110-20 N 19 '51
 Walt Whitman, age 36 bw 38:
  113 Je 20 '55
The enigma of Hitler. Dali 6:44
 Ap 17 '39 bw 19:65 S 24 '45
Enjoying snow scene. bw Chiang
 Kai-Shek 33:8 O 13 '52
Enkyo bridge. woodcut Hiroshige
 31:67 D 31 '51
Entombment of Christ See Jesus
 Christ--Entombment
Epernou, Duke of
 Van Dyck. Charles I, King of
  England, accompanied by

 Duke of Epernou 41:189 N
  12 '56
Epiphany at Bethlehem, Connec-
 ticut. Ford 17:38-9 D 25
 '44
Epping, Franc
 Scrubwoman sculpture bw 7:37
  Jy 17 '39
Epstein, Jacob, sculptor
 Adam bw 33:66 N 3 '52
 Albert Einstein bust bw 33:70
  N 3 '52
 Consummatum est (It is fin-
  ished) bw 3:88 N 15 '37;
  33:68 N 3 '52
 Genesis bw 3:92 N 15 '37
 J.B. Priestley bw 3:90 N 15 '37
 Judith Margulies bust bw 33:
  66 N 3 '52
 Lucifer bw 33:66 N 3 '52
 Mother and child bw 6:83 My
  22 '39
 Nerenska bw 3:90 N 15 '37
 Professor Franz Boas bw 3:
  90 N 15 '37
 Rita bw 3:90 N 15 '37
 Rosemary bw 3:90 N 15 '37
 Sally Ryan bw 3:90 N 15 '37
 Social consciousness bw 33:
  65 N 3 '52
 Artist at work photog bw 33:
  65-6 N 3 '52 port.
Equestrians See also Godiva,
 Lady; Horses; Hunters and
 Hunting
 Ataturk, sculpture bw, An-
  kara 8:76 Ap 8 '40
 Battle of Blenheim Brussel's
  tapestry 24:34-5 Ap 19 '48
 "Book of Hours" of the Duc
  de Berry 24:38-50 Ja 5 '48
 Brueghel, P., the elder.
  Horsemen, detail in Mas-
  sacre of the innocent 35:
  34 D 27 '54
 Callahan. The search 35:86
  S 28 '53
 The circuit rider bw 39:78
  D 26 '55
 Daumier. Don Quixote 40:
  74-5 My 28 '56

Degas. Jockey on race horse*
wax sculpture 39:121 O 31
'55

Dressage, steps and tricks,
18th century bw 21:53-5 O
14 '53

El Greco. St. Martin and the
beggar 33:91 O 27 '52

Elysian Field's amusement
park,* Hoboken, N.J. 32:
117 Ap 7 '52

General Andrew Jackson e-
questrian statue, Independence, Kansas (copy of Kansas City statue) 39:89 O 3
'55

General Lee memorial,
Gettysburg, Va. bw 4:35
Je 27 '38

General Zachary Taylor bw
22:116 Je 9 '47

Gericault. Officer of the imperial guard 35:62 Ag 17
'53

Hurd. Landscape with polo
players 7:26 Jy 24 '39

Knight and horse armor,
German, 15th century pho-
tog 40:184-5 Ap 9 '56

Lee, D. The runaway bw 3:47
S 20 '37

Lieutenant Ulysses S. Grant,
Mexican War, 1847 22:119
Je 9 '47

Marini. Horse and rider lithograph 33:85 Jy 14 '52
sculpture bw 22:102 My 22
'50

Martorell. St. George killing
the dragon 33:91 O 27 '52

Melicov. Girl on a horse
sculpture bw 5:5 N 7 '38

Miller. A Sioux on the warpath 36:78-9 Mr 8 '54

Milles. Folke Filbyter sculpture bw 2:32 F 22 '37

Mills. Andrew Jackson equestrian statue bw 19:10 S 24
'45

Palmer. Once around the ring
22:97 Ap 21 '47

Parthenon sculptures bw 35:
154-5 O 26 '53

Paul Revere sculpture bw 18:
66 Ja 15 '45

Puget. Alexander the Great
on his horse, Bucephalus,
riding over foes bw 39:86
N 14 '55

Ranney. Retreat 27:42 Jy 4
'49

Raphael. St. George and the
dragon 33:37 D 29 '52

Rembrandt. The Polish rider
3:36 D 27 '37

Remington. Bronco buster
sculpture bw 13:72 S 14 '42

Remington. Cavalry charge
on the southern plains 13:
76 S 14 '42

Remington. Cheyenne sculpture bw 13:72 S 14 '42

Remington. Cowboy bw 5:29
O 31 '38

Remington. The discovery 36:
77 Mr 8 '54

Remington. Fired on 9:77 D
9 '40

Remington. The outlaw sculpture bw 13:72 S 14 '42

Remington. The rattlesnake
sculpture bw 13:72 S 14
'42

Remington. The scalp sculpture bw 13:72 S.14 '42

Ryder. Death on a pale horse
5:36 O 31 '38; 15:67 S 20
'43

St. Acacius santo, woodcarving bw 24:58 My 17 '48

Saint-Gaudens. General
Sherman bw 24:109 Mr 15
'48

Sully. Washington at Trenton
29:Cover Jy 3 '50

Van Dyck. Charles I, King
of England, accompanied
by Duke of Epernou 41:
189 N 12 '56

Velazquez. Don Baltasar
Carlos 31:71 O 1 '51

Washington on his white horse
woodcarving, U.S., mid-
19th century 31:69 Jy 2 '51
Will Rogers statue bw, Fort
Worth 28:25 Ja 23 '50
William Henry Harrison statue
bw, Cincinnati, Ohio 38:91
Mr 28 '55
Wimar. Indians pursued by
American dragoons 27:43
Jy 4 '49
Young. Pony express sculp-
ture bw 10:79 F 17 '41
Equinox. sculpture bw Lipton 29:
150 S 18 '50
Erasmus, Desiderius
Erasmus bw 24:60 Je 14 '48
Holbein. Erasmus bw 16:66
Ja 10 '44
Erechtheum, Athens photog bw
18:57 Ja 1 '45
Ericson, Lief
Lief Ericson statue bw, Ice-
land 8:21 Ap 22 '40
Ericsson, John
John Ericsson bw 39:113 O 17
'55
Eridu pottery, neolithic photog
40:81 Ap 16 '56
Erma. Bernatschke 10:47 F 3
'41
Ernst, Jimmy
Jimmy Ernst photog bw 30:34
Ja 15 '51 port.
Ernst, Max
Above the clouds walks the
moonlight montage bw 34:
25 My 25 '53
Collage bw 25:163 N 8 '48
The elephant Celebes 1:27 D
14 '36
"Microbe" paintings: small-
size surrealist pictures 32:
58-9 Ja 21 '52
Woman, old man and flower
bw 19:64 S 24 '45
Monsters bw 32:61 Ja 21 '52
(sculpture)
Max Ernst photog bw 5:72 D
12 '38; 32:58, 61-2 Ja 21
'52 port.

Erwitt, Elliott
Elliott Erwitt photog 38:133 F
14 '55
Esau selling his birthright.
Murillo 41:73 D 10 '56
Escher, Maurits
Self-portrait drawing bw 30:
19 My 7 '51
Escardivol, Montserrat
Typewriter "paintings" 35:10-
2 Jy 20 '53
Esherick, Joseph, architect
Grill home, Oakland 27:51 S
5 '49
Esherick, William
Oblivion sculpture bw 9:54 Ag
12 '40
Eskimo figures stone carving
bw 36:67-9 My 24 '54
Eskimo myths and legends. Elg-
struem 20:8-10 Ja 14 '46
Espalargues, Pere
Life of Christ retablo, 1490
4:29 F 7 '38
Espaliered figure. sculpture
bw Callery 33:143 N 17
'52
L'Estaque. bw Braque 26:82
My 2 '49
L'Estaque. bw Cezanne 26:82 My
2 '49
Este, Beatrice d'
Leonardo da Vinci. Beatrice
d'Este bw 7:17 Jy 17 '39
Esteve, Maurice
Young woman with a bag 17:
76 N 13 '44
Artist at work photog bw 17:
74 N 13 '44 port.
Ester's feast. Rembrandt 41:74
D 10 '56
Etchings
Alken. Leading the field
aquatint bw 6:38 F 6 '39
Bayeux tapestry, etching of
40:88-9 Mr 26 '56
Bone. Gothic cathedral,
Spain bw 1:45 D 7 '36
Boxing match, c1810 6:39
F 6 '39
Chagall. Moses on Mount

Sinai bw 38:97 Je 13 '55
Durer. St. Jerome 34:76 F 23
'53
Isaiah during Babylonian cap-
tivity* bw 38:97 Je 13 '55
Marin. Chartre cathedral bw
29:62 Jy 10 '50
Mathews, C. "At home on the
Diligence," c1822 31:111
N 19 '51
Rembrandt. Sacrifice of Isaac
bw 6:54 Ja 30 '39
Roberts, P. Isaac Britton,
boxer bw 6:42 F 6 '39
Roualt. Madonna and Child,
Miserere series bw 34:56
F 2 '53
Eternal and angels. Giotto 4:30
F 7 '38
The eternal city. bw Blume 3:
20 D 6 '37
Eternal springtime. sculpture
bw Rodin 6:57 Mr 20 '39
Eternal vigilance, England,
Middle Ages. Castellon 30:
90 Mr 12 '51
Eternity. Hall 24:86 Mr 8 '48
Etnier, Stephen
Adolescence 6:27 F 13 '39
Passing tow 23:68-9 Jy 14 '47
Eton Hall, country house of
Duke of Westminster, Eng-
land photog bw 15:101 N
15 '43
Etruscan safety pin c600 B.C.
bw 6:52 Mr 20 '39
Etruscan warriors ceramics
bw, c600 B.C. 6:51 Mr 20
'39
Eugenie, Consort of Napoleon III,
Emperor of the French
Empress Eugenie bw 31:163
N 19 '51
Napoleon III and Eugenie
photog bw 25:91 N 22 '48
Eurich, Richard
Air fight over Portland 26:46
F 28 '49
Dunkirk beaches 26:43 F 14
'49
Invasion of North Africa* 29:
90-1 N 6 '50
Preparation for Normandy in-
vasion* 35:85 O 26 '53
Raid at Bruneval* 29:93 O 30
'50
Raid at Dieppe* 29:92 O 30 '50
Survivors from a torpedoed
ship 26:54-5 Mr 21 '49
Withdrawal from Dunkirk 10:
65 F 24 '41; 26:44-5 F 14
'49
Europa See Mythological
Themes--Europa
European War, 1914-1918 See
War Themes--European War
Evacuation from Corunna, Spain*
Peninsular War, 1809
print 26:43 F 14 '49
Evander showing Aeneas the site
of Rome (The tree wise-
men). Giorgione 39:170 O
24 '55
Evans, Bergen
Bergen Evans photog bw 22:
75 My 5 '47
Evans, Edith
Edith Evans photog bw 33:82
O 6 '52
Evans, Lemuel
Lemuel Evans bw 25:105 Jy
26 '48
Evans, Randolph, architect
$5000 dream house plan,
photog bw 3:13-4 D 13 '37
Eve See Adam and Eve
Evening. bw Burchfield 8:69 My
27 '40
An evening in Maine. Pittman
18:70 F 19 '45
Evening in Roscommon. Bohrod
11:94 N 10 '41
Eventide--October: The village
inn. Currier and Ives
print 9:32 D 30 '40
Evergood, Philip
Art on the beach bw 3:126 O
4 '37
Philip Evergood photog bw
3:126 O 4 '37 port.
Philip Evergood. in group
photog 29:172-3 O 16

Evergood, Philip (cont。)
'50 port。
Self-portrait bw 15:13 O 25
'43 port。
Evergreen, 1840, Greek revival
plantation house, Louisiana
photog 32:78-9 Je 9 '52
The evolution of culture in Mexi-
co。 mural Orozco 25:70 N
22 '48
Evolution of spring。 mosaic
Morado 41:104 D 3 '56
Evzone ("well-girdled"), Greek
Soldier photog bw 9:Cover
D 16 '40
Ewers
Persian bronze ewer, 8th
century 20:92 Je 24 '46
Rock crystal carved ewer,
Vienna, c1800 25:129 D 6
'48
Eworth, Hans
Philip and Mary bw 41:104
O 29 '56
Execution of Charles I, King of
England drawing bw 41:204
N 12 '56
Execution of Mary Stuart, Queen
of Scots, Fotheringay
castle* bw 41:150-1 N 5 '56
Execution of Maximilian, Emper-
or of Mexico, June 19 1867*
bw 4:52 Ap 11 '38
Execution of officers of Schell's
guards, Wesel, 1809 bw 15:
96 N 22 '43
Execution Wall, Paris。 Davis,
G.R. 19:54 Jy 16 '45
Executive mansions, 48 states
photogs bw 10:22-3 Ja 20
'41
The exhumation of the mastodon。
Peale, C.W。 6:28 Je 19 '39
Existentialist Painting
Patrix。 Clown bw 20:64 Je 17
'46
Exit from theater。 Daumier 7:56
O 9 '39
Exodus。 Hall 24:86 Mr 8 '48
Exotic landscape。 Rousseau 33:
95 O 27 '52

The expectant volcano。 Ernst 32:
58 Ja 21 '52
Expectation。 sculpture bw Bor-
gatta 37:101 D 6 '54
Explosion。 sculpture bw Cherry
22:140 Je 16 '47
The eye。 Magritte 1:25 D 14 '36
bw 19:64-5 S 24 '45
Eye of Horus
Necklace with Eye of Horus
pendant, Egypt 24:81 Ja 19
'48
Eyre, John
Sidney in 1809 bw 12:78 F 9
'42
Ezaki, Kehei
Japanese capturing Guam* 28:
68 F 27 '50

F

"Fables for Our Time" written
and illustrated by Thurber
bw 24:80 Ap 19 '48
Faces, reversible。 drawings bw
Whistler, R。 22:22-3 Mr
31 '47
Facist Art
"The Third Rome:" columns,
sculpture, mosaic, mural
photogs bw 27:111-4 N 21
'49
Factories See Industrial
Scenes
Factory workers。 Beardon 21:
64 Jy 22 '46
Faience
Five-tiered necklace, Egypt,
c1000 B.C。 9:93 D 9 '40
Isis holding son, Horus Blue
faience, Egypt 41:114 N
26 '56
Fair Play (horse) statue bw 3:
88 N 1 '37
Fairbanks, Charles W。
Charles Fairbanks photog bw
9:9 Ag 5 '40
The Fairman Rogers four-in-
hand。 Eakins 16:74 My
15 '44
Fairs See also Holidays and
Festivals

Architecture of famous U.S. fairs, 1853-1939 bw 6:34-5 Mr 13 '39

Golden Gate International Exposition, San Francisco, 1938
American and old master exhibit of world art 6:26-32 F 13 '39
Buildings--airview photogs bw 5:18 O 31 '38
Sculpture, controversial bw 4:14 F 21 '38
Sculpture, Court of the Pacific 5:70-1 D 5 '38

New York World's Fair, 1938
Airview photog bw 5:18 O 31 '38
Architecture, sculpture, exhibits 6:33-49 Mr 13 '39 bw 7:54 Jy 3 '39 night views 7:37-40 Ag 7 '39
Billings, H. Mobile three-dimensional mural, Ford Building 6:42 Mr 13 '39
Emblems, model, sculpture bw 4:11 Ja 31 '38
Manship. Figures; sun dial sculpture bw 4:14-5 Ja 31 '38
Old masters in art exhibit 6:38-9 My 29 '39

Paris Exposition, 1937
Buildings bw 3:69 Jy 26 '37
Sculpture on national buildings bw 3:70 Ag 9 '37
Falangist emblem: five yoked arrows photog bw 3:101 N 1 37; 31:63 Ag 27 '51
Fall morning. Boyd 23:98 N 10 '47
The fall of Rome. bw 16:62 Mr 20 '44
Fall of the Bastille, 1789* engraving bw 3:32 Jy 5 '37
Fall plowing. bw Wood, G. 14:57 Ja 18 '43
Fallen angel. bw Burlin 26:84 F 21 '49

Fallingwater, Bear Run, Pa. photog, bw Wright, archt. 21:94 Ag 12 '46
False perspective. bw Hogarth 1:27 D 14 '36
Falter, John
Quality of mercy poster 26:101 F 21 '49
Family Groups See also Children; Holy Family; Mother and Child
Bellows. Elinor, Jean and Anna 11:77 O 6 '41 bw 16:79 Ap 24 '44
A century of family portraits in America 25:90-4 O 18 '48
Copley. Sir Silliam Pepperell and his family 41:73 D 10 '56
Croce. Mozart family, 1780 40:117 Ap 23 '56
Curry. Father and mother bw 1:29 N 23 '36
Fragonard. The reconciliation 16:63 Ja 10 '44
George III of England, Queen Charlotte, and children* 25:106 S 13 '48
Ghirlandaio. Frencesco Sassetti and his son Teodore 2:43 Je 28 '37
Glackens. Family portrait 41:160-1 D 24 '56
Hooch. Family group 27:70 O 24 '49
Hovenden. Breaking the home ties 9:76 D 9 '40; 27:60 Ag 29 '49
Horne. The Stehlis of Zurich 25:91 O 18 '48
Husband and wife, misericord, wood carving bw 37:79-80 S 27 '54
Jackson. The family 41:70 Jy 9 '56
Jarvis. Black Hawk and son 36:73 Mr 8 '54
Johnson, E. The Hatches of New York, 1871 25:91 O 14 '48

Family Groups (cont.)

Johnston. The James Mc-
Cormick family 9:76 D 9
'40

Laurent. The river sculpture
bw 10:68 Je 2 '41

Lincoln family (Abraham Lincoln, wife, and three sons)
bw 23:45 Ag 25 '47

Marcks. Grandmother and
grandchild bw 28:71 F 6 '50

Moore, H. Family sculpture
bw 24:95 Ap 12 '48

Moore, H. Family group
sculpture bw 22:78 Ja 20
'47

Nollekens. Family in a park
25:98 S 13 '48

Peale, Rembrandt. The artist's
daughters 12:65 Mr 20 '42

Poor. March sun (The artist's
family) 12:61 Je 15 '42

Raeburn. The sisters 9:48 Jy
29 '40

Rembrandt. A married couple
24:76 Je 14 '48

Rossi. The Astors of New
York, 1870 25:92-3 O 18
'48

Sargent. Daughters of Edward
Boit 36:96-7 My 17 '54

Sargent. Mrs. Phipps and
grandson 25:94 O 18 '48

Sargent. The Sitwell family
bw 25:172 D 6 '48

Sargent. The Wyndham sisters
("The Three Graces") 23:
79 N 17 '47

Savage. The Washington family 6:27 Je 19 '39

Swallow. As the earth sings
sculpture bw 14:42 Mr 8
'43

Two sisters, American primitive 36:95 Je 28 '54

Van Eyck. Giovanni Arnolfini
and wife 33:36 D 29 '52

Victoria, Queen of England,
Prince Albert and children
bw 23:76 O 20 '47

Vuillard. The meal 37:76 N
1 '54

Vuillard. Painter's family
(mother and sister) 37:75
N 1 '54

The Wedgwood family 25:98 S
13 '48

Westin. King Charles XIV of
Sweden and his family* bw
33:92 D 1 '52

Wickey. Little brother and
sister sculpture bw 12:54
F 23 '42

Zoffany. A colonial family 25:
99 S 13 '48

Family of Man, photography ex-
hibit, Museum of Modern
Art. Steichen 38:132-43
F 14 '55

The family of saltimbanques.
Picasso 23:93 O 13 '47 bw
5:29 O 10 '38

Family portrait (Artist's family
and friends). Glackens 41:
160-1 D 24 '56

Family portrait. Greene 29:64
O 23 '50

Family portrait. drawing bw
Levy, E. 37:93 Jy 12 '54

Family portrait. Valadon 28:91
Ja 16 '50

Family reunion 30:154-5 Mr 19
'51

Family reunion. Sharon 33:76
Jy 21 '52

Fancy dress. Greenham 3:27 D
20 '37

Fantasy. Grilo 36:79 My 31 '54

Faraday, Michael
Michael Faraday bw 25:106
N 22 '48

Farm at Jas de Bouffan. Cezanne 32:83 F 25 '52

Farm in autumn. watercolor
Dehn 11:41 Ag 11 '41

The farmer and the raincloud.
Cowles 24:75 F 9 '48

Farmyards and Farm Buildings
Alger. Red Barns 16:46 Ja
3 '44

Burchfield. Evening bw 8:
69 My 27 '40

Chagall. The trough 22:58 My
5 '47

Currier and Ives print. Holiday in the country: troublesome flies 9:32 D 30 '40

Curry. Line storm 1:30 N 23
'36 bw 15:19 N 29 '43

Curry. Sanctuary 1:30 N 23
'36 bw 15:19 N 29 '43

Curry. The tornado bw 15:19
N 29 '43

Curry. Tornado over Kansas
1:29 N 23 '36; 21:73 N 25
'46

Hicks. Residence of David
Twining in 1787 9:76 D 9
'40

Hurd. Riverbank farm* 23:78
Ag 18 '47

Lalk. They're cute when
they're small 10:78 Mr 31
'41

Lee, D. Mexican farmhouse
22:74 My 12 '47

Levy, M. Old barn 16:45 Ja 3
'44

Lucioni. Clouds over Equinox
3:48 Jy 19 '37

Lucioni. Vermont classic 3:49
Jy 19 '37

Marten van Bergen farmhouse,
Leeds, New York 39:55 Jy
18 '55

Mount. Bargaining for a horse
18:65 Je 25 '45

Mount. Dance of the haymakers
18:67 Je 25 '45

Mount. Long Island farmhouses
18:68 Je 25 '45

Mount. The truant gamblers
18:66 Je 25 '45

Mount. Who'll turn the grindstone 12:73 Ap 20'42; 18:65
Je 25 '45

O'Keefe. White barn 4:30 F 14
'38

Renoir. Farmhouse at Les
Collettes 32:97 My 19 '52

Repin. Recruit's farewell 14:
46 Mr 29 '43

Wills. Colonial farmhouse

sketch, photog, plan 21:73
Ag 26 '46

Farnol, Jeffrey
Jeffrey Farnol photog bw 3:114
N 1 '37

Farnsworth, Jerry
The dancer 5:30 S 19 '38

Farnsworth, Lucy
Lucy Farnsworth bw 29:70 Ag
21 '50

Farnsworth Art Museum, Rock-
land, Maine
Exhibit of paintings of Maine
29:70-3 Ag 21 '50

Farouk Collection of Art
Royal treasures of the deposed
king of Egypt 33:88-95 N
24 '52

Farragut, David Glasgow
Currier and Ives print.
Farragut's victory at New
Orleans, April 18, 1862
21:73 S 2 '46
David Farragut, admiral
photog bw 14:76 F 15 '43

Farrell, James T.
James T. Farrell caricature
bw 23:83 S 1 '47

Fascist Symbols See Emblems
and Decorations

Fasola, Roberto
Pliepipedi (three dimensional)
paintings bw 41:188-9 N
26 '56
Roberto Fasola photog bw 41:
188 N 26 '56 port.

Fat running tiger. sculpture bw
Hardy 37:123 O 11 '54

Fates
Manship. Three fates under
tree of life, sundial bw 4:
14 Ja 31 '38

Father and mother. bw Curry 1:
29 N 23 '36

Faulkner, Barry
Oregon history mural, State
Capitol, Salem 7:44-5 Ag
14 '39
Barry Faulkner photog bw 7:
45 Ag 14 '39 port.

Faulkner, William, author
    Dance, 1921 cartoon bw 35:
        133 S 23 '53
    William Faulkner caricature
        bw 23:82 S 1 '47 port.
    William Faulkner--portraits,
        locale of his novels photogs
        bw 33:118-9 S 28 '53 port.
Faure, Jules
    Jules Faure photog bw 4:14
        Mr 28 '38
Faust and Marguerite bw 27:23
        Jy 25 '49
Favrile Glass
    Tiffany. Vases and dishes 40:
        92-3 Mr 5 '56
Fay, Frank
    Beaton. Frank Fay in "Harvey"
        drawing 21:7 Jy 22 '46
Fayetteville, Arkansas, Art
    Center photog 34:148 My
    18 '53
Fazzini, Pericle, sculptor
    Altarpiece bw 32:70 Mr 10 '52
    Elliptical nude* bw 32:68 Mr.
        10 '52
    Figures bw 32:65 Mr 10 '52
    Triangular bust bw 32:66 Mr
        10 '52
    Artist at work photog bw 27:
        50 Ag 1 '49 port.
    Pericle Fazzini photog bw 32:
        70 Mr 10 '52
Feake, Elizabeth
    Elizabeth Feake and baby
        Mary, American primitive,
        Massachusetts, 1675 bw 5:
        28 O 31 '38
Feasts See Holidays and Festi-
    vals
Feathered serpent. sculpture bw,
    Toltec 28:62 Ja 9 '50
Featherwork, Inca
    Coca bag bw 36:26 Ap 5 '54
    Crown, gold with plumes 36:
        102-3 Ap 12 '54
    Earplugs, feathers on wood
        36:101 Ap 12 '54
    Textile, detail 36:105 Ap 12
        '54
Fede, Lucrezia del

Sarto. Lucrezia del Fede 29:
    109 S 11 '50
Federal Art Project See United
    States Works Project Admini-
    stration
Federal Eagle See Emblems
    and Decorations
Feikema, Feike
    Feike Fiekema photog bw 24:
        131 Mr 8 '48
Feininger, Andreas, photographer
    Experimental art photographs
        13:8-9, 11 O 5 '42
    Freight yards* bw 31:92 N
        12 '51
    Manhattan moon* bw 24:15 My
        10 '48
    New York dimout 14:73-7 F 1
        '43
    New York harbor bw 31:90 N
        12 '51
Feininger, Lux
    The emerald coast 31:94-5 N
        12 '51
    Jersey harbor bw 31:90 N 12
        '51
    Old engine 31:93 N 12 '51
Feininger, Lyonel
    Big wheel locomotive 31:92-3
        N 12 '51
    The church 14:45 Mr 8 '43
    Church of Gelmeroda 31:96 N
        12 '51
    City at night 31:91 N 12 '51
    Dunes and breakwater 31:92-
        3 N 12 '51
    Glorious victory of the sloop,
        Maria 26:87 F 21 '49
    Stars above the town bw 31:
        89 N 12 '51
    Yachts 31:95 N 12 '51
    Lyonel Feininger photog bw
        15:12 O 25 '43 port.
    Self-portrait bw 15:12 O 25
        '43 port.
Feininger Family
    Lyonel Feininger, and his
        sons, Andreas and Lux
        photog bw 31:89 N 12 '51
Feke, Robert, attributed (also
    attributed to John Green-

wood)
Benjamin Franklin, c1784 40:
78 Ja 9 '56
Feliz of Cantalice, Saint
Murillo. Christ giving bread
to St. Felix of Cantalice
bw 39:94 O 10 '55
Fenollosa, Ernest
Ernest Fenollosa photog bw
9:54 Jy 22 '40
Fenwick, Elizabeth
Elizabeth Fenwick photog
bw 22:78 Je 2 '47
Ferber, Edna
Edna Ferber in "Royal Fam-
ily" photogs bw 9:46-8 S
23 '40
Ryan. Edna Ferber sculpture
bw 8:94 Je 24 '40
Ferber, Herbert See Silvers,
Herbert Ferber
Ferdinand, King of Spain
King Ferdinand, in "Missal
of King Ferdinand," manu-
script, Italy, 15th century
32:87 Ap 14 '52
Ferdinando Francesco II of
Gravinia
Ferdinando bw 28:21 My 8 '50
Ferguson Company, H.K., wall-
less factory, Corpus
Christi, Texas. photogs bw
28:10-2 Ja 9 '50
Fernstand photog bw 35:16 D 14
'53
Ferren, John
Abstraction, ink on orlon 37:
162 N 22 '54
Artist and his work photog 37:
162 N 22 '54 port.
Ferris, Jean Leon Gerome
Betsy Ross bw 32:58 F 18 '52
Fertility sculpture bw 4:14 F 21
'38
Festival Figures See Figures--
Holiday, Festival, Advertising
Festivals See Holidays and
Festivals
A fete at Rambouillet. Fragonard
29:87 N 27 '50
Fete champetre. Giorgione 23:52

Ag 4 '47; 39:170-1 O 24 '55
Fete galante. Lancret 29:86 N
27 '50
Feuerharm, Kurt
Meat market 30:36 Ja 15 '51
Fielding, Henry
His book "Tom Jones" illus-
trated: Tom comes to
London bw 25:109 S 13 '48
Fields, Lew
Lew Fields photog bw 14:41 F
22 '43
Fiene, Ernest
Cattle roundup mural, Depart-
ment of the Interior, Wash-
ington, D.C. 10:43 Ja 27
'41
Hudson navigation boat 12:76
Ap 20 '42
Kitchen table 7:25 Ag 28 '39
Razing old New York post
office bw 8:69 My 27 '40
Walkowitz bw 16:79 F 21 '44
Ernest Fiene. in group photog
29:172-3 O 16 '50 port.
Fiesole, Giovanni da See Angel-
ico, Fra
Fiesta costumes. Lee, D. 22:75
My 12 '47
Fight for the water hole, Reming-
ton 13:75 S 14 '42
Fighter. sculpture bw Brown,
Joseph 26:114 Je 20 '49
Fighter for freedom, War in
Spain, 1936. Weber 16:78
Je 12 '44
Figure, female. sculpture bw
Moore, H. 22:78 Ja 20 '47
Figure. sculpture bw Silvers 29:
147 S 18 '50
Figure, abstract. sculpture bw
Weber 19:84 Ag 20 '45
Figure organization. bw Benton
6:70 Ap 24 '39
Figure outdoors. Kroll 3:26 D
20 '37
Figureheads
Bellamy eagle figurehead,
from frigate, Lancaster
wood carving 38:Cover Ap
18 '55

Figureheads (cont.)
    Jenny Lind woodcarving, U.S.,
        19th century 31:70 Jy 2 '51
    Martin. Home from the sea
        9:91 N 11 '40
    New Guinea canoe prow, Sepik
        River woodcarving 21:82
        N 4 '46
    Solomon Islands canoe prow
        photog 21:82 N 4 '46
Figures. sculpture Couturier
    29:101 D 11 '50
Figures. sculpture bw Fazzini
    32:65 Mr 10 '52
Figures. sculpture bw Nadelman
    24:119 My 24 '48
Figures, Garden
    Cast iron "American Gothic"
        Greek figures photogs bw
        12:11 My 11 '42
Figures--Holiday, Festival, Ad-
    vertising
    Ancestor figure, Baluba tribe,
        Africa bw 33:117 S 8 '52
    Ancestral spirit figure, New
        Hebrides woodcarving 21:
        83 N 4 '46
    Buddha figure, Ceylon photog
        bw 40:28 Je 11 '56
    Buddha riding Kanthaka, Cey-
        long photog bw 40:27 Je 11
        '56
    Buddha's float, Kandy, Ceylon
        photog bw 40:30 Je 11 '56
    Buddhist guardian images,
        temple, Peiping 38:65 Ap 4
        '55
    Cigar store Indian 38:62 Ja 3
        '55
    Dogon statue, African,
        multiple-view bw 33:124-5
        S 8 '52
    Elves and toys parade figures
        photog 37:34 D 20 '54
    Fertility figure, paleolithic,
        France 39:76, 79 D 12 '55
    Fire fallas, Valencia Spain
        photog 38:51-2 My 2 '55
    Garuda bird floats, Cambodia
        photog 40:212 Ap 9 '56
    Inca religious figure, c1550

        bw 36:25 Ap 5 '54
    Paul Bunyan bw 27:104-6 Jy
        11 '49
    Rama-Lila pageant figures,
        gods and devils, New Del-
        hi photogs 30:90-5 S 12 '51
    St. George and the dragon,
        Portugal photog bw 23:28
        Ag 11 '47
    Santo nino perdido bw 17:128
        S 11 '44
    Taoist deities, two figures
        photog bw 38:70 Ap 4 '55
    Tomb figures, Japanese 30:
        70 My 28 '51
Figures at the shore. Taubes
    12:46 Mr 9 '42
Figurines See also Carving,
    Wood
    Andean cast gold goddess,
        Quimbaya 36:103 Ap 12 '54
    Andean copper figure, painted,
        c100 36:101 Ap 12 '54
    Etruscan goddess, bronze 40:
        63 F 13 '56
    Inca pottery vessels 36:104
        Ap 12 '54
    Pre-Columbian ceramic fig-
        ures, Mexico 18:49 Je 4
        '45
    Prehistoric pottery figurines,
        neolithic 40:74, 81 Ap 16
        '56
    Victorian nymph lamp, U.S.
        40:86 Mr 5 '56
    Warrior, bronze, Etruscan,
        c450 B.C. 40:62-3 F 13
        '56
Filbyter, Folke. sculpture bw
    Milles 2:32 F 22 '37
Fildes, Luke
    Edward VII of England 35:82
        N 23 '53
    George V of England 28:62 My
        29 '50; 35:83 N 23 '53
    The empty chair (Dicken's
        study) bw 25:84 D 27 '48
        (drawing)
Fillmore, Millard
    Millard Fillmore bw 9:8 Ag
        5 '40

Finck, Furman
Recollections of an English
abbey 39:113 S 12 '55
The finding of Moses. Giordano
41:71 D 10 '56
The finding of Moses. bw Vero-
nese 40:104 F 20 '56
Fine Arts Section See United
States Treasury Department.
Fine Arts Section
Fineman, Freda
Woman painter* 24:73 Ap 5
'48
Finger Painting
Shaw. Finger paintings bw 11:
39-41 Jy 28 '41
Fink, Herbert L.
Man 25:100 D 6 '48
Artist and his work photog bw
25:98 D 6 '48 port.
The fire eater. bw Morado 20:58
Je 3 '46
Fire-eater. Watkins, F.C. 26:
86 F 21 '49
Fire engine
Hand pumped fire engine, U.S.,
1843 photog 39:62-3 Ag 29
'55
Fire of the warehouse of Henry
Webb and Company, Balti-
more, 1827 6:28 Je 19 '39
Firearms See Weapons
Firechief. Dubuffet 33:96 O 27
'52
Fired on. Remington 9:77 D 9
'40
Fireplaces
Jackson. Ceiling-suspended,
spherical fireplace photog
bw 39:100 D 12 '55
U.S. contemporary fireplaces
photogs 35:139-42 D 7 '53
U.S. colonial fireplace: field-
stone hearth, 1660 38:123
Ap 18 '55
Fires
Great fire, London 41:71 N 19
'56
Haines. At high tide 12:39 Mr
2 '42
Haines. Journey's end 12:40

Mr 2 '42
McCrady. Small town fire 3:
41 O 18 '37
Manwaring. City silhouette,
from a balcony at head-
quarters, London fire
forces 12:40 Mr 2 '42
North-Taylor. Harrow school
speech room, October,
1940 12:39 Mr 2 '42
Orr. Ack-ack guns in action
12:40 Mr 2 '42
Ranney. Prairie fire 27:42 Jy
4 '49
Rosoman. House collapsing
on two firemen, Shoe Lane
12:40 Mr 2 '42; 26:49 F 28
'49
Summers. Forest fire, after
Demishoff-Uralsky 10:77
Mr 31 '41
Turpin. Getting to work 12:40
Mr 2 '42
World War bombing fires,
London 12:38-40 Mr 2 '42
Fireworks
Coronation festivities for
Alexander II, Czar of Rus-
sias, 1856* 38:66-7 Ja 31
'55
Firpo, Luis
Bellows. Dempsey and Firpo
bw 6:58 Mr 27 '39
The first American Thanksgiv-
ing. Brownscombe 13:77
N 23 '42
The First Bible of Charles the
Bold, page of 34:81 F 23
'53
First born. sculpture bw Borgat-
ta 37:102 D 6 '54
The first communion dress.
Ford 17:41 D 25 '44
First Furniture Company
Knockdown furniture for chil-
dren photog bw 37:41 D
20 '54
First landing of Americans in
Japan, July 14 1853 9:48
O 28 '40

First meeting house of North
    Church, Salem, Mass.
    Davidson 13:80 N 23 '42
The First Nowell. Kester 23:49
    D 22 '47
First robin. Junkin 10:67 My 26
    '41
"First-Rate" (ship) England, 17th
    century, cross-section,
    print 41:84 O 29 '56
Fischer, Anton Otto
    "George W. Campbell," coast
    guard cutter in the Atlantic
    15:59-69 Jy 5 '43
    The North Atlantic 14:75-6 F
    8 '43
    Artist at work; home; family
    photogs bw 15:71-3 Jy 5 '43
    port.
Fish See also Animals--
    Imaginery
    Australian native artist. But-
    terfish tree bark 21:78 N
    4 '46
    Bonnard. Fish 17:75 N 13 '44
    Cherry. Silly fish sculpture
    bw 22:138-9 Je 16 '47
    Fish, mobile, Northland shop-
    ping center, Detroit 37:82
    Ag 30 '54
    Hartley. Give us this day 32:
    87 Je 16 '52
    Lawrence, W. G. The sailfish
    6:29 F 2 '39
    Lawrence, W. G. The white
    marlin 6:29 F 2 '39
    Milles. Fish sculpture bw 34:
    102 Mr 30 '53
    Outerbridge. Fish mobile 29:
    63 D 18 '50
    Rafinesque. Fish, described
    by Audubon drawing bw 30:
    51 Ja 29 '51
    Rock codfish, Eskimo stone
    carving bw 36:70 My 24 '54
    Rosenthal, B. Fish sculpture
    bw 34:134 Ap 6 '53
    Sacred cod, 1760, State House,
    Boston sculpture 38:118 Ap
    18 '55
    Vagis. Fish rock sculpture bw

40:123 Je 11 '56
    Waugh. Fish engraved glass
    bw 7:32 S 18 '39
    White. Flying fish 22:84 Mr
    10 '47
    Zao Wou-Ki. Spectral fish 36:
    104 F 22 '54
Fish, Hamilton
    Hamilton Fish 19:88 S 24 '45
Fish kite. Kuniyoshi 30:36 Ja 15
    '51
Fish market. di Gioia 20:78 F
    18 '46
Fisher, Mary
    Mary Fisher in Mission to
    Turkey, 1657 bw 33:96 S
    29 '52
Fisher and Fisher, architects
    Ideal Cement Company,
    Boettcher, Colorado, in-
    dustrial design photog 36:
    33 Ja 4 '54
Fisher girl. bw Hals 6:58 Mr 27
    '39
Fishermen and Fishing
    Agnew. A day in port 23:98 N
    10 '47
    Albright, A. Anglers bw 16:
    64 Mr 27 '44
    Albright, I. Heavy the oar to
    him who is tired, heavy
    the coat, heavy the sea 16:
    68 Mr 27 '44
    Bellows. The big dory 29:71
    Ag 21 '50
    Bingham. Fishing 38:72 Mr
    28 '55
    Brandt. Purse seiner 11:76 O
    27 '41
    Brazilian fishermen riding
    turtles underwater* bw,
    Japanese illustration, 1853
    25:8 Ag 2 '48
    Corbino. Fishermen 8:66 My
    27 '40
    Covarrubias. Balinese fisher-
    men 3:48 S 27 '37
    Cowles. Fisherman's dream
    24:77 F 9 '48
    Currier and Ives print. A-
    merican winter sports:

Trout fishing on Chateaugay Lake 9:27 D 30 '40

Durfee. Fishermen's wharf 28:87 Mr 20 '50

Eakins. Shad fishing at Gloucester 16:73 My 15 '44

Hunting and fishing, illumination, Flemish, 15th century 22:78-80 My 26 '47

Lee, D. Landscape with fishermen bw 3:47 S 20 '37

Mount. Eel spearing at Setauket 18:66 Je 25 '45

Newton. Fishing captain 24:72 Ap 5 '48

Peirce, W. Mike fishes in Maine 19:85 N 12 '45

Pleissner. Trout fishing 25:66-7 Ag 23 '48

Shokler. Net menders 16:45 Ja 3 '44

Sokole. Sunday fishing 23:68 Jy 14 '47

Stuempfig. Sturgeon 25:101 S 20 '48

White. Indians fishing, c1585* 22:81 Mr 10 '47

Fishers for souls. Van der Venne 24:64-5 Je 14 '48

Fisk, Jim
Jim Fisk photog bw 3:42 Ag 2 '37; 30:68 Je 11 '51

Fitzgerald, F. Scott
F. Scott Fitzgerald caricature bw 23:82 S 1 '47
Scott Fitgerald, writer and his family photogs bw 30:83-5 Ja 15 '51

Fiume, Salvatore
Isle of statues 29:107 D 11 '50
Murals on Andrea Doria, Italian steamship 34:58-9 Je 22 '53

Five graces, circus bandwagon photog 20:51 F 4 '46

Five that escaped. sculpture bw 24:96 Ap 12 '48

527 Wellar. Wolfkill 10:58 Je 16 '41

Flabella photog bw 5:41 D 25 '38

Flack, Marjorie

"Adolphus" illustrations bw 11:84 D 15 '41

Flag raising, Mt. Suribachi, Iwo Jima. sculpture bw, Washington D.C. de Welden 37:128-33 S 20 '54

Flag raising, Mt. Suribachi. photog bw Rosenthal 18:17 Mr 26 '45

Flagg, James Montgomery
Emily Post drawing bw 20:66 My 6 '46
George Bernard Shaw caricature bw 41:104B Ag 6 '56
Webby (H. T. Webster) bw 33:51 O 6 '52

Flags
Banners of teutonic knights, 1410 bw 17:86 Ag 28 '44
Confederate flag, U.S. 31:64 O 15 '51
Kigu banner, Tibet 6:25 Je 12 '39
State flags of the 48 states of the U.S. 15:77-82 D 6 '43
U.S.--first American flag, 1777 17:57 S 4 '44
U.S.--first American navy flag, 1775 17:57 S 4 '44
U.S.--George Washington's flag 17:57 S 4 '44

Flames are flowers. Ernst 32:59 Ja 21 '52

Flannagan, John
Jonah and the whale sculpture bw 24:95 Ap 12 '48

Flannagan, John Bernard
Triumph of the egg bw 6:82 My 22 '39

Flannery, Vaughn
Item 9, Man O'War 8:65 My 27 '40
Maryland hunt 5:73 D 12 '38
Night paddocks 10:74 Ap 14 '41
Old Pimlico race track 32:70-2 My 5 '52

Flappers
Held. Flapper cartoon bw 28:48 Ja 2 '50

Flappers (cont.)
  Wickey. Eleventh Avenue
    flapper sculpture bw 12:
    54 F 23 '42
Flare. Ernst 32:58 Ja 21 '52
Flasks See Bottles and Flasks
Flashy autoes. Reinhardt 32:90
    Mr 24 '52
Flax-scutching, U.S. 19th cen-
    tury 31:72-3 Jy 2 '51
The fleet's in. bw Cadmus 2:44
    Mr 29 '37
Flemish games. bw Brueghel,
    P., the elder 31:94 Ag 20
    '51
Flemish proverbs. Brueghel, P.,
    the elder 24:74-5 Mr 22
    '48
Flight into Egypt
  Angelico. The flight into
    Egypt 21:Cover, 54 D 23
    '46
  Bellini. Flight into Egypt 16:
    70 Ap 10 '44
  Brueghel, P., the elder.
    Arrival of Joseph and Mary
    in Bethlehem 37:Cover, 30-
    3 D 27 '54
  Flight into Egypt, gilded wood-
    carving, Flemish, 15th
    century bw 5:49 N 28 '38
  Ford. Flight into Egypt 5:31
    D 25 '38
  Giotto. Flight into Egypt 25:
    44-5 D 27 '48
  Lu Hung Nien. The flight into
    Egypt 11:45 D 22 '41 scroll
    bw 11:49 D 22 '41
  Tintoretto. Flight into Egypt
    31:33 D 24 '51
  Zurburan. Flight into Egypt
    4:42 My 16 '38
"Flight into Space," illustrations.
    Osborn 35:90 Ag 31 '53
Flivver. Sterne 31:54 Ag 27 '51
Floating angel. sculpture Barlach
    41:140 N 5 '56
Floating figure. bw Lachaise 6:
    82 My 22 '39
Floating ice. Bellows 12:75 Ap
    20 '42

Floating palaces. MacIver 33:94-
    5 S 15 '52
Floats See Figures; Parades
The flood. engraving bw Dore
    6:47 Ja 16 '39
The flood. fresco Michelangelo
    27:40-3 D 26 '49 bw 21:63
    Jy 1 '46
Flood refugees. Corbino 4:28 Je
    13 '38
Flood survivors. Tobey 8:46 F
    12 '40
Floods
  Currier and Ives print. High
    water 21:73 S 2 '46
  Curry. Hoover and the flood
    8:59-9 My 6 '40
  Curry. The Mississippi 13:
    96 N 9 '42
  Curry. Sanctuary 1:30 N 23
    '36 bw 15:19 N 29 '43
  Harrington. Deep south 8:46
    F 12 '40
Flora. bw Rembrandt 28:58 Ja
    30 '50
Flora. sculpture bw Maillol 8:
    108 Ap 15 '40
Flora. sculpture bw, Victorian
    10:121 Ap 21 '41
Florence, Italy
  Florence, airview photog bw
    15:26-7 Ag 9 '43
  Giotto's tower photog bw 25:
    57 D 27 '48
  Horse racing on the streets of
    Florence. Cassone paint-
    ing, Florence, 1417 15:
    67 S 20 '43
Florian's cafe, Venice 30:108
    Ap 30 '51
Florida
  Emett. Skin-diving, Florida
    Cartoon 37:46 Jy 5 '54
  Haberman. Pompano, Flori-
    da 24:73 Ap 5 '48
  Covarrubias. Florida, picture
    map 20:52-3 F 4 '46 (map)
The florist. Koch 16:77 Ap 24
    '44
Flower, Forrest
  Indians stealing horses in

the Black Hawk war 25:59
N 29 '48

Flower girl. Modigliani 33:92 O
27 '52

Flower of youth. sculpture bw
11:145 O 13 '41

Flower Stalls
Davis, G. R. Flower stalls,
Paris 19:49 Jy 16 '45
Paris street scene 35:88 O
26 '53

Flowers
Benton. Pussy cat and roses
6:71 Ap 24 '39
Braque. Anemones 26:83 My
2 '49
Braque. Sunflowers 26:86 My
2 '49
Cezanne. Flowers and organ-
ges 32:79 F 25 '52
Churchill. Still life 20:49 Ja
7 '46
Davis, G. R. Flowers 14:46
Ap 19 '43
De Martelly. Tulip farm 25:
68 Ag 23 '48
Gauguin. Tahitian women with
red mango blossoms 21:61
Jy 29 '46
Knaths. Basket bouquet 30:35
Ja 15 '51
Koch. The florist 16:77 Ap
24 '44
Kuniyoshi. Boquet and stove
26:86 F 21 '49
Lasky. Flowers bw 3:87 S 27
'37
Lee, D. Wild flowers of Michi-
gan 25:68 Ag 23 '48
Matisse. Still life: fern 33:94
O 27 '52
O'Keefe. Calla lillies 4:30 F
14 '38
O'Keefe. Horses head with
pink rose 4:29 F 14 '38
Renoir. Gabrielle with roses
32:95 My 19 '52
Roualt. Boquet 34:61 F 2 '53
Tamayo. Indian women and
baskets of flowers* mural
34:103 Mr 16 '53

Todd. Flower paintings 38:95-
101 Ap 11 '55
Van Gogh. Sunflowers bw 27:
82 O 10 '49
Wood, G. Wild flowers lithograph 7:25 Ag 28 '39

Floyd, William
William Floyd bw 15:8 Jy 5
'43

Fluorescent Paintings See
"Black Light" Painting

Flushing pheasant. watercolor
Pleissner 21:68 O 7 '46

Flute player. sculpture bw
Marcks 28:71 F 6 '50

The flute player. Temayo 20:59
Je 3 '46

The flying Cadonas. Curry 1:31
N 23 '36

Flying harrows. Boggs 28:83 Mr
20 '50

Flying saucers drawings 39:177-
8 D 5 '55

Flying squirrels. Audubon 9:
115 O 21 '40

Folly Cove Designers
Hand blocked Yanke textiles,
Cape Anne, Mass. 19:80-
3 N 26 '45

Food for the dead* wall painting
bw, Tomb of Ptah-Iruk,
Egypt, 2500 B.C. 24:77 Ja
19 '48

The foolish virgins. bw Morado
20:58 Je 3 '46

Football See Games and Sports
--Football

For internal use only. Davis, S.
22:81 F 17 '47

Forbidden City, Peiping, air
view photog bw 3:55 Ag 23
'37

Ford, Mrs. Ellsworth
Carroll. Mrs. Ellsworth
Ford bw 8:120 My 13 '40

Ford, Henry
Ford collection of American
antiques, Greenfield Vil-
lage, Dearborn, Michigan
photogs bw 6:46 Ja 2 '39

Ford, Henry (cont.)
  Henry Ford: associates; home
    photogs bw 2:28-31 My 31
    '37
Ford, Lauren
  Adoration 17:33 D 25 '44
  Baptism of Arnauld 17:35 D
    25 '44
  Boyhood of Jesus in New Eng-
    land setting--etchings,
    paintings 5:28-32 D 25 '38
  The celestial mother (Blessed
    Catherine Laboure) 17:40
    D 25 '44
  The country doctor 3:28 D
    20 '37
  Epiphany at Bethlehem, Con-
    necticut 17:38-9 D 25 '44
  The first communion dress 17:
    41 D 25 '44
  Guardian angel 10:71 Ap 14
    41; 17:42 D 25 '44
  Madonna and Child 17:Cover D
    25 '44
  No room in the inn 5:27 Jy 4
    '38
  Resurrection 17:34 D 25 '44
  St. Francis 17:36 D 25 '44
  St. Germaine 27:37 D 25 '44
  The star of Bethlehem 7:25 D
    25 '39
  Vision at dusk 17:44 D 25 '44
  Vision of LaSalette 17:43 D 25
    '44
  Artist at work photogs bw 5:
    26 Jy 4 '38 port.
Ford Motor Company, geodesic
    dome, River Rouge. photog
    bw Fuller 34:67-70 Je 8 '53
The forest. Hall 24:86 Mr 8 '48
Forest fire, after Demishoff-
    Uralsky. Summers 10:77
    Mr 31 '41
The Forest of Arden. Ryder 30:
    90 F 26 '51
Forestier, Amedee
  Treaty of Ghent 41:72-3 Jy 2
    '56
The forge. Goya 3:37 D 27 '37
Forgery of Works of Art
  Chirico. Square* (declared

forgery by artist; genuine
  by Court) bw 30:71 Mr 5
  '51
Holbein. Portrait of a man,*
  copy of bw 39:147 S 26 '55
Leonardo da Vinci. Mona
  Lisa, 7 forgeries and o-
  riginal bw 39:141 S 26 '55
Malskat. Forged frescoes,
  Lubeck church bw 34:49-50
  Ja 12 '53
Pinson-Berthet. Forged paint-
  ings of Vlaminck and Utril-
  lo bw 30:70 Ap 9 '51
Rembrandt. Philosopher with
  an open book, forgery
  previously attributed to
  Rembrandt bw 39:142-3
  S 26 '55
Ryder, Seascape* bw 30:94-5
  F 26 '51
Salon of fakes, Paris bw 39:
  141-4 S 26 '55
Tiara of Saitaphernes, gold
  relief bw 39:144 S 26 '55
Van Gogh. Study by candle-
  light (self-portrait) bw,
  work of artist once con-
  sidered a forgery 27:27 D
  19 '49; 29:17 O 9 '50
Van Meergeren. Forged paint-
  ings bw 23:145 N 17 '47
Vermeer. Isaac baptizing
  Jacob bw 23:145 N 17 '47
Vlaminck. Village scene* bw
  30:69 Ap 9 '51
Fornasetti, Piero
  Signs of zodiac, on Andrea
  Doria, Italian steamship
  34:61 Je 22 '53
Forrest, Yvonne, sculptor
  Artist at work photog bw 21:
  105 Jy 8 '46 port.
Fort Davis, Texas. Lester 38:
  73 Je 6 '55
Fort Laramie, Wyoming, 1837.
  Miller 27:44-5 Jy 4 '49;
  39:75 N 28 '55
Fort Sacsahuamen, Cuzco,
  Peru photog bw 19:102-3
  S 24 '45

Fort Sumter, Bombardment of
bw 39:182 S 12 '55

Fortifications of Sebastapol bw
11:15 D 15 '41

Fortune telling. Mount 18:68 Je
25 '45

Forty-niners working sluice box
photog bw 24:44 F 2 '48

"The 47 Ronin," scenes from.
prints Hiroshige; Hokusai
15:53-6 N 1 '43 hero prints
bw 18:97 Ap 16 '45

Forty-two kids. Bellows 20:80
Mr 25 '46

Forum Romanum photog bw 17:
95 S 4 '44

Foster, John
Richard Mather, first American woodcut 38:121 Ap 18
'55

Foster, Marian (Mariana, pseudonym)
"Miss Flora McFlimsey," illustrations bw 33:84 S 22
'52
Artist at work photog bw 33:
83 S 22 '52 port.

Foubert, E.L.
Nude bw 11:61 O 27 '41

Fougasse See Bird, Kenneth

Foujita, Tsuguharu
Kiki bw 34:14 Je 29 '53
Pearl Harbor attack 28:67 F
27 '50
Tsuguharu Foujita photog bw
34:12 Je 29 '53 port.

Foundries
Fredenthal. Molten ore 25:
65 Ag 23 '48; 34:80 Ja 5 '53

The founding fathers at the Federal Convention, U.S.,
c1850. Rossiter 39:58-9
Jy 4 '55

The fount. sculpture bw Dobson
25:103 S 27 '48

Fountain of life in The Garden of
Eden. Bosch 11:56 S 8 '41

Fountains
Carved stone fountain, Baroque (copy), Gunston Hall,
Va. photog bw 11:119 D 15
'41

Dragon head fountain, Fushimi
Shrine sculpture bw 18:91
F 19 '45

Face fountain, Villa d'Este,
Italy photog 28:78 My 8
'50

Fish, mobile in fountain,
Northland shopping center,
Detroit photog 37:82 Ag
30 '54

Fountain, Forum Mussolini,
Imperial Square, Rome
photog bw 4:33 My 9 '38

Fountain, Place de la Concorde, Paris photog 8:62
Je 3 '40 bw 2:70 Je 14 '37

Milles. Fountain of faith
sculpture bw 34:99-101 Mr
30 '53 plaster models bw
bw 25:70-2 Ag 30 '48

Milles. Orpheus fountain,
Stockholm bw 2:28-9 F 22
'37 copy bw 2:30 F 22 '37

Milles. The wedding of the
Mississippi and the Mis-
souri, St. Louis bw 2:
Cover, 26 F 22 '37; 8:110-
2 Je 10 '40

Rosenthal, B. Fountain of the
sea bw 34:134 Ap 6 '53

Sharrer. Man at fountain 28:
88 Mr 20 '50

Water organ, Villa d'Este,
Italy photog 28:79 My 8
'50

Wood. Paris observatory
fountain bw 14:57 Ja 18 '43

Four A.M. Pittman 18:69 F 19
'45

The four humors, Middle Ages
bw 22:84 Ap 7 '47

Four occupations. bw Chiang
Kai-Shek 33:6-7 O 13 '52

Four peaches. Kuniyoshi 29:172-
3 O 16 '50

Four seasons. Japanese, 16th
century screen 34:98-9
Ap 20 '53

The four seasons of life: childhood, youth, middle age, old age. Currier and Ives print 9:30-1 D 30 '40

Four soldiers. sculpture bw Smith, D 22:78 S 22 '52

"The Four Zoas," illustrations. watercolors Blake 36:66 Ap 19 '54

Foure, Adolphe
Rotheneufs family history, rock sculpture, Brittany coast bw 39:14-5 Jy 25 '55
Adolphe Foure photog bw 39: 14 Jy 25 '55 port.

Fourment, Helene
Rubens. Helene Fourment, the artist's wife, c1635 29:84 N 27 '50

Fourth of July
Emett. Fourth of July 37: Cover Jy 5 '54
Fourth of July, Philadelphia, 1876 engraving bw 25:49 Jy 5 '48
Fourth of July, greeting cards, early 1900's 31:34-5 Jy 2 '51
Fourth of July picnic, Weymouth Landing, Mass., 19th century 31:74-5 Jy 2 '51
Howland. Fourth of July parade, Walpole, N.H., c 1848 25:46-7 Jy 5 '48
Krimmel. Fourth of July celebration in Centre Square, Philadelphia 25: 48 Jy 5 '48; 39:62 Ag 29 '55
Spencer. The picnic--or the Fourth of July, a day to be remembered 25:48 Jy 5 '48

Fox, Charles James
Charles Fox bw 25:113 S 13 '48

Fox, Fontaine, cartoonist
Toonerville trolley, final cartoon bw 38:92 F 21 '55
Fontaine Fox photog bw 38:92

F 21 '55

Fox, George
Fox in America bw 33:97 S 29 '52
George Fox bw 33:95 S 29 '52

Fox and geese quilt pattern 11: 62 S 22 '41

Foxes
Audubon. The cross fox 9:115 O 21 '40
Audubon. Red fox 30:48 Ja 29 '51
Fox, Fushimi shrine sculpture bw 19:91 F 19 '45
Sacred foxes of Shinto folklore bw 31:58 D 31 '51
Schwerzmann. Fox ice sculpture bw 6:6 Ja 16 '39

The foxhunt. bw Sample 18:44 Ja 1 '45

Fragments from yesterday. Ellis 28:86 Mr 20 '50

Fragonard, Jean Honore
A fete at Rambouillet 29:87 N 27 '50
Monsieur de la Breteche. bw 3:43 N 29 '37
The reconcilliation. bw 16:63 Ja 10 '44
The shady grove 5:35 S 26 '38
The swing. 23:79 S 15 '47
Jean Honore Fragonard bw 5:34 S 26 '38 port.

France
Arms of France 22:69 My 26 '47
Fall of the Bastille, Paris, July 14, 1789 prints, map 3:32, 35 Jy 5 '37
Hagnauer. Street fighting in Paris, 1848 25:88-9 N 22 '48
Mob storming the Bastille, July 14, 1789* bw 31:78 Jy 30 '51
A new constitution, Paris, 1848 25:89 N 22 '48
Paris street barricades, street fighting, rebuilding of Paris bw 31:80 Jy 30 '51

Francesco di Giorgio Martini
  The meeting of Dido and Aen-
    eas 35:150-1 N 16 '53
Francis, Saint
  Bellini. St. Francis in ecs-
    tasy 3:34-5 D 27 '37; 16:64
    Ap 10 '44
  Bercot. St. Francis 28:74 Je
    19 '50
  Domenico Veneziano. The
    stigmatization of St. Fran-
    cis 1:48 D 28 '36; bw 16:
    68 Ap 10 '44
  Ford. St. Francis 17:36 D
    25 '44
  Giorgione. Castelfranco Ma-
    donna 39:166 O 24 '55
  Giotto. Death of St. Francis
    fresco bw 16:68 Ap 10 '44
  Giotto and pupils. Story of
    St. Francis of Assisi fres-
    coes 16:65-71 Ap 10 '44
  Portinari. St. Francis preach-
    ing to birds* bw 27:76 Jy
    4 '49
  St. Francis bw 16:66 Ap 10
    '44
  St. Francis of Assisi bw 22:
    70 Ap 7 '47; statue bw,
    Assisi, Italy 35:104 Ag 24
    '53
  St. Francis renouncing world-
    ly possessions* bw 16:65
    Ap 10 '44
  Umlauf. St. Francis sculpture
    bw 27:145 O 17 '49
  Van Eyck, J. St. Francis re-
    ceiving the stigmata 4:30
    F 7 '38
Francis I, King of France
  Clouet. Francis I 35:50 Ag 17
    '53
Francis II, King of France
  Francis II, king of France,
    and his queen, Mary Stu-
    art* bw 41:149 N 5 '56
Francis Joseph I, Emperor of
    Austria
  Franz Joseph bw 4:13 Mr 28
    '38; 24:29 Mr 8 '48 photog
    bw 2:14 Mr 22 '37; 26:128

Mr 28 '49
Franz Joseph and Archduke
  Maximilian photog bw 25:
  91 N 22 '48
François, Andre
  "The Tattooed Sailor," book
    of cartoons bw 35:109 S
    21 '53
Frankish jewelry--pin and
  plaque, 7th century 33:130
  O 20 '52
Frankie and Johnny. mural de-
  tail Benton 2:36 Mr 1 '37
Franklin, Benjamin
  Benjamin Franklin 39:63 Jy
    4 '55; c1767 40:79 Ja 9
    '56; c1780 40:79 Ja 9 '56
    bw 15:8 Jy 5 '43
  Benjamin Franklin glassware,
    American flask 40:82 Ja
    9 '56
  Benjamin Franklin medallions
    40:82 Ja 9 '56
  Benjamin Franklin miniature
    40:82 Ja 9 '56
  Benjamin Franklin portrait
    on snuff box cover 40:82
    Ja 9 '56
  Benjamin Franklin print,
    1780 40:80 Ja 9 '56
  Benjamin Franklin terra cot-
    ta statue bw, France 6:
    52 Mr 20 '39
  Benjamin Franklin water-
    color 40:79 Ja 9 '56
  Benjamin Franklin as a vol-
    unteer fireman bw 6:100
    Ap 24 '39
  Benjamin Franklin before the
    House of Commons, Lon-
    don, 1766 bw 25:110 S 13
    '48
  Benjamin Franklin crowns
    Mirabeau print 40:80 Ja
    9 '56
  Benjamin Franklin's birth-
    place, Boston, 1706 bw
    40:73 Ja 9 '56
  Caffieri. Benjamin Frank-
    lin bust bw (copy) 40:82
    Ja 9 '56

Franklin, Benjamin (cont.)
 Duplessis. Benjamin Franklin.
  1778 40:72 Ja 9 '56
 Feke (or Greenwood), attributed. Benjamin Franklin,
  c1784 40:78 Ja 9 '56
 George Washington and Benjamin Franklin printed
  cotton textile, England,
  1782 40:82 Ja 9 '56
 "Poor Richard's Almanac,"
  illustrations for mottoes.
  steel engravings bw Pelton
  40:74-5 Ja 9 '56
 West. Benjamin Franklin and
  the lightning 40:81 Ja 9 '56
  bw 6:26 Je 19 '39
 Zorach. Benjamin Franklin
  statue bw 8:93 Ap 1 '40
Franklin, Maud
 Whistler. Arrangement in
  black and white 36:94 My
  17 '54
Frasconi, Antonio, woodcutter
 The storm is coming 37:85
  O 18 '54
 Sunrise--Fulton Fishmarket
  37:86-7 O 18 '54
 Artist at work photogs bw 37:
  84 O 18 '54 port.
Freake, Elizabeth Clarke
 Mrs. Freake and Baby Mary,
  American primitive, Mas-
  sachusetts, 1675 bw 5:28
  O 31 '38
Fredenthal, David
 Molten ore 25:65 Ag 23 '48;
  34:80 Ja 5 '53
 Night landing on New Britain
  bw 17:48-56 Ag 21 '44
 Thirst 21:80 N 25 '46
 "Winesberg, Ohio," illustra-
  tion of characters and
  scenes in Anderson's book
  bw 20:74-9 Je 10 '46
 Yugoslavia after World war--
  scenes and portraits 20:50-
  62 Ja 28 '46
 Russian soldiers; partisans--
  in Yugoslavia bw 18:83-9
  F 5 '45 (drawings)

 David Fredenthal. in group
  photog 32:87 Mr 17 '52
  port.
Frederick I, Barbarossa, Emper-
 or of the Holy Roman Em-
 pire
 Frederick Barbarossa bw 22:
  84 My 26 '47
Frederick II, the Great, King of
 Prussia
 Frederick the Great bw 8:24
  Ap 22 '40; 13:105 O 5 '42;
  23:88 S 15 '47; 28:65 Mr
  6 '50
 Frederick and staff, Battle
  of Zorndorf, 1758 bw 15:
  95 N 22 '43
 German army reviewed by
  Frederick the Great, 1779
  bw 15:96 N 22 '43
Frederick William I, King of
 Prussia
 Frederick Wilhelm bw 28:65
  Mr 6 '50
Freedman, Benedict
 Benedict Freedman photog bw
  22:82 Je 2 '47
Freedman, Nancy
 Nancy Freedman photog bw
  22:82 Je 2 '47
Freedom
 Crawford. Armed freedom
  sculpture, Capitol dome,
  Washington, D.C. 16:56
  Mr 20 '44 cast bw 19:9 S
  24 '45
Freedom of the press. Castellon
 30:94 Mr 12 '51
Freemasons
 Baker. George Washington in
  masonic dress bw 26:56
  Mr 28 '49
 Kempton. Harry Truman in
  masonic dress 26:54 Mr
  28 '49
 Masonic initiation, France,
  18th century bw 23:76-7
  S 15 '47
Fremont, John Charles
 General Fremont photog bw
  14:6 My 31 '43

French, Chester Daniel, sculptor
  Abraham Lincoln, statue, Lincoln Memorial, Washington, D.C. bw 5:58 Jy 11 '38; 20:Cover F 11 '46
  The angel of Death and the sculptor bw 6:57 Mr 20 '39
  John Harvard, Harvard University bw 10:Cover My 5 '41
  Minute men bw 7:10 O 23 '39
French, Jared
  Cavalrymen crossing a river mural, Parcel Post Building, Richmond, Va. 10:44 Ja 27 '41
  Origins of food mural, details bw 6:62-3 F 27 '39
  Artist and his work photog bw 6:62 F 27 '39 port.
The French Academy
  Jean Cocteau in uniform of French Academy photog 39:158 N 7 '55
  Meeting of the French Academy photog bw 3:64 D 20 '37
French girl.* Davis, F. 19:52 Jy 16 '45
French Huguenots attack Catholic priests* bw 24:60 Je 14 '48
French Revolution See France
French revolutionary calendar bw 18:43 Ja 1 '45
Frescoes See Mural Paintings
Freund, Rudolf
  Animals in winter: squirrel, rabbit, weasel and others 25:76-80 N 29 '48
  Bees--anatomy; in hive; predators 33:62-7 Ag 11 '52
  Legendary animals; basilisk, gorgon, griffin, manticore, su, unicorn, yale 30:115-9 Ap 23 '51
  Mushrooms--non-poisonous and poisonous 31:90-1 Ag 13 '51
Freund, Will

The reach 39:116 S 12 '55
Frick, Henry Clay
  Frick collection of painting masterpieces 3:Cover, 30-8 D 27 '37
  Henry Clay Frick photog bw 3:30 D 27 '37
Friend, Shirley
  Artist at work photog bw 41: 83 Ag 13 '56
A friend's ranch. Metcalfe 29: 72 Jy 17 '50
Friezes See Sculpture
Frishmuth, Mrs. William D.
  Eakins. Mrs. William D. Frishmuth 16:75 My 15 '44
Frith, Mary
  Mary Frith, smoking a pipe, 17th century 24:82 Mr 22 '48
Frobel, Friedrich
  Friedrich Frobel bw 2:26 My 10 '37
Frogs
  Chapin. Frog sculpture bw 5:7 N 28 '38
  Frogs and monkeys woodcarving bw, Bali 15:115 O 25 '43
  Peacock. American frogs-- 6 pictures 7:46 Jy 10 '39
  Pre-Columbian gold frog 18: 49 Je 4 '45
Frohman, Charles
  Charles Frohman photog bw 31:117 N 19 '51
A frolic at the old homestead. sculpture bw Rogers 6:7 Mr 6 '39
Fromelles (France) dressing station. watercolor Hitler 1:42 N 30 '36
Front Street, Hamilton, Bermuda. bw Davis, F. 14: 6 Je 28 '43
Frontier and Western Themes
  Bingham. Daniel Boone escorting a band of pioneers into the western country 6:28 Je 19 '39

Frontier & Western Themes (cont.)
  Bingham. Fur traders descending the Missouri 28:76-7 Mr 6 '50
  Bodmer. Encampment of the travellers 15:88 Ag 30 '43
  Chadwick. Placer mining in California 6:29 Je 19 '39; 27:48 Jy 4 '49
  Colman. Emigrant train 6:29 Je 19 '39
  Colman. Ships of the plains 39:74 N 28 '55
  Conway. Oklahoma land rush mural 30:78-9 Mr 5 '51
  Curry. Homestead 7:36 D 25 '39
  Curry. Oklahoma land rush 7:36 D 25 '39 bw 15:19 N 29 '43
  Faulkner, B. Oregon history, settlers mural, State Capitol, Salem 7:44-5 Ag 14 '39
  Hahn. Central Pacific Station, Sacramento, California, 1870 39:83 N 28 '55
  Hurd. Old pioneers mural 10:46 Ja 27 '41
  Killing of Jane McCrea 29:49 Jy 3 '50
  Laurent. Spanning the continent sculpture bw 10:68 Je 2 '41
  Lea. The nesters mural 10:46 Ja 27 '41
  Lester. Fort Davis, Texas 38:73 Je 6 '55
  Leutze. "Westward the course of empire" 36:76 Mr 8 '54
  Lewis and Clark expedition on Columbia River bw 12:98 My 25 '42
  Lockwood. Daniel Boone's arrival in Kentucky mural 10:46 Ja 27 '41
  Miller, A. J. Fort Laramie, Wyoming, 1837 27:44-5 Jy 4 '49; 39:75 N 28 '55
  Miller, A. J. Trapper, 1837 bw 27:40 Jy 4 '49

  Nahl. Sunday morning in the mines 27:49 Jy 4 '49
  The opening of the West: famous paintings depicting 27:40-50 Jy 4 '49
  Poor. Surveying new lands 2:36 Ja 4 '37
  Ranney. Emigrant train bw 27:40 Jy 4 '49
  Ranney. Prairie fire 27:42 Jy 4 '49
  Ranney. Retreat 27:42 Jy 4 '49
  Refrigier. Oklahoma's development mural 30:78 Mr 5 '51
  Remington. Attack on the supply wagon 13:76 S 14 '42
  Remington. Cavalry charge on the southern plains 13:76 S 14 '42
  Remington. The discovery 36:77 Mr 8 '54
  Remington. Fight for the water hole 13:75 S 14 '42
  Remington. The sentinel 13:74 S 14 '42
  Russell. In without knocking 39:86 N 14 '55
  Russell. Lewis and Clark expedition mural bw 33:65 N 10 '52
  Schwarz. On the Oregon trail mural bw 7:45 Ag 14 '39
  Scott. Western magazine covers and illustrations bw 12:68 Je 29 '42
  Solid comfort. lithograph 27:49 Jy 4 '49
  Vanderlyn. Death of Jane McCrea 29:49 Jy 3 '50
  Wimar. Attack on an emigrant train 27:43 Jy 4 '49
  Wimar. Indians pursued by American dragoons 27:43 Jy 4 '49
  Young. Pony express sculpture bw 10:79 F 17 '41
Frost, Robert
  Robert Frost photog bw 9:

102 O 14 '40

Fruit

Albright, I. Wherefore now
ariseth the illusion of the
third dimension 16:66-7 Mr
27 '44

Arcimboldo, School of Summer (Reclining woman of
fruit and vegetables) bw 7:
24 Ag 28 '39

Blanch. Basket and fruit 7:26
Ag 28 '39

Brackman. Composition in
life and still life 5:29 S 19
'38

Brackman. Still life with
mask 8:60 F 5 '40

Braque. Pitcher and basket
of fruit 26:83 My 2 '49

Braque. Still life: grapes and
bananas 33:95 O 27 '52

Braque. Still life with grapes
38:109 My 23 '55

Braque. Sugar bowl with fruit
26:83 My 2 '49

Cezanne. Flowers and oranges
32:79 F 25 '52

Cezanne. Still life with apples
2:46 Ap 12 '37

De Bry. Fruits of India drawing bw 24:87 My 22 '48

Hynckes. Basket of fruit 29:
102 D 11 '50

Kuniyoshi. Four peaches 29:
172-3 O 16 '50

Monet. Still life 29:90 N 27
'50

Peale, J. Fruit in a bowl 12:
66 Mr 20 '42

Peale, Raphaelle. Melons 12:
66 Mr 20 '42

Rosenthal, D. Girls and bananas 15:68 N 22 '43

Smith, T. Still life: fish and
fruit 25:100 D 6 '48

Fruit basket. woodcarving Mc-
Intire 38:63 My 30 '55

Fruit peddler, Korea. Kidd 29:
70-1 O 9 '50

La frutera. sculpture bw Cohn
10:59 Je 16 '41

Fry Christopher
Eisenstadt. Christopher Fry
photog bw 32:100 Ja 14 '52

Fuad I, King of Egypt
De Laszlo. King Fuad I of
Egypt bw 16:85 Ap 10 '44

Fuchs, Emil
Emily Post, age 26 20:64 My
6 '46

Fuchs, Feodor
Custer's last charge bw 24:
12 Je 21 '48

Fudo, King of Japan
King Fudo 34:100 Ap 20 '53

Fujikawa, Eiko
Nudes bw 32:101 Je 23 '52
Artist and her work bw 32:
101 Je 23 '52 port.

Full moon. sculpture bw Lippold
28:59 Je 12 '50

Full moon, empty earth. Ernst
32:59 Ja 21 '52

Fuller, Margaret
Margaret Fuller, transcen-
dentalist bw 17:65 Jy 31
'44

Fuller, R. Buckminster, architect and designer
Dymaxion world: map drawn
to show time scale and di-
rection, corrected con-
figuration 14:41-55 Mr 1
'43

Fuller house: round, aluminum, suspended from
mast bw 20:73-4, 76 Ap
1 '46

Geodesic dome, Ford Motor
Company, River Rouge bw
34:67-70 Je 8 '53

R. Buckminster Fuller photog
bw 14:41 Mr 1 '43; 34:70
Je 8 '53 port.

Fuller, Sue
String composition 27:77 O
31 '49

Fulton, Robert
Self-portrait 39:67 Jy 18 '55

Fulton Fishmarket, New York
   City
   Frasconi. Sunrise--Fulton
     Fishmarket woodcut 37:86-
     7 O 18 '54
Fulwider, Edwin L.
   Dead head 6:30 F 13 '39
Funck, John, architect
   Heckendorf home, Modesto,
     Calif photog bw 19:115 O
     22 '45
Funeral. Rouault 34:61 F 2 '53
Funeral procession. Pilipili
   34:107 My 4 '53
Fur traders descending the
   Missouri. Bingham 28:76-
   7 Mr 6 '50
Fur-lined teacup. bw Oppen-
   heim, M. 1:24 D 14 '36;
   32:108 Ap 28 '52
Furman, Iris
   Artist at work photog bw 10:
     79 Mr 31 '41 port.
Furniture
   "America's best" designed
     29:90-1 D 25 '50
   Antique reproductions.
     Tacchi 37:91-2 O 25 '54
   Chippendale. Chinese parlor;
     tables, sofa, side chairs,
     screen, Du Pont Museum
     38:68-9 My 30 '55
   Eighteenth century American
     Furniture: commode, desk,
     secretaries, tilt-top table
     38:66-7 My 30 '55
   Eighteenth century English
     furniture: Adam, Chippen-
     dale, Hepplewhite, Shera-
     ton 23:70-80 Ag 25 '47
   Eighteenth century furniture
     --rooms and individual
     pieces 7:45 Jy 31 '39
   Grecian parlor--Duncan Phyfe
     furniture: chairs, sofa,
     tables 39:60-1 Ag 29 '55
   Louis XV drawing room 27:
     56-7 O 3 '49
   Mission style, U.S. bw 40:61
     Ja 16 '56
   Revolutionary period furniture,

     U.S. 38:56-69 My 30 '55
   Shakers' gathering room,
     c1850 39:103 O 17 '55
   Thorne miniature rooms,
     period furniture and interi-
     ors 3:38-42 N 29 '37
   U.S. Colonial furniture 38:
     108-31 Ap 18 '55; adapted
     from Old World 38:126-7
     Ap 18 '55

  Contemporary
   Adapted from past styles:
     beds, mirrors, chairs,
     tables, lamps--original
     and modern design bw 35:
     15-8 D 14 '53
   Furniture for modern living:
     Swedish modern; 18th cen-
     tury; modern; regency 7:
     45-9 Jy 31 '39
   Iron furniture for indoor use
     bw 32:68-70 F 11 '52
   Jackson. Ceiling suspended
     furniture: day bed, chair
     bw 39:100 D 12 '55
   Japanese interiors; Japa-
     nese-style American fur-
     niture 31:60-1, 69 D 31
     '51
   Japanese-style furniture:
     tables, couch, chaise,
     seating piece, cushions
     bw 37:72-3 D 27 '54
   Knoll Associates furniture
     34:72-6 Mr 2 '53
   McCobb iron, canvas, and
     rubber washable furniture
     34:74-6 My 18 '53
   Miller "Trade Secrets" house
     34:8-10 Ja 5 '53
   Modern furniture--bedroom,
     living room, children's
     room 36:72-3 Mr 29 '54
   Modern furniture--four
     rooms, $1,800 bw 30:89-
     94 My 14 '51
   Modern furniture of 6 top
     designers bw 25:115-8 N
     15 '48
   Nelson furniture: chairs,

cabinet, desk, lamp, tables bw 25:116-7 N 15 '48

Risom furniture: chair, tables, sideboard bw 25:118 N 15 '48

Robsjohn furniture: tables, chairs, chest, ottoman, desk bw 25:116-7 N 15 '48; modern living room 27:60-1 O 3 '49

Rooms and individual pieces 7:45-9 Jy 31 '39

Sanders module furniture-- interchangeable units bw 21:128-9 S 23 '46

Space-saving furniture: tables, desks, hassocks, chests bw 33:33-6 D 22 '52

Suspended furniture: stairway, legless day-bed, chair, spherical fireplace bw 39: 99-100 D 12 '55

Surrealist furniture exhibit, Galerie des Beaux Arts, Paris bw 4:57 F 7 '38

Wormley furniture: chairs, cabinet, desk, sofas, tables bw 25:116-7 N 15 '48

Pre-fabricated
  Chair kit bw 40:117-20 Ap 16 '56
  Grabe prefabricated living room bw 26:110-2 Mr 14 '49

Regency
  Living room, dining area, bedroom bw 7:45-9 Jy 31 '39

Swedish Modern
  Malmsten furniture bw 7:45 Jy 31 '39
  Ruhtenberg furniture bw 5:36-8 D 12 '38

Victorian
  Age of gilded opulence, U.S.: desks, chairs, lamps, bedroom 40:86-91 Mr 5 '56

  Belton Victorian parlor 39: 102 O 17 '55
  U.S. pre-Civil War furniture 39:102 O 17 '55
  Victorian quilted rocking chair, iron flower pot drawing bw 27:59 Ag 29 '49

Beds
  Brass bed bw 35:18 D 14 '53
  Jackson. Ceiling suspended day-bed bw 39:100 D 12 '55
  Trundle bed bw 35:18 D 14 '53

Cabinets and Cupboards
  Chippendale Chinese-style china cabinet bw 23:75 Ag 25 '47
  Colonial spice cabinet, U.S., 1679 38:126 Ap 18 '55
  Cupboard, England, 15th century 22:79 My 26 '47

Chairs
  African stool bw 40:125 F 6 '56
  Andreef and Guillon. Parachute cord chairs bw 34: 105-7 Mr 23 '53
  Bertoia. Chairs 34:75 Mr 2 '53
  Brewster chair, U.S., Colonial 38:127 Ap 18 '55
  Brodovitch. Knockdown wood-cord chair bw 28:98 My 8 '50
  Chippendale. Chinese-style chair bw 23:75 Ag 25 '47
  Chippendale. Ribbon-back chair bw 23:75 Ag 25 '47
  Eames. Armless "shell" chair bw 28:98-9 My 8 '50
  Eames. Molded plywood chair bw 29:152 S 11 '50
  Eames. Molded plywood resilient chair bw 20:49 My 20 '46
  Guillon. Parachute cord chair bw 34:105-7 Mr 23

Chairs (cont.)
   '53
    Hepplewhite. Shield-back
      chair bw 23:77 Ag 25 '47
    Hitchcock. Contemporary
      production of 1826-40
      chair 28:118-20 My 1 '50
    Home-assembled chairs 40:
      117 Ap 16 '56
    Jefferson. Revolving chair
      with writing arm bw 14:
      73 Ap 12 '43
    Knoll. Chairs 34:72-3 Mr 2
      '53
    Knoll. Simplified form-fitting
      chair bw 20:47-8 My 20
      '46
    Knorr. Curved metal chair
      bw 28:99 My 8 '50
    Legless, ceiling-suspended
      chair bw 39:100 D 12 '55
    Middle Ages chair, North
      Italy 22:79 My 26 '47
    Mies van der Rohe. Chairs
      34:74 Mr 2 '53
    Noguchi. Rocking stool bw
      40:122, 125 F 6 '56
    Palace chair bw 35:17 D 14
      '53
    Phyfe. Lyre-back chair 39:
      61 Ag 29 '55
    Phyfe. Spread-eagle splat
      chair 39:60 Ag 29 '55
    Pratt. Occasional chair bw
      28:99 My 8 '50
    Queen Anne chairs--3 styles
      38:64 My 30 '55
    Robsjohn-Gibbings. Walnut
      arm chair 29:90 D 25 '50
    Rope seat chair 40:117 Ap 16
      '56
    Saarinen, Eero. Chairs 34:
      74 Mr 2 '53
    Saarinen, Eero. Easy chair
      bw 35:16 D 14 '53
    Saarinen, Eero. Fabric-cov-
      ered plastic shell chair 25:
      115 N 15 '48
    Shaker two- and three-slat
      maple chairs, 1850 39:103
      O 17 '55

    Sheehan. Windsor chair bw
      35:18 D 14 '53
    Sheraton. Arm and side
      chairs bw 23:78 Ag 25 '47
    South Seas saddle-shaped
      stool, with arm for grat-
      ing coconuts bw 21:79 N
      4 '46
    Victorian gilded rattan cor-
      ner chair, lyre-back 40:
      91 Mr 5 '56
    Victorian ladder-back rattan
      chair 40:91 Mr 5 '56
    Victorian quilted rocking
      chair drawing bw 27:59 Ag
      29 '49
    Victorian swivel chair, cast
      iron 40:90 Mr 5 '56
    Windsor chairs, stools, set-
      tees 38:64-5 My 30 '55
    Wormley. Morris chair bw
      35:17 D 14 '53

Chaises
    Belgiojoso-Peressutti-Rog-
      ers. Chaise 34:72-3 Mr
      2 '53
    Van Keppel-Green. Tubular
      steel chaise 29:90 D 25
      '50

Chests
    Covered chest, England, 1590
      31:69 S 3 '51
    Shaker cupboard, pine, 1850
      39:103 O 17 '55
    U.S. Colonial dower chest
      38:127 Ap 18 '55

Children's
    First Furniture Company.
      Knockdown furniture bw
      37:41 D 20 '54

Chimney Piece
    Chippendale. Chimney piece
      bw 23:75 Ag 25 '47

Commodes
    Thomas. Elliptical commode,
      Boston, c1880 38:66-7 My

30 '55

Cradles
Windsor cradle 38:65 My 30
'55

Desks
"Bombe" desk, Massachu-
setts, c1760 38:67 My 30
'55

Lamps
Bubble lamp bw 35:16-7 D 14
'53
Noguchi. Decorative lamps
32:114-5 Mr 10 '52
Sculptured bronze lamps bw
21:103-6 N 18 '46
Thurston. Hanging lamp bw
35:18 D 14 '53
Tiffany glass lamps 40:92-3
Mr 5 '56
Victorian nymph lamp, bronze
U.S. 40:86 Mr 5 '56

Mirrors
Early American gilded mirror, eagle, dolphin, and
shell decoration 17:57 S
4 '44
McCobb. Wrought iron mir-
ror 35:15 D 14 '53
Mirrors bw 35:16 D 14 '53

Screens
Bertoia. Metal screen 37:62
O 25 '54
Buddha, Amida, Lord of
Light, screen, Japanese,
13th century 34:99 Ap 20
'53
Cedar screen, Tlingit Indian,
Alaska, c1825 41:53 Jy 16
'56
Four seasons, Japanese
screen, 16th century 34:
98-9 Ap 20 '53
Wind God, Japanese screen,
17th century 34:100-1 Ap
20 '53

Secretaries
Bureau bookcase, England
18th century bw 23:79 Ag
25 '47
Goddard. Block-front secretary, U.S., c1759 38:66-
7 My 30 '55
Mahogany secretary, eagle
and landscape decoration,
c1790 17:59 S 4 '44
Seymour. Tambour secre-
tary, "American Hepple-
white," Boston, 18th cen-
tury 38:67 My 30 '55
Sheraton. Cylinder desk and
bookcase bw 23:78 Ag 25
'47

Sideboards
Sheraton. Sideboard with
candleholder 23:78 Ag 25
'47

Sofas
Chippendale. Decorated sofa
bw 23:75 Ag 25 '47
Hepplewhite. Window seat
bw 23:76 Ag 25 '47
Modern sofa, Tecno, Italy
bw 38:84 Je 27 '55
Pahlmann. Walnut sofa bw
35:16 D 14 '53
Phyfe. Upholstered sofa with
reeding and carving 39:
60-1 Ag 29 '55
Saarinen, Eero. Ottoman
34:72-3 Mr 2 '53
Victorian circular sofa, U.S.
40:91 Mr 5 '56

Stoves
Dunce-cap stove, U.S., 1816
39:63 Ag 29 '55
Iron cook stoves, U.S. 38:
62-3 Ja 3 '55
Iron stove, Shaker, 1850 39:
103 O 17 '55
Porcelain stove, white and
gold, Prague bw 27:55
Jy 18 '49

Stoves (cont.)
　Tile stove, Moravian, Old
　　Salem, N.C. bw 37:167 O
　　25 '54

Tables
　Card table, American, 18th
　　century 38:71 My 30 '55
　Chippendale. Piecrust table,
　　18th century 38:66 My 30
　　'55
　Hepplewhite. Pembroke table,
　　inlaid, with spade foot bw
　　23:77 Ag 25 '47
　Hepplewhite. Shaving table bw
　　23:76 Ag 25 '47
　Knoll, F. Tables 34:72-5 Mr
　　2 '53
　Nelson, G. Lazy susan table
　　bw 35:16 D 14 '53
　Phyfe. Folding mahogany
　　table, eagle and acanthus
　　carving 39:60 Ag 29 '55
　Phyfe. Tambour sewing table,
　　with brass lion-paw feet
　　39:61 Ag 29 '55
　Robsjohn-Gibbings. Coffee
　　table bw 35:17 D 14 '53
　Trestle table, Shaker, 1850
　　39:103 O 17 '55
　Trestle table, U.S. colonial,
　　1650 38:126-7 Ap 18 '55
　Tripod table bw 35:17 D 14 '53

Whatnot
　Spool-turned whatnot, Victori-
　　an 40:90-1 Mr 5 '56
Furniture Remodeling
　Hunt. Redesigned and redeco-
　　rated furniture bw 13:49-52
　　N 2 '42
Fushimi Shrine sculpture bw 18:
　91 F 19 '45
Fust, Johann
　Johann Fust bw 36:85 Mr 1
　　'54
Futility of a well-ordered life.
　ceramics bw Aitken 3:94
　O 11 '37
Fyton, Jane
　Gainsborough, attributed.

Miss Jane Fyton bw 17:92
　Jy 17 '44

G

G.A.R. encampment, Minneapo-
　lis, 1884 bw 41:20-1 Ag 20
　'56
G.A.R. grand review, Washing-
　ton, D.C., 1892 41:22-3
　Ag 20 '56
G.A.R. parade, Philadelphia,
　1868 bw 41:21 Ag 20 '56
Gabo, Naum, sculptor
　Construction* plastic thread
　　sculpture 33:93 O 27 '52
　The unknown political prison-
　　er bw 34:40 Je 1 '53
Gabriel, archangle See also
　　Mary, Virgin--Annuncia-
　　tion
　Angel Gabriel mosaic, Santa
　　Sophia 29:58 D 25 '50
Gabrielle (Mrs. Conrad Slade)
　Renoir. Seventeen paintings
　　of Gabrielle, Renoir's
　　model bw 13:38, 40 Ag 3
　　'42
Gabrielle and Jean. Renoir 32:
　91 My 19 '52
Gabrielle and roses. Renoir 32:
　95 My 19 '52
Gainsborough, Thomas
　The blue boy (Jonathan But-
　　tall) 4:26 Ja 24 '38
　The cottage door 5:43 S 12
　　'38
　The Honorable Frances Duns-
　　combe 3:32 D 27 '37
　The Honorable Mrs. Graham
　　25:96 S 13 '48
　Karl Friedrich Abel 4:27 Ja
　　24 '38
　Miss Jane Fyton bw 17:92 Jy
　　17 '44 (attributed)
　View in Suffolk 13:94 N 9 '42
　Viscount Downe bw 6:58 Mr
　　27 '39
　Thomas Gainsborough bw 4:
　　23 Ja 24 '38; 5:42 S 12
　　'38 port.

A gala day. Munnings 23:85 N 17
'47
"Galatea" (ship) U.S. clipper 39:
107-8 O 17 '55
Galaxy. space-sculpture bw
Kiesler 32:79 My 26 '52
Galerie des Beaux Arts, Paris
Surrealist furniture exhibit
photogs bw 4:57 F 7 '38
The gallant offering. Steen 24:78
Je 14 '48
Gallatin, Albert
Albert Gallatin bw 10:26 Mr 3
'41; 13:97 O 5 '42
Stuart. Albert Gallatin bw 4:
42 My 2 '38
Gallatin, Albert Eugene
Abstractions bw 4:42 My 2 '38
Gallatin collection of cubist
and abstract art 4:42-4 My
2 '38
Portraits of modern artists in
their studios: Braque, Le-
ger, Matisse, Miro, Mon-
drian, Picasso bw 4:45 My
2 '38 photog.
Leger. Albert Eugene Galla-
tin drawing bw 4:42 My 2
'38 port.
Galleries and Museums See also
Art Galleries and Museums
Latest acquisitions of six ma-
jor museums in U.S.A. 29:
40-7 Jy 31 '50
Gallery of the Louvre. Morse 17:
62 D 18 '44
Gallic cock. sculpture bw La-
mont, F. 14:42 Mr 8 '43
Galvan, Jesus Guerrero
La vigorina 4:30 Mr 14 '38
Galvez, Cristina
Female figure leather-sculp-
ture 36:81 My 31 '54
Gambier, Lord
Forestier. Treaty of Ghent
41:72-3 Jy 2 '56
The game. Bigaud 23:60 S 1 '47
Games and Sports See also
Fishermen and Fishing;
Horse Racing; Hunters and
Hunting

Corcos. Games in America
31:94-5 Ag 20 '51
Brueghel, P., the elder.
Children's games 29:30-1
D 25 '50 bw 31:94 Ag 20 '51
Mount. Raffling for the goose
18:66 Je 25 '45
Roper's gymnasium, 1840 bw
6:41 F 6 '39
Sporting prints, 19th century,
from "Four Centuries of
Sporting Prints" exhibit
6:38-42 F 6 '39

Backgammon
Backgammon, Middle Ages*
bw 22:74 My 26 '47

Baseball
Baseball, 1870* bw 6:41 F 6
'39
Baseball game,* Polo Grounds,
New York City 32:117 Ap 7
'52
Baseball players, miseri-
cord woodcarving bw 37:82
S 27 '54
Brown, Joseph. The hurler
bw 12:90 My 19 '41
Davis, F. Softball game in
Hyde Park,* London 16:
66-7 Ap 3 '44; 31:79 O 29
'51
Dufy. Ball game 30:65 Ja 22
'51
Laning. Joe di Maggio tying
the record bw 11:64 N 10
'41
Steinberg. Baseball-scenes,
players drawings 39:56-66
Jy 11 '55
Thomas, B. The minors--the
York White Roses vs the
Trenton Packers 10:51 Je
23 '41

Bicycling
Burden. Ridin' high 25:99 D
6 '48

Billiards
    Braque. Billiard table 33:94
        O 27 '52
    Martin, F. Service club 11:
        62 Jy 7 '41
    Smith, D. Billiard player bw
        33:78 S 22 '52

Bowling
    Hooch. The game of skittles
        13:95 N 9 '42; 24:72 Je 14
        '48
    Thomas, B. Pastime bowling
        alley 10:52 Je 23 '41

Boxing
    Bellows. Dempsey and Firpo
        bw 6:58 Mr 27 '39
    Bellows. Stag at Sharkey's 5:
        38 O 31 '38; 26:85 F 21 '49
    Boxing match, 1810 etching
        6:39 F 6 '39
    Brown, Joseph. Fighter sculp-
        ture bw 26:114 Je 20 '49
    Brown, Joseph. Right upper-
        cut sculpture bw 12:90 My
        19 '41
    Eakins. Between rounds 16:
        76 My 15 '44
    Martin, F. A lad from the
        fleet 8:67 My 27 '40
    Martin, F. Lullaby 16:76 Ap
        24 '44
    Mili. Louis knockdown by Joe
        Walcott photog bw 24:16 My
        10 '48
    Roberts, P. Isaac Bitton,
        boxer etching bw 6:42 F 6
        '39
    Young, J. Richard Humph-
        reys, boxer mezzotint bw
        6:42 F 6 '39
    Young, M. The knockdown
        sculpture bw 10:79 F 17 '41
    Young, M. Right to the jaw
        sculpture bw 10:79 F 17
        '41

Bubble Blowing
    Chardin. Bubble blower bw 6:
        58 Mr 27 '39

Chardin. Soap bubbles 5:37 S
    26 '38
Manet. Boy blowing bubbles
    29:89 N 27 '50

Bullfighting
    Gargallo. Picador sculpture
        bw 24:95 Ap 12 '48
    Goya. Bullfight 7:35 Jy 31 '39
    O'Hara. Bullfight woodcut 37:
        88 O 18 '54

Cards
    Bingham. Raftsmen playing
        cards 7:41 S 11 '39 draw-
        ing bw 7:40 S 11 '39
    Cezanne. The card players
        2:47 Ap 12 '37; 32:84-5 F
        22 '52
    Poker game bw 35:31 S 14 '53

Chess
    Ernst. Abstract chessmen bw
        photog 32:62 Ja 21 '52
    Chessmen, ivory and ceramic
        from oriental and western
        carving photog bw 8:48-9
        Ja 29 '40
    Duchamp. Chess players 32:
        102 Ap 28 '52
    Lucas van Leyden. Chess
        players 24:76 Mr 22 '48

Cockfighting
    Cockfighting, 1870 32:115 Ap
        7 '52
    Cockfighting, Balinese
        frieze, relief sculpture bw
        3:51 S 27 '37

Croquet
    Leech. A nice game for two
        or more lithograph 6:40
        F 6 '39

Dice
    Bigaud. The game 23:60 S
        1 '47
    Binford. The crap shooter
        10:67 My 26 '41

Egyptian dice, c30 B.C. bw
6:53 Mr 20 '39

Discus
  Myron. Discobolus sculpture
    bw 5:46 D 25 '38

Football
  Brown, W. Football paintings
    from photographs 41:14-5
    O 8 '56
  Football player, misericord
    woodcarving bw 37:82 S 27
    '54
  Princeton-Yale football game,
    1879 bw 21:85 S 23 '46
  Rogers, J. Football sculpture
    bw 6:8 Mr 6 '39
  Zorach. Linesman sculpture
    bw 8:92 Ap 1 '40

Go
  Japanese envoys playing go,
    1860* bw 12:86 F 23 '42

Golf
  Eisenhower. Bobby Jones 34:
    74 Mr 23 '53
  Goodman, J. The defeat of
    Bobby Jones 7:33 S 4 '39

Handball
  Shahn. Handball 37:98-9 O 4
    '54

Jousting
  Jousting 22:69 My 26 '47
  Knight's activities illustration
    bw 22:68 My 26 '47

Polo
  Hurd. Landscape with polo
    players 7:26 Jy 24 '39

Pool
  Jones, B. Bill's poolroom 10:
    58 Je 16 '41

Quoits
  Rowlandson. Quoits 25:102 S
    13 '48

Roque
  Sample. Roque 3:43 N 15 '37

Rowing
  American championship scull-
    ing race bw 6:41 F 6 '39
  Cremonini. Two rowers 38:
    72-3 Ja 17 '55
  Eakins. Max Schmitt in a
    single scull bw 5:33 O 31
    '38; 16:72 My 15 '44
  Eakins. Turning the stake
    boat. 15:68 S 20 '43
  Lady gondoliers' race, Venice,
    Renaissance bw 23:59 Ag
    4 '47

Rugby
  Rugby on the village green,
    1810 6:39 F 6 '39

Running
  Bragg. Jackson, the Ameri-
    can deer, 1862 6:40 F 6
    '39

Shooting
  Bingham. Shooting for the
    beef 6:28 Je 19 '39
  Miller, B. The shooting
    gallery bw 5:30 O 31 '38

Skating
  Homer. Skating in Central
    Park, 1860 32:118 Ap 7
    '52
  Lee, D. Winter in the Cats-
    kills bw 3:47 S 20 '37
  Regnier. Ice skater litho-
    graph 6:40 F 6 '39

Skiing
  Zhaba. Skiers (copy by Miro-
    nova) 14:46 Mr 29 '43
Skittles See Bowling
Stilts
  Pierce. Stilts woodcut 37:89
    O 18 '54

Games (cont.)
Swimming
  Bellows. Forty-two kids 20:
    80 Mr 25 '46
  Bohrod. Chicago beach 25:62-
    3 Jy 26 '48
  Cadmus. Coney Island 2:45 Mr
    29 '37
  Emett. Skin-diving, Florida
    cartoon 37:46 Jy 5 '54
  Marsh. Swimming in the Hud-
    son 6:25 Ja 9 '39
  Peirce, W. Maine swimming
    hole bw 18:44 Ja 1 '45

Swinging
  Fragonard. The swing 23:79
    S 15 '47

Tennis
  Lawn tennis game, c1870 32:
    118 Ap 7 '52
  Tennis game, France, 18th
    century bw 23:77 S 15 '47

Tops
  Rosenthal, D. Tops 15:65 N
    22 '43

Wrestling
  Brown, Joseph. Hammerlock
    sculpture bw 12:90 My 19
    '41
  Wickey. Kids wrestling sculp-
    ture bw 12:53 F 23 '42
  Wrestler vase, Sumerian bw
    5:59 Ag 15 '38
Gandhi, Mohandas Karamchand
  Mahatma Ghandi statue bw,
    Durga temple, Madras 24:
    29 Ap 5 '48; family; friends,
    photogs bw 24:27-31 F 9 '48
Ganine, Peter
  Chess set ceramics bw 8:48-
    9 Ja 29 '40
Gann, Dolly
  Dolly Gann photog bw 9:11 Ag
    5 '40
Gansevoort, Madgalena (Douw,
  Magdalena; Girl with red shoes)
  American primitive 38:115 Ap

18 '55
Ganso, Emil
  Bearsville meadows 5:26 Ag
    29 '38
  Nudes bw 2:32 F 1 '37
  The village church 2:34 F 1
    '37
  Emil Ganso photog bw 2:32 F
    1 '37 port.
Garafulic, Lily
  Metal figure sculpture 36:80
    My 31 '54
Garbage man eating his lunch.
  sculpture bw Wickey 12:54
  F 23 '42
Garber and Associates, archi-
  tects
  Cincinnati public library bw
    38:91 Mr 28 '55
Garbisch (Edgar W.) collection
  of early American primi-
  tives 36:95-6 Je 28 '54
Garbo, Greta
  Steichen. Greta Garbo, 1928
    photog bw 38:Cover Ja 10
    '55
Garbousova, Raya
  Halsman. Raya Garbousova
    photog bw 16:50 Mr 13 '44
Garcia, Juan
  General Garcia photog bw 4:
    23 Je 13 '38
Garconniere
  Hexagonal garconniere, Hou-
    mas House, Louisiana
    photog 32:74 Je 9 '52
Gardanne. Cezanne 32:86 F 22
  '52
Garden, Mary
  Parks. Mary Garden photog
    bw 34:16 Mr 16 '53
Garden in Carthage. Lee, D. 33:
  112 N 10 '52
Garden of delights. Bosch 27:
  75-82 N 14 '49
Garden of Eden See also Adam
  and Eve
  Auguste. Garden of Eden 28:
    101 Mr 13 '50
  Bosch. Garden of Eden
    (Garden of Paradise) 11:

56 S 8 '41; 27:76 N 14 '49

Garden of Eden, stained glass, Chartre cathedral 22:73 Ap 7 '47

Michelangelo. Garden of Eden 27:35-6 D 26 '49

Garden sculpture
  Greek figures, cast iron, American gothic gardens, New England 12:11 My 11 '42
  Maillol. Garden piece sculpture bw 2:51 Ja 4 '37
  "Outdoor sculpture, then and now--1850-1941," exhibit, Arden Gallery bw 10:118-21 Ap 21 '41

Gardening, illumination, Flemish, 15th century 22:79 My 26 '47

Gardens See also Parks
  The Alhambra, Spain photogs 33:52 Ag 18 '52
  Davis, G. R. Luxembourg gardens, Paris 19:48 Jy 16 '45
  Gunston Hall garden, Virginia photog 11:121 D 15 '41
  Hooch. Game of skittles 13:95 N 9 '42; 24:72 Je 14 '48
  Hooch. Garden scene bw 3:112 O 18 '37
  Italian gardens, Renaissance villas, Italy photogs 28:73-9 My 8 '50
  McLaughlin gardens, Quebec photog bw 9:109 S 9 '40
  Millroad topiary garden, Lake Forest, Illinois photogs bw 11:62-6 N 3 '41
  Palazzo Colonna, Rome photog bw 18:94-5 Mr 5 '45
  San Juan Capistrano mission photog 40:46 Ja 16 '56
  Tuileries gardens, Paris photog 8:57 Je 3 '40
  Villa Borghese, Rome photog bw 17:98 S 4 '44
  Vuillard. Gardens 37:75 N 1 '54
  Yoshimura. Japanese house,

Museum of Modern Art photogs bw 37:71-2, 74 Ag 23 '54

Gardner, Mrs.
  Sargent. Mrs. Jack Gardner 41:161 D 24 '56

Gargallo, Pau
  Picador sculpture bw 24:95 Ap 12 '48

Gargoyle, Notre Dame, Paris photog bw 27:43 N 14 '49

Garrett, Pat
  Pat Garrett photog bw 11:68 Ag 4 '41

Garibaldi, Giuseppe
  Garibaldi photog bw 15:18 Ag 9 '43
  Garibaldi and Mazzini meet, 1883* bw 15:19 Ag 9 '43
  Garibaldi and Victor Emmanuel II bw 15:21 Ag 9 '43; 20:28 Je 24 '46

Garner, John Nance
  Vice-President and Mrs Garner photog bw 9:11 Ag 5 '40

Garneray, L.
  Battle of Lake Erie 9:48 O 28 '40

Garnier, Jean Louis Charles
  Opera house, Paris photog 8:62 Je 3 '40

Garrick, David
  Hogarth. David Garrick and his wife 21:82 D 16 '46

Garrison house. domestic architecture, U.S. Wills 21:74 Ag 26 '46

Garter, Order of
  The Great George 26:72 F 7 '49; 35:74 N 23 '53
  Order of the Garter 26:73 F 7 '49

Garuda
  Man-bird, Hinduism 38:69 F 7 '55
  Religious float, Cambodia 40:212 Ap 9 '56

Gasoline Alley. cartoons bw King, F. O. 12:62 F 16 '42

Gates, Horatio
General Horatio Gates bw 29:
52 Jy 3 '50
Gateways and Doors See also
Arches
Brandenberg Gate, Berlin,
1945 photog bw 19:21 Jy
23 '45
Bronze doors, scenes from
New Testament, Beneven-
to cathedral, 12th century
bw 17:58 Jy 24 '44
Classic tavern doorway, a-
canthus on pilasters,
Massachusetts, 1750 bw
6:53 Mr 20 '39
Doorway, Grant (Ebenezer)
house, East Windsor,
Connecticut, 1757 photog
bw 15:15 D 6 '43
Harvard gate, Harvard Uni-
versity photog bw 10:89 My
5 '41
Iron gates, New Orleans
photogs bw 12:8-9, 11 Ap
6 '42
Mnesikles. Propylaea, gateway
to Acropolis, Athens pho-
tog bw 18:56 Ja 1 '45
St. John's gateway, Cambridge,
England photog bw 15:97
S 20 '43
Trinity College, great gate-
way, Cambridge, England
photog bw 15:96 S 20 '43
Gatto, Joe
Circus bw 25:76 N 8 '48
Columbus discovers America
25:72 N 8 '48
Jungle cafe 25:72 N 8 '48
Joe Gatto photogs bw 25:73 N
8 '48 port.
Gauchos
Campos. Argentina: paintings
of pampas; gauchos 4:34-5
Je 20 '38
Gauguin, Paul
Annah the Javanese 29:112 S
11 '50
Back from the forest, Tahiti
bw 6:58 Mr 27 '39

Brittany landscape 21:62 Jy
29 '46
Ia orana Maria 7:26 D 25 '39
bw 13:51 S 14 '42
Man with an ax 37:127 D 13
'54
No te aha oe riri 11:58 S 8 '41
Peasants and angel mural 28:
93 My 1 '50
Picking lemons 21:64 Jy 29
'46
Schneklud--Cellist 21:62 Jy
29 '46
The seed of Areois 21:63 Jy
29 '46
The swineherd, Brittany 21:
62 Jy 29 '46
Tahitian landscape 21:63 Jy
29 '46
Tahitian women with red man-
go blossoms 21:61 Jy 29
'46
Under the pandanus 21:63 Jy
29 '46
We greet you, Mary See Ia
orana Maria
Why are you jealous (angry)
See No te aha oe riri
Swan 33:85 Jy 14 '52 (litho-
graph)
Derelict,* c1890 21:60 Jy 29
'46 (sculpture)
Paul Gauguin photog bw 21:
60 Jy 29 '46 port.
Self-portrait, 1891 bw 13:51
S 14 '42 port.
Self-portrait, age 45, 1892
bw 29:112 S 11 '50
Gautreau, Madame
Sargent. Madame X (Madame
Gautreau) 36:96 My 17 '54
bw 6:54 Mr 20 '39
Gazagnaire, Jean and Hellen,
textile designers
Artists at work photog bw 37:
124 O 25 '54 port.
Gazelles
Manship. Dancer and gazel-
les sculpture bw 7:37 Jy
31 '39

Geddes, Norman Bel
  Norman Bel Geddes photog
    bw 12:53 Ja 12 '42
Gee, David
  Lady Godiva bw 25:164 N 15
    '48
Gee, Yun
  Central Park lake 16:46 Ja 3
    '44
Geese on Cape Cod. Ripley 29:
    126 D 4 '50
Geese
  Scott. Brent in Strangford
    lough 7:53 N 13 '39
  Scott. Grey-lag geese alight-
    ing 7:53 N 13 '39
  Scott. Lesser whitefront
    preening 7:54 N 13 '39
  Scott. Pinkfeet flying 1:43 D
    21 '36
  Scott. Pinkfeet flying at dusk
    1:42 D 21 '36
  Wright. The golden egg sculp-
    ture bw 29:124 Ag 28 '50
Geisel, Theodore S. (Dr. Seuss,
    pseudonym)
  "And to Think that I saw it on
    Mulberry Street," illustra-
    tions from his book 11:85
    D 15 '41
  "Thidwick the Big-hearted
    Moose," illustrations from
    his book bw 25:26-7 N 22
    '48
Gem Saloon, New York, c1850
    32:117 Ap 7 '52
Gemini. sculpture bw Maldarelli
    22:139 Mr 24 '47
Gems
  Abraham Lincoln, carved
    black sapphire 34:99 F 9
    '53
  Black Prince ruby 2:40 Mr
    15 '37
  Catherine the Great's sapphire
    32:68 Mr 17 '52
  Cullinan diamond 2:40-1 Mr
    15 '37
  Diamond chalice of Pope Pius
    IX 32:84 Ap 14 '52
  Diamond, 426-carat, uncut,

  World's ninth largest 40:
    57 F 20 '56
  Harry Winston collection of
    historic gems 32:67-8 Mr
    17 '52
  Hope diamond 32:67-8 Mr 17
    '52
  Idol's Eye, diamond 32:67 Mr
    17 '52
  Jonker diamond 32:67-8 Mr
    17 '52
  Koh-i-nur diamond 2:40-1 Mr
    15 '37
  Pearl of Asia, Shah Jahan's
    gift to Mumtaz Mahal 33:
    34 D 29 '52
  Roman cameo, sardonyx, c60
    B.C. bw 9:94 D 9 '40
  Royal Spanish emerald 32:68
    Mr 17 '52
  Ruby, rare gem 32:68 Mr 17
    '52
  Star of the East, diamond 32:
    67-8 Mr 17 '52
The General Armstrong sur-
    rounded, 1814. Leutze 9:
    48 O 28 '40
General attack on Hong Kong.
    Yamaguchi 28:70 F 27 '50
General Custer's death struggle
    lithograph bw 24:13 Je 21
    '48
General Doubleday crossing the
    Potomac, 1863. Henry 6:
    29 Je 19 '39
General Motor's Technical Cen-
    ter, Warren, Mich.
    photogs Saarinen, Eero,
    archt 40:102-5 My 21 '56
General store, New Salem, Ill.
    Phillips, A.F. 36:81 F
    15 '54
Genesis. sculpture bw Epstein
    3:92 N 15 '37
Genevieve, Saint
  St. Genevieve bw 31:76 Jy
    30 '51
Genghis Khan bw 13:104 O 5
    '42
The genius of America. bw
    Yvon 33:44 S 29 '52

The genius of mirth. sculpture
bw Crawford 19:9 S 24 '45
"Genoa" (locomotive)standard
American eight-wheeler,
1872 photog 39:82-3 N 28
'55
Genthe, Arnold, photographer
Autochromes (color photo-
graphs) of 1907: Dancer;
Country scene; Otis Skin-
ner in "Kismet" 28:11 Ja
2 '50
Geodesic Dome
Fuller. Ford Motor Company,
River Rouge photog bw 34:
67-70 Je 8 '53
The George See George, Saint
"The George" (ship) Salem
square-rigger, c1790 38:
68 My 30 '55
George, Saint
Giorgione. Castelfranco Ma-
donna 39:166 O 24 '55
Great George, Knight of the
Garter emblem sculpture
21:72 F 7 '49; 35:74 N 23
'53
Martorell. St. George killing
the dragon 33:91 O 27 '52
Raphael. St. George and the
dragon 33:37 D 29 '52
St. George and the dragon,
parade figure, Portugal
photog bw 23:28 Ag 11 '47
George III, King of England
King George III bw 9:34 D 9
'40
George III, Queen Charlotte,
and children* 25:106 S 13
'48
George V, King of England
Fildes. George V of England
28:62 My 29 '50; 35:83 N
23 '53
George V photog bw 23:72 O
20 '47
George V, tomb effigy, St.
George's chapel, Windsor
castle bw 6:22 Ap 3 '39;
36:44 F 8 '54
George VI, King of England

George VI photog bw 23:72 O
20 '47
George VI, "Time" cover
portrait 17:62 D 11 '44
Kelly. George VI of England
35:83 N 23 '53
"George N. Campbell," coast
guard cutter in the At-
lantic. Fischer 15:59-69
Jy 5 '43
Georgia jungle. Brook 10:52 Ja
13 '41; 21:74 N 25 '46 bw
16:79 Ap 24 '44
"Georgics," illustrations. bw
Maillol 8:109 Ap 15 '40
Gerard, François
Madame Recamier 10:74 Ap
28 '41
Gerasimov, Alexander Mikhailo-
vich
Nudes bw 40:166 Ap 9 '56
Stalin bw 40:165 Ap 9 '56
Alexandr Gerasimov photog
bw 40:165-8 Ap 9 '56 port.
Gergely, Tibor
"Topsy Turvy Circus," illus-
trations 11:85 D 15 '41
Gericault, Theodore
Officer of the imperial guard
35:62 Ag 17 '53
Germain, George
Lord George Germain bw 29:
37 Jy 3 '50
Germaine, Saint
Ford. St. Germain 17:37 D
25 '44
German army review by Fred-
erick the Great, 1779 bw
15:96 N 22 '43
German prisoners, Paris.
Davis, F 19:53 Jy 16 '45
Germantown, Battle of
The Chew House 29:50 Jy 3
'50
Germany
Military scenes and portraits,
Frederick the Great to
present bw 8:24-5 Ap 22
'40
Parliament in Frankfort,
1848 bw 25:86 N 22 '48

Portraits and historical
scenes of General Staff
Corps bw 15:93-101 N 22 '43
Swastika emblem, 1939 photog
bw 9:68 Ag 19 '40

Gerny, George
Big utopia sculpture bw 21:
101 Jy 8 '46
Artist and his work photog
bw 21:101 Jy 8 '46 port.

Gerry, Elbridge
Elbridge Gerry 39:62 Jy 4 '55
bw 9:8 Ag 5 '40; 15:8 Jy 5 '43

Gethsemane See also Jesus
Christ--Gethsemane
Garden of Gethsemane photog
20:59 Ap 1 '46

Getting to work. Turpin. 12:40
Mr 2 '42

Gettysburg
Alabaman's monument photog
bw 4:35 Je 27 '38
Crowd assembled for Gettys-
burg address, November
19, 1863 photog bw 11:105
N 10 '41
General Lee memorial,
equestrian statue bw 4:35
Je 27 '38
Gettysburg 13:62 Jy 6 '42
Victory monument photog bw
4:36 Je 27 '38

Gheeraerts, Marcus, the younger
Sir Walter Raleigh 41:71 D
10 '56

Ghent, Belgium
The Count of Flanders castle
photog bw 22:Cover My
26 '47
Forestier. Treaty of Ghent
41:72-3 Jy 2 '56
Guildhalls, Middle Ages
photog bw 22:82-3 My 26
'47

Ghent altarpiece, Cathedral of
Bavon. Van Eyck, Jan and
Hubert 26:58-69 Ap 18 '49

Ghika (Hadjikyriakos, Nicholas)
Great landscape of Hydra 29:
105 D 11 '50

Ghirlandaio, Domenico

Amerigo Vespucci bw 37:106
O 11 '54
Francesco Sassetti and his
son Teodoro 2:43 Je 28 '37

Ghost over the trees. bw Sedlacek 2:57 Ap 26 '37

Ghost town. watercolor Dehn 11:
43 Ag 11 '41

Ghost town. cartoons Emett 37:
48-9 Jy 5 '54

Ghost town hotel. Guy 16:46 Ja
3 '44

G I Joe. cartoon bw Breger 15:
12-4 Jy 12 '43

Giacometti, Alberto, sculptor
Figure bw 31:151 N 5 '51
Head bw 31:153 N 5 '51
Nude 33:93 O 27 '52
Sculptures of animals bw 31:
152 N 5 '51
Artist and his work photogs
bw 31:152 N 5 '51

Giant Bible of Admont, page 34:
78, 82 F 23 '53

Giant cypress tree, Oaxaca,
Mexico. Lee, D. 22:75 My
12 '47

Gibbon, Edward
Edward Gibbon bw 25:113 S
13 '48

Gibson, Charles Dana
Gibson girl bw 5:29 O 31 '38;
13:133-4, 138 O 12 '42;
26:30 Ja 3 '49 (drawings)
Home for the holidays bw 28:
17 Ja 2 '50 (drawing)
Presentation to the King and
Queen of England bw 23:
88-9 N 17 '47 (drawing)
The social push bw 28:17 Ja
2 '50 (drawing)
Charles Dana Gibson; wife;
home photogs bw 13:122-
4 O 12 '42

Gide, Andre
Andre Gide photogs bw 23:51
N 24 '47

Gies, Ludwig, sculptor
Crucifixion bw 3:72 Ag 16
'37

Gies, Ludwig (cont.)
   Artist and his work photog 36:
      144 My 10 '54 port.
Gifford, Sanford Robinson
   Healy. Sanford Gifford in
      Arch of Titus 33:89 S 15 '52
Gift (art object). bw Ray 34:25
   My 25 '53
Gigaku mask, Japan, 8th century
   30:71 My 28 '51
Gilbert, A.C., toy designer and
   manufacturer
   Erector sets; American Flyer
      trains photogs bw 21:67 N
      18 '46
Gilbert, Humphrey
   Polar map, showing sea pas-
      sage from America to China,
      1582 18:61 My 21 '45
Gilbert, Jean B. A.
   John Quincy Adams, age 77 41:
      72 Jy 2 '56
Gilbert and Sullivan land.
   Corcos 25:86-7 O 11 '48
Gilcrease (Thomas) collection of
   American Indian and
   frontier art 36:71-9 Mr 8
   '54
Gilded mask. sculpture bw Weber,
   M. 19:84 Ag 20 '45
Gilding the acrobats. Cadmus
   2:47 Mr 29 '37
Gillam, Bernhard
   James G. Blaine, political
      cartoon bw 31:20 O 22 '51
Gillray, James
   Old lady of Threadneedle
      Street, 1797 cartoon bw 21:
      99 O 21 '46
Gin lane. bw Hogarth 20:66 My
   27 '46; 21:83 D 16 '46
Giordano, Luca
   The finding of Moses 41:71 D
      10 '56
Giorgione (Giorgio Barbarelli)
   Adultress brought before
      Christ (painted with Piom-
      bo and Titian) 39:169 O 24
      '55
   Castelfranco Madonna (Ma-
      donna with St. Francis and

St. George) 39:166 O 24
   '55
The concert (The musicians)
   (painted with Titian) 39:168-
   9 O 24 '55
Concert champetre (Fete
   champetre; Pastoral sym-
   phony) 23:52 Ag 4 '47; 39:
   170-1 O 24 '55
Sleeping Venus 41:104-5 O 22
   '56 bw 40:103 F 20 '56
The tempest 39:166-7 O 24
   '55
The three wisemen (Evander
   showing Aeneas the site of
   Rome; Three philosophers)
   39:170 O 24 '55
Self-portrait (copy) 39:165 O
   24 '55 port.
Giotto
   Ethernal and angels 4:30 F 7
      '38
   Lives of Christ and Mary,
      Arena chapel, Padua, 14th
      century frescoes 25:Cover,
      34-57 D 27 '48
   Madonna and Child bw 13:47
      D 28 '42
   St. Francis of Assisi, San
      Francesco church, Assisi
      frescoes 16:65-71 Ap 10
      '44
   G otto's tower, Florence
      photog bw 25:57 D 27 '48
      (architecture)
   Giotto (?) bw 25:57 D 27 '48
      port.
Giraffes
   The giraffe parade, tapestry,
      Flemish, c1525 24:76-7
      Mr 22 '48
   Giraffes mobiles, Northland
      shopping center, Detroit
      37:81 Ag 30 '54
   Mochi. Giraffes paper cut-
      outs 34:18, 20 Mr 9 '53
   Priebe. The piebald giraffe
      21:79 N 25 '46
   Rosenthal, B. Giraffes sculp-
      ture bw 34:134 Ap 6 '53
Girard, Alexander

Alexander Girard photog bw
27:119 O 24 '49

Girl. sculpture bw Kruger 39:
187 N 14 '55

Girl. sculpture bw Laurent 10:
67 Je 2 '41

Girl before a mirror. Picasso
23:96 O 13 '47; 25:58 O 11
'48

Girl combing her hair. Renoir
37:66 Ag 9 '54

Girl in red. Albright, M. 16:
65 Mr 27 '44

The girl in red. Carroll, J. 8:
120 My 13 '40

Girl juggling. woodcut Seong
Moy 37:88 O 18 '54

Girl on a horse. sculpture bw
Melicov 5:5 N 7 '38

Girl perplexed. wood carving bw
Steig 6:36 Ap 10 '39

Girl playing with ball. sculpture
bw 3:72 Ag 16 '37

Girl resting. Boucher 41:104-5
O 22 '56

Girl washing hair. sculpture bw
Laurent 10:64 Je 2 '41

Girl washing her hair. sculpture
bw Robus 6:83 My 22 '39

Girl with a wand. Austin, D. 19:
82 O 1 '45

Girl with cock. bw Picasso 8:59
Mr 4 '40

Girl with mountain snow. Baylinson 16:46 Ja 3 '44

Girl with red shoes (Magdalena
Douw), American primitive
38:115 Ap 18 '55

Girls and bananas. Rosenthal, D.
15:68 N 22 '43

Gischia, Leon
Egg plants 17:76 N 13 '44
Artist at work photog bw 17:
74 N 13 '44 port.

Giselle. bw Davis, G. R. 22:94
Ap 21 '47

Gisze, George
Holbein. Merchant Gisze 24:
70 Mr 22 '48

Give us this day. Hartley 32:87
Je 16 '52

Giza, Egypt
Great Pyramid (Pyramid of
Khufu) models, showing
steps in construction bw 19:
75-80 D 3 '45
Pyramids, including Great
Pyramid, photog bw 24:75
Ja 19 '48
Sphinx photog 41:107 N 26 '65
bw 13:Cover O 19 '42

Glackens, William
Nude with apple 9:78 D 9 '40;
38:74 Mr 28 '55

Gladstone, William Ewart
William Gladstone 24:71 My
24 '48 photog bw 4:60 Ap 4
'38; 9:115 S 9 '40

Glamis castle, Scotland photog
bw 3:67 Jy 19 '37; 22:95
My 5 '47

Glanzman, Lew
Bob Hope, as the masters
might paint him: Daumier,
Dore, Goya, Picasso, Rem-
brandt cartoons bw 21:119
O 21 '46

Glasgow, Ellen
Ellen Glasgow photog bw 17:
14 Ag 14 '44

Glasier, Marshall
Three babes in the Wisconsin
woods 25:58 N 29 '48

Glaspell, Susan
Susan Glaspell photog bw 9:72
Jy 15 '40

Glass blowers, New Jersey
engraving 39:59 Jy 18 '55

Glass making, Middle Ages bw
22:82 My 26 '47

Glass Painting
Fasola. Poliepipedi (three dimensional) paintings 41:
188-9 N 26 '56
Pereira. Paintings on glass
layers 34:73-5 Ja 26 '53
Portrait plate, Venetian,
15th century 37:55 Ag 2
'54

Glass Staining
Bourges cathedral: Three
apostles 22:72-3 Ap 7 '47

Glass Staining (cont.)
Chartres cathedral: Angel;
Ascension of Christ; Garden
of Eden; Good Samaritan;
Virgin and Child 22:71-3 Ap
7 '47

Contemporary
Battle of Britain window, Westminster Abbey 26:58 F 7 '49
Bonawit. Life of Christ window
6:31 Ap 3 '39
Burnham. Battle of Lexington
bw 16:96 Ja 10 '44
Burnham. Religious law win-
dows and details 6:32 Ap 3
'39
Ciampi. Facade, Corpus
Christi Roman Catholic
church, San Francisco 38:
68-9 Ap 11 '55
Connick. Rose window 6:31 Ap
3 '39
D'Ascenzo. Stained glass
window, Maryland church
6:31 Ap 3 '39
Devils in church vestments
and scenes, Anti-Religious
Museum, Moscow bw 11:
121 O 13 '41
Le Compte. Window, St.
George's Episcopal church,
Mt. Savage, Md. 38:65 Ap
11 '55
Loire. Window with dove of
Holy Spirit 38:66 Ap 11 '55
Matisse. Stained glass, Do-
minican chapel, Vence,
France, 31:108 N 26 '51
Meistermann. Window designs
radio station, Cologne 36:
146 My 10 '54
Nicolas. Life of Christ, Fair-
mont church, Cleveland
12:52-3 Ap 6 '42
Pied Piper of Hamilin bw 16:
125 My 29 '44
Pinart. Stained glass photog
bw 37:124 O 25 '54
Roualt. Christ 28:75 Je 19 '50
Sowers. Window. St. George's

Episcopal church, Durham,
N.H. 38:64 Ap 11 '55
Stained glass church windows
by modern artists of
France 28:74-5 Je 19 '50
Stained glass in United States
renaissance 6:30-2 Ap 3
'39
Willet. Window, Westwood
Community Presbyterian
church, Los Angeles 38:
66-7 Ap 11 '55
Glassware, American
Amber whisky flask, eagle de-
sign, c1850 17:59 S 4 '44
Amelung. Salt holder 39:59
Jy 18 '55
Amelung. Wineglass 39:58 Jy
18 '55
"America's Best" designed
goblets and glasses 29:89
D 25 '50
Audubon. Bird plates, Steuben
glass bw 23:19 N 10 '47
Benjamin Franklin flask 40:
82 Ja 9 '56
Bullseye window pane 39:58
Jy 18 '55
Columbia blown flask 39:58-
9 Jy 18 '55
Eighteenth and early nine-
teenth century glass 39:58-
9 Jy 18 '55
Ludlow bottle 39:58-9 Jy 18
'55
Ohio flat bowl 39:58 Jy 18 '55
Ohio "Grandfather" flask 39:
58 Jy 18 '55
Ohio three-mold decanter 39:
59 Jy 18 '55
Pittsburgh creamer 39:59 Jy
18 '55
Sandwich pressed glass bowl
39:58 Jy 18 '55
Stiegel. "Daisy-diamond"
blown flask 39:58-9 Jy 18
'55
Stiegel. Sugarbowl 39:58 Jy
18 '55
Stiegel. Tumbler. enameled
39:58 Jy 18 '55

Glassware

Tiffany. Lamps, shades, vases, dishes 40:92-3 Mr 5 '56

Victorian vases and dishes, bric-a-brac 40:90-1 Mr 5 '56

Waugh. Merry-go-round bowl, Steuben glass bw 23:18 N 10 '47

Waugh, Zodiac bowl, compass bowl; pigeon, fish figures; sugar and creamer bw 7:32 S 18 '39

Wistarberg candlestick 39:58-9 Jy 18 '55

Wistarberg (South Jersey) sugar bowl 39:58-9 Jy 18 '55

Wistarberg-type (South Jersey) "Lily pad" pitcher 39:58 Jy 18 '55

Glassware, Swedish
National Museum, Stockholm, exhibit: vases, bowls, decanters, graal-decorated ware bw 17:65-8 Ag 7 '44

Glassware, Venetian
Venetian bulls eye glass 37:56 Ag 2 '54

Venetian glass 37:53-8 Ag 2 '54

Wedding cup, 15th century. Barovier 37:55 Ag 2 '54

Work of the renaissance: pitcher; enamelled goblet 23:50 Ag 4 '47

The gleaners. Millet, F. F. 25:96-7 N 22 '48

"Gleason's Pictorial Drawing-Room Companion," first illustrated weekly in U.S., 1851-59 woodcuts bw 31:14-5 Ag 6 '51

Glockendon, Albrecht
Manuscript calendar, 1527 bw 18:42 Ja 1 '45

The glorious first of June, 1794 24:67 My 10 '48

Glorious victory of the sloop, Maria. Feininger, Lyonel 26:87 F 21 '49

Glover, John
My harvest home, Tasmania bw 12:78 F 9 '42

The glutton. Tamayo 34:102 Mr 16 '53

Gneisenau, August (?)
A. Gneisenau bw 15:96 N 22 '43

Go See Games and Sports--Go

Goats
Goat, Sumerian statuette, inlaid gold, Ur 40:92 Je 4 '56

Hardy. Billy sculpture bw 37:124 O 11 '54

Maldarelli. Goat sculpture bw 22:138 Mr 24 '47

Maldarelli. Long-horn Bill sculpture bw 22:139 Mr 24 '47

Persian goat charm, bronze, c1000 B.C. bw 20:90 Je 24 '46

Gobelin Tapestry
Louis XIV wins the Battle of Dole, 1674 bw 5:15 S 5 '38

Osterly Park wall coverings, England photog 23:71 Ag 25 '47

Rosecliff, Newport photog bw 11:83 Ag 18 '41

Goblets and Glasses
African carved ceremonial goblet, Bushongo tribe bw 33:120 S 8 '52

Amelung. Wineglass 39:58 Jy 18 '55

"America's Best" designed glassware 29:89 D 25 '50

Stiegel. Enamelled tumbler 39:58 Jy 18 '55

Sumerian gold tumbler 40:85 Je 4 '56

Venetian goblet, enamelled, c1475 bw 23:50 Ag 4 '47

Venetian glass, modern 37:53 Ag 2 '54

Viennese carved quartz goblets, c1800 25:129 D 6 '48

Goblin sculpture, Japanese, 1215 34:95 Ap 20 '53

God

Blake. God creating Adam
print bw 6:45 Ja 16 '39
Blake. God creating Eve print
bw 6:45 Ja 16 '39
Coypel. God the father* ceiling mural, Royal chapel,
Versaille 23:86 S 15 '47
Giotto. Eternal and angels
4:30 F 7 '38
Michelangelo. Creation of the
world, Sistine chapel
frescoes 21:62-9 My 1 '46;
27:27-36 D 26 '49
Michelangelo. God fresco detail bw 21:69 Jy 1 '46
Michelangelo. God creating
the sky and the water fres-
co 27:28 D 26 '49
Michelangelo. God creating the
sun and the moon 27:28-9
D 26 '49
Michelangelo. God separating
day from night 27:27 D 26
'49
Milles. God of Peace sculp-
ture bw 2:27 F 22 '37
Schnorr. Jacob's ladder en-
graving bw 6:55 Ja 30 '39
Van Coxie. God and Adam
tapestry 35:94 D 14 '53
Van Eyck brothers. The Lord
26:64-5, 69 Ap 18 '49
Van Leyden. Adam and Eve
driven from Eden bw 6:46
Ja 16 '39
God Rest You Merry, Gentlemen.
Peirce, W. 23:56 D 22 '47
Goddard, John, Furniture design-
er
Block-front secretary, U.S.,
c1759 38:66-7 My 30 '55
Goddesses See Gods and Goddes-
ses
Goddesses. bw Moore, A 35:162
O 26 '53
Godeberta, Saint
Christus. St. Elgius and St.
Godeberta 37:65 Ag 9 '54
Godiva, Lady
Collier. Lady Godiva bw 25:

160 N 15 '48
Gee. Lady Godiva bw 25:164
N 15 '48
Lady Godiva engraving bw,
England 25:164 N 15 '48
Lady Godiva bw, France 25:
164 N 15 '48
Lady Godiva statue bw, Cov-
entry 27:40 N 7 '49
Landseer. Lady Godiva bw
25:160 N 15 '48
Madame Wharton as Lady
Godiva bw 25:164 N 15 '48
Vinck. Lady Godiva bw 25:164
N 15 '48
Gods and Goddesses See also
names of religions, as
Buddha and Buddhism;
Confucius and Confucian-
ism; Hinduism; Jainism;
and Mythological Themes

Cambodia
Goddess sculpture bw, Angkor-Wat bw 5:35 Ag 1 '38

China
Two dieties fresco bw, 12th
century 35:152-5 O 5 '53

Egypt
Amen gold statue 41:115 N 26
'56
Amen, Temple of
Karnak photog bw 24:79 Ja
19 '48
Luxor photog bw 24:79 Ja
19 '48
Thebes photog 41:116 N 26
'56
Harakhte 41:115 N 26 '56 tomb
painting 24:82 Ja 19 '48
Hathor 41:114 N 26 '56 tomb
painting 24:82 Ja 19 '48
Horus, the hawk god, basalt
bw c350 B.C. 6:53 Mr 20
'39
Isis holding her son, Horus
statue, blue faience 41:
114 N 26 '50
Isis, motherhood goddess,

tomb painting 24:82 Ja 19
'48

Nut, portrait with symbols 41:
114-5 N 26 '56

Osiris 41:114 N 26 '56

Ubasti, cat goddess, 6th century B.C. bw 5:16 Ag 29
'38; 13:92 N 9 '42

Eskimo
Elgstroem. Eskimo myths and
legends 20:8-10 Ja 14 '46

Etruria
Etruscan goddess bronze 40:
63 F 13 '56

Japan
Hachiman, god of war photog
bw 17:24 N 27 '44

Oyamakui-No-Mikoto, warrior
god sculpture bw 18:95 F
19 '45

Wind god, 17th century 34:100
Ap 20 '53

Mexico
Quetzalcoatl, feathered serpent, sculpture bw Toltec
28:62 Ja 9 '50
mosaic mask bw 24:84 Mr
22 '48

Temple, Teotihuacan photog
bw 4:57 Ap 11 '38; 22:100
F 24 '47

Tlaloc sculpture bw 28:62 Ja
9 '50

Persia
Mithras, sun god, sculptured
head bw: Roman, 2nd cen-
tury 37:56 O 11 '54

Sky god and sun god, bronze
harness ornaments, c1000
B.C. bw 20:90 Je 24 '46

Ur
Abu, Sumerian God, "Lord of
Vegetation," and wife
statue 40:89 Je 4 '56

Georg, Edouard

Nativity with birds bw 27:55
D 26 '49

Edouard Georg photog bw 27:
55 D 26 '49 port.

Goertschacher, Urban
Ecce Homo bw 9:108-9 D 2 '40

Goethe, Johann Wolfgang von
Goethe--portraits; home,
Weimar bw 27:22-3 Jy 25
'49

Goff, Bruce, architect
Chapel, University of Oklahoma, bw 30:16-7 Ap 30 '51

Round house, Aurora, Ill.
plan, photogs 30:70-5 Mr
19 '51

Space and saucer house 39:
155-6 S 19 '55

Ultra-modern house, Norman,
Okla. bw 24:72-4 Je 28 '48

Goin' home. bw Benton 5:9 D 12
'38

Going to town. Liguore 1:44 N
30 '36

Gold case. mural Poor 2:36 Ja
4 '37

Gold diggers, Ararat, 1854.
bw Roper 12:78 F 9 '42

Goldberg, Rube
Cartoons bw 17:76 N 27 '44

The golden Buddha, Gyantze
temple, Tibet 6:26 Je 12
'39

Golden Buddha, Marble temple,
Bangkok 31:35 D 31 '51

Golden Buddha, Shwe Dagon
Pagoda, Rangoon sculp-
ture 38:Cover Mr 7 '55

Golden Buddha, Wat Bovornives
monastery, Bangkok sculp-
ture 38:80 Mr 7 '55

Golden city. Zao Wou-Ki 36:102-
3 F 22 '54

Golden eagle. Audubon 3:40 Jy
12 '37

Golden egg. sculpture bw
Wright, P. 29:124 Ag 28
'50

Golden Fleece, Order of 26:73
F 7 '49

Golden Gate bridge. Chamberlain, R. 23:98 N 10 '47

Golden Gate International Exposition See Fairs

Golden hair. Bonnard 25:54 Jy 26 '48

Golden Meru, cremation altar, Thailand photogs bw 28: 132, 138-41 Ap 17 '50

The golden thrones, New Delhi photog bw 10:81 Ja 27 '41

The golden tower, Buddhist shrine, Tibet photog 6:26 Je 12 '39

Goldfish and sculpture. Matisse 25:60 O 11 '48

Goldfish pond. Churchill 20:48 Ja 7 '46

Goldsmithing See also Armor; Jewelry

Christ and saints, altarpiece, Basel cathedral gold relief 33:38-9 D 29 '52

Cross, emerald-studded, c1580 40:38 Ja 9 '56

Jamnitzer. Silver-gilt basin, with cupids, kings, continents, Nurnberg, 17th century bw 31:20-1 S 24 '51

Rouchomovski. Tiara of Saltaphernes, gold relief bw 39: 144 S 26 '55

Snuffboxes, gifts to Duke of Wellington 26:72 F 7 '49

Zadok collection of chalices bw 32:77 Ja 14 '52

Goldsmithing, Anglian

Coins, buckles, clasps, plaques, 7th century 31:84 Jy 16 '51

Goldsmithing, Egyptian

Dagger, Tutankamen's tomb, c1375 B.C. 24:81 Ja 19 '48

Mummy finger-sheaths 24:81 Ja 19 '48

Mummy mask of Tutankamen 24:81 Ja 19 '48

Winged serpent amulet, c1375 B.C. 24:81 Ja 19 '48

Goldsmithing, England

Salt of State jewelled 2:42

Mr 15 '37

Goldsmithing, Italian

Cellini. Rospigliosi cup bw 6:53 Mr 20 '39; 31:26 O 15 '51

Cellini. Salt cellar, c1540 31: 18-9 S 24 '51

Cup, 16th century 37:64 Ag 9 '54

Goldsmithing, Persian

Persian gold and enamelled plate 33:43 D 29 '52

Goldsmithing, Pre-Columbian

Figures; ornaments: bird, crab, frog, alligator; lip plug 18:49 Je 4 '45

Jewelry and other ornaments: breastplates, ear plugs, crown, pendant 36:102-4 Ap 12 '54

Llama, c1550 bw 36:25-6 Ap 5 '54

Pin, Chiriqui, Panama 33: 130 O 20 '52

Pin, Cocle, Panama 33:130 O 20 '52

Goldsmithing, Sumerian

Bull's head 40:92-3 Je 4 '56

Goat 40:92 Je 4 '56

Head dress 40:93 Je 4 '56

Helmet 40:93 Je 4 '56

Tumbler, fluted 40:85 Je 4 '56

Goldsmithing, United States

Spiegel. Gold pap spoon with bells 38:116 Ap 18 '55

Gomata, feet of Jain statue, Mysore photog bw 9:73 N 25 '40; 10:103 My 12 '41

Good King Wenceslas. Lee, D. 23:45 D 22 '47

Good shepherd. sculpture bw Sister Mary Thomasita 35: 157 O 12 '53

Golf See Games and Sports-- Golf

Gomez, Edward

The unknown political prisoner sculpture bw 34:42 Je 1 '53

Gompers, Samuel

Samuel Gompers photog bw
33:33 D 8 '52

Gonne, Maude See McBride,
Maude (Gonne)

Good Samaritan, stained glass,
Chartre cathedral 22:73
Ap 7 '47

Goodhue, Bertram G. archt.
Nebraska State Capitol, 1922
5:30 O 31 '38

Goodin, Peggy
Peggy Goodin photog bw 22:
81 Je 2 '47

Goodman, Charles M., archt.
Contemporary house, Alex-
andria, Va. photogs, plan
bw 31:123 S 10 '51

Goodman, Johnny
The defeat of Bobby Jones 7:
33 S 4 '39

Goop. drawing bw Burgess 31:
37 O 1 '51

Gorgon See Animals, Imaginary --Gorgon

Gorilla. sculpture bw Jonas 12:
89 Mr 23 '42

Goring Art Collection, cached
paintings and sculptures
bw 18:41-2 Je 11 '45

Gorky, Arshile
Artist and family photog bw
24:91 F 16 '48 port.

Gorsline, Douglas
Thomas Wolfe 10:47 F 3 '41

Gospels See Manuscripts

The gossips. Pittman 18:70 F
19 '45

Gothic cathedral. etching bw Bone
1:45 D 7 '36

Gottlieb, Adolf
Vigil 25:63 O 11 '48

Gottlieb, Adolph
Artist at work on stained
glass photog 38:67 Ap 11 '55
port.
Gottlieb photog bw 30:34 Ja 15
'51 port.

Gould, Allan
Source of power mural, post
office, Greenville, Ky. 10:
45 Ja 27 '41

Gould, Chester
Dick Tracy, cartoons bw 17:
43-4 Ag 14 '44
Chester Gould photog bw 17:
46 Ag 14 '44

Gould, Jay
Jay Gould photog bw 13:142 D
7 '42; 30:68 Je 11 '51
Jay Gould's flight to Jersey
cartoon bw 13:142 D 7 '42
Nast. Gould and Drew, 1869
bw 13:142 D 7 '42

Gown. drawing Ingres 34:86 My
11 '53

Goya, Francisco de
Bullfight 7:35 Jy 31 '39
The forge 3:37 D 27 '37
Don Manuel Osorio de Zuniga
2:41 Je 28 '37
The Duchess of Alba 4:44 My
16 '38 bw 26:86 Mr 28 '49
The maja clothed 29:107 S 11
'50
The maja nude 29:106-7 S 11
'50
Maria Luisa, Queen of Spain
31:63 O 1 '51
Marquesa de la Solana bw 16:
65 Ja 10 '44
El pelele (The manikin) tapes-
try cartoon 40:73 My 28
'56
Portrait 37:63 Ag 9 '54
The witches' Sabbath murals
31:64-5 O 1 '51
Goya bw 4:40 My 16 '38 port.
Self-portrait, age 69, 1815
bw 29:106 S 11 '50 port.

Goyen, Jan Josephsz van
Dutch scene* bw 11:54 N 10
'41

Gozzoli, Benozzo
Journey of the Magi, chapel,
Medici-Riccardi palace,
Florence, 1459 19:Cover,
43-5 D 24 '45

Graal-decorated glass, Sweden
bw 17:67 Ag 7 '44

Graf Spee defeat. Wilkinson
24:68 My 10 '48

Graham, Cecelia
  A South American woman
    grinding corn sculpture bw
    4:14 F 21 '38; 5:70 D 5 '38
  Artist at work photog bw 9:
    62 Ag 5 '41 port.
Graham, Mary (Cathcart)
  Gainsborough. The Honorable
    Mrs. Graham 25:96 S 13
    '48
Graham Galleries, New York
    City
  Peale exhibit: paintings of
    five Peale's: Charles Will-
    son, James, Rembrandt,
    Mrs. Rembrandt, Raphaelle
    12:64-6 Mr 20 '42
Grahame, Kenneth
  Kenneth Grahame photog bw
    27:69 N 21 '49
Gramercy park. Bellows 20:79
    Mr 25 '46
The Grand Canal, Venice: Shy-
    lock. Turner 5:44 S 12 '38
Grand Canyon. cartoon Emett
    37: 50 Jy 5 '54
Grand Central station. Sloan 7:
    46 D 11 '39
Grande Jatte. Seurat 31:60-2 Jy
    23 '51
Grand Union hotel, Saratoga
    Springs, New York
  Grand Union hotel lobby bw
    33:43-4 S 29 '52
"Grandfather" clock, Chinese
    Chippendale case, Phila-
    delphia, c1770. photog
    Rittenhouse 39:64 Jy 18 '55
"Grandfather" flask Ohio glass-
    ware 39:58 Jy 18 '55
Grandson David. Eisenhower 28:
    151 Ap 17 '50
Granet, François Marius
  Ingres. Granet the artist 34:
    90 My 11 '53 port.
Grant, Gordon
  Kennebunkport, Maine, 1825
    mural bw 18:34 Ap 2 '45
Grant, Ulysses Simpson
  Boyle. General Ulysses Simp-
    son Grant bw 6:31 Je 19 '39

General Grant, G.O.P. cam-
    paign poster, 1868 40:69
    Ja 30 '56
General Ulysses S. Grant
    photog bw 14:76 F 15 '43;
    23:57 N 3 '47
Grant and his family, 1885
    photog bw 23:57 N 3 '47
Lt. Ulysses S. Grant, Mexi-
    can War, 1847 bw 22:119
    Je 9 '47
Ulysses S. Grant cartoon
    opposing third term, 1880
    8:10-1 Ap 22 '40
Ulysses S. Grant political
    cartoons 1880 40:70 Ja
    30 '56 bw 31:19 O 22 '51;
    37:14 Jy 5 '54
Granting charters,* England,
    Middle Ages bw 22:81 My
    26 '47
Granvella, Antoine Perrenot de
  Titian. Antoine Perrenot de
    Granvella 7:55 O 9 '39
Graphic Arts See Prints; and
    names of graphic arts tech-
    niques, as Engravings;
    Etchings; Lithographs;
    Woodcuts
Grard, Georges
  Nude sculpture bw 41:84 O 8
    '56
Grasshopper. sculpture bw Rudy
    15:82 D 20 '43
Gratz, Rebecca
  Sully. Rebecca Gratz 41:158
    D 24 '56
The grave of William Penn.
    Hicks 17:72 O 16 '44
Graves, Morris
  Han bronze 35:88 S 28 '53
  Little known bird of the inner
    eye 25:64 O 11 '48
  Preening sparrow 35:88 S 28
    '53
  Morris Graves photog 35:88
    S 28 '53 port.
Gray, Cleve
  Cypresses 33:93 S 15 '52
Gray, Thomas
  Literary locale of his poem,

"Elegy in a Country Church-
yard" photog bw 14:77-83
Je 14 '43
Great Caesar's ghost. bw Bacon,
P. 6:58 My 8 '39
The great concert. bw Dufy 34:
36 Ap 13 '53
Great fire, London 41:171-2 N
19 '56
Great George, Knight of the
Garter emblem, diamond
and gold encrusted 26:72 F
7 '49; 35:74 N 23 '53
"Great Harry" (ship) ("Henry
Grace a Dieu") English,
1514 24:66 My 10 '48; 41:
78 O 29 '56
Great landscape of Hydra. Ghika
29:105 D 11 '50
Great palace, Amsterdam photog
bw 5:29 S 5 '38
Great Pyramid See Pyramids
The great race meeting. Wootton,
J. 25:102-3 S 13 '48
The great red dragon and the
woman clothed with sun.
watercolor bw Blake 10:94
Je 9 '41
Great wall of China photog bw 3:
56 Ag 23 '37
Greaves, Derrick
The spaghetti eaters bw 40:
166 Ap 23 '56
Derrick Greaves photog bw
40:164 Ap 23 '56 port.
Greco, Emilio
Pinocchio sculpture, Collodi,
Italy 40:127 Je 4 '56
Greece
Delacroix. Massacre at Scio
25:86 N 22 '48
Perlin. Greek priest, peas-
ant, partisan drawings bw
17:35 S 4 '44
Greek Catholic church, Uzhorod,
Czechoslovakia photog bw
3:100 N 8 '37
Greek phalanx opposing Persian
hordes bw 13:108 O 5 '42
Greek revival furniture, U.S.--
Duncan Phyfe and other

photogs 39:60-1 Ag 29 '55
Greek revival interior.* water-
color Davis, A.J. 39:60-
1 Ag 29 '55
Greek slave. sculpture, plaster
model bw Powers 33:97 S
15 '52
"Greek slave" exhibited, New
York, 1887 bw 19:8 S 24
'45; 27:56 Ag 29 '49
Greeley, Horace
Horace Greeley photog bw 7:
50 Ag 28 '39; 14:7 My 31
'43
Nast. Horace Greeley, politi-
cal cartoon bw 31:20 O 22
'51
Green, Henry See Yorke,
Henry
Greenaway, Kate
"A Day in a Child's Life,"
illustrations from her book
bw 18:87-8 Ap 9 '45
Illustrations from her books
23:87-92 D 1 '47
"Queen of the Pirate Isle,"
illustrations of Harte's
book 23:88 D 1 '47
Greenbaum, Dorothea
Acrobat sculpture bw 4:62
Ap 25 '38
Greenbow, Rose O'Neal
Mrs. Rose O'Neal Greenbow
photog bw 11:96 N 10 '41
Greene, Graham
Graham Greene photog bw 29:
51 O 30 '50
Greene, Nathaniel
Nathaniel Greene bw 29:52 Jy
3 '50
Greene, Stephen
The burial 29:65 O 23 '50
Christ and the money changers
29:64-5 O 23 '50
The deposition 29:65 O 23 '50
bw 27:149 O 17 '49
The doll 28:89 Mr 20 '50
Family portrait 29:64 O 23
'50
Resurrection 33:99 O 27 '52
Stephen Greene, photog bw

Greene, Stephen (cont.)
    29:64 O 23 '50
Greenham, Robert D.
    Fancy dress 3:27 D 20 '37
Greenland
    Thomas. Greenland at war
      15:77-8 S 6 '43
    Wolf. Greenland at war draw-
      ings bw 15:76 S 6 '43
Greenough, Horatio, sculptor
    George Washington statue,
      nude to waist bw 5:5 N 7
      '38; 19:9 S 24 '45
    Sears children bw 37:41 O 25
      '54
Greenwood, Greek revival
    plantation, Louisiana, 1830
    photog 32:82-3 Je 9 '52
Greenwood, John
    Benjamin Franklin, attributed
      (also attributed to Robert
      Feke), c1784 40:78 Ja 9 '56
    Sea captains carousing in Su-
      rinam, 1758 26:84-5 F 28
      '49 port.
Greenwood, Walter
    Walter Greenwood and his wife
      photog bw 3:114 O 11 '37
Gregarti, Guido
    Saint Pius X, official portrait
      36:99 My 31 '54
Gregory, Saint
    Bazaine. St. Gregory stained
      glass 28:74 Je 19 '50
    St. Gregory 22:70 Ap 7 '47
Gregory, Waylande
    Electron children terra cotta
      sculptures bw, New York
      World's Fair, 1939 6:36
      Mr 13 '39
Greuze, Jean Baptiste
    The broken eggs 5:36 S 26 '38
    Jean Greuze bw 5:34 S 26 '38
      port.
Grey, Charles
    Earl Grey 24:70 My 24 '48
Grey, Jane
    Lady Jane Grey bw 32:24 F
      18 '52
Grey-lag geese alighting. Scott
    7:53 N 13 '39

Grief. sculpture bw Saint-Gau-
    dens 24:110 Mr 15 '48
Griffin See Animals, Imagin-
    ary--Griffins
Grilles See Ironwork
Grilo, Sarah
    Fantasy 36:79 My 31 '54
Gris, Juan
    The guitar player bw 26:86 Ja
      10 '49
Gromaire, Marcel
    Balloons 33:96 O 27 '52
The groom. Brueghel, P., the
    elder 7:56 O 9 '39
Gropius, Walter
    Walter Gropius photog bw 10:
      96 My 5 '41
Gropper, William
    Civilization bw 8:71 My 27
      '40
    Horseman 20:79 F 18 '46
    Pearl Harbor 16:78 Je 12 '44
    The Senate 2:24 F 1 '37
    William Gropper photog bw
      2:32 F 1 '37; 16:76 Je 12
      '44
Gros, Antoine
    Bonaparte at Arcola 10:74 Ap
      28 '41
Gross, Anthony
    Hurricane fighter plane 26:
      60 Mr 21 '49
    Medical orderlies 26:60 Mr
      21 '49
Gross, Chaim, sculptor
    Acrobats 2 sculptures 30:66-
      7 Ja 8 '51
    Balancing dancers* bw 30:65
      Ja 8 '51
    Billowing bather bw 30:65 Ja
      8 '51
    Bouncing baby bw 30:65 Ja 8
      '51
    Hand stand bw 7:37 Jy 17 '39
    I found my love 30:63 Ja 8
      '51
    Mother and child bw 5:7 N
      28 '38
    War bride 30:63 Ja 8 '51
    Artist at work 30:63 Ja 8
      '51 port.

Chaim Gross. in group photog
29:172-3 O 16 '50 port.
Newman. Chaim Gross photog
bw 20:11 F 4 '46
Grossenheider, Richard P.
White footed mouse 21:86 O
28 '46
Grosvenor, Thelma
"Love Stories," book, by
Mary Roberts Rinehart, il-
lustrations bw 20:56 F 25
'46
Grosz, George
Approaching storm 12:76 Ap
20 '42
The blue chair 7:26 Ag 28 '39
Dante's "Inferno," illustra-
tions bw 15:12-4 D 13 '43
I was always present 16:77 Je
12 '44
Nude bw 28:24 Ja 23 '50
Artist and his work photog bw
16:76 Je 12 '44 port.
Newman. George Grosz
photog bw 20:10 F 4 '46
port.
Grotenrath, Ruth
My Wisconsin 25:58 N 29 '48
Groth, John
Barrage 16:78 Je 12 '44
Artist at work photog bw 16:
76 Je 12 '44 port.
John Groth. in group photog
29:172-3 O 16 '50 port.
Ground swell. Hopper 8:66 My
27 '40; 28:104-5 Ap 17 '50
Group of myselves. bw Cloar
24:79-82 Ja 26 '48
Grove, Katherine
Portrait 25:101 D 6 '48
Artist at work photog bw 25:
103 D 6 '48 port.
Grover, Beatrice
"Broad Stripes and Bright
Stars," illustrations bw
11:84 D 15 '41
Gruen, Victor, Associates, ar-
chitects
Northland shopping center,
Detroit 37:81-3 Ag 30 '54
Grunewald, Matthias

Isenheim altarpiece, 16th
century 30:74-85 Mr 26 '51
Self-portrait drawing bw 30:
74 Mr 26 '51 port.
Self-portrait as St. Paul,
Isenheim altarpiece 30:80
Mr 26 '51 port.
Gruenther, Alfred M.
Biddle. Major General Alfred
M. Gruenther drawing bw
16:14 Ja 3 '44
Gryphons See Animals, Imagin-
ary--Griffins
Guadalcanal
Shepler. World War in Gua-
dalcanal 15:50-3 D 27 '43
Guardi, Francesco
San Pietro di Castello, Ven-
ice 29:87 N 27 '50
Santa Maria della Salute 35:
152-3 N 16 '53
Guardian angel. Ford 10:71 Ap
14 '41; 17:42 D 25 '44
Guardian figures: warriors,
horses, camels. sculpture
bw Ming dynasty, China
3:57 Ag 23 '37
Guardian image, Chinese Bud-
dhist temple, Peiping 38:
65 Ap 4 '55
Guardian king sculpture, Japan,
13th century 30:73 My 28
'51
Guardian of law sculpture bw,
U.S. Supreme Court Build-
ing, Washington, D.C.
30:104 Mr 12 '51
Guareschi, Giovannino, cartoonist
Political cartoons bw 33:116
N 10 '52
Giovannino Guereschi photogs
bw 33:115 N 10 '52; 36:59-
60 Je 14 '54 port.
Self-portrait cartoon 36:59
Je 14 '54 port.
Guernica. fresco bw Picasso
3:64 Jy 26 '37
Guernica, Spain
Sacred oak of Guernica
photog bw 2:61 My 10 '37

"Guerriere" (ship)
  Birch. Constitution and
    Guerriere 9:47 O 28 '41
  Constitution firing on Guerri-
    ere lithograph, 1812 23:69
    O 27 '47
Guest, Edgar A.
  Edgar Guest photog bw 7:64
    O 23 '39
Guildhalls, Middle Ages, Ghent
    photog bw 22:82-3 My 26
    '47
Guildsmen inspect weights and
    measures, Middle Ages
    bw 22:82 My 26 '47
Guillon, Jacques, furniture de-
    signer
  Chair, parachute cord bw 34:
    105-7 Mr 23 '53
Guinan, Texas
  Texas Guinan photog bw 19:
    67 Ag 27 '45; 28:67 Ja 2 '50
Guitar Players See Musicians
    and Musical Instruments--
    Guitar
Gukei Sumiyoshi
  In and around Kyoto 31:66-7
    D 31 '51
Gulbenkian, Calouste Sarkis
  Calouste Gulbenkian photog
    bw 29:80 N 27 '50
  Gulbenkian collection of paint-
    ings loaned to National
    Gallery of Art, Washington,
    D.C. 29:81-90 N 27 '50
The gulf stream. Homer 2:26 Ja
    11 '37; 5:36 O 31 '38
Gulliver in Lilliput. bw illustra-
    tion for Swift's "Gulliver's
    Travels" 25:109 S 13 '48
Gulls in flight. sculpture bw
    Burlingame 10:120 Ap 21
    '41
Gunnarson, Oscar
  Residents of Linsborg, Kansas
    sculpture bw 40:14-5 Ja
    23 '56
Guns See Weapons--Firearms
Gunston Hall, Virginia photogs
    bw 11:118-21 D 15 '41
Gustavus Adolphus, King of

Sweden bw 13:104 O 5 '42
Guston, Philip
  Holiday 20:92 My 27 '46
  If this be not I 20:92 My 27
    '46
  Lemonade and doughnuts 20:
    92 My 27 '46
  Sentimental moment 20:91 My
    27 '46
  Artist and his work photog bw
    20:90 My 27 '46 port.
Gutenberg, Johannes
  Johannes Gutenberg bw 34:84
    F 23 '53 print bw 36:85
    Mr 1 '54
  Laning. Gutenberg printing
    Bible* mural panel 9:66 S
    30 '40 bw 33:92 O 20 '52
Gutenfels castle, Germany, 12th
    century photog bw 8:45 Je
    3 '40
Guthrie, A. B., Jr.
  A. B. Guthrie photog bw 23:
    92 S 1 '47
Guthrie, James
  Great statesmen of World
    War I* 24:29 Ap 19 '48
Gutkin, Ann
  Ann Gutkin, model, painted
    by New York City painters
    5:29-30 S 19 '38
Guy, James
  Ghost town hotel 16:46 Ja 3
    '44
Gwathmey, Robert
  Hoeing 16:78 Ap 24 '44
  Woman at table 38:74 Mr 28
    '55
Gwinnett, Button
  Button Gwinnett bw 15:8 Jy
    5 '43
Gwyn, Nell
  Nell Gwyn 41:166-7 N 19 '56
Gy-Ant-Wachia
  Humphries. "Jack of Dia-
    monds," playing card 38:
    Cover My 30 '55

H
Haarlem, Netherlands
  Ruysdael. View of Haarlem

24:74-5 Je 14 '48
Haas, Ernst
Image of a magic city, New
York City photogs 35:108-
20 S 14 '53
Haas, Lillian Henkel
Carroll. Mrs. Haas bw 8:121
My 13 '40
Haberman, Philip W.
Pompano, Florida 24:73 Ap
5 '48
Habsburg coat of arms 27:61 O
24 '49
Habsburg collection of painting
masterpieces 27:61-72 O
24 '49
Hachiman, Japanese god of war,
masked photog bw 17:28 N
27 '44
Hacker, Arthur
Wet night in Piccadilly Circus
23:85 N 17 '47
Hadjikyriakos, Nicholas See
Ghika
Hagenauer, Nikolas
Isenheim altarpiece statues:
Sts. Anthony, Augustine,
Jerome; Christ and dis-
ciples 30:80-1 Mr 26 '51
Hagia Sophia See Santa Sophia
Hagnauer
Street fights in Paris, 1848
25:88-9 N 22 '48
Hahn, William
Central Pacific station, Sacra-
mento, 1870 39:83 N 28 '55
Haines, W. S.
At high tide 12:39 Mr 2 '42
Journey's end 12:40 Mr 2 '42
Hairdresser's window. Sloan 27:
61 Ag 29 '49
Haiti
Benedetto. Calling the loa 8:
35 Ja 1 '40
Haitian couple. Cortor 28:101 Mr
13 '50
Halberd See Weapons--Halberd
Hale, Edward Everett
Edward Everett Hale bw 17:65
Jy 31 '44 statue bw 21:14 D
9 '46

Hale, Nathan
Nathan Hale statue bw, Yale
University 12:64 Je 1 '42;
31:85 Jy 2 '51
Halifax, Lord
Lord Halifax bw 26:98 Mr 14
'49
Hall, Carl
Eternity 24:86 Mr 8 '48
Exodus 24:86 Mr 8 '48
The forest 24:86 Mr 8 '48
Kites 24:86-7 Mr 8 '48
Moon dance 24:86 Mr 8 '48
Morning wreath 24:86 Mr 8
'48
Artist at work photogs bw 24:
84 Mr 8 '48 port.
Hall, Lyman
Lyman Hall bw 15:8 Jy 5 '43
Hall of Fame, U.S. Capitol
photog bw 2:23 Je 14 '37
Halle, Raymond
Slap that bass sculpture bw
10:59 Je 16 '41
Haller, Herman
Young girl with arms raised
sculpture bw 26:114 Je 20
'49
Halles building, Bruges photog
33:62 S 15 '52
Halliday, Brett
Brett Halliday photog bw 22:
20 Mr 10 '47
Halliday, Edward
The State apartments, Chats-
worth bw 9:59 Ag 12 '40
Hallsthammar, Carl
Venus in red cherry sculp-
ture bw 2:42 Mr 8 '37
Artist at work photog bw 2:42
Mr 8 '37 port.
Hals, Frans
The bohemian 35:60 Ag 17 '53
bw 9:6 S 30 '40
Claes Duyst van Voorhoot
2:43 Je 28 '37
Fisher girl bw 6:58 Mr 27
'39
Hille Bobbe (Malle Babbe,
witch of Haarlem) 24:71
Mr 22 '48

Hals, Frans (cont.)
  Man with beer keg 6:39 My
    29 '39
  Portrait of a gentlemen 5:34
    Ag 29 '38
  Portrait of a young man bw 31:
    23 S 3 '51
  Sara Andriesdr, Hessix 29:84
    N 27 '50
  Self-portrait bw 5:30 Ag 29
    '38 port.
Hals, Frans, School of
  Portrait bw 11:54 N 10 '41
Halsall, William Formby
  The Mayflower upon her ar-
    rival 13:76 N 23 '42
Halsman, Philippe, photographer
  Master musicians in the
    United States--portraits bw
    16:43-50 Mr 13 '44
  Salvador Dali bw 25:4-5 Ag 9
    '48
  Surrealist portraits of Jean
    Cocteau bw 26:18-20 F 7
    '49
Hamam, Grand Vizier to King
    Ahasuerus of the Persians
  Rembrandt. Esther's feast 41:
    74 D 10 '56
Hamburg, Germany, housing
    project photog bw 36:148 My
    10 '54
Hamby, William, architect
  William Hamby photog bw 26:
    93 My 2 '49 port.
Hamilton, Alexander
  Alexander Hamilton 39:58 Jy
    4 '55 bw 16:47 Ja 17 '44;
    16:54 F 7 '44; 31:106 N 5
    '51
  Hamilton-Burr duel bw 14:62
    Ap 12 '43
  Riggs. Hamilton-Burr duel
    23:69 Jy 7 '47
  Trumbull. Alexander Hamil-
    ton, 1805 23:64 Jy 7 '47
Hamilton, Elizabeth (Schuyler)
  Betsy Schuyler (Mrs. Alex-
    ander Hamilton) bw 23:66
    Jy 7 '47

Hamilton, Emma
  Romney. Emma Hamilton bw
    10:41 Ap 7 '41
  Romney. Lady Hamilton as
    "Nature" 3:33 D 27 '37
Hamilton, Ian
  Sargent. Sir Ian Hamilton
    23:80 N 17 '47
Hamlin, Hannibal
  Hannibal Hamlin photog bw 9:
    8 Ag 5 '40; 14:75 F 15 '43
Hammer-heads
  Denslow. "The Wonderful
    Wizard of Oz," illustra-
    tions 35:59 D 28 '53
Hammerlock. sculpture bw
  Brown, Joe 12:90 My 19
    '41
Hammerstein, Oscar II
  Oscar Hammerstein photog
    bw 16:82 Mr 6 '44; 28:103
    My 15 '50; 33:53 D 29 '52
Hammurabi
  Code of Hammurabi, cast bw
    24:147 Mr 15 '48 stone
    replica bw 37:94 D 13 '54
Hampton, John
  John Hampton bw 41:184 N
    12 '56
Han bronze. Graves 35:88 S 28
    '53
Hancock, John
  John Hancock bw 15:8 Jy 5
    '43
Hancock, Winfield Scott
  Winfield Scott Hancock bw
    14:7 My 31 '43
Hand, Learned
  Judge Learned Hand photog
    bw 21:116 N 4 '46; 30:102
    Mr 12 '51
Hand stand. sculpture bw Gross,
    C. 7:37 Jy 17 '39
Handball See Games and
    Sports--Handball
Handbills, G.O.P., 1888 40:71
    Ja 30 '56
Handel, George
  George Handel bw 4:20 Ap
    18 '38
Hands

Michelangelo. Creation of
Adam, fresco detail 27:
30-1 D 26 '49
Handy, Margaret
Wyeth. Dr. Margaret Handy
41:62-3 D 24 '36
Handy, W. C.
W. C. Handy photog bw 5:59
O 3 '38
Hanford, Ben
Ben Hanford, Socialist party
poster bw 24:105 Ja 19
'48
Haniwa
Japanese tomb figures sculp-
ture 30:70 My 28 '51
Hanmer, Thomas
Van Dyck, A. Sir Thomas
Hanmer 15:66 S 20 '43
Hansen, Lee
Young Lincoln sculpture bw
9:130 S 9 '40
Lee Hansen photog bw 9:130
S 9 '40 port.
Hanson, Gertrude
Genealogy rug, hooked rug
28:89 Ap 3 '50
Harakhte, tomb painting, Egypt
24:82 Ja 19 '48
Haraszty, Eszter
Eszter Haraszty photog 34:
76 Mr 2 '53 port.
Harbors
Churchill. Scene in Canne
harbor 20:46 Ja 7 '46
Dufy. New York harbor 30:66
Ja 22 '51
Feininger, Lux. Jersey har-
bor bw 31:90 N 12 '51
General Washington' arrival
in New York harbor for in-
auguration, * c1800 31:61
Jy 2 '51
Miller, B. San Francisco
harbor in war 15:73-4 Jy
12 '43
Reindel. New England harbor
3:36 Ag 9 '37
Revington. Monhegan Harbor,
Maine 29:72 Ag 21 '50
Salmon. Boston harbor--Long

and Central wharves, 1832
6:29 Je 19 '39
Hardiman, Alfred Frank, sculp-
tor
England's royal lion 2:Cover
43 Ja 25 '37
Artist at work photog bw 2:
Cover, 43 Ja 25 '37 port.
Harding, George
Jungle 19:63 O 8 '45
Hardwick Hall, English country
house, 17th century 19:
105 O 29 '45
Hardwicke, Sir Cecil
Beaton. Sir Cecil Hardwicke
in "Candida" 21:9 Jy 22
'46
Hardy, Thomas
Literary local of Hardy
photogs bw 14:77-83 Je
14 '43
Hardy, Tom, sculptor
Billy bw 37:124 O 11 '54
Bison bw 37:124 O 11 '54
Fat running tiger bw 37:124
O 11 '54
Horse bw 37:123 O 11 '54
Tall cow bw 37:124 O 11 '54
Artist at work photogs bw
37:123 O 11 '54 port.
Hare, David
Newman. David Hare photog
bw 35:20 D 7 '53 port.
Silvers. Portrait of David
Hare sculpture bw 29:146
S 18 '50 port.
Hari, Mata
Mata Hari--portraits, 1905-
15; home bw 7:6-8 D 18
'39
Hark! The Herald Angels Sing.
Stark 23:55 D 22 '47
Harkavy, Minna, sculptor
Dancing figure, lamp design
bw 21:103 N 18 '46
Two men bw 32:78 Ja 7 '52
Harlech castle, Wales photog
40:90 Mr 19 '56
Harlem dancers. sculpture bw
Kane, M. 9:54 Ag 12 '40

Harlow house, Plymouth, Mas-
    sachusetts, 1677: Central
    room with fireplace,
    scullery 18:54, 57 My 7 '45
Harnett, William
    Emblems of peace 7:25 Ag
        28 '39
    Old models 27:60 Ag 29 '49
    Trophy of the hunt 10:74 Ap
        14 '41
Harold, the Saxon 40:86 Mr 26
    '56
Harp Players See Musicians
    and Musical Instruments--
    Harp
Harpoon, whalers' photog 39:
    109 O 17 '55
Harpsichords See Musicians
    and Musical Instruments--
    Harpsichords
Harriman, Edward Henry
    Pach brothers. Edward Har-
        riman photog bw 3:17 O 25
        '37
Harriman, Mrs. J. Borden
    Mrs. J. Borden Harriman
        photog bw 28:66 Ja 2 '50
Harrington, Oliver Wendell
    Deep south 8:46 F 12 '40
Harris, Harwell, architect
    Hilltop home, La Jolla,
        Calif bw 19:114 O 22 '45
    "Inverted gable" roof house,
        San Francisco 27:50 S 5
        '49
Harris, Raymond
    Artist and his work photog bw
        35:114 Jy 13 '53 port.
Harris, Roy
    Roy Harris photog bw 15:101
        O 25 '43
Harrison, Benjamin
    Benjamin Harrison bw 15:8
        Jy 5 '43; 16:50 F 28 '44
Harrison, Wallace
    Concrete bungalow, housing
        project bw 27:103-4 O 10
        '49
    Harrison and Abramovitz.
        Republic National bank,
        Dallas, Texas 38:61, 63 F

28 '55
    U.S. Embassy, Rio de
        Janeiro 34:45 Je 22 '53
    Rockefeller center bw 22:34
        My 26 '47
    United Nations--General As-
        sembly Building bw 33:113-
        9 N 3 '52
    Wallace K. Harrison photog
        bw 22:34 My 26 '47; 27:
        103 O 10 '49; 33:113 N 3
        '52 port.
Harrison, William Henry
    General Harrison, equestrian
        statue, Cincinnati, Ohio
        bw 38:91 Mr 28 '55
Harrow School speech room,
    October, 1940. North-
    Taylor 12:39 Mr 2 '42
Harsanyi, Charles
    Manana Island 29:73 Ag 21 '50
Hart, Albert Bushnell
    Albert Bushnell Hart photog
        bw 10:97 My 5 '41
Hart, John
    John Hart, signer of the
        Declaration of Independ-
        ence bw 15:9 Jy 5 '43
Hart, Lorenz
    Lorenz Hart photog bw 15:103
        My 15 '50
Hart, Moss
    Moss Hart photog bw 15:64
        N 29 '43; 21:50 O 7 '46
Hart, William M.
    Chocorua Mountain, New
        Hampshire 19:83 S 10 '45
Hart, William S.
    William S. Hart statue bw 2:
        48 Mr 15 '37
Harte, Bret
    Greenaway. "Queen of the
        Pirate Isle," title page
        illustration 23:88 D 1 '47
Hartford, Connecticut
    Church. The Hooker party
        migrates to Hartford,
        Connecticut, 1636 13:82
        N 23 '42
    Church. Quest for freedom
        bw 24:70 Je 14 '48

Hartley, Marsden
  Albert Pinkham Ryder bw 30:
    101 F 26 '51
  Give us this day 32:87 Je 16
    '52
  Log jam 32:86 Je 16 '52
  The lost Felice 32:89 Je 16
    '52
  Robin Hood cove, Maine 32:
    88 Je 16 '52
  Smelt Brook falls 13:96 N 9
    '42
  Storm clouds 32:85 Je 16 '52
  Waldenstein peaks 32:86 Je
    16 '52
  The wave 32:88 Je 16'52
  Lynes. Marsden Hartley
    photog bw 32:84 Je 16 '52
    port.
Hartley, Master
  Romney. Master Hartley bw
    6:58 Mr 27 '39
Harvard, John
  French. John Harvard statue
    bw, Harvard University
    10:Cover My 5 '41
Harvest. Jones, Joe 13:46 Ag 31
  '42; 21:77 N 25 '46
Harvest festival. Corbino 4:28
  Je 13 '38
Harvesting illumination, Flemish
  15th century 22:80 My 26
  '47
Hastings, Battle of
  Bayeux tapestry bw 16:8-10
    Je 26 '44
  French chronicle, 15th cen-
    tury 40:86 Mr 26 '56
Hatch, Don, architecture
  Ranch house of Pedro Penzi-
    ni, Caracas, Venezuela
    37:127 S 13 '53
The Hatches of New York, 1871.
  Johnson, E. 25:91 O 18
  '48
Hatfield, Anderson
  Craven. Captain (Devil Anse)
    Hatfield bw 16:114 My 22
    '44
Hatfield Family, West Virginia,
  Feuding Hatfields of West

  Virginia photog bw 31:13
    S 10 '51
  Portraits and scenes of Hat-
    field-McCoy feud bw 16:
    108-16 My 22 '44
Hatfield house, English country
  house, 17th century 19:
  106 O 29 '45; 41:156-7 N
  5 '56
Hathor, Egypt 41:115 N 26 '56
  tomb painting 24:82 Ja 19 '48
Hatshepsut, Queen of Egypt
  sculpture 41:111 N 26 '56
  black granite sculpture 9:
  93 D 9 '40
  Hatshepsut's temple, Delrel-
    Bahri, Egypt photog bw
    24:78-9 Ja 19 '48
  Thebes photog 41:110-1
    N 26 '56
Hattorf, Alvin
  Seventh and Canal 10:68 My
    26 '41
Haubourdin, France, February,
  1916. watercolor Hitler
  1:42 N 30 '36
Hausmann, Raoul
  Montage bw 34:25 My 25 '53
Haussonville, Louise
  Ingres. Portrait of La Com-
    tesse D'Haussonville 3:
    Cover D 27 '37
Havana siesta. Lee, D. 22:73
  My 12 '47
Havell, Robert
  View of Sing Sing 19:85 S 10
    '45
Hawkins, John
  Sir John Hawkins 41:80 O 29:
    56; 41:165 N 5 '56
Hawks
  Hazard. "Hook," the hawk,
    illustrations bw 40:155-
    60 Mr 19 '56
  Horus, the hawk god, Egypt,
    c350 B.C. bw 6:53 Mr 20
    '39
Hawthorne
  Lewicki. Hawthorne bloom-
    ing at Christmas, German
    legend 33:82 D 1 '52

Hawthorne, Nathaniel
House of the Seven Gables,
Salem, Massachusetts,
1668 photog bw 15:13 D 6
'43
Hay, John
John Hay 19:88 S 24 '45 bw 3:
12 D 27 '37; 10:27 Mr 3
'41; 14:76 F 15 '43
Hayden, D. B.
Ear, surrealist 23:98 N 10
'47
D. B. Hayden photog bw 23:
101 N 10 '47 port.
Hayden, Palmer
Baptizing day 21:65 Jy 22 '46
Haydn, Joseph
Joseph Haydn bw 36:51 Je 28
'54
Haydn's tomb photog bw 36:
54 Je 28 '54
Hayes, Rutherford Birchard
Rutherford B. Hayes photog
bw 16:50 F 28 '44
Swearing in of President
Hayes, 1876 print bw 40:
69 Ja 30 '56
Hayward, Brooke
Philipp, R. Brooke Hayward
bw 8:62 Ap 8 '40
Hazard, Durfee
"Hook," the hawk, illustra-
tions bw 40:155-60 Mr 19
'56
Hazford Rupert LXXXI, prize
Hereford. Lea 26:81 Ap 25
'49
Head. Picasso 33:93 O 27 '52
Head. Sculpture bw Barthe 21:
62 Jy 22 '46
Head. Inca trophy head, ceramic
36:104 Ap 12 '54
Head. sculpture bw Brancusi 2:
51 Ap 5 '37
Head. sculpture bw Marini 22:
99 My 22 '50
Head. sculpture bw Olmec, Mexi-
co c50 B.C., plaster cast
28:89 My 29 '50
Head. sculpture bw, Greece 350
B.C. Praxitiles 7:37 Jy

31 '39
Head in a state of rhythm.
drawing Tchelitchew 30:
11 Ja 29 '51
Head of a boy. sculpture bw
Bishop, E. 21:62 Jy 22 '46
Head of a girl. lithograph
Cox, Jan 33:86 Jy 14 '52
Head of a little girl. sculpture
bw Salemme 7:36 Jy 17
'39
Head of a woman. sculpture bw
Maillol 38:110 My 23 '55
Head of Prometheus. sculpture
bw Brancusi 39:135 D 5
'55
Head of woman, rock sculpture,
Vagis photog bw 40:123
Je 11 '53
Headache. woodcarving bw
Steig 6:35 Ap 10 '39
Headdresses
African antelope headdress,
Bambara, Sudan photog bw
33:118 S 8 '52
Lady with headdress,*
France, c1700 bw 23:75
S 15 '47
Maya headdress, Bonampak
mural 27:80-4 N 21 '49
South Seas fibre, with sur-
mounted stylized face
photog 21:76 N 4 '46
Sumerian headdress: Queen
Shubad of Ur, 2600 B.C.
bw 33:12 N 10 '52; 40:93
Je 4 '56
Headrests
Baluba headrest, Africa
photog bw 33:120 S 8 '52
Heade, Martin Johnson
Mary Rebecca Clark 41:161
D 24 '56
Heads. sculpture bw Carpenko
32:12 F 11 '52
Heads sculpture bw Prehistoric
Northwest U.S. 32:98-9
My 5 '52
Heads, Jericho, plastered or-
namented human skulls,
5000 B.C. photogs bw

34:119 My 11 '53
Healing the sick. bw Nagler 8:
41 Mr 25 '40
Healy, George Peter Alexander
Abraham Lincoln bw 6:22 Ap
3 '39
Arch of Titus, Rome 33:89 S
15 '52
Webster replying to Hayne,
January 26-7, 1830 16:54
F 21 '44
Self-portrait in Arch of Titus
33:89 S 15 '52
Hearst, George
George Hearst photog bw 31:
26 Ag 27 '51
Hearst, Phoebe Apperson (Mrs.
George)
Phoebe Hearst photog bw 31:
26 Ag 27 '51
Hearst, William Randolph
Herford. "The yellow peril,"
cartoon bw 31:27 Ag 27
'51
San Simeon, Hearst estate,
California photogs bw 31:
28-9 Ag 27 '51
William Randolph Hearst
photogs bw 31:23-31 Ag
27 '51
"Yellow Kid," 1898 carica-
ture bw 31:27 Ag 27 '51
Hearst art collection--art and
antique objects sold at
Gimbels photogs bw 10:
28-9 F 10 '41
Monastery, Spanish, 12th
century photogs 36:40 Ja
25 '54
Warehouse treasures to be
sold: armor, sculpture,
tapestries, other photogs
bw 5:47-9 N 28 '38
Heaven See also Biblical and
Christian Themes
Elwell. I dreamt St. Peter
sat for his portrait bw 22:
40 My 19 '47
Heaven sculpture bw, Abbey
church, Vezelay, France
22:78 Ap 7 '47

Heavy the oar to him who is
tired, heavy the coat,
heavy the sea. Albright,
I. 16:68 Mr 27 '44
Hebuterne, Jeanne
Modigliani. Mme Jeanne
Hebuterne 29:113 S 11 '50
Hecate's court. bw Bacon, P.
6:58 My 8 '39
Hecht, Zoltan
Summer sea 16:45 Ja 3 '44
Hedin, Sven
Milles. Sven Hedin sculpture
bw 2:32 F 22 '37
Hegel, Georg Wilhelm Friedrich
Georg Hegel bw 25:64 O 18
'48
Heggen, Thomas
Thomas Heggen photog bw 22:
76 Je 2 '47; 24:128 Mr 8
'48
Hegh, Hugh
Unto one of the least of these
8:44 F 12 '40
Heifers See Cattle
Heifitz, Jascha
Heifitz with Helen Keller
photog bw 4:20 F 28 '38
Heiliger, Bernhard, sculptor
Artist and his work photog
36:145 My 10 '54 port.
Heinz, H. J., Vinegar Factory,
Pittsburgh. Skidmore,
Owings and Merrill pho-
tog 36:35 Ja 4 '54
Held, Anna
Anna Held photog bw 28:64
Ja 2 '50; 31:117 N 19 '51
Held, John, Jr., cartoonist
Artist and his work photog
28:48 Ja 2 '50
Helen, Consort of Victor Em-
manuel III, King of Italy
Helen photog bw 15:104 Ag
23 '43
Helicopter. Lee 16:77 Ap 24
'44
Heliolab, S. C. Johnson and
Son, Research laboratory,
Racine, Wisconsin.
Wright photogs 29:8-10

Heliolab (cont.)
  D 11 '50
Hell
  Bosch. Hell, triptych panel,
    with details 27:77-82 N
    14 '49
  Dore. Dante's "Inferno," il-
    lustrations bw 15:12-3 D
    13 '43
  Grosz. Dante's "Inferno,"
    illustrations bw 15:12-3
    D 13 '43
  Hell, with Devil sculpture bw,
    Abbey church, Vezelay,
    France 22:78 Ap 7 '47
  Michelangelo. Last judgment
    fresco 27:44-8 D 26 '49
Hell on the border, hooked rug
    pattern 8:45 Ja 29 '40
Hellman, Lillian
  Lillian Hellman photog bw 21:
    50 O 7 '46
Helmers, Peter
  Hollywood--surrealist satiri-
    cal drawings bw 16:12-4 F
    21 '44
Helmets See Armor--Head-
  coverings
Heloise and Abelard sculpture bw
    22:77 Ap 7 '47
Hemingway, Ernest
  Ernest Hemingway, caricature
    bw 23:82 S 1 '47
  Ernest Hemingway photog bw
    2:76 My 31 '37; 17:14 Ag
    14 '44; 33:Cover, 34 S 1
    '52 age 37 to present; fam-
    ily; wives 26:86-101 Ja 10
    '49
  Writer and his bride, Martha
    Gellhorn; locale of "For
    Whom the Bell Tolls"
    photogs bw 10:49-57 Ja 6
    '41
Hemy, C. Napier
  Plymouth Hooker 23:84 N 17
    '47
Hendricks, Thomas A.
  Thomas Hendricks photog bw
    9:9 Ag 5 '40
Hendrickson, Russell

Winter reflections 32:70 Ja
    14 '52
Henning, Rudolph
  Eakins. The cello player
    (Rudolph Henning) 16:75 My
    15 '44
Henri, Robert
  Mary 12:60 Je 15 '42
  Robert Henri photog bw 26:71
    Je 20 '49 port.
  Henri de Valois bw 17:86 Ag 28
    '44
Henry, Edward Lampson
  The 9:45 accommodation,
    Stratford, Connecticut 6:
    30 Je 19 '39
Henry, Patrick
  "Give me liberty, or give me
    death," 1775 bw 14:62 Ap
    12 '43
  Patrick Henry before the
    Virginia Assembly, 1775
    bw 25:110 S 13 '48
  St. John Churchyard, Rich-
    mond, Virginia, scene of
    speech 6:28 Je 19 '39
    photog bw 11:104 N 10 '41
Henry I, King of England
  Henry I's coronation, 1100 bw
    40:100 Mr 26 '56
Henry II, King of England
  Henry II, sculpture, capital,
    French, 12th century bw
    40:107 Mr 26 '56
Henry V, King of England bw
    40:179 Ap 9 '56
Henry VII, King of England bw
    41:85 O 29 '56
Henry VIII, King of England
  Henry VIII, after Holbein bw
    41:77 O 29 '56
  Henry VIII meeting Francis
    I, King of France, on
    field of cloth of gold* bw
    41:86-7 O 29 '56
  Wives of Henry VIII-por-
    traits bw 41:88 O 29 '56
Henry IV, King of France
  Henry IV's conversion to
    Catholicism bw 24:61 Je
    14 '48

"Henry Grace a Dïeu" (ship)
(Great Harry) English,
1514 24:66 My 10 48; 41:
78 O 29 '56
Henry the Navigator, Prince of
Portugal 24:76 Mr 22 '48
bw 23:27 Ag 11 '47
Henry the Pious, 1514.
Cranach 40:104 My 7 '56
Hentrich, H., architect
Office buildings, Dusseldorf,
Germany photog bw 36:152
My 10 '54
Hepburn, Katharine
Brook. Katharine Hepburn
8:46 Ja 22 '40
Hepplewhite, George, furniture
and interior designer
Drawing room design bw 23:
77 Ag 25 '47
Furniture: chair, window
seat, tables, urn, tea cad-
dies photogs bw 23:76-7
Ag 25 '47
Heraldry See also Emblems
and Decorations
Hardiman. British lion(leop-
ard) sculpture 2:Cover,
43 Ja 25 '37

Coats and Shields of Arms
Bradford, William bw 19:57
N 26 '45
Brewster, William bw 19:57
N 26 '45
Bruce family, 13th century
22:69 My 26 '47
Chandos family 22:69 My 26
'47
Columbus, Christopher 39:
122 O 10 '55
Cornwall family 22:69 My 26
'47
Coucy family 22:69 My 26 '47
De Warenne family 22:69 My
26 '47
Dunois family 22:69 My 26 '47
England, arms of 22:69 My
26 '47
France, arms of 22:69 My 26
'47

Habsburg 27:61 O 24 '49
Holmes, Sherlock bw 16:82
My 1 '44
Howland, John bw 19:56 N 26
45
Iran, arms of 20:34 Ap 8 '46
Kyrell family 40:187 Ap 9 '56
Luttrell, Sir Geoffrey 40:186
Ap 9 '56
Marlborough 24:34 Ap 19 '48
Massachusetts. McIntire
woodcarving 38:63 My 30
'55
Mortimer family 22:69 My
26 '47
Northumberland family 22:69
My 26 '47
Percy family 22:69 My 26 '47
Richard II, King of England
22:69 My 26 '47
Sigismund August, II, King
of Poland 35:92 D 14 '53
Tilley, Edward bw 19:56 N
26 '45
Washington, George bw 30:
107 F 19 '51
Wodwylle family 40:187 Ap
9 '56
Herbin, Auguste
Noel bw 27:57 D 26 '49
Herbs
Herb garden 32:73 Ap 7 '52
Twelve most used herbs 32:
74-5 Ap 7 '52
Hercules See Mythological
Themes--Hercules
Herdsmen leading cattle,* bas-
relief, Egypt 41:109 N 26
'56
Hereford map of the world,
c1280. bw De Haldingham
22:85 Ap 7 '47
Herford, Oliver
"The yellow peril," (W.R.
Hearst) cartoon bw 31:27
Ag 27 '51
Herkimer, Nicholas
General Herkimer directing
Oriskany battle bw 19:
106 N 12 '45

Hermaphrodite sculpture bw,
    Louvre 11:78 Ag 18 '41
Hermitage, Greek revival plan-
    tation house, Louisiana,
    1812 photog 32:78 Je 9 '52;
    porch, central hall, stair-
    way 18:52 My 7 '45 bw hall
    and stairway 13:65 Jy 6 '42
A hero. watercolor Rey 2:34 F
    22 '37
Herod ordering Magi to find
    new-born Christ, relief
    from Ulm cathedral 35:28
    D 28 '53
Herold, David
    David Herold photog bw 4:46
    F 14 '38
Herron, David
    St. Louis cemetery, New Or-
    leans 20:80 F 18 '46
Hersey, John
    John Hersey photog bw 14:8
    Je 28 '43
Hertford, Isabella
    Hoppner. Isabella, Marchio-
    ness of Hertford 4:27 Ja
    24 '38
Herzen, Alexander
    Alexander Herzen photog bw
    31:110 O 29 '51
Herzog, Maurice
    Karsh. Maurice Herzog
    photog bw 37:133 O 4 '54
Hesler, Alexander
    A. Lincoln, presidential cam-
    paign portrait photog bw
    12:51 Ja 5 '42
Hess, Emil, designer
    Artist at work photog bw 37:
    160 N 22 '54 port.
Hess, Rudolf
    Rudolf Hess 28:55 F 6 '50
Hesselius, John
    Charles Calvert of Maryland
    9:75 D 9 '40; 26:84 F 28
    '49
Hessix, Sara
    Hals. Sara Andriesdr. Hessix
    29:84 N 27 '50
Hestia
    Parthenon sculptures (Elgin

marbles) bw 35:158 O 26
    '53
Het Loo palace, Netherlands,
    air view photog bw 5:29 S
    5 '38
Hewes, Joseph
    Joseph Hewes bw 15:9 Jy 5
    '43
Heyward, Thomas, Jr.
    Thomas Heyward, Jr. bw 15:
    9 Jy 5 '43
Hickel, Karl
    The House of Commons, Lon-
    don, c1776 bw 29:53 Jy 3
    '50
Hickock, James Butler ("Wild
    Bill")
    Wild Bill Hickock photog bw
    7:51 Ag 28 '39; 16:110 Ap
    10 '44 statue bw 11:102
    O 6 '41
Hicks, Edward
    The grave of William Penn 17:
    72 O 16 '44
    The peaceable kingdom 17:72
    O 16 '44
    Penn treating with the Indi-
    ans, 1682 24:71 Je 14 '48;
    36:78 Mr 8 '54
    The residence of David
    Twining in 1787 9:76 D 9
    '40
    Washington at the Delaware,
    1776 29:46 Jy 10 '50
Hicks, Elias
    Elias Hicks bw 33:96 S 29
    '52
Hicks, Granville
    Granville Hicks photogs bw
    22:95 Mr 17 '47
Hickson, Richard
    Song in the night 30:36 Ja 15
    '51
    Self-portrait in Song in the
    Night 30:36 Ja 15 '51 port.
Higgins, Daniel P.
    Pope; Eggers; Higgins. Jef-
    ferson memorial, Wash-
    ington, D.C. photog 23:
    49 Jy 7 '47 bw 14:Cover
    Ap 12 '43

Higgins, Eugene
  Dickinson. Eugene Higgins
    10:48 F 3 '41 port.
High water. Currier and Ives
    print 21:73 S 2 '46
High water in winter. Cowles
    24:76 F 9 '48
High yaller. Marsh 2:34 F 1 '37
    bw 10:70 Ap 14 '41
Highway design, Los Angeles--
    four-level freeway cross-
    over photog 36:33 Ja 4 '54
Highway robbery. print Hiro-
    shige 15:53 N 1 '43
Hill, Ruby
  Beaton. Ruby Hill in "St.
    Louis Woman" drawing 21:
    7 Jy 22 '46
Hill, Thomas
  Driving the golden spike, May
    10, 1869 27:50-1 Jy 4 '49
Hille Bobbe, the witch of Haar-
    lem (Malle Babbe). Hals
    24:71 Mr 22 '48
Hilliard, Nicholas
  Miniature painting: Lady of
    the court;* Lover;* Young
    man* 41:147 N 5 '56
Hillmer, Jack, architect
  Hillmer and Callister. Hall
    house, Marin County, Calif.
    27:46-7 S 5 '49
Hilltop landscape. Lee, L. 32:69
    Ja 14 '52
Himalayas
  Lea. C-47 flies over the
    hump 35:56 N 2 '53
Himmler, Heinrich
  Heinrich Himmler, "Time"
    cover portrait 17:66 D 11
    '44
Hindu woman. bw Sheets 20:80 Ja
    21 '46
Hinduism
  Demon with sword and snake
    sculpture bw 9:73 N 25 '40
  Four-armed goddess, onyx
    sculpture bw 9:72 D 16 '40
  Gods and goddesses: Brahma,
    Vishnu, Rama, Kali and
    others 38:68-9 F 7 '55

Indrajith, festival figure 30:
    93 F 12 '51
Jagannath, temple of photog
    bw 3:61 Ag 16 '37
Krishna bw 29:160 D 11 '50
Kumbhakarna, festival figure
    30:92 F 12 '51
Lakshmi statue bw 24:29 Ap
    5 '48
Ravana, demon king, festival
    figure 30:92 F 12 '51
Sacred word "OM" 38:57 F 7
    '55
Sarasvati statue bw 24:29 Ap
    5 '48
Siva 38:67-8 F 7 '55
  temple of, South India 38:
    65-6 F 7 '55
  tower, with statues of Siva,
    Madras 27:98-9 S 12
    '49
Hine, Lewis
  Child worker in a cotton mill,
    1908 photog bw 28:82 Ja
    2 '50
Hines, Duncan
  Duncan Hines photog bw 21:
    16 Jy 8 '46
Hingham, Massachusetts, old
    ship meeting house 38:128-
    9 Ap 18 '55
Hinman, Frank, Jr.
  Day break 23:99 N 10 '47
  Frank Hinman, Jr. photog
    bw 23:101 N 10 '47 port.
Hippopotamuses
  Jonas. Hippopotamus sculp-
    ture bw 12:89 Mr 23 '42
  Lotus decorated hippopota-
    mus, Egypt, c1950 B.C.
    ceramic 6:53 Mr 20 '39
  Mochi. Hippopotamus paper
    cutout 34:19 Mr 9 '53
Hiroshige, Ando
  Enkyo bridge 31:67 D 31 '51
  "The 47 Ronin," scenes
    from 15:53-6 N 1 '43
  hero prints bw 18:97 Ap
    16 '45
  Highway robbery, 1840,
    scene from "The 47 Ronin"

Hiroshige, Ando (cont.)
  print 15:53 N 1 '43
Hirsch, Joseph
  Nine men 30:37 Ja 15 '51
  Walkowitz pastel bw 16:80 F
    21 '44
Hirschfeld, Albert
  Fifth Avenue Cinema Theater
    mural--caricature of mo-
    tion picture stars cartoons
    bw 36:20-1 My 17 '54
  Howard Lindsay and Russell
    Crouse, scenes from their
    plays caricatures bw 21:
    116-7 N 11 '46
His master's voice, Victor
  Company trademark. bw
  Barraud 33:92 N 17 '52
"Historia Anglorum," illumina-
  tions, 13th century 40:98
  Mr 26 '56
Historic Houses See also Liter-
  ary Landmarks and Locale;
  The White House
  Adams House, Quincy, Mass.,
    18th century photogs 41:70-
    5 Jy 2 '56 bw 22:76 Je 23
    '47
  John Alden House, Duxbury,
    Mass., 1653 photog bw 11:
    87 S 8 '41
  Benjamin Franklin's birth-
    place, Boston, 1706 bw
    40:73 Ja 9 '56
  Birthplaces of U.S. Presi-
    dents bw 6:6-8 F 20 '39
  Executive mansions, 48 states
    bw 10:22-3 Ja 20 '41
  Hyde Park, New York. photogs
    White, archt. 28:89-92 Ja
    2 '50 bw 6:61-7 My 29 '39;
    20:89-92 Ap 15 '46
  Monticello, Virginia. Jeffer-
    son, archt. photog bw 14:
    65 Ap 12 '43
  Mount Vernon, Virginia photog
    bw 5:28 O 31 '38
  Phillips, A.F. Lincoln land-
    marks, New Salem, Illi-
    nois 36:79-81 F 15 '54
  Stratford Hall, Lee home,

  Virginia bw 13:57 Jy 6
    '42; 21:66-8 Ag 19 '46
  Strawberry Hill, home of
    Horace Walpole needle-
    point bw 17:118 O 23 '44
  Wood, G. Birthplace of
    Herbert Hoover 14:55 Ja
    18 '43
Historical Themes See also
  War Themes; names of
  countries, as United
  States; names of persons
  and groups, as Washing-
  ton, George; Pilgrims
  Bayeux tapestry, etching of
    40:88-9 Mr 26 '56 photog
    bw 16:8-10 Je 26 '44
  Carreno. Birth of the Ameri-
    can nations bw 10:106-7
    Mr 17 '41
  Brumidi. Ceiling, corridor
    paintings, Senate, Wash-
    ington, D.C. 31:56 Jy 2
    '51
  Brumidi. Fresco, Dome,
    U.S. Capitol, Washing-
    ton, D.C. 31:52-3 Jy 2
    '51
  The giraffe parade tapestry,
    Flemish, c1525 24:76-7
    Mr 22 '48
  Delacroix. Liberty leading
    the people 25:84 N 22 '48
  Forestier. Treaty of Ghent
    41:72-3 Jy 2 '56
  Perry's arrival in Japan,
    1853 bw 19:58 S 17 '45
  Puritan triumph at Naseby*
    bw 41:200 N 12 '56
  Removal of the Acadians
    from Nova Scotia, 1755
    bw 9:112 S 9 '40
  Vespucci in Brazil, 17th cen-
    tury drawing bw 37:110 O
    11 '54
History of Missouri. mural
  Benton 2:35-7 Mr 1 '37
Hitching post, iron figure, U.S.,
  1860 photog 39:106 O 17
  '55
Hitchcock, Alfred

Penn. Alfred Hitchcock photog
bw 24:15 My 10 '48
Hitchcock, Lambert, furniture
designer
Contemporary production of
1826-40 chair, Riverton,
Conn photog 28:118-20 My
1 '50
Hitler, Adolf
Battleship Wien 7:53 O 30 '39
Fromelles (France) dressing
station watercolor 1:42 N
30 '36
Haubourdin, France, February 1916 watercolor 1:42
N 30 '36
House with white fence watercolor 1:43 N 30 '36
Old abbey at Messines, Belgium watercolor 1:43 N 30
'36
Roman ruins* and other paintings 7:53-4 O 30 '39
Adolph Hitler caricature bw,
from Loyalist Spain 3:112
S 20 '37 port.
Dali. The enigma of Hitler 6:
44 Ap 17 '39 bw 19:65 S 24
'45 port.
Hommel. Adolf Hitler, Su-
preme Commander of the
German Army bw 9:97 S 23
'40 port.
Hoyer. Hitler addressing his
first followers in Munich
cellar, 1919* bw 7:43 S
25 '39 port.
Lanzinger. Adolf Hitler, as
knight 24:73 My 3 '48 bw
11:73 Ag 18 '41 port.
Picture album of Hitler's early years photogs bw 9:61-8
Ag 19 '40 port.
Hittin' the sack. Lea 12:58 My
25 '42
Hivlyn, Ann
Vanderlyn. Mrs. Ann Hivlyn
bw 9:74 D 9 '40
Hobart, Garret A.
Garret Hobart photog bw 9:9
Ag 5 '40

Hobo clown (Emmett Kelly).
MacIver 23:43 Jy 21 '47
Hoboes
Bacon, P. Wanderlus 20:80
F 18 '46
McCubbin. Down on his luck
bw 12:79 F 9 '42
Hochelaga
Jacques Cartier and Chief
Hochelaga, * 1535 bw 9:
112 S 9 '40
Hoeing. Gwathmey 16:78 Ap 24
'44
Hofer, Karl
The wind 5:73 D 12 '38
Artist and his work photog
36:143 My 10 '54 port.
Karl Hofer photog bw 5:72 D
12 '38 port.
Hoffman, Bernard
Carl Sandburg photog bw 4:
Cover F 21 '38
Hoffman's slough. tempera
Wyeth, A. 24:104 My 17
'48
Hofmann, Hans
Red table 33:98 O 27 '52
Hofmann, Josef
Josef Hofmann; wife; inven-
tions photogs bw 3:71-2,
74 N 15 '37 hands photogs
bw 10:8-11 Ja 6 '41
Hog killing, detail from Arrival
of Joseph and Mary at
Bethlehem. Brueghel, P.,
the elder 37:32 D 27 '54
Hogarth, William
Calais gate 21:81 D 16 '46
The dance (Masked ball at
Wansted) 21:81 D 16 '46;
25:99 S 13 '48
David Garrick and his wife
21:82 D 16 '46
False perspective bw 1:27
D 14 '36
Gin lane bw 20:66 My 27 '46;
21:83 D 16 '46
Marriage a la mode, six
scenes 21:80 D 16 '46
Night bw 21:78 D 16 '46
Noon bw 21:78 D 16 '46

Hogarth, William (cont.)
  Scene in a tavern bw 35:31 S
    14 '53
  The shrimp girl 21:79 D 16 '46
  Sigismonda bw 7:61 S 18 '39
  Self-portrait: Artist at work bw
    21:77 D 16 '46 port.
  Self-portrait in Calais gate 21:
    81 D 16 '46 port.
Hogfeldt, Robert
  Gnomes, pixies, trolls--comic
    watercolors 17:56-7 Jy 3 '44
Hogs killing a rattlesnake bw 15:
  19 N 29 '43 watercolor bw
  15:18 N 29 '43
Hogue, Alexandre
  Drouth-stricken area 2:60 Je
    21 '37
  Drouth survivors bw 2:61 Je 21
    '37
  Dust bowl 2:60 Je 21 '37
  Spindletop, Texas oil gusher
    10:40 F 10 '41
  Alexandre Hogue photogs bw
    10:41 F 10 '41 port.
  Self-portrait bw 2:61 Je 21 '37
    port.
Hokinson, Helen E.
  "New Yorker" cover 21:69-70
    Jy 15 '46
Hokusai
  "The 47 Ronin," prints 15:54-
    5 N 1 '43 hero prints bw
    18:97 Ap 16 '45
Holabird, William
  Holabird and Roche. Tacoma
    Building, 1887, Chicago
    bw 40:99 Mr 5 '56
  Holabird and Root. Three bed-
    room country house plan
    bw 9:82 Jy 1 '40
  Holabird, Root and Burgee.
    Armour's Pharmaceutical
    Center, Kankakee, Ill. 36:
    31 Ja 4 '54
Holbein, Hans, the younger
  The ambassadors 24:82 Mr 22
    '48
  Catherine Howard, Queen of
    England 7:34 Jy 31 '39
  Erasmus bw 16:66 Ja 10 '44

  Merchant Gisze, 1532 24:70
    Mr 22 '48
  Portrait of a man aged 54 bw
    39:147 S 26 '55
  Portrait of a young merchant
    bw 39:147 S 26 '55
  Sir Thomas More 3:33 D 27
    '37
  Self-portrait, 1542 5:40 Jy 11
    '38 port.
Holidays and Festivals See also
  Parades; and names of spe-
  cific holidays, as Christ-
  mas; Fourth of July
  Beckmann. Carnival 21:79 N
    25 '46
  Bellini. The Corpus Christi
    procession 23:54-5 Ag 4
    '47
  Brueghel, P., the elder. The
    wedding dance 4:22 Ap 11
    '38 bw 35:31 S 14 '53
  Celebration of coronation of
    Alexander II, Czar of Rus-
    sia, 1856* 38:64-5 Ja 31
    '55
  Corbino. Harvest festival 4:
    28 Je 13 '38
  Covarrubias. Balinese festi-
    val* 3:49 S 27 '37
  Currier and Ives print. Holi-
    day in the country: trouble-
    some flies 9:32 D 30 '40
  Dodd. Carnival 27:64 S 26 '49
  Du Bois, G. Carnival inter-
    lude 8:61 Ap 29 '40
  The feast of the Passover en-
    graving bw 6:55 Ja 30 '39
  Festival in Antwerp, 16th cen-
    tury bw 4:52-3 My 23 '38
  Fragonard. A fete at Rambou-
    illet 29:87 N 27 '50
  Guston. Holiday 20:92 My 27 '46
  Lancret. Fete galante 29:86
    N 27 '50
  Martin, F. Celebration 9:92
    N 11 '40
  Mock war, Venice, Renais-
    sance bw 23:59 Ag 4 '47
  Morado. The foolish virgins
    bw 20:58 Je 3 '46

Peirce, W. Country fair 3:34
Ag 30 '37; 21:74 N 25 '46
Pickens. Carnival 28:88 Mr
20 '50
Priebe. Carnival interlude 23:
71 N 24 '47
Rubens. The feast of Venus
27:66-7 O 24 '49
Sharon. May-Day party 33:75
Jy 21 '52
Spring festival on the Yellow
River, Ch'ing Ming scroll,
c1500 31:44-9 D 31 '51
Spring festival, Ming dynasty,
17th century 15:64 O 11 '43
Steen. Baptismal party 24:77
Je 14 '48
Victoria's diamond jubilee,
1897 bw 13:76 N 16 '42
Victoria's golden jubilee bw
32:22 F 18 '52
Wedding of Doge and the sea,*
Venice, Renaissance bw 23:
59 Ag 4 '47
Wedding scene,* England,
c1550 41:146 N 5 '56
Wood, G. Arbor day 14:56 Ja
18 '43
Holliday, Judy
Beaton. Judy Holliday in
"Born Yesterday" drawing
21:7 Jy 22 '46
Holloway, Wittich
Oil storage tanks, Wilmington,
N.C.* 34:79 Ja 5 '53
Holly quilt pattern bw 11:64 S
22 '41
Hollywood. Benton 5:74-5 D 12
'38
Hollywood
Emett. Evening, Hollywood
cartoon 37:52-3 Jy 5 '54
Helmers. Hollywood--surrea-
list satirical drawings bw
16:12-4 F 21 '44
Lee, D. Artist's impressions
of Hollywood 19:84-9 O 15
'45
Holmes, Oliver Wendell, 1902-
1932
Charles Evans Hughes and

Oliver Wendell Holmes in
court robes photog bw 25:
38 S 6 '48
Justice Holmes photog bw 23:
118 N 4 '46
Holmes, Sherlock
Coat of arms; memorabilia bw
16:82 My 1 '44
Illustrations for by Steele;
Doyle's father; Paget bw
16:77, 79 My 1 '44
Holy Family See also Flight into
Egypt; Jesus Christ--Ador-
ation
Brueghel, P., the elder.
Arrival of Joseph and Mary
at Bethlehem 37:Cover, 30-
3 D 27 '54
El Greco. The Holy family 15:
65 S 20 '43
Holy family, painted terra
cotta, Italy, c1400 bw 6:53
Mr 20 '39
Lippi. Holy family with St.
Margaret and St. John 1:
45 D 28 '36
Mantegna. The holy family,
c1500 40:106 My 7 '56
Ribera. Holy family with St.
Catherine 4:42 My 16 '38
Rubens. Holy family 6:39 My
29 '39
Tintoretto. Holy family, de-
tail from Nativity 31:
Cover D 24 '51
Holy Ghost descends on apostles.*
Giotto 25:54 D 27 '48
Holy Land
Shrines and scenes of Holy
Land photogs 20:52-63 Ap
1 '46
Strabo. Map of the Holy Land
20:53 Ap 1 '46 (map)
Holy rollers. bw Curry 15:18 N
29 '43
Holy sepulchre, Jerusalem pho-
tog bw 31:62 D 24 '51
Holy trinity. Santero painting,
altarpiece, Mission San
Jose, Laguna, N. Mex
photog 40:48-9 Ja 16 '56

Holyrood chapel photog bw 24:67
    Je 14 '48
Holyrood House photog bw 3:67
    Jy 19 '37
Holzschuher, Hieronymus
    Durer. Hieronymus Holzschu-
    her bw 19:25 D 31 '45
Homage to the Eiffel Tower.
    Chagall 22:58 My 5 '47
Home for Christmas. bw Nichols
    5:9 D 12 '38
Home for the holidays. drawing
    bw Gibson 28:17 Ja 2 '50
Home from the sea. Martin, F.
    9:91 N 11 '40
Homer, Winslow
    Driftwood 2:27 Ja 11 '37
    Eight bells 12:60 Je 15 '42
    The gulf stream 2:26 Ja 11
        '37; 5:36 O 31 '38
    Kissing the moon bw 6:82-3
        My 22 '39
    The lookout--"All's Well" 9:
        52 Jy 22 '40
    New England country school
        6:30 Je 19 '39
    Portrait of a girl* 41:160 D
        24 '56
    Prisoners from the front 5:33
        O 31 '38
    Skating in Central Park, 1860
        32:118 Ap 7 '52
    Watching the breakers bw 6:58
        Mr 27 '39
    Weaning the calf 41:72-3 D 10
        '53
    The wreck 2:26 Ja 11 '37
    Confederate pickets reconnoi-
        tering* bw 5:29 O 31 '38
        (drawing)
    West Point hop* bw 6:2 Ja 2
        '39 (drawing)
    Winslow Homer bw 5:29 O 31
        '38 port.
Homestead. Curry 7:36 D 25 '39
Hommel, Conrad
    Adolf Hitler, Supreme Com-
        mander of the German Army
        bw 9:97 S 23 '40
Hondius atlas world map, 1641 bw
    13:59 Ag 3 '42

Hong Kong
    Yamaguchi. General attack on
        Hong Kong 28:70 F 27 '50
Honored guests. Klaussen 26:59
    Mr 28 '49
The honors of Scotland: crown,
    sword, others photog bw
    3:67 Jy 19 '37
Hooch, Pieter de
    Family group 27:70 O 24 '49
    Game of skittle 13:95 N 9 '42;
        24:72 Je 14 '48
    Garden scene bw 3:112 O 18
        '37
    Interior 37:63 Ag 9 '54
    The linen cupboard 24:77 Je
        14 '48
Hood, John
    John Hood bw 25:30 O 25 '48
Hooft, Martha Visser't
    Tumblers and pigeons 30:36-7
        Ja 15 '51
"Hook," the hawk, illustrations
    from animated motion pic-
    ture. Durfee 40:155-8,
    160 Mr 19 '56
The Hooker party migrates to
    Hartford, Connecticut,
    1636. Church 13:82 N 23
    '42
Hooper, William
    William Hooper bw 15:9 Jy 5
        '43
Hooton, Earnest Albert
    Professor Hooton photog bw 2:
        25 Ap 12 '37; 3:95-6 N 15
        '37; 7:60-1 Ag 7 '39
Hoover, Herbert
    Curry. Hoover and the flood
        8:58-9 My 6 '40
    Wood, G. Birthplace of Her-
        bert Hoover 14:55 Ja 18 '43
Hope, Bob
    Glanzman. Bob Hope, as
        masters might paint him:
        Daumier, Dore, Goya, Pi-
        casso, Rembrandt cartoon
        bw 21:119 O 21 '46
Hope diamond, gemstone 32:67-
    8 Mr 17 '52
Hopkins, Stephen

Stephen Hopkins bw 15:9 Jy 5 '43

Hopkinson, Francis
Francis Hopkinson bw 15:9 Jy 5 '43

Hopper, Edward
Cape Cod afternoon bw 2:44 My 3 '37
Chop suey 28:102 Ap 17 '50
The city 20:80 F 18 '46
Corner saloon 28:101 Ap 17 '50
Drug store 28:103 Ap 17 '50
Early Sunday morning 27:62 Ag 29 '49
Ground swell 8:66 My 27 '40; 28:104-5 Ap 17 '50
Hotel room 2:47 My 3 '37
House by the railroad 2:47 My 3 '37
Lighthouse at two lights, Maine 2:46 My 3 '37; 21:74 N 25 '46
Manhattan bridge loop 28:102-3 Ap 17 '50
The Martha McKeen of Wellfleet 23:70 Jy14 '47
Night windows 28:103 Ap 17 '50
Office at night 28:102 Ap 17 '50
Seven A.M. 28:101 Ap 17 '50
The Sheridan theater 2:46 My 3 '37
Tables for ladies 2:45 My 3 '37
Two on the aisle 28:103 Ap 17 '50
Edward Hopper photog bw 2:44 My 3 '37; 28:100 Ap 17 '50 port.

Hoppner, John
Duke of Bedford bw 11:54 N 10 '41
Isabella, Marchioness of Hertford 4:27 Ja 24 '38

Hord, Donal, sculptor
Artist at work photog bw 9:82 O 21 '40

Horne, Dietler
The Stehlis of Zurich, 1874 25:91 O 18 '48

"Hornet" (ship)
Lea. Hornet's last day 15:42-9

Ag 2 '43
Lea. Portraits and scenes aboard U.S.S. Hornet 14: 50-8 Mr 22 '43

Horowitz, Vladimir
Vladimir Horowitz photog bw 16:49 Mr 13 '44

Horse and rider. lithograph Marini 33:85 Jy 14 '52
Horse and rider. sculpture bw Marini 22:102 My 22 '50
The horse fair. Bonheur 6:55 Mr 20 '39
Horse Armor See Armor
Horse Racing
Degas. At the races 40:74-5 My 28 '56
Degas. Jockey on race horse* sculpture, wax model 39: 121 O 31 '55
Flannery. Old Pimlico race track 32:70-2 My 5 '52
Horse race in the streets of Florence, cassone painting, 1417 15:67 S 20 '43
Marsh. The steeplechase 40: 83 F 6 '56
Peirce, W. Maine trotting race 3:34 Ag 30 '37
Racing horses and charioteers terra cotta, Etruscan, c550 40:59 F 13 '56
Toulouse-Lautrec. The jockey drawing bw 28:96 My 15 '50
Trotting match, Union course, 1858 39:106 O 17 '55
Wootton. The great race meeting 25:102-3 S 13 '48
Horseman. Gropper 20:79 F 18 '46
Horsemen See Equestrians
Horses See also Equestrians; Wagons and Carts
Avilov. Communication troops 14:47 Mr 29 '43
Bellows. The sand team 20: 81 Mr 25 '46
Bellows. The white horse 20: 81 Mr 25 '46
Blythe. The Pittsburgh horse market 9:76 D 9 '40

Bonheur. The horse fair 6:55 Mr 20 '39

Brook. Pasture at Elk 10:52 Ja 13 '41

Buddha riding Kanthaka, festival figure, Ceylon photog bw 40:27Je 11 '56

Burchfield. November evening 26:86-7 F 21 '49

Cowles. The farmer and the rain cloud 24:75 F 9 '48

Du Bois, W. "The Great Geppy," illustrations 8:60 Ap 29 '40

Eakins. The Fairman Roger's four-in-hand 16:74 My 15 '44

Fair play sculpture bw 3:88 N 1 '37

Flannery. Item 9, Man O' War 8:65 My 27 '40

Flannery. Night paddocks 10: 74 Ap 14 '41

Guardian figures, China, Ming dynasty sculpture bw 3:57 Ag 23 '37

Hardy. Horse sculpture bw 37: 123 O 11 '54

Horse, China, 4th century B.C. woodcarving 40:99 Ja 9 '56

Horse, China, T'ang ceramic 33:101 O 27 '52

Horse, ivory whip handle, Egypt, 1350 B.C. bw 6:52 Mr 20 '39

Horses, bronze urn, Greek, 6th century 37:87 S 13 '54

Horses, Greek, c800 B.C. sculpture bw 6:52 Mr 20 '39

Horses, Greek, 5th century B.C. sculpture bw 6:52 Mr 20 '39

Horses, Cro-Magnon cave painting, Montignac, France 22:65-8 F 24 '47

Horses, paleolithic cave painting, France 39:86 D 12 '55

Horses, paleolithic stone carving, 39:89 N 7 '55; 39:85 D 12 '55

Horses, Gallery of St. Mark's,

Venice sculpture 35:33 D 28 '53

Jackson, Harry. Blue horse 41:70 Jy 9 '56

Lebrun. Centurion's horse 30: 35 Ja 15 '51

Lee, D. The widow 8:66 My 27 '40

McCrady. Woman mounting a horse 3:42 O 18 '37

Metcalfe. Horses 29:72 Jy 17 '50

Mount. Bargaining for a horse 18:65 Je 25 '45

Muybridge. Galloping horse, photog winning Stanford bet, 1872 bw 11:10 O 20 '41

Peirce, W. After the show 12: 74 Ap 20 '42

Puget. Alexander on his horse, Bucephalas, riding over foes 39:86 N 14 '55

Reeves. Armed (race horse) 24:101 Ap 12 '48

Remington. Bronco buster 13: 73 S 14 '42

Remington. Cavalry charge on the southern plains 13: 76 S 14 '42

Remington. Navajos at the water hole 13:74 S 14 '42

Ryder. In the stable 30:88 F 26 '51

Sample. Janitor's holiday 3: 44 N 15 '37; 21:74 N 25 '46

Simkhovitch. Back country 11: 40 D 29 '41

Snyder. Oil 10:77 Mr 31 '41

Tiepolo. The building of the Trojan horse 9:48 Jy 29 '40

Toulouse-Lautrec. Horses* drawing bw 36:110 Ap 26 '54

Toulouse-Lautrec. In the circus--Fernando the ringmaster 11:59 S 8 '41

Wood horse, harnessmaker's dummy photog 39:104 O 17 '55

Horses and figures. drypoint bw

Picasso 23:93 O 13 '47
Horse's head with pink rose.
O'Keefe 4:29 F 14 '38
Horseshoe Falls. Church 26:78-
9 Je 6 '49
Horton, Mildred McAfee
Clemens. Mildred McAfee
Horton of Wellesley 23:93
O 27 '47
Horus
Eye of Horus necklace, Egypt
24:81 Ja 19 '48
Horus, the hawk god, basalt
bw c350 B.C. 6:53 Mr 20
'39
Isis holding son, Horus, ceram-
ic statue, blue faience 41:
114 N 26 '56
Hotel. bw Thomas, B. 10:53 Je
23 '41
Hotel de France. Davis, S. 22:80
F 17 '47
Hotel du Tertre. Utrillo 28:92-3
Ja 16 '50
Hotel room. Hopper 2:47 My 3 '37
Hotel valet. bw Soutine 9:67 O 14
'40
Hotels, architecture
Cincinnati Terrace Plaza Ho-
tel, store-top photogs 25:
83 S 20 '48
Hotel, Atami, Japan--rotating
top story photogs bw 40:111
F 6 '56
Mexico City hotels: Casa-
Latino-Americana; Reforma
photogs bw 21:98 F 24 '47
Stone. El Panama, Panama
City photogs 32:50-7 Ja 7
'52
Wright. Imperial Hotel, Tokyo
photog bw 21:93 Ag 12 '46
Houdon, Jean Antoine
Voltaire sculpture bw (copy)
12:15 Je 8 '42
Houmas House, Greek revival
plantation house, Louisiana,
1840 photog 32:74 Je 9 '52
Hountouaji, Bruno
St. Peter and the cock sculp-
ture bw 29:63 S 4 '50

The hour of the hyena (Mussolini)
cartoon bw, from "Punch"
26:55 F 14 '49
House by the railroad. Hopper
2:47 My 3 '37
House collapsing on two firemen,
Shoe Lane. Rosoman 12:40
Mr 2 '42; 26:49 F 28 '49
House furnishings design photog
bw 37:83-6 Jy 26 '54
A house in a village. Hyppolite
23:58 S 1 '47
House in the trees. Cezanne 37:
66 Ag 9 '54
House of Commons, England
Benjamin Franklin before the
House of Commons, 1766
bw 25:110 S 13 '48
Hickel. The House of Com-
mons 29:53 Jy 3 '50
House of Emil Zola at Medan.
Cezanne 2:47 Ap 12 '37
House of Lords, England
Pitt stricken in House of
Lords* 25:107 S 13 '48
House of Mallarme. Vuillard 37:
77 N 1 '54
House of mystery. Burchfield 1:
25 D 28 '36
House of Seven Gables, Salem,
Massachusetts, 1668 photog
bw 9:101 O 14 '40; 15:13
D 6 '43
House on the hill. McCrady 3:40
O 18 '37
House with white fence. water-
color Hitler 1:43 N 30 '36
Houseboat, Kashmir Lake photog
bw 10:90 My 12 '41
Houses See also Architecture,
Domestic; Historic Houses;
Literary Landmarks and
Locale
Bohrod. Merrillan night 11:94
N 10 '41
Burchfield. Six o'clock 1:26 D
28 '36
Cornelius. 'Long the Pennsy
line 28:90 Mr 20 '50
Dehn. The three red houses
11:41 Ag 11 '41

Houses (cont.)
 Dodd. Lumpkin Street 27:63
  S 26 '49
 Du Bois, Y. Wanamaker
  House 8:62 Ap 29 '40
 Emett. American dream house
  37:43 Jy 5 '54
 Hitler. Haubordin, France,
  February 1916 watercolor
  1:42 N 30 '36
 Kallem. Country tenement 24:
  103 Je 28 '48
 Kane, J. Schenley mansion
  2:46 My 17 '37
 Kingman. Victorian mansion,*
  Provincetown, Mass. 30:
  101 My 14 '51
 Raczka. The blue bench 28:90
  Mr 20 '50
 Stuempfig. Two houses 25:100
  S 20 '48
 Terry. The snail, surrealist
  architectural model bw 1:
  24 D 14 '36
 Thomas. Deserted house 10:
  52 Je 23 '41
 Thomas. New castle bw 10:53
  Je 23 '41
 Van Gogh. Houses at Auvers
  7:35 Jy 31 '39; 25:80 N 1
  '48
 Vlaminck. Houses at Chatou
  33:97 O 27 '52
 Volpi. Houses 36:82 My 31 '54
 Whitaker. Pink house 16:45 Ja
  3 '44
 Wyeth, A. Deserted house 35:
  80-1 Jy 27 '53
 Wyeth, N. C. Mrs. Cushman's
  house 20:79 Je 17 '46
Houses at Chatou. Vlaminck 33:
  97 O 27 '52
Housman, Alfred Edward
 Locale of Housman's writing
  photog bw 14:77-83 Je 14
  '43
Houston, Texas, skyline photog
  bw 40:100-1 My 21 '56
Houston, Nora
 Jubilate deo omnis terra 10:
  68 My 26 '41

Houston, Sam
 General Sam Houston photog
  bw 6:39 Ap 10 '39
Houtondji, Felicien
 Mary meeting Jesus sculpture
  bw 29:63 S 4 '50
Hovannes, John
 Music and ballet lamp design
  sculpture bw 21:103 N 18
  '46
Hovenden, Thomas
 Breaking home ties 9:76 D 9
  '40; 27:60 Ag 29 '49
Hovhaness, Alan
 Composer Hovhaness photog
  bw 40:142 My 21 '56
Howard, Catherine, Consort of
  Henry VIII, King of England
 Catherine Howard bw 41:88 O
  29 '56
 Holbein. Catherine Howard 7:
  34 Jy 31 '39
Howard, Norman
 Battle of Jutland, May 31,
  1916 bw 3:90 S 13 '37
Howard, Sidney
 Sidney Howard photog bw 2:82
  Je 28 '37
Howe, George, architect
 Howe and Brown. Two-story
  house photogs, plan bw 9:
  83 Jy 1 '40
House, William
 William House bw 29:53 Jy 3
  '50
Howl of the weather. Remington
  13:74-5 S 14 '42
Howland, Alfred Cornelius
 Fourth of July parade,* Wal-
  pole, New Hampshire,
  c1848 25:46-7 Jy 5 '48
Howland, John, coat of arms bw
  19:56 N 26 '45
Hoxie, Vinnie Ream
 Abraham Lincoln sculpture bw
  18:Cover Je 18 '45
Hoyer, H. O.
 Hitler addressing his first
  followers in a Munich cel-
  lar, 1919* bw 7:43 S 25
  '39

Huber, Wolfgang
  The agony in Gethsemane,
    c1530 39:28 D 26 '55
Huck Finn. mural detail. Benton
  2:36 Mr 1 '37; 21:74 N 25
  '46
Hudson, Thomas
  General John Burgoyne bw 28:
    56 Mr 6 '50
Hudson autumn. Mitchell 20:77
  F 18 '46
Hudson navigation boat 12:76 Ap
  20 '42
Hudson River
  Currier and Ives print. A night
    on the Hudson: Through at
    daylight 9:34 D 30 '40
  Klitgaard. View of Kingston 5:
    25 Ag 22 '38
  Lee, D. Hudson river excur-
    sion 3:46 S 20 '37
  Outing on the Hudson, c1870 9:
    76 D 9 '40
  Smith, D. Hudson river land-
    scape sculpture bw 33:76 S
    22 '52
  Wall. Hudson river from West-
    point 19:83 S 10 '45
Hudson River Bracketed
  "Hudson River Bracketed" ar-
    chitecture: hexagonal house,
    Barrytown photog bw 7:63
    O 2 '39
  "Hudson River Bracketed"
    Tuscan villa print, 1855 39:
    99 O 17 '55
Hudson River houses: bracketed,
  rustic-pointed, octagonal
  photog bw 7:62-3 O 2 '39
Hudson River School: landscape
  panoramas, Catskill Moun-
  tains 19:82-6 S 10 '45
Hughes, Charles Evans
  Charles Evans Hughes 19:88 S
    24 '45 photog bw 14:7 My 31
    '43
  Charles Evans Hughes--family;
    biographical scenes photogs
    bw 2:30-7 Mr 8 '37; 25:35 S
    6 '48
  Poor. Charles Evans Hughes

in Gold case mural 2:36 Ja
  4 '37
Hughes, Langston
  Langston Hughes bw 5:58 O 3
    '38
Hughes, Toni, toy designer
  Plastic carnival toys, Museum
    of Modern Art exhibit 29:
    32-3 D 25 '50
Hugo, Victor
  Rodin. Victor Hugo sculpture
    bw 38:20 My 9 '55
  Victor Hugo on the "Rock of
    Exiles," Jersey Isle pho-
    tog bw 25:99 N 22 '48
Hui Tsung, Emperor of China
  Ladies preparing newly woven
    silk, Sung dynasty, 12th
    century (copy after Chang
    Hsuan) 15:66-7 O 11 '43
Hull, Cordell
  Cordell Hull photog bw 19:89
    S 24 '45
Hull, John, silversmith
  Hull and Sanderson. Com-
    munion cup 38:117 Ap 18
    '55
  Hull and Sanderson. Dram
    cup 38:116 Ap 18 '55
Hull, Isaac
  Stuart, G. Sir Isaac Hull 23:
    69 O 27 '47
Hultberg, John
  Yellow sky 39:114-5 S 12 '55
Human pool tables. Marsh 6:26
  Ja 9 '39
Humbert I, King of Italy photog
  bw 15:21 Ag 9 '43; 15:104
  Ag 23 '43
Humboldt river, Elko County,
  Nevada print bw 26:101 Ap
  18 '49
Hummingbirds
  Audubon. Ruby-throated hum-
    mingbird 3:41 Jy 12 '37
  Peterson. Ruby-throated and
    other hummingbirds 25:78-
    80 Jy 26 '48
Humors
  The four humors, Middle
    Ages bw 22:84 Ap 7 '47

Humphrey, Maud
  A busy day, advertising pos-
    ter, c1900 28:40 Ja 2 '50
Humphreys, J. Y., Philadelphia
  card maker, 18th century
  Historical playing cards 38:
    Cover My 30 '55
Humphreys, Richard
  Young, J. Richard Humphreys,
    boxer mezzotint bw 6:42 F
    6 '39
Hungerford, Cy
  War posters to prevent sabo-
    tage 10:12-4 Mr 24 '41
Hunt, Peter
  Redesigned and redecorated
    furniture photogs bw 13:49-
    52 N 2 '42
  Peter Hunt photog bw 13:48 N
    2 '42 port.
Hunt, Richard Morris, architect
  Biltmore, North Carolina 28:
    89-92 Ja 2 '50
  The Breakers, Newport, Rhode
    Island 31:46-9 Jy 23 '51
Hunter, Margaret King, architect
  Center-kitchen house 41:
    34-6 D 24 '56
Hunters and Hunting
  Alken. Leading the field aqua-
    tint bw 6:38 F 6 '39
  Amino. Hunter sculpture 37:
    162 N 22 '54
  Brown. Buffalo hunter litho-
    graph bw 39:20 D 12 '55
  Brussel-Smith. Hunting inci-
    dents wood engravings 39:
    190-201 N 14 '55
  The buffalo hunter 39:111 N 21
    '55
  Chilean hunter,* Japanese il-
    lustration, 1853 bw 25:8 Ag
    2 '48
  De Bry. Deer hunt, after Le
    Moyne engraving bw 22:85
    Mr 10 '47
  Duke of Weimar returns from
    the hunt bw 27:22 Jy 25 '49
  Eskimo hunter stone carving
    36:68 My 24 '54
  Flannery. Maryland hunt 5:73

    D 12 '38
  Hippo hunt on the Nile bas-
    relief, Egyptian, Fifth
    dynasty 41:84 O 1 '56
  Hunt of the Amazons mosaic,
    Early Christian 28:78 Mr
    27 '50
  Hunting and fishing illumina-
    tions, Flemish, 15th cen-
    tury 22:78-80 My 26 '47
  King Peroz I hunting ibexes,
    Persian gilded silver dish,
    Sasanian dynasty, 224-637
    20:92 Je 24 '46
  Kroll. Hunter in the hills 14:
    43 Mr 8 '43
  Leech. A delicate compliment
    print bw 6:38 F 6 '39
  Leech. Hunting prints bw 6:
    38 F 6 '39
  Lion hunt bas-relief, Assyri-
    an bw 32:154 Ap 14 '52
  Lorjou. The hunt* 29:101 D
    11 '50
  Master of fox hounds photog
    bw 9:26 D 30 '40
  Munnings. Duke of Windsor,
    fox hunter, 1921 28:122 My
    22 '50
  Pleissner. Decoying broadbill
    watercolor 21:64 O 7 '46
  Pleissner. Dove shoot 21:65
    O 7 '46
  Pleissner. Flushing pheasant
    watercolor 21:68 O 7 '46
  Pleissner. Jumping woodcock
    watercolor 21:65 O 7 '46
  Pleissner. Pushing for rail
    watercolor 21:68 O 7 '46
  Pleissner. Rigging decoys*
    watercolor 21:63 O 7 '46
  Pleissner. Shooting grouse
    watercolor 21:64 O 7 '46
  Pleissner. Walking up on
    quail watercolor 21:66-7
    O 7 '46
  Renoir. The hunter 32:98 My
    19 '52
  Ripley. Coots on the open sea
    29:127 D 4 '50
  Ripley. Geese on Cape Cod

29:126 D 4 '50

Ripley. Hunting turkeys* 29:
123 D 4 '50

Ripley. Pheasants in New England 29:124-5 D 4 '50

Ripley. Quail in Georgia 29:
126 D 4 '50

Ripley. Woodcock in Canada
29:127 D 4 '50

Rubens. A bear hunt drawing
bw 6:58 Mr 27 '39

Rubens. Diana of the hunt 40:
112 My 7 '56

Sample. The fox hunt bw 18:44
Ja 1 '45

Unicorn hunt tapestry, France,
16th century 22:70-2 My 26
'47

Watteau. Return from the hunt
23:82-3 S 15 '47

Huntington Art Gallery, San Marino, California

England's greatest portraits in
America, 18th century 4:23-
9 Ja 24 '38

English landscape painting in
America 5:42-4 S 12 '38

Hurd, Nathaniel

Copley. Nathaniel Hurd 15:68
S 20 '43 port.

Hurd, Peter

Ascension Island scenes,
World War 18:62-3 Ap 30
'45

Bar-X ranch, New Mexico 23:
76-7 Ag 18 '47

Bob Crosby, rodeo champion
bw 20:59 My 13 '46

Boy from the plains 7:26 Jy 24
'39

Cloudburst 23:77 Ag 18 '47

Desert windmill water tank*
23:75 Ag 18 '47

The dry river 7:25 Jy 24 '39;
21:76 N 25 '46 bw 11:9 N 17
'41

An early meeting on the Oklahoma prairie mural 30:78-9
Mr 5 '51

Eighth U.S. army air force;
operations 15:58-64 Jy 26
'43

Enemy action bw 14:7 Je 28 '43

Lady bronc rider 7:26 Jy 24
'39

Landscape with polo players
7:26 Jy 24 '39

Marine training base 11:61 Jy
7 '41

Mirage 23:77 Ag 18 '47

Old pioneers mural, Post Office, Big Springs, Texas
10:46 Ja 27 '41

Return from Rouen 14:52-3 Je
21 '43 bw 14:6 Je 28' 43

Riverbank farm* 23:78 Ag 18
'47

The windmill crew 14:46 Mr 8
'43

Sketchbook bw 14:73 F 15 '43;
16:12-4 Je 19 '44 (drawings)

Artist at work photog 26:66 Mr
14 '49 bw 11:60 Jy 7 '41;
14:66 F 15 '43 port.

Peter Hurd photog bw 11:67
Ag 4 '41; 23:74 Ag 18 '47
age 35 7:24 Jy 24 '39 in
uniform 14:8 Je 28 '43
port.

Wyeth, H. Peter Hurd, the
artist's husband 10:48 F
3 '41

The hurler. sculpture bw Brown,
Joseph 12:90 My 19 '41

Hurricane fighter plane. Gross,
A. 26:60 Mr 21 '49

Husain, Grandson of Mohammed
Tomb, replica, photog 38:87
My 9 '55

Husgen, Wilhelm

Doris Husgen, the artist's
daughter--31 heads, annual
sculpture bw 32:120 Je 2
'52

Huss, John

Burning of John Huss, 1415
bw 24:29 Mr 8 '48; 27:59
Ag 1 '49

John Huss bw 24:60 Je 14 '48

Hutton, Barbara
  Berti. Barbara Hutton sculp-
    ture bw 4:23 Jy 18 '38
Huxley, Aldous
  Aldous Huxley photog bw 4:60
    Ap 4 '38; 22:53, 60 Mr 24
    '47
Huxley, Julian Sorell
  Julian Huxley photog bw 14:31-
    4 My 17 '43; 22:53, 58 Mr
    24 '47; 27:66 O 31 '49
Huxley, Thomas
  Self-portrait drawing bw 22:
    54 Mr 24 '47
Huxley, Mrs. Thomas
  Mrs. Thomas Huxley photog
    bw 22:54 Mr 24 '47
Hvalfjordur, Iceland. bw Coale
  13:92-3 Jy 13 '42
Hyde Park, London
  Davis. Softball in Hyde Park*
    16:66-7 Ap 3 '44; 31:79 O
    29 '51
Hyde Park, New York, Greek re-
    vival architecture. photog
    White, archt. 28:89-92 Ja 2
    '50 bw 6:61-7 My 29 '39;
    20:89-92 Ap 15 '46
Hyderabad, Throne of the Nizam
  of photog bw 2:56 Mr 22
  '37
Hynckes, Raoul
  Basket of fruit 29:102 D 11 '50
Hypnotist and woman patient* bw
  23:76 S 15 '47
The hypochondriac. Smith, J.G.
  12:45 Mr 9 '42
Hyppolite, Hector
  A house in the village 23:61 S
    1 '47
  Artist at work photog bw 23:
    58 S 1 '47 port.

                    I

I found my love. sculpture Gross,
  C. 30:63 Ja 8 '51
I Tatti, Bernard Berenson's
  home, Italy photogs bw 26:
  158-60 Ap 11 '39
I was always present. Grosz 16:
  77 Je 12 '44

Ia orana Maria (We greet you
    Mary). Guaguin 7:26 D 25
    '39 bw 13:51 S 14 '42
Ibexes
  King Peroz I hunting ibexes,
    Persian gilded silver dish,
    Sasanian dynasty, 224-637
    20:92 Je 14 '46
Ice sculpture See Sculpture--
    Ice
Ice skater. lithograph Regnier
    6:40 F 6 '39
Icon
  Three-faced Christ bw 11:120
    O 13 '41
Ideal Cement Company, Boettch-
    er, Colorado. Fisher and
    Fisher, archt. 36:33 Ja 4
    '54
Idle hour park. Bohrod 11:62 Jy
    7 '41 bw 14:6 Je 28 '43
Idols and Images See Biblical
    and Christian Themes; Fig-
    ures; Gods and Goddesses
Idol's Eye, gemstone, diamond
    32:67 Mr 17 '52
If this be not I. Guston 20:92 My
    27 '46
Ife chief, bronze scarified head,
    Nigeria, c1350 bw 33:116
    S 8 '52
Ignatius of Loyola, Saint
  St. Ignatius bw 24:61 Je 14
    '48; 39:43 D 26 '55
Ikaris, Nikolaos
  The unknown political prison-
    er sculpture bw 34:42 Je 1
    '53
Ilic, Boza
  Sounding the terrain of New
    Belgrade 29:105 D 11 '50
Illuminations See also Manu-
    scripts
  Adam and Eve, Codex Paulin-
    us 34:77 F 23 '53
  Arming of Henry V, King of
    England, "Book of Hours,"
    15th century 40:178 Ap 9
    '56
  The ascension, 16th century
    manuscript 18:62 Ap 2 '45

At Christ's tomb 18:61 Ap 2 '45

Battle of Hastings, French chronicle, 15th century 40: 86 Mr 26 '56

The betrayal, Psalter, 13th century 18:59 Ap 2 '45

Descent from the cross 18:60 Ap 2 '45

The descent into hell, 14th century manuscript 18:60 Ap 2 '45

Doubting Thomas 18:61 Ap 2 '45

The entry into Jerusalem, 11th century manuscript 18:58 Ap 2 '45

Harvesting, Flemish, 15th century 22:80 My 26 '47

Jesus before Pilate, Flemish, 15th century 18:59 Ap 2 '45

Jesus crowned with thorns, 11th century 18:59 Ap 2 '45

Limbourg. "Book of Hours" of the Duc de Berry 24:38-50 Ja 5 '48

Matthew working on gospel, German, 13th century 22: 82 Ap 7 '47

Memling. June, calendar page, c1478 bw 18:42 Ja 1 '45

"Missal of Ferdinand," Italy, 15th century 32:87 Ap 14 '52

Persian illuminations, 14th and 15th century 20:91 Je 24 '46

The resurrection, Saxon lectionary, 13th century 18: 60-1 Ap 2 '45

Richard II's Bible, historiated letters 34:80 F 23 '53

Travels of Marco Polo, 15th century bw 23:48-9 Ag 4 '47

"Tres Riches Heures" du Duc de Berri 24:38-50 Ja 5 '48

Virgil's "Aeneid" 32:86 Ap 14 '52

"Illustrated London News"
Illustrations from first century of publication, 1842-1942 bw 13:71-8 N 16 '42

Illustrations See Also Allegorical and Symbolical Themes; Biblical and Christian Themes; Illuminations; Literary Themes; Mythological Themes

Alajalov. "Cinderella" bw 15: 79-80 S 13 '43

Bacon, P. "Buttons" bw 6:61 My 8 '39

Bemelmans. "Madeline" bw 7:6-7 S 4 '39

Birch. "Little Lord Fauntleroy" bw 27:71 D 5 '49

Blake. "The Four Zoas" watercolors 36:66 Ap 19 '54

Blake. "Songs of Innocence," title page bw 36:66 Ap 19 '54

Botticelli. Birth of Venus 41: 103 O 22 '56

Browne. "Nicholas Nickleby" bw 23:2-3 D 22 '47

Brussel-Smith. Hunting incidents wood engravings 39: 190-201 N 14 '55

"Candide" bw 23:88 S 15 '47

Chamberlain. "My Confession"
I. 41:Cover, 68-82 Jy 23 '56
II. 41:52-9 Jy 30 '56
III. 41:64-72 Ag 6 '56

Children's book illustrations 11:84-6 D 15 '41

Christmas carols, illustrated by American artists 23:42-58 D 22 '47

Christy. "The Man in Lower Ten" bw 20:56 F 25 '46

"Classic of Filial Piety," Confucian scripture 38:73 Ap 4 '55

Cornwell. "The Robe" 23:91-4 D 8 '47

Cruikshank. "Oliver Twist" bw 25:78 D 27 '48

Curry. Magazine illustrations and cover for "Wayside Tales," "St. Nicholas," "Country Gentleman" bw 15:18 N 29 '43

Illustrations (cont.)

Denslow. "The Wonderful Wizard of Oz" 35:52-9 D 28 '53

Dewitt. "The Story of the Mississippi" 11:85 D 15 '41

Dodgson. "Alice's Adventures in Wonderland" bw 20:100-1 Ap 15 '46

Dore. "Inferno" bw 15:12-3 D 13 '43

Dore. "Journey for Our Time," humorous Russian history bw 30:108-13 Mr 5 '51

Dore. Satan brooding, for "Paradise Lost" bw 24:76 F 2 '48

Du Bois. "The Bear Party" 29:44-9 D 25 '49

Du Bois. "The Flying Locomotive" 11:86 D 15 '41

Du Bois. "The Great Geppy" 8:60 Ap 29 '40

Du Bois. "Lion" 39:60-2 Jy 25 '55

Eichenberg. "Jane Eyre" wood engravings bw 15:100-1 N 29 '43

Eichenberg. "Wuthering Heights" wood engravings bw 15:102-3 N 29 '43

Flack. "Adolphus" bw 11:84 D 15 '41

Foster. "Miss Flora McFlimsey" books bw 33:84 S 22 '52

Geisel. "And to think that I saw it on Mulberry Street" 11:85 D 15 '41

Geisel. Thidwick the Big-Hearted Moose bw 25:26-7 N 22 '48

Gergely. "Topsy Turvy Circus" 11:85 D 15 '41

Greenaway. "A Day in a Child's Life" bw 18:87-8 Ap 9 '45

Greenaway. Illustrations from her books 23:87-92 D 1 '47

Greenaway. "Queen of the Pirate Isle," title page 23:88

D 1 '47

Grosvenor. "Love Stories" bw 20:56 F 25 '46

Grosz. "Inferno" bw 15:12-3 D 13 '43

Grover. "Broad Stripes and Bright Stars" bw 11:84 D 15 '41

"Gulliver's Travels" bw 25:109 S 13 '48

"Harper's Weekly," representative illustrations 6:2-4 Ja 2 '39

Hazard. "Hook," the hawk bw 40:155-60 Mr 19 '56

"Illustrated London News," illustrations from first century of publication, 1842-1942 bw 13:71-8 N 16 '42

Julian. "Piccoli" 35:197-200 D 7 '53

Kleiman. UNESCO's "What is Race" 34:101-2 My 18 '53

Knight. "Eloise" 39:149 D 12 '55

Lantz. "The Matchlock Gun" lithographs 11:85 D 15 '41

Lear. Alphabet--written and illustrated bw 32:6-8 Mr 24 '52

Leech. "A Christmas Carol" bw 25:78 D 27 '48

"Lief the Lucky" bw 11:84 D 15 '41

Low. "Mother Goose Riddle Rhymes," rebus book 36:6-7 Ap 19 '54

McCloskey. "Blueberries for Sal" bw 25:69-71 D 27 '48

McGuffey's Readers bw 13:90-2 Jy 20 '42

Maillol. "Daphnis and Chloe" bw 8:108 Ap 15 '40

Maillol. "Geogics" bw 8:109 Ap 15 '40

"Mrs. Malaprop" bw 25:109 S 13 '48

Martin. "Old Mother Hubbard" bw 20:104-5 Ap 15 '46

"Meriken Shinshi," Japanese history of U.S., 1853 bw

25:6-8 Ag 2 '48

Ogden. "The Night Before Christmas" 31:96-100 D 10 '51

Osborn. "Flight into Space" 35:90 Ag 31 '53

Paget. Sherlock Holmes stories bw 16:77 My 1 '44

Pelton. "Poor Richard's Almanac" steel engravings bw 40:74-5 Ja 9 '56

Potter. "Tale of Peter Rabbit" bw 33:113-4 D 8 '52

Potter. "Tale of Tom Kitten" bw 33:113-4 D 8 '52

Price. "The Lancashire Lad" bw 8:110-1 My 6 '40

Psalms, Canterbury Psalter 34:80 F 23 '53

Pyle. "Robin Hood" bw 20:78 Je 17 '46

Ralph. "Circular Staircase" bw 20:56 F 25 '46

Reisman. "Anna Karenina" 8: 46-9 F 5 '40

Richardson's "Clarissa" bw 25:109 S 13 '48

"The Rivals" bw 25:109 S 13 '48

"Robinson Crusoe" bw 25:109 S 13 '48

Scott. Western magazine covers and illustrations bw 12: 68 Je 29 '42

"She" bw 15:8 D 27 '43

Shepard. "The Wind in the Willows" bw 27:69 N 21 '49

Shepard. "Winnie-the-Pooh" and other Milne books bw 30:75-6 F 19 '51; 40:117-22 F 27 '56

Sickles. "The Bridges of Toko-Ri" 35:58 Jy 6 '53

Steele. "Sherlock Holmes" bw 16:77 My 1 '44

"The Sorrows of Young Werther" bw 27:22 Jy 25 '49

Stern. "A Child's Book of Prayers" 11:85 D 15 '41

"Ten Nights in a Barroom" bw 32:63-4 Mr 17 '52

Tenniel. "Alice in Wonderland" bw 29:22 N 6 '50; 30:85-7 Je 18 '51

Thurber. "Fables for our Time" bw 24:80 Ap 19 '48

"Tom Jones" bw 25:109 S 13 '48

"Treatise on Rural Economy" 15th century 22:78-80 My 26 '47

White. De Bry's "Voyages" bw 18:60 My 21 '45

Williams, Garth. "Little Fur Family" 21:59-61 D 2 '46

Williams, Gluyas. "Chips Off the Old Benchley" bw 27: 24-9 O 10 '49

Wilson. "Anthony Adverse" 18: 57 Ap 23 '45

Wilson. "Iron Men and Wooden Ships" 18:55 Ap 23 '45

Wilson. "The Last of the Mohicans" 18:58 Ap 23 '45

Wilson. "The Man Without a Country" 18:58 Ap 23 '45

Wilson. "Ranging the Maine Coast" 18:57 Ap 23 '45

Wilson. "Robinson Crusoe" 18:55 Ap 23 '45

Wilson. "Treasure Island" 18: 56 Ap 23 '45

Wilson. "Two Years Before the Mast" 18:60 Ap 23 '45

Wilson. "The Village Blacksmith" 18:59 Ap 23 '45

Wright. "Uncle Remus' Stories" bw 29:124 Ag 28 '50

Wyeth, N.C. "Drums" 20:81 Je 17 '46

Wyeth, N.C. "Robin Hood" 20:81 Je 17 '46

Wyeth, N.C. "Scottish Chiefs" 20:81 Je 17 '46

Wyeth, N.C. "The Yearling" 20:81 Je 17 '46

Wyss, J.E. "The Swiss Family Robinson" 37:50-61 D 27 '54

Ilunga. Witch doctors 34:107 My 4 '53

Ilunga and Pilipili. Birds, bugs
    and foliage frieze 34:106-
    7 My 4 '53
Imaginary Animals See Animals,
    Imaginary
Imaginary Beings See also
    Witches and Witchcraft
Brauner. Kabyline in move-
    ment 1:26 D 14 '36
Chagall. The juggler 22:57 My
    5 '47
Denslow. Illustrations for
    "The Wonderful Wizard of
    Oz" 35:52-9 D 28 '53
Goblin sculpture, Japanese,
    1215 34:95 Ap 20 '53
Half-man, half-toad statue bw
    35:39 Jy 27 '53
Kinnaras, woman-bird of Hin-
    duism 38:68-9 F 7 '55
Man-bats on the moon, 1835
    bw 23:16 Jy 21 '47
Milles. Buddha of the sea
    sculpture bw 2:32 F 22 '37
Nagas, snake-gods of Hindu-
    ism 38:69 F 7 '55
Ogres drawings bw 36:114 Ap
    26 '54
Imai, Taiho
Artist and his work photog 32:
    99 Je 23 '52 port.
Immigrants, Castle Garden, New
    York, c1870 bw 16:50 Ja
    17 '44
Immigration
Brinkmann. Ellis Island scenes
    bw 6:60-1 Mr 13 '39
An imperial lady, China 15:65 O
    11 '43
Imperial crown of India photog 2:
    41 Mr 15 '37
Imperial Palace, Moscow photogs
    38:62-5 Ja 31 '55
Imperial Theatre, Moscow
Gala performance, 1856* 38:
    64 Ja 31 '55
In and around Kyoto. Sumiyoshi
    Gukei 31:66-7 D 31 '51
In memoriam. Burchfield 1:27 D
    28 '36
In Montmartre. Davis, G. R. 19:

54 Jy 16 '55
In Squeaker Cove. De Martini 29:
    72 Ag 21 '50
In the box. Cassatt 36:98 My 17
    '54
In the circus--Fernando the ring-
    master. Toulouse-Lautrec
    11:59 S 8 '41
In the ring. Marin 29:64 Jy 10
    '50
In the salon: Rue des Moulins,
    detail. Toulouse-Lautrec
    28:100 My 15 '50
In the stable. Ryder 30:88 F 26
    '51
In the Wintergarden. bw Manet
    24:68 Mr 22 '48
In without knocking. Russell, C.
    M. 39:86 N 14 '55
Inaugurations
General Washington's arrival
    in New York harbor for in-
    auguration* 31:61 Jy 2 '51
Incas See also Art, Pre-Colum-
    bian
Machu Picchu ruins, Peru
    photog 25:55 Ag 2 '48 bw
    19:101-9 S 24 '45
India See also Art, Indian (East
    Indian)
Architecture, sculpture, car-
    riages photogs bw 9:69-73
    N 25 '40
Buddha, reclining figure, A-
    janta Caves bw 38:80 Mr 7
    '55
Buddhist temple of Boodhnath,
    Nepal photog bw 38:43 Mr
    28 '55
De Bry. Animals and fruit of
    India drawings bw 24:87 Mr
    22 '48
Golden Buddha, Shwe Dagon
    Pagoda, Rangoon 38:Cover
    Mr 7 '55
Jain temple, Calcutta photog
    bw 12:86 Mr 16 '42
Observatory, Delhi photog bw
    12:91 Mr 16 '42
Observatory, Jaipur photog bw
    9:70 N 25 '40

Rama-Lila pageant, giant effigies of gods and devils, New Delhi photogs 30:90-5 F 12 '51

Schnier. India sculpture bw 5: 70 D 5 '38

Sheets. Village of Begampur--scenes and portraits 20:80-3 Ja 21 '46

Sheets. India famine scenes 18:60-1 Ap 30 '45

Shwe Dagon Pagoda, Rangoon photogs bw 26:64 My 9 '49; 38:88-9 Mr 7 '55

Siva temple, South India photog 38:65-6 F 7 '55

Star of India photog bw 16:62 Ja 24 '44

Temples, parade floats of Jagannath (Vishnu) photogs bw 3:60-1 Ag 16 '37

Indian Idol
Sri Sri Iswari Bhuba Neswari Thak Urani sculpture bw 2: 57 My 10 '37

Indian Lascars
Sawyers. Indian Lascars--12 portraits drawings 16:63-4 Ja 24 '44

Indian maiden's ghost. Brown 26: 80 Je 6 '49

Indian mutiny, Lucknow Garrison, 1857* bw 7:71 S 25 '39

Indian rope trick* bw 10:81 Je 16 '41

Indians, Mexico
Castellanos. The aunts 4:30 Mr 14 '38

Rivera. Sellers waiting 4:29 Mr 14 '38

Tamayo. Indian women and baskets of flowers* mural 34:103 Mr 16 '53

Indians, North America See also subjects, as Battle of the Little Big Horn

Andre. Indians and soldiers in a tavern* drawing bw 35:92 S 28 '53

Blakelock. Pipe dance bw 5: 29 O 31 '38

Bodmer. Camp of the Gros Ventres of the prairies 15: 88 Ag 30 '43

Bodmer. Interior of an Indian hut, Mandan tribe* 27:45 Jy 4 '49

Bodmer. Pehriska-Ruhpa, war chief of the Minnetaree tribe, Dakota lithograph 27: 41 Jy 4 '49

Brownscombe. The first American Thanksgiving 13: 77 N 23 '42

The buffalo hunter 39:111 N 21 '55

Catlin. Red Jacket, Seneca·chief 36:72 Mr 8 '54

Chappel. Pocahontas saving Capt. Smith* bw 31:154 D 3 '51

Chief Keokuk and son, 1812 print bw 21:106 S 30 '46

Cigar store Indian, wood carving 38:62 Ja 3 '55

Curtis. Sacred Navaho ritual photog bw 31:12 S 10 '51

De Bry. Deer hunt, after Le Moyne bw 22:85 Mr 10 '47

De Bry. Drying meat, after Le Moyne bw 22:85 Mr 10 '47

Drowne. Indian, weathervane 38:121 Ap 18 '55

Elizabeth Ross 36:73 Mr 8 '54

Emett. Albuquerque Indians rain dance cartoon 37:51 Jy 5 '54

Flower. Indians stealing horses in the Black Hawk War 25:39 N 29 '48

Gilcrease collection of American Indian and frontier art 36:71-9 Mr 8 '54

Hicks. Penn treating with the Indians, 1682 24:71 Je 14 '48; 36:78 Mr 8 '54

Humphreys. Historical playing cards: Indian portraits --Brant, Joseph; Gy-antwachia; Red Jacket 38:Cover My 30 '55

Indians, No. American (cont.)

Jacques Cartier and Chief
Hochelaga, 1535* bw 9:112
S 9 '40

Jarvis. Black Hawk and son,
Sauk and Fox chief 36:73
Mr 8 '54

Keokuk chief and son, 1812
print bw 21:106 S 30 '46

Laning. The corn dance 6:44
My 1 '39

Le Clear. Red Jacket's grandson 36:73 Mr 8 '54

Marin. Corn dance 29:64 Jy 10
'50

Miller, A. J. Fort Laramie,
Wyoming, 1837 27:44-5 Jy
4 '49; 39:75 N 28 '55

Miller, A. J. A Sioux on the
warpath 36:78-9 Mr 8 '54

Milles. God of peace sculpture
bw 2:27 F 22 '37

Nahl. Governor Caleb Lyon's
1856 Indian treaty* 36:78
Mr 8 '54

New World cannibals,* 16th
century engraving bw 41:
181 N 12 '56

Parsons. Cunne Shote, Cherokee chief 36:75 Mr 8 '54

Pilgrims first Thanksgiving*
bw 19:52 N 26 '54

Remington. Cheyenne sculpture bw 13:72 S 14 '42

Remington. The discovery 36:
77 Mr 8 '54

Remington. Howl of the weather
13:74-5 S 14 '42

Remington. Navahos at the
waterhole 13:74 S 14 '42

Remington. The scalp sculpture bw 13:72 S 14 '42

Russell. Lewis and Clark expedition bw 33:65 N 10 '52

Russell. The Navahos 24:65
Mr 1 '48

Vanderlyn. Death of Jane Mc-
Crea 29:49 Jy 3 '50

West. Death of General Wolfe
5:31 O 31 '38; 25:106-7 S
13 '48 bw 7:70 S 25 '39; 9:
112 S 9 '40

West. Penn's treaty with the
Indians 6:27 Je 19 '39

White, J. Indians of Virginia
bw 18:60 My 21 '45

White, J. Indians--series of
watercolors, c1585 22:81-
5 Mr 10 '47

Wimar. Attack on an emigrant
train 27:43 Jy 4 '49

Wimar. Indians pursued by
American dragoons 27:43
Jy 4 '49

Indians, South American

Chilean hunter,* Japanese illustration, 1853 bw 25:8 Ag
2 '48

De Bry. Indian market drawing bw 24:86 Mr 22 '48

De Bry. Tree dwellers* drawing bw 24:87 Mr 22 '48

Graham. A South American
woman grinding corn sculpture bw 4:14 F 21 '38; 5:70
D 5 '38

Poleo. Marketgoers, Venezuela 36:79 My 31 '54

Indrajith, Hindu festival figure
30:93 F 12 '51

Industrial Themes See also
Railroads

Artzybasheff. Machine tools
34:59-61 Ja 5 '53

Dehn. Iron mines, Ironwood,
Michigan* 34:78 Ja 5 '53

Demuth. My Egypt (grain ele-
vators) 38:75 Mr 28 '55

Fredenthal. Molten ore 25:65
Ag 23 '48; 34:80 Ja 5 '53

Gould. Source of power mural
10:45 Ja 27 '41

Holloway. Oil storage tanks,
Wilmington, N.C. 34:79
Ja 5 '53

McCrady. Oil refinery, Baton Rouge, La. 34:80 Ja 5
'53

Nack. Refinery 28:86 Mr 20
'50

Poor. Tennessee Valley Authority 2:36 Ja 4 '37

Sample. Norris Dam bw 3:42
    N 15 '37
Sample. The Schuylkill River
    34:78-9 Ja 5 '53
Sample. Shell factory 11:63 Jy
    7 '41 bw 14:7 Je 28 '43
Schneider iron works, Le
    Creusot, France, c1848
    25:95 N 22 '48
Sheeler. City interior 5:43 Ag
    8 '38
Sheeler. Upper deck 5:44 Ag
    8 '38
Wheel shop, Hangtown, Cali-
    fornia, c1850 31:74 Jy 2 '51;
    39:104 O 17 '55
Ines, Saint
El Greco. The Virgin with
    Santa Ines and Santa Tecla
    7:26 D 25 '39
Infanta Margarita Theresa.
    Velazquez 27:72 O 24 '49
Ingersoll, Sturgis
Watkins, F. C. Sturgis Inger-
    soll 38:71 Mr 28 '55
Ingestre Hall, Staffordshire,
    England, photogs bw 8:88-
    92 Je 3 '40
Ingram, A. J.
Tanks through minefield* 26:
    59 Mr 21 '49
Ingres, Jean Auguste Dominique
Bather of Valpincon 41:Cover
    O 22 '56
Granet the painter 34:90 My
    11 '53
Mlle Riviere 34:87 My 11 '53
Odalisque 34:88-9 My11 '53
Portrait of la Comtesse
    D'Haussonville 3:Cover D
    27 '37
Turkish bath 10:73 Ap 28 '41;
    41:107 O 22 '56
Gown 34:86 My 11 '53 (draw-
    ings)
Mme Lucièn Bonaparte 34:91
    My 11 '53 (drawings)
Nicolo Paganini at 37 bw 36:
    128 N 16 '53 (drawings)
Slave 34:86 My 11 '53 (draw-
    ings)

Self-portrait bw 34:86 My 11
    '53 port.
Self-portrait, age 85 bw 10:
    72 Ap 28 '41 port.
Inkstands
Coney. Silver inkstand, Bos-
    ton, c1700 bw 6:52 Mr 20
    '39
Silver inkstand, U.S., 1770's
    41:67 Jy 2 '56
Inman, Henry
Picnic in the Catskills 27:57
    Ag 29 '49
Inness, George
The coming storm 12:59 Je
    15 '42
Peace and plenty 5:34-5 O 31
    '38 detail bw 19:82 S 10 '45
St. Peter's basilica 33:90 S
    15 '52
George Inness bw 19:82 S 10
    '45 photog bw 5:28 O 31
    '38 port.
Innocent III plaque, U.S. Capitol
    bw 30:74 F 5 '51
Inns See Barrooms, Inns and
    Taverns
Inokuma, Genichiro
Artist and his work photog
    32:100, 103 Je 23 '52 port.
Inquisitive model. Patrick 11:73
    O 27 '41
Insane
Manacled mentally ill, c1841*
    bw 22:80 Ja 13 '47
Institute of Contemporary Art,
    Boston
Exhibit of main trends in U.S.
    art since 1913. Armory
    Show 26:84-9 F 21 '49
"L'Insurgente" (ship)
Constellation capturing L'In-
    surgente, 1799 bw 23:72
    O 27 '47
Interior Design See also Archi-
    tecture; Furniture

Colonial
Eighteenth century kitchen
    38:127 Ap 18 '55

Colonial (cont.)
  Harlow House, 1677, Ply-
    mouth, Mass--central room
    with fireplace, scullery 18:
    54-7 My 7 '45
  Seventeenth century parlor 38:
    126 Ap 18 '55
  Whipple House, 1683, Ipswich,
    Mass.--main bedroom 18:
    58 My 7 '45

Contemporary
  Bond and Miller. Southern
    house 31:117 F 21 '55
  Brown, E. West coast orient-
    al 38:120-1 F 21 '55
  Clark, G. Northeast town
    house 38:116-7 F 21 '55
  Kahn. House, Palo Alto, Cali-
    fornia 37:120-2 N 15 '54
  Knoll. Interior, Dallas Muse-
    um of Fine Arts 34:72-3
    Mr 2 '53
  Pahlmann. "Momentum" stu-
    dio apartment 27:58-9 O 3
    '49
  Robsjohn-Gibbings. Modern
    living room 27:60-1 O 3
    '49
  Rooms decorated around a
    single painting 3:43 N 29 '37
  Sedwick. Southwest style house
    38:114-5 F 21 '55
  Swanson. Nordic modern
    house, midwest 38:118-9 F
    21 '55
  Three styles of decoration 27:
    55-61 S 26 '49
  Widmann. "Trade secrets"
    house 34:8-10 Ja 5 '53

English
  Adam. Kedleston 23:136 S 8
    '47
  Adam. Osterly Park; Syon
    House 23:71-4 Ag 25 '47
  Ham House, 17th century 41:
    160 N 5 '56
  Hardwicke Hall, Elizabethan
    41:160 N 5 '56
  Hepplewhite. Drawing room bw

    23:77 Ag 25 '47
  Jones, I. Double cube room,
    Wilton House 41:161 N 5 '56

French
  French salon, 18th century 31:
    66-7 S 3 '51
  McClelland. Louis XV drawing
    room 27:56-7 O 3 '49

Georgian
  Mount Pleasant, Philadelphia,
    1761--parlor 18:54 My 7
    '45

Italian
  Fornasetti. Andrea Dorea
    stateroom, steamship 34:
    61 Je 22 '53

Victorian
  Campbell House, St. Louis,
    1851--Victorian double par-
    lor 18:55 My 7 '45
  Gould mansion, New York
    City bw 13:140-1 D 7 '42
  Victorian era decoration 40:
    86-93 Mr 5 '56
Interior landscape with trachea.
    drawing Tchelitchew 30:10
    Ja 29 '51
Interiors See also specific
    rooms, as Kitchens; Stu-
    dios
  Burchfield. Christmas morn-
    ing bw 1:29 D 28 '36
  Christus. St. Elgius and St.
    Godberta 37:65 Ag 9 '54
  Cortor. The room number
    five 28:85 Mr 20 '50
  Country store, reassembled
    at Webb Museum, Shel-
    burne, Vt. 35:52-3 Jy 6
    '53
  Cranach. Cardinal Albrecht
    as Saint Hieronymus 5:39
    Jy 11 '38
  Cress. Interior shadows 39:
    115 S 12 '55
  Currier and Ives print. The
    four seasons of life:

Middle age; Old age 9:31 D
  30 '40
Da Silva. Azulejos 29:104 D
  11 '50
Davis, A. J. Greek revival in-
  terior, 1845 watercolor 39:
  60-1 Ag 29 '55
Degas. Cotton market in New
  Orleans 10:74 Ap 28 '41
English country houses, 14th
  16th, 18th centuries photogs
  19:100-1, 105-6 O 29 '45
Ford, Celestial mother 17:40
  D 25 '44
Ford. The first communion
  dress 17:41 D 25 '44
Greuze. The broken eggs 5:
  36 S 26 '38
Hogarth. The dance (Masked
  ball at Wanstead) 21:81 D
  16 '46; 25:99 S 13 '48
Hogarth. Marriage a la mode
  21:80 D 16 '46
Hooch. Interior 37:63 Ag 9 '54
Hooch. The linen cupboard 24:
  77 Je 14 '48
Hopper. Hotel room 2:47 My
  3 '37
Hovenden. Breaking home ties
  9:76 D 9 '40; 27:60 Ag 29
  '49
Johnson. The Hatches of New
  York, 1871 25:91 O 14 '48
Lawrence, J. Interior 21:64
  Jy 22 '46
Leutze. Cromwell and Milton
  27:58 Ag 29 '49
Lochner. St. Jerome in his
  study 41:74 D 10 '56
Matisse. Red interior 31:116
  N 26 '51
Mrs. William Cooper 31:70-1
  Jy 2 '51
Mount. Winding-up 18:68 Je
  25 '45
Pittman. Charleston houses
  pastels 22:68-72 Ap 14 '47
Pittman. Four A.M. 18:69 F
  19 '45
Pittman. The gossips 18:70 F
  19 '45

Pittman. Miss Pat and Miss
  Eva Lion 18:69 F 19 '45
Pittman. Summer evening 18:
  70 F 19 '45
Poisson. Toilette 23:60 S 1 '47
Rembrandt. Meditating phil-
  osopher bw 39:142-3 S 26
  '55
Rembrandt. The painter's
  study bw 29:104 S 11 '50
Rosenthal. Nude at table 15:
  67 N 22 '43
Rossi. The Astors of New York
  25:92-3 O 18 '48
Sharon. Afternoon refresh-
  ment 33:76 Jy 21 '52
Sheeler. City interior 5:43 Ag
  8 '38
Singier. Provencal interior
  lithograph 33:86 Jy 14 '52
Solman. Sunlit windows bw
  36:90 Ja 25 '54
Steen. Baptismal party 24:77
  Je 14 '48
Steen. The gallant offering
  24:78 Je 14 '48
Steen. The world upside down
  27:70 O 24 '49
Teniers. Interior of a public
  house 4:22 Ap 11 '38
Thon. Reverie 20:98 Ap 29 '46
Van Eyck, J. The annuncia-
  tion bw 13:42 D 28 '42
Van Eyck, J. Giovanni Arnol-
  fini and his wife 33:36 D
  29 '52
Van Gogh. Night cafe 2:34 F
  15 '37; 27:85 O 10 '49
Van Gogh. The potato eaters
  27:83 O 10 '49 bw 41:67 O
  1 '56
Vermeer. Woman weighing
  gold 24:73 Je 14 '48; 5:31
  Ag 29 '38
Vermeer. A young lady with
  a pearl necklace 24:77 Mr
  22 '48 bw 19:25 D 31 '45
Wyeth, A. Arthur Cleveland
  24:103 My 17 '48
Wyeth, A. Henry Teel 24:105
  My 17 '48

Wyeth, A. Interior 35:81 Jy
27 '53
Yankee pedlar 31:74 Jy 2 '51
Internal protection sculpture,
translucent plastic, New
York's World's Fair bw 6:
38 Mr 13 '39
International Exhibition of
Modern Art See Armory Show
International mobile. sculpture
bw Calder 26:112 Je 20 '49
The invasion of Leyte. Sample
19:66-7 O 8 '45
Inventions
Old inventions of the nineteenth
century bw 26:16-8 Je 20
'49
Patent models from U.S.
Patent Office, photogs bw
8:14-6 Ap 15 '40
Ionic Columns
Athena Victorious temple,
Athens. photog bw Calli-
crates, archt. 18:56 Ja 1
'45
Erechtheum, Athens photog bw
18:58-9 Ja 1 '45
Iran
Coat of arms bw 20:34 Ap 8
'46
Historical portraits and
scenes bw 20:34 Ap 8 '46
Mitchell. World War scenes
18:58-9 Ap 30 '45
Mosque of the Shah, Isfahan,
Iran photog 38:72 My 9 '55
Irenaeus of Lyons, Saint
St. Irenaeus bw 27:20 N 7 '49
The iron horse. mural Daugherty
3:50 O 25 '37
Iron mines, Ironwood, Michigan.*
Dehn 34:78 Ja 5 '53
Iron work
Chair, swivel, Victorian cast-
iron photog 40:90 Mr 5 '56
Fence, Bangalore, India photog
bw 10:95 My 12 '41
Figure, hitching post, U.S.,
1860 photog 39:106 O 17 '55
Flower pot, Victorian drawing
bw 27:59 Ag 29 '49

Furniture, wrought-iron:
chairs, tables, and other
articles. Tempestini;
Bloom; Landrum photog bw
32:68-70 F 11 '52
Greek figures, gothic gardens,
New England 12:11 My 11
'42
Grill, patio, Seville photog
33:50 Ag 18 '52
Grill, Polish eagles and
horsemen, Cracow photog
bw 17:84 Ag 28 '44
Grills, gates, New Orleans,
19th century photogs bw 12:
8-9, 11 Ap 6 '42
White eagles of Poland photog
bw 5:54 Ag 29 '38
Irradiation. Ernst 32:58 Ja 21
'52
Irvin, Rea
Eustace Tilley, "New Yorker"
magazine trade-mark 21:
68 Jy 15 '46
Irving, Washington
Memorial with bust bw 17:63
O 30 '44
Washington Irving; home; lit-
erary locale photogs bw
17:63-71 O 30 '44
Rip Van Winkle locale photog
bw 33:67-77 Jy 7 '52
Irwin, May
Otis Skinner and May Irwin,
1884 photog bw 26:76 Je 6
'49
Isaac baptizing Jacob (forged
Vermeer) bw. Van Meer-
geren 23:145 N 17 '47
Isaiah during Babylonian captiv-
ity* etching bw 38:97 Je
13 '55
Isaiah scroll bw 34:83 F 23 '53
Isenheim altarpiece, Colmar.
Grunewald; Hagenauer,
sculptor 30:74-85 Mr 26 '51
Isham, Ralph
Ralph Isham photog bw 2:81
Je 21 '37
Isherwood, Christopher
Christopher Isherwood photog

bw 22:60 Mr 24 '47
Isis
  Isis, tomb painting 24:82 Ja
    19 '48
  Isis holding her son, Horus
    statue blue faience 41:114
    N 26 '56
Isle of statues. Fiume 29:107 D
  11 '50
Isola Bella, garden, Italy photog
  28:74 My 8 '50
Israelites in slavery. bw engrav-
  ing Schnorr 6:55 Ja 30 '39
It is finished. sculpture bw Ep-
  stein 3:88 N 15 '37; 33:68
  N 3 '52
L'Italienne. Corot 24:65 Mr 1 '48
Italy
  Biddle. Italian front, 1944--
    scenes, portraits drawings
    bw 16:13-7 Ja 3 '44
  Craig. World War scenes 18:
    56-7 Ap 30 '45
  Craig. Scenes of Italy's war
    damage 19:73-6 S 17 '45
  Fasces emblem, Mussolini's
    office, Rome photog bw 2:
    57 Ap 5 '37
  Gardens of Renaissance villas
    photogs 28:73-9 My 8 '50
  Historical scenes and por-
    traits; air views bw 15:18-
    27 Ag 9 '43
  Laning. Paintings of Italy's
    war damage 19:69-72 S 17
    '45
  U.S. artists paintings and
    sculpture of Italian scenes
    and art: 1830-70, and post-
    World War II 33:88-96 S
    15 '52
Item 9, Man O'War. Flannery 8:
  65 My 27 '40
Ithaca, New York, amateur art-
  ists' paintings 26:68-70 Ap
  4 '49
Ivan III, the Great, Grand Prince
  of Muscovy
  Ivan III bw 14:93 Mr 29 '43
Ivan IV, the Terrible, Czar of
  Russia

Ivan IV bw 18:91 Mr 12 '45
Ives, James
  James Ives photog bw 9:35 D
    30 '40
Ivory Carving See Carving--
  Ivory

                    J

Jack, J. Louis
  Operations 23:99 N 10 '47
  J. Louis Jack photog bw 23:
    101 N 10 '47 port.
Jackson, Andrew
  Andrew Jackson daguerro-
    type, 1845 bw 23:57 N 3 '47
  Andrew Jackson political car-
    toon bw 31:18 O 22 '51;
    37:14 Jy 5 '54
  General Andrew Jackson
    equestrian statue, Independ-
    ence, Kansas (copy of Kan-
    sas City statue) bw 39:89
    O 3 '55
  Mills. Andrew Jackson eques-
    trian statue bw 19:10 S 24
    '45
  Waldo. Andrew Jackson bw 6:
    31 Je 19 '39
Jackson, Charles
  Charles Jackson photogs bw
    22:95 Mr 17 '47
Jackson, Harry
  Afternoon in the bar 41:74-6
    Jy 9 '56
  Blue horse 41:70 Jy 9 '56
  The family 41:70 Jy 9 '56
  Artist at work photogs 41:71-
    6 Jy 9 '56 port.
Jackson, Harry, furniture de-
  signer
  Fireplace, spherical, ceiling-
    suspended photog bw 39:
    100 D 12 '55
  Legless, ceiling-suspended,
    furniture: day bed, chair
    photogs bw 39:100 D 12
    '55
  Stairways, spoke-shaped
    spiral photog bw 39:99 D
    12 '55

Jackson, Huson, architect
  Jackson and Callender. Hillside house photogs, plan
    bw 23:62-3 Jy 21 '47
Jackson House, 1664 photog
    15:13 D 6 '43
Jackson, William H., photographer
  Jackson, photographer photog
    bw 6:32 Je 5 '39 port.
Jackson, the American deer.
    Bragg 6:40 F 6 '39
Jacobs, George
  Harrison. The trial of George
    Jacobs 13:78 N 23 '42
Jacobs, Jay Wesley
  Harry Truman 19:59 N 26 '45
Jacob's ladder bw 30:20 Ja 8 '51
Jacob's ladder. engraving bw
    Schnorr 6:55 Ja 30 '39
Jacona, adobe, New Mexico.
    photogs Clark, archt. 26:
    64-5 Mr 14 '49
Jacques, Francis
  Upland game birds 9:57-8 N
    4 '40
  Wild ducks 5:25-8 N 7 '38
Jade Buddha sculpture, Circular
    City, Peiping 20:68 Ap 29
    '46
Jadwiga, Queen of Poland, tomb
    effigy bw 17:86 Ag 28 '44
Jaenisch, Hans
  Artist at work photog 30:145
    My 10 '54 port.
Jagannath, temple of photog bw
    3:61 Ag 16 '37
Jainism
  Gomata, feet of statue, Mysore photog bw 9:73 N 25
    '40; 10:103 My 12 '41
  Jain temple, Calcutta photog
    bw 12:86 Mr 16 '42
Jam session. lithograph bw
    Von Physter 5:55 Ag 8 '38
James, Alexander
  Danny, the artist's son 10:48
    F 3 '41
  Michael, 1942, the artist's
    son bw 30:149 My 21 '51
  Self-portrait bw 30:149 My

21 '51 port.
James, Daniel
  James, William, Jr. Daniel
    James bw 30:149 My 21 '51
James, Henry
  James, William. Henry James
    bw 30:149 My 21 '51
  Henry James photog bw 22:56
    Mr 24 '47
James, Jesse
  Benton. Jesse James mural
    detail bw 6:70 Ap 24 '39
  Jesse James--portraits,
    birthplace; family bw 6:42-
    3 Ja 30 '39
James, Michael, sculptor
  Annunciation bw 30:146 My 21
    '51
  Crucifixion bw 30:144 My 21
    '51
  Pieta bw 30:144 My 21 '51
  Prophet bw 30:143 My 21 '51
  Resurrection bw 30:146 My 21
    '51
  Artist at work photog bw 30:
    143 My 21 '51 port.
  James, A. Michael, 1942,
    bw 30:149 My 21 '51 port.
James, William, psychologist,
    1842-1910
  Self-portrait, 1867 bw 30:149
    My 21 '51
James, William, newphew of
    William James, the psychologist
  Henry James bw 30:149 My
    21 '51
James, William, Jr.
  Daniel James bw 30:149 My
    21 '51
James I, King of England
  Castellon. The law and the
    king 30:94 Mr 12 '51
  James I 41:180 N 12 '56 bw
    34:84 F 23 '53
  Mary, Queen of Scots, age
    25, and her son 41:153 N
    5 '56
James II, King of England
    41:171 N 19 '56
Jamieson, Mitchell

Embarkation port--World War paintings 14:70-2 My 3 '43
Seascape bw 38:83 F 28 '55
Sicily invasion--World War 15:78-9 D 27 '43
Mitchell Jamieson photog bw 15:84 D 27 '43 port.
Jamnitzer, Christopher, goldsmith
Silver-gilt basin, with cupid, kings, continents, Nurnberg, 17th century bw 31:20-1 S 24 '51
"Jane Eyre," illustrations, wood engravings bw. Eichenberg 15:100-1 N 29 '43
Janeway, Carol, ceramicist
Decorative tiles; plates 19:12-4 Jy 23 '45
Janitor's holiday. Sample 3:44 N 15 '37; 21:74 N 25 '46
January. bw Wood, G. 14:57 Ja 18 '43
Japan
Amitabha Buddha, Kamakura sculpture 38:91 Mr 7 '55
Battle scroll, 4 sections 9:51 Jy 22 '40
Buddhist altar, with ancestor tablets photog bw 3:41 Ag 30 '37
First Japanese missions to America, 1860 drawings bw 12:86 F 23 '42
First landing of Americans in Japan, July 14 1853 9:48 O 28 '40
Floats of Gion Matsuri festival, July 17 and July 24 photogs 17:64-5 S 18 '44
Hachiman, god of war, masked photog bw 17:28 N 27 '44
Oyamakui-No-Mikoto, Japanese war god with bow and arrow sculpture bw 18:95 F 19 '45
Perry's arrival in Japan, 1853 bw 19:58 S 17 '45
Sanu-San-Gen-Do temple, Kyoto photog bw 20:52-3 Je 17 '46
Sekiguchi war prints: Japanese conquest of China, Sino-Japanese War, 1894-5 3:25-32 D 6 '37
U.S.S. Constitution and Vincennes in Japan, 1846 9:48 O 28 '40
Japanese artists' World War II scenes 39:52-3 Ag 15 '55
Japanese envoys playing go, 1860* bw 12:86 F 23 '42
Jars and Jugs
American Indian jars: Santa Clara, Socorro, Tewa, Zia, Zuni 40:55 Ja 16 '56
Inca figurine ceramic jug 36:104 Ap 12 '54
Mayan, Tzakol period, jar 22:56 Je 30 '47
Persian Kashan jug, 12th century 20:92 Je 24 '46
Prehistoric jar fragment, neolithic 40:76 Ap 16 '56
Sumerian calcite urn 40:85 Je 4 '56
U.S. colonial jug, ceramic Maine, 1667 38:126 Ap 18 '55
U.S. sgraffito jug, 1781 39:57 Jy 18 '55
U.S. stoneware jug, early 19th century 39:56 Jy 18 '55
Jarvis, John Wesley
Black Hawk and son, Sauk and Fox chief 36:73 Mr 8 '54
Jasper, Frances Cropsey
Frances Cropsey Jasper bw 19:82 S 10 '45 port.
Jasper's rescue of American civilians from the British, 1779* engraving 13:58 Jy 6 '42
Jay, John
John Jay 39:64 Jy 4 '55 bw 10:26 Mr 3 '41; 19:84 S 24 '45
Je veux la tete de Jokanaan. sculpture bw Martins 11:157 D 8 '41

The jealous lover of Lone Green Valley. Benton 6:71 Ap 24 '39

Jean. Carroll 11:78 O 6 '41

Jean in blue. Speicher 11:77 O 6 '41

Jean in pink organdy. Carroll 11:78 O 6 '41

Jean in pink dress. bw Bellows 11:76 O 6 '41

Jean sewing. Renoir 32:94 My 19 '52

Jean with a doll. bw Bellows 11:76 O 6 '41

Jean with blue book and apple. bw Bellows 11:76 O 6 '41

Jeanneret, Charles Edouard (Le Corbusier), architect
Swiss students' dormitory, University of Paris photog bw 22:35 My 26 '47
Le Corbusier photog bw 22:35 My 26 '47 port.

Jefferson, Joe
Jefferson as Rip van Winkle photog bw 31:116 N 19 '51
Jefferson with Helen Keller photog bw 4:20 F 28 '38
Sargent. Joseph Jefferson bw 6:31 Je 19 '39

Jefferson, Thomas, architect
Ash Lawn, Virginia photog bw 14:70 Ap 12 '43
Ice House, Montpelier photog bw 14:70 Ap 12 '43
Monticello, Virginia, photog bw 14:65 Ap 12 '43
Oak Hill, Virginia photog bw 14:70 Ap 12 '43
Privy, Poplar Forest photog bw 14:70 Ap 12 '43
University of Virginia photog bw 14:71 Ap 12 '43
library, dormitories photogs 2:48-9 Je 7 '37
Virginia State Capitol, model photog bw 14:70 Ap 12 '43
Revolving chair, with writing arm photog bw 14:73 Ap 12 '43 (furniture design)
Borglum. Mt. Rushmore National Memorial, South Dakota photog 4:26 Je 27 '38 bw 3:104 O 4 '37; 7:19 Jy 17 '39 port.
Brown, Mather. Jefferson as minister to France, 1786 14:64 Ap 12 '43 port.
Peale, C. W. Jefferson as Secretary of State 14:63 Ap 12 '43 port.
Stuart. Jefferson as President, 1805 14:64 Ap 12 '43 port.
Thomas Jefferson 31:98 N 5 '51; 39:64 Jy 4 '55 bw 15:104 S 13 '43; 16:42 Ja 31 '44; 19:84 S 24 '45 political cartoon bw 31:18 O 22 '51 port.
Thomas Jefferson, playing card, "King of Clubs." Humphreys 38:Cover My 30 '55 port.
Thomas Jefferson sculpture bw 9:8 Ag 5 '40 plaque, U.S. Capitol bw 30:74 F 5 '51 port.

Jefferson Memorial, Washington, D.C. Pope; Eggers; Higgins photog 23:49 Jy 7 '47 bw 14:Cover Ap 12 '43

Jelke trial. bw Marsh 37:48 Jy 26 '54

Jellicoe, John Rushworth
Earl Jellicoe bust bw, Trafalgar Square 25:93 N 15 '48

Jenkins, George, theater designer
"I Remember Mama," sets bw 17:104-5 N 20 '44

Jennifer. Simkhovitch 10:47 F 3 '41

Jennings, John
John Jennings photog bw 24:22 My 17 '48

Jennys, J. William
Mrs. Constant Storrs, 1802 bw 9:74 D 9 '40

Jensen, Cecil
Colonel M'Cosmic cartoon bw 12:28-9 My 11 '42

Jeremiah
  Michelangelo. The prophet
    Jeremiah fresco 7:55 N 20
    '39; 21:68 Jy 1 '46
Jericho
  Battle of Jericho illumination,
    Bible of St. Paul's Outside
    the Walls 34:79 F 23 '53
  Jericho heads, plastered, orna-
    mented human skulls, 5000
    B.C. bw 34:119 My 11 '53
  Ruins of Jericho photog 20:56
    Ap 1 '46
Jerome, Jennie
  Jennie Jerome 28:73-4 F 27
    '50
Jerome, Leonard
  Leonard Jerome 28:73 F 27
    '50
Jerome, Saint
  Durer. St. Jerome etching 34:
    76 F 23 '53
  El Greco. St. Jerome 37:64 Ag
    9 '54
  El Greco. St. Jerome as a
    cardinal 3:31 D 27 '37
  Hagenauer. St. Jerome, statue,
    Isenheim altarpiece 30:81
    Mr 26 '51
  Lochner. St. Jerome in his
    study 41:74 D 10 '56
  St. Jerome bw 22:70 Ap 7 '47
  St. Jerome translating the
    scriptures, France, 15th
    century 4:30 F 7 '38
Jersey harbor. Feininger, Lux
  31:90 N 12 '51
"Jervis Bay" (ship)
  Wilkinson. The Jervis Bay 24:
    68 My 10 '48
Jesus Christ

                Adoration
  Adoration, after Botticelli bw
    11:61 O 27 '41
  Adoration of the Magi, relief,
    Ulm cathedral 35:28 D 28
    '53
  Botticelli. Adoration of the
    Magi 13:44-5 D 28 '42
  Breinen. Silent Night, Holy

  Night 23:50-1 D 22 '47
  Brueghel, P., the elder. A-
    doration of the kings 37:34-
    5, 38-9 D 27 '54
  Ch'en, L. The adoration of the
    Magi 11:44 D 22 '41
  Ford. Adoration 17:33, 36 D
    25 '44
  Lippi. Adoration of the child
    19:44 D 24 '45
  Lucas van Leyden. The adora-
    tion of the Magi 11:56 S
    8 '41
  Piero di Cosimo. Adoration of
    the Child 7:33 Jy 31 '39
  Tintoretto. Adoration of the
    kings 31:33 D 24 '51
  Titian. Adoration of the Magi
    1:45 D 28 '36

                Appearances
  Ryder. Christ appearing to
    Mary 30:88 F 26 '51

                Ascension
  The ascension, illumination,
    16th century 18:62 Ap 2 '45
  Ascension of Christ, stained
    glass, Le Mans cathedral,
    France, 12th century 22:
    71 Ap 7 '47
  Blake. Ascension of Christ
    watercolor 36:64 Ap 19 '54
  Giotto. Ascension of Christ
    25:54-5 D 27 '48
  Tintoretto. Ascension of
    Christ 31:49 D 24 '51

                Baptism
  Giotto. Baptism of Christ 25:
    46-7 D 27 '48
  Piero della Francesca. The
    baptism 39:20-1 D 26 '55
  Tintoretto. Baptism of Christ
    31:36 D 24 '51
  Veronese. Baptism of Christ
    16:70 Ap 10 '44

  Bearing the Cross See
  Procession to Calvary

Betrayal

Angelico. The betrayal 21:58
D 23 '46

The betrayal, illumination,
Psalter, 13th century 18:
59 Ap 2 '45

Bosch. The betrayal 6:38 My
29 '39

Giotto. Judas betrays Christ
25:48 D 27 '48

Giotto. Judas' kiss 25:50-1 D
27 '48

Crowned with Thorns

Bosch. The crowning with
thorns 31:69 O 1 '51

Giotto. Christ crowned with
thorns 25:51 D 27 '48

Jesus crowned with thorns,
illumination, 11th century
18:59 Ap 2 '45

Crucifixion

Antonella da Messina. The
crucifixion 7:51 N 20 '39;
39:29 D 26 '55

Bellows. The crucifixion 9:78
D 9 '40

Blake. The crucifixion watercolor 36:61 Ap 19 '54

Cranach. Crucifixion 1:47 D
28 '36

Crucifix, Cordova cathedral
photog 33:61 Ag 18 '52

Gies. Crucifixion sculpture
bw 3:72 Ag 18 '37

Giotto. Crucifixion 25:52-3 D
27 '48

Grunewald. Crucifixion 30:75-
7 Mr 26 '51

Hegh. Unto one of the least of
these 8:44 F 12 '40

James, M. Crucifixion bw 30:
144 My 21 '51

Johnson, W. H. Mount calvary
21:65 Jy 22 '46

Mantegna. The crucifixion 35:
57 Ag 17 '53

Mestrovic. Crucifix sculpture
bw 27:145 O 17 '49

Nagler. The crucifixion 8:40

Mr 25 '40

Nicolas. The crucifixion 12:53
Ap 6 '42

Sangre de Cristo, santo, wood
carving bw 24:58 My 17 '48

Tintoretto. Crucifixion 31:44-
6 D 24 '51

Tolman. Double crucifix, wood
carving, Church of the
Blessed Sacrament, Hol-
yoke, Mass bw 35:93 Jy 6
'53

Van Eyck, J. Christ on the
cross, the Blessed Virgin,
and St. John 24:69 Mr 22
'48

Werden crucifix, 11th century
39:Cover D 26 '55

Deposition

Blake. The deposition watercolor 36:62 Ap 19 '54

Descent from the cross, illumination 18:60 Ap 2 '45

Greene. The deposition 29:65
O 23 '50 bw 27:149 O 17
'49

Grunewald. Deposition 30:76-
7 Mr 26 '51

Lorenzetti. Descent from the
cross fresco 39:30 D 26
'55

Descent into Hell

Descent into Hell, illumination, 14th century 18:60 Ap
2 '45

Disciples

Barlach. The reunion (Christ
and Thomas) 41:137 N 5 '56

Christ and St. John sculpture
bw, German, 14th-15th
century 15:64 S 20 '43

Christ between Peter and
Paul mosaic, Early Chris-
tian 28:68 Mr 27 '50

Christ blessing an apostle
fresco, bw, Rome, 4th
century 40:148 Ap 23 '56

Hagenauer. Christ and dis-

ciples 30:80-1 Mr 26 '51

Emmaus
Rembrandt. Supper at Emmaus 11:78 D 1 '41; 35:61 Ag 17 '53; 39:30 D 26 '55
Van Meergeren. Christ at Emmaus bw (forged Vermeer) 23:148 N 17 '47

Enthroned
Christ enthroned fresco bw 9:53 Jy 22 '40
Christ enthroned illumination, Canterbury Psalter 34:80 F 23 '53

Entombment
Angelico. The entombment 16:71 Ap 10 '44; 21:60 D 23 '46
Blake. The sepulchre watercolor 36:60 Ap 19 '54
Titian. Entombment of Christ bw 11:81 D 1 '41

Entry into Jerusalem
Dore. Christ's entry into Jerusalem bw 23:44 S 22 '47
The entry into Jerusalem, illumination, 11th century 18:58 Ap 2 '45
Giotto. The entry into Jerusalem 25:46-7 D 27 '48

Gethsemane
El Greco. The agony in the garden bw 28:92 Ap 24 '50
Giotto. Gethsemane 25:50-1 D 27 '48
Huber. The agony in Gethsemane 39:28 D 26 '55
Scharl. Gethsemane bw 27:149 O 17 '49
Tintoretto. Gethsemane 31:41 D 24 '51
Vitti. Christ on the Mount of Olives 1:46 D 28 '36

Last Supper
Giotto. Last supper 25:48-9

D 27 '48
Leonardo da Vinci. The last supper bw 7:17 Jy 17 '39; 22:54-6 Je 9 '47
Nagler. Last supper bw 8:41 Mr 25 '40
Nicolas. The last supper 12:52 Ap 6 '42
Tintoretto. The last supper 31:40 D 24 '51; 39:26-7 D 26 '55
Vas. The last supper bw 29:66 S 4 '50
Warnecke. The last supper bw 39:119 S 19 '55

Life of Christ
Bonawit. Life of Christ stained glass window 6:31 Ap 3 '39
Christ story frieze bw, Notre Dame, Paris 22:83 Ap 7 '47
Espalargues. Life of Christ retablo, 1490 4:29 F 7 '38
Ford. Boyhood of Jesus in New England setting etchings, paintings 5:28-31 D 25 '38
Giotto. Lives of Christ and Mary fresco, Arena chapel, Padua, 14th century 25: Cover, 34-57 D 27 '48
Master of Cologne. Life of Christ 24:72-3 Mr 22 '48
Nicolas. Life of Christ stained glass 12:52-3 Ap 6 '42
Pettus collection of Chinese Christian art 11:41-8 D 22 '41

Mary's at the Tomb
Angelico. At the sepulcher 21:61 D 23 '46
At Christ's tomb illumination 18:61 Ap 2 '45
Blake. Mary's at the tomb watercolor 36:62-3 Ap 19 '54

Miracles

Angelico. The raising of Lazarus 21:55 D 23 '46

Christ healing the blind, c500 39:25 D 26 '55

Delacroix. Christ on the Sea of Galilea 39:23 D 26 '55

Duccio. Resurrection of Lazarus 1:46 D 28 '36

Giotto. Wedding at Cana 25:47 D 27 '48

Giotto. Raising of Lazarus 25: 46 D 27 '48

Jesus stills the tempest, China 11:48 D 22 '41

Nagler. Healing the sick bw 8: 41 Mr 25 '40

Rembrandt. Storm on the Sea of Galilee 1:31 N 30 '36

Tintoretto. Miracle of the loaves and the fishes 31:39 D 24 '51

Tintoretto. Resurrection of Lazarus 31:38 D 24 '51

Nativity

Angelico. The nativity 21:53 D 23 '46

Corregio. Nativity bw 40:101 F 20 '56

Dore. The birth of Christ engraving bw 7:24 D 25 '39

Ford. Nativity in New England 5:28-9 D 25 '38

Giotto. The nativity 25:Cover, 42-3 D 27 '48

Georg. Nativity with birds bw 27:55 D 26 '49

Grunewald. Nativity 30:82-3 Mr 26 '51

Lu Hung Nien. The birth of Jesus 11:41 D 22 '41

Luini. The nativity 13:43 D 28 '42

Morand. Nativity at Saint-Paul de Vence bw 27:56 D 29 '49

Nativity, illumination, Missal of Ferdinand, Italy, 15th century 32:87 Ap 14 '52

Nativity, relief, Ulm cathedral 35:28 D 28 '53

Tintoretto. Nativity 31:Cover, 31-2 D 24 '51

Van der Goes. The nativity 39: 18-9 D 26 '55

Passion

Thomasita. Eighth station of the cross sculpture 35:157 O 12 '53

Pieta

Giotto. Pieta 25:52 D 27 '48

James, M. Pieta sculpture bw 30:144 My 21 '51

Mestrovic. P eta sculpture bw 22:131 Je 2 '47

Michelangelo. Pieta sculpture bw 5:46 D 25 '38

Pieta of Avignon 35:57 Ag 17 '53

Rembrandt. Lamentation over Christ bw 6:58 Mr 27 '39

Portrait

Christ of the depths, underwater memorial, Portofino, Italy bw 37:151-2 S 13 '54; 29:48 Ag 22 '55

Christ story, frieze bw, Notre Dame, Paris 22:83 Ap 7 '47

Christ the redeemer statue bw, Rio de Janiero harbor 10: 60 Ja 6 '41

Cranach. Christ and the pope* woodcuts, anti-papist series bw 24:60-1 Je 14 '48

Dix, O. Veronica's veil lithograph 33:84 Jy 14 '52

Ecce Home tapestry, Flemish 15th century bw 5:48 N 28 '38

Epstein. It is finished (Consummatum est) sculpture bw 3:88 N 15 '37; 33:68 N 3 '52

Goertschacher. Ecce Homo bw 9:108-9 D 2 '40

Head of Christ mosaic, Chora church, Istanbul 29:54 D 25 '50

Jesus Christ 29:160 D 11 '50

Jesus Christ, tabernacle, gold jewelled and enamelled, 1403 33:32 D 29 '52

Jesus Christ wood statue, painted, Atotonilco, Mexico 28:62 Ja 9 '50

Ossorio. Jesus Christ altar fresco, Philippines 30:15 Ap 30 '51

Roualt. Christ stained glass 28:75 Je 19 '50

Roualt. The crown of thorns 39:28 D 26 '55

Ryan. Thou sayest it bw 8:94 Je 24 '40

Three-faced Christ icon bw 11:120 O 13 '41

Presentation in the Temple

Ford. Christ in the temple 5: 32 D 25 '38

Giotto. Christ in the temple, age 12 25:46 D 27 '48

Giotto. Presentation in the temple 25:43 D 27 '48

Van Meergeren. Christ in the temple bw 23:146 N 17 '47

Procession to Calvary

Angelico. Christ bearing the cross 21:59 D 23 '46

Giotto. Christ bearing the cross 25:52 D 27 '48

Houtondji. Mary meeting Jesus bw 29:63 S 4 '50

Tintoretto. Procession to Calvary 31:43 D 24 '51

Resurrection

Blake. Resurrection watercolor 36:62 Ap 19 '54

Ford. Resurrection 17:34 D 25 '44

Giotto. Resurrection 25:54 D 27 '48

Greene. Resurrection 33:99 O 27 '52

Grunewald. Resurrection 30: 83-5 Mr 26 '51

James, M. Resurrection sculpture bw 30:146 My 21 '51

Nicolas. The resurrection stained glass 12:53 Ap 6 '42

Piero della Francesca. Resurrection 39:30-1 D 26 '55

Reinhardt. Resurrection 28: 84 Mr 20 '50

Resurrection, Illumination, Lectionary, Saxony, 13th century 18:60-1 Ap 2 '45

Resurrection, illumination, Missal of Ferdinand, Italy, 15th century 32:87 Ap 14 '52

Tintoretto. Resurrection of Christ 31:47-8 D 24 '51

Teachings

Christ teaching, Chartre cathedral, 13th century sculpture 39:21 D 26 '55

Duccio. The calling of the apostles Peter and Andrew 39:22 D 26 '55

Giorgione; del Piombo; Titian. Adultress brought before Christ 39:169 O 24 '55

Giotto. Driving out the money changers 25:47 D 27 '48

Greene. Christ and the money changers 29:64-5 O 23 '50

Lu Hung Nien. Jesus and the woman at the well 11:46 D 22 '41

Murillo. Christ giving bread to St. Felix of Cantalice bw 39:94 O 10 '55

Van Meergeren. Christ and the adulterous woman bw 23:148 N 17 '47

Veronese. Christ and the centurion 7:53 O 9 '39

Temptation

Duccio. Temptation of Christ bw 4:28 F 7 '38

Tintoretto. The temptation in the wilderness 31:36 D 24 '51; 39:20 D 26 '55

Transfiguration
Bellini. The transfiguration 39:
   24-5 D 26 '55
Raphael. Transfiguration bw 5:
   46 D 25 '38; 8:26 F 26 '40

Trial
Ecco Homo tapestry, Flemish,
   15th century bw 5:48 N 28
   '38
Giotto. Christ before Pilate*
   25:51 D 27 '48
Goertschacher. Ecce Homo bw
   9:108-9 D 2 '40
Jesus before Pilate, illumination, Flemish, 15th century·
   18:59 Ap 2 '45
Tintoretto. Christ before Pilate
   31:42 D 24 '51

Washington Apostles' Feet
Giotto. Jesus washing the dis-
   ciples' feet 25:48 D 27 '48
Jesus washing his disciples
   feet, China 11:47 D 22 '41
Jeune femme se poudrant (Made-
   leine Knobloch). bw Seurat
   31:64 Jy 23 '51
Jewelry See also Crowns; Gems;
   Goldsmithing; Silversmith-
   ing
Ancient jewelry museum copies
   33:130 O 20 '52
Bed spread, jewelled with
   10,000 stones, India 33:67
   D 1 '52
Buckle, Hallstatt, Austria, 500
   B.C. 33:130 O 20 '52
Burgundy belt ornament, 6th
   century 33:120 O 20 '52
Celtic jewelry bw 37:88 S 13
   '54
Coronation ring of England 2:
   38 Mr 15 '37
Easter egg, Russian, jewelled
   6:5 Ap 3 '39
Frankish plaque 33:130 O 20
   '52
Key of St. Peter, jewelled,
   16th century 32:85 Ap 14 '52
Manuscript cover, gold and

jewelled, St. Gall, Switzer-
   land, 9th century 18:57 Ap
   2 '45
Orbs, king's and queen's, Eng-
   land 2:38 Mr 15 '37
Queen Shubad's jewelry: head-
   dress, necklace, earrings,
   Ur, c2500 B.C. bw 33:12
   N 10 '52 pin, 33:130 O 20
   '52
Septre, royal, England 2:39
   Mr 15 '37
Sword, jewelled, of State,
   England 2:39 Mr 15 '37
Tabernacle, gold jewelled and
   enamelled, 1403 33:32 D
   29 '52

Bracelets
Archer's wrist guard, American Indian 40:54 Ja 16 '56
Cambodian bracelet, with Gods
   and dancers bw 5:35 Ag 1
   '38
Egyptian scarab bracelet 24:
   81 Ja 19 '48
Indian, American, turquoise
   bracelet 40:54 Ja 16 '56
Iron Age bracelet, 1000 B.C.
   33:130 O 20 '52

Brooches and Pins
Avaric pin, 7th century 33:130
   O 20 '52
Celtic pin 33:130 O 20 '52
Etruscan gold brooch, c650 B.
   C. 40:60 F 13 '56
Frankish pin, 7th century 33:
   130 O 20 '52
Gothic pin, 5th-7th century 33:
   130 O 20 '52
Iron Age pin, c1000 B.C. 33:
   130 O 20 '52
Persian votive pin, 900 B.C.
   33:130 O 20 '52
Pope Leo XIII's diamond
   brooch, 1887 32:84 Ap 14
   '52
Queen Shubad's pin, Sumeri-
   an, Ur, 2500 B.C. 33:130
   O 20 '52

Scythian pin, 5th century 33:
130 O 20 '52
Topaz brooch, 1851 32:84 Ap
14 '52

Crosses
Byzantine cross, 6th century
33:130 O 20 '52
Gold cross, emerald studded,
c1580 40:38 Ja 9 '56
Jewelled historic crosses, Vatican 32:82-3 Ap 14 '52

Earrings and Earplugs
Ashanti earrings, West Africa
33:130 O 20 '52
Greek figurine earrings, 5th
century B.C. 6:52 Mr 20 '39
Inca earplugs, feathers on
wood 36:101 Ap 12 '54
Inca earplugs, gold with turquoise mosaic 36:104 Ap 12
'54
Queen Shubad's earrings, Sumerian, Ur, 2500 B.C. bw
33:12 N 10 '52

Pendants and Necklaces
Egyptian Eye of Horus pendant
24:81 Ja 19 '48
Egyptian five-tiered faience
necklace, c1000 B.C. 9:93
D 9 '40
Etruscan gold necklace, stone
inset, c60 B.C. bw 9:94 D
9 '40
Iceland pendant 33:130 O 20 '52
Inca pendant, shell inlaid with
gold 36:104 Ap 12 '54
Indian, American, necklaces:
turquoise, shell, silver
squash blossom 40:54 Ja 16
'56
Medieval pendant 33:130 O 20
'52
Medieval pendant, pearled, Italy,
16th century 37:64 Ag 9 '54
Moorish necklace, gold filigree
and cloisonne, Hispano-Mo-
resque, c1340 bw 9:94 D 9
'40

Paleolithic pendant, with incised cow bw 39:91 N 7 '55
Queen Shubad's necklace, Sumerian, Ur, 2500 B.C. 33:
130 O 20 '52 bw 33:12 N 10
'52

Tiaras
Diamond tiara, Napoleon's
gift to Josephine 33:34 D 29
'52
Emerald and diamond tiara,
Napoleon's gift to Marie-
Louise 38:45 Ja 31 '55
Tiara of Pope Pius IX bw 6:39
Ap 10 '39
Tiara of Saitaphernes, gold
relief. bw Rouchomovski
39:144 S 26 '55
Jimmu, First Emperor of Japan
statue bw 7:49 Jy 10 '39
Jingo, Empress of Japan bw 3:24
D 6 '37
Jitterbug. sculpture bw Mazoff
10:59 Je 16 '41
Joachim
Giotto. Story of Joachim and
Anna, fresco 25:36-7 D 27
'48
Joad, C. E. M.
C.E.M. Joad photogs bw 14:
31-4 My 17 '43
Joan of Arc
Davis, G. R. Joan of Arc
statue, Paris 19:49 Jy 16
'45
Joan of Arc bw 22:84 My 26
'47
Joan of Arc statue bw, Rheims
cathedral 40:190 Ap 9 '56
Joan of Arc in armor bw 14:7
Ja 4 '43
Rox. Joan of Arc sculpture
bw 27:146 O 17 '49
Rubens. Joan of Arc 41:74 D
10 '53
Job
Ben-Shmuel. Job sculpture
bw 14:42 Mr 8 '43
Job, Richard II's Bible 34:80
F 23 '53

Job (cont.)
   Velazquez. Job (Seneca) 11:57
      S 8 '41
The jockey. drawing bw Toulouse-
   Lautrec 28:96 My 15 '50
Jockey. sculpture bw Rudy 15:82
   D 20 '43
Jockey on race horse.* sculpture,
   wax Degas 39:121 O 31 '55
Joconde, La See Mona Lisa
Jodhpur palace, India photog bw
   9:70 N 25 '40
Joe. war cartoon bw Mauldin 16:
   8-10 Ja 17 '44
Jogues, Isaac
   Father Isaac Jogues sculpture
      bw 19:104 N 12 '45
John, Saint, the Baptist
   Christ and St. John sculpture
      bw, German, 14th-15th cen-
      turies 15:64 S 20 '43
   Grunewald. St. John 30:76, 78
      Mr 26 '51
   Head of St. John, mosaic,
      Santa Sophia 29:60 D 25 '50
   Leonardo da Vinci. Madonna of
      the rocks 7:54 N 20 '39
   Lippi, Filippino. Holy family,
      with Margaret and St. John
      1:45 D 28 '36
   Lippi, Fra Filippo. Adoration
      of the Child 19:44 D 24 '45
   Previtali. Madonna with St.
      John and St. Catherine 6:32
      F 13 '39
   Ribera. St. John, the Baptist
      41:72 D 10 '56
   Sarto. The Virgin and Child
      with St. John 41:72 D 10 '56
   Van Eyck, J. Christ on the
      cross, the blessed Virgin,
      and St. John 24:69 Mr 22 '48
   Van Eyck brothers. St. John
      the Baptist 26:65 Ap 18 '49
John, Saint, the Evangelist
   St. John, the Evangelist, Gos-
      pel Book of Charlemagne
      34:87 F 23 '53
   Lurcat. St. John's revelation
      tapestry 28:76 Je 19 '50
John and Priscilla. bw Millet, F.

   D. 11:85 S 8 '41
John III, Sobieski, King of Poland
   bw 5:55 Ag 29 '38
John Brown goes to his hanging.
   Pippin 21:64 Jy 22 '46
John Frederick I, the Magnani-
   mous, Elector of Saxony
   Cranach. Luther and his
      friends 24:63 Je 14 '48
Johnie. Weedon 10:47 F 3 '41
John, Augustus
   Madame Guilhermina Suggia
      bw 16:79 Ap 24 '44
   Sean O'Casey bw 37:68 Jy 26
      '54
   Eisenstadt. Augustus John
      photog bw 32:Cover Ja 14
      '52 port.
   Painter Augustus John photog
      bw 5:72 D 12 '38 port.
Johns, Veronica Parker
   Veronica Johns photog bw 22:
      21 Mr 10 '47
Johnson, Andrew
   Andrew Johnson bw 16:62 F 21
      '44 photog bw 9:8 Ag 5 '40;
      14:76 F 15 '43
Johnson, Eastman
   The blacksmith shop 41:71 D
      10 '56
   The Hatches of New York,
      1871 25:91 O 14 '48
   Old Kentucky home 5:32 O 31
      '38
Johnson, Floyd
   Backstreet city bw 32:91 Mr
      17 '52
   Floyd Johnson photog bw 32:
      91 Mr 17 '52 port.
Johnson, Louisa Catherine See
   Adams, Louisa Catherine
Johnson, Philip C., architect
   Glass house, New Canaan, Ct.
      photogs 27:94-6 S 26 '49
   Philip C. Johnson photog bw
      27:94-6 S 26 '49 port.
Johnson, Richard M.
   Richard M. Johnson bw 9:8
      Ag 5 '40
Johnson, S.C., and Son Admini-
   stration Building, Racine,

Wis., Wright, archt. photogs
bw 6:15 My 8 '39

Johnson, Samuel
Reynolds. Samuel Johnson 25:
108 S 13 '48
Rowlandson. Johnson and Bos-
well caricature bw 29:93
D 4 '50
Samuel Johnson bw 30:126 F
12 '51
Samuel Johnson, engraving in
"Dictionary," 1785, from
Reynold's painting bw 38:
166 My 2 '55

Johnson, Sargent
Chester sculpture bw 21:63 Jy
22 '46

Johnson, T. Laughton
Twenty great battles of the
world mural bw, West Point
mess hall 11:4 N 24 '41

Johnson, William
Sir William Johnson statue bw
Johnstown 19:104 N 12 '45

Johnson, William H.
Mount Calvary 21:65 Jy 22 '46

Johnson, William S.
William S. Johnson bw 16:47
Ja 17 '44

Johnston, Joshua
The James McCormick family
9:76 D 9 '40

Jonah and the Whale
Flannagan. Jonah and the whale
sculpture bw 24:95-6 Ap 12 '48
Jonah and the whale, Giant
Bible of Admont 34:82 F 23
'53
Jonah and the whale, Manuscript of Ferdinand, Italy,
15th century 32:87 Ap 14 '52
Milles. Jonah and the whale
sculpture bw 2:32 F 22 '37
Trace. Jonah in the whale ceramics bw 9:129 N 11 '40

Jonas, Louis Paul, sculptor
Babirusa bw 12:89 Mr 23 '42
Gorilla bw 12:89 Mr 23 '42
Grizzly bear and cubs bw 12:
90 Mr 23 '42
Hippopotamus bw 12:89 Mr 23

'42
Mother and baby zebra bw 12:
90 Mr 23 '42
Panda bw 12:90 Mr 23 '42
Louis Jonas photogs bw 12:86
Mr 23 '42 port.

Jones, A. Quincy, architect
Palo Alto, California, house
photogs 37:120-2 N 15 '54

Jones, Amy
Portrait of sis 10:47 F 3 '41

Jones, Benjamin
Bill's poolroom 10:58 Je 16
'41

Jones, Bobby
Eisenhower. Bobby Jones 34:
74 Mr 23 '53
Goodman, J. The defeat of
Bobby Jones 7:3 S 4 '39

Jones, Casey See Jones, John
Luther

Jones, Inigo, architect
Double cube room, Wilton
House, England photog 41:
161 N 5 '56

Jones, James
Locale of his book, "From
Here to Eternity" photogs
bw 37:155 O 18 '54

Jones, Joe
Dust storm 8:66 My 27 '40
Harvest 13:46 Ag 31 '42; 21:77
N 25 '46

Jones, John Luther (Casey Jones)
Casey in his cab photog bw 12:
63 Ja 28 '42
Casey Jones photog bw 12:61
Ja 28 '42
Locomotive "382" (Casey Jones'
locomotive) photog bw 12:
63 Ja 28 '42

Jones, John Paul
John Paul Jones bw 19:88 Ag
27 '45

Jones, Robert Edmond, theater
designer
"Lute Song," set and costume
designs 20:54-5 Mr 4 '46
Robert Edmond Jones photog
bw 20:54 Mr 4 '46 port.

Jonker diamond, gemstone 32:
      67-8 Mr 17 '52
Jordaens, Jacob
      The king drinks bw 6:23 Ja 23
      '39
Jordan, Olaf
      Cossack division soldiers,
      World War* 28:67 F 20 '50
Jordania, Noah
      Noah Jordania photog bw 31:
      111 O 29 '31
Jordy. bw Philipp, R. 8:62 Ap 8
      '40
Jorn, Aster
      Return to the detested city
      lithograph 33:85 Jy 14 '52
Joseph, Saint
      Kratina. St. Joseph sculpture
      bw 27:146 O 17 '49
Joseph interprets pharoah's
      dreams. engraving bw
      Schnorr 6:55 Ja 30 '39
Joshua
      Joshua, Bible of St. Paul's
      Outside the Walls 34:79 F
      23 '53
Jour d'ete. bw Morisot 40:148
      Ap 23 '56
Journey of the Magi. fresco Goz-
      zoli 19:Cover, 43-5 D 24
      '45
Journey of the Queen of Sheba.
      The Virgil Master 35:150-
      1 N 16 '53
Journey's end. Haines 12:40 Mr
      2 '42
Jousting See Games and Sports --
      Jousting
Joyce, Peggy Hopkins
      Peggy Hopkins Joyce photog bw
      28:67 Ja 2 '50
Jubilate deo omnis terra 10:68
      My 26 '41
Judaism See also Biblical and
      Christian Themes
      Chagall. Rabbi of Vitebsk 22:
      58 My 5 '47
      Star of David, emblem 38:57
      F 7 '55
      Torah cases, silver photog bw
      4:47 Ap 18 '38

Torah scrolls photog 29:160 S
      11 '50 bw 36:75 My 24 '54
Weber. The rabbi 19:86 Ag
      20 '45
Weber. Two patriarchs 33:99
      O 27 '52
Judas Iscariot See Jesus Christ
      --Betrayal
Jude, Saint
      El Greco. St. Jude bw 39:77
      Ag 8 '55
Judges See Lawyers and Judges
Judgment day. bw Reiss 32:88
      Mr 17 '52
Judgment day, sculpture, Abbey
      church, Vezelay, France
      bw 22:78 Ap 7 '47
Judgment of Paris See Mytho-
      logical Themes--Paris
Judith and Holofernes. Mantegna
      4:28 Mr 21 '38 bw 26:160
      Ap 11 '49
Judson, Sylvia Shaw
      Winter, Spring, Summer,
      Autumn sculpture bw 10:
      118-9 Ap 21 '41
The juggler. Chagall 22:57 My 5
      '47
Jugs See Jars and Jugs
Juin, Alphonse
      Karsh. Alphonse Juin photog
      bw 37:136 O 4 '54
Jule-Nissen, illustration of the
      Christmas legend. Le-
      wicki 39:64 D 19 '55
Julian, Paul
      "Piccoli," illustrations 35:
      197-200 D 7 '53
July 4th, 5th and 6th. Martin,
      F. 9:91 N 11 '40 bw 15:13
      O 25 '43
Jumping woodcock. watercolor
      Pleissner 21:65 O 7 '46
June. calendar page, c1478 bw
      Memling 18:42 Ja 1 '45
Juneau, Alaska. Appel 16:76
      Ap 24 '44
Jungle. Harding 19:63 O 8 '45
Jungle cafe. Gatto 25:72 N 8
      '48
Junk, Chines photog bw 24:102

Je 21 '48

Junk sailing under Brooklyn
bridge.* bw Kingman 30:
100 My 14 '51

Junkin, Marion
First robin 10:67 My 26 '41

Jupiter See Mythological
Themes--Jupiter

"Jupiter" (locomotive) Central
Pacific photog bw 25:14 S
27 '48

Justinian, Byzantine Emperor
Castellon. Justinian's codification, Constantinople, 527
A.D. 30:90 Mr 12 '51
Justinian, plaque, U.S. Congress bw 30:74 F 5 '51
Justinian in Virgin and Child
mosaic, Santa Sophia 29:
56-7 D 25 '50

K

Kaaba
Black Stone set in Kaaba
photogs bw 2:62-3 Mr 15
'37; 38:92 My 9 '55
Great mosque of Mecca, showing Kaaba photog 38:76 My
9 '55

Kabyline in movement. Brauner
1:26 D 14 '36

Kahn, Albert, architect
Albert Kahn photog bw 7:64
O 23 '39 port

Kahn, Matt, interior designer
Palo Alto, California, house
photog 37:120-2 N 15 '54

Kaiser Friedrich Museum, Berlin photog bw 24:68 Mr 29
'48
Masterpieces from collection
hidden in salt mine in
World War II 24:68-80 Mr
22 '48 bw 19:24-5 D 31 '45

Kakemono See also Scrolls
Jakuchu. Roosters 31:66 D 31
'51

Kalidahs, illustrations from
"Wonderful Wizard of Oz."
Denslow 35:54 D 28 '53

Kallem, Henry

Country tenement 24:103 Je 28
'48

Kalulu
Stanley and Kalulu 2 drawings
bw 7:60 Ag 14 '39

Kandinsky, Wassily
Painting number one 28:61 Ja
2 '50
Wassily Kandinsky, c1913
photog bw 28:61 Ja 2 '50
port.

Kane, John
Nine mile run seen from Cal-
vary 2:47 My 17 '37
Schenley mansion 2:46 My 17
'37
Turtle Creek valley 2:46 My
17 '37
Artist at work photog bw 2:44
My 17 '37 port.
Self-portrait 2:45 My 17 '37
port.

Kane, Margaret Brassler, sculptor Harlem dancers bw 9:
54 Ag 12 '40
Undersea ballet bas-relief bw
7:36-7 Jy 17 '39

Kangaroos
Kangaroo, treebark, Australian native art 21:78 N 4 '46
Shepard. Kanga, illustration
from "Winnie-the-Pooh"
bw 30:76 F 19 '51

Kansas
Curry. Tornado over Kansas
1:29 N 23 '36; 21:73 N 25
'46

Kanthaka
Buddha riding Kanthaka, festival figure, Ceylon photog
bw 40:27 Je 11 '56

Kantor, Morris
Cathedral woods 29:72-3 Ag
21 '50
Lighthouse bw 6:45 My 1 '39
Walkowitz bw 16:79 F 21 '44
Morris Kantor photog bw 6:
26 F 13 '39

Kaplan, Marmor, Micheline
Artist at work photog bw 37:
134 O 25 '54 port.

Kaptan, Hasan
  Hasan Kaptan, child artist,
    at work photog 32:85 My 12
    '52
Karasz, Ilonka
  "New Yorker" cover 21:71 Jy
    15 '46
Karfiol, Bernard
  The awakening 10:73 Ap 14 '41
  Making music bw 9:68 O 14 '40
  Bernard Karfiol. in group
    photog bw 32:87 Mr 17 '52
    port.
Karnak temple of Amen, Egypt
    photog bw 24:79 Ja 19 '48
Karsh, Yousef, photographer
  Artists and statesmen, por-
    traits bw 29:72-9 Ag 7 '50
  Contemporary artists of
    France: architects, musici-
    ans, painters, writers bw
    37:129-36 O 4 '54
  George Bernard Shaw bw 16:
    Cover F 7 '44; 22:40 My
    19 '47; 41:104A Ag 6 '56
  Leaders of Britain bw 16:
    Cover, 87-95 F 7 '44
Kasagi, Sueo
  Nude sculpture 32:100 Je 23
    '52
Kashan ceramics--dish and jug,
    Persian, 12th century 20:
    92 Je 24 '46
Katherine, wife of Henry the
    Pious. Cranach 40:105 My
    7 '56
Katkov, Norman
  Norman Katkov and family
    photog bw 23:125 Mr 8 '48
Katzman, Herbert
  Paris bw 32:88 Mr 17 '52
  Artist and his work photog bw
    32:87 Mr 17 '52 port.
Kaufman, George
  George Kaufman photog bw 21:
    50 O 7 '46
Kaus, Max
  Artist and his work photog 30:
    145 My 10 '54 port.
Kawabata, Minoru
  Artist and his work photog 32:

  100 Je 23 '52 port.
Keck, George Fred, architect
  George Keck photog bw 26:93
    My 2 '49 port.
Kedleston, Great Marble Hall,
    classic revival, English
    country house. Adam, R.,
    design photog 23:136 S 8 '47
Keelboat, U.S. frontier 39:80 N
    28 '55
Keller, Helen
  Helen Keller photogs bw 4:
    20-1 F 28 '38
Kelley, Florence
  Florence Kelley photog bw
    16:56 F 14 '44
Kelly, Emmett
  MacIver. Hobo clown (Em-
    mett Kelly) 23:43 Jy 21 '47
Kelly, Gerald
  George VI of England 35:83 N
    23 '53
  Somerset Maugham, 1933 bw
    11:76 D 1 '41
Kelly, Harold Osman
  Barn dance 29:71 Jy 17 '50
  Old western crossroads 29:71
    Jy 17 '50
  Harold Kelly photog bw 29:70
    Jy 17 '50 port.
Kelly, Walt, cartoonist
  Pogo bw 37:134 N 22 '54
  Pogofenokee-land 32:12-3 My
    12 '52
  "Uncle Pogo's So-So Stories"
    bw 34:20-1 My 11 '53
Kelsey, Muriel, sculptor
  Artist at work photog bw 21:
    102 Jy 8 '46 port.
Kemble, E. W.
  William Jennings Bryan politi-
    cal cartoon bw 31:20 O 22
    '51
Kemble, Fanny
  Fanny Kemble in Romeo and
    Juliet engraving bw 31:110
    N 19 '51
Kempton, Greta
  Harry Truman as a masonic
    Grand Master 26:54 Mr
    28 '49; 39:105 O 24 '55

Kenmore mansion, Fredericks-
    burg, Virginia--ceiling dec-
    oration, architectural de-
    tail 38:62 My 30 '55
Kennebunkport, Maine, 1825.
    mural bw Grant, G. 18:34 Ap
    2 '45
Kennelly, Ardyth
    Ardyth Kennelly photog bw 28:
    35 Ja 30 '50
Kenneth II, King of Scotland bw
    30:20 Ja 8 '51
Kennington, Eric
    British home guard volunteer*
    26:48 F 21 '49
    Night flyer at readiness 26:44
    F 28 '49
    RAF fighter pilots of World
    War II 26:45 F 28 '49
    Spirit of the British sailor*
    (Stoker Martin) 24:60 My
    10 '48
Kensett, John Frederick
    Landscape 19:84 S 10 '45
    John Kensett bw 19:82 S 10
    '45 port.
Kent, Adaline
    Musician sculpture bw 5:70 D
    5 '38
Kent, Frank R.
    Frank R. Kent photog bw 2:60
    Mr 22 '37
Kent, Rockwell
    Auto accidents and causes bw
    5:42, 46-7 Jy 4 '38
    Below Black Head 29:71 Ag 21
    '50
    End of world theories bw 3:
    55-6 N 1 '37
    Our America, Salamina din-
    ner service 9:76, 78 S 9 '40
    (ceramic design)
    Angel bw 5:9 D 12 '38 (wood-
    cut)
    Rockwell Kent photog bw 5:43
    Jy 4 '38 port.
Kentucky
    Lockwood. Daniel Boone's ar-
    rival in Kentucky mural 10:
    46 Ja 27 '41
    Kentucky in "The Adventures

of Col. Daniel Boone" bw
    18:66 My 21 '45
Keppel, Mrs.
    Mrs. Keppel 23:98 N 17 '47
Keokuk, chief, and son, 1812
    print bw 21:106 S 30 '46
Kerkam, Earl
    Artist and his work, photog
    bw 35:114 Jy 13 '53 port.
Kern, Jerome
    Jerome Kern photog bw 18:30
    Ja 1 '45
Kerrigan, Edward, architect
    Kerrigan and King. U.S. em-
    bassy, Brussels bw 34:47
    Ap 20 '53
Kester, Leonard
    The First Nowell 23:49 D 22
    '47
Ket, Kick
    Self-portrait bw 38:40 Ja 10
    '55
Kettering, Charles Francis
    Charles Kettering: portraits,
    home, inventions, associ-
    ates photogs bw 3:60 O 18
    '37; 3:74 O 25 '37
Key of St. Peter, jewelled, 16th
    century 32:85 Ap 14 '52
Khafre, King of Egypt, c2560
    B.C. sculpture 41:108 N
    26 '56
Khamernebti II, Queen of Egypt
    Mycernus and his Queen,
    Khamernebti II sculpture
    bw, c2000 B.C. 9:50 Jy
    22 '40
Kharj, El, palace of Ibn Saud
    photog bw 14:77 My 31 '43
Khufu (Cheops), Pharoah of
    Egypt
    Seated Pharoah sculpture bw
    36:22 Je 14 '54
Khufu pyramid, Giza, models
    showing steps in construc-
    tion bw 19:75-80 D 3 '45
Kidd, Steven R.
    Fruit peddler, Korea 29:70-
    1.O 9 '50
    On a back street 29:70 O 9
    '50

Kidd, Steven R. (cont.)
Oxcart and jeep 29:70 O 9 '50
Young girl, Korea 29:71 O 9
'50
Kids wrestling. sculpture bw
Wickey 12:53 F 23 '42
Kierkegaard, Soren
Soren Kierkegaard bw 20:59 Je
17 '46
Kiesler, Frederick, architect
Endless house, egg shaped
model and plan bw 32:82 My
26 '52
Galaxy bw 32:79 My 26 '52
(sculpture)
Kigu banner, Tibet, showing
Buddha as Messiah 6:25 Je
12 '39
Kiki, model See Prin, Alice
Kilchurn castle, Scotland photog
bw 29:90 Jy 17 '50
Kineglyph
Amdendola. Sculpture for the
blind bw 21:102 N 11 '46
King, Austin A.
Austin A. King photog bw 7:51
Ag 28 '39
King, Charles Bird
Charles Frances Adams, 1829
41:75 Jy 2 '56
Mrs. Charles Frances Adams
(Abigail Brooks Adams),
1829 41:75 Jy 2 '56
King, Ernest
Admiral Ernest King, "Time"
cover portrait 17:61 D 11
'41
King, Frank O., cartoonist
Gasoline Alley bw 12:62 F 16
'42
Frank King photog bw 12:62 F
16 '42 port.
King, Leland, architect
Kerrigan and King. U.S. em-
bassy, Brussels bw 34:47 Ap
20 '53
King, Rufus
Rufus King bw 16:47 Ja 17 '44
King, William
William King bw 9:8 Ag 5 '40
The king and queen surrounded

by swift nudes. Duchamp
32:103 Ap 28 '52
The king drinks. bw Jordaens 6:
23 Ja 23 '39
King of the Bushongo, carved
wood head, Africa c1800
bw 33:123 F 8 '52
Kingman, Dong
Junk sailing under Brooklyn
bridge* bw 30:100 My 14
'51
Landscape* 30:102 My 14 '51
New York's Chinatown* 30:102
My 14 '51
Victorian mansion, Province-
town, Mass.* 30:101 My
14 '51
The wire 11:76 O 27 '41
"A Report to the Department
of State" 38:66-70 F 14 '55
(drawings)
Artist and wife photog bw 30:
100 My 14 '51 port.
Artist at work photog bw 11:
72 O 27 '41 port.
Kinigstein, Jonah
Devil's aide bw 32:88 Mr 17
'52
Jonah Kinigstein photog bw 32:
87 Mr 17 '52 port.
Kipling, Rudyard
Beerbohm. Rudyard Kipling
caricature bw 23:88 N 17
'47; 33:126 S 22 '52
Kirby, Rollin
Prohibitionist caricature bw
20:67 My 27 '46
Kircher, Athanasius (?)
Glass to focus sun's rays on
enemy ships drawing bw,
17th century 19:80 Jy 23
'45
Kirkland, Wallace, photographer
Nature photographs bw 33:20-
1 S 22 '52
Wallace Kirkland photog bw
33:20 S 22 '52 port.
Kisling, Moise
Kiki bw 34:14 Je 29 '53
Maria Lani bw 19:14 D 3 '45
Walkowitz bw 16:77 F 21 '44

The kiss. Chagall 33:96 O 27 '52
The kiss. sculpture bw Brancusi 28:63 Ja 2 '50
The kiss. sculpture bw Rodin 26: 7-9 Je 27 '49
The kiss. sculpture bw Whitney 7:45 S 11 '39
Kiss in a shipwreck. bw 11:61 O 27 '41
Kissing the moon. bw Homer 6: 82-3 My 22 '39
The kitchen. Vuillard 40:71 My 28 '56
Kitchen table. Fiene 7:25 Ag 28 '39
Kitchen, Williamsburg. Sheeler 5:44 Ag 8 '38
Kitchens
    Lee, D. Thanksgiving bw 3:44 S 20 '37
    U.S. farmhouse kitchen, c1820 photog 39:54 Jy 18 '55
    Wood, G. Dinner for threshers 13:46-7 Ag 31 '42; 21:77 N 25 '46
    Wyeth, A. Interior 35:81 Jy 27 '53
Kites
    Bell. Tetrahedral kite photog bw 10:79 My 12 '41
    Chinese-American kites: animal, flag, geometric forms photogs bw 10:79-82 My 12 '41
    Hall. Kites 24:86-7 Mr 8 '48
    Kuniyoshi. Fish kite 30:36 Ja 15 '51
    West. Benjamin Franklin and the lightning 40:81 Ja 9 '56 bw 6:26 Je 19 '39
Kittredge, George Lyman
    George Lyman Kittredge photog bw 5:75 D 5 '38
Klaussen, Bjarne
    Honored guests 26:59 Mr 28 '49
    Artist at work, at home 26:59-60 Mr 28 '49 port.
Klee, Paul
    Nearly hit 38:61 Mr 14 '55
Kleiman, Jean Eakin
    "What is Race," UNESCO

publication, illustrations 34:101-2 My 18 '53
Klein, Jeanette
    Calisthenics ceramics bw 9: 131 N 11 '40
Klein, Morton
    Quiet mill pond 16:46 Ja 3 '44
Klimsch, Fritz
    Nude sculpture bw 9:96-7 S 23 '40
Klinghoffer, Clara
    Hendrik van Loon 10:47 F 3 '41
Klitgaard, Georgina
    View of Kingston 5:25 Ag 22 '38
Klonis, Bernard
    Bernard Klonis. in group photog 29:172-3 O 16 '50 port.
Knaths, Karl
    Basket bouquet 30:35 Ja 15 '51
Kneeling figure, sculpture McWilliams 25:101 S 27 '48
Kneeling figure. sculpture bw Maillol 7:37 Jy 31 '39
Kneeling girl. sculpture bw Marini 22:102 My 22 '50
Kneeling nude. sculpture bw Dalton 32:77 Ja 7 '52
Kneeling woman. sculpture Lehmbruck 25:47 Ag 16 '48 bw 7:55 O 30 '39 bw in Armory Show 26:89 F 21 '49
Kneeling woman. sculpture bw Stackpole 9:97, 80 O 21 '40
Knight, Dame Laura
    Balloon site bw 24:82 My 3 '48
Knight, Hilary
    "Eloise," illustrations 39:149 D 12 '55
Knight, Ridgeway
    Rural courtship bw 36:84 Mr 8 '54
Knights See also Armor; Emblems and Decorations
    Banners of Teutonic knights, 1410 bw 17:86 Ag 28 '44
    El Greco. Portrait of a knight 31:70 O 1 '51

Giotto. St. Francis giving his
cloak to a poor knight 16:69
Ap 10 '44
Illustrations of knights' activi-
ties bw 22:68 My 26 '47
Knight of the Holy Ghost: robe
and hat, France 35:96-7 D
14 '53
Lanzinger. Adolf Hitler as
knight 24:73 My 3 '48 bw 11:
73 Ag 18 '41
Millais. Knight errant* bw 9:
64 S 2 '40
Order of Teutonic Knights bw
15:94 N 22 '43
Van Dyck, A. Portrait of a
knight 27:65 O 24 '49
Van Eyck brothers. Knights of
Christ 26:62 Ap 18 '49
Knights of Labor
Founding officers, 1869 photog
bw 33:33 D 8 '52
Knipschild, Robert
Lavender circle bw 32:88 Mr
17 '56
Robert Knipschild photog bw
32:87 Mr 17 '52 port.
Knives
Bowie knife photog 39:76 N 28
'55
Inca gold ceremonial knife,
Chibcha 36:103 Ap 12 '54
The knockwon. sculpture bw
Young, M. 10:79 F 17 '41
Knole, English country house,
13th century 19:106 O 29
'45
Knoll, Florence, furniture de-
signer
Tables photog 34:72-5 Mr 2 '53
Florence Knoll photog 34:73
Mr 2 '53 port.
Knoll, Hans, furniture and interi-
or designer
Knoll room, Dallas Museum of
Fine Arts photog 34:72-3
Mr 2 '53
Simplified, form-fitting chairs
photog bw 20:47-8 My 20 '46
Hans Knoll photog 34:73 Mr 2
'53 port.

Knorr, Don, furniture designer
Chairs, curved metal photog
bw 28:99 My 8 '50
Knox, John
Wilkie. Preaching of John
Knox 24:66 Je 14 '48
Kobo Daishi, Buddhist priest,
9th century 34:96-7 Ap 20
'53
Koch, Carl, architect
Acorn house, prefabricated
photogs 26:70-2 Ja 24 '49
Carl Koch photog bw 26:93 My
2 '49 port.
Koch, John
Children painting* 29:Cover D
25 '50
Convalescent 18:76 My 14 '45
The florist.16:77 Ap 24 '44
Mrs. Doubleday and children
25:94 O 18 '48
Mrs. Theodore Roosevelt and
family bw 41:78 Ag 13 '56
Koch, Pyke
Resting chimney sweep 3:26
D 20 '37
Koch, Richard, architect
"LIFE" house for 2-3,000 in-
come family photogs bw
5:35 D 12 '38
Koeffler, Camilla See Ylla
Koerner, Henry
Looking 24:78 My 10 '48
My parents 24:77 My 10 '48
The prophet 24:78 My 10 '48
Vanity Fair 24:78-9 My 10 '48
Henry Koerner photog bw 24:
77 My 10 '48 port.
Koh-i-nur diamond, gemstone 2:
40-1 Mr 15 '37
Kolbe, Georg
The large sitting woman sculp-
ture bw 31:81 S 24 '51
Kollektivhuset, Stockholm.
photog bw Markelius, ar-
chitect 22:34 My 26 '47
Kollwitz, Kaethe
Ernst Barlach in death* bw
41:140 N 5 '56 (drawing)
Komainu, mythical animal,
Kyoto sculpture bw 18:91

F 19 '45

Konigshover, Jon, architect
Pacifica House photob bw 32:
131 Mr 17 '52
Jon Konigshofer photog bw 32:
132 Mr 17 '52 port.

Koran, 8th century 38:73 My 9
'55

Korea
Korean scenes and portraits,
1945 29:70-2 O 9 '50

Korolkov, Sergei Grigorievich
Russian scenes bw 27:114-30
S 26 '49

Kosa, Emil, Jr.
Mountains could talk 11:74 O
27 '41
Artist at work photog bw 11:
72 O 27 '41 port.

Kosciusko refusing the sword*
bw 17:86 Ag 28 '44

Kossuth, Louis
Louis Kossuth, 1848 photog bw
25:86 N 22 '48

Koun, Takamura
Monkey sculpture, Japan, 1893
30:74 My 28 '51

Koussevitzky, Sergei
Sergei Koussevitzky conducting
photog bw 11:76 S 1 '41;
18:78 Ja 29 '45
Sergei Koussevitzky conducting; family; home photog
8:42-6 F 26 '40 bw 16:55
Ap 24 '44

Krans, Olof
Bishop Hill, Illinois: portraits
and scenes of communal
settlers bw 16:10-2 Ja 31
'44
Self-portrait bw 16:12 Ja 31
'44 port.

Kratina, George
St. Joseph sculpture bw 27:
146 O 17 '49

Krause, Herman
Wolf by the lake 10:78 Mr 31
'41

Kravchenko, Victor
Victor Kravchenko photog bw
26:26-7 F 14 '49

The Kremlin, Moscow
The Kremlin photog 14:89 Mr
29 '43 bw 21:12-4 Jy 15
'46
Kremlin, 12th century bw 23:
31 O 6 '47
Kremlin plan, drawing, air
view bw 8:40-1 Ja 29 '40
Leydenfrost. The Kremlin
bw 23:36 O 6 '47

Kress collection of art 35:148-
60 N 16 '53

Krimmel, John Lewis
Fourth of July celebration in
Centre Square, Philadel-
phia 25:48 Jy 5 '48; 39:62
Ag 29 '55

Krishna bw 29:160 D 11 '50

Kroeber, Alfred Louis
A. L. Kroeber photog bw 28:
19 Ja 9 '50

Krogh, Per
Peace and freedom mural bw,
UN General Assembly
Building 33:114 N 3 '52
Venus bw 34:14 Je 29 '53

"Krokodil," Russian humor
magazine
Cartoons of the U.S.A. 27:
145-6 D 12 '49

Kroll, Leon
Adolescent girl 24:69 Je 28
'48
Ann in white scarf 5:30 S 19
'38
Figure outdoors 3:26 D 20 '37
Hunter in the hills 14:43 Mr
8 '43
Marie-Claude's birthday bw
10:70 Ap 14 '41
Nude back 24:67 Je 28 '48
Nude in blue 24:68 Je 28 '48
The pool 24:68 Je 28 '48
Quarry on the Cape 23:70 Jy
14 '47
The road from the cove bw
16:79 Ap 24 '44
Seated nude 24:68 Je 28 '48
Triumph of justice mural,
Attorney General's Office,
Washington, D.C. 4:38

Kroll, Leon (cont.)
  Ap 25 '38
  Self-portrait 24:67 Je 28 '48
    port.
Kronberg castle, Denmark, air
  view photog bw 8:45 Je 3 '40
Kruger, Louise, sculptor
  Boy bw 39:189 N 14 '55
  Crow bw 39:189 N 14 '55
  Girl bw 39:187 N 14 '55
  Louise Kruger photog bw 39:
    187 N 14 '55 port.
Krupp, Alfred
  Alfred Krupp portraits, statue
    bw 19:81, 87 Ag 27 '45
Krylov See Kukrynisky
Ku Yuan
  Yenan art academy woodcut bw
    18:60 Ap 9 '45
Kuan Yin See also Buddha and
    Buddhism
  Kuan Yin fresco, Chinese,
    10th century bw 35:155 O 5
    '53
  Kuan Yin sculpture bw 38:91
    Mr 7 '55
  Kuan Yin sculpture, Chinese,
    12th century 41:73 S 3 '56
  Kuan Yin, the compassionate
    lord woodcarving, China,
    12th century bw 9:50 Jy 22
    '40
  Kwannon statues bw, Temple
    of Sanu-San-Gen-Do, Kyoto
    20:52-3 Je 17 '46
  Seated Kuan Yin, Yuan dynasty,
    13th century 15:65 O 11 '43
Kubicek, Juro
  Artist and his work photog 36:
    144 My 10 '54 port.
Kublai Khan bw 3:54 Ag 23 '37
Kuffner, Baroness de
  Amethyst bw 21:101 Jy 1 '46
Kuhn, Hans
  Artist and his work photog 36:
    144 My 10 '54 port.
Kuhn, Walt
  The blue clown 26:88 F 21 '49
Kuhr, Fritz
  Artist and his work photog 36:
    145 My 10 '54 port.

Kukrynisky (pseudonym of 3 Rus-
    sian cartoonists: Kupria-
    nov; Krylov; Sokolov)
  Anti-German (Nazi) war car-
    toons bw 14:4-7 Mr 29 '43
Kumbhakarna, Hindu festival
    figure photog 30:92 F 12 '51
Kuniyoshi, Yasuo
  Boquet and stove 26:86 F 21
    '49
  Fish kite 30:36 Ja 15 '51
  Four peaches 29:172-3 O 16
    '50
  Objects on a sofa 6:28 F 13 '39
  Artist and wife photog bw 5:27
    Ag 29 '38 port.
  Yasuo Kuniyoshi. in group
    photog 29:172-3 O 16 '50 bw
    32:87 Mr 17 '52 port.
Kuprianov See Kukrynisky
Kurka, Robert
  Robert Kurka, composer
    photog bw 40:147 My 21 '56
Kutuzov, Mikhail
  General Kutozov, 1805 bw 14:
    94 Mr 29 '43
Kwannon See Kuan Yin
Kyrell Family coat of arms 40:
    187 Ap 9 '56

                    L

Labor and Laborers See Work
    and Workers
Laboure, Catherine
  Ford. The celestial mother
    (Blessed Catherine Laboure)
    17:40 D 25 '44
The lacemaker. Vermeer 35:55
    Ag 17 '53
Lachaise, Gaston, sculptor
  Floating figure bw 6:82 My 22
    '39
  Head of John Marin bronze 38:
    110 My 23 '55
A lad from the fleet. Martin, F.
    8:67 My 27 '40
Ladies preparing newly woven
    silk. Chang Hsuan (copy
    by Hui Tsung) 15:66-7 O
    11 '43
The lady and the unicorn tapes-

try, French, 16th century
22:70-2 My 26 '47

Lady at the tea table (Mrs. Robert
Riddle). Cassatt 38:74 Mr
28 '55

Lady bronc rider. Hurd 7:26 Jy
24 '39

Lady Godiva See Godiva, Lady

Lady Jean. Bellows 7:58 N 20 '39
bw 11:76 O 6 '41

The lady on the hill. Priebe 23:
70 N 24 '47

Lady with a pearl necklace. Vermeer 24:77 Mr 22 '48 bw
19:25 D 31 '45

Lady with a headdress,* France,
c1700 bw 23:75 S 15 '47

La Farge, Marie
Marie La Farge, 1840 bw 32:
51 Ap 21 '52

Lafayette, Marie Joseph
Houdon. Marquis de Lafayette
bust bw 19:42 Jy 9 '45
Marquis de Lafayette bw 29:
52 Jy 3 '50
Morse. Lafayette 17:61 D 18
'44 bw 5:28 O 31 '38; 6:26
Je 19 '39

"Lafayette" (locomotive) Baltimore and Ohio, 1837 photog
bw 25:12 S 27 '48

Lafayette Hotel. Sloan 7:46 D 11
'39

La Follette, Robert Marion,
1855-1925
"Old Bob" La Follette
photog bw 28:81 Ja 2 '50

Lagriffe, Henri
French resistance martyrs,
memorial, Auxerre, France
sculpture bw 26:35 Ap 18
'49

La Guardia, Fiorello
Wheelock. Mayor La Guardia
sculpture bw 7:37 Jy 17 '39

Lahey, Richard
My wife 6:28 F 13 '39

Laidler, Graham ("Pont,"
pseudonym), cartoonist
"British Character," cartoon
book bw 5:58-9 D 19 '38

Laing, Hugh
Davis, G. R. Dancer, Hugh
Laing 16:78 Mr 20 '44

Lake Lugano. Churchill 20:50
Ja 7 '46

Lake Erie, Battle of. Garneray
9:48 O 28 '40; 31:54 Jy 2
'51

Lake resort. Blanch 25:66 Ag 23
'48

Lake through the locusts. Lucioni 3:49 Jy 19 '37

Laks, Victor
Artist and his work photog bw
37:124 O 25 '54 port.

Lakshmi, Hindu goddess statue
bw 24:29 Ap 5 '48

Lalk, Millie
They're cute when they're
small 10:78 Mr 31 '41
Artist at work photog bw 10:
79 Mr 31 '41 port.

Lamasary, Tibet, Great Assembly Hall photog 24:76-7 F
16 '48

Lamb of God
Crunewald. Lamb of God
30:79 Mr 26 '51
Van Eyck brothers. Lamb of
God 26:59 Ap 18 '49

Lambert, Jack, sculptor
Harry Truman caricature bw
21:32 O 7 '46

Lamentation over Christ. bw
Rembrandt 6:58 Mr 27 '39

Lamont, Daniel
Daniel Lamont political cartoon, 1888 40:70-1 Ja 30
'56

Lamont, Frances
Gallic cock sculpture bw 14:
42 Mr 8 '43

Lamps See also Furniture--
Lamps
Street lamp, U.S., c1800 39:
62 Jy 18 '55

Lamy, Jean
Father Jean Lamy statue bw,
Santa Fe, N. Mex 30:122
Mr 19 '51

Lancret, Nicholas
  Fete galante 39:86 N 27 '50
Lancut castle, Poland photog bw
  5:53 Ag 29 '38; 17:85 Ag 28
  '44
Landberg, Nils, glass maker
  Crystal decanter, Swedish
  glass photog bw 17:66 Ag 7
  '44
Landing of Cartier in Canada,
  1534 24:78 Mr 22 '48
Landing of the Pilgrims.
  Rothermel 13:76 N 23 '42
  bw 19:56 N 26 '45
Landon, Alfred M.
  Alf Landon photog bw 14:7 My
  31 '43
Landowska, Wanda
  Halsman. Wanda Landowska
  photog bw 16:50 Mr 13 '44
Landowski, Paul
  Christ the redeemer statue
  bw, Rio De Janeiro 10:60
  Ja 6 '41
Landscape.* Courbet 24:66 Mr 1
  '48
Landscape. Kensett 19:84 S 10 '45
Landscape.* Kingman 30:102 My
  14 '51
Landscape. Parrish 18:45 Ja 1
  '45
Landscape, Ohio, 1945. Shahn
  37:98 O 4 '54
Landscape Architecture See also
  Gardens; Parks
  Japanese landscaping photogs
  31:58-69 D 31 '51
  Stedman. Palo Alto, Californ-
  ia, house photogs 37:120-2
  N 15 '54
  Traditional and modern
  gardens--8 plans for differ-
  ent income levels 6:25-6 Mr
  20 '39
Landscape in Abruzzi. Perlin 28:
  91 Mr 20 '50
Landscape near Chicago. Bohrod
  2:24 F 1 '37
Landscape with a mill near Ornans. Courbet 26:64 My 30
  '49

Landscape with fishermen. bw
  Lee, D. 3:47 S 20 '37
Landscape with goat cart.
  Nottingham 10:68 My 26 '41
Landscape with polo players.
  Hurd 7:26 Jy 24 '39
Landscape with raft. Doughty 19:
  84 S 10 '45
Landscape with willows. Eaton
  16:45 Ja 3 '44
Landscapes See also Agricultur-
  al Themes; Beach Scenes;
  Bridges; Clouds; Moun-
  tains; Storms; Trees. Also,
  names of artists, and Cur-
  rier and Ives prints
Allston. Elijah fed by ravens
  19:84 S 10 '45
Anderson, D. City at night
  32:68-9 Ja 14 '52
Appel. Juneau, Alaska 16:76
  Ap 24 '44
Austin. Beast enchanted 19:82
  O 1 '45
Bellini. St. Francis in ecstacy
  3:34-5 D 27 '37
Bellini. The transfiguration
  39:24-5 D 26 '55
Bellows. The white horse 20:
  81 Mr 25 '46
Benton. Moonlight on the O-
  sage bw 6:70 Ap 24 '39
Billings. The descent bw 8:70
  My 27 '40
Bingham. Fur traders de-
  scending the Missouri. 28:
  76-7 Mr 6 '50
Blakelock. Moonlight 23:101 S
  8 '47
Blume. Lilies 8:67 My 27 '40
Bodmer. Bellevue 15:88 Ag
  30 '43
Bodmer. Camp of the Gros
  Ventres of the prairies 15:
  88 Ag 30 '43
Bodmer. Encampment of the
  travellers 15:88 Ag 30 '43
Bodmer. Missouri River 15:
  87 Ag 30 '43
Bodmer. White castels on the
  upper Missouri 15:87 Ag

30 '43

Bone. Cudillero, Spain 1:43 D 7 '36

Bonnard. The Riviera 25:54-5 Jy 26 '48

Bouche. Train through the night club-car mural 11:50 Ag 18 '41

Bowen. After the heat of the day 23:84 N 17 '47

Boyd. Fall morning 23:98 N 10 '47

Braque. L'Estaque bw 26:82 My 2 '49

Brook. Georgia jungle 10:52 Ja 13 '41; 21:74 N 25 '46

Brook. Pasture at Elk 10:52 Ja 13 '41

Burchfield. November evening 26:86-7 F 21 '49

Burchfield. Over the dam 1:28 D 28 '36

Burchfield. Road and rain 1: 26 D 28 '36

Cadmus. Puerto de Andraitx 2:46 Mr 29 '37

Canaletto. The Thames 25: 100-1 S 13 '48

Casilear. Lake George bw 5: 28 O 31 '38

Cezanne. L'Estaque bw 26:82 My 2 '49

Cezanne. Farm at Jas de Bouf-fan 32:83 F 25 '52

Cezanne. House of Emil Zola at Medan 2:47 Ap 12 '37

Cezanne. Mont Sainte-Victoire 11:77 D 1 '41; 26:66 F 7 '49; 32:83 F 25 '52

Cezanne. The turn in the road (Bend in the road) 25:78-9 N 1 '48; 40:76 My 28 '56

Chavannes. Summer 15:66 S 20 '43

Chiang- Kai-Shek. Chinese landscapes 33:5-8 O 13 '52

Ch'ing Ming scroll, c1500 31: 44-9 D 31 '51

Church. The Hooker party migrates to Hartford, Conn. 13:82 N 23 '42

Churchgoing, York Springs, Pennsylvania, 19th century 31:73 Jy 2 '51

Churchill. Landscape paintings of Italy and England 20: 45-50 Ja 7 '46

Churchill. Mont Sainte-Victoire 26:66 F 7 '49

Cole, T. The Catskill mountains 9:77 D 9 '40

Cole, T. Mountain sunrise 19: 86 S 10 '45

Constable. View on the Stour near Dedham 5:44 S 12 '38

Contemporary New England and New York landscapes 23:67-70 Jy 14 '47

Corot. View of Naples 25:96 N 22 '48

Craig. Rivals 11:74 O 27 '41

Crist. Shanksville 16:45 Ja 3 '44

Crome ("Old Crome"). The edge of the commons 5:43 S 12 '38

Cropsey. View of Catskill house 19:84 S 10 '45

Curry. Wisconsin landscape 8:65 My 27 '40

Cuyp. The travelers' halt 41: 72-3 D 10 '56

Day. The transfixed hour 10: 68 My 26 '41

Dehn. Landscape paintings watercolors 11:41-4 Ag 11 '41

De Martelly. No more mowing 13:48 Ag 31 '42

Diego. Besieged city 20:81 Mr 11 '46

Dodd. Carnival 27:64 S 26 '49

Dodd. View of Athens 27:64-5 S 26 '49

Dufy. Charles River 30:65 Ja 22 '51

Durand. View of Rutland, Vermont 19:85 S 10 '45

Eagle and pines, Kano School, Japan, 17th century 31:66-7 D 31 '51

Eakins. Max Schmitt in a

single scull bw 16:72 My 15 '44

Egidio. Lake Lacar, Argentina bw 30:147 Je 11 '51

Eilshemius. Delaware Water Gap village bw 7:51 N 6 '39

Eisenhower. Adobe building 28:151 Ap 17 '50

El Greco. View and plan of Toledo. 28:88-9 Ap 24 '50

El Greco. View of Toledo 4: 41 My 16 '38

English landscape painting in America 5:42-4 S 12 '38

Fiene. Hudson River navigation boat 12:76 Ap 20 '42

Flannery. Night paddocks 10: 74 Ap 14 '41

Ford. The country doctor 3: 28 D 20 '37

Fragonard. A fete at Rambouillet 29:87 N 27 '50

Fragonard. The shady grove 5:35 S 26 '38

Gainsborough. The cottage door 5:43 S 12 '38

Gainsborough. View in Suffolk 13:94 N 9 '42

Ganso. Bearsville meadows 5: 26 Ag 29 '38

Ganso. The village church 2: 24 F 1 '37

Gauguin. Brittany landscape 21:62 Jy 29 '46

Gauguin. No te aha oe riri 11: 58 S 8 '41

Gauguin. The swineherd, Brittany 21:62 Jy 29 '46

Gauguin. Tahitian landscape 21:63 Jy 29 '46

Ghika. Great landscape of Hydra 29:105 D 11 '50

Giorgione. Concert champetre (Fete champetre; Pastoral symphony) 23:52 Ag 4 '47; 39:170-1 O 24 '55

Gozzoli. Journey of the Magi fresco 19:Cover, 43-5 D 24 '45

Gukei. In and around Kyoto 31: 66-7 D 31 '51

Hall. Landscape paintings 24: 85-7 Mr 8 '48

Hartley. Robin Hood cove, Maine 32:88 Je 16 '52

Havell. View of Sing Sing 19: 85 S 10 '45

Hicks. The grave of William Penn 17:72 O 16 '44

Hicks. The peaceable kingdom 17:72 O 16 '44

Hinman. Daybreak 23:99 N 10 '47

Hogarth. False perspective bw 1:27 D 14 '36

Homer. Weaning the calf 41: 72-3 D 10 '53

Homer. The wreck 2:26 Ja 11 '37

Houston. Jubilate deo omnis terra 10:68 My 26 '41

Hudson River school: Landscape panoramas, Catskill mountains 19:82-6 S 10 '45

Hurd. The dry river, New Mexico 21:76 N 25 '46

Hurd. New Mexico landscapes 23:75-8 Ag 18 '47

Hurd. The windmill crew 14: 46 Mr 8 '43

Inman. Picnic in the Catskills 27:57 Ag 29 '49

Inness. The coming storm 12: 59 Je 15 '42

Inness. St. Peter's basilica 33:90 S 15 '52

Junkin. First robin 10:67 My 26 '41

Kane, J. Landscape paintings of the Pittsburgh area 2: 46-7 My 17 '37

Kantor. Cathedral woods 29: 72-3 Ag 21 '50

Kingman. The wire 11:76 O 27 '41

Klein. Quiet mill pont 16:46 Ja 3 '44

Klitgaard. View of Kingston 5:25 Ag 22 '38

Koerner. My parents 24:77 My 10 '48

Kosa. Mountains could talk

11:74 O 27 '41

Krause. Wolf by the lake 10:
78 Mr 31 '41

Kroll. Hunter in the hills 14:
43 Mr 8 '43

Kroll. Quarry on the Cape 23:
70 Jy 14 '47

Lancret. Fete galante 29:86 N
27 '50

Lee, D. The bath 10:73 Ap 14
'41

Lee, D. Country wedding 14:
45 Mr 8 '43

Lee, D. Helicopter 16:77 Ap
24 '44

Lee, D. Noon 3:46 S 20 '37;
21:74 N 25 '46

Lee, D. Paintings of Mexico
22:72-8 My 12 '47

Lee, D. Pastoral 5:25 Ag 22
'38

Lee, D. The widow 8:66 My 27
'40

Lee, L. Hilltop landscape 32:
69 Ja 14 '52

Leonardo da Vinci. Mona Lisa
35:51 Ag 17 '53; 39:141 S
26 '55

Limbourg brothers. "Book of
Hours" of the Duke de Berry
24:38-50 Ja 5 '48

Lucioni. Vermont classic 3:49
Jy 19 '37

Lutz. Railroad crossing 11:75
O 27 '41

Magritte. Mental calculus 1:
26 D 14 '36

Manet. Luncheon on the grass
bw 12:44 Mr 9 '42

Marin. New England village
29:63 Jy 10 '50

Masaccio. The tribute money
fresco 39:22-3 D 26 '55

May Yuan. Bare willows and
distant mountains 15:62 O
11 '43

Meeker. Bayou Teche 28:78 Mr
6 '50

Metcalfe. Horses 29:72 Jy 17
'50

Miller, A. J. Fort Laramie,

Wyoming, 1837 27:44-5 Jy
4 '49

Miller, A. J. Scenic grandeur
of the West 27:46-7 Jy 4 '49

Mitchell. Hudson autumn 20:
77 F 18 '46

Miyamoto. Battle of Nicholson
28:70 F 27 '50

Monet. Rouen 5:26 O 10 '38

Moran, T. Western landscape
19:86 S 10 '45

Morse. Allegorical landscape
showing New York Univer-
sity 17:62 D 18 '44

Moses. Winter is here bw 25:
77 O 25 '48

Mount. Long Island farm-
houses 18:68 Je 25 '45

Palencia. Twilight in Castile
29:102 D 11 '50

Patiner and Massys. The
temptation of St. Anthony
31:62-3 O 1 '51

Penniman. Meeting house hill,
Roxbury, in 1790 13:80 N
23 '42

Phillips, A. F. Lincoln landmarks, New Salem, Illinois
36:79-81 F 15 '54

Pittman. An evening in Maine
18:70 F 19 '45

Poussin. Parnassus bw 25:78
O 11 '48

Raphael. Creation of Eve 27:
119 D 12 '49

Reindel. Net menders 3:36 Ag
9 '37

Reindel. Storm over Menemsha 3:35 Ag 9 '37

Rembrandt. The mill 5:33 Ag
29 '38

Remington. Fight for the water
hole 13:75 S 14 '42

Renoir. Farmhouse at Les
Collettes 32:97 My 19 '52

Renoir. Monet at Argenteuil
32:93 My 19 '52

Rosenthal. The source 15:67
N 22 '43

Roualt. The quarry 34:58-9 F
2 '53

Landscapes (cont.)

Rousseau, H. The dream 29: 110-1 S 11 '50

Rousseau, H. The waterfall 11:58 S 8 '41

Ruysdael, Jacob. View of Haarlem 24:74-5 Je 14 '48

Sample. Janitor's holiday 3: 44 N 15 '37; 21:74 N 25 '46

Scarseth. Milking time 10:78 Mr 31 '41

Schwarz. Sandgate, Vermont 16:46 Ja 3 '44

Sepeshy. New England siesta 8:66 My 27 '40

Seurat. A Sunday afternoon on the Island of La Grande Jatte 31:60-2 Jy 23 '51

Simkhovitch. Back country 11: 40 D 29 '41

Simkhovitch. Winter in Connecticut 11:40 D 29 '41

Steamboat rounding Indian Mounds near Natchez, * 1850 39:81 N 28 '55

Sugden. Wisconsin scene 10: 77 Mr 31 '41

Taubes. Summer evening 8: 39 Ja 15 '40

Thomas, B. Ohio landscape, Lancaster, Ohio 22:62-3 Je 16 '47

Thomas, B. Scotland's River Tay 17:61 O 9 '44; 31:80 O 29 '51

The travellers, Ming Dynasty, 16th century, after Kuo Hsi 15:68 O 11 '43

Tung Yuan. Clear weather in the valley 15:66-7 O 11 '43

Turner. Rain, steam and speed 25:96 N 22 '48

Ucello, School of. The triumph of Death bw 4:28 F 7 '38

Van Eyck brothers. The virgin martyrs 26:60-1 Ap 18 '49

Van Gogh. Entrance to the public gardens at Arles 38: 109 My 23 '55

Van Gogh. Road with cypresses 2:33 F 15 '37

Van Gogh. Stairway at Auvers 13:95 N 9 '42

Van Gogh. Vegetable gardens, Arles 27:83 O 10 '49

Varga. Road to Danbury 10: 72 Ap 14 '41

Wartik. Mountain landscape 39:136-7 N 21 '55

Watteau. Reunion on the country 40:110-1 My 7 '56

Wilson. River scene: Bathers and cattle 5:43 S 12 '38

Wood, G. Arbor Day 14:56 Ja 18 '43

Wood, G. Birthplace of Herbert Hoover 14:55 Ja 18 '43

Wood, G. Death on Ridge Road 14:55 Ja 18 '43

Wood, G. The midnight ride of Paul Revere 14:54 Ja 18 '43

Wood, G. Spring in the country 14:56 Ja 18 '43

Wood, G. Spring in town 14: 56 Ja 18 '43

Wood, G. Spring turning 2: 34-5 F 8 '37

Wood, G. Stone City, Iowa 14: 54 Ja 18 '43 bw 21:104 S 30 '46

Wootton. The great race meeting 25:102-3 S 13 '48

Wyeth, A. Blue dump 24:104 My 17 '48

Wyeth, A. Hoffman's Slough 24:104 My 17 '48

Wyeth, A. Public sale 24:105 My 17 '48

Zao Wou-Ki. Birds and rocks 33:87 Jy 14 '52

Zao Wou-Ki. Green landscape* 36:104 F 22 '54

Landseer, Edwin

Lady Godiva bw 25:160 N 15 '48

Lane, Harry

Autumn still life 16:45 Ja 3 '44

Lange, Joseph
  Wolfgang Mozart, unfinished
    portrait bw 40:127 Ap 23
    '56
The Lange boy. bw Manet 6:58
    Mr 27 '39
Langer, William L.
  William L. Langer photog bw
    10:96 My 5 '41
Langtry, Lily
  Lily Langtry photog bw 23:76
    N 17 '47; 31:117 N 19 '51
Lani, Maria
  Maria Lani, model, portraits
    by contemporary Parisian
    artists photog bw 19:14-6
    D 3 '45
Laning, Edward
  The corn dance 6:44 My 1 '39
  Gutenberg printing Bible*
    mural bw 9:66 S 30 '40; 33:
    92 O 20 '52
  History of printing 6 panels of
    mural, New York Public
    Library 9:65-6 S 30 '40
  Italy's war damage 19:69-72 S
    17 '45
  Joe di Maggio tying the record
    11:64 N 10 '41
  Learning to read mural lu-
    nette 9:65 S 30 '40
  Medieval manuscripts mural
    panel 9:65 S 30 '40
  Moses on Mt. Sinai mural
    panel 9:65 S 30 '40
  New York stock exchange,
    October 24, 1929 bw 8:78
    F 26 '40
  Santa Fe Railway at war 13:
    92-4 D 7 '42
  The student mural lunette 9:
    66 S 30 '40
  T. R. in Panama 6:44-5 My
    15 '39
  Walkowitz bw 16:79 F 21 '44
  Prometheus drawing bw, de-
    tail for mural 9:65 S 30 '40
    (drawing)
  Artist at work photog bw 9:64
    S 30 '40 port.
Lantz, Paul

Dan Cathey 10:47 F 3 '41
"The Matchlock Gun," illus-
    tration 11:85 D 15 '41
    (lithograph)
Lanyamek castle, Czechoslo-
    vakia photog bw 3:100 S 27
    '37
Lanzinger, Hubert
  Adolf Hitler as knight 24:73
    My 3 '48 bw 11:73 Ag 18
    '41
Lao Tze, scroll portrait, Sung
    dynasty 38:72 Ap 4 '55
Laocoon sculpture bw, Greek
    5:46 D 25 '38
Lapiths, Battle of the
  Battle of the Lapiths and Cen-
    taurs sculpture detail bw,
    Parthenon, Elgin Marbles
    35:158-9 O 26 '53
Larence, Jacob
  Cafe scene 20:77 F 18 '46
The large sitting woman, sculp-
    ture bw Kolbe 31:81 S 24
    '51
La Salle, Rene
  La Salle claiming Mississippi
    for France, 1682 bw 9:112
    S 9 '40
Las Casas, Bartolome de
  Father Las Casas bw 37:113
    O 11 '54
Lashley, Karl S.
  Karl Lashley photog bw 11:43
    O 13 '41
Lasker, Joseph
  El candy store 28:84 Mr 20
    '50
Lasky, Bessie
  Flowers bw 3:87 S 27 '37
  Artist at work photog bw 3:
    87 S 27 '37 port.
Last Judgment
  Angelico. The last judgment
    21:56-7 D 23 '46
  Ford. Resurrection 17:34 D
    25 '44
  Giotto. Last judgment fres-
    co, Arena Chapel, Padua
    25:56 D 27 '48

Last Judgment (cont.)
    Michelangelo. The last judg-
        ment fresco, Sistine Chapel
        27:44-8 D 26 '49 full paint-
        ing 27:44-5 D 26 '49
"The Last of the Mohicans," illus-
    trations, Wilson, E.A. 18:
    58 Ap 23 '45
The Last Supper See Jesus
    Christ--Last Supper
Latham, Barbara
    Barbara Latham photog 26:66
        Mr 14 '49 port.
Latona See Mythological Themes
    --Latona
Lauda, Jan
    Seal sculpture bw 41:84 O 8 '56
Laughing old woman. sculpture
    Barlach 41:138 N 5 '56
Laughton, Charles
    Martin, F. Charles Laughton
        as Captain Kidd 19:62 N 5
        '45
Laundering and Launderesses
    Boccacci. Laundress* bw 29:
        15 O 30 '50
    Lee, D. Washing pool, Mexi-
        co 22:76 My 12 '47
Laurencin, Marie
    Mili. Marie Laurencin, age
        64 photog 27:90 D 12 '49
        port.
Laurens, Henri
    Maria Lani sculpture bw 19:14
        D 3 '45
Laurent, Robert, sculptor
    Le cygne bw 10:64 Je 2 '41
    Girl bw 10:67 Je 2 '41
    Girl washing hair bw 10:64
        Je 2 '41
    Pelleas and Melisande bw 10:
        67 Je 2 '41
    The river bw 10:68 Je 2 '41
    Spanning the continent, model
        bw 10:68 Je 2 '41
    Artist at work photog bw 10:
        68 Je 2 '41 port.
Lavender circle. Knipschild 32:
    88 Mr 17 '52
Lavery, John
    Winston Churchill, 1916 bw

24:95 Mr 15 '48
Lavinia with a fan, the artist's
    daughter. Titian 40:107
    My 7 '56
Law, John
    John Law bw 23:77 S 15 '47
The law and the king, England,
    16th century. Castellon 30:
    94 Mr 12 '51
Lawn tennis game, c1870* 32:118
    Ap 7 '52
Lawrence, David
    David Lawrence photog bw 2:
        60 Mr 22 '37
Lawrence, Jacob
    Interior 21:64 Jy 22 '46
    Jacob Lawrence. in group
        photog bw 32:87 Mr 17 '52
        port.
Lawrence, Thomas
    The Calmady children (Nature)
        6:55 Mr 20 '39
    Lady Elizabeth Conyngham 6:
        38 My 29 '39
    Pinkie (Sarah Moulton-Bar-
        rett) 4:25 Ja 24 '38
    Sir Thomas Lawrence bw 4:
        23 Ja 24 '38 port.
Lawrence, Thomas Edward
    (Lawrence of Arabia)
    T. E. Lawrence 24:53 Ap 26
        '48
Lawrence, W. Goodby
    The sailfish 6:29 F 2 '39
    The white marlin 6:29 F 2 '39
Lawrie, Lee
    Atlas sculpture, Rockefeller
        Center, New York City
        photog 4:52 Je 27 '38
Lawyers and Judges See also
    Court Roome Scenes; Le-
    gal Themes
    Curry. U.S. Supreme Court
        murals bw 1:28 N 23 '36
    Daumier. Three lawyers 38:
        108 My 23 '55
    De Castro. Zemayas 41:71
        D 10 '56
    Roualt. The judges 34:61 F
        2 '53
    Roualt. Three judges 25:60

O 11 '48

U.S. Supreme Court, 1790-
1940: Portraits of 80 justices serving on Court in
150 years bw 8:48-9 F 12
'40 in 1865 photogs bw 14:
76 F 15 '43

William Stoughton, Judge,
1692 bw 27:76 S 26 '49

Lawyers as artists 24:72-3 Ap
5 '48

Lazarus

Duccio. Resurrection of Lazarus 1:46 D 28 '36

Giotto. Raising of Lazarus
25:46 D 27 '48

Tintoretto. Resurrection of
Lazarus 31:38 D 24 '51

Lazuk, Alexander

Taubes. Alexander Lazuk 10:
47 F 3 '41

Le Clear, Thomas

Red Jacket's grandson 36:73
Mr 8 '54

Le Compte, Rowan and Irene

Stained glass window, St.
George's Episcopal church,
Mt. Savage, Md. 38:65 Ap
11 '55

Le Corbusier See also Jeanneret, Charles E.

Karsh. Le Corbusier photog
bw 37:132 O 4 '54

Le Douanier See Rousseau,
Henri

Le Moyne de Morgues, Jacque

Map of Skull creek, near Hil-
tonhead, S.C., 1564 en-
graving bw 22:80 Mr 10 '47

Le Roux, Bartholomew, silversmith Sugar caster, U.S.
colonial 38:117 Ap 18 '55

Lea, Tom

ATC (Air Transport Command)
route scenes 18:43-6 Ap 30
'45

At sun-up* 28:74 F 20 '50

Between watches* 28:74 F 20
'50

Bruce Bieber, Top Sergeant
11:64 Jy 7 '41

C-47 flies over the Hump 35:
56 N 2 '53

China patriarch 17:63 Jy 10
'44

Destroyer base bw 14:7 Je 28
'43

The empty places* 18:43 Ap
30 '45

Hazford Rupert LXXXI, prize
Hereford 26:81 Ap 25 '49

Hittin' the sack 12:58 My 25
'42

Hornet's last day 15:42-9 Ag
2 '43

Portraits and scenes aboard
U.S.S. Hornet 14:50-8 Mr
22 '43

Lookout on flying bridge 12:55
My 25 '42

The nesters mural, Post office, Washington, D.C. 10:
46 Ja 27 '41

North Atlantic patrol--scenes
and portraits 12:54-61 My
25 '42

Peleliu invasion, September
15, 1944 18:61-7 Je 11 '45

Placentia Bay, Newfoundland
28:74 F 20 '50

Sinking of Wasp 14:48-9 Ap 5
'43

Soldiers at work--3 portraits
12:44 Ap 27 '42

Tin can skipper 12:55 My 25
'42

Tossing the cans 12:55 My 25
'42 bw 14:6 Je 28 '43

Bert Balchen bw 16:70 My 29
'44 (drawing)

Claire Chennault bw 16:72 My
29 '44 (drawing)

Jimmy Doolittle bw 16:68 My
29 '44 (drawing)

Tom Lea photog bw 11:60 Jy
7 '41; 12:53 My 25 '42 in
uniform 14:8 Je 28 '43
port.

Lead Belly photogs 2:38 Ap 19
'37

Leading the field. aquatint bw
Alken 6:38 F 6 '39

Leake, Eugene
    Nonie 10:47 F 3 '41
Leander and Hero, sculpture bw
    Tasq 11:146 O 13 '41
Leaning tower of Pisa photog bw
    18:107-8 Je 18 '45
Lear, Edward
    Alphabet--written and illus-
        trated bw 32:6-8 Mr 24 '52
    Edward Lear photog bw 32:7
        Mr 24 '52 port.
Learning to read, mural lunette ·
    Laning 9:65 S 30 '40
Leather Work
    American Indian fringed jacket
        photog 39:75-6 N 28 '55
    Galvez. Female figure, leather
        sculpture 36:81 My 31 '54
    Hunting pouch, U.S. colonial
        photog 38:60 My 30 '55
    Western saddles--7 types
        photogs 40:50-1 Ja 16 '56
Lebrun, Rico
    Centurion's horse 30:35 Ja 15
        '51
Leda See Mythological Themes--
    Leda
Lee, Ann
    Mrs. Richard Lee 21:70 Ag
        19 '46
Lee, Ann Hill Carter
    Mrs. Henry Adams 21:72 Ag
        19 '46
Lee, Arthur, 1740-1792
    Arthur Lee 21:71 Ag 19 '46
Lee, Charles
    Washington and Lee at the
        Battle of Monmouth bw 29:
        51 Jy 3 '50
Lee, Doris
    The artist's impressions of
        Hollywood 19:84-9 O 15 '45
    The bath 10:73 Ap 14 '41
    Catastrophe 3:45 S 20 '37
    Country wedding 14:45 Mr 8
        '43
    Garden in Carthage 33:112 N
        10 '52
    Good King Wenceslas 23:45 D
        22 '47
    "The Harvey Girls," scenes

    from the moving picture
        19:83-6 D 3 '45
    Helicopter 16:77 Ap 24 '44
    Hudson River excursion 3:46
        S 20 '37
    Landscape with fishermen bw
        3:47 S 20 '37
    Market in Tunis 33:112 N 10
        '52
    Mexico: scenes and portraits
        as record of trip 22:72-8
        My 12 '47
    Noon 3:46 S 20 '37; 21:74 N
        25 '46
    North Africa 33:110-1 N 10
        '52
    Oasis 33:109 N 10 '52
    "Oklahoma," scenes from the
        moving picture 16:83-4 Mr
        6 '44
    Parade of passers-by, Mar-
        rakesh 33:110-1 N 10 '52
    Pastoral 5:25 Ag 22 '38
    The runaway bw 3:47 S 20 '37
    "Show Boat," scenes 7:48-9
        N 27 '39
    Snake charmer 33:109 N 10
        '52
    Thanksgiving bw 3:44 S 20 '37
    The widow 8:66 My 27 '40
    Wildflowers of Michigan 25:
        68 Ag 23 '48
    Winter in the Catskills bw 3:
        47 S 20 '37
    Christmas tree bw 19:9 D 24
        '45 (drawing)
    Artist at work photog bw 16:
        82 Mr 6 '44 port.
    Doris Lee photog bw 3:44, 47
        S 20 '37; 5:72 D 12 '38 port.
Lee, Edna
    Edna Lee photog bw 24:22 My
        17 '48
Lee, Ezra
    Sergeant Lee in "American
        Turtle," first U.S. sub-
        marine, c1776 drawing
        bw 22:82 Ja 13 '47
Lee, Gypsy Rose
    Gypsy Rose Lee photog bw
        11:110 O 6 '41

Lee, Hannah Ludwell
  Mrs. Thomas Lee 21:71 Ag
    19 '46
Lee, Henry ("Light Horse Harry")
  Henry Lee 21:72 Ag 19 '56
Lee, Jeremiah, Mansion, Marble-
    head, 1768 photog bw 15:13
    D 6 '43
Lee, Laetitia Corbin
  Mrs. Richard Lee, II 21:70 Ag
    19 '46
Lee, "Light Horse Harry" See
  Lee, Henry
Lee, Lowell
  Hilltop landscape 32:69 Ja 14
    '52
Lee, Manfred B.
  Lee and Dannay (Ellery Queen)
    photog bw 15:70 N 22 '43
  Manfred B. Lee photog bw 22:
    21 Mr 10 '47
Lee, Mary Ann Randolph Custis
  Mrs. Robert E. Lee 21:72 Ag
    19 '46
Lee, Richard, 1640-1664
  Richard Lee 21:70 Ag 19 '46
Lee, Richard, II, 1647-1715
  Richard Lee, II 21:70 Ag 19 '46
Lee, Richard Henry,
  Richard Henry Lee 21:71 Ag
    19 '46
Lee, Robert Edward
  General Lee memorial eques-
    trian statue, Gettysburg bw
    4:35 Je 27 '38
  General Robert E. Lee, Com-
    mander in Chief of Confed-
    erate Forces 21:69 Ag 19
    '46
  General Robert E. Lee's tomb,
    Lexington, Va. photog bw
    9:62 Ag 5 '40
  Robert E. Lee, in full-dress
    lieutenant's uniform after
    West Point graduation 21:72
    Ag 19 '56
"Lee, Robert E." (Mississippi
    steamboat)
  Currier and Ives print. Low
    water 21:72 S 2 '46
Lee, Thomas, 1690-1750

  Thomas Lee 21:71 Ag 19 '46
Leech, John
  "A Christmas Carol," illus-
    trations bw 25:78 D 27 '48
  A delicate compliment bw 6:
    38 F 6 '39 (lithographs)
  Don't move there. We shall
    clear you bw 6:38 F 6 '39
  A nice game for two or more
    6:40 F 6 '39
  A ride home after a blank day
    bw 6:38 F 6 '39
Legal Themes See also Court
    Room Scenes; Lawyers and
    Judges
  Castellon. History of western
    law, scenes from 30:87-97
    Mr 12 '51
  Code of Hammurabi
    Cast bw 24:147 Mr 15 '48
    Stone replica bw 37:94 D
      13 '54
  Du Bois. New evidence 26:68
    Je 20 '49
  Guardian of Law, U.S. Su-
    preme Court Building,
    Washington, D.C. sculp-
    ture bw 30:104 Mr 12 '51
  Kroll. Triumph of justice
    mural 4:38 Ap 25 '38
  Lycurgus plaque, U.S. Capi-
    tol bw 30:74 F 5 '51
The legend. Austin 19:81 O 1 '45
Legend of St. Mark mosaic, St.
    Mark's, Venice 35:34 D
    28 '53
Legends See Mythological
    Themes
Leger, Fernand
  The city 4:44 My 2 '38
  Maria Lani bw 19:15 D 3 '45
  Siphon 33:96 O 27 '52
  Litany of the Virgin, Assy
    church, France 28:73 Je
    19 '50 (mosaics)
  Artist and his work photog 39:
    141 N 14 '55 port.
  Gallatin. Fernand Leger
    photog bw 4:45 My 2 '38
    port.

Leger, Fernand (cont.)
  Mili. Fernand Leger, age 68
    photog 27:88 D 12 '49 port.
Legong, Balinese dancer. draw-
  ing Covarrubias 3:46 S 27
  '37
Lehman family collection, Met-
  ropolitan Museum 37:63-7
  Ag 9 '54
Lehmann, Lotte
  Halsman. Lotte Lehmann
    photog bw 16:45 Mr 13 '44
  Lotte Lehmann photogs bw 30:
    72 Mr 5 '51
Lehmbruck, Wilhelm, sculptor
  Kneeling woman 25:47 Ag 16
    '48 bw 7:55 O 30 '39 bw in
    Armory Show 26:89 F 21
    '49
  Standing youth 25:47 Ag 16 '48
Leicester, Robert Dudley, Earl of
  Queen Elizabeth and Earl of
    Leicester dancing a lavolta*
    41:148 N 5 '56
Leighton, E. Blair
  St. Elizabeth 23:84 N 17 '47
Leighton, Frederic
  Self-portrait bw 35:162 O 26
    '53 port.
Leighton, Scott
  Mr. Morgan and Mr. Vander-
    bilt in a sleigh 6:31 Je 19
    '39
Leith-Ross, Harry
  Summer showers 16:46 Ja 3
    '44
Lekberg, Barbara, sculptor
  Artist at work photog bw 37:
    160 N 22 '54 port.
Lemonade and doughnuts. Guston
    20:92 My 27 '46
Lenin, Nicolai
  Lenin and Stalin sculpture bw
    6:17 Ja 30 '39
  Nikolai Lenin photog bw 31:
    116 O 29 '51
Lenin library, Moscow photog bw
    14:84 Mr 29 '43
Leningrad Pavillion photog 14:90
    Mr 29 '43
Lenox ceramics 9:76-9 S 9 '40;

29:89 D 25 '50
Lentelli, Leo
  American beauties sculpture
    bw 6:Cover Mr 13 '39
Leonard, Jonathan Norton
  "Flight into Space," illustrated
    by Osborn 35:90 Ag 31 '53
Leonardo da Vinci
  Beatrice d'Este bw 7:17 Jy 17
    '39
  The last supper bw 7:17 Jy 17
    '39; 22:54-6 Je 9 '47
  Madonna of the rocks 7:54 N
    20 '39
  Mona Lisa (La Gioconde) bw
    35:51 Ag 17 '53 original
    and 7 forgeries bw 39:141
    S 26 '55
  The musician bw 7:17 Jy 17
    '39
  Anatomical drawings bw 7:16
    Jy 17 '39 (drawings)
  Basillica models from da
    Vinci sketches bw 7:16-8
    Jy 17 '39 (drawings)
  Flying machine design--basis
    of modern toy 39:63 O 3
    '55 (drawings)
Leopards
  Mochi. Leopards paper cut-
    outs 34:19 Mr 9 '53
Leopold, Wilhelm
  Teniers. Archduke Leopold in
    his gallery 27:62-3 O 24
    '49
Lepanto
  Veronese. Battle of Lepanto
    23:58 Ag 4 '47
Leprince, Jean-Baptiste
  Little farmer feeding chickens
    bw 3:43 N 29 '37
Lesser white front preening.
  Scott 7:54 N 13 '39
Lester, William
  Fort Davis, Texas 38:73 Je
    6 '55
Letty. Philipp, R. 8:63 Ap 8
    '40
Leutze, Emanuel
  Cromwell and Milton 27:58
    Ag 29 '49

The General Armstrong surrounded, 1814 9:48 O 28 '40
Washington crossing the Delaware bw 5:28 O 31 '38; 6:54 Mr 20 '39; 18:17 Mr 26 '45; 22:118 F 17 '47
"Westward the course of empire" 36:76 Mr 8 '54

Levee at New Orleans. Currier and Ives print 21:71 S 2 '46

Lever house, New York City. Skidmore, Owings and Merrill, archts. photogs 32:44-5 Je 2 '52

Levi, Carlo
Artist at work photog bw 27:50 Ag 1 '49 port.

Levi, Julian
Beached 10:73 Ap 14 '41
Tarring nets 20:78 F 18 '46

Levine, Jack
String quartette 14:43 Mr 8 '43; 26:86 F 21 '49
Jack Levine. in group photog bw 32:87 Mr 17 '52 port.

Levitan, Israel, sculptor
Artist and his work photog bw 36:92 Ja 25 '54 port.

Levitt, Alfred, architect
Contemporary house, Jericho, New York photogs, plan bw 31:124 S 10 '51

Levitt, William J.
Levitt houses, 1948-50 photogs bw 28:141 My 22 '50
Levittown house photog bw 26:74 Ja 31 '49
William J. Levitt photog bw 25:75 Ag 23 '48; 26:74 Ja 31 '49

Levy, Edgar
Family portrait sketch bw 37:93 Jy 12 '54 port.
Artist's family photog bw 37:93 Jy 12 '54

Levy, Martha
Old barn 16:45 Ja 3 '44

Levy, Mme. Michel
Manet. Mme. Michel Levy 5:25 O 10 '38

Lewandowski, Edmund
Three kings bw 27:56 D 29 '49

Lewicki, James
Christmas customs and legends of many lands, Christmas cards 19:74-6 D 17 '45; 33:82-7 D 1 '52; 39:60-71 D 19 '55
Scenes from coast-to-coast camping trip, U.S. 31:97-101 Jy 9 '51 (drawings)

Lewis, Clive Staples
C. S. Lewis photog bw 24:80 F 2 '48

Lewis, John
Peale, C. W. John Lewis, c1775 12:66 Mr 20 '42

Lewis, John L., labor leader
Wolverton. John L. Lewis caricature bw 22:14-5 My 5 '47

Lewis, Sinclair
Sinclair Lewis caricature bw 23:82 S 1 '47
Sinclair Lewis photogs bw 2:82 Je 28 '37; 17:14 Ag 14 '44; 30:69 Ja 22 '51 age 53, in "It Can't Happen Here" 5:30-1 Ag 8 '38 age 64 28:54 Ja 2 '50
"Main Street" locale, Sauk Centre, Minn. photogs bw 22:100-1 Je 23 '47

Lewis and Clark Expedition on Columbia River bw 12:98 My 25 '42

Lewis and Clark Expedition, mural bw Russell 33:65 N 10 '52

Lexington, Battle of. stained glass bw Burnham 16:96 Ja 10 '44

Leydenfrost, A.
The Kremlin bw 23:36 O 6 '47
U.N. headquarters, plan bw 22:32-3 My 26 '47

Leyte
Sample. Cathedral encampment Leyte 35:56 N 2 '53
Sample. Invasion of Leyte 19:66-7 O 8 '45
Vidar. Leyte* 39:56 Ag 15 '55

Li T'ang, attributed
  Man on a water buffalo return-
    ing intoxicated from a vil-
    lage feast, 12th century 15:
    65 O 11 '43
Liberale, Saint
  Giorgione. Castelfranco Ma-
    donna 39:166 O 24 '55
Liberty, State of See Statue of
  Liberty
Liberty enlightening the world.
    sculpture bw Bartholdi 17:
    93 O 2 '44 bw 10:6 Je 23 '41
Liberty leading the people.
    Delacroix 25:84 N 22 '48
Library steps, folding into table.
    bw Sheraton, designer 23:
    78 Ag 25 '47
Lie, Jonas
  Smuggler's cove 4:26 Je 13 '38
Liebes, Dorothy
  Dorothy Liebes photog 23:93
    N 24 '47
Liedloff, Helen
  Artist and her work photog bw
    38:89 Ja 25 '54 port.
LIFE (magazine)
  Art competition for men in the
    armed services 13:31-6 Jy
    6 '42 paintings as Christ-
    mas cards bw 13:138-9, 141
    O 19 '42
  Defense paintings by 7 major
    American artists 11:60-4 Jy
    7 '41
  House for $2-3,000 income
    family photog bw 5:35 D 12
    '38
  Ten years of American paint-
    ing: 25 paintings reproduced
    in LIFE, 1936-46 21:72-80
    N 25 '46
  War art of World War II by ma-
    jor American artists 11:60-
    4 Jy 7 '41; 15:49-84 D 27 '43;
    18:42-67 Ap 30 '45; 19:58-70
    O 8 '45
Life in the country: The morning
    ride. Currier and Ives print
    9:29 D 30 '40
Life of Christ. fresco Giotto 25:

Cover, 34-57 D 27 '48
Life of Christ. Master of Cologne
    24:72-3 Mr 22 '48
Life of Christ. fresco Tintoretto
    31:Cover, 30-49 D 24 '51
Life of Jesus sculpture bw,
    Riverside church, New York
    City 19:74 D 24 '45
Lifelines. drawing bw Bone 10:64
    F 24 '41
Light Brigade charge bw 11:15 D
    15 '41
The light in the mirror. Du Bois,
    G. 26:68 Je 20 '49
Lighthouses
  De Martini. Lighthouse point
    23:69 My 14 '47
  Hopper. Lighthouse at two
    lights, Maine 2:46 My 3 '37;
    21:74 N 25 '46
  Kantor. Lighthouse bw 6:45
    My 1 '39
  Scott. Lighthouse drawing bw
    7:52 N 13 '39
  Thon. The outpost 20:97 Ap
    29 '46
Lighting, Architectural and Dec-
    orative
  Fluorescent wheels of light,
    Bank, Dusseldorf, Germany
    photog bw 36:152 My 10 '54
  Luminous panels photogs bw
    30:105-6 Je 18 '51
  Neon light chains, meeting
    hall, Frankfort, Germany
    photog bw 36:150 My 10 '54
  Noguchi. Decorative lamps
    32:114-5 Mr 10 '52
Lightning
  Curry. Line storm 1:30 N 23
    '36 bw 15:19 N 29 '43
  West. Benjamin Franklin and
    the lightning 40:81 Ja 9 '56
    bw 6:26 Je 19 '39
Liguore, Donald
  Going to town 1:44 N 30 '36
Lilies. Blume 8:67 My 27 '40
Lillie, Gordon ("Pawnee Bill")
  Major Lillie photog bw 16:
    109 Ap 10 '44

Lilliput
  "Gulliver in Lilliput," illus-
    tration bw 25:109 S 13 '48
"Lily pad" pitcher, Wistarber-
  type, American glassware
  39:58 Jy 18 '55
Lily-pad vase, Favrile glass,
  Tiffany 40:92-3 Mr 5 '56
Limbourg, Pol de, and brothers,
  Jean and Herman
  Calendar pages, "Tres Riches
    Heures du Duc de Berri"
    24:38-50 Ja 5 '48
Limestone quarry. Meeker, D.
  32:69 Ja 14 '52
Limoges Enamel
  Mumtaz Mahal's marriage cup,
    silver and enamel, France,
    17th century 25:129 D 6 '48
Lincoln, Abraham
  Abraham Lincoln bw 25:101 Jy
    26 '48
  Abraham Lincoln photog.bw,
    1846 (first portrait) 4:40 F
    14 '38 July 4, 1856 6:72 Je
    12 '39 April 9, 1865 (last
    portrait) 4:43 F 14 '38
  Abraham Lincoln and wartime
    associates photogs bw 14:
    75-6 F 15 '43
  Abraham Lincoln at Antietam
    battlefield photogs bw 3:83-
    5 S 20 '37
  Abraham Lincoln, head carved
    black sapphire 34:99 F 9 '53
  Abraham Lincoln, photographs
    from Lorant's "The Life of
    Abraham Lincoln," 1846-
    1865, including 3 Mathew
    Brady photographs bw 38:22-
    3 F 14 '55
  Abraham Lincoln, photographs
    from Lorant's "Lincoln, His
    Life in Photographs," 1846-
    1865 bw 12:50-5 Ja 5 '42
  Abraham Lincoln sculpture bw
    18:Cover Ja 18 '45
  Abraham Lincoln sculpture
    Rotunda, Capitol, Washing-
    ton, D.C. 31:48 Jy 2 '51
  Borglum. Abraham Lincoln,

Mt. Rushmore National
  Memorial sculpture 4:26 Je
  27 '38 bw 3:104 O 4 '37; 7:
  19 Jy 17 '39; 18:Cover Je
  18 '45
Brady. A. Lincoln, February
  9, 1864 photog bw 14:75 F
  15 '43
Byers. Abraham Lincoln, age
  49 photog bw 24:111 F 9 '48
Currier and Ives print. Assassination of President Lincoln bw 5:7 Jy 11 '38
Currier and Ive print. The Republican party going to the
  right house bw 31:18 O 22
  '51
French. Abraham Lincoln
  statue bw, Lincoln Memorial 20:Cover F 11 '46 bw 5:
  58 Jy 11 '38
Hansen. Young Lincoln sculpture bw 9:130 S 9 '40
Healy. Abraham Lincoln bw
  6:22 Ap 3 '39
Hoxie. Abraham Lincoln
  sculpture bw 18:Cover Je
  18 '45
Lincoln and his family: Biographical portraits photogs
  bw 4:40-7 F 14 '38
Lincoln as a presidential can-
  didate, 1860 photog bw 22:
  62 F 3 '47
Lincoln backdrop in auditorium, 1860 40:68 Ja 30 '56
Lincoln family, wife and three
  sons bw 23:45 Ag 25 '47
Lincoln's death* bw 11:108 N
  10 '41
Phillips, A. F. Lincoln landmarks, New Salem, Illi-
  nois 36:79-81 F 15 '54
Tenniel. Anti-Lincoln cartoons; caricatures; death
  tribute bw 6:8-11 F 13 '39
Wheelock. The tragic Lin-
  coln statue bw 8:117 My
  20 '40

Lincoln Memorial, Washington,
    D.C. Bacon, H., archt;
    French, sculptor 20:Cover
    F 11 '46 bw 5:58 Jy 11 '38
Lincoln, Joseph C.
    Joseph C. Lincoln photog bw
    9:73 Jy 15 '40
Lincoln, Mary Todd See also
    Lincoln, Abraham
    Mary Todd Lincoln photog bw
    14:76 F 15 '43 as a girl 4:
    41 F 14 '38
Lincoln, Robert
    Robert Lincoln photogs bw 23:
    45 Ag 25 '47
Lincoln, Tad
    Tad Lincoln photog bw 7:50 Ag
    28 '39
Lind, Jenny
    Jenny Lind figurehead, U.S.,
    19th century 31:70 Jy 2 '51
Lind, Kenneth C., architect
    Lind and Vagtborg. California
    cabin photogs, plan bw 23:
    45-6 Jy 28 '47
Lindbergh, Anne
    Despiau. Anne Lindbergh head
    bw 24:95 Ap 12 '48
Lindey, Alexander
    Still life* 24:72 Ap 5 '48
Lindsay, Howard
    Hirschfeld. Lindsay and
    Crouse caricature bw 21:
    116 N 11 '46
    Howard Lindsay photog bw 21:
    120 N 11 '46
Line storm. Curry 1:30 N 23 '36
    bw 15:19 N 29 '43
The linen cupboard. Hooch 24:77
    Je 14 '48
Linesman. sculpture bw Zorach
    8:92 Ap 1 '40
Lingayen Gulf invasion.* Turn-
    bull, J. 39:57 Ag 15 '55
"Lion," illustrations. Du Bois,
    W. 39:60-2 Jy 25 '55
Lions See also Animals,
    Imaginary
    Bone. Court of Lions, the
    Alhambra 1:44 D 7 '36
    Cranch. Cardinal Albrecht as

St. Hieronymus 5:39 Jy 11
    '38
Denslow. The cowardly lion
    35:54-9 D 28 '53
Durer. St. Jerome etching
    34:76 F 23 '53
El Greco. The Virgin with
    Santa Ines and Santa Tecla
    7:26 D 25 '39
Hardiman. England's royal
    lion sculpture bw 2:Cover,
    43 Ja 25 '37
Hicks. The peaceable kingdom
    17:72 O 16 '44
Lion of Flanders, banner
    photog 33:62 S 15 '52
Lion of Gate of Heaven, Peip-
    ing sculpture 20:75 Ap 29
    '46 bw 3:54-5 Ag 23 '37
Lion of Peiping bronze bw 3:
    55 Ag 23 '37
Lions, bronze urn, Greek,
    6th century 37:87 S 13 '54
Lions, sculpture Mandalay 38:
    86 Mr 7 '55
St. Jerome translating the
    scriptures, France, 15th
    century 4:30 F 7 '38
Winged lion of Brazil photog
    bw 10:61 Ja 6 '41
Wright. Androcles and the
    lion sculpture bw 29:124 Ag
    28 '50
Lip Plug, Aztec gold serpent 18:
    49 Je 4 '45
Lippi, Filippino
    Holy family with St. Margaret
    and St. John 1:45 D 28 '36
Lippi, Fra Filippo
    Adoration of the Child fresco
    19:44 D 24 '45
    Madonna and Child 13:46 D 28
    '42
    Madonna and Child and two
    angels 29:108 S 11 '50
    Self-portrait, age 35, 1441
    bw 29:109 S 11 '50 port.
Lipmann, Walter
    Walter Lippmann photog bw
    2:61 Mr 22 '37
Lippold, Richard, sculptor

Full moon bw 28:59 Je 12 '50

New moon light bw 28:60 Je 12 '50

The new one bw 28:60 Je 12 '50

The unknown political prisoner bw 34:40 Je 1 '53

Variations within a sphere, No. 10: The sun 41:90 Jy 30 '56

Richard Lippold photog 41:90 Jy 30 '56 port.

Lipton, Seymour, sculptor

Equinox bw 29:150 S 18 '50

Moloch bw 24:95 Ap 12 '48

Moloch I bw 29:150 S 18 '50

Seymour Lipton photog bw 29:150 S 18 '50 port.

Lisbeth, the artist's sister. Rembrandt 1:33 N 30 '36

Literary Landmarks and Locale
See also Illustrations; and names of authors

American literary locale, colonial to contemporary photogs bw 33:67-77 Jy 7 '52

Anderson, Sherwood
Fredenthal. Clyde, Ohio, portraits and scenes as setting for "Winesburg, Ohio" photogs bw 20:74-9 Je 10 '46

Benet, Stephen Vincent
Locale of "John Brown's Body" photogs bw 33:76-7 Jy 7 '52

Bronte sisters
Portraits; settings bw 15:95-9 N 29 '43

Brook Farm, near Boston photog bw 9:95 O 14 '40

Cather, Willa
Nebraska, Quebec, and New Mexico scenes and friends depicted in books bw 30:112-23 Mr 19 '51

Chaucer
Locale of "Canterbury Tales" photogs bw 14:77 Je 14 '43

Clemens, Samuel Langhorne

Locale of "Life on the Mississippi" photogs bw 33:75 Jy 7 '52

Locale of "Tom Sawyer" in Hannibal, Missouri photogs bw 9:90-1 Jy 15 '40

Scenes of books photogs bw 16:89-99 My 8 '44

Coffee house, England, 18th century 25:104 S 13 '48

Corcos. Gilbert and Sullivan land 25:86-7 O 11 '48

Dodgson, Charles L.
Original "Alice" photog bw 6:27 Jy 11 '38

Doyle, Arthur Conan
Locale of "Hound of the Baskervilles" photog bw 14:82 Je 14 '43

Sherlock Holmes memorabilia photog bw 16:77 My 1 '44

Du Maurier, Daphne
Menabilly House, English manor setting for Manderley, in "Rebecca" photogs bw 17:122-3 S 11 '44

Elsinore castle, Denmark photog bw 2:74 Je 28 '37

Emerson, Ralph Waldo
Home, memorabilia photogs bw 9:94-5 O 14 '40

English literary locale, Chaucer to contemporary photogs bw 14:77-83 Je 14 '43

Existentialist literature, Paris: Sartre, Beauvoir, and others photogs bw 20:64 Je 17 '46

Faulkner, William
Locale and characters depicted in his novels photogs bw 33:118-9 S 28 '53

Gray, Thomas
Locale of "Elegy Written in a Country Churchyard" photog bw 14:78

Literary Landmarks
  Gray, Thomas (cont.)
    Je 14 '43
  Hardy, Thomas
    Stonehenge, locale of "Tess
      of the D'Urbervilles"
      photogs bw 14:80 Je 14 '43
  Hemingway, Ernest
    Locale of "For Whom the
      Bells Toll" photogs bw
      10:52-7 Ja 6 '41
  House of Seven Gables, Salem,
    Massachusetts, 1668 photog
    bw 9:101 O 14 '40; 15:13 D
    6 '43
  Housman, Alfred Edward
    Locale of "Shropshire Lad"
      photogs bw 14:81 Je 14
      '43
  Irving, Washington
    Hudson River valley locale
      of writings photogs bw
      17:63-71 O 30 '44
    Locale of "Rip Van Winkle"
      photog bw 33:67, 73 Jy
      7 '52
    Locale of "The Legend of
      Sleepy Hollow" photog bw
      9:93 O 14 '40
  Jones, James
    Locale of "From Here to
      Eternity," Schofield
      Barracks, and other
      Honolulu scenes photogs
      bw 37:155 O 18 '54
  Lewis, Sinclair
    Locale of "Main Street,"
      scenes and portraits in
      Sauk Centre, Minnesota
      photogs bw 22:100-1 Je
      23 '47
  Longfellow, Henry Wadsworth
    New England literary locale;
      home, Craigie House
      photogs bw 9:98-9 O 14
      '40; 33:70 Jy 7 '52
  Marquand, John P.
    Locale and true-life char-
      acters of "Wickford Point"
      photogs bw 25:42 N 8 '48
  Milne, A. A.

    The world of Pooh photogs
      bw 40:115-20 F 27 '56
  New England literary land-
    scape; locale discussed in
    Brook's literary histories
    photogs bw 9:93-103 O 14
    '40
  Potter, Beatrix
    Locale of Peter Rabbit Land
      photogs bw 33:113 D8 '52
  Sunnyside, home of Washing-
    ton Irving photog bw 17:64-
    5 O 30 '44
  Thoreau, Henry David
    Walden Pond literary locale
      photog bw 9:95 O 14 '40
  Tintagel castle, Cornwall,
    England, legendary birth-
    place of King Arthur photog
    40:90-1 Mr 19 '56 bw 14:
    76 Je 14 '43
  Toplady, Augustus
    Locale of "Rock of Ages"
      photog bw 14:83 Je 14
      '43
  Whitman, Walt
    Locale of "Leaves of Grass"
      photogs bw 38:113-21 Je
      20 '55
  Whittier, John Greenleaf
    "Snowbound" farm house
      photog bw 9:100 O 14 '40
  Willison, George
    Locale of pilgrim myths
      and facts, from "Saints
      and Strangers" photogs
      bw 19:51 N 26 '45
  Wolfe, Thomas
    Locale of autobiographical
      novels: "Look Home-
      ward Angel," "Of Time
      and the River; Ashe-
      ville, N.C. as "Alta-
      mont" photogs bw 19:59-
      61 D 24 '45
    Locale of novels 33:69, 71
      Jy 7 '52; 41:178-9 S 17
      '56; 41:168-9 S 24 '56
  Wordsworth, William
    Lake country literary lo-
      cale photogs bw 29:82

Jy 17 '50

Locale of "Daffodils" photog bw 14:79 Je 14 '43

Literary Themes See also Allegorical Themes; Biblical and Christian Themes; Illustrations; Mythological Themes; and names of characters, as Holmes, Sherlock

Albright brothers. Picture of Dorian Gray bw 16:70-1 Mr 27 '44; 18:99-105 Mr 19 '45

Benton. Frankie and Johnny mural detail 2:36 Mr 1 '37

Benton. Huck Finn mural detail 2:36 Mr 1 '37; 21:74 N 25 '46

Daumier. Don Quixote 40:74-5 My 28 '56

Don Quixote, Gobelin tapestry, c1714 21:82-3 S 30 '46 bw 6:17 Je 19 '39

Don Quixote and Sancho Panza sculpture bw, Madrid 31: 58 Ag 27 '51

Greco. Pinocchio sculpture bw, Italy 40:127 Je 4 '56

Grimm and Anderson fairy story characters Salzburg marionettes 33:Cover, 68-73 D 29 '52

Koerner. Vanity Fair 24:78-9 My 10 '48

LoMedico. Aesop fable lamp design bw 21:106 N 18 '46

"Message to Garcia" photogs bw 4:23 Je 13 '38

Mount. Who'll turn the grindstone 12:73 Ap 20 '42; 18: 65 Je 25 '45

Pied Piper of Hamilin stained glass bw 16:125 My 29 '44

Robinson. Judson Stoddard, from Edgar Lee Master's poem 20:79 F 18 '46

Ryder. The temple of the mind (E. A. Poe) 30:91 F 26 '51

Solovey the brigand ice sculpture bw 6:7 Ja 16 '39

Uncle Tom's Cabin posters 41:60 S 3 '56

Van Dyck. Rinaldo and Armida, from Tasso's "Jerusalem Delivered" 4:21 Ap 11 '38

Venturi. Pinocchio sculpture bw 40:128 Je 4 '56

Waugh. Author's sketch of characters in his book "Decline and Fall" bw 20:58 Ap 8 '46

Wright, P. Androcles and the lion sculpture bw 29:124 Ag 28 '50

Wright, P. Brer Rabbit hitting Tar-Baby sculpture bw 29: 124 Ag 28 '50

Wright, P. "How the elephant got his trunk" sculpture bw 29:122 Ag 28 '50

Shakespeare

Ariel sculpture bw, Dome, Bank of England, London 21:101 O 21 '46

Puck sculpture bw, Folger Shakespeare Library, Washington, D.C. 4:33 Ap 25 '38

Rogers. Romeo and Juliet sculpture bw 6:7 Mr 6 '39

Ryder. The forest of Arden 30:90 F 26 '51

Turner, J.M.W. The Grand Canal, Venice: Shylock 5: 44 S 12 '38

Lithographs See also Currier and Ives prints

Ackerman. Temperance poster 39:72-3 D 26 '55

Battle of the Big Horn bw 24: 13 Je 21 '48

Bellows. Nude study bw 20:78 Mr 25 '46

Bodmer. Pehriska-Ruhpa 27: 41 Jy 4 '49

Bornet. Niagara Falls, 1855 26:77 Ap 18 '49

Brown, M. Buffalo hunter bw 39:20 D 12 '55

Cincinnati Art Museum International exhibit of color lithographs 33:84-7 Jy 14 '52

Lithographs (cont.)
  Cloar. Group of myselves bw
    24:79-82 Ja 26 '48
  Cox, Jan. Head of a girl 33:
    86 Jy 14 '52
  Dix, O. Veronica's veil 33:84
    Jy 14 '52
  Gauguin. Swan 33:85 Jy 14 '52
  General Custer's death strug-
    gle 24:13 Je 21 '48
  German army destruction in
    Belgium, * World War bw
    24:66-7 My 24 '48
  Jorn. Return to the detested
    city 33:85 Jy 14 '52
  Lantz. "Matchlock Gun" illus-
    trations 11:85 D 15 '41
  Leech. English sporting prints
    6:38-40 F 6 '39
  Marini. Horse and rider 33:85
    Jy 14 '52
  Matisse. Persian girl 31:110
    N 26 '51
  Moore, H. Prometheus 33:86
    Jy 14 '52
  Oliviera. The arena 33:84 Jy
    14 '52
  Picasso. Departure 33:84 Jy
    14 '52
  Regnier. Ice skater 6:40 F 6 '39
  San Francisco, 1816 40:49 Ja
    16 '56
  Santa Fe, New Mexico, 1849
    40:49 Ja 16 '56
  Singier. Provencal interior
    33:86 Jy 14 '52
  Solid comfort 27:49 Jy 4 '49
  Sporting prints, 19th century
    6:38-42 F 6 '39
  Svanberg. The vigilant heart
    33:86 Jy 14 '52
  Von Physter. Destiny bw 5:55
    Ag 8 '38
  Von Physter. Jam session bw
    5:55 Ag 8 '38
  Wood, G. Tree planting bw 14:
    57 Ja 18 '43
  Wood, G. Wild flowers 7:25 Ag
    28 '39
  Zao Wou-Ki. Birds and rocks
    33:87 Jy 14 '52

Little, Robert A., architect
  Home of the architect photogs
    34:113-6 Je 15 '53
Little bather standing. sculpture
  bw Maillol 8:106 Ap 15 '40
The little bridge. Cezanne 32:82
  F 25 '52
Little brother and sister. sculp-
  ture bw Wickey 12:54 F 23
  '42
Little farmer feeding chickens.
  bw Leprince 3:43 N 29 '37
"Little Fur Family," illustra-
  tions. Williams, G. 21:59-
  61 D 2 '46
Little girls. sculpture bw Wickey
  12:53 F 23 '42
Little known bird of the inner eye.
  Graves 25:64 O 11 '48
"Little Lord Fauntleroy," illus-
  trations. bw Birch, R. 27:
  71 D 5 '49
Litvinoff, Max
  Max Litvinoff, "Time" cover
    portrait 17:65 D 11 '44
Liu Te-hwa.
  Moonlight march woodcut bw
    18:59 Ap 9 '45
Living American Art, Inc.
  Color prints distributed 2:32-
    5 F 1 '37
Livingston, Crawford
  Crawford Livingston water-
    color bw 2:72 My 31 '37
Livingston, Philip
  Philip Livingston bw 15:9 Jy
    5 '43
Livingstone, David, explorer
  David Livingstone bw 7:60 Ag
    14 '39
  Stanley meeting Livingstone
    bw 7:60 Ag 14 '39
Ljungdahl, Goesta
  Albert Einstein photog 4:48
    Ap 11 '38
Llama
  Llama gold ornament, Inca
    c1550 bw 36:25-6 Ap 5 '54
  Pottery vessel, Inca 36:104
    Ap 12 '54
Llewellyn, William

Queen Mary of England, coronation portrait 28:66 My 29 '50

Lloyd George, David

David Lloyd George 24:53 Ap 26 '48 photog bw 2:61 My 10 '37

David Lloyd George in Big Four at Versailles photog bw 33:41 D 22 '52

Loading cotton by moonlight. Currier and Ives print 21:71 S 2 '46

Lochner, Stefan

St. Jerome in his study 41:74 D 10 '56

Locke, John

John Locke bw 25:119 S 13 '48

Lockwood, Ward

Corner grocery, Taos 6:30 F 13 '39

Daniel Boone's arrival in Kentucky mural, Post Office, Lexington, Ky. 10:46 Ja 27 '41

Locomotives See Railroads; and names of locomotives, as Atlantic, Dewitt Clinton, Jupiter, Lafayette, 119, 382, 999, Tom Thumb

Lodge, Henry Cabot

Senator Lodge, c1917 photog bw 16:52 F 28 '44

Loewy, Raymond, architect and industrial designer

Coral Gables, Youth Center sketch, floor plan bw 21:137 Mr 17 '47

Desert house, Palm Springs, Calif. photog bw 22:113-7 Mr 24 '47

Good design in objects of daily use: bottles, lamps, chairs, houses, automobiles 26:110-2 My 2 '49

Redesigned humans bw 25:16-7 D 13 '48 (drawings)

Raymond Loewy photog bw 22:114-5 Mr 24 '47; 26:110-2 My 2 '49 port.

Log Cabins See Cabins

Log jam. Hartley 32:86 Je 16 '52

Logan, Joshua

Joshua Logan photogs bw 15:103 My 15 '50; 26:102-18 My 9 '49

Loire, Gabriel

Window with dove of holy spirit stained glass 38:66 Ap 11 '55

Lombard crown of Italy photog bw 15:19 Ag 9 '43

LoMedico, Thomas

Aesop fable lamp design bw 21:106 N 18 '46

London See also Bank of England

Bohrod. Paddington Station, London 31:78 O 29 '51

Bone. Whitehall, thoroughfare of empire 24:60 My 10 '48

Canaletto. The Thames 25:100-1 S 13 '48

Davis, F. Softball game in Hyde Park* 16:66-7 Ap 3 '44; 31:79 O 29 '51

Great Fire, London 41:171 N 19 '56

Hacker. Wet night in Piccadilly Circus 23:85 N 17 '47

Hogarth. Drawings and paintings of eighteenth century London 21:77-83 D 16 '46

The mall, 18th century 25:100 S 13 '48

The rotunda, Ranelagh Gardens, 18th century 25:100 S 13 '48

Whistler. Old Battersea bridge 12:62 Je 15 '42

Whistler. Old Battersea bridge (Symphony in Brown and Silver) 36:94-5 My 17 '54

London blitz, September 7, 1940. Mills 26:50 F 28 '49

London slum, c1850. bw Dore 4:52 My 23 '38

Long, Huey

McCready. The shooting of Huey Long 6:49 Je 26 '39

Long, Huey (cont.)
  bw 21:121 D 9 '46
'Long the Pennsy Line 28:90 Mr
  20 '50
Longfellow, Henry Wadsworth
  Henry Wadsworth Longfellow
    photog bw 11:91 S 8 '41
  Longfellow and his daughter in
    Healy. Arch of Titus 33:89
    S 15 '52
  New England literary locale;
    home, Craigie House pho-
    togs bw 9:98-9 O 14 '40;
    33:70 Jy 7 '52
Long-Horn Bill. sculpture bw
  Maldarelli 22:139 Mr 24'47
Long Island farmhouses. Mount
  18:68 Je 25 '45
Long Island sound. Bouche 8:68
  My 27 '40
Longstaff, John
  Sir John Longstaff photog bw
    3:126 O 4 '37 port.
Looking. Koerner 24:78 My 10
  '48
Looking up at distant Miao Kao
  terrace on the way home
  from the third recluse pool.
  bw Chiang Kai-Shek 33:5 O
  13 '52
Looking westwards. Ernst 32:59
  Ja 21 '52
The lookout--"All's Well" 9:52 Jy
  22 '40
Lookout on flying bridge. Lea 12:
  55 My 25 '42
Loomis, Andrew
  Dionne quintuplets 18:45 Ja 1
    '45
Loos, Anita
  Anita Loos photog bw 21:50 O
    7 '46; 28:67 Ja 2 '50
Lopez, Carlos
  Waiting for train 25:66 Ag 23
    '48
The lord. Van Eyck brothers 26:
  64-5, 69 Ap 18 '49
Loredano, Leonardo
  Bellini. Leonardo Loredano,
    Doge of Venice 23:46 Ag 4
    '47

Lorenzetti, Pietro
  Descent from the cross fres-
    co, Lower Church of St.
    Francis, Assisi 39:30 D
    26 '55
Lorenzini, Carlo
  (Collodi, Pseudonym)
  Collodi bw 40:127 Je 4 '56
Lorenzo da Viterbo
  The marriage of the Virgin
    fresco bw, 15th century
    21:103 O 28 '46
Lorenzo Monaco, precursor of
  Assumption of the Virgin 1:48
    D 28 '36
Lorge, Irving
  Irving Lorge photog bw 30:132
    F 12 '51
Lorjou, Bernard
  The hunt* 29:101 D 11 '50
Los Angeles
  Highway design, four-level
    freeway crossover photog
    36:33 Ja 4 '54
  Joseph Wolfskill's lemon and
    orange groves, 1880 bw
    15:102-3 N 22 '43
Los Angeles County Museum
  Conservative and modern
    paintings, exhibit of local
    artists bw 22:40 Je 16 '47
The lost Felice. Hartley 32:89
  Je 16 '52
The lost penny. Benton 7:26 Ag
  28 '39
Lot
  Rubens. Departure of Lot and
    his family from Sodom 4:
    24 Ap 11 '38
Louis, Joe
  Mili. Louis knockdown by Joe
    Walcott photog bw 24:16 My
    10 '48
Louis, Saint
  St. Louis burying dead in
    Palestine during Crusades
    mural bw, Luxembourg
    palace, Paris 21:41 O
    21 '46
Louis IX, King of France bw 22:
  84 My 26 '47

Louis XIV wins the battle of Dole,
  1674 Gobelin tapestry bw
  5:15 S 5 '38
Louis XV, King of France
  Rigaud. Louis XV, age 20 23:
    80 S 15 '47
  Van Loo. Louis XV bw 5:39 S
    26 '38
Louis IV, of Hesse photog bw 23:
  72 O 20 '47
Louis of Anjou
  Donatello. San Lucovico gilded
    bronze statue, 13th century
    27:106-7 S 19 '49
Louisiana
  Plantation houses: Greek re-
    vival, steamboat gothic
    photogs 32:72-83 Je 9 '52
Louisiana Purchase bw 14:62 Ap
  12 '43
Louisiana swamp landscape. car-
  toon Emett 37:46 Jy 5 '54
Louise, Crown Princess of
    Sweden caricature bw 26:44
    F 21 '49
The Louvre, Paris
  Art collection 35:50-62 Ag 17
    '53
  Famous sculptures and paint-
    ings returned from wartime
    storage photogs bw 19:48-
    50 Jy 30 '45
  Morse. Gallery of the Louvre
    17:62 D 18 '44
  Pissarro. The Louvre, morn-
    ing 13:94 N 9 '42
  Reconstruction of the Louvre,
    18th century bw 31:78 Jy 30
    '51
Love disarmed. bw Boucher 12:
  44 Mr 9 '42
Love song on a snow bed. Ernst
  32:59 Ja 21 '52
The lovers. Picasso 23:95 O 13
  '47
Lovers in the cornfield. Benedet-
  to 21:77 N 25 '46
Low, David, cartoonist
  "Very well, alone" bw 26:63 F
    21 '49
  David Low photog bw 27:59 O

17 '49   port.
  Eisenstadt. David Low photog
    bw 32:101 Ja 14 '52 port.
  Karsh. David Low photog bw
    16:95 F 7 '44 port.
Low, Joseph
  "Mother Goose Riddle Rhymes,"
    rebus book 36:6-7 Ap 19 '54
Low, Juliette
  Juliette Low photog bw 32:110
    Mr 24 '52
Low water. Currier and Ives
  print 21:72 S 2 '46
Low water in the Mississippi.
  Currier and Ives print 9:33
  D 30 '40
Lowell, James Russell
  James Russell Lowell bw 10:
    26 Mr 3 '41
Lowes, John Livingston
  John Livingston Lowes photog
    bw 10:96 My 5 '41
Lowinger, Linda
  Concerto in color 10:58 Je 16
    '41
Loxodrome photog bw 9:61 Jy 15
    '40
Loy, Myrna
  Weinbreiner. Myrna Loy
    sculpture bw 3:46 O 11 '37
Loyola, Ignatius of, Saint
  St. Ignatius bw 24:61 Je 14 '48;
    39:43 D 26 '55
Lu Hung Nien
  An angel summons the shep-
    herds 11:43 D 22 '41
  The annunciation 11:42 D 22
    '41 bw 29:66 S 4 '50
  The birth of Jesus 11:41 D 22
    '41
  The flight into Egypt 11:45 D
    22 '41 scroll painting bw
    11:49 D 22 '41
  Jesus and the woman at the
    well 11:46 D 22 '41
  Joseph at the inn scroll paint-
    ing bw 11:49 D 22 '41
  Lu Hung Nien photog bw 11:
    40 D 22 '41 port.
Lubin, Leo
  Smokers* 29:105 D 11 '50

Lucas van Leyden
  The adoration of the Magi 11:
    56 S 8 '41
  Chess players 24:76 Mr 22 '48
  Adam and Eve driven from
    Eden bw 6:46 Ja 16 '39 (en-
    gravings)
  Cain slaying Abel bw 6:46 Ja
    16 '39 (engravings)
  Eve giving Adam the apple bw
    6:46 Ja 16 '39 (engravings)
Luce, Molly
  Vegetable garden* 13:45 Ag 31
    '42
Lucerna in dry dock,* Bone 26:
    57 Mr 21 '49
Lucifer. sculpture bw Epstein 33:
    66 N 3 '52
Lucioni, Luigi
  The artist's Vermont home*
    bw 3:46 Jy 19 '37
  Clouds over Equinox 3:48 Jy
    19 '37
  Lake through the locusts 3:49
    Jy 19 '37
  Red buildings in sunlight 3:48
    Jy 19 '37; 21:74 N 25 '46
  Tree in landscape 3:47 Jy 19
    '37
  Vermont classic 3:49 Jy 19 '37
  Artist at work photogs bw 3:
    46 Jy 19 '37 port.
Lucius, Florence
  Davidson. Florence Lucius
    bust bw 10:108 Mr 17 '41
    port.
  Florence Lucius photog bw 10:
    108 Mr 17 '41 port.
Lucretia See Mythological
    Themes--Lucretia
Ludgin collection of contemporary
    American painting 33:98-9
    O 27 '52
Ludlow bottle, glassware, U.S.
    39:58-9 Jy 18 '55
Ludlow castle, Shropshire, Eng-
    land photog 40:91 Mr 19 '56
Ludovico, San (Louis of Anjou)
  Donatello. San Ludovico gilded
    bronze statue, 13th century
    27:106-7 S 19 '49

Ludwig, Emil
  Emil Ludwig photog bw 3:67 D
    20 '37
Luini, Bernardino
  Body of St. Catherine borne by
    angels to Sinai fresco bw 6:
    32 F 13 '39
  The nativity 13:43 D 28 '42
Luke, Saint
  St. Luke, Gospel Book of
    Charlemagne 34:87 F 23 '53
Luks, George
  Ann Pratt 41:162 D 24 '56
  The spielers 12:61 Je 15 '42
Lull. bw Cloar 32:88 Mr 17 '52
Lull. Ernst 32:59 Ja 21 '52
Lullaby. Martin, F. 16:76 Ap 24
    '44
Lumpkin Street. Dodd 27:63 S 26
    '49
Lunch table. bw Claesz 7:24 Ag
    28 '39
Luncheon of the boating party.
    Renoir 32:94 My 19 '52; 38:
    110 My 23 '55
Luncheon on the grass. bw Ma-
    net 12:44 Mr 9 '42
Lurcat, Jean, tapestry designer
    Nazi warfare satire 21:81 S 30
    '46
  Tapestries, Assy church,
    France 28:76 Je 19 '50
  Artist at work photog bw 21:80
    S 30 '46 port.
Lusitania launching, 1913 23:86
    N 17 '47
Lustron house photog bw 26:75
    Ja 31 '49
Lute players See Musicians and
    Musical Instruments--Lute
Luther, Martin
  Church doors where 95 theses
    posted, Wittenberg photog
    bw 24:62 Je 14 '48
  Cranach. Luther and his
    friends 24:63 Je 14 '48
  Luther throwing inkpot at the
    Devil* bw 24:84 F 2 '48
  Luther's study, Paulus church,
    Worms photog bw 17:83 D
    4 '44

Luther's study, Warburg castle
photog bw 24:62 Je 14 '48
Martin Luther bw 34:84 F 23
'53; 39:42 D 26 '55; 41:76 O
29 '54
Lutherbaum engraving, c1800 35:
154 S 21 '53
Luti, Benedetto
Apotheosis of Pope Martin V
bw 18:91 Mr 5 '45
The Lutine Bell, Lloyd's, London
photog bw 8:96 Je 3 '40
Luttrell, Geoffrey
Luttrell coat of arms 40:186
Ap 9 '56
Lutz, Dan
Railroad crossing 11:75 O 27
'41
Luxembourg garden, Paris. Da-
vis, G.R. 19:48 Jy 16 '45
Luxor temple of Amen, Egypt
photog bw 24:79 Ja 19 '48
Luxury, calm, and voluptuous-
ness. Matisse 28:59 Ja 2
'50
Lycurgus plaque, U.S. Capitol
bw 30:74 F 5 '51
Lynch, Thomas, Jr.
Thomas Lynch, Jr. bw 15:9
Jy 5 '43
Lynes, George Platt, photogra-
pher
Marsden Hartley, 1943 bw 32:
84 Je 16 '52
Portraits of writers bw 27:16-
7 O 10 '49
Cadmus. George Platt Lynes
10:48 F 3 '41 port.
Lynes, Russell
Russell Lynes photog bw 26:
99 Ap 11 '49
Lynnewood Hall, Elkins Park,
Pa. photogs bw 17:91-3 Jy
17 '44
Lyon, Caleb
Nahl. Governor Caleb Lyon's
1856 Indian treaty* 36:78
Mr 8 '54
Lyon, Congressman
Congressman Lyon bw 16:56
F 7 '44

Lyon, Mary
Mary Lyon bw 23:90 O 27 '47
Lyre clock, Boston, 1815. Sawin
and Dyer 17:58 S 4 '44
Lyre Players See Musicians and
Musical Instruments--Lyres

M
Ma jolie. Picasso 25:59 O 11 '48
Maar, Dora
Picasso. Dora Maar bw 23:
100 O 13 '47
Macarena Virgin, religious fig-
ure, Seville, 17th century
photogs 33:56-7 Ag 18 '52
MacArthur, Charles
Charles MacArthur photog bw
21:50 O 7 '46
MacArthur, Douglas
Stephens, T. E. General Doug-
las MacArthur, age 70 29:
Cover Ag 28 '50
McBean, Angus, photographer
Surrealist portraits of English
actresses bw 4:4-7 My 16
'38
McBride, Clifford, cartoonist
Napoleon and Uncle Elby bw
17:12-4 D 4 '44
Artist at work photog bw 17:
12-4 D 4 '44 port.
McBride, Katherine
Clemens. Katherine McBride
of Bryn Mawr 23:94 O 27
'47
McBride, Maude Gonne
Maude Gonne McBride photog
bw 2:75 My 24 '37
McClellan, George
General and Mrs. McClellan
photog bw 11:99 N 10 '41
General George McClellan
photog bw 14:76 F 15 '43;
14:6 My 31 '43
McClelland, Nancy, interior de-
signer
Louis XV drawing room
photogs 27:56-7 O 3 '49
Nancy McClelland photog bw
27:55 O 3 '49 port.

McCloskey, Robert
"Blueberries for Sal," illustrations bw 25:69-71 D 27 '48

McCloy, Helen
Helen McCloy photog bw 22:20 Mr 10 '47

McCobb, Paul, furniture designer
Wrought iron mirror photog bw 35:15 D 14 '53

McCombe, Leonard, photographer
Examples of news photographs bw 28:12-4 Ap 10 '50
Startled starling* bw 24:16 My 10 '48
Leonard McCombe photog bw 28:12 Ap 10 '50 port.

McCormick, James
Johnston. The James McCormick family 9:76 D 9 '40

McCoy, John T., Jr.
Air training in the army 14:50-1 My 24 '43
Airplanes of the U.S. navy 9:71-4 O 28 '40

McCoy Family, West Virginia
Portraits and scenes of Hatfield-McCoy feud bw 16:108-16 My 22 '44

McCrady, John
House on the hill 3:40 O 18 '37
Oil refinery, Baton Rouge* 34:80 Ja 5 '53
Small town fire 3:41 O 18 '37
The shooting of Huey Long 6:49 Je 26 '39 bw 21:121 D 9 '46
Swing Low, Sweet Chariot 3:39 O 18 '37
Woman mounting a horse 3:42 O 18 '37
Artist at work photog bw 3:38 O 18 '37 port.
Self-portrait 3:40 O 18 '37 port.

McCreery, James
Products of Missouri mural, Post Office, Monett, Mo. 10:45 Ja 27 '41

McCubbin, Frederick
Down on his luck bw 12:79 F 9 '42

McCully, E. Walbridge

E. Walbridge McCully bw 22:21 Mr 10 '47

MacDonald, Betty
Betty MacDonald; family; home photogs bw 20:134-7 Mr 18 '46

Macdonald, John A.
John Macdonald photog bw 9:115 S 9 '40

MacDonald, Pirie, photographer
Portraits of famous men bw 13:12-3 Ja 11 '43
Pirie MacDonald photog bw 14:15 Ja 11 '43 port.

Mace See also Weapons--Mace
Mace, Canadian Parliament photog bw 9:103 S 9 '40
Mace, House of Commons, England photog 2:39 Mr 15 '37 bw 16:81 My 22 '41
Silver gilt mace, House of Lords, England photog bw 31:65 N 19 '51

McGee, Thomas
Florence McGee, the artist's wife 10:47 F 3 '41

McGlynn, Thomas
Artist at work photog bw 2:30 F 22 '37 port.

McGuffey, William Holmes
McGuffey Reader, pages from bw 13:90-2 Jy 20 '42

McGuire, Dorothy Hackett (Mrs. John Swope)
Clemens. Dorothy McGuire 21:57 S 2 '46

Machine tools. drawings
Artzybasheff 34:59-61 Ja 5 '53

Machinery See also Industrial Themes
Atom-smasher 3:37 Ag 30 '37
Duchamp. Chocolate grinder drawing 32:103 Ap 28 '52
Duchamp. Coffee grinder drawing 32:103 Ap 28 '52
Osver. Cranes 30:38 Ja 15 '51
Sheeler. Upper deck 5:44 Ag 8 '38
Sterne. Mechanical inventions

31:51 Ag 27 '51
Machu Picchu, Cuzco, Peru
    Inca ruins photog 25:55 Ag 2
        '48 bw 19:101-9 S 24 '45
McIntire, Samuel, wood carver
    Arms of Massachusetts 38:63
        My 30 '55
    Cornucopia 38:63 My 30 '55
    Fruit basket 38:63 My 30 '55
    Pierce house, decoration 38:
        63 My 30 '55
        Chippendale staircase 38:
        62 My 30 '55
    U.S. eagle 38:63 My 30 '55
McIntosh, Millicent Carey
    Clemens. Millicent Cary Mc-
        Intosh of Barnard 23:92 O
        27 '47
    Rand. Mrs. Millicent McIn-
        tosh 10:48 F 3 '41
McIntyre, Peter
    Disabled landing craft* 28:
        57 F 6 '50
MacIver, Loren
    Floating palaces 33:94-5 S 15
        '52
    Hobo clown (Emmett Kelly) 23:
        43 Jy 21 '47
McKay, Claude
    Claude McKay photog bw 5:58
        O 3 '38
McKay, Donald
    Donald McKay, 1854 photog bw
        39:107 O 17 '55
McKean, Thomas
    Thomas McKean bw 15:9 Jy
        5 '43
MacKenzie, William Lyon
    MacKenzie of Canada bw 9:114
        S 9 '40
Mackey, John W.
    Borglum. John Mackey statue
        bw 12:110 My 11 '42
McKim, Mead and White, archts.
    American shingle style house,
        Bristol, R.I. photog 40:98
        My 5 '56
    Madison Square Garden photog
        bw 5:29 O 31 '38
    McKim, Mead and White group
        photog bw 5:29 O 31 '38 port.

McKinley, William
    William McKinley statue bw
        23:38 Ag 11 '47
McLaughlin Gardens, Quebec
    photog bw 9:109 S 9 '40
MacLeish, Archibald
    Archibald MacLeish, at grad-
        uation from college, 1915
        photog bw 14:7 Ap 26 '43
McMillan, John
    Night services led by John
        McMillan, priest bw 39:77
        D 26 '55
Macnamara, Francis
    Brockhurst. Francis Macna-
        mara 10:48 F 3 '41
McPherson, Aimee Semple
    Evangelist McPherson photog
        bw 28:67 Ja 2 '50
McReynolds, James C.
    Poor. Gold case mural
        2:36 Ja 4 '37
McSorley's bar. Bouche 10:73 Ap
        14 '41
McSorley's bar. Sloan 7:46 D 11
        '39; 26:85 F 21 '49
McWilliams, F. F.
    Kneeling figure sculpture 25:
        101 S 27 '48
Madame X (Madame Gautreau).
        Sargent 36:96 My 17 '54
        bw 6:54 Mr 20 '39
La Madeleine, Paris. Davis, G.
        R. 19:46 Jy 16 '45
Madero, Francisco Indalegio
    President Madero of Mexico
        photog bw 4:53 Ap 11 '38
Madison, Dolly
    Peale, R. Dolly Madison 41:
        158-9 D 24 '56
Madison, James
    James Madison 16:54 Mr 6
        '44; 31:98 N 5 '51; 39:58 Jy
        4 '55 bw 16:47 Ja 17 '44;
        19:84 S 24 '45
Madison Square Garden. photog
        bw McKim, Mead and
        White, archts. 5:29 O 31
        '38
Madison (Wisconsin) from the
        air. Colescott 32:70 Ja 14 '52

Madonna See Mary, Virgin

Madonna. woodcarving bw Taylor 9:55 Ag 12 '40

Madonna della sedia. bw Raphael 6:31 F 13 '39

Madonna of Port Lligat. Dali 29: 48 D 18 '50

Madonna of the chair (Madonna della sedia). bw Raphael 6: 31 F 13 '39

Madonna of the pinks. Raphael 6: 61 My 22 '39

Madonna of the rocks. Leonardo da Vinci 7:54 N 20 '39

Madonna with St. John and St. Catherine. bw Previtali 6: 32 F 13 '39

Maeck, Philippe
  Shanties, Rïo de Janeiro 36: 84 My 31 '54

Magi See also Jesus Christ-- Adoration
  Lewandowski, Three kings bw 27:56 D 29 '49

Magin David (star of David), sym- bol of Judaism 38:57 F 7 '55

Magic Lantern Slides
  Beale. Illustrations from stories, 1875-1900 bw 8:4- 6 Ja 8 '40

Magna Carta
  Castellon. Magna Carta 30:92- 3 Ma 12 '51
  Signing of the Magna Carta, 1215 bw 22:98 Mr 24 '47

Magritte, Rene
  The eye 1:25 D 14 '46 bw 19: 64-5 S 24 '45
  Mental calculus 1:26 D 14 '36

Mahal, Mumtaz
  Mumtax Mahal's marriage cup, silver and enamel, France, 17th century 25:129 D 6 '48
  Taj Mahal, Agra, tomb of Mumtaz aerial photog bw 16: 94 Je 5 '44

Mahmal, pyramid-shaped litter photog bw 2:60-1 Mr 15 '37

Maid of mist. De Grailly 26:79 Je 6 '49

Maid of Sargossa bw 14:6 Ja 4 '43

The maids of honor. Velazquez 7:57 N 20 '39; 31:61 O 1 '51

Mailbox art. bw cartoon Emett 37:47 Jy 5 '54

Maillol, Aristide
  Drawing of a girl bw 2:50 Ja 4 '37 (drawing)
        Sculptures
  Action in chains bw 8:108 Ap 15 '40
  Applegirl bw 2:51 Ja 4 '37
  Flora bw 8:108 Ap 15 '40
  Garden piece bw 2:51 Ja 4 '37
  Head of a woman, bronze 38: 110 My23 '55
  Kneeling figure bw 7:37 Jy 31 '39
  Little bather standing bw 8: 106 Ap 15 '40
  The Mediterranean bw 8:106- 7 Ap 15 '40
  The three graces 25:101 S 27 '48
  Torso of a girl bw 8:109 Ap 15 '40
  Torso of a young woman bw 8: 107 Ap 15 '40
  Venus with a necklace bw 7: 63 S 18 '39
  Woman bw 2:51 Ja 4 '37
  "Daphnis and Chloe," illustra- tions bw 8:108 Ap 15 '40 (wood engravings)
  Virgil's "Georgics," illustra- tions bw 8:109 Ap 15 '40 (wood engravings)
  Aristido Maillol photog bw 2: 50 Ja 4 '37; 8:106 Ap 15 '40 port.

Main street. mural panel Cadmus 2:45 Mr 29 '37 detail 21:74 N 25 '46

Maine
  Hartley. Paintings of Maine 32:85-9 Je 9 '52
  Monhegan Island--scenery in paintings of famous Ameri- can artists 29:70-3 Ag 21 '50
  Pittman. An evening in Maine 18:70 F 19 '45

"Maine" (ship)

Chapman. U.S.S. Maine 9:49
O 28 '40

Maine swimming hole. bw Peirce,
W. 18:44 Ja 1 '45

Maine trotting race. Peirce, W.
3:34 Ag 30 '37

The maja clothed. Goya 29:107 S
11 '50

The maja nude. Goya 29:106-7 S
11 '50

Majestic tenement. bw Ozver 22:
78 F 17 '47

Majolica pottery 37:66-7 Ag 9 '54

Major disturbance. Ernst 32:59
Ja 21 '52

Majors, Bob
Practice landing 13:32 Jy 6 '42

Makara, fish of Hinduism 38:68
F 7 '55

Making music. bw Karfiol 9:68 O
14 '40

Making-up. Davis, G. R. 16:77 Mr
20 '44

Malahide castle, Ireland photog
bw 29:101 D 4 '50

Malaprop, Mrs.
Mrs. Malaprop, illustration
for Sheridan's "The Rivals"
bw 25:109 S 13 '48

Maldarelli, Oronzio, sculpture
The caress bw 22:140 Mr 24
'47

Gemini bw 22:139 Mr 24 '47

Goat bw 22:138 Mr 24 '47

Long-horn Bill bw 22:139 Mr
24 '47

Mother and child bw 22:137 Mr
24 '47

Rumba dancer bw 22:138 Mr
24 '47

"Male Call." cartoon bw Caniff
14:10-2 Mr 1 '43

Malinche in Cortes and the Indians bw 21:46 D 16 '46

The Mall, London, 18th century
25:100 S 13 '48

Mallards in sunshine. Scott 1:41
D 21 '36

Mallards settling. Scott 1:43 D
21 '36

Mallarme, Stephane

Vuillard. House of Mallarme
37:77 N 1 '54

Malmsten, Carl, furniture designer
Swedish modern furniture photog bw 7:45 Jy 31 '39

Malraux, Andre
Karsh. Andre Malraux photog
bw 37:129 O 4 '54

Malskat, Lothar
Forged frescoes, Lubeck
church bw 34:49-50 Ja 12
'53

Mama, papa is wounded. Tanguy
19:65 S 24 '45

Mammoth, Magdalenian stone
carving 39:86 N 7 '55

Man, Improved Design for
Artzybasheff. Machine tools
34:59-61 Ja 5 '53
Loewy. Redesigned humans bw
25:16-7 D 13 '48

Man, Cro-Magnon cave painting,
Montignac, France bw 22:
64 F 24 '47

Man and his passions. sculpture
bw Santiano 11:147 O 13
'41

The man and the mannequin
(Portrait of Paul Cezanne).
Degas 29:88 N 27 '50

Man at fountain. Sharrer 28:88
Mr 20 '50

Man at gathering. woodcarving
bw Steig 6:36 Ap 10 '39

Man in a green coat. Soutine 33:
93 O 27 '52

"The Man in Lower Ten," illustrations. bw Christy 20:
56 F 25 '46

Man on a water buffalo returning
intoxicated from a village
feast, 12th century. Li
T'ang, attributed 15:65 O
11 '43

The man with a hoe. Millet, J.
F. 9:46-7 Jy 29 '40

Man with a wine glass. Velazquez 7:34 Jy 31 '39

Man with an ax. Gauguin 37:127
D 13 '54

Man with beer keg. Hals 6:39 My
    29 '39
Man with a book. sculpture bw
    Stea 4:62 Ap 25 '38
Man with glove. Titian 11:83 D 1
    '41
Man with golden helmet. bw
    Rembrandt 19:24 D 31 '45
Man with pink. Massys 4:23 Ap
    11 '38
Man with pink. bw Van Eyck, J.
    19:25 D 31 '45
"The Man Without a Country,"
    illustrations. Wilson, E. A.
    18:58 Ap 23 '45
Manana Island. Harsanyi 29:73
    Ag 21 '50
Manayunk. Stuempfig 25:64 O 11
    '48
Manca, Albino
    Nejla Ates, nude statue bw
    38:129 Je 6 '55
Mandel, Howard
    Artist at work photog bw 21:
    105 Jy 8 '46 port.
Mandolin Players See Musicians
    and Musical Instruments--
    Mandolins
Mandrill and maidens. Reinhardt
    32:89 Mr 24 '52
Manet, Edouard
    Boy blowing bubbles 29:89 N
    27 '50
    In the wintergarden bw 24:68
    Mr 22 '48
    The Lange boy bw 6:58 Mr 27
    '39
    Luncheon on the grass bw 12:
    44 Mr 9 '42
    Mme. Michel Levy 5:25 O 10
    '38
    Olympia 35:58 Ag 17 '53; 41:
    105 O 22 '56
    Reclining young woman 40:71
    My 28 '56
    Edouard Manet photog bw 5:
    24 O 10 '38 port.
Mangravite, Peppino
    Peppino Mangravite. in group
    photog 29:172-3 O 16 '50
    port.

Manhattan. Dufy 30:66 Ja 22 '51
Manhattan bridge loop. Hopper
    28:102-3 Ap 17 '50
Manhattan No. 2. watercolor
    Marin 29:65 Jy 10 '50
The manikin (El pelele). tapestry
    cartoon Goya 40:73 My 28
    '56
Mankind. sculpture bw Noguchi
    21:13 N 11 '46
Manley, Marion I, architect
    Weed and Manley. University
    of Miami, functional mod-
    ern building, Florida
    photogs bw 25:72-3 D 27
    '48
Mann, Erika
    Erika Mann bw 3:80 Ag 9 '37
Mann, Thomas
    Thomas Mann; family; home
    photogs 6:56-9 Ap 17 '39
Manners, William
    William Manners photog bw
    22:20 Mr 10 '47
Manolete photogs bw 20:105-8
    Ap 29 '46
Man's existence. sculpture bw
    Noguchi 21:13 N 11 '46
Mansfield, Josie
    Josie Mansfield photog bw 3:
    42 Ag 2 '37
Manship, Paul, sculptor
    Dancer and gazelles bw 7:37
    Jy 31 '39
    Day bw 4:15 Ja 31 '38
    Night bw 4:14 Ja 31 '38
    Sundial: three fates under tree
    of life bw 4:14 Ja 31 '38
    Soldiers* bw 32:77 Ja 7 '52
    Artist and his work photog
    bw 4:14-5 Ja 31 '38 port.
Mantegna, Andrea
    The crucifixion 35:57 Ag 17
    '53
    The holy family 40:106 My 7
    '56
    Judith and Holofernes 4:28
    Mr 21 '38 bw 26:160 Ap
    11 '49
    Andrea Mantegna bw 4:26
    Mr 21 '38 port.

Manticore See Animals,
Imaginary--Manticore
Manuel, Jorge
Members of El Greco's family
bw 28:96 Ap 24 '50
Manufacturers Trust Company,
Fifth Avenue Office, New
York City. Skidmore, Ow-
ings and Merrill, archts.
photog 37:62 O 25 '54
Manuscript Cover
The Four Gospels, gold and
jewelled, St. Gall, Switzer-
land, 9th century 18:57 Ap
2 '45
Manuscripts See also Illumina-
tions
Bible of St. Paul's Outside the
Walls 34:79 F 23 '53
"Book of Hours," 15th century
40:178 Ap 9 '56
Canterbury Gospels bw 18:80
My 14 '45
Canterbury Psalter 34:80 F
23 '53
Chaucer's "Canterbury Tales,"
Flemish, 15th century bw
22:75 Ap 7 '47
Codex Paulinus 34:77, 88 F 23
'53
Dead Sea scrolls bw 34:95-6
Je 15 '53; 41:41 Jy 23 '56
First Bible of Charles the
Bald 34:81 F 23 '53
Giant Bible of Admont 34:78,
82 F 23 '53
Gospel Book of Charlemagne
34:87 F 23 '53
Gospel Book of Johannes von
Troppau 34:86 F 23 '53
Gospel of Matthew, German,
13th century 22:82 Ap 7 '47
Historia Anglorum, 13th cen-
tury 40:98 Mr 26 '56
Isaiah scroll bw 34:83 F 23 '53
Missal of Ferdinand, Italy,
15th century 32:87 Ap 14 '52
Morgan Library exhibit of manu-
scripts: "The Written Word"
18:57-62 Ap 2 '45
Newton collection of rare books

and manuscripts bw 10:86-
8 Je 9 '41
Pietro de Crescenzi. "Treat-
ise on Rural Economy,"
Flemish, 15th century 22:
78-80 My 26 '47
Psalter of Ingeborg 34:78, 85
F 23 '53
Richard II's Bible 34:80 F 23
'53
Rustam. Persian manuscript
20:91 Je 24 '46
Tatsuta. Manuscript on horn
34:102 F 23 '53
"Tres Riches Heures du Duc
de Berri" 24:38-50 Ja 5
'48
Virgil's "Aeneid," from Ab-
bey of St. Denis, 5th cen-
tury 32:86 Ap 14 '52
Manwaring, H. N.
City silhouette from a balcony
at headquarters, London
Fire Forces 12:40 Mr 2 '42
Manzu, Giacomo, sculptor
Cardinal bw 41:102 Ag 6 '56
Crouching girl bw 41:102-3
Ag 6 '56
Dancers bw 41:101 Ag 6 '56
Artist and his work photog bw
41:102-3 Ag 6 '56 port.
Maori Art See Art, South Seas
Maps
Brazil, French map, 1547 24:
79 Mr 22 '48
Canada, French map, 1547
24:78 Mr 22 '48
Caribbean area, French map,
1547 24:79 Mr 22 '48
Castillo del Oro, Venezuela,
1529 bw 33:32 D 29 '52
Covarrubias. Bali 3:50 S 27
'37
Covarrubias. Trust Territory
of the Pacific 26:96 Ap 25
'49
Drake's voyage, 1585 18:64
My 21 '45
Gilbert. Polar map, 1582
18:61 My 21 '45

Maps (cont.)
  Strabo. Holyland 20:53 Ap 1
    '46
  Venice, Italy, 1500 bw 23:48-
    9 Ag 4 '47
  Waldseemuller. Atlantic
    Ocean, 1513 bw 18:61 My
    21 '45

  America
  Covarrubias. Florida 20:52-
    3 F 4 '46
  Kentucky in "The Adventures
    of Col. Daniel Boone" bw
    18:66 My 21 '45
  Le Moyne de Morgues. Skull
    creek, near Hiltonhead,
    S.C., 1564 bw 22:80 Mr 10
    '47
  New England, 1634 bw 18:67
    My 21 '45
  New World, 1507 37:101 O 11
    '54
  Pennsylvania in "History of
    Pennsylvania," 1698 bw 18:
    66 My 21 '45
  St. Augustine, Florida, first
    city map 18:64 My21 '45
  United States of America,
    London, 1783 6:43 Je 5 '39
  Virginia in "Capt. John
    Smith's Adventures" 18:67
    My 21 '45

  France
  Palloy. Plan of the Bastille,
    1789 3:35 Jy 5 '37
  Paris, earliest bw 31:76 Jy 30
    '51
  Paris, medieval, 1548 bw 31:
    76 Jy 30 '51

  World
  De Haldingham. Hereford map
    of the world, c1280 bw 22:
    85 Ap 7 '47
  First maps of round world:
    Ptolemy, 150 A.D., to Hon-.
    dius Atlas, 1641 bw 13:58-9
    Ag 3 '42
  Fuller. Dymaxion world 14:41-

    55 Mr 1 '43
  Ptolemy, 150 bw 13:58 Ag 3
    '42
  Ribero, 1529 bw 13:59 Ag 3
    '42
  Rosello, 1532 18:62-3 My 21
    '45
  Waldseemuller. World map,
    1507 bw 13:58-9 Ag 3 '42
  World map, 1527 bw 18:65 My
    21 '45
  Wright-Molyneux. World map,
    mercator projection, 1600
    bw 18:65 My 21 '45
Marca-Relli, Corrado
  Seated man, * collage 39:112
    S 12 '55
March of Time. cartoon bw
    Sapajou 28:65 F 27 '50
March sun. Poor 12:61 Je 15 '42
Marchenilla castle, Spain photog
    33:53 Ag 18 '52
Marching into Concord. engrav-
    ing Doolittle 29:41 Jy 3 '50
Marcier, Emeric
  Blind leading the blind 36:83
    My 31 '54
Marcks, Gerhard, sculptor
  Calling crane bw 28:71 F 6
    '50
  Flute player 28:71 F 6 '50
  Girl reading bw 28:71 F 6 '50
  Girl swimmer bw 28:71 F 6
    '50
  Grandmother and grandchild
    28:71 F 6 '50
  Melusine II 28:71 F 6 '50
  Statues, Catherine church, Lu-
    beck bw 28:72 F 6 '50
  Gerhard Marcks photog bw 28:
    72 F 6 '50 port.
Marco Polo
  Travels of Marco Polo,
    manuscript, 15th century
    bw 23:48-9 Ag 4 '47
Marcus, Alan D.
  Dam* 24:73 Ap 5 '48
Marcy, William
  William Marcy 19:86 S 24
    '45
Margaret, Saint

Lippi, Filippino. Holy family
with St. Margaret and St.
John 1:45 D 28 '36
Margarita Theresa, daughter of
Philip IV, King of Spain
Velazquez. Infanta Margarita
Theresa 27:72 O 24 '49
Margherita, Consort of Humbert
I, King of Italy
Margherita and son photogs bw
15:104 Ag 23 '43
Queen Margherita bw 15:110
Ag 23 '43
Margulies, Judith
Epstein. Judith Margulies
sculpture bw 33:66 N 3 '52
Marguelies, Walter, interior de-
signer
Plastic furniture and fabrics
photog 33:104-5 S 8 '52
Designer Marguelies at home
photog 33:104-5 S 8 '52 port.
Marguerite, the artist's daughter,
age 15. Matisse 31:111 N
26 '51
Maria Alexandrovna, Consort of
Alexander II, Czar of Russia
Maria Alexandrovna miniature
38:60 Ja 31 '55
Maria Luisa, Queen of Spain
Goya. Maria Luisa, Queen of
Spain 31:63 O 1 '51
Mariana See Foster, Marian
Marie Antoinett, Queen of France
bw 31:78 Jy 30 '51
Marie Claude's birthday. bw
Kroll 10:70 Ap 14 '41
Marienburg castle, Germany
photogs bw 19:116 N 19 '45
Marin, John, watercolorist
Boat and sea 29:63 Jy 10 '50
Corn dance 29:64 Jy 10 '50
In the ring 29:64 Jy 10 '50
Manhattan No. 2 29:65 Jy 10
'50
New England village 29:63 Jy
10 '50
Chartre cathedral bw 29:62 Jy
10 '50 (etching)
Artist and his work photog bw
29:62 Jy 10 '50 port.

Lachaise. Head of John Mar-
in, bronze 38:110 My 23
'55 port.
"Marin-Marie," French World
War artist
Battle at Oran* 26:50 Mr 7 '49
British bombardment at Da-
kar* 26:50 Mr 7 '49
Marine training base. Hurd 11:
61 Jy 7 '41
Marine Paintings See Seascapes
Marini, Marino, sculptor
Dancer bw 22:99 My 22 '50
Head bw 22:99 My 22 '50
Horse and rider bw 22:102 My
22 '50
Kneeling girl bw 22:102 My 22
'50
Three graces bw 22:99 My 22
'50
Horse and rider 33:85 Jy 14
'52 (lithograph)
Marino Marini and wife photog
bw 28:99 My 22 '50 port.
Marion, Francis
General Marion inviting a
British officer to dinner*
13:59 Jy 6 '42
Marionette. Romero 4:29 Mr 14
'38
Marionettes See Dolls and Pup-
pets
Mark, Saint
Legend of St. Mark mosaics,
St. Mark's, Venice 35:34 D
28 '53
St. Mark, illumination, Gos-
pel Book of Charlemagne
34:87 F 23 '53
Tintoretto. Abduction of body
of St. Mark 23:51 Ag 4 '47
Markelius, Sven, architect
Kollektivhuset, Stockholm
photog bw 22:34 My 26 '47
Sven Markelius photog bw 22:
34 My 26 '47 port.
Marketgoers, Venezuela. Poleo
36:79 My 31 '54
Markets See Shops and Markets
Marlborough, Sara, Duchess of
Duchess of Marlborough 24:

Marlborough, Sarah (cont.)
    35 Ap 19 '48 bw 25:12 S 13
    '48
Marlborough, Caroline, Fourth
    Duchess of
    Reynolds. Caroline, Duchess
    of Marlborough 24:36 Ap
    19 '48
Marlborough, Duke of
    Duke of Marlborough 24:34
    Ap 19 '48; 41:171 N 19 '56
    Duke of Marlborough in Battle
    of Blenheim tapestry,
    Brussels 24:34-5 Ap 19 '48
Marlborough, Duke of, 1704
    Churchill, J. Marlborough
    pavilion mural, Chartwell,
    Kent, England 35:81 N 23
    '53
Marlborough coat of arms 24:34
    Ap 19 '48
Marquand, John P.
    J. P. Marquand photogs bw
    10:63 Mr 24 '41; 17:65-73 Jy
    31 '44
    "Wickford Point" locale 25:42
    N 8 '48
Marquand rug, Persia, 16th cen-
    tury 31:68-9 S 3 '51
Marrakesh. Churchill 29:96 N 6
    '50
Marriage a la mode, six scenes.
    Hogarth. 21:80 D 16 '46
Marriage of the Virgin See
    Mary, Virgin--Marriage
Mars See Mythological Themes--
    Mars
Marsh, Reginald
    Airhole 6:26 Ja 9 '39
    The Bowery 40:84 F 6 '56
    Brazil scenes, World War II
    18:64-5 Ap 30 '45
    Cheesecake 6:25 Je 9 '39
    The death of Dillinger 8:70 Mr
    11 '40 bw 37:48 Jy 26 '54
    High yaller 2:34 F 1 '37 bw 10:
    70 Ap 14 '41
    Human pool tables 6:26 Ja 9
    '39
    Jelke trial bw 37:48 Jy 26 '54
    Mink and Mannequin 40:83 F

6 '56
    Monday night at Met 40:82 F
    6 '56
    Pip and Flip 40:80-1 F 6 '56
    Sorting mail mural 2:33 Ja 4
    '37
    The steeplechase 40:83 F 6
    '56
    Swimming in the Hudson 6:25
    Ja 9 '39
    Transfer of mail from liner
    to tugboat mural 2:33 Ja 4
    '37
    Twenty cent movie 12:75 Ap
    20 '42; 21:77 N 25 '46
    Vaudeville teams, from "New
    York Daily News" cartoon
    bw 40:86 F 6 '56
    The village bw 5:30 O 31 '38
    Walkowitz bw 16:79 F 21 '44
    Fire, drawn at age 7 bw 40:
    86 F 6 '56 (drawing)
    Television backstage bw 37:
    47 Jy 26 '54
    Artist at work photog bw 2:
    32 Ja 4 '37; 6:24 Ja 9 '39;
    40:85, 88 F 6 '56 port.
    Artist's family, father and
    step-mother photog bw 40:
    88 F 6 '56 port.
    Reginald Marsh photog bw 2:
    32 Ja 4 '37; 37:48 Jy 26
    '54 in group 29:172-3 O 16
    '50 port.
    Self-portrait, age 35 40:81 F
    6 '56 port.
Marshall, George C.
    General Marshall, "Time"
    cover portrait 17:60 D 11
    '44
Marshall, James
    James Marshall photog bw 24:
    44 F 2 '48
Marshall, John
    Chief Justice Marshall 39:64
    Jy 4 '55 bw 18:87 Ja 22 '45;
    23:118 N 4 '46; 39:57 D
    26 '55
Marshall, Thomas
    Thomas Marshall photog bw
    9:9 Ag 5 '40

Marta. Schnakenberg 10:48 F 3
'41

Martel, Charles
Charles Martel bw 22:70 Ap 7
'47

Martha and Mary. sculpture bw
Edmondson 3:79 N 1 '37

The Martha McKeen of Wellfleet.
Hopper 23:70 Jy 14 '47

Martin, Saint
El Greco. St. Martin and the
beggar 33:91 O 27 '52

Martin, David Stone
Flectrification mural, Post
Office, Lenoir City, Tenn.
10:44 Ja 27 '41

Martin, Fletcher
Celebration 9:92 N 11 '40
Charles Laughton as Captain
Kidd 19:62 N 5 '45
Home from the sea 9:91 N 11
'40
July 4th, 5th and 6th 9:91 N
11 '40 bw 15:13 O 25 '43
A lad from the fleet 8:67 My
27 '40
Lullaby 16:76 Ap 24 '44
North Africa: scenes and por-
traits of World War II in
Algeria and Tunisia 15:60-
7 D 27 '43
Service club 11:62 Jy 7 '41
Sylvia Sidney 19:61 S 10 '45
Tomorrow and tomorrow 9:
92 N 11 '40
Trouble in Frisco 9:92 N 11
'40 bw 5:30 O 31 '38
Yvonne de Carlo 19:65 D 24
'45
St. Lo battleground, Normandy
bw 17:22-3 Ag 7 '44 (draw-
ing)
Sketchbook: North Africa in
World War II 15:82-3 D 27
'43 (drawings)
Artist and his work photog bw
9:90 N 11 '40; 15:13 O 25
'43 port.
Fletcher Martin photog bw 11:
60 Jy 7 '41; 15:84 D 27 '43
in uniform 14:8 Je 28 '43

port.
Self-portraits bw 15:12 O 25
'43 port.

Martin, John
Red Sea return* bw 6:52-3 F
20 '39
Parting of the Red Sea* bw 38:
98-9 Je 13 '55 (engraving)

Martin, Luther
Luther Martin 39:62 Jy 4 '55

Martin, Sarah Catherine
"Old Mother Hubbard," illustrations for her manu-
script bw 20:104-5 Ap 15
'46

Martin V, Pope
Luti. Apotheosis of Pope
Martin V bw 18:91 Mr 5 '45

Martinez, Ricardo
The astronomer 20:60 Je 3 '46

Martins, Maria, sculptor
Je veux la tete de Jokanaan bw
11:157 D 8 '41
Artist and her work photog bw
11:154-7 D 8 '41 port.

Martins da Silveira, Elisa
Procession, church festival,
Brazil 36:82-3 My 31 '54

Martorell, Bernardo
St. George killing the dragon
33:91 O 27 '52

Marx, Karl
Karl Marx photog bw 25:63 O
18 '48; 25:91 N 22 '48

Marx collection of modern European art 33:92-3 O 27 '52

Mary. Henri 12:60 Je 15 '42

Mary, Virgin See also Flight
into Egypt; Holy Family;
Jesus Christ--Nativity
Cousino. Virgin Mary bw 31:
163 N 19 '51
Dali. Madonna of Port Lligat
29:48 D 18 '50
Giotto. Life of the Virgin fres-
co, Arena chapel 25:Cover,
34-57 D 27 '48
Houtondji, Mary meeting
Jesus sculpture bw 29:63
S 4 '50

Macarena Virgin, religious fig-
ure, Seville, 17th century
photogs 33:56-7 Ag 18 '52
Our lady of risk sculpture bw,
Cistercian abbey of Boquen,
Brittany 28:80 Jy 10 '50
Our lady of sorrows, santo
woodcarving bw 24:60 My
17 '48
Previtali. Madonna with St.
John and St. Catherine bw
6:32 F 13 '39
Taylor. Madonna woodcarving
bw 9:55 Ag 12 '40
Van Eyck brothers. Virgin
Mary 26:64 Ap 18 '49
Virgin mother sculpture bw,
Little Company of Mary
Hospital; Chicago 39:67 D
26 '55
Weeping Virgin woodcarving
bw, German, 15th century
15:64 S 20 '43

Annunciation
Angelico. The annunciation 21:
52 D 23 '46
Bouts. The annunciation 1:45
D 28 '36
Duccio. The annunciation 1:46
D 28 '36
Ford. Annunciation 5:29 D 25
'38
Giotto. Annunciation 25:40 D
27 '48
Grunewald. Annunciation, in
Isenheim altarpiece 30:82
Mr 26 '51
James, M. Annunciation
sculpture bw 30:146 My 21
'51
Lu Hung Nien. The annuncia-
tion 11:42 D 22 '41 bw 29:
66 S 4 '50
Tintoretto. Annunciation 31:
30-1 D 24 '51
Van Eyck, J. The annunciation
bw 13:42 D 28 '42

Appearances
Ford. The vision at dusk 17:

44 D 25 '44
Vision of La Salette 17:43 D
25 '44

Assumption
El Greco. The assumption of
the Virgin 11:54 S 8 '41;
28:90 Ap 24 '50; 29:50 O
30 '50
Lorenzo Monaco, precursor
of. Assumption of the Virgin 1:48 D 28 '36

Coronation
Conrad von Soest. Coronation
of the Virgin 1:48 D 28 '36

Madonna and Child
Bellini. Madonna and Child
37:64 Ag 9 '54 bw 24:67 Ja
26 '48
Cimabue. Madonna with angels
35:56 Ag 17 '53
Crivelli. Madonna and Child
2:42 Je 28 '37
Durer. Madonna and Child
with St. Anne 5:40 Jy 11 '38
El Greco. The Virgin with
Santa Ines and Santa Tecla
7:26 D 25 '39
Ford. Madonna and Child 17:
Cover D 25 '44
Gauguin. Ia orana Maria (We
greet you, Mary) 7:26 D
25 '39 bw 13:51 S 14 '42
Giorgione. Castelfranco Ma-
donna 39:166 O 24 '55
Giotto. Madonna and Child bw
13:47 D 28 '42
Leonardo da Vinci. Madonna
of the rocks 7:54 N 20 '39
Lippi, Fra Filippo. Madonna
and Child 13:46 D 28 '42
Lippi, Fra Filippo. Madonna
and Child with two angels
29:108 S 11 '50
Madonna and Child, Mada-
gascar artist bw 29:66 S
4 '50
Madonna and Child mosaic,
St. Mark's, Venice 35:

Cover D 28 '53

Madonna and Child, tabernacle, gold jewelled and enamelled, 1403 33:32 D 29 '52

Madonna and Child, woodcarving, France, 13th century 22:80 Ap 7 '47

Matisse. Madonna and Child drawing bw 36:113 Ap 26 '54

Raphael. Alba Madonna 13: Cover D 28 '42

Raphael. La belle jardiniere bw 19:50 Jy 30 '45

Raphael Madonna and Child (Small Cowper Madonna) 4: 27 Mr 21 '38

Raphael. Madonna and Child and two saints bw 19:24 D 31 '45

Raphael. Madonna of the chair bw 6:31 F 13 '39

Raphael. Madonna of the pinks 6:61 My 22 '39

Raphael. Sistine Madonna 40: 113 My 7 '56

Rouault. Madonna and Child, Miserere etching bw 34:56 F 2 '53

Sarto. The Virgin and Child with St. John 41:72 D 10 '56

Signorelli. Madonna and Child with saints 35:154 N 16 '53

Tintoretto. Madonna and Child bw 24:68 Ja 26 '48

Van Eyck, J. Madonna and Child with saint and angel 40:108-9 My 7 '56

Virgin and Child mosaic, Santa Sophia 29:56-7 D 25 '50

Virgin and Child sculpture, Spain, 13th century 4:29 F 21 '38

Virgin and Child stained glass, Chartre cathedral 22:72 Ap 7 '47

Marriage

Giotto. Marriage of the Virgin 25:39 D 27 '48

Lorenzo da Viterbo. The mar-
riage of the Virgin fresco bw 21:103 O 28 '46

Nativity

Giotto. Birth of Mary 25:39 D 27 '48

Pieta See Jesus Christ-- Pieta

Presentation in the Temple

Cima. Presentation of Mary 40:107 My 7 '56

Mary, Magdalene, Saint

El Greco. The penitent Magdalene 7:55 O 9 '39 bw 6: 58 Mr 27 '39

Ryder. Christ appearing to Mary 30:88 F 26 '51

Wesley. Mary Magdalene bw 29:63 S 4 '50

Mary, Consort of George V, King of England

Needlepoint rug, 1948 28:95 My 8 '50

Dick. Queen Mary, tomb effigy, Windsor Castle bw 36:44 F 8 '54 port.

Llewellyn. Queen Mary, coronation portrait 28:67 My 29 '50 port.

Mary, Queen of England photog bw 23:72 O 20 '47

Mary I, Queen of England ("Bloody Mary")

Eworth. Philip and Mary bw 41:104 O 29 '56

Mary I bw 32:24 F 18 '52

Mary II, Queen of England bw 32: 24 F 18 '52

Mary Stuart, Queen of Scots

Execution of Mary Stuart, Queen of Scots, Fotheringay castle* bw 41:150-1 N 5 '56

Francis II, King of France and his queen, Mary Stuart* bw 41:149 N 5 '56

Mary, Queen of Scots, age 25, and her son 41:153 N 5 '56

Wilkie. Preaching of John Knox 24:66 Je 14 '48

Maryland hunt. Flannery 5:73 D
    12 '38
Masaccio
    The tribute money fresco,
        Brancacci chapel, Church of
        the Carmine, Florence 39:
        22-3 D 26 '55
Masaryk, Thomas Garrigue
    Thomas Masaryk--portraits,
        statue, home bw 3:100-1 S
        27 '37
Masefield, John
    Macdonald. John Masefield,
        1933 photog bw 14:12 Ja 11
        '43
Masha See Stern, Marie
Masks
    African Baluba funeral mask
        bw 33:124 S 8 '52
    African Serufo animal mask,
        Ivory Coast bw 33:118-9 S
        8 '52
    Aztec mosaic mask of Quetz-
        alcoatl, c1519 bw 24:84 Mr
        22 '48
    Brackman. Still life with mask
        8:60 F 5 '40
    Cellini. Gold mask, on salt
        cellar, c1540 bw 31:19 S
        24 '51
    Egyptian girl, Middle Kingdom
        41:109 N 26 '56
    Egyptian mummy mask of
        Tutankhamen, inlaid gold
        24:81 Ja 19 '48
    Greek masks, Theater of Di-
        onysus, Athens photog bw
        18:55 Ja 1 '45
    Inca gold mask 36:102-3 Ap 12
        '54
    Japanese black-nosed demon
        with scaly monsters in hair
        31:68 D 31 '51
    Japanese Gigaku mask, 8th
        century 30:71 My 28 '51
    Japanese masked god of war,
        Hachiman 17:28 N 27 '44
    Japanese mask, 7th century
        34:94 Ap 20 '53
    Mask cups, 18th century 25:
        129 D 6 '48

    Maya masks, Bonampak mur-
        als, 320-987 27:82 N 21
        '49
    Mexican stone mummy (?)
        mask, c1350 18:49 Je 4 '45
    South Sea Island wooden masks
        21:79, 81 N 4 '46
    Tibetan mask, with tiara of
        skulls 38:93 Mr 7 '55
    Weber, M. Gilded mask sculp-
        ture bw 19:84 Ag 20 '45
    Willi. Swiss contemporary
        masks, fastnacht spirits
        and furies bw 22:8-10 Ja
        13 '47
Mason, Elizabeth (Heltzhoover)
    Stuart. Mrs. John Thomson
        Mason bw 6:58 Mr 27 '39
Mason, F. Van Wyck
    Van Wyck Mason photog bw
        24:22 My 17 '48
Mason, George
    George Mason 39:62 Jy 4 '55
        plaque, U.S. Capitol bw
        30:74 F 5 '51
Mason, George, IV
    George Mason IV bw 11:118
        D 15 '41
Mason, James
    J. Arthur Rank caricature bw
        22:34 Ja 6 '47
    Self-portrait caricature bw
        22:34 Ja 6 '47 port.
Mason children (David, Joanna,
    Abigail), c1670, American
    Primitive 38:111 Ap 18 '55
Masons, Society of See Free-
    masons
Masquerade. bw Acuna 9:67 O
    14 '40
Massachusetts
    Fourth of July picnic, Wey-
        mouth Landing, Mass.,
        19th century 31:74-5 Jy 2
        '51
    McIntire. Massachusetts coat
        of arms woodcarving 38:
        63 My 30 '55
Massachusetts Institute of Tech-
    nology, Cambridge Mass.
    Saarinen, Eero. Auditorium

38:79-81 Mr 14 '55
Saarinen, Fero. Chapel 39:
114-5 D 26 '55
Massacre at Scio. Delacroix 25:
86 N 22 '48
Massacre of the innocents. Brue-
ghel, P., the elder 37:36-7
D 27 '54
Massacre of the innocents, copy.
Brueghel, P., the younger
24:65 Je 14 '48
Massacre of the innocents. Tin-
toretto 31:34-5 D 24 '51
Massys, Quentin
Man with pink 4:23 Ap 11 '38
The temptation of St. Anthony,
painted with Patiner 31:62-
3 O 1 '51
Quentin Massys bw 4:20 Ap 11
'38   port.
Master Hartley. bw Romney 6:
58 Mr 27 '39
Master of Cologne
Life of Christ 24:72-3 Mr 22 '48
Mather, Cotton
Reverend Cotton Mather bw
13:74 N 23 '42
Mather, Increase
Reverend Increase Mather bw
13:74 N 23 '42
Mather, Richard
Foster. Richard Mather first
American woodcut 38:121
Ap 18 '55
Reverend Richard Mather bw
13:74 N 23 '42
Mathews, Charles
"At Home in the Diligence,"
characterizations, c1852
etching 31:111 N 19 '51
Mathews, Elden
Clouds and shadows 32:69 Ja
14 '52
Matilda, Queen of England bw
32:24 F 18 '52
"Matildas" (tanks). Cole, L. 28:
73 F 20 '50
Matisse, Henri
Black table 31:115 N 26 '51
Dancer seated in an armchair
17:75 N 13 '44

Goldfish and sculpture 25:60
O 11 '48
Luxury, calm and voluptuous-
ness 28:59 Ja 2 '50
Mme. Matisse 31:115 N 26 '51
Marguerite, the artist's
daughter, age 15 31:111 N
26 '51
Maria Lani bw 19:14 D 3 '45
Mural design (last work) 37:
42 D 13 '54
Odalisque 31:112-3 N 26 '51
Red interior 31:116 N 36 '51
Red studio 31:114-5 N 26 '51
Spanish girl 37:66 Ag 9 '54
Still life, fern 33:94 O 27 '52
Studio, Quai St. Michel 38:
109 My 23 '55
Dominican chapel, Vence,
France glasswork, tile
photogs 31:108 N 26 '51
(decorative arts)
Madonna and Child bw 36:113
Ap 26 '54 (drawing)
Persian girl bw 31:110 N 26
'51 (lithograph)
Artist at work photog bw 17:
74 N 13 '44; 31:109 N 26
'51; 37:44 D 13 '54   port.
Artist's family (wife, Amelie;
2 sons, Pierre and Jean)
photog bw 37:43 D 13 '54
port.
Blumenfeld. Henri Matisse,
age 70 photog bw 7:4 Jy 3
'39 port.
Gallatin. Artist in his studio
photog bw 4:45 My 2 '38 port.
Henri Matisse, 1912 photog
bw 28:59 Ja 2 '50 port.
Henri Matisse in Dominican
chapel, Vence, France
photog 31:108 N 26 '51 port.
Mili. Henri Matisse, age 80
photog 27:87 D 12 '49 port.
Self-portrait, age 37 31:115
N 26 '51 port.
Matisse, Mme Henri
Matisse, H. Mme Matisse
31:115 N 26 '51

Matisse, Marguerite
  Matisse, H. Marguerite, the
    artist's daughter, age 15 31:
    111 N 26 '51
Matriarch. woodcarving bw Stein
    6:36 Ap 10 '39
Matter, Herbert
  Herbert Matter photog 34:76
    Mr 2 '53 port.
Matteson, Tompkins
  Harrison. The trial of George
    Jacobs 13:78 N 23 '42
Matthew, Saint
  Matthew working on Gospel, *
    illumination, German, 13th
    century 22:82 Ap 7 '47
  St. Matthew, Gospel Book of
    Charlemagne 34:87 F 23 '53
  St. Matthew, Gospel Book of
    Johannes 34:86 F 23 '53
Matthew 6:19 or "Lay not up for
    yourselves treasures upon
    earth." Sample 8:66 My 27
    '40
Mattson, Henry
  Night and the sea 6:44 My 1 '39
    1942 16:78 Ap 24 '44
  Henry Mattson photog bw 15:13
    O 25 '43 port.
  Self-portrait, 1923 bw 15:13
    O 25 '43 port.
Maugham, Somerset
  Kelly, G. Somerset Maugham,
    1933 bw 11:76 D 1 '41
  Somerset Maugham photog bw
    9:56 D 2 '40; 13:50 S 14 '42
    age 75 26:71 Ap 18 '49
  Somerset Maugham in Martha's
    Vineyard, Mass. photogs
    bw 17:122-5 S 18 '44
Mauldin, Willliam, cartoonist
  European tour 35:17 Ag 17 '53
  Joe bw 16:8-10 Ja 17 '44
  Ox roasting ceremony in St.
    Keverne 34:36-7 Je 15 '53
  Up front bw 18:49-53 F 5 '45
  Vacation in U.S. 37:92-8 Ag 23
    '54
  Bill Mauldin photog bw 18:49
    F 5 '45 port.
Maurin, A.

Amerigo Vespucci bw 37:106 O
    11 '54
Maurin, Hugues
  Artist at work photog bw 37:123
    O 25 '54 port.
Maurois, Andre
  Andre Maurois photog bw 10:
    62 Ja 6 '41; 24:118-9 Ja 19
    '48
  Karsh. Andre Maurois photog
    bw 37:130 O 4 '54
Mavrina, Tatiana Alexeyevna
  Churches of Russia--11 paint-
    ings 17:64-8 N 27 '44
Max Schmitt in a single scull. bw
    Eakins 5:33 O 31 '38; 16:
    72 My 15 '44
Maximilian, Emperor of Mexico
  Execution of Maximilian, June
    19, 1867* bw 4:52 Ap 11 '38
  Franz Joseph and Maximilian
    photog bw 25:91 N 22 '48
  Maximilian bw 4:52 Ap 11 '38
May, Cliff, architect
  Ranch house, Montecito, Calif.
    photog 40:58-9 Ja 16 '56
May Yuan
  Bare willows and distant moun-
    tains 15:62 O 11 '43
Mayan Art See Art, Pre-Colum-
    bian
Mayans
  Bonampak murals, 320-987
    27:80-4 N 21 '49
Maybeck, Bernard, architect
  Berkeley, California, homes
    photogs bw 24:147, 150 My
    17 '48
  Christian Science church,
    Berkeley, Calif. photog bw
    24:142 My 17 '48
  Palace of Fine Arts, San
    Francisco photog bw 24:141
    My 17 '48
  Bernard Maybeck 24:141, 153
    My 17 '48 port.
May day party. Sharon 33:75 Jy
    21 '52
Mayerling--portraits and scenes
    photogs bw 26:127-33 Mr
    28 '49

Mayflower Compact
Moran, P. Signing the Compact
13:75 N 23 '42
Signing of Mayflower Compact
bw 25:130 N 29 '48
The Mayflower upon her arrival.
Halsall 13:76 N 23 '42
Maynor, Dorothy
Dorothy Mayner bw 7:41-2 D
11 '39
Mayo
Kili bw 34:14 Je 29 '53
Mazoff, Milton
Jitterbug sculpture bw 10:59
Je 16 '41
Mazzini, Giuseppe
Garibaldi and Mazzini meet,
1833* bw 15:19 Ag 9 '43
Garibaldi Mazzini photog bw
15:18 Ag 9 '43; 25:86 N 22
'48
The meal. Vuillard 37:77 N 1 '54
Meat market. Feuerherm 30:36
Ja 15 '51
Mecca, Great Mosque of photogs
38:76 My 9'55 bw 2:62-3
Mr 15 '37
Mechanical inventions. Sterne
31:51 Ag 27 '51
Medallions
Benjamin Franklin 40:82 Ja 9
'56
Medals See Coins and Medals
Medical cooperative. woodcut bw
Yen Han 18:60 Ap 9 '45
Medical orderlies. Gross, A. 26:
60 Mr 21 '49
Medical Themes
Eakins The Agnew clinic 16:
75 My 15 '44
First use of ether photog bw
25:91 N 22 '48
Florence Nightingale tending
sick in Crimean war bw 11:
15 D 15 '41; 13:71 N 16 '42
Ford. The country doctor 3:28
D 20 '37
Head bath, 19th century bw
25:82 Ag 9 '48
Jack. Operation 23:99 N 10 '47
Koch. Convalescent 18:76 My

14 '45
Palmer, W. C. Medical his-
tory scenes mural, Queens
General Hospital, New
York 3:40-2 O 11 '37
Rain bath, France, 1860 bw
25:82 Ag 9 '48
Rembrandt. Anatomy lesson of
Professor Tulp 1:30 N 30
'36
Sample. Ward room bw 3:42 N
15 '37
Soyer. Doctor's office 4:27 Je
13 '38
Stretcher party. drawing bw
unknown Marine artist 15:
81 D 27 '43
Medici, Giovanni de'
Raphael. Pope Leo X, and two
cousins bw 4:33 Mr 21 '38
Medici, Giuliano de'
Raphael. Giuliano de' Medici
2:42 Je 28 '37
Medici, Lorenzo de' (The Mag-
nificent)
Lorenzo de' Medici bw 4:33
Mr 21 '38 bust bw 12:12 Je
8 '42
Verrocchio. Lorenzo de' Me-
dici terra cotta 38:95 F 21
'55
Medici chapel altar photog 19:43
D 24 '55
Medici-Riccardi Palace, Flor-
ence Gozzoli. Journey of
the Magi fresco 19:Cover,
43-51 D 24 '45
Medieval lady. woodcut Reder
37:88 O 18 '54
Meditating philosopher. bw
Rembrandt 39:142-3 S 26
'55
The Mediterranean. sculpture bw
Maillol 8:106-7 Ap 15 '40
Meeker, Dean
Limestone quarry, Devil's
Lake, Wisconsin 32:69 Ja
14 '52
Meeker, Joseph Rusling
Bayou teche 28:78 Mr 6 '50

Meeting house hill, Roxbury, in
    1790. Penniman 13:80 N 23
    '42
The meeting of Dido and Aeneas.
    Frencesco di Giorgio Mar-
    tini 35:150-1 N 16 '53
Meigs, Walter
    One man four pots bw 32:91 Mr
    17 '52
    Walter Meigs photog bw 32:91
    Mr 17 '52 port.
Meiji, Emperor of Japan photog
    bw 3:24 D 6 '37
Meistermann, Georg, stained
    glass design
    Stained glass windows, radio
    station, Cologne, Germany
    36:146 My 10 '54
    Georg Meistermann photog 36:
    146 My 10 '54 port.
Melanchthon, Philipp
    Philipp Melanchthon in Cran-
    ach. Luther and his friends
    24:63 Je 14 '48
Melanesian Art See Art, South
    Seas
Melbourne, William Lamb
    Lord Melbourne 24:71 My 24
    '48
Melcarth, Edward
    Coney Island 28:88 Mr 20 '50
Melchior, Lauritz
    Halsman. Lauritz Melchior
    photog bw 16:45 Mr 13 '44
Melicov, Diana
    Girl on a horse sculpture bw
    5:5 N 7 '38
Melons. Peale, Raphaelle 12:66
    Mr 20 '42
Melting horizon. Pereira 34:73
    Ja 26 '53
Melton (James) collection of
    antique automobiles photogs
    bw 13:8-11 Jy 27 '42
Meltsner, Paul
    Mother and child 16:46 Ja 3 '44
Melville, Herman
    Herman Melville, 1844 bw 40:
    57 Je 25 '56   photog bw 31:
    111 N 5 '51
Memling, Hans

June, calendar page bw 18:42
    Ja 1 '45
St. Ursala legend, Shrine of
    St. Ursala, Bruges 34:81-
    6 Ap 6 '53
Memorials and Monuments See
    also Tombs; and forms of
    memorials, as Arches
Alabamans' monument, Gettys-
    burg bw 4:35 Je 27 '38
Borglum. Mt. Rushmore Na-
    tional Memorial photogs
    4:26 Je 27 '38 bw 3:104 O
    4 '37 complete with 4 units
    bw 7:19 Jy 17 '39 Detail,
    Lincoln bw 18:Cover Je 18
    '45 Detail, Washington
    bw 11:103 O 6 '41
Borglum. Sacco-Vanzetti
    memorial plaque bw 3:24 S
    6 '37
Bunker Hill monument photog
    bw 18:67 Ja 15 '45
Christ of the depths, under-
    water memorial, Italy
    sculpture bw 29:48 Ag 22
    '55; 37:151-2 S 13 '54
French. The angel of death
    and the sculptor sculpture
    bw 6:57 Mr 20 '39
Churchill knight, 1644 photog
    bw 9:92 N 18 '40
Geographical center of North
    America, reputed, obelisk,
    North Dakota photog bw 11:
    99 O 6 '41
Homestead steel strike me-
    morial, 1892 photog bw
    20:21 F 4 '46
Irving memorial with bust bw
    17:63 O 30 '44
Jefferson memorial, Washing-
    ton, D.C. Pope; Eggers;
    Higgins photog 23:49 Jy 7
    '47 bw 14:Cover Ap 12 '43
La Griffe and Moutard.
    French resistance martyrs
    memorial, Auxerre, France
    photog bw 26:35 Ap 18 '49
Lee memorial, equestrian
    statue, Gettysburg bw 4:

35 Je 27 '38

Lincoln memorial, Washington, D.C. Bacon, H., archt. French, sculptor photog 20: Cover F 11 '46 bw 5:58 Jy 11 '38

Moerdyk. Piet Retief memorial, Pretoria bw 28:25-6 Ja 16 '50

Reformation monument, Geneva sculpture bw 20:31-2 Mr 18 '46

Russian monument, Mukden photog bw 20:30 Mr 25 '46

Roosevelt memorial, Grosvenor Square, London. Dick sculpture bw 24:32-3 Ap 26 '48

Saarinen, Eero. Gateway to the West, memorial arch design bw 24:113 Mr 8 '48

Seattle obelisk memorial to World War dead photog bw 13:31 Ag 31 '42

Strauss memorial, Vienna sculpture bw 20:92 Mr 4 '46

Unknown political prisoner, monument competition 34: 39-42 Je 1 '53

Victory monument, Gettysburg photog bw 4:36 Je 27 '38

European War, 1914-18
Aisne-Marne memorial, Chateau-Thierry photog bw 17:35 S 18 '44

Carentan European War dead memorial, France photog bw 17:19 Jy 3 '44

Douaumont Hill monument, Verdun photog bw 17:34 S 18 '44

German war memorials photogs bw 7:10-3 S 25 '39

Hermann, the war man monument, Teutoburger photog bw 17:85 O 9 '44

Indian troops in World War I, Suez Canal sculpture 31:82 O 22 '51

Pantheon of war, 402 foot can-

vas by 128 French artists 35:55-6 Ag 10 '53

U.S. war memorials in France photogs bw 3:22-3 Ag 30 '37

World War, 1939-45
Bradford. Mosaics, chapel, near Cambridge, England 35:38 Ag 24 '53

De Weldon. Flag raising at Mt. Suribachi, Iwo Jima, Marine memorial, Washington, D.C. photogs bw 37:128-33 S 20 '54

RAF heroes memorial, Battle of Britain window, stained glass, Westminster Abbey, London 26:58 F 7 '49

Memories of New York. ink drawing Bielenberg 10:58 Je 16 '41

Mencken, Henry Louis
H. L. Mencken photogs bw 28:119 My 15 '50; 40:75 F 20 '56

Penn. George Jean Nathan and H. L. Mencken photog bw 24:14 My 10 '48

Mendelsohn, Eric, architect Synagogue, St. Louis photogs bw 30:15 Ap 30 '51

Mendes-France, Lily
Self-portrait bw 37:85 Jy 19 '54

Mendes-France, Pierre
Premier Mendes-France in Le cow-boy political cartoon bw 37:70 D 6 '54

Mengs, Raphael, attributed
Jean Jacques Casanova, 1767 bw 35:47 Jy 27 '53

Menken, Adah
Alexander Dumas and Adah Menken photog bw 31:116 N 19 '51

Menkes, Zygmunt
Martyrdom of Warsaw 35:55 N 2 '53

Walkowitz bw 16:79 F 21 '44

Mennin, Peter
    Composer Mennin photog bw
        40:141 My 21 '56
Mental calculus. Magritte 1:26
    D 14 '36
Menuhin, Yehudi
    Halsman. Menuhin photog bw
        16:43 Mr 13 '44
    Menuhin--portraits; family
        photogs bw 7:27-8 D 25 '39
Mercer, William
    Battle of Princeton, 1776 29:
        46 Jy 3 '50
Merchant Gisze. Holbein 24:70
    Mr 22 '48
Merenptah, sarcophagus statue
    bw 24:85 Ja 19 '48
Mergenthaler, Edward
    Solarium 10:57 Je 16 '41
Mergenthaler, Ottmar
    Laning. Mechanical typeset-
        ting mural panel 9:66 S 30
        '40
Menorah photog bw 38:89 Je 13
    '55
Meridian. bw Waugh, F.J. 3:24
    D 20 '37
"Meriken Shinshi," illustrated
    Japanese history of the U.S.
    drawings bw 25:6-8 Ag 2
    '48
Merkurov
    Stalin (copy) sculpture bw 14:
        90 Mr 29 '43
Mermaids
    Milles. Buddha of the sea sculp-
        ture bw 2:32 F 22 '37
Merrillan night. Bohrod 11:94 N
    10 '41
"Merrimac" (ship)
    Davidson. Monitor and Merri-
        mac, 1862 9:49 O 28 '40
Merry Christmas of Rosette. bw
    Robin 27:57 D 26 '49
Merry-Go-Rounds
    Davis, G. R. Carousel 22:96
        Ap 21 '47
    Davis, G.R. Merry-go-rounds
        19:48 Jy 16 '45
    Marsh. The steeplechase 40:
        83 F 6 '56

    Pearlstein. Merry-go-round
        10:57 Je 16 '41
    Waugh. Merry-go-round bowl,
        Steuben glass bw 23:18 N
        10 '47
Merwin, Hester
    Nancy 10:47 F 3 '41
Meserve (Frederick W.) collec-
    tion of photographs
    Prints of the 1880's bw 13:10-
        3 O 19 '42
Mesmer, Anton
    Anton Mesmer photog bw 27:
        90 Jy 25 '49
Mesopotamian Art See Art,
    Mesopotamian
Mess line. Miller, B. 11:63 Jy
    7 '41 bw 14:6 Je 28 '43
Mestovic, Ivan, sculptor
    Atlantide bw 22:135 Je 2 '47
    Crucifix bw 27:145 O 17 '49
    Mother and child bw 22:132 Je
        2 '47
    Torso 25:101 S 27 '48
    Vestal virgin bw 22:132 Je 2
        '47
    Ivan Mestrovic photog bw 22:
        131 Je 2 '47 port.
Metal work See also Armor;
    Enamels; Jewelry; and type of
    metal, as Copper; Goldsmith-
    ing; Iron Work; Pewter;
    Silversmithing
    Bertoia. Metal screen 37:62 O
        25 '54
    Carved sword hilt, 22 scenes
        from Bible, Italy, c1600
        bw 6:53 Mr 20 '39
    Metal screen, Massachusetts
        Institute of Technology
        chapel photog 39:114-5 D
        26 '55
Metalious, Grace
    Grace Metalious photogs bw
        41:104 N 12 '56
Metcalfe, Augusta
    A friend's ranch 29:72 Jy 17
        '50
    Horses 29:72 Jy 17 '50
    Augusta Metcalfe photog bw
        29:70 Jy 17 '50 port.

The metro. Dubuffet 33:96 O 27
    '52
Metropolitan Museum of Art,
    New York City
  Artists for Victory, exhibit of
    modern American artists
    14:42-7 Mr 8 '43
  First U.S. painting competi-
    tion 30:34-8 Ja 15 '51
  Lehman family collection 37:
    63-7 Ag 9 '54
  Life in America, 1616-1916
    6:26-31 Je 19 '39
  Treasures from collection:
    paintings, sculpture, art
    objects 6:51-7 Mr 20 '39
Metropolitan Opera House, New
    York City
  Marsh. Monday night at Met
    40:82 F 6 '56
Metternich, Klemens von
  Prince Metternich, 1848 photog
    bw 25:91 N 22 '48
Mexican farm house. Lee, D. 22:
    74 My 12 '47
Mexico
  Cortes capturing Mexico City,
    August 13, 1521 bw 4:52
    Ap 11 '38; 21:46 D 16 '46
  Execution of Maximilian,
    June 19, 1867* bw 4:52 Ap
    11 '38
  Historical scenes and portraits
    bw 4:50-9 Ap 11 '38
  Lee, D. Chapultepec Park,
    Mexico City 22:76-7 My 12 '47
  Lee, D. Mexico: scenes and
    portraits as record of trip
    22:72-8 My 12 '47
  Ninos heroes, Battle of Cha-
    pultepec, 1847 bw 22:47 Mr
    17 '47
  Orozco. The evolution of cul-
    ture in Mexico 25:70 N 22 '48
  Pena. Chapultepec Park, Mex-
    ico City* drawing bw 20:58
    Je 3 '46
  Rivera. History of Mexico,*
    mural, Del Prado Hotel bw
    23:104-6 N 3 '47
  Rivera. Man's dependence on

    water, Water storage tank,
    Mexico City 31:73 S 17 '51
  Rosenthal. Portraits and
    scenes in Mexico 15:65-8
    N 22 '43
  Storming of Chapultepec
    castle, September 13, 1847
    bw 4:52 Ap 11 '38; 22:122
    Je 9 '47
  Walker, J. Chapultepec 13:
    60-1 Jy 6 '42
Mexico City
  Modern hotel architecture--
    Casa Latino-Americana;
    Reforma photogs bw 21:98
    F 24 '47
  National Lottery Building
    photog bw 21:98 F 24 '47
  University of Mexico photogs
    41:102-13 D 3 '56
Meyers, William H.
  California naval war, 1847:
    scenes of U.S. Navy in the
    Pacific, Mexican War 7:
    43-4 Ag 28 '39
Mice
  Bufano. Mouse sculpture bw
    17:106 D 4 '44
  Denslow. Mice, illustrations
    from "Wonderful Wizard
    of Oz" 35:55 D 28 '53
  Grossenheider. White footed
    mouse 21:86-8 O 28 '46
Michael, Emperor of Russia,
    1613 bw 14:93 Mr 29 '43
Michael, Saint, the Archangel
  St. Michael mural, door of
    church compound, Gondar,
    Ethiopia 39:88 N 21 '55
  Signorelli. Madonna and
    Child with saints 35:154 N
    16 '53
  Van Eyck, J. Archangel
    Michael and unidentified donor
    Altarpiece panel 40:109 My 7 '56
Michel, Alfonso
  The yellow cage 20:60 Je 3 '46
Michel, Robert
  Devil's Island scenes, French
    penal colony, Guiana 4:
    47-8 Ap 4 '38

Michelangelo
  Charon in The last judgment
    27:47 D 26 '48
  Creation, Sistine chapel fres-
    coes 21:62-9 Jy 1 '46; 27:
    25-49 D 26 '49
  The creation of Adam fresco
    11:77 D 1 '41; 21:66-7 Jy
    1 '46; 27:30-1 D 26 '49
  Creation of Eve fresco 27:32-
    3 D 26 '49 bw 21:67 Jy 1
    '46
  The Delphic sibyl fresco 21:
    65 Jy 1 '46
  Drunkenness of Noah fresco bw
    21:64 Jy 1 '46
  The flood fresco 27:40-3 D 26
    '49 bw 21:63 Jy 1 '46
  Garden of Eden 27:35-6 D 26
    '41
  God, fresco detail bw 21:69
    Jy 1 '46
  God creating the sky and the
    water fresco 27:28 D 26 '49
  God creating the sun and the
    moon fresco 27:28-9 D 26
    '49
  God separating the day from
    the night (Fourth day of
    creation) fresco 27:27 D 26
    '49
  Jeremiah fresco 7:55 N 20 '39;
    21:68 Jy 1 '46
  The last judgment fresco 27:44-
    8 D 26 '49 full painting 27:
    44-5 D 26 '49
  Noah's sacrifice fresco 27:34
    D 26 '49
  Satin in The last judgment bw
    24:78 F 2 '48
  Sistine chapel frescoes
    Ceiling frescoes: Creation,
      Fall of man, Flood 21:
      62-9 Jy 1 '46
    Ceiling and Altar frescoes:
      including The last judg-
      ment 27:25-49 D 26 '49
  The temptation and the expul-
    sion fresco bw 21:64 Jy 1
    '46
  Dome, St. Peter's, Rome

  photogs 20:31-3, 36-7 Mr
    11 '46; 27:49 Ag 1 '49 (ar-
    chitecture)
  Avenging angel bw 27:26 D 26
    '49 (drawings)
  Figure bw 28:91 Je 26 '50
    (drawings)
  Bound slave bw 27:99 D 5 '49
    (sculpture)
  David bw 26:104 Ja 24 '49
    (sculpture)
  Pieta bw 5:46 D 25 '38 (sculp-
    ture)
  Volterra. Michelangelo,
    bronze head from death
    mask bw 27:49 D 26 '48
    port.
Michener, James A.
  Mr. and Mrs. Michener
    photog bw 39:55 N 7 '55
Michigan
  Benton. Communists and fas-
    cists in Michigan drawings
    bw 3:22-5 Jy 26 '37
  Paintings of Michigan 25:65-8
    Ag 23 '48
Michnick, David
  Peasant mother and child
    sculpture bw 4:62 Ap 25 '38
"Microbe" paintings. Ernst 32:
    58-9 Ja 21 '52
Middleditch, Edward
  Edward Middleditch photog bw
    40:164 Ap 23 '56 port.
Middleton, Arthur
  Arthur Middleton bw 15:9 Jy
    5 '43
Middleton, David
  Straight-line drawings bw 8:
    43-4 Mr 18 '40
  David Middleton photog bw 8:
    43 Mr 18 '40 port.
The midnight ride of Paul Re-
    vere. Wood, G. 3:28 D 20
    '37; 14:54 Ja 18 '43
Mies van der Rohe, Ludwig,
    architect and designer
  Chairs photog 34:74 Mr 2 '53
Mieszko I, King of Poland
  King Mieszko I bw 17:86 Ag
    28 '44

Mike, the artist's son, Peirce,
W. 19:86 N 12 '45
Mike fishes in Maine. Peirce, W.
19:85 N 12 '45
Mikoun, Mika
Maria Lani sculptured head
bw 19:14 D 3 '45
Miles, Richard
Bishop Richard Miles bw 27:
150 S 19 '49
Milhaud, Darius
Karsh. Darius Milhaud
photog bw 37:134 O 4 '54
Mili, Gjon, photographer
Louis knockdown by Joe Wal-
cott bw 24:16 My 10 '48
Picasso flashlight drawings
in dark bw 28:10-2 Ja 30
'50
Portraits of 9 Parisian artists:
founders of "Modernism"
27: 82-92 D 12 '49
Provence in stone 35:76-86 Jy
13 '53
Milk glass hands, Victorian glass-
ware, U.S. 40:91 Mr 5 '56
Milking time. Scarseth 10:78 Mr
31 '41
Milky Way. Stephens, D.O. 3:49-
51 N 8 '37
The mill. Rembrandt 5:33 Ag 29
'38
Mill, John Stuart
John Stuart Mill photog bw 22:
100 Mr 24 '47
Millroad topiary garden, Lake
Forest, Illinois photogs bw
11:62-6 N 3 '41
Millais, John Everett
Knight errant* bw 9:64 S 2 '40
Millay, Edna St. Vincent
Edna St. Vincent Millay, 1942
bw 13:100 O 19 '42
Miller, Alfred Jacob
Fort Laramie, Wyoming, 1837
watercolor 27:44-5 Jy 4 '49;
39:75 N 28 '55
Scenic grandeur of the West
27:46-7 Jy 4 '49
A Sioux on the warpath 36:78-9
Mr 8 '54

Trapper bw 27:40 Jy 4 '49
Miller, Barse
Beach party 11:73 O 27 '41
bw 9:79 D 9 '40
Mess line 11:63 Jy 7 '41 bw
14:6 Je 28 '43
The shooting gallery bw 5:30
O 31 '38
San Francisco harbor in war
15:73-4 Jy 12 '43
U.S. Supply lines' heroes,
World War 12:72-7 My 11
'42
Barse Miller photog bw 11:60
Jy 7 '41; 12:72 My 11 '42
port.
Miller, Herman, furniture de-
signer
Furniture in Trade secrets
house photogs 34:8-10 Ja 5
'55
Miller, Kenneth Hayes
Walkowitz bw 16:77 F 21 '44
Kenneth Hayes Miller, in
group photog 29:172-3 O 16
'50 port.
Miller, Lewis
Folk scenes, Pennsylvania
and New York states, c1825
watercolors 39:60-1 Jy 18
'55
Self-portrait watercolor 39:
60 Jy 18 '55 port.
Miller, Mary and John R., in-
terior designers
U.S. contemporary southern
house 38:117 F 21 '55
Miller, Richard
Artist at work photog bw 9:72
Jy 15 '40 port.
Miller, Robert
Soldiers of the U.S. army,
World War II cartoons bw
31:85-6 D 10 '51
Milles, Carl, sculptor
Buddha of the sea bw 2:32 F
22 '37
Europa and the bull bw 2:32
F 22 '37
Filbyter Folke bw 2:32 F 22
'37

Milles, Carl (cont.)
  Fountain of faith bw 34:99-101
    Mr 30 '53 plaster models
    bw 25:70-2 Ag 30 '48
  God of peace, St. Paul bw 2:
    27 F 22 '37
  Jonah and the whale bw 2:32
    F 22 '37
  Naiad and dolphin bw 2:32 F 22
    '37
  Orpheus fountain, Stockholm
    bw 2:28-9 F 22 '37 copy bw
    2:30 F 22 '37
  Siren and fishes bw 2:32 F 22
    '37
  Sven Hedin, model bw 2:32 F
    22 '37
  Swedenborg, model bw 2:32 F
    22 '37
  Two dancers bw 2:32 F 22 '37
  The wedding of the Mississip-
    pi and the Missouri, foun-
    tain, St. Louis 2:Cover, 26
    F 22 '37 bw 8:110-2 Je 10
    '40
  Carl Milles photogs bw 2:26-
    31 F 22 '37; 8:110 Je 10 '40;
    34:102 Mr 30 '53   port.
  Home of the artist photog bw
    34:102 Mr 30 '53 port.
Millet, Francis Davis
  John and Priscilla bw 11:85 S
    8 '41
Millet, Jean François
  The gleaners 25:96-7 N 22 '48
  The man with a hoe 9:46-7 Jy
    29 '40
Millikan, Robert Andrews
  Robert Millikan photog bw 11:
    42 O 13 '41
The millinery shop. Degas 39:119
  N 7 '55
Millman, Edward
  Bilibrid prison, Manila 19:67
    O S '45
  Santo Tomas University, Ma-
    nila 19:66 O 8 '45
  St. Louis Post Office histori-
    cal mural, painted with Si-
    porin 13:71-4 O 12 '42
  Artist teaching photog 34:148-

  9 My 18 '53 port.
Mills See Windmills
Mills, Anne
  Anne Mills, English seaman
    bw 14:7 Ja 4 '43
Mills, Clark
  Andrew Jackson equestrian
    statue bw 19:10 S 24 '45
Mills, Reginald
  London blitz, September 7,
    1940 26:50 F 28 '49
Milne, A(lan) A(lexander)
  Shepard. "Winnie-the-Pooh"
    illustrations bw 30:75-6 F
    19 '51; 40:115-20 F 27 '56
Milo of Crotona sculpture bw 20:
  8 My 20 '46
Milton, John
  Leutze. Cromwell and Milton
    27:58 Ag 29 '49
Minamoto-no-Yoritomo, 12th
  century Japanese general
  34:96 Ap 20 '53
Minerva See Mythological
  Themes--Minerva
Mines and Mining
  Anderson, G. Deposition of
    the miner 35:87 S 28 '53
  Baizerman. The miner sculp-
    ture bw 25:157 O 4 '48
  Chadwick. Placer mining in
    California 6:29 Je 19 '39;
    27:48 Jy 4 '49
  De Bry. Silver mountain, 16th
    century silver mine, Peru
    drawing bw 24:86 Mr 22 '48
  Dehn. Iron mines, Ironwood,
    Michigan* 34:78 Ja 5 '53
  Forty-niners working sluice
    box photog bw 24:44 F 2
    '48
  Meeker, D. Limestone quarry,
    Devil's Lake, Wis. 32:69
    Ja 14 '52
  Nahl. Sunday morning in the
    mines 27:49 Jy 4 '49
  Roper. Gold diggers, Ararat,
    1854 bw 12:78 F 9 '42
  Roualt. The quarry 34:58-9 F
    2 '53
  Solid comfort lithograph 27:

49 Jy 4 '49

Woman mine workers, England 1842 bw 25:94 N 22 '48

Mineature Objects

Boschi. Paintings on pinheads: Juan Peron; Lake Lacarno bw 30:146-7 Je 11 '51

Boyer. Pinhead paintings and sculpture bw 20:14-6 Mr 25 '46

Carved sword hilt, 22 scenes from Bible, Italy, c1600 bw 6:53 Mr 20 '39

Tatsuta. Microscopic writing bw 34:102 F 23 '53

Thorne miniature rooms, period furniture and interior decoration, Chicago Art Institute 3:38-42 N 29 '37

Miniature Painting (Portraits) See also Illuminations; Manuscripts

Alexander II, Czar of Russia 38:60 Ja 31 '55

Benjamin Franklin 40:82 Ja 9 '56

Hilliard. Lady of the court* 41:147 N 5 '56

Hilliard. Lover* 41:147 N 5 '56

Hilliard. Young man* 41:147 N 5 '56

Maria Alexandrovna 38:60 Ja 31 '55

Mrs. John Quincy Adams, 1797 41:72 Jy 2 '56

Oliver. Young girl* 41:147 N 5 '56

Peale, C. W. Portrait of a woman* bw 6:52 Mr 20 '39

Voilles. Czarina of Russia and children 33:35 D 29 '52

Minin rousing the Russians bw 14:93 Mr 29 '43

Mink. Audubon 9:115 O 21 '40

Mink and Mannequin. Marsh 40:83 F 6 '56

Minnesota

Dehn. Threshing in Minnesota 11:42 Ag 11 '41

The minors--The York White Roses

vs. The Trenton Packers. Thomas, B. 10:51 Je 23 '41

Minstrels, U.S.

Minstrel show performers, portraits bw 11:74 Ag 25 '41

Minutemen

Captain John Parker sculpture bw, Lexington Common 9:13 Ag 19 '40

French. Minutemen sculpture bw 7:10 O 23 '39

Mirabeau, Honore

Benjamin Franklin crowns Mirabeau print 40:80 Ja 9 '56

The miracle of Dunquerque--arrival at Dover. bw Bone 10:64 F 24 '41

Miracles See also Jesus Christ Miracles

Botticelli. Three miracles of St. Zenobias bw 21:104 O 28 '46

Dix, O. Veronica's veil lithograph 33:84 Jy 14 '52

Giotto. St. Francis receiving the stigmata bw 16:65-71 Ap 10 '44

St. Denis walking with his head in his hands* bw 31:76 Jy 30 '51

Veneziano. The stigmatization of St. Francis 1:48 D 28 '36

Mirage. Hurd 23:77 Ag 18 '47

Mirandola, Pico della

Pico della Mirandola bw 23:60 Ag 4 '47

Miro, Joan

Collage bw 25:163 N 8 '48

Dog barking at the moon 4:44 My 2 '38

Person throwing a stone at a bird 25:60 O 11 '48 bw 19:65 S 24 '45

Personages with a star 33:97 O 27 '52

Ricart 33:92 O 27 '52

Yellow moon 33:96 O 27 '52

Rug photog 33:93 O 27 '52

Miro, Joan (cont.)
   (textile design)
   Artist in his studio photog 39:
      143 N 14 '55 port.
   Gallatin. Artist in his studio
      photog bw 4:45 My 2 '38
      port.
Miroku, bronze sculpture, Japan,
   c666 30:72 My 28 '51
Mironova
   Skiers (copy, after Zhaba) 14:
      46 Mr 29 '43
A mirror for friends. Ernst 32:
   59 Ja 21 '52
Mirror Hook
   Eagle mirror hook, U.S.,
      c1784 bw 17:56 S 4 '44
Mirrors See also Furniture--
   Mirrors
   Greek two-piece bronze mirror
      bw 6:53 Mr 20 '39
Miserere Series
   Roualt. Madonna and Child
      etching bw 34:56 F 2 '53
Misericords woodcarvings bw
   37:79-82 S 27 '54
"Miss Flora McFlimsey," illus-
   trations by author, Marian
   Foster bw 33:84 S 22 '52
Miss Pat and Miss Eva Lion
   Pittman 18:69 F 19 '45
Missal of Ferdinand, manuscript,
   Italy, 15th century 32:87
   Ap 14 '52
Missions
   Old Spanish missions, U.S.
      southwest: Walls, corredor,
      tower, doors, photogs 40:
      46-9, 56-7 Ja 16 '56
   Our Lady of Ascensions, New
      Mexico photog 24:85 Mr 22
      '48
   San Carlos Borromeo, Carmel,
      California, bell tower photog
      40:56 Ja 16 '56
   San Fernando, San Fernando,
      California photogs 40:56-7
      Ja 16 '56
   San Jose, Laguna, New Mexico,
      Holy Trinity, santero altar-
      piece photog 40:48-9 Ja 16
      '56
   San Juan Capistrano, San Juan
      Capistrano, California,
      garden photog 40:46 Ja 16
      '56
   San Xavier Del Bac, Arizona
      photog 26:74 Mr 14 '49
The Mississippi. Curry 13:96 N
   9 '42
Mississippi River
   Benton. Cotton loading on the
      Mississippi bw 6:70 Ap 24
      '39
   Bingham. Raftsmen playing
      cards 7:41 S 11 '39 draw-
      ings bw 7:40 S 11 '39
   Currier and Ives prints. Dis-
      covery, and other scenes
      of the Mississippi 21:70-4
      S 2 '46
   Currier and Ives print. Low
      water on the Mississippi 9:
      33 D 30 '40
   Locale of Clemen's "Life on
      the Mississippi" photogs bw
      33:75 Jy 7 '52
   Momberger. Wooding up, on
      the Mississippi engraving
      28:73 Mr 6 '50
   Paintings and prints of the
      Mississippi, exhibit, City
      Art Museum of St. Louis
      28:73-8 Mr 6 '50
   Powell. De Soto's discovery
      of the Mississippi bw 24:88
      Mr 22 '48
   Steamboat rounding Indian
      Mounds near Natchez, 1850
      39:81 N 28 '55
Mississippi River boatman. draw-
   ing bw Bingham 28:76 Mr 6
   '50
Mississippi River steamboat,
   1882 photog 39:80 N 28 '55
Mississippi steamboat.* Bunn 9:
   71 O 14 '40
Missouri
   Benton. History of Missouri
      mural, State House, Jeff-
      erson City, Mo. 2:35-7 Mr
      1 '37

McCrerry. Products of Missouri mural, Post Office, Monett, Mo. 10:45 Ja 27 '41

Millman and Siporin. Historical mural, Post Office, St. Louis 13:71-4 O 12 '42

Missouri River

Bingham. Fur traders descending the Missouri 28:76-7 Mr 6 '50

Bodmer. Missouri River 15: 87 Ag 30 '43

Bodmer. White castels on the upper Missouri 15:87 Ag 30 '43

Mist over the marshes. bw Vogelein 18:44 Ja 1 '45

Mr. Churchill and his friends overthrowing Hitler and his. Hafi Musavir el Malk 35:70 N 9 '53

Mr. John Nobody woodcarving, misericord bw 37:80 S 27 '54

Mr. Morgan and Mr. Vanderbilt in a sleigh, 1885. bw Leighton, S. 6:31 Je 19 '39

Mr. X. Rouault 34:59 F 2 '53

Mistletoe

Lewicki. Gathering mistletoe for Christmas 33:84 D 1 '52

Mrs. McCormick's general store, Catskill, New York 6:28 Je 19 '39

Mistress and maid. Vermeer 3: 33 D 27 '37

Mitchell, Bruce

Hudson autumn 20:77 F 18 '46

Iran in World War II 18:58-9 Ap 30 '45

Mitchell, John

John Mitchell, leader of United Mine Workers photog bw 33:33 D 8 '52

Mithras sculptured head, Roman 2nd century 37:53 O 11 '54

Mitropoulas, Dimitri

Dimitri Mitropoulas photogs bw 20:57-8 F 18 '46

Miwa, Chosei

Cavite navy yard attack, December 10 '41* 28:68 F 27 '50

Miyamoto, Saburo

Battle of Nicholson 28:70 F 27 '50

Japanese paratroops at Palembang* 28:69 F 27 '50

Mnesikles

Propylaea, gateway to Acropolis, Athens, photog bw 18:56 Ja 1 '45

Mobiles See names of artists, as Billings, Henry; Calder, Alexander; Outerbridge; Donald

Northland shopping center mobiles, Detroit, Michigan photogs 37:81-2 Ag 30 '54

Mochi, Ugo

Animals paper cutouts 34:18-20 Mr 9 '53

Mocking birds. Peterson 20:72-5 Ap 8 '46

Model on pink chair. Renoir 37: 66 Ag 9 '54

The Model T decade. mural Daugherty 3:49 O 25 '37

Modena Cathedral relief, Italy 12th century photog bw 40: 93 Mr 19 '56

Modigliani, Amedeo

Flower girl 33:92 O 27 '52

Mme Jeanne Hebuterne 29:113 S 11 '50

Portrait of a boy with red hair 40:72 My 28 '56

Portrait of a man* 24:67 Mr 1 '48

Self-portrait, age 35, 1919 bw 29:112 S 11 '50 port.

Module--interchangeable furniture units. photog bw Sanders 21:128-9 S 23 '46

Moerdyk, Gerard, architect

Piet Retief memorial, Pretoria photog bw 28:25-6 Ja 16 '50

Moffat, John

Henry Fox Talbot, 1860 photog bw 2:5 Mr 29 '37

Mohammed and Mohammedanism
  Islam symbol, creed of the one
      God 38:57 F 7 '55
  Kaaba
    Black Stone set in Kaaba
      photogs bw 2:62-3 Mr 17 '37;
      38:92 My 9 '55
    Great Mosque of Mecca
      showing Kaaba photog 38:76
      My 9 '55
    Mecca, Great Mosque of pho-
      togs 38:76 My 9 '55 bw 2:
      62-3 Mr 15 '37
  Mohammed bw 29:160 D 11 '50
Mohammed the Eunich, King of
    Persia bw 20:34 Ap 8 '46
The Mojave desert. watercolor
    Dehn 11:44 Ag 11 '41
"The Molly Maguires," 1870 bw
    33:33 D 8 '52
Molnar, George
  Statues cartoons bw 37:23 Ag
    30 '54
Moloch. sculpture bw. Lipton 24:
    95 Ap 12 '48
Moloch I. sculpture bw Lipton 29:
    150 S 18 '50
Molten ore. Fredenthal 25:65 Ag
    23 '48
Momberger, William
  Wooding up, on the Mississippi
    engraving 28:73 Mr 6 '50
"Momentum" furniture. Pahlmann
    27:58-9 O 3 '49
Mommer, Paul
  Studio interior bw 36:92 Ja 25 '54
  Artist and his work photog bw
    36:92 Ja 25 '54 port.
Mona Lisa (La Gioconde). Leo-
    nardo da Vinci bw 35:51
    Ag 17 '53 original and 7
    forgeries bw 39:141 S 26 '55
  Decker. Fanny Brice as Mona
    Lisa bw 4:34 Ap 18 '38
Mona Lisa with moustache. Du-
    champ 32:102 Ap 28 '52
Monasteries
  Cistercian monastery, Clair-
    vaux, France photog bw 22:
    75 Ap 7 '47
  St. George monastery, Pales-

tine photog bw 20:63 Ap 1
    '46
  Spanish monastery, 12th cen-
    tury, moved to Miami
    Beach, Florida photog bw
    36:60 Ja 25 '54
  Valamo monastery, Finland
    airview photog bw 7:72 O
    30 '39
  Wat Bovornives, Bangkok
    photog 38:80 Mr 7 '55
Monday night at Met. Marsh 40:
    82 F 6 '56
Mondrian, Piet
  Composition 19:6 Jy 2 '45; 19:
    6-7 Jy 2 '45; 33:96 O 27 '52
  Composition in red and white
    19:6 Jy 2 '45
  Composition in white and blue
    (3 paintings) 19:7 Jy 2 '45
  Composition in white and red
    19:6 Jy 2 '45
  Gallatin. Artist in his studio
    photog bw 4:45 My 2 '38
    port.
  Newman. Piet Mondrian photog
    bw 20:11 F 4 '46 port.
  Piet Mondrian; studio photogs
    bw 19:8 Jy 2 '45 port.
Monet, Claude
  Rouen 5:26 O 10 '38
  Still life 29:90 N 27 '50
  Claude Monet photog bw 5:24
    O 10 '38 port.
  Renoir. Monet at Argenteuil
    32:93 My 19 '52 port.
Monhegan Harbor, Maine. Rev-
    ington 29:72 Ag 21 '50
Monhegan Island, Maine: scenery
    in paintings of famous A-
    merican artists 29:70-3 Ag
    21 '50
"Monitor" (ship)
  Launching of the Monitor, *
    Greenpoint, L.I. 39:113 O
    17 '55
Monitor and the Merrimac, 1862.
    Davidson 9:49 O 28 '40
Monkeys See also Animals,
    Imaginary--Monkeys
  Frogs and monkey woodcarv-

ing bw, Bali 15:115 O 25
'43
Moselio. Ape sculpture bw 3:
42 N 22 '37
Reinhardt. Mandrill and
maidens 32:89 Mr 24 '52
Rousseau. Exotic landscape
33:95 O 27 '52
Seurat. Grande Jatte 31:60-2
Jy 23 '51
Takamura. Monkey sculpture
30:74 My 28 '51
The monocle. sculpture bw Cal-
der 24:95 Ap 12 '48
Monoliths
Vigeland. Oslo monolith sculp-
ture bw 25:52 O 25 '48
"Monongahela" (ship)
Salvage of the U.S.S. Monon-
gahela, 1867 9:49 O 28 '40
Monroe, James
James Monroe bw 6:31 Je 19
'39; 8:102 Je 3 '40; 10:26
Mr 3 '41; 19:84 S 24 '45
Monroe, Keith
The unknown political prisoner
sculpture bw 34:40 Je 1 '53
Monsters See Animals, Imagin-
ary
Mont St. Michel, Benedictine ab-
bey, 1203 photog 26:72 Je
13 '49 bw 22:67 Ap 7 '47
Mont Sainte-Victoire 11:77 D 1
'41; 26:66 F 7 '49; 32:82 F
25 '52
Mont Sainte-Victoire. Churchill
26:66 F 7 '49
Montage
Ernst. Above the clouds walks
the moonlight bw 34:25 My
25 '53
Hausmann. Montage bw 34:25
My 25 '53
Picabia. Portrait bw 34:25 My
25 '53
"Montagne" (ship) French, 1794
The glorious first of June 24:
67 My 10 '48
Montagu, Mary
Lady Mary Montague bw 25:112
S 13 '48

Montaigne, Michel Eyquem
Montaigne bw 31:78 Jy 30 '51
Montanarini, Luigi
Artist at work 27:47 Ag 1 '49
port.
Monte Alban, Mexico, temple
photog bw 22:100 F 24 '47
Montenegro, Roberto
The slaughter wall 4:29 Mr 14
'38
Monteux, Pierre
Pierre Monteux photogs bw 26:
154-5 My 23 '49
Montezuma in chains bw 21:46 D
16 '46
Montgomery, Bernard
Sir Bernard Montgomery,
"Time" cover portrait 17:
62 D 11 '44
Montgomery, Richard
Trumbull. Death of General
Montgomery 29:42-3 Jy 3
'50
Monticello, Virginia. photog bw
Jefferson, archt. 14:65 Ap
12 '43
Montmartre. bw Curry 15:18 N
29 '43
Montmartre steps.* Davis, G.R.
19:55 Jy 16 '45
Montsee war memorial, 1914-8,
Neo-Greek temple photog
bw 3:23 Ag 30 '37
Monuments See Memorials and
Monuments
Moon. rock sculpture bw Vagis
40:123 Je 11 '56
Moon dance. Hall 24:86 Mr 8 '48
Mooney, Tom
Tom Mooney, age 54 photog
bw 4:62 Ja 10 '38
Moonlight. Blakelock 23:101 S 8
'47
Moonlight. Thomas, B. 14:46 Mr
8 '43
Moonlight. Sterne 28:82 Mr 20
'50
Moonlight march. woodcut bw
Liu Te-hwa 18:59 Ap 9 '45
Moonlight on the Osage. bw Bent-
on 6:70 Ap 24 '39

Moore, A. Goddesses bw 35:162 O 26 '53

Moore, Catharine T.
Catharine Moore bw 31:96 D 10 '51

Moore, Charles Herbert
The old bridge 19:84 S 10 '45

Moore, Clement C.
Clement Moore bw 31:96 D 10 '51
"The Night Before Christmas," Moore's poem, printed and illustrated by author's daughter, Mary Moore Ogden 31:96-100 D 10 '51

Moore, George
Beerbohm. Mr. W. B. Yeats presenting Mr. George Moore to the Queen of the Fairies bw 23:89 N 17 '47

Moore, Henry
Tube shelter perspective, 1941 chalk and water colors 26:56 Mr 21 '49
Prometheus 33:86 Jy 14 '52 (lithograph)
Bird basket, wood bw 22:78 Ja 20 '47 (sculpture)
Composition, wood bw 22:79 Ja 20 '47 (sculpture)
Family bw 24:95 Ap 12 '48 (sculpture)
Family group, bronze bw 22:78 Ja 20 '47 (sculpture)
Figure (female), marble bw 22:78 Ja 20 '47 (sculpture)
Mother and child bw 33:86 O 2 '52 (sculpture)
Reclining figure, wood bw 22:78-9 Ja 20 '47 (sculpture)
Three standing figures 25:100 S 27 '48 (sculpture)
Artist and his work photog bw 22:77 Ja 20 '47 port.

Moore, Madiline
Madiline bw 14:8 Ja 4 '43

Moore, Marianne
Lynes. Marianne Moor photog bw 27:16 O 10 '49

Moose
Giesel (Dr. Seuss). "Thidwick the Big-hearted Moose" bw 25:26-7 N 22 '48

Morado, Chavez
The fire eater bw 20:58 Je 3 '46
The foolish virgins bw 20:58 Je 3 '46
Evolution of spring 41:104 D 3 '56 (mosaic)

Moran, Earl
Calendar girls 18:46 Ja 1 '45 bw 9:4 D 30 '40
Earl Moran photogs bw 9:6 D 30 '40 port.

Moran, Edward
Embarkation of the pilgrims from Southampton, 1620 13:75 N 23 '42 bw 24:68-9 Je 14 '48

Moran, Percy
Signing the Compact 13:75 N 23 '42

Moran, Thomas
Western landscape 19:86 S 10 '45
Thomas, Moran bw 19:82 S 10 '45 port.

Morand, Guillemette
Nativity at Saint-Paul de Vence bw 27:56 D 29 '49

More, Thomas
Holbein. Sir Thomas More 3:33 D 27 '37

Moretti, Giuseppe
Vulcan sculpture bw 3:63 N 29 '37

Morey, Charles R.
Charles Morey photog bw 11:43 O 13 '41

Morgan, John Pierpont
J. P. Morgan 26:122 Ap 25 '49 photog bw 8:14-7 Mr 11 '40; 10:10 My 19 '41
Leighton. Mr. Morgan and Mr. Vanderbilt in a sleigh 6:31 Je 19 '39
Pach brothers. J. P. Morgan photog bw 3:17 O 25 '37

Morgan, John Pierpont, Jr.
J. P. Morgan, Jr. photog bw 26:123 Ap 25 '49

Morgan, Thomas Hunt
  Thomas Hunt Morgan photogs
    bw 3:69 S 13 '37
Morgan Library, New York City
  "The Written Word," exhibit
    of illuminated manuscripts
    18:57-62 Ap 2 '45
Morison, Samuel Eliot
  Samuel Eliot Morison photog
    bw 40:57 Je 25 '56
Morisot, Berthe
  Jour d'ete (Summer's day) bw
    40:148 Ap 23 '56
Morley, Christopher
  Christopher Morley photog bw
    16:82 My 1 '44
Morley, John
  John Morley 24:53 Ap 26 '48
Mormons
  Young, M. This is the place
    sculpture bw 10:79 F 17 '41
Morning. sculpture bw Bates 14:
    42 Mr 8 '43
Morning in Port-au-Prince. Bene-
    detto 8:36 Ja 1 '40
"Morning Star" (ship)
  Currier and Ives print. Queen
    of the West vs. Morning
    Star 21:74 S 2 '46
Morning wreath. Hall 24:86 Mr 8
    '48
Morris, George L. K.
  Unequal combat bw 26:84 F 21
    '49
Morris, Gouverneur
  Gouverneur Morris 39:62 Jy 4
    '55 bw 16:47 Ja 17 '44
Morris, Lewis
  Lewis Morris bw 15:9 Jy 5 '43
Morris, Robert
  Robert Morris bw 15:9 Jy 5 '43
Morse, Jared, architect
  Cullen and Foreman Building,
    Grand Junction, Colo. --
    revolving building photog bw
    38:133 F 7 '55
  Jared Morse photog bw 38:133
    F 7 '55 port.
Morse, Lucretia Pickering
    (Walker)
  Morse, S. F. B. Mrs. S. F. B.

Morse and her two children
    17:59 D 18 '44
Morse, Samuel Finley Breese
  Allegorical landscape showing
    New York University 17:62
    D 18 '44
  David Curtis De Forest 17:60
    D 18 '44
  Eli Whitney 38:66 Ag 29 '55
    bw 6:31 Je 19 '39
  Gallery of the Louvre 17:62 D
    18 '44
  Lafayette 17:61 D 18 '44 bw 5:
    28 O 31 '38; 6:26 Je 19 '39
  Miss Emma Gordon Shields
    17:60 D 18 '44
  Mrs. David Curtis De Forest
    17:60 D 18 '44
  Mrs. S. F. B. Morse and her
    two children 17:59 D 18 '44
  The Reverend Nathaniel Bowen
    17:60 D 18 '44
  Sketches from the artist's
    sketchbook bw 17:63 D 18
    '44 (drawings)
  S. F. B. Morse, daguerrotype,
    age 59 bw 5:28 O 31 '38
    port.
  S. F. B. Morse and his family
    photog bw 17:58 D 18 '44
    port.
  Self-portrait, age 23 12:59 Je
    15 '42 port.
Mortar and pestle, wood, U.S.
    colonial photog 38:119 Ap
    18 '55
Mortimer Family shield of arms
    22:69 My 26 '47
Morton, John
  John Morton bw 15:9 Jy 5 '43
Morton, Levi P.
  Levi Morton 9:9 Ag 5 '40
Mosaics
  Adam and Eve, vestibule, St.
    Mark's, Venice 35:34 D 28
    '53
  Creation of the world, vesti-
    bule, St. Mark's, Venice
    35:34 D 28 '53
  Earplugs, Inca, gold with
    turquoise inlay 36:104 Ap

Mosaics (cont.)
12 '54
Floor mosaic, human figures,
Greek, Troy (Hissarlik),
Turkey bw 13:102 N 16 '42
Gold purse lid, Anglian, inlaid
with glass, 7th century 31:
84 Jy 16 '51
Legend of St. Mark, St. Mark's,
Venice 35:34 D 28 '53
Madonna and Child, St. Mark's,
Venice 35:Cover D 28 '53
Pendant, Inca, skull inlaid
with gold and stones 36:104
Ap 12 '54
Quetzalcoatl mask, Aztec,
c1519 bw 24:84 Mr 22 '48
Royal standard of Ur, panels,
Sumerian 40:90-1 Je 4 '56
Saracenic mosaic, Palace of
Farouk I, Egypt bw 16:88 Ap
10 '44
Sumerian war chariot and
armed soldiers bw 40:80 Je
4 '56

Byzantine and Early Christian
Angel 28:68 Mr 27 '50
Angel Gabriel 29:58 D 25 '50
Child's head 28:68 Mr 27 '50
Christ between Peter and Paul
28:68 Mr 27 '50
Head of Christ, Chora church,
Istanbul 29:54 D 25 '50
Helios 28:71 Mr 27 '50
Hunt of the Amazons 28:78 Mr
27 '50
Pope John VII 28:69 Mr 27 '50
St. John the Baptist 29:60 D
25 '50
St. Peter's, Rome, mosaics
28:68-71 Mr 27 '50
Santa Sophia, Istanbul, mosaics
29:56-60 D 25 '50
Virgin and child 29:56-7 D 25
'50

Contemporary
Bradford. Mosacis, chapel,
England 35:38 Ag 24 '53
Leger. Litany of the Virgin,

Assy church, France 28:73
Je 19 '50
Morado. Evolution of spring
41:104 D 3 '56
Moscow See also The Kremlin
Imperial palace--Interiors:
Angulous Hall, Golden
Room; Exteriors: Red Porch
38:62-5 Ja 31 '55
Imperial theater, gala per-
formance, 1856 38:64 Ja
31 '55
Ouspensky cathedral 38:62-3
Ja 31 '55
Red Square army review pho-
tog bw 3:73 D6 '37
St. Basil's cathedral 38:60-1
Ja 31 '55
Timbered outpost, Moscow
c1240-1480 bw 14:93 Mr 29
'43
Moselio, Simon
Ape sculpture bw 3:42 N 22
'37
Moses
Chagall. Moses on Sinai etch-
ing bw 38:97 Je 13 '55
Dore. The brazen serpent bw
4:48 Ap 18 '38; 23:45 S 22
'47
Dore. Moses receiving the ten
commandments engraving
bw 4:48 Ap 18 '38; 6:53 F
20 '39
Giordano. The finding of
Moses 41:71 D 10 '56
Laning. Moses on Mt. Sinai
9:65 S 30 '40
Moses bw 29:160 D 11 '50
Moses, Giant Bible of Admont
34:78 F 23 '53
Moses, plaque, U.S. Congress,
bw 30:74 F 5 '51
Moses, Psalter of Ingeborg
34:78 F 23 '53
Moses sculpture, Ulm cathedral, Germany 35:31 D 28
'53
Perkins. Moses sculpture bw
21:62 Jy 22 '46
Schnorr. Moses discovered

in the bullrushes engraving
bw 6:55 Ja 30 '39

The story of Moses bw 6:52-3
F 20 '39

Tiepolo. Moses spurns the
crown of Pharoah 35:153 N
16 '53

Veronese. The finding of
Moses bw 40:104 F 20 '56

Moses, Anna Mary (Robertson)
("Grandma Moses")

Sugaring-off bw 25:77 O 25 '48

Winter is here bw 25:77 O 25
'48

Grandma Moses photog 25:76
O 25 '48 port. bw 41:152 D
24 '56 port.

Mosler, Henry

Betsy Ross bw 32:58 F 18 '52

Mosques

Blue mosque, Istanbul photogs
bw 8:82-3 Ap 8 '40

Dome of the Rock, Jerusalem
(Mosque of Omar) photog
6:54 My 15 '39; 20:58 Ap 1
'46; 38:78-9 My 9 '55 bw 31:
61 D 24 '51

Great Mosque of Mecca photog
38:76 My 9 '55 bw 2:62-3
Mr 15 '37

Moslem mosque, Seringapatam,
India photog bw 10:94 My 12 '41

Mosque of the Shah, Isfahan, Iran
photog 38:72 My 9 '55

Mother (Arrangement in grey and
black, no. 1). bw Whistler
5:29 O 31 '38

Mother and Child See also Chil-
dren; Family Groups;
Mary, Virgin--Madonna and
Child

Bellows. Emma and her children 11:77 O 6 '41

Carpenko. Mother and child
woodcarving bw 32:14 F 11
'52

Cassatt. Before the window 12:
56 Ja 19 '42

Cassatt. Mother and child 12:
56 Ja 19 '42; 36:99 My 17 '54

Cassatt. The toilet 12:55 Ja 19
'42

Cassatt. Young mother sewing
12:56 Ja 19 '42

Conway. Mother and child bw
27:55 D 26 '49; 30:79 Mr 5
'51

De Creeft. Maternity sculpture
bw 14:42 Mr 8 '43

Epstein. Mother and child
sculpture bw 6:83 My 22 '39

Eskimo mother and child
stone carving bw 36:67 My
24 '54

Gross, C. Bouncing baby sculpture bw 30:65 Ja 8 '51

Gross, C. Mother and child
sculpture bw 5:7 N 28 '38

Hovenden. Breaking home ties
9:76 D 9 '40; 27:60 Ag 29
'49

Isis holding her son, Horus
statue blue faience, Egypt
41:114 N 26 '56

Koch. Mrs. Doubleday and
children 25:94 O 18 '48

Koch. Mrs. Theodore Roosevelt and family bw 41:78 Ag
13 '56

Maldarelli. Mother and child
sculpture bw 22:137 Mr 24
'47

Mary, Queen of Scots, and
her son 41:153 N 5 '56

Meltsner. Mother and child 16:
46 Ja 3 '44

Mestrovic. Mother and child
sculpture bw 22:132 Je 2 '47

Michnick. Peasant mother and
child sculpture bw 4:62 Ap
25 '38

Mrs. Freake and Baby Mary,
American primitive, Mass-
achusetts, 1675 bw 5:28 O
31 '38

Moore, H. Mother and child
sculpture bw 33:86 O 2 '52

Morse, S.F.B. Mrs. S.F.B.
Morse and her two chil-
dren 17:59 D 18 '44

Peirce. Alzira cuts Mike's
hair* 19:83 N 12 '45

Mother and Child (cont.)
  Renoir. Mme Charpentier and
    her children 3:47 Jy 5 '37
  Renoir. Mme Renoir and Pierre
    32:94 My 19 '52
  Repin. Recruit's farewell 14:
    46 Mr 29 '43
  Sargent. Mrs. Saint-Gaudens
    and son 25:94 O 18 '48
  Smith. Mother and child, on
    "Good Housekeeping" covers
    bw 12:57 Ja 19 '42
  Tynys. Mother and child sculp-
    ture bw 28:98 Mr 13 '50
  Van Gogh. Mother and child*
    24:67 Mr 1 '48
  Wilson, J. Mother and child
    21:65 Jy 22 '46
  Zorach. Mother and child
    sculpture bw 7:37 Jy 17 '39;
    8:92-3 Ap 1 '40; 32:77 Ja 7
    '52
"Mother Goose Riddle Rhymes,"
  rebus book. Low, J. 36:6-7
  Ap 19 '54
Motherwell, Robert
  Robert Motherwell photog bw
    30:34 Ja 15 '51 port.
Motion in Art See also Perspec-
  tive
  Duchamp. Nude descending a
    staircase 28:60 Ja 2 '50;
    32:102 Ap 28 '52 bw 26:89 F
    21 '49; 32:100 Ap 28 '52
  Rattner. Transcendence 27:62
    Ag 29 '49
Motion Pictures
  Marsh. Twenty cent movie 12:
    75 Ap 20 '42; 21:77 N 25 '46
  Taubes. "The Birth of a Na-
    tion" is filmed by Griffith
    8:40-1 Ja 15 '40
Motley, John Lothrop
  John Motley bw 10:26 Mr 3 '41
Mott, Lucretia
  Lucretia Mott photog bw 33:97
    S 29 '52
Moulin de la Galette. Picasso 8:
  57 Mr 4 '40
Moulin de la Galette. Utrillo 28:
  94 Ja 16 '50

Moulin Rouge, Paris See also
  Toulouse-Lautrec, H.
  Bonnard. At the Moulin Rouge
    25:53 Jy 26 '48
  Toulouse-Lautrec. At the
    Moulin Rouge 28:98-9 My
    15 '50
  Toulouse-Lautrec. The dance
    at Moulin Rouge 28:99 My
    15 '50
Moulton-Barrett, Sarah
  Lawrence, T. Pinkie (Sarah
    Moulton-Barrett) 4:25 Ja
    24 '38
Mount, William Sidney
  Bargaining for a horse 18:65
    Je 25 '45
  A barroom oracle relates 18:
    66 Je 25 '45
  The breakdown (A bar room
    scene) 18:67 Je 25 '45
  Dance of the haymakers 18:67
    Je 25 '45
  Eel spearing at Setauket 18:66
    Je 25 '45
  Fortune telling 18:68 Je 25
    '45
  Long Island farmhouses 18:68
    Je 25 '45
  The power of music 18:66 Je
    25 '45
  Raffling for a goose 18:66 Je
    25 '45
  Reading the Tribune 18:65 Je
    25 '45
  Ringing the pig 18:66 Je 25 '45
  The truant gamblers 18:66 Je
    25 '45
  Who'll turn the grindstone 12:
    73 Ap 20 '42; 18:65 Je 25
    '45
  Winding up 18:68 Je 25 '45
  William Sidney Mount; home
    photogs bw 18:64 Je 25 '45
Mount Calvary. Johnson, W.H.
  21:65 Jy 22 '46
Mount Corcoran. Bierstadt 27:
  59 Ag 29 '49
Mount Eisenhower. bw Eisen-
  hower 26:44 F 21 '49

Mount of Olivcs See also Jesus
　Christ--Gethsemane
Mount of Olives, Jerusalem
　photog 20:58 Ap 1 '46
Mount Pleasant, Georgian man-
　sion, Philadelphia--eight-
　enth century parlor photog
　18:54 My 7 '45
Mount Rushmore National Memo-
　rial, Black Hills, S. Dak.
　photogs Borglum, sculptor
　4:26 Je 27 '38 bw 3:104 O 4
　'37 complete with 4 units bw
　7:19 Jy 17 '39 Detail Lin-
　coln bw 18:Cover Je 18 '45
　Detail, Washington bw 11:
　103 O 6 '41
Mount Vernon, Washington's
　home, Virginia photog bw
　5:28 O 31 '38
Mountain landscape. Wartik 39:
　136-7 N 21 '55
Mountain mountain on the wall,
　who is most beautiful of us
　all. Frnst 32:59 Ja 21 '52
Mountain of heresy, triptych de-
　tail. Bosch 27:81 N 14 '49
Mountain sheep. sculpture bw
　prehistoric, Northwest,
　U.S. 32:100 My 5 '52
Mountain sunrise, Cole, T. 19:
　86 S 10 '45
Mountains.
　Bierstadt. Thunderstorm in
　　the Rockies 19:86 S 10 '45
　Church. Scene in the Catskills
　　19:84 S 10 '45
　Cole, T. The Catskill moun-
　　tains 9:77 D 9 '40
　Cropsey. View of Catskill
　　house 19:84 S 10 '45
　Dehn. Sopris Peak 11:43 Ag 11
　　'41
　Dehn. Yosemite 11:44 Ag 11 '41
　Dore. The Scottish highlands 7:
　　33 Jy 31 '39
　Hart, W. M. Chocorua Moun-
　　tain, New Hampshire 19:83
　　S 10 '45
　Hartley. Waldenstein peaks 32:
　　86 Je 16 '52

　Hudson River School: land-
　　scape panoramas, Catskill
　　Mountains 19:82-6 S 10 '45
　Hurd. The dry river 7:25 Jy
　　24 '39; 21:76 N 25 '46 bw
　　11:9 N 17 '41
　Lea. C-47 flies over the Hump
　　35:56 N 2 '53
　May Yuan. Bare willows and
　　distant mountains 15:62 O
　　11 '43
　Moran, T. Western landscape
　　19:86 S 10 '45
　Waldo. Sierra peaks bw 22:40
　　Je 16 '47
Mountains could talk. Kosa 11:74
　O 27 '41
Mountbatten, Louis Alexander
　Louis Mountbatten photog bw
　　23:72 O 20 '47
Mountbatten, Philip
　Philip Mountbatten photogs 23:
　　71-6 O 20 '47
Mourning dove. sculpture bw
　Fdmondson 3:79 N 1 '37
Moutard, Robert, architect
　La Griffe and Moutard.
　　French resistance martyrs
　　memorial, Auxerre, France
　　photog bw 26:35 Ap 18 '49
Mozart, Wolfgang
　Croce. Mozart family, 1780
　　40:117 Ap 23 '56
　Lange. Wolfgang Mozart, un-
　　finished portrait bw 40:127
　　Ap 23 '56
　Mozart, in his mid-20's 40:
　　113 Ap 23 '56
　Mozart presented at Austrian
　　court bw 40:121 Ap 23 '56
Mozert, Zoe
　Nude 18:46 Ja 1 '45
Mrs. Cushman's house. Wyeth,
　N.C. 20:79 Je 17 '46
Mrs. Feake and Baby Mary, A-
　merican primitive, Massa-
　chusetts, 1675 bw 5:28 O
　31 '38
Mrs. T in cream silk. Bellows
　20:79 Mr 25 '46

Mueller, Hans Alexander
  Wood engravings 7:71-2 D 4
    '39
Mugs
  German ceramic beer mug,
    14th century 22:80 My 26
    '47
  Oxford College silver mugs bw
    3:77 D 13 '37
Muiden castle, Holland photogs
  28:122-3 Mr 6 '50
Muiderslot (Lock castle), Holland,
  c1200 photogs bw 8:45 Je 3
    '40
Mulatto from Alvarado. Soriano
  20:60 Je 3 '46
Mulk, Haji Musavir el
  Mr. Churchill and his friends
    overthrowing Hitler and his
    35:70 N 9 '53
Mullen, Brian
  Daily occurence in the Channel
    26:53 Mr 7 '49
Mullins, Priscilla
  John Alden and Priscilla Mull-
    ins out riding* bw 25:131
    N 29 '48
  Millet, F. D. John and Pris-
    cilla bw 11:85 S 8 '41
Mulvaney, John
  Custer's last rally bw 24:12
    Je 21 '48
Mummers, Middle Ages* bw 22:
  74 My 26 '47
Munch, Charles
  Charles Munch photog bw 27:
    61 O 17 '49
Munchkins, illustrations from
  "The Wonderful Wizard of
  Oz." Denslow 35:53 D 28
    '53
Munnings, Alfred James
  Duke of Windsor, fox hunter,
    1921 28:122 My 22 '50
  A gala day 23:85 N 17 '47
  Procession to Ascot 28:120-1
    My 22 '50
Munsell color tree photog 17:46
  Jy 3 '44
Muraba, Ibn Saud's palace, Riad
  photog bw 14:72-3 My 31 '43

Mural assistant. Bouche 6:28 F
  13 '39
Mural Painting and Decoration
  Baker, E.H. Economic ac-
    tivities in the days of the
    Naragansett planters, Post
    Office, Wakefield, R.I. 10:
    44 Ja 27 '41
  Benton. History of Missouri,
    with details 2:35-7 N 25 '46
    Jesse James, detail bw 6:
    70 Ap 24 '39
  Biddle. U.S. Justice Depart-
    ment murals, Washington,
    D.C.: Society freed through
    justice; tenement 2:34-5 Ja
    4 '37
  Billings, Henry. Mobile three-
    dimensional mural, Ford
    Building, New York's
    World's Fair 6:42 Mr 13
    '39
  Bohrod. Clinton in winter,
    Post Office, Clinton, Ill.
    10:45 Ja 27 '41
  Bouche. Railroad club-car
    murals 11:49-50 Ag 18 '41
  Brumidi. Capitol Building
    murals, Washington, D.C.
    31:52-6 Jy 2 '51
  Byzantine mural, Christ en-
    throned bw, Spain, c1150
    9:53 Jy 22 '40
  Cadmus. Main street 2:45 Mr
    29 '37 detail 21:74 N 25
    '46
  Cezanne. Classic goddess,
    1860* bw 32:78 F 25 '52
  Conway. Oklahoma land rush*
    30: 78-9 Mr 5 '51
  Curry. John Brown, Kansas
    State Capitol Building bw
    15:20 N 29 '43 mural study
    7:35 D 25 '39
  Curry. U.S. Supreme Court
    mural, Washington, D.C.
    bw 1:28 N 23 '36
  Daugherty. Fairfield Court
    history of transportation
    mural, Stamford, Ct. 3:
    49-50 O 25 '37

Early Christian and Roman frescoes, Vatican grottoes 28:65-78 Mr 27 '50

Faulkner, B. Oregon history, State Capitol, Salem 7:44-5 Ag 14 '39

Fiene. Cattle roundup, U.S. Department of the Interior, Washington, D.C. 10:43 Ja 27 '41

Fiume. Murals, Andrea Dorea, Italian steamship 34:58-9 Je 22 '53

Food for the dead,* Tomb of Ptah-Iruk, Egypt, 2500 B.C. bw 24:77 Ja 19 '48

French. Cavalrymen crossing a river, Parcel Post Building, Richmond, Va. 10:44 Ja 27 '41

French. Origins of food, details bw 6:62-3 F 27 '39

Gauguin. Peasants and angel 28:93 My 1 '50

Giotto. Lives of Christ and Mary, Arena chapel frescoes, Padua, 14th century 25:Cover, 34-57 D 27 '48

Giotto and pupils. Story of St. Francis of Assisi, San Francesco church frescoes, Assisi 16:65-71 Ap 10 '44

Gould. Source of power, Post Office, Greenville, Ky. 10:45 Ja 27 '41

Goya. The witches sabbath 31:64-5 O 1 '51

Gozzoli. Journey of the Magi, Medici-Riccardi chapel frescoes 19:Cover, 43-5 D 24 '45

Grant, G. Kennebunkport, Me. 1825 bw 18:34 Ap 2 '45

Haitian artists. Primitive murals, cathedral, Port-au-Prince 33:64-5 D 22 '52

Hirschfield. Cartoon caricatures of motion picture stars, Fifth Avenue Cinema Theater, New York City bw 36:20-1 My 17 '54

Hurd. An early meeting on the Oklahoma prairie 30:78-9 Mr 5 '51

Hurd. Old pioneers, Post Office, Big Springs, Texas 10:46 Ja 27 '41

Inca hammered gold mural 36:102-3 Ap 12 '54

Indian, North American, Governor's Room fresco, San Fernando Mission, Calif. 40:56-7 Ja 16 '56

Johnson, T.L. Twenty great battles of the world, West Point mess hall bw 11:4 N 24 '41

Krohg. Peace and freedom, United Nations Security Council, General Assembly Building, New York City bw 33:114 N 3 '52

Kroll. Triumph of justice Attorney General's office, Washington, D.C. 4:38 Ap 25 '38

Kuan Yin fresco bw, Chinese, 10th century 35:155 O 5 '53

Laning. History of printing, New York Public Library 9:65-6 S 30 '40

Lea. The nesters, Post Office, Washington, D.C.10:46 Ja 27 '41

Lippi, Fra Filippo. Adoration of the Child fresco 19:44 D 24 '45

Lockwood. Daniel Boone's arrival in Kentucky, Post Office, Lexington, Ky. 10:46 Ja 27 '41

Lord Buddha's farewell* fresco, Persian-Chinese 6:26 Je 12 '39

Lorenzetti. Descent from the cross fresco, Lower Church of St. Francis, Assisi 39:30 D 26 '55

Lorenzo da Viterbo. Marriage of the Virgin fresco bw 21:103 O 28 '46

Luini. Body of St. Catherine borne by angels to Sinai fresco bw 6:32 F 13 '39

Malskat. Lubeck church murals--forgeries 34:49-50 Ja 12 '53

McCreery. Products of Missouri, Post Office, Monett, Mo. 10:45 Ja 27 '41

Marsh. Postal activities murals, U.S. Post Office Department, Washington, D.C. 2:33 Ja 4 '37

Martins, D. S. Electrification, Post Office, Lenoir City, Tenn. 10:44 Ja 27 '41

Masaccio. The tribute money, Brancacci chapel fresco, Florence 39:22-3 D 26 '55

Matisse. Mural design (last work) 37:42 D 13 '54

Mayan mural, Bonampak 27:80-4 N 21 '49

Medieval mural by teen agers for museum exhibit, Carnegie Institution, Pittsburgh 35:76 S 21 '53

Michelangelo. Sistine chapel fresco, ceiling 21:62-9 Jy 1 '46 ceiling and altar 27:25-49 D 26 '49

Millman and Siporin. Historical mural, Post Office, St. Louis, Mo. 13:71-4 O 12 '42

Mural prizewinners in commissions for public building decoration, Fine Arts Section, U.S. Treasury Department 10:42-6 Ja 27 '43

Nbebele tribe, South Africa, decorated exterior dwelling walls 34:173 My 4 '53

Oklahoma history paintings, for mural, First National Bank, Tulsa, Okla. 30:78 Mr 5 '51

Orozco. Evolution of culture in Mexico, Normal School, Mexico City 25:70 N 22 '48

Palmer, W.C. Medical history

scenes, Queen's General Hospital, New York 3:40-2 O 11 '37

Picasso. Guernica fresco bw 3:64 Jy 26 '37

Piero della Francesca. Story of the true cross, San Francesco chapel fresco, Arezzo 20:60-8 Ap 22 '46

Pinturicchio. Life of Aenaes Piccolomini (Pius II), Piccolomini Library frescoes, Siena 22:73-6 Mr 3 '47

Poor. U.S Justice Department, Washington, D.C. 2:36 Ja 4 '37

Portinari. St. Francis preaching to birds bw 27:76 Jy 4 '49

Raphael. Battle of Milvian Bridge, Vatican fresco bw 39:39 D 26 '55

Refrigier. Oklahoma's development* 30:78 Mr 5 '51

Rivera. Cortes conquest of Mexico, Palace of Cortes, Cuernavaca, Mexico 6:41 Ja 23 '39

Rivera. History of Mexico,* bw, Del Prado Hotel, Mexico City 23:104-6 N 3 '47

Rivera. Man's dependence on water, Water Storage Tank, Mexico City 31:73 S 17 '51

Rivera. Nudes bw Ciro's, Hotel Reforma, Mexico City 16:78 F 28 '44; 23:106 N 3 '47

Rivera. Pan-American unity,* San Francisco Junior College 10:52-6 Mr 3 '41

Roman frescoes, St. Peter's, Rome 28:71 Mr 27 '50

Russell. Lewis and Clark expedition bw 33:65 N 10 '52

St. Louis burying dead in Palestine during Crusades,* Luxembourg palace, Paris bw 21:41 O 21 '46

St. Michael, door of church compound, Gondar, Ethi-

opia 39:88 N 21 '55

Sant' Angelo in Formis frescoes, 11th century 17:62
Jy 24 '44

Santa Chiara frescoes, Naples,
14th and 18th centuries 17:
60-2 Jy 24 '44

Savoy chapel fresco, St. Stephen's, Venice bw 21:51 N
11 '46

Schwarz. On the Oregon trail
bw 7:45 Ag 14 '39

Shinn. Plaza Hotel, c1910 21:
88 N 18 '46

Stuart, J.E.B. French cavalrymen crossing a river 10:
44 Ja 27 '41

Tamayo. Indian woman and
baskets of flowers* 34:103
Mr 16 '53

Tintoretto. Life of Christ,
School of San Rocco, Venice
31:Cover, 30-49 D 24 '51

Tomb murals of Ramesis II,
c1100 B.C. 24:83 Ja 19 '48

Two dieties fresco bw Chinese,
12th century 35:152, 155 O
5 '53

Van Duzer. Growth of Tulsa,
Oklahoma* 30:78 Mr 5 '51

Veronese. Villa Maser frescoes 29:58-65 Jy 24 '50

Muraviev, Apostal
Count Maraviev bw 31:110 O
29 '51

Murder of Archbishop Thomas a
Beckett 40:98 Mr 26 '56

Murder of Marcus Whitman, 1847*
print bw 39:74-5 D 26 '55

Murillo, Bartolome Estaban
Christ giving bread to St. Felix
of Cantalice bw 39:94 O 10
'55

Esau selling his brighright 41:
73 D 10 '56

St. Thomas of Villanueva dividing his clothing among
beggar boys 4:42 My 16 '38

Murillo bw 4:40 My 16 '38 port.

Murphy and Mackey, architects

Catholic church of the Resurrection, St. Louis, Mo.
photog 39:114 D 26 '55

Murphy-Dolan Crowd
L. G. Murphy and J. J. Dolan
photog bw 11:68 Ag 4 '41

Muse of music. sculpture bw
Stanley 9:82 O 21 '40

"Museum Director's Choice" of
art objects in collection

1. Finley, David E., National
Gallery, Washington, D.C.
Verrocchio. Lorenzo de'
Medici terra cotta 38:95
F 21 '55

2. Morley, Grace, San Francisco Museum of Art
Klee. Nearly hit 38:61 Mr
14 '55

3. Robinson, Frederick B.,
Springfield (Mass.) Muse-
um of Fine Arts
Chardin. Still life 38:125
My 2 '55

4. Bywaters, Jerry, Dallas
Museum of Fine Arts
Lester. Fort Davis, Texas
38:73 Je 6 '55

5. Rich, Daniel Catton, Art
Institute of Chicago
Degas. The millinery shop
39:119 N 7 '55

6. Story, Mrs. Ala, Museum
of Art, Santa Barbara,
Calif.
The buffalo hunter, unknown
artist, U.S. c1830-40 39:
111 N 21 '55

7. Colt, Thomas C., Jr.
Portland (Oreg.) Art Mu-
seum. Horse woodcarving,
China, 4th century B.C.
40:99 Ja 9 '56

8. Williams, Hermann, Jr.,
Corcoran Gallery of Art
Cassatt. Woman with a dog
40:67 Ja 23 '56

9. Washburn, Gordon, Car-
negie Institute. Blythe.
Post office 40:125 Je 4 '56

Museum Director's Choice (cont.)
   10. Bach, Otto Karl, Denver
       Art Museum
       Carved cedar screen, Tlin-
       git Indian, Alaska, c1825
       41:53 Jy 16 '56
Museum of Modern Art, New York
   City
   Architecture exhibit: Japanese
       house. bw Yoshimura,
       archt. 37:71-4 Ag 23 '54
   "Art in Our Time" opening
       exhibit 6:82-5 My 22 '39
   Furniture exhibit: Prize win-
       ning furniture for mass
       production 28:98-100 My 8
       '50
   Photography exhibit: "The Ex-
       act Instant," news photo-
       graphs of the past 100 years
       bw 26:12-4 F 21 '49
   Photography exhibit: "Forgot-
       ten Photographs" bw 31:12-
       4 S 10 '51
   Photography exhibit: "In and
       Out of Focus" 24:14-6 My
       10 '48
   Poster exhibit: "Artists for
       Victory," war posters 13:
       54-7 D 21 '42
   Poster exhibit: World War
       poster contest--Latin and
       North America bw 13:12-5
       N 2 '42
   Toy exhibit: Hughes. Plastic
       carnival toys photogs 29:
       32-3 D 25 '50
Museums See Galleries and
   Museums
Mushrooms
   Freund. Nonpoisonous and
       poisonous mushrooms 31:
       90-1 Ag 13 '51
Music, Antonio
   Antonio Music photog bw 36:
       110 Ap 26 '54 port.
Musicians and Musical Instruments
   Benton. The Jealous Lover of
       Lone Green Valley 6:71 Ap
       24 '39
   Bermudez. Musicians* 36:80-

   1 My 31 '54
   Caravaggio. Musicians bw 32:
       47 Je 9 '52
   David. First Bible of Charles
       the Bold 34:81 F 23 '53
   Davis, G. R. The music les-
       son 14:46 Ap 19 '43
   Dufy. The great concert bw
       34:136 Ap 13 '53
   Dufy. Orchestra* bw 36:113
       Ap 26 '54
   Eakins. Professionals at re-
       hearsal 16:74 My 15 '44
   Famous musicians--candid
       camera shots at rehearsals
       with Philadelphia orches-
       tra bw 14:45-50 Ja 18 '43
   Giorgione. Concert champetre
       23:52 Ag 4 '47; 39:170-1
       O 24 '55
   Giorgione and Titian. The con-
       cert 39:168-9 O 24 '55
   Halsman. Master musicians
       in the United States bw 16:
       43-50 Mr 13 '44
   Kent. Musician sculpture bw
       5:70 D 5 '38
   Kinnaras, woman-bird. Hindu
       mythology 38:68-9 F 7 '55
   Leonardo da Vinci. The mu-
       sician bw 7:17 Jy 17 '39
   Levine. String quartette 14:
       43 Mr 8 '43; 26:86 F 21 '49
   Peirce, W. The twins' con-
       cert 19:84 N 12 '45
   Picasso. The three musicians
       4:43 My 23 '38
   Sample. Band concert 3:44 N
       15 '37
   Sarasvati, Hindu goddess of
       rhythm statue bw 24:29 Ap
       5 '48
   Shahn. German band 37:97 O
       4 '54
   Tamayo. Musicians 34:101
       Mr 16 '53
   Taubes. Rehearsal 4:25 Je
       13 '38
   Ter Borch. The concert 24:
       80 Mr 22 '48
   Ven Eyck brothers. Musici-

ans, Ghent altarpiece 26:65
Ap 16 '49
Von Physter. Destiny litho-
graph bw 5:55 Ag 8 '38
Von Physter. Jam session lith-
ograph bw 5:55 Ag 8 '38
Weber. Two musicians 19:86
Ag 20 '45
Willard, A.M. Spirit of '76
bw 9:55 Ag 5 '40

Accordion
Davis, G.R. The music lesson
14:46 Ap 19 '43
Karfiol. Making music bw 9:
68 O 14 '40
Picasso. Accordionist bw 26:
82 My 2 '49

Bagpipes
Bosch. Hell, detail from Garden of Delights triptych 27:
82 N 14 '39

Cello
Adams, W. Gregor Piatigor-
sky 16:75 Ap 24 '44
Eakins. The cello player 16:
75 My 15 '44
Gauguin. Schneklud--Cellist
21:62 Jy 29 '46
John. Madame Guilhermina
Suggia bw 16:79 Ap 24 '44

Churinga
Churinga, paleolithic noisemaker photog 39:79 D 12 '55

Drum
Drum, New Hebrides photog
21:81 N 4 '46
U.S. military drum, Revolu-
tionary War photog 38:58
My 30 '55

Flute
Harnett. Emblems of peace 7:
25 Ag 28 '39
Marcks. Flute player sculp-
ture bw 28:71 F 6 '50
Tamayo. The flute player 20:

59 Je 3 '46
Taubes. Rehearsal 4:25 Je 13
'38

Guitar
Brackman. Still life with gui-
tar 8:60 F 5 '40
Braque. Guitarist bw 26:82
My 2 '49
Degas. Artist's father listen-
ing to guitarist, Pagans 25:
79 N 1 '48
Gris. The guitar player bw
26:86 Ja 10 '49
Lantz. Dan Cathey 10:47 F 3
'41
Steig. Guitarist woodcarving
bw 6:35-6 Ap 10 '39

Harp
Chagall. Song of David 33:99 O
6 '52
Lawrence, T. Lady Elizabeth
Conyngham 6:38 My 29 '39
Vodicka. Song of David sculp-
ture bw 41:76 S 10 '56

Harpsichord
Giorgione and Titian. The
concert 39:168-9 O 24 '55

Lute
Holbein. The ambassadors
24:82 Mr 22 '48
Memling. Shrine of St. Ursala, detail 34:84 Ap 6 '53

Lyre
Stanley. Muse of Music sculpture bw 9:82 O 21 '40

Mandolin
Braque. Compote dish, bottle and mandolin 26:85 My
2 '49
Braque. Still life, 1908 bw
26:82 My 2 '49
Still life with pink background
26:84 My 2 '49
Braque. Woman with mando-
lin 25:75 O 11 '48

Peirce, W. Bill plays an old
  mandolin 19:85 N 12 '45
Picasso. Woman with mando-
  lin 8:58 Mr 4 '40
Tamayo. Musicians 34:101
  Mr 16 '53

                 Organ
Leutze. Cromwell and Milton
  27:58 Ag 29 '49
Memling. Organ, Shrine of St.
  Ursala detail 34:85 Ap 6
  '53
Rosenthal. Sacred music 15:
  66 N 22 '43

                 Piano
Pittman. Miss Pat and Miss
  Eva Lion 18:69 F 19 '45

                Psaltery
Memling. Psaltery, Shrine of
  St. Ursala detail 34:82 Ap
  6 '53

                Singers
Calder. Singer sculpture bw
  33:88 Ag 25 '52
Davis, G. R. Caroler 23:Cover
  D 22 '47
Eakins. The concert singer 16:
  74 My 15 '44

                 Spinet
Ter Borch. The concert 24:80
  Mr 22 '48

                Trumpet
Harnett. Old models 27:60 Ag
  29 '49
Trumpeters and masked men,
  Mayan murals, Bonampak
  27:82 N 21 '49

             Viola da Gamba
Gainsborough. Karl Friedrich
  Abel 4:27 Ja 24 '38

             Viola d'Amour
Ter Borch. The concert 24:80
  Mr 22 '48

                 Violin
Benton. Jealous Lover of Lone
  Green Valley 6:71 Ap 24
  '39
Grunewald. Nativity panel,
  Isenheim altarpiece 30:82,
  84 Mr 26 '51
Harnett. Old models 27:60 Ag
  29 '49
Memling. Shrine of St. Ursala
  detail 34:83 Ap 6 '53
Mount. The power of music 18:
  66 Je 25 '45
Musk ox, Eskimo stone carving
  bw 36:70 My 24 '54
Mussolini, Benito
Blume. The eternal city bw
  3:20 D 6 '37
The hour of the hyena cartoon
  bw, from "Punch" 26:55 F
  14 '49
Mulk. Mr. Churchill and his
  friends overthrowing Hitler and his 35:70 N 9 '53
Mussolini caricature bw,
  Loyalist Spain 3:112 S 20
  '37
Mustard pot. silver, U.S. Colonial Van Dyck 38:117 Ap
  18 '55
Muybridge, Eadweard, photographer Galloping horse
  photog winning Stanford
  bet, 1872 bw 11:10 O 20
  '41
"Instantaneous" photographs
  of animals, zoopraxiscope
  bw 11:10-3 O 20 '41
Mwenze
Tropical forest 34:106 My 4
  '53
Mwenze photog 34:106 My 4
  '53 port.
"My Confession," Mexican War
  memoirs, written and illustrated by Chamberlain.
  I. 41:Cover, 68-82 Jy 23
      '56
  II. 41:52-9 Jy 30 '56
  III. 41:64-72 Ag 6 '56

My Egypt (grain elevator). De-
    muth 38:75 Mr 28 '55
My harvest home, Tasmania. bw
    Glover 12:78 F 9 '42
My mother. Bellows 11:60 S 8 '41
My neighbor, Mr. Lounsberry.
    bw Biddle 9:79 D 9 '40
My parents. Koerner 24:77 My
    10 '48
My wife. Lahey 6:28 F 13 '39
My wife and I. Philipp, R. 8:64
    Ap 8 '40
My Wisconsin. Grotenrath 25:58
    N 29 '48
Mycernus, King of Egypt
    Mycernus and his Queen,
        Khamernebti II, c2000 B.C.
        sculpture bw 9:50 Jy 22 '40
Myron
    Discobolus sculpture bw 5:46
        D 25 '38
Mysore palace, India photog 41:
    177 N 5 '56   bw 10:94-5 My
    12 '41   night view 9:73 N 25
    '40
Mystic Painting
    Blake. The four Zoas 36:60-4
        Ap 19 '54
    Davies, A.B. Afterthoughts of
        earth bw 16:79 Ap 24 '44
    Graves. Little known bird of
        the inner eye 25:64 O 11 '48
    Mystic painters, Northwest
        U.S. 35:84-9 S 28 '53
    Ryder. Death on a pale horse
        5:36 O 31 '38; 15:67 S 20 '43
    Ryder. The temple of the mind
        30:91 F 26 '51
Mythological Themes See also
        Animals, Imaginary; Gods
        and Goddesses; Imaginary
        Beings; Literary Themes
    Brown. Niagara Falls legends
        26:80 Je 6 '49
    Carpaccio. St. Ursala legend
        23:56-7 Ag 4 '47
    Cozanne. Classic goddess*
        mural bw 32:78 F 25 '52
    Chavannes. The sacred grove
        bw 28:88 Ja 16 '50
    Elgstroem. Eskimo myths and

    legends 20:8-10 Ja 14 '46
    Helios mosaic, Early Chris-
        tian 28:71 Mr 27 '50
    Memling. St. Ursala legend
        34:81-6 Ap 6 '53
    Poussin. Parnassus bw 25:78
        O 11 '48
    Rembrandt. Flora bw 28:58 Ja
        30 '50
    Sumerian myths inlaid panel
        40:88 Je 4 '56
    Volga titan, ice sculpture bw
        6:7 Ja 16 '39
    Wright. The golden egg bw
        29:124 Ag 28 '50

                 Actaeon
    Titian. Diana and Actaeon 41:
        106-7 O 22 '56

                 Adonis
    Titian. Venus and Adonis 4:
        29 Mr 21 '38

                 Aeneas
    Francesco di Giorgio Martini.
        The meeting of Dido and
        Aeneas 35:150-1 N 16 '53
    Giorgione. Evander showing
        Aeneas the site of Rome
        39:170 O 24 '55
    Virgil's "Aeneid," illuminated
        manuscript, 5th century
        32:86 Ap 14 '52

                 Amazons
    Courbet. The amazon (Louise
        Colet) 26:61 My 30 '49
    Hunt of the amazons mosaic,
        Early Christian 28:78 Mr
        27 '50
    Queen Penthesileia in battle*
        bw 14:6 Ja 4 '43

                 Androcles
    Wright. Androcles and the
        lion sculpture bw 29:124
        Ag 28 '50

                 Antaeus
    Pollaiuolo. Hercules slaying

Mythological Themes
    Antaeus (cont.)
    Antaeus sculpture bw 6:32
    F 13 '39

Antiope
Titian. Jupiter and Antiope bw
    12:44 Mr 9 '42

Ariadne
Tintoretto. Bacchus and Ariad-
    ne bw 12:44 Mr 9 '42

Atlantide
Mestrovic. Atlantide sculpture
    bw 22:135 Je 2 '47

Bacchus
Bacchus, mask cup, 18th cen-
    tury 25:129 D 6 '48
Poussin. The triumph of
    Bacchus 7:53 O 9 '39
Satyr holding Bacchus sculpture
    bw, Rome, 3rd century 28:
    76 Mr 27 '50
Tintoretto. Bacchus and Ari-
    adne bw 12:44 Mr 9 '42

Callisto
Boucher. Jupiter, in the guise
    of Diana, and Callisto 5:36
    S 26 '38

Cerberus
Milles. Cerberus, detail in
    Orpheus Fountain, Stockholm
    sculpture bw 2:29 F 22 '37

Ceres
Demeter sculpture bw, Greek
    bronze, 4th century 35:41 D
    21 '53
Demeter sculpture bw, Greek,
    Parthenon (Elgin Marbles)
    35:157 O 26 '53
"Queen of Clubs" playing card
    38:Cover My 30 '55

Charon
Michelangelo. Charon, detail
    in The last judgment fresco

27:47 D 26 '48

Danae
Correggio. Awakened Danae
    41:105 O 22 '56
Rubens. Danae receiving the
    golden shower 4:24 Ap 11
    '38 bw 12:44 Mr 9 '42
Titian. Danae 27:69 O 24 '49
    bw 17:80 Jy 31 '44

Diana
Rubens. Diana of the hunt 40:
    112 My 7 '56
Saint-Gaudens. Diana sculpture
    bw 4:27 My 30 '38; 24:112
    Mr 15 '48
Sanford. Diana sculpture bw
    10:120 Ap 21 '41
Titian. Diana and Actaeon 41:
    106-7 O 22 '56

Dido
Franceso di Giorgio. The meet-
    ing of Dido and Aeneas 35:
    150 N 16 '53
Rubens. Death of Dido bw 16:
    65 Ja 10 '44

Europa
Austin. Europa and the bull 19:
    81 O 1 '45
Derujinsky. The rape of Eu-
    ropa sculpture bw 6:36 Mr
    13 '39
Milles. Europa and the bull
    sculpture bw 2:32 F 22 '37
Peirce, W. Europa and the
    bull 22:95 Ap 21 '47
Rembrandt. The rape of Europa
    6:39 My 29 '39
Titian. The rape of Europa bw
    26:160 Ap 11 '49

The Graces
Boucher. Cupid and three
    graces bw 29:81 N 27 '50
Ceschiatti. Three graces sculp-
    ture 36:82 My 31 '54
Maillol. The three graces
    sculpture 25:101 S 27 '48

The Graces (cont.)

Marini. Three graces sculpture bw 22:99 My 22 '50
Rubens. Three graces 41:107 O 22 '56

Hercules

Hercules bronze statue bw, Greek, 500 B.C. 6:52 Mr 20 '39
Hercules slaying henchmen of King Busiris,* detail from vase, Etruscan, c530 B.C. 40:64 F 13 '56
Pollaiuolo. Hercules slaying Antaeus sculpture bw 6:32 F 13 '39
Veronese. Allegory of Virtue and Vice (The choice of Hercules) 3:38 D 27 '37

Jupiter

Boucher. Jupiter in the guise of Diana, and Callisto 5:36 S 26 '38
Jupiter giving apple to Minerva bas-relief, Bank of England bw 21:99 O 21 '46
Titian. Jupiter and Antiope bw 12:44 Mr 9 '42
Zeus bust bw 5:46 D 25 '38

Justitia

"Queen of Diamonds" playing card 38:Cover My 30 '55

Latona

Rinehart. Latona and her children bw 19:10 S 24 '45

Leda

Correggio. Leda and the swan bw 19:25 D 31 '45
Dali. Leda atomica bw 25:5 Ag 9 '48
Wright. Leda and the swan sculpture bw 29:122 Ag 28 '50

Lucretia

Cranach. Lucretia. 24:78 Mr 22 '48
Titian. Tarquin and Lucretia 27:68 O 24 '49
Tintoretto. Lucretia and Tarquinius 28:73 Je 5 '50

Mars

Ares sculpture bw, Greek, Parthenon 35:157 O 26 '53
Veronese. Mars and Venus 23:53 Ag 4 '47

Minerva

Jupiter giving apple to Minerva bas-relief, Bank of England bw 21:99 O 21 '46
Phidias, attributed. Pallas Athene sculpture bw 5:46 D 25 '38; 14:6 Ja 4 '43
"Queen of Spades" playing card 38:Cover My 30 '55
Rembrandt. Pallas Athena 29:85 N 27 '50

Neptune

Cellini. Saltcellar, c1540 goldsmithing 31:18-9 S 24 '51

Nymphs

Cellin. Saltcellar, c1540 goldsmithing 31:18-9 S 24 '51
Lamp, bronze, U.S. Victorian 40:86 Mr 5 '56
Milles. Naiad and dolphin sculpture bw 2:32 F 22 '37
Milles. Wedding of the Mississippi and the Missouri sculpture bw 2:26 F 22 '37
Rubens. Nymphs pursued by satyrs 31:64-5 O 1 '51

Orpheus

Milles. Orpheus fountain, Stockholm bw 2:28-9 F 22 '37 copy bw 2:30 F 22 '37

Pan

Williams. Pan gilded bronze bw 10:118-9 Ap 21 '41

Paris

Cranach. The judgment of
Paris 13:93 N 9 '42
Judgment of Paris, bronze box,
Etruscan, 4th century bw
40:65 F 13 '56
Judgment of Paris sculpture bw,
Bank of England 21:99 O 14
'46
Renoir. Judgment of Paris 32:
97 My 19 '52

Persephone

Benton. Persephone bw 6:39
F 20 '39

Prometheus

Brancusi. Head of Prometheus
39:135 D 5 '55
Laning. Prometheus, mural
cartoon detail bw 9:65 S
30 '40
Moore, H. Prometheus lithograph 33:86 Jy 14 '52

Psyche

David, J.L. Cupid and Psyche
bw 4:42 My 2 '38
Psyche, White Rock trademark
drawing bw 22:14 Je 30 '47

Romulus and Remus

Romulus and Remus statue
27:45 Ag 1 '49

Satyrs

Rubens. Nymphs pursued by
satyrs 31:64-5 O 1 '51
Satyr, mask cup, 18th century
25:129 D 6 '48
Satyr abducting a maiden terra
cotta, Etruscan, 5th century
B.C. 40:60 F 13 '56
Satyr holding Bacchus sculpture, Rome, 3rd century 28:
76 Mr 27 '50
Satyrs tapestry 35:92 D 14 '53

Sirens

Delvaux. The sirens 29:102-3
D 11 '50; 33:97 O 27 '52

Draper. Ulysses and the sirens 23:85 N 17 '47
Milles. Siren and fishes sculpture bw 2:32 F 22 '37
Ryder. Siegfried and the Rhine
maidens 30:87 F 26 '51

Tarquin

Tintoretto. Lucretia and Tarquinius 28:73 Je 5 '50
Titian. Tarquin and Lucretia
27:68 O 24 '49

Tellus

Cellini. Saltcellar, c1540
goldsmithing 31:18-9 S 24
'51

Tritons

Milles. Triton, detail of Wedding of the Mississippi and
the Missouri sculpture bw
2:Cover, 26 F 22 '37
Milles. Tritons sculpture bw
34:102 Mr 30 '53

Venus

Aphrodite sculpture bw 5:51
Ag 15 '38
Aphrodite sculpture bw,
Hearst collection 10:28 F
10 '41
Baizerman. Aphrodite sculpture bw 25:158 O 4 '48
Botticelli. The birth of Venus
7:52 N 20 '39; 41:103 O 22
'56 bw 6:31 F 13 '39; 12:
44 Mr 9 '42
Boucher. The toilet of Venus
23:85 S 15 '47 bw 16:68 Ja
10 '44; 33:2 D 29 '52
Dufy. Aphrodite 39:144 N 14
'55
Giorgione. Sleeping Venus
41:104-5 O 22 '56 bw 40:
103 F 20 '56
Hallsthammar. Venus in red
cherry ksculpture bw 2:42
Mr 8 '37
Krohg. Venus bw 34:14 Je 29
'53

Maillol. Venus with a necklace sculpture bw 7:63 S 18 '39

"Queen of Hearts" playing card 38:Cover My 30 '55

Rubens. The feast of Venus 27: 66-7 O 24 '49

Titian. Venus and Adonis 4:29 Mr 21 '38

Titian. Venus and organ player 24:76 Mr 22 '48

Velazquez. Venus and Cupid (Venus at the mirror) 41: 104 O 22 '56

Venus sculpture bw 34:137-8 Ap 27 '53

Venus de Milo sculpture bw, Greek 19:48 Jy 30 '45; 35: 51 Ag 17 '53

Venus Genetrix sculpture bw, Rome, Sabratha 5:66 D 12 '38

Veronese. Mars and Venus 23: 53 Ag 4 '47

Williams. Venus and Manhattan sculpture bw 27:100 D 19 '49

Vulcan

Moretti. Vulcan sculpture bw 3:63 N 29 '37

N

Nack, Kenneth
Refinery 28:86 Mr 20 '50

Nadelman, Elie, sculptor
Figures bw 24:119-20 My 24 '48
Elie Nadelman photog bw 24: 120 My 24 '48 port.

Nagler, Fred
The crucifixion 8:40 Mr 25 '40
Healing the sick bw 8:41 Mr 25 '40
Last supper bw 8:41 Mr 25 '40
Fred Nagler photog bw 8:41 Mr 25 '40 port.

Nahl, Charles Christian
Governor Caleb Lyon's 1856 Indian treaty* 36:78 Mr 8 '54

Sunday morning in the mines 27:49 Jy 4 '49

Naiads See Mythological Themes
--Nymphs

Nakamura, Kerichi
Off Malaya* 28:68-9 F 27 '50

Nalpas, Albert
New poster 39:117 S 12 '55

Nancy. Merwin 10:47 F 3 '41

Naples
Corot. View of Naples 25:96 N 22 '48

Napoleon I, Emperor of the French
Canova. Napoleon sculpture 1: 33 D 7 '36
David. Napoleon as first consul bw 16:68 Ja 10 '44
Gros. Bonaparte at Arcola 10:74 Ap 28 '41
Napoleon bw 13:105 O 5 '42
plaque bw, U.S. Congress 30:74 F 5 '51
Napoleon visiting tomb of Frederick the Great bw 15: 96 N 22 '43
Napoleon's plan to invade England, 1799-1805 bw 2:57 Mr 29 '37; 9:8-11 S 30 '40
Napoleon's tomb, Les Invalides, Paris photog bw 9:15 Ag 5 '40
Vereshchagin. The 1812 Series: Napoleon in Russia bw 12:61-8 F 2 '42

Napoleon III, Emperor of the French
Bismark and Napoleon III bw 8:24 Ap 22 '40
Battle of Magenta, June 4, 1859 bw 15:20 Ag 9 '43
Battle of Solferino, June 24, 1859 bw 15:20 Ag 9 '43
Napoleon and Eugenie photog bw 25:91 N 22 '48
Napoleon and Uncle Elby. cartoons bw McBride 17:12-4 D 4 '44
La Napoule, castle, Canne photog bw 31:119 O 15 '51

Nasby, Petroleum B.
   Petroleum Nasby bw 16:92 My
     8 '44
Nash, Ogden
   Ogden Nash photogs bw 31:132
     O 29 '51
Nash, Paul
   Dead sea 26:46 F 28 '49
Nassau Hall, Princeton Univer-
     sity bw 21:84, 88 S 23 '46
Nast, Thomas, cartoonist
   Communism and working
     people,* 1874 bw 25:68 O
     18 '48
   Confederate cavalry raiding
     Kentucky* bw 6:3 Ja 2 '39
   Gould and Drew, 1869 bw 13:
     142 D 7 '42
   Horace Greeley, political car-
     toon bw 31:20 O 22 '51
Natanson, Thadee
   Vuillard. Thadee Natanson
     and his wife 37:78 N 1 '54
Nathan, George Jean
   George Jean Nathan photogs
     bw 8:52, 54 Mr 11 '40
   Penn. George Jean Nathan and
     H.L. Mencken photog bw 24:
     14 My 10 '48
Natinguerra, Bartoli
   Office worker* bw 29:16 O 30
     '50
Nation, Carry
   Carry Nation, with hatchet
     photog bw 28:65 Ja 2 '50
National Association of Home
     Builders Trade Secrets house
     photogs 34:8-10 Ja 5 '53
National Gallery of Art, Washing-
     ton, D.C.
   Both (Ralph H.) collection of
     renaissance paintings given
     to National Gallery 24:66-7
     Ja 26 '48
   Garbisch collection of early
     American primitives 36:95-
     6 Ja 28 '54
National Monuments See also
     Memorials and Monuments
   Dinosaur Park, South Dakota--
     concrete dinosaurs bw 11:

     102 O 6 '41
   Hyde Park, New York. White,
     archt. 28:89-92 Ja 2 '50
     bw 6:61-7 My 29 '39; 20:
     89-92 Ap 15 '46
National Museum, Stockholm
   Swedish glass: decanters,
     vases, bowls 17:65-8 Ag 7
     '44
Nativity See Jesus Christ--
     Nativity
Nattier, Jean Marc
   Mademoiselle de Beaujolais
     41:71 D 10 '56
Nature. Lawrence 6:55 Mr 20 '39
Natwick, Mildred
   Beaton. Mildred Natwick in
     Candida drawing 21:9 Jy
     22 '46
Navaho Indian blankets photogs
     40:54 Ja 16 '56
The Navahos. Russell 24:65 Mr
     1 '48
Navajos at the water hole. Re-
     mington 13:74 S 14 '42
Naylor, James
   Tongue boring of James Nay-
     lor bw 33:96 S 29 '52
Nazi Emblem See Emblems and
     Decorations
Ndebele Tribes, South Africa
   Painting of exterior walls of
     dwelling 34:173 My 4 '53
Neagle, Richard
   Portrait of a classmate sculp-
     ture bw 10:59 Je 16 '41
Nearly hit. Klee 38:61 Mr 14 '55
Nebraska, University of
   Modern U.S. Art--51st annual
     exhibit 10:70-5 Ap 14 '41
Necklaces See Jewelry--Pend-
     ants and Necklaces
Needlepoint See Embroidery
Nefertiti, Queen of Egypt,
     sculpture bw 41:121 N 26
     '56
Negroes
   Archer. Waiting for the de-
     parture 10:68 My 26 '41
   Beardon. Factory workers
     21:64 Jy 22 '46

Binford. The crap shooter 10:
67 My 26 '41

Binford. The razor fight bw
13:140 N 16 '42

Brook. Georgia jungle 10:52
Ja 13 '41; 21:74 N 25 '46
bw 16:79 Ap 24 '44

Burden. Ridin' high 25:99 D 6
'48

Cortor. Southern gate 21:63 Jy
22 '46

Currier and Ives. My Old Kentucky Home 41:60 S 3 '56

Curry. The Mississippi 13:96
N 9 '42

Harrington. Deep south 8:46
F 12 '40

Hesselius. Charles Calvert of
Maryland 9:75 D 9 '40; 26:
84 F 28 '49

Homer. The gulf stream 2:26
Ja 11 '37; 5:36 O 31 '38

Johnson, E. Old Kentucky
Home 5:32 O 31 '38

McCrady. Woman mounting a
horse 3:42 O 18 '37

Manet. Olympia 35:58-9 Ag 17
'53; 41:105 O 22 '56

Marsh. High yaller 2:34 F 1
'37; bw 10:7 Ap 14 '41

Mount. The power of music 18:
66 Je 25 '45

Savage, E. The Washington
family 6:27 Je 19 '39

Toulouse-Lautrec. The black
countess 28:97 My 15 '50

Toulouse-Lautrec. Dancing
clown drawing bw 28:96 My
15 '50

Wilson, J. Mother and child
21:65 Jy 22 '46

Negulesco, Jean
Life study bw 16:68 Je 19 '44
Artist at work photogs bw 16:
65-8 Je 19 '44 port.

Neighboring pews. sculpture bw
Rogers 6:6 Mr 6 '39

Nelson, George, furniture designer
Modern furniture: chairs,
cabinet, desk, lamp, tables

photogs bw 25:116-7 N 15
'48
Table, lazy susan photog bw
35:16 D 14 '53
George Nelson photog bw 25:
117 N 15 '48 port.

Nelson, Horatio
Death of Nelson at Trafalgar,*
1805 bw 7:70 S 25 '39
Horatio Nelson 24:65 My 10
'48 bust bw 7:14 O 30 '39
statue 24:76 My 3 '48

Nelson, Thomas
Thomas Nelson bw 15:9 Jy 5
'43

Nelson, William Rockhill
William Rockhill Nelson photog bw 7:52 O 9 '39

Nelson (William Rockhill) Gallery of Art, Kansas City
Master paintings from collection 7:53-7·O 9 '39

Neo-Greek Architecture
Barney and Wright houses,
Nantucket photog bw 3:39
Ag 9 '37

Neptune See also Mythological
Themes--Neptune
Temple of Neptune, Greek,
Doric, photog bw 16:12 Je
5 '44

Nerenska. sculpture bw Epstein
3:90 N 15 '37

Nero head bw 5:51 Ag 15 '38

Nessler, Charles
Charles Nessler photog bw 30:
37 F 5 '51

The nesters. mural Lea 10:46
Ja 27 '41

Net menders. Reindel 3:36 Ag
9 '37

Net menders. Shokler 16:45 Ja
3 '44

Netsukes 37:15 Jy 2 '54

"Neuart" German statue bw 9:72
D 16 '40

Neutra, Richard, architect
California desert house photog bw 26:146-7 Ap 11 '49
Lakeside home photog bw 26:
148 Ap 11 '49

Neutra, Richard (cont.)
  Lewin House, Santa Monica,
    Calif. photog bw 19:115 O
    22 '45
Nevins, Allan
  Allan Nevins photog bw 28:79
    Ja 2 '50
Nevinson, C.R.W.
  Suburbia, 1939 bw 9:59 Ag 12
    '40
Nevsky, Alexander
  Nevsky's court, bw 14:93 Mr
    29 '43
"New Berlin Group"
  Artists and their work 36:144-
    5 My 10 '54
New castle. bw Thomas 10:53 Je
  23 '41
A new constitution, Paris, 1848.
  Champin 25:89 N 22 '48
New England, map, 1634 bw 18:
  67 My 21 '45
New England country school.
  Homer 6:30 Je 19 '39
New England country store.
  Wood, T. 6:30 Je 19 '39
New England harbor. Reindel 3:
  36 Ag 9 '37
New England literary landscape
  photogs bw 9:93-103 O 14
  '40
New England siesta. Sepeshy 8:
  66 My 27 '40
New England village. Marin 29:
  63 Jy 10 '50
New evidence. Du Bois, G. 26:
  68 Je 20 '49
New Guinea Art See Art--South
  Seas
New Hampshire
  Hart, W.M. Chocorua Moun-
    tain, New Hampshire 19:83 S
    10 '45
New Hebrides Art See Art--
  South Seas
New Mexico
  Hurd. New Mexico landscapes
    23:75-8 Ag 18 '47
New moon light. sculpture bw
  Lippold 28:60 Je 12 '50
The new one. sculpture bw Lip-

pold 28:60 Je 12 '50
New Orleans
  Currier and Ives print. Levee
    at New Orleans 21:71 S 2
    '46
  Currier and Ives print. New
    Orleans, c1850 bw 21:70 S
    2 '46
  Emett. New Orleans cartoon
    37:47 Jy 5 '54
  La Prete house--ironwork
    grill, gates photogs bw 12:8-
    11 Ap 6 '42
New poster. Nalpas 39:117 S 12
  '55
New York City See also specific
    locations and buildings, as
    Statue of Liberty
  Baseball game,* Pologrounds
    32:117 Ap 7 '52
  Bellows. Gramercy park 20:
    79 Mr 25 '46
  Bielenberg. Memories of New
    York drawing bw 10:58 Je
    16 '41
  Binford. New York harbor in
    wartime 17:55-60 N 20 '44
  Burgiss. New York City, 1717
    drawing bw 38:112-4 Ap 18
    '55
  Cadmus. Coney Island 2:45
    Mr 29 '37
  Congdon. Black city 30:109 Ap
    30 '51
  Davis, S. New York under
    gaslight 22:80 F 17 '47
  Du Bois, Y. East River 8:62
    Ap 29 '40
  Dufy. Brooklyn bridge 30:64-
    5 Ja 22 '51
  Dufy. Manhattan 30:66 Ja 22
    '51
  Dufy. New York City scenes
    30:64-7 Ja 22 '51
  Dufy. New York harbor 30:66
    Ja 22 '51
  Dufy. New York parade 30:64
    Ja 22 '51
  Dufy. Times Square 30:65 Ja
    22 '51
  Emett. New York, Third Ave-

nue cartoon 37:42 Jy 5 '54

Feininger, A. Manhattan moon* photog bw 24:15 My 10 '48

Feininger, A. New York dim-out photog 14:73-7 F 1 '43

Feininger, A. New York harbor photog bw 31:90 N 12 '51

Feininger, L. City at night 31: 91 N 12 '51

Fiene. Razing old New York post office bw 8:69 My 27 '40

Frasconi. Sunrise--Fulton Fish Market woodcut 37:86-7 O 18 '54

Gee. Central Park lake 16:46 Ja 3 '44

Haas. "Images of the Magic City" photogs 35:108-20 S 14 '53

Homer. Skating in Central Park, 1860 32:118 Ap 7 '52

Hopper. Early Sunday morning 27:62 Ag 29 '49

Hopper. Manhattan bridge loop 28:102-3 Ap 17 '50

Hopper. Night windows 28:103 Ap 17 '50

Kingman. Junk sailing under Brooklyn bridge* bw 30:100 My 14 '51

Kingman. New York's Chinatown* 30:102 My 14 '51

Laning. New York stock exchange, October 24, 1929 bw 8:78 F 26 '40

Manhattan skyline after sundown photog 31:110 S 17 '51

Manufacturers Trust Company, Fifth Avenue office. Skidmore, Owens and Merrill, archts. photog 37:62 O 25 '54

Marin. Manhattan No. 2 29:65 Jy 10 '50

Marsh. The Bowery 40:84 F 6 '56

Marsh. The village 5:30 O 31 '38

New York City skyline, eleven views, 1878-1932 photogs bw 13:12-5 Ag 31 '42

Night views of the City photogs bw 10:8-11 Ja 27 '41

Rockefeller Center. Harrison, archt. photog bw 22:34 My 26 '47

Sloan. Back yards, Greenwich Village bw 5:29 O 31 '38

Sloan. The City from Greenwich Village 7:46 D 11 '39

Sloan. Grand Central Station 7:46 D 11 '39

Sloan. The white way 7:46 D 11 '39

Sterne. New York skyscraper 31:51 Ag 27 '51

Waugh, C. Sunday in Central Park bw 5:56 N 28 '38

Weinstock. East River Drive 16:45 Ja 3 '44

New York Public Library
Laning. History of printing mural 9:65-6 S 30 '40

New York World's Fair, 1938
See Fairs

"New Yorker" magazine
Cartoons--war album bw 13: 97-103 D 7 '42

Covers 21:68-72 Jy 15 '46

Trademark: Irvin. Eustace Tilley 21:68 Jy 15 '46

Newburgh in winter. Dehn 11:41 Ag 11 '41

Newfoundland. bw Coale 13:90-1 Jy 13 '42

Newman, Arnold, photographer
Marc Chagall bw 22:56 My 5 '47

Portraits of artists 35:19-20 D 7 '53

Portraits of modern artists of U.S. bw 20:10-2 F 4 '46

Newman, Barnett
Barnett Newman photog bw 30:34 Ja 15 '51 port.

Newman, Harry Shaw
Cosgrave. Harry Shaw Newman 24:19 Ja 19 '48

Harry Shaw Newman photog bw 24:19 Ja 19 '48

Newton, A. Edward
A. Edward Newton photog bw 10:86 Je 9 '41

Newton (A. Edward) collection of rare books and manuscripts photogs bw 10:86-8 Je 9 '41

Newton, Carl F.
Fishing captain 24:72 Ap 5 '48

Newton, Isaac
Sir Isaac Newton bw 25:122 S 13 '48

Niagara Falls
Bornet. Niagara Falls lithograph 26:77 Je 6 '49
Boy drowning in Falls, 1873* bw 26:76 Je 6 '49
Brown, J. F. Sacrifice of Indian maiden 26:80 Je 6 '49
Chambers. Trapper 26:78 Je 6 '49
Church. Horseshoe Falls 26: 78-9 Je 6 '49
De Grailly. Maid of mist 26: 79 Je 6 '49
De Martelly. Niagara Falls* 26:79 Je 6 '49
Emett. Niagara Falls cartoon 37:45 Jy 5 '54
Monsieur Blondin, tight-rope walker, spanning Niagara Gorge, 1859* print 26:80 Je 6 '49
Trumbull. Rainbow 26:78 Je 6 '49

A nice game for two or more. Leech lithograph 6:40 F 6 '39

Nicholas I, Czar of Russia bw 14: 95 Mr 29 '43

Nicholas II, Czar of Russia
Czar and royal family sun on Siberia rooftop photog bw 14:97 Mr 29 '43
Czar and royal family with Edward VII of England and his family photog bw 14:96 Mr 29 '43
Czar in court costume photog bw 14:96 Mr 29 '43

Nicholas, Saint

Lewicki, St. Nicholas parading at Christmas 33:85 D 1 '52

"Nicholas Nickleby," illustrations bw Browne (Phiz) 23:2-3 D 22 '47

Nichols, Dale
Home for Christmas bw 5:9 D 12 '38

Nicolas, Joep, stained glass worker
Stained glass panels, Fairmount church, Cleveland 12:52-3 Ap 6 '42

Nicolay, John G.
John Nicolay photog bw 14:76 F 15 '43

Niebuhr, Reinhold
Reinhold Niebuhr photog bw 24:80 F 2 '48

Niemeyer, Oscar, architect
Church of St. Francis, Belo Horizonte, Brazil photogs bw 25:76-7 Jy 4 '49
Education and Health Building, Rio de Janeiro photog bw 22:35 My 26 '47
House of the architect, Rio de Janeiro photog bw 13:134 O 26 '42
Oscar Niemeyer photog bw 22: 35 My 26 '47 port.

Night. bw. Hogarth 21:78 D 16 '46

Night. sculpture bw Manship 4: 15 Ja 31 '38

Night (Unknown soldier). sculpture bw 25:158 O 4 '48

Night and clouds. Ryder 13:96 N 9 '42

Night and the sea. Mattson 6:44 My 1 '39

"The Night Before Christmas" ("Visit from St. Nicholas"), illustrations. Ogden 31:96-100 D 10 '51

Night cafe. Van Gogh 2:34 F 15 '37; 27:85 O 10 '49

Night flyer at readiness. Kennington 26:44 F 28 '49

Night forest. bw Oscar 32:88 Mr
    17 '52
Night life. Sloan 38:72-3 Mr 28
    '55
A night on the Hudson: Through
    at daylight. Currier and
    Ives print 9:34 D 30 '40
Night paddocks. Flannery 10:74
    Ap 14 '41
Night scenes
    Anderson, D. City at night 32:
        68-9 Ja 14 '52
    Benedetto. Calling the loa 8:
        35 Ja 1 '40
    Blakelock. Moonlight 23:101 S
        8 '47
    Bohrod. Evening in Roscom-
        mon 11:94 N 10 '41
    Bohrod. Merrillan night 11:94
        N 10 '41
    Bohrod. Rainy night 11:93 N 10
        '41
    Bohrod. Taverns at night 11:93
        N 10 '41
    Bouche. Train through the
        night 11:50 Ag 18 '41
    Burchfield. Six o'clock 1:26 D
        28 '36
    Covarrubies. Balinese festi-
        val* 3:49 S 27 '37
    Currier and Ives print. Ameri-
        can winter scene: Evening
        9:27 D 30 '40
    Currier and Ives print. Even-
        tide--October: The village
        inn 9:32 D 30 '40
    Day. The transfixed hour 10:
        68 My 26 '41
    Dodd. Beach house 27:64 S 26
        '49
    Dodd. Savannah 27:64 S 26 '49
    Feininger, L. City at night 31:
        91 N 12 '51
    Hacker. Wet night in Picca-
        dilly Circus 23:85 N 17 '47
    Hall. Moon dance 24:86 Mr 8
        '48
    Hicks. Washington at the Dela-
        ware 29:46 Jy 10 '50
    Homer. The lookout--"All's
        well" 9:52 Jy 22 '40

    Hopper, Drug Store 28:103 Ap
        17 '50
    Krause. Wolf by the lake 10:
        78 Mr 31 '41
    McCrady. Swing Low, Sweet
        Chariot 3:39 O 18 '37
    Miller, B. Beach party 11:73
        O 27 '41 bw 9:79 D 9 '40
    Pittman. An evening in Maine
        18:70 F 19 '45
    Remington. Around the camp-
        fire 13:75 S 14 '42
    Remington. Fired on 9:77 D 9
        '40
    Remington. The sentinel 13:
        74 S 14 '42
    Ryder. Siegfried and the Rhine
        maidens 30:87 F 26 '51
    Ryder. The temple of the
        mind 30:91 F 26 '51
    Ryder. Under a cloud 30:88-9
        F 26 '51
    Sample. Band concert 3:44 N
        15 '37
    Van Gogh. Night cafe 2:34 F
        15 '37; 27:85 O 10 '49
    Whistler. Southampton waters
        36:94-5 My 17 '54
    Wood, F. The midnight ride
        of Paul Revere 3:28 D 20
        '37; 14:54 Ja 18 '43
Night watch. bw Rembrandt 21:
    106 O 28 '46
Night windows. Hopper 28:103 Ap
    17 '50
Nightfall. Wyeth, N.C. 20:80 Je
    17 '46
Nightingale, Florence
    Florence Nightingale photog
        bw 14:95 Mr 29 '43
    Florence Nightingale tending
        sick in Crimean war bw 11:
        15 D 15 '41; 13:71 N 16 '42
Nijinsky, Vaslav
    Nijinsky, and his wife; in "Le
        Spectre de la Rose" photogs
        19:63-70 S 10 '45
Nike of Samothrace sculpture bw
    Greece, c306 B.C. 19:49
        Jy 30 '45

Nine dragons, Sung dynasty, 1244
　　Ch'em Jung 15:66-7 O 11 '43
The 9:45 accommodation, Strat-
　　ford, Connecticut. Henry,
　　E. L. 6:30 Je 19 '39
Nine men. Hirsch 30:37 Ja 15 '51
Nine mile run seen from Calvary.
　　Kane, J. 2:47 My 17 '37
1942. Mattson 16:78 Ap 24 '44
Nine de Guevara, Fernando, Car-
　　dinal El Greco. Don Fernando
　　Nino de Guevara 28:93 Ap 24
　　'50
Ninos Heroes, Battle of Chapulte-
　　pec, 1847. Portraits bw 22:
　　47 Mr 17 '47
Nithart, Mathis Gothart See
　　Grunewald Matthias
No more mowing. De Martelly 13:
　　48 Ag 31 '42
No room in the inn. Ford, L. 5:
　　27 Jy 4 '38
No te aha oe riri (Why are you
　　jealous; angry). Gauguin 11:
　　58 S 8 '41
Noah
　　Michelangelo. Drunkenness of
　　Noah fresco detail bw 21:
　　64 Jy 1 '46
　　Michelangelo. Noah's sacri-
　　fice 27:34 D 26 '49
Noble, Thomas Satterwhite
　　Witch hill (The Salem martyr)
　　13:79 N 23 '42
La noble pastorale. Beauvois
　　tapestry bw Boucher 4:28 Ja
　　28 '38
"Nocturnes" of J. Whistler See
　　Old Battersea Bridge; South-
　　ampton waters
Noel. bw Herbin 27:57 D 26 '49
Noel, Tony
　　Progress sculpture bw 11:144
　　O 13 '41
Noel, the artist's son. Davis, G.
　　R. 14:45 Ap 19 '43
Nofret, Queen of Egypt See also
　　Nefertiti
　　Nofret, wife of Rahotep, Prince
　　of Egypt 41:109 N 26 '56
　　Nofret, portrait statue 24:76

Ja 19 '48
Nofretari, Queen of Egypt, tomb
　　painting 24:182 Ja 19 '48
Noguchi, Isamu
　　Decorative lamps photogs 32:
　　114-5 Mr10 '52 furniture
　　design
　　Rocking stool photog bw 40:
　　122, 125 F 6 '56 furniture
　　design
　　Mankind bw 21:12 N 11 '46
　　sculpture
　　Man's existence bw 21:13 N 11
　　'46 sculpture
　　"King Lear," London produc-
　　tion--costumes, properties
　　bw 39:64 Ag 8 '55 theater
　　design
　　Isamu Noguchi photog 32:114
　　Mr 10 '52 bw 21:12, 15 N
　　11 '46
Nollekens, Joseph Francis
　　Family in a park 25:98 S 13
　　'48
Nonie. Leake 10:47 F 3 '41
Noon. bw Hogarth 21:78 D 16 '46
Noon. Lee, D. 3:46 S 20 '37; 21:
　　74 N 25 '46
Norkin, Sam, cartoonist
　　Caricatures of servicemen bw
　　14:108-9 Ja 25 '43
Norling, Ernest R.
　　Marcus Whitman bw 15:100 S
　　27 '43
Norris, Ben
　　Army planes in Hawaii water-
　　colors 13:51 N 9 '42
Norris, Charles
　　Charles and Kathleen Norris
　　photog bw 15:79 Jy 12 '43
Norris, Kathleen
　　Charles and Kathleen Norris
　　photog bw 15:79 Jy 12 '43
Norris Dam. bw Sample 3:42 N
　　15 '37
North. De Stael 38:108 My 23
　　'55
North Africa. Lee, D. 33:110-1
　　N 10 '52
North Africa--scenes and por-
　　traits of World War II in

Algeria and Tunisia. Martin,
    F. 15:60-7 D 27 '43
"North Carolina" (ship) Billings
    11:60 Jy 7 '41 bw 14:7 Je 28
    '43
North Church, Salem, Massachu-
    setts Davidson. First meeting
    house of North Church 13:
    80 N 23 '42
North Carolina Museum of Art,
    Raleigh, North Carolina
    Million-dollar collection of
    15th to 19th century paint-
    ings 41:70-8 D 10 '56
North-Taylor, Philip
    Harrow School speech room,
    October 1940 12:39 Mr 2 '42
"Northern Belle" (Mississippi
    steamboat). Bunn 9:72 O 14
    '40
Northland, shopping center, De-
    troit, Michigan. Victor Gru-
    en Associates, archt.
    photogs 37:81-3 Ag 30 '54
Northumberland Family shield of
    arms 22:69 My 26 '47
Notornis (bird) bw 26:106 Mr 21
    '49
Notre Dame cathedral, Paris
    photog 8:60-1 Je 3 '40 bw 2:
    70 Je 14 '37 Christ story
    frieze bw 22:83 Ap 7 '47
Nottingham, Elizabeth
    Landscape with goat cart 10:
    68 My 26 '41
Nova Scotia morning. Cowles 24:
    77 F 9 '48
Novar, Louis
    The butcher 1:44 N 30 '36
November evening. Burchfield
    26:86-7 F 21 '49
Nowicki, Matthew, architect
    Fair Grounds Building, Raleigh,
    North Carolina photog 36:
    34-5 Ja 4 '54
Noyes, Eliot, architect
    Bubble house, sprayed concrete
    photog bw 36:75-8 F 22 '54
    Eliot Noyes photog bw 36:78 F
    22 '54 port.
Nudes See also Bathers and

Bathing
Austin. The legend 19:81 O 1
    '45
Austin. The sisters 19:81 O 1
    '45
The awakening of sex sculp-
    ture bw 11:145 O 13 '41
Baizerman. Aphrodite sculp-
    ture bw 25:158 O 4 '48
Barnard. The struggle of two
    natures in man bw 6:57 Mr
    20 '39
Bellows. Nude study litho-
    graph bw 20:78 Mr 25 '46
Bellows. Two women 20:81 Mr
    25 '46
Benton. Figure organization
    bw 6:70 Ap 24 '39
Benton. Hollywood 5:74-5 D
    12 '38
Benton. Persephone bw 6:39
    F 20 '39
Blumenfeld. The spirit of the
    chair photog bw 24:14 My
    10 '48
Bonnard. Cabinet de toilette
    24:56 Jy 26 '48
Boru. Sentimental letter cer-
    amics bw 9:130 N 11 '40
Bosch. The garden of delights
    triptych 27:75-82 N 14 '49
Botticelli. Birth of Venus 7:
    52 N 20 '39; 41:103 O 22
    '56 bw 6:31 F 13 '39; 12:44
    Mr 9 '42
Boucher. Love disarmed bw
    12:44 Mr 9 '42
Boucher. Girl resting 41:104-
    5 O 22 '56
Boucher. Nude drawing 40:
    70 My 28 '56
Brackman. Autumn light 8:59
    F 5 '40
Brackman. Composition in
    life and still life 5:29 S 19
    '38
Braque. Woman with basket
    of fruit 26:84 My 2 '49
Brockman. Nude 5:30 S 19 '38
Brook. Bacchante 5:30 S 19
    '38

Brook. Summer wind 10:51 Ja 13 '41

Bush. Mae West 1:33 D 7 '36

Callery. Reclining figure bw 26:114 Je 20 '49

Canova. Napoleon 1:33 D 7 '36

Cash. Standing nudes sculpture bw 9:55 Ag 12 '40

Castellanos. The aunts 4:30 Mr 14 '38

Chabas. September morn bw 2:53 My 24 '37; 21:90 D 23 '46; 29:96 N 27 '50

Clemens. South wind 8:67 My 27 '40; 21:75 N 25 '46

Corot. Nude bw 40:168 Ap 9 '56

Corregio. Awakened Danae 41: 105 O 22 '56

Cortor. Southern gate 21:63 Jy 22 '46

Courbet. Woman with parrot 6:56 Mr 20 '39

Covarrubias. Balinese girl 3: 47 S 27 '37

Cowles. The parade 12:45 Mr 9 '42; 21:75 N 25 '46

Cranach. Eve with serpent 11: 57 S 8 '41

Cranach. The judgment of Paris 13:93 N 9 '42

Cranach. Lucretia 24:78 Mr 22 '48

Dali. Leda atomica bw 25:5 Ag 9 '48

Dalton. Kneeling nude sculpture bw 32:77 Ja 7 '52

Davey. Nude* 12:45 Mr 9 '42

David. Cupid and Psyche bw 4:42 My 2 '38

Davies, A. B. Afterthoughts of earth bw 16:79 Ap 24 '44

Davis, G. R. Odalisque 14:45 Ap 19 '43

Davis, G. R. Seated figure 14: 46 Ap 19 '43; 21:75 N 25 '46

Dobson. The fount sculpture bw 25:103 S 27 '48

Donatello. David sculpture bw 5:35 Ag 29 '38

Duchamp. Nude descending a staircase 28:60 Ja 2 '50; 32:102 Ap 28 '52 bw 26:89 F 21 '49; 32:100 Ap 28 '52

Eakins. William Rush carving his allegorical figure of Schuylkill River 16:73 My 15 '44 bw 5:29 O 31 '38

Epstein. Adam sculpture bw 33:66 N 3 '52

Epstein. Genesis sculpture bw 3:92 N 15 '37

Fazzini. Elliptical nude* bw 32:68 Mr 10 '52

Fertility sculpture bw 4:14 F 21 '38

Flower of youth sculpture bw 11:145 O 13 '41

Fourbert. Nude bw 11:61 O 27 '41

Fujikawa. Nudes bw 32:101 Je 23 '52

Ganso. Nudes bw 2:32 F 1 '37

Gauguin. Annah the Javanese 29:112 S 11 '50

Gauguin. Tahitian women with red mango blossoms 21:61 Jy 29 '46

Gerasimov. Nudes bw 40:165 Ap 9 '56

Gerny. Big utopia sculpture bw 21:101 Jy 8 '46

Giacommeti. Nude sculpture 33:93 O 27 '52

Giorgione. Sleeping Venus 41: 104-5 O 22 '56 bw 40:103 F 20 '56

Glackens. Nude with apple 9: 78 D 9 '40; 38:74 Mr 28 '55

Goya. The maja nude 29:106-7 S 11 '50

Grard. Nude sculpture bw 41: 84 O 8 '56

Gregory. Electron children sculpture bw 6:36-7 Mr 13 '39

Gross, C. I found my love 30: 63 Ja 8 '51

Gross, C. War bride 30:63 Ja 8 '51

Grosz. Nude bw 28:24 Ja 23 '50

Haller. Young girl with arms raised sculpture bw 26:114 Je 20 '49

Hallsthammar. Venus in red cherry sculpture bw 2:42 Mr 8 '37

Ingres. Odalisque 34:88-9 My 11 '53

Kane, M.B. Undersea ballet bas-relief bw 7:36-7 Jy 17 '39

Karfiol. The awakening 10:73 Ap 14 '41

Kasagi. Nude sculpture bw 32: 100 Je 23 '52

Kiss in a shipwreck bw 11:61 O 27 '41

Klein. Calisthenics ceramic bw 9:131 N 11 '40

Klimsch. Nude sculpture bw 9:96-7 S 23 '40

Kolbe. The large sitting woman sculpture bw 31:81 S 24 '51

Kroll. Adolescent girl 24:69 Je 28 '48

Kroll. Ann in white scarf 5:30 S 19 '38

Kroll. Nude back 24:67 Je 28 '48

Kroll. Nude in blue 24:68 Je 28 '48

Kroll. Seated nude 24:68 Je 28 '48

La Chaise. Floating figure bw 6:82 My 22 '39

Laurent. Le cygne sculpture bw 10:64 Je 2 '41

Laurent. Girl sculpture bw 10:67 Je 2 '41

Laurent. Girl washing hair sculpture bw 10:64 Je 2 '41

Laurent. Pelleas and Melisande sculpture bw 10:67 Je 2 '41

Laurent. The river sculpture bw 10:68 Je 2 '41

Lehmbruck. Kneeling woman sculpture 25:47 Ag 16 '48 bw 7:55 O 30 '39 in Armory show bw 26:89 F 21 '49

Lehmbruck. Standing youth sculpture 25:47 Ag 16 '48

Lentelli. American beauties sculpture bw 6:Cover Mr 13 39

Maillol. Action in chains sculpture bw 8:108 Ap 15 '40

Maillol. Kneeling figure sculpture bw 7:37 Jy 31 '39

Maillol. The Mediterranean sculpture bw 8:106-7 Ap 15 '40

Maillol. The three graces sculpture bw 25:101 S 27 '48

Maillol. Torso of a girl sculpture bw 8:109 Ap 15 '40

Maillol. Torso of a young woman sculpture bw 8:107 Ap 15 '40

Maillol. Venus with a necklace sculpture bw 7:63 S 18 '39

Maldarelli. The caress sculpture bw 22:140 Mr 24 '47

Maldarelli. Gemini sculpture bw 22:139 Mr 24 '47

Manca. Nejla Ates statue bw 38:129 Je 6 '55

Manet. Luncheon on the grass bw 12:44 Mr 9 '42

Manet. Olympia 35:58-9 Ag 17 '53; 41:105 O 22 '56

Marcks. Girl swimmer sculpture bw 28:71 F 6 '50

Martinez. The astronomer 20:60 Je 3 '46

Martins, N. Je veux la tete de Jokanaan sculpture bw 11:157 D S '41

Matisse. Luxury, calm and voluptuousness 28:59 Ja 2 '50

Matisse. Odalisque 31:112-3 N 26 '51

Mestrovic. Atlantide sculpture bw 22:135 Je 2 '47

Michelangelo. David sculpture bw 26:104 Ja 24 '49

Michelangelo. Sistine chapel frescoes 21:62-9 Jy 1 '46; 27:25-49 D 26 '49

Millais. Knight errant* bw 9: 64 S 2 '40

Milles. Two dancers sculpture bw 2:32 F 22 '37

Mozert. Nude 18:46 Ja 1 '45

Negulesco. Life study bw 10: 68 Je 19 '44

Noel. Progress sculpture bw 11:144 O 13 '41

Parrish. The dinky bird bw 5: 29 O 31 '38

Patrick. Inquisitive model 11: 73 O 27 '41

Paulus. Nude study 25:100 D 6 '48

Philipp, R. Jordy bw 8:62 Ap 8 '40

Philipp, R. Letty 8:63 Ap 8 '40

Philipp, R. Nude bw 6:45 My 1 '39

Picasso. Standing nude 8:58 Mr 4 '40

Picasso. La vie 8:57 Mr 4 '40

Pisano. Nude bw 41:102 O 22 '56

Praxiteles, copy after. Nude sculpture bw 41:102 O 22 '56

Raphael. Creation of Eve 27: 119 D 12 '49

Reder. Wounded woman sculpture bw 26:113 Je 20 '49

Rembrandt. The painter's study bw 29:104 S 11 '50

Renoir. Judgment of Paris 32: 97 My 19 '52

Renoir. Nude 9:48 Jy 29 '40 bw 12:44 Mr 9 '42

Rivera. Nudes mural bw, Ciro's, Hotel Reforma, Mexico City 16:78 F 28 '44; 23:106 N 3 '47

Robin. Merry Christmas of Rosette bw 27:57 D 26 '49

Rodin. Eternal springtime sculpture bw 6:57 Mr 20 '39

Rodin. Honore de Balzac sculpture bw 38:22 My 9 '55

Rodin. The kiss 26:7-9 Je 27 '49

Rodin. The thinker sculpture

bw 6:57 Mr 20 '39

Rosenthal. Between two screens 12:46 Mr 9 '42

Rosenthal. Nude at table 15:67 N 22 '43

Rousseau. The dream 29:110-1 S 11 '50

Rubens. Danae receiving the golden shower 4:24 Ap 11 '38 bw 12:44 Mr 9 '42

Rubens. Death of Dido bw 16: 65 Ja 10 '44

Rubens. The feast of Venus 27:66-7 O 24 '49

Rubens. Nymphs pursued by satyrs 31:64-5 O 1 '51

Rubens. Three graces 41:107 O 22 '56

Santiano. Man and his passions sculpture bw 11:147 O 13 '41

Sargent. Egyptian girl 36:97 My 17 '54

Shimada. Seated nude bw 28: 104 Ja 23 '50

Sloan. Nude and chief blanket 7:45 D 11 '39

Sloan. Susanna in Santa Fe 7: 44 D 11 '39

Smith. The hypochondriac 12: 45 Mr 9 '42

Soyer. Nude* 12:45 Mr 9 '42

Stella bw 6:47 Mr 13 '39

Taubes. At the shore 12:46 Mr 9 '42

Tasq. Leander and Hero sculpture bw 11:146 O 13 '41

Thorak. Dancer sculpture bw 9:96 S 23 '40

Tintoretto. Bacchus and Ariadne bw 12:44 Mr 9 '42

Tintoretto. Lucretia and Tarquinius 28:73 Je 5 '50

Titian. Danae 27:69 O 24 '49 bw 17:80 Jy 31 '44

Titian. Diana and Actaeon 41: 106-7 O 22 '56

Titian. Jupiter and Antiope bw 12:44 Mr 9 '42

Titian. Venus with organ

player 24:76 Mr 22 '48
Velazquez. Venus and Cupid
(Venus at the mirror) 41:104
O 22 '56
Venus de Milo sculpture bw,
Greek 19:48 Jy 30 '45; 35:51
Ag 17 '53
Vos. The birth of a nation sculp-
ture bw 3:71 Ag 9 '37
Weber. Tranquillity 19:85 Ag
20 '45; 21:78 N 25 '46
Sheeler. Spring sculpture 25:
101 S 27 '48
Whitney, G. The kiss sculpture
bw 7:45 S 11 '39
Young, M. Alkmena 10:79 F
17 '41
Zamoyski. Figures sculpture
bw 26:97 F 14 '49
Zorach. Conflict sculpture bw
8:92-3 Ap 1 '40
Zorach. Youth 9:54 Ag 12 '40
bw 8:90-1 Ap 1 '40
"Number 18" (locomotive) Union
Pacific, 1874 photog bw 25:
14 S 27 '48
Number nine. Pollock 27:42-3 Ag
8 '49; detail bw 41:58 Ag 27
'56
"Number 999" (locomotive) 1893
photog bw 25:14 S 27 '48
"Number 119" (locomotive) Union
Pacific, 1869 photog bw 25:
14 S 27 '48
Number seventeen. Pollock 27:43
Ag 8 '49
Number 10, Downing Street
photogs bw 3:90-1 S 20 '37
Number twelve. Pollock 27:42 Ag
8 '49
Number 23. Kenzo Okada 40:75
My 28 '56
Nunes del Prado, Carrasco
The embrace 36:81 My 31 '54
Nuns and children. bw Chamber
37:123 O 25 '54
Nusa, Japanese staff with in-
scribed streamers photog
bw 18:94 F 19 '45
Nut, Egyptian sky goddess 41:114-
5 N 26 '56

Nye, Bill
Bill Nye photog bw 11:91 S 8
'41
Nymphs See Mythological
Themes--Nymphs

O

O Little Town of Bethlehem.
Thomas 23:46 D 22 '47
Oak Alley, Greek revival planta-
tion house, Louisiana. pho-
tog Swainey, archt. 32:76-
7 Je 9 '52
Oak Hill, Virginia. photog bw
Jefferson, archt. 14:70 Ap
12 '43
Oakley, Annie
Annie Oakley photog bw 16:110
Ap 10 '44; 22:67, 75 Ap 28
'47
Oasis. Lee, D. 33:109 N 10 '52
Oates, Titus
Titus Oates drawing bw 41:
176 N 19 '56
Oaxaca, Mexico
Blue pottery photog 6:34 Ja 23
'39
Lee, D. Giant cypress tree 22:
75 My 12 '47
Lee, D. Park at Oaxaca 22:75
My 12 '47
Obelisks
Black obelisk of Shalmaneser
bw 24:147 Mr 15 '48
Lincoln's tomb, Springfield,
Ill. photog bw 32:113 Je 23
'52
Marker of claimed "center of
North America," South Da-
kota photog bw 11:99 O 6
'41
Obelisk, Place de la Concorde,
Paris photog 8:62 Je 3 '40
Seattle, Washington, obelisk
memorial to World War
dead photog bw 13:31 Ag
31 '42
Oberon, Merle
Brook. Merle Oberon as
George Sand 18:69 F 5 '45

Obin, Philome
    The cacos of Leconte 23:61 S
    1 '47
Object of destruction. bw 34:24 My
    25 '53
Ojects on a sofa. Kuniyoshi 6:28
    F 13 '39
Oblivion. sculpture bw Esherick
    9:54 Ag 12 '40
O'Brady, Gertrude
    Louis Dreyfus home, Bedford
    Village, New York bw 41:
    78 Ag 13 '56
Obregon, Alvaro
    General Obregon photog bw 24:
    14 Ja 12 '48
Observatories
    Observatoire, Paris bw 31:78
    Jy 30 '51
    Indian observatory, Delhi,
    perforated walled circles
    to mark stars photog bw 12:
    91 Mr 16 '42
    Indian observatory, Jaipur,
    18th century photog bw 9:70
    N 25 '40
    Mayan observatory, Chichen
    Itza, Yucatan photog 22:60
    Je 30 '47
O'Casey, Sean
    John. Sean O'Casey bw 37:68
    Jy 26 '54
Octagonal church, Holyoke, Mass.
    photog bw 35:88 Jy 6 '53
Octagonal houses, Hudson River
    Valley photogs bw 7:62 O 2
    '39
The odalisque. Davis, G. R. 14:
    45 Ap 19 '43
Odalisque. Ingres 34:88-9 My 11
    '53
Odalisque. Matisse 31:112-3 N
    26 '51
O'Dell, Scott
    Scott O'Dell photog bw 24:22
    My 17 '48
Oecolampadius, John
    John Oecolampadius in
    Cranach. Luther and his
    friends 24:63 Je 14 '48
Office at night. Hopper 28:102 Ap

    17 '50
Office Buildings
    Aetna Life Insurance Company
    Building, Hartford, Conn.
    photog bw 41:78 Ag 13 '56
    Brazil contemporary office
    buildings: Education and
    Health Ministry; ABI (Bra-
    zilian Associated Press)
    Building; Social Security
    Building photogs bw 13:132-
    4 O 26 '42
    Burnham. Flatiron Building,
    New York City, 1902 photog
    40:99 Mr 5 '56
    Dow. Dow Office Building,
    Midland, Mich. photog bw
    3:50 N 15 '37
    "Gateway Center," Pittsburgh
    photog 36:32 Ja 4 '54
    Harrison. Rockefeller Center,
    New York City photog bw
    22:34 My 26 '47
    Harrison and Abramovitz.
    Republican National Bank,
    Dallas, Texas photog 38:61-
    3 F 28 '55
    Hentrich. Office Building, Dus-
    seldorf, Germany photog
    bw 36:152 My 10 '54
    Holabird and Roche. Tacoma
    Building, Chicago, 1887 bw
    40:99 Mr 5 '56
    Morse. Cullen and Foreman
    Building, Grand Junction,
    Colo. photog 38:133 F 7 '55
    Niemeyer. Education and
    Health Building, Rio de Ja-
    neiro photog bw 13:132-4 O
    26 '42
    Skidmore, Owings and Mer-
    rill. Lever house, New
    York City photogs 32:44-5
    Je 2 '52
    Sullivan and Adler. Guaranty
    Building, Buffalo, 1895
    photog 40:102 Mr 5 '56
    Wright, S.C. Johnson and Son
    Administration Building,
    Racine, Wis. photogs bw
    6:15 My 8 '39

Officer of the imperial guard.
Gericault 35:62 Ag 17 '53

Ogden, Mary Moore
"The Night Before Christmas,"
illustrations of her father's
poem. 31:96-100 D 10 '51

Ogres See Imaginary Beings

O'Hara, Frederick
Bullfight woodcut 37:88 O 18
'54

Ohio
Shahn. Landscape, Ohio, 1945
37:98 O 4 '54
Thomas. Ohio landscape 22:
62-3 Je 16 '47

Ohio glassware, American,
c1815: flat bowl; decanter,
three-mold; "grandfather"
flask 39:58-9 Jy 18 '55

Oil. Snyder 10:77 Mr 31 '41

Oil, Texas. cartoon Emett 37:
46-7 Jy 5 '54

Oil Wells
Hogue. Spindletop, Texas Oil
gusher 10:40 F 10 '41

Okada, Kenzo
Number 23 40:75 My 28 '56

O'Keefe, Georgia
Adobe, New Mexico* bw 4:31
F 14 '38
Calla lillies 4:30 F 14 '38
Cross by the sea 4:30 F 14 '38
Horses head with pink rose 4:
29 F 14 '38
White barn 4:30 F 14 '38
Georgia O'Keefe photog bw 4:
28 F 14 '38; 25:63 D 6 '48:
26:67 Mr 14 '49; 41:152 D
24 '56
Speicher. Georgia O'Keefe,
1908 bw 25:63 D 6 '48
Stieglitz. Georgia O'Keefe
photogs bw 14:9 Ap 5 '43

Oklahoma
Mural of Oklahoma History,
art competition 30:78-9 Mr
5 '51
Van Duzer. Growth of Tulsa,
Oklahoma* mural 30:78 Mr
5 '51

"Oklahoma," scenes from the mo-

tion picture. Lee, D. 16:
83-4 Mr 6 '44

Oklahoma land rush. Curry 7:36
D 25 '39 bw 15:19 N 29 '43

Oklahoma land rush.* mural
Conway 30:78-9 Mr 5 '51

Oklahoma Territory land rush,
1893 photog bw 31:100 N 5
'51

Oklahoma's development.* mural
Refrigier 30:78 Mr 5 '51

Old abbey at Messines, Belgium.
Hitler 1:43 N 30 '36

"Old Abe," eagle mascot of 8th
Wisconsin regiment, U.S.
Civil War photog bw 39:186
S 12 '55

Old barn. Levy, M. 16:45 Ja 3
'44

Old Battersea bridge. Whistler
12:62 Je 15 '42

Old Battersea bridge (Symphony
in Brown and Silver) 36:
94-5 My 17 '54

The old bridge. Moore, C.H.
19:84 S 10 '45

Old church, Rockport, Mass.
Dufy 30:63 Ja 22 '51

Old engine. Feininger, Lux 31:
93 N 12 '51

Old Feather store, Boston, 1820-
5 13:81 N 23 '42

"Old Ironsides" (ship) See
"Constitution"

The old Jew. bw Picasso 40:168
Ap 9 '56

Old Kentucky Home. Currier and
Ives print 41:60 S 3 '56

Old Kentucky Home. Johnson, E.
5:32 O 31 '38

"Old Lady of Threadneedle
Street," 1797. cartoon bw
Gillray 21:99 O 21 '46

Old models. Harnett 27:60 Ag
29 '49

"Old Mother Hubbard," written
and illustrated by Martin
bw 20:104-5 Ap 15 '46

Old North Church, Boston photog
bw 20:122 Ap 22 '46

Old Parr. Rubens 7:54 O 9 '39

Old pioneers, mural Hurd 10:46
    Ja 27 '41
Old Richmond. Banks 10:68 My
    26 '41
Old Ship Meeting House, Hingham,
    Massachusetts, 1681 photog
    38:128-9 Ap 18 '55
Old school ties, 32 English
    schools 8:73-4 Je 3 '40
Old western crossroads. Kelly,
    H.O. 29:71 Jy 17 '50
Old woman cutting her nails.
    Rembrandt 6:56 Mr 20 '39
Old woman with rosary. Cezanne
    28:62 Ja 2 '50
Olinsky, Ivan
    Abram Poole 10:48 F 3 '41
Olive grove at La Dragoniere.
    Churchill 20:47 Ja 7 '46
Oliver, Isaac
    Young girl miniature painting
    41:147 N 5 '56
"Oliver Twist"
    Cruikshank. Oliver asking for
    more illustration bw 25:78
    D 27 '48
Oliviera, Nathan
    The arena lithograph 33:84 Jy
    14 '52
Olmec head, Mexico, c50 B.C.,
    plaster cast 28:89 My 29 '50
Olmsted, Fred, sculptor
    Artist at work photog bw 9:44
    Jy 29 '40 port.
Olympia. Manet 35:58-9 Ag 17
    '53; 41:105 O 22 '56
Olympias, Consort of Philip of
    Macedonia bw 39:90 N 14 '55
Olympic Games symbol: sacred
    torch of Greece, five linked
    rings 41:150-1 N 26 '56
"OM" sacred word, emblem,
    Hinduism 38:57 F 7 '55
On a back street. Kidd 29:70 O 9
    '50
On Lexington Green. engraving
    Doolittle 29:40 Jy 3 '50
On stage four. print bw Riggs 3:
    46 S 13 '37
On the defensive. Billings 29:172-
    3 O 16 '50

On the Oregon Trail. mural bw
    Schwarz 7:45 Ag 14 '39
On the shores of Lake Como.
    Churchill 20:45 Ja 7 '46
On watch. sculpture bw Creeft
    24:95 Ap 12 '48
Once around the ring. Palmer,
    W.C. 22:97 Ap 21 '47
One man four pots. bw Meigs 32:
    91 Mr 17 '52
Oneida stone, Utica, New York
    photog bw 19:104 N 12 '45
O'Neil, Kitty
    Kitty O'Neil, dancer bw 11:74
    Ag 25 '41
O'Neill, Eugene
    Eugene O'Neill photogs bw 21:
    50 O 7 '46; 21:102 O 14 '46
The open window. Bonnard 38:
    107 My 23 '55
The opening of the fifth seal.
    El Greco 28:87 Ap 24 '50
Opera House, Paris, 1862.
    Garnier, archt. photog 8:62
    Je 3 '40
Opera House, Vienna photog 39:
    156-60 N 14 '55 Rebuild-
    ing 38:157, 160 Je 13 '55
The operatic star. bw Degas 6:7
    Ap 17 '39
Operation. Jack 23:99 N 10 '47
Opium smokers, San Francisco,
    1892. photog bw Taber 31:
    13 S 10 '51
Oppenheim, E. Phillips
    E. Phillips Oppenheim photog
    bw 6:18 Mr 27 '39
Oppenheim, Meret
    Fur-lined teacup bw 1:24 D
    14 '36; 32:108 Ap 28 '52
The optimist. bw Bacon, P. 6:
    57 My 8 '39
Orbs, king's and queen's, Eng-
    land photog 2:38 Mr 15 '37
Order No. 11. Bingham 7:41 S
    11 '39
Orders and Decorations See
    Emblems and Decorations
Ore boats, Soo Locks, Michigan.
    Pleissner 25:65 Ag 23
    '48

Oregon
  Faulkner, B. Oregon history
    murals, State Capitol,
    Salem 7:44-5 Ag 14 '39
  Hall. Oregon landscapes 24:
    85-7 Mr 8 '48
  Schwarz. On the Oregon Trail
    mural bw 7:45 Ag 14 '39
Organ Players See Musicians
  and Musical Instruments--
  Organ
Orlando, Vittorio Emanuele
  Vittorio Orlando in Big Four
    at Versailles photog bw 15:
    22 Ag 9 '43; 33:41 D 22 '52
Orne, Joseph
  Washington Street, Salem,
    Massachusetts, 1765 13:80
    N 23 '42
Orpen, William
  Duke of Windsor, 1922 28:114
    My 22 '50
  Winston Churchill, 1915 bw 24:
    94 Mr 15 '48
  Woodrow Wilson 16:49 F 28 '44
Orozco, Jose Clemente
  The evolution of culture in
    Mexico mural, Normal
    School, Mexico City 25:70
    N 22 '48
Orpheus See Mythological
  Themes--Orpheus
Orr, J. W.
  Ack-ack guns in action 12:40
    Mr 2 '42
Orrefors glass bw 17:65 Ag 7 '44
Osborn, Robert, cartoonist
  "Bores" bw 31:115 S 3 '51
  Dilbert bw 14:8-10 My 17 '43
  The hangover, bw 33:Cover,
    106-7 Jy 7 '52
  Snobs bw 29:86-7 N 20 '50
  "War is no Damned Good,"
    cartoon book 22:14-6 Ja 27
    '47
Oscar, Charlie
  Night forest bw 32:88 Mr 17
    '52
  Charlie Oscar photog bw 32:
    87 Mr 17 '52 port.
Osiris 41:114 N 26 '56

Osorio de Zuniga, Manuel
  Goya. Don Manuel Osorio de
    Zuniga 2:41 Je 28 '37
Osorkon II, King of Egyps kneel-
  ing statue bw 39:155 N 14
    '55
Ossorio, Alfonso
  Altar fresco, Catholic church,
    Negros Island, Philippines
    30:15 Ap 30 '51
Osterly Park, England
  Adam, R. Rooms, interior
    design 23:71-4 Ag 25 '47
  Gobelin tapestry wall cover-
    ings photog 23:71 Ag 25 '47
Osver, Arthur
  Cranes (machinery) 30:38 Ja
    15 '51
  Majestic tenement bw 22:78 F
    17 '47
Ottakar, II, King of Bohemia bw
    24:28 Mr 8 '48
Otter, Eskimo stone carving bw
    36:70 My 24 '54
Ottoman See Furniture--Sofas
Ouch. sculpture bw Aul   10:59
    Je 16 '41
Our America, ceramics, dinner
  service. Kent, R. 9:76 S
    9 '40
Our Lady of Ascension mission,
  New Mexico photog 24:85
    Mr 22 '48
Our Lady of Risk sculpture bw,
  Cistercian abbey of Boquen,
  Brittany 29:80 Jy 10 '50
Our Lady of Sorrows, santo,
  wood carving bw 24:60 My
    17 '48
Ouspensky cathedral, Moscow
    38:62-3 Ja 31 '55
Outcry. sculpture bw Vodicka 41:
    76 S 10 '56
Outerbridge, Donald
  Fish, magnetic mobile 29:63
    D 18 '50
Outing on the Hudson, c1870 9:
    76 D 9 '40
The outlaw. sculpture bw Rem-
  ington 13:72 S 14 '42
Outline. Mochi 34:18-20 Mr 9 '53

The outpost. Thon 20:97 Ap 29
    '46
Outside the big tent. Bellows 12:
    62 Je 15 '42
Over the dam. Burchfield 1:28 D
    28 '36
Overseas highway. Crawford 6:
    27 F 13 '39
The overseas highway. Lee, D.
    22:72 My 12 '47
Owls
    Bosch. The heretical owl,
        triptych detail 27:80 N 14
        '49
    Hals. Hille Bobbe 24:71 Mr 22
        '48
    Owl sculpture bw, prehistoric
        Northwest U.S. 32:97 My
        5 '52
    Thurber. Owl bw 24:80 Ap 19
        '48
Owl's Head. Thon 20:98 Ap 29 '46
Oz, Wonderful Wizard of. illus-
    trations Denslow 35:52-9 D
    28 '53
Oxcart and jeep. Kidd 29:70 O 9
    '50
Oyamakui-No-Mikoto, Japanese
    warrior god, with bow and
    arrow sculpture bw 18:95
    F 19 '45

                    P
P B M hauled to rest. bw Sample
    14:6 Je 28 '43
Paca, William
    William Paca bw 15:9 Jy 5 '43
Pach Brothers, photographers
    Portraits of great Americans
        bw 3:16-9 O 25 '37
Pacifica. sculpture bw Stackpole
    5:71 D 5 '38
Pacifica House. photog bw
    Konigshofer, archt. 32:131
    Mr 17 '52
Paderewski, Ignaz
    Ignaz Paderewski photog bw
        17:94 Ag 28 '44
Padma-Sambhava in Amitabha
    Buddha 8:31 Ja 8 '40

Paganini, Nicolo
    Delacroix. Nicolo Paganini,
        at 50 bw 36:128 N 16 '53
    Ingre. Nicolo Paganini, at 37
        drawing bw 36:128 N 16 '53
Pagans, Lorenzo
    Degas. Artist's father listen-
        ing to guitarist, Pagans
        25:79 N 1 '48
Page, Homer
    Girl walking photog bw 24:14·
        My 10 '48
Page, Sophie
    Page, W. Sophie Page, the
        artist's wife 33:90-1 S 15
        '52
Page, William
    Sophie Page, the artist's wife
        33:90-1 S 15 '52
Paget, Sidney
    Sherlock Holmes stories il-
        lustrations bw 16:77 My 1
        '44
Pagodas
    Pagodas of Peiping photogs
        20:72-3 Ap 29 '46
    Shwe Dagon pagoda, Rangoon
        photog bw 26:64 My 9 '49;
        28:88-9 Mr 7 '55; Buddha
        statues bw 26:65 My 9 '49
Pahlmann, William, furniture
    and interior designer
    "Momentum" furniture, studio
        apartment photogs 27:58-9
        O 3 '49
    Walnut sofa photog bw 35:16
        D 14 '53
    William Pahlmann photog bw
        27:55 O 3 '49 port.
Paine, Robert Treat
    Robert Treat Paine bw 15:9
        Jy 5 '43
The painter's study. bw Rem-
    brandt 29:104 S 11 '50
Painting, 1948. De Kooning 25:
    62 O 11 '48
Painting number one. Kandinsky
    28:61 Ja 2 '50
Palaces See also Palazzo
    Blenheim palace, England.
        Vanbrugh, archt. photog

24:32 Ap 19 '48

Bone. Whitehall, thoroughfare of empire 24:60 My 10
'48

Congdon. Venetian palace 30:
108 Ap 30 '51

Doge's palace, Venice, Senate
chamber photog bw 23:50
Ag 4 '47

El Kharj palace, Saudi Arabia
photog bw 14:77 My 31 '43

Farouk I palace, Egypt photogs
bw 16:85-91 Ap 10 '44

Het Loo, Great palace, Amsterdam airview photogs bw
5:29 S 5 '38

Imperial palace, Moscow 38:
62-5 Ja 31 '55

Jodhpur palace, India photog
bw 9:70 N 25 '40

MacIver. Floating palaces 33:
94-5 S 15 '52

Medici-Riccardi palace,
Florence

Gozzoli. Journey of the Magi
fresco 19:Cover 43-51 D
24 '45

Muraba, Ibn Saud's palace,
Riad, Saudi Arabia photog
bw 14:72-3 My 31 '43

Mysore palace, India photog
bw 10:94-5 My 12 '41 night
view 9:73 N 25 '40

Palace of Darius, Persepolis
photog bw 20:34 Ap 8 '46

Peiping summer palace photogs
bw 3:58 Ag 23 '37

Peterhoff palace, 1715 photog
bw 14:83 Mr 29 '43

Petra palace, Trans-Jordan
photogs 27:68-9 O 31 '49

Pitti palace, Florence photog
bw 4:31 Mr 21 '38

Royal palace of Iran, Teheran
photogs bw 20:35 Ap 8 '46

Schonbrunn palace, Vienna
photog bw 26:133 Mr 28 '49

Versaille airview photogs 8:
64 Je 3 '40 bw 5:39 S 26 '38
Royal chapel 23:86 S 15 '47

Whitehall 41:168 N 19 '56

Palace of Fine Arts, San Francisco. Maybeck, archt.
photog bw 24:141 My 17 '48

Palanquin, carved silver, Seville
photog 33:56-7 Ag 18 '52

Palazzo Colonna, Rome
Interiors, sculpture and painting, exterior, gardens
photogs bw 18:87 Mr 5 '45
art gallery 27:53 Ag 1 '49

Palencia, Benjamin
Twilight in Castile 29:102 D
11 '50

Palenque, Chiapas, Mexico
Temple of the inscriptions,
Mayan photog bw 34:70-1
Ap 27 '53
Temple of the sun, Mayan
photog 22:55 Je 30 '47

Palladian Style
Waldershare Park, English
country house photog bw
19:98 O 29 '45

Palladio, Andrea, architect
The Villa Maser, Italy 29:58-
65 Jy 24 '50

Pallas Athena. Rembrandt 29:85
N 27 '50

Pallas Athene. statue bw Phidias, attributed 5:46 D 25
'38; 14:6 Ja 4 '43

Palloy, P. F.
Map of Bastille, Paris, 1789
3:35 Jy 5 '37

Palm Sunday. stained glass
Nicolas 12:52 Ap 6 '42

Palmer, Joseph, sculptor
Palmer grave marker bw 22:
81 Ja 13 '47

Palmer, William Charles
Medical history scenes: Con-
trolled medicine; Uncon-
trolled medicine; Discovery
of antitoxin mural,
Queen's General Hospital,
New York 3:40-2 O 11 '37
Once around the ring 22:97
Ap 21 '47
Summer pleasures 4:26 Je
13 '38

Palmerston, Henry John
　Viscount Palmerston 24:71 My
　　24 '48
Palomar telescope 3:52 N 8 '37
Palos Christopher Columbus
　memorial
　Christopher Columbus, La
　　Rabida monastery 39:121
　　O 10 '55
　Whitney. Christopher Colum-
　　bus statue 39:118 O 10 '55
Pan See Mythological Themes--
　Pan
El Panama hotel, Panama City.
　photogs Stone, archt 32:50-
　7 Ja 7 '52
Panama Canal
　Laning. T. R. in Panama 6:
　　44-5 My 15 '39
Pan-American unity. mural
　Rivera 10:52-6 Mr 3 '41
Panda Bear, Giant
　Jonas. Pandas sculpture bw
　　12:90 Mr 23 '42
Pani, Mario, architect
　Artist and his work (Plaza
　　hotel, Mexico City) photog
　　bw 22:99 F 24 '47 port.
Pankhurst, Emmeline
　Emmeline Pankhurst photog bw
　　23:91 N 17 '47
Pantheon, Rome photog bw 16:12
　Je 5 '44
Pantheon of war, 402 foot canvas.
　French artists 35:55-6 Ag
　10 '53
Panthers
　Memorial to Indian troops in
　　World War I, Suez Canal
　　photog 31:82 O 22 '51
　Tons. Panther tapestry 35:98-
　　9 D 14 '53
Paoli massacre of continental
　soldiers print bw 35:92 S
　28 '53
Paola Adorno. Van Dyck, A. 3:33
　D 27 '37
Paper cutouts. Mochi 34:18-20 Mr
　9 '53
Papiers Colles See Collage
Papineau, Louis Joseph

Louis Papineau bw 9:114 S 9
　'40
Parachutes
　Billings. The descent bw 8:70
　　My 27 '40
　Majors. Practice landing 13:
　　32 Jy 6 '42
Parades See also Holidays and
　Festivals
　Bazile. Parade* 28:101 Mr 13
　　'50
　Bellini. The Corpus Christi
　　procession 23:54-5 Ag 4 '47
　Benevento. Circus parade 1:44
　　N 30 '36
　Celebration of coronation of
　　Alexander II, Czar of Rus-
　　sias, 1856* 38:64-5 Ja 31
　　'55
　Cowles. The parade 12:45 Mr
　　9 '42; 21:75 N 25 '46
　Dufaut. Church procession*
　　mural 33:64-5 D 22 '52
　Dufy. New York parade 30:64
　　Ja 22 '51
　Edward VII, England, review-
　　ing troops, 1903* 23:82-3
　　N 17 '47
　Float of Ganesa in Rama-Lila
　　pageant, New Delhi 30:94
　　F 12 '51
　Floats of Gion Matsuri festival,
　　July 17 and July 24, Japan
　　photogs 17:64-5 S 18 '44
　G.A.R. parade, Philadelphia,
　　1868 photog bw 41:21 Ag
　　20 '56
　G.A.R. grand review, Wash-
　　ington, D.C., 1892 41:22-
　　3 Ag 20 '56
　Gozzoli. Journey of the Magi
　　fresco 19:Cover, 43-5 D
　　24 '45
　Howland. Fourth of July pa-
　　rade, Walpole, New Hamp-
　　shire, c1848* 25:46-7 Jy
　　5 '48
　Labor parade, New York City,
　　1871 bw 33:32 D 8 '52
　Lee, D. Parade of passers-
　　by, Marakesh 33:110-1 N

10 '52

Martins da Silveira. Procession, church festival, Brazil 36:82-3 My 31 '54

Mayan procession, Bonampak
mural 27:82-3 N 21 '49

Parade of Jagannath, Puri,
India photogs bw 3:60-1 Ag
16 '37

Salisbury. Silver jubilee at
St. Paul's 28:68-9 My 29
'50

Steinberg. American parade
31:52-3 Ag 27 '51

"Paradise Lost," illustrations.
bw Dore 24:76 F 2 '48

Parakeets
Audubon. Carolina parakeets
7:60 N 27 '39

Paris See Mythological Themes--
Paris

Paris, France
Buildings, monuments, gar-
dens photogs 8:56-64 Je 3
'40
Chagall. Homage to the Eiffel
Tower 22:58 My 5 '47
Curry. Montmartre bw 15:18
N 29 '43
Davis, F. and G. R. Paris,
1945--scenes and people
since liberation 19:46-55 Jy
16 '45
Davis, G. R. Paris street
scene 35:88 O 26 '53
Davis, S. Place Pas de Loup
22:80 F 17 '47
Fifteenth century Paris bw 31:
76 Jy 30 '51
French revolution: Paris street
barricades, street fighting,
rebuilding of Paris bw 31:
80 Jy 30 '51
Hagnauer. Street fights in
Paris, 1848 25:88-9 N 22 '48
Katzman. Paris bw 32:88 Mr
17 '52
New republic, May 4 1848 25:89
N 22 '48
Observatoire bw, Renaissance
31:78 Jy 30 '51

Pissarro. The Louvre, morning 13:94 N 9 '42

Pissarro. St. Lazare station
33:94 O 27 '52

Renoir. The Pont Neuf 32:92
My 19 '52

Russian cavalry in Paris,
1814 bw 14:95 Mr 29 '43

Utrillo. Place du Tertre,
Montmartre drawing bw 28:
89 Ja 16 '50

Utrillo. Sacre-Coeur et Rue
Saint-Rustique 28:93 Ja 16
'50

Earliest Paris, mud-and-
wattle huts, print bw 31:76
Jy 30 '51 maps

Medieval Paris, 1548 bw 31:
76 Jy 30 '51 maps

Paris Exposition, 1937 See
Fairs

Paris Observatory fountain bw.
Wood, G. 14:57 Ja 18 '43

The park. Dike 16:45 Ja 3 '44

Park at Oaxaca, Mexico. Lee, D.
22:75 My 12 '47

Parker, Alton B.
Alton B. Parker photog bw
14:7 My 31 '43

Parker, Gilbert
Gilbert Parker photog bw 7:
82 S 25 '39

Parker, John
Captain John Parker statue
bw, Lexington Common 9:
13 Ag 19 '40

Parker, Matthew
Matthew Parker bw 34:84 F 23
'53

Parker Pen Factory, Jonesville,
Wis. photog 36:33 Ja 4 '54

Parks See also Gardens
Bellows. Gramercy park 20:
79 Mr 25 '46
Bohrod. Idle hour park 11:62
Jy 7 '41 bw 14:6 Je 28 '43
Davis, F. Softball game in
Hyde Park, London* 16:66-
7 Ap 3 '44; 31:79 O 29 '51
Elysian Fields amusement
park,* Hoboken, N.J. 32:

Parks (cont.)
117 Ap 7 '52
Gee. Central Park lake 16:46
Ja 3 '44
Homer. Skating in Central
Park, 1860 32:118 Ap 7 '52
Nollekens. Family in a park
25:98 S 13 '48
Pena. Chapultepec park draw-
ing bw 20:58 Je 3 '46
Seurat. A Sunday afternoon on
the Island of La Grande-
Jatte 31:60-2 Jy 23 '51
Parks, Gordon, photographer
Mary Garden photog bw 34:16
Mr 16 '53
Photographs bw 34:14-6 Mr 16
'53
Parliament, England
Benjamin Franklin before the
House of Commons, 1776
bw 25:110 S 13 '48
Dissolution of Parliament by
Cromwell, 1653* bw 41:162-
3 N 19 '56
Hickel. The House of Com-
mons, c1776 bw 29:53 Jy 3
'50
House of Commons, House of
Lords--as they would be
under Napoleon cartoon bw
9:11 S 30 '40
King Charles I and Parliament*
drawing bw 41:186 N 12 '56
Oliver Cromwell addressing
Parliament bw 24:93 Je 14
'48
Opening of Parliament by Queen
Victoria, January 24, 1846
bw 13:76 N 16 '42
Parliament called by Edward I*
bw 22:81 My 26 '47
Pitt stricken in the House of
Lords* 25:107 S 13 '48
Queen Elizabeth I and Parlia-
ment* engraving bw 41:170
N 5 '56
Parliament Buildings. photogs
Barry, archt. 24:49 Ap 26
'48 bw 16:81 My 22 '44
House of Lords remodelled

photog 31:60 N 19 '51
Parliament in Frankfort, 1848 bw
25:86 N 22 '48
Parnassus. bw Poussin 25:78 O
11 '48
Parr, Catherine
Catherine Parr bw 41:88 O 29
'56
Parrish, Maxfield
The dinky bird bw 5:29 O 31
'38
Landscape 18:45 Ja 1 '45
Parson Weems' fable. Wood, G.
8:32-3 F 19 '40 bw 14:58
Ja 18 '43
Parsons, Francis
Cunne Shote, Cherokee chief
36:75 Mr 8 '54
Partch, Virgil
Cartoons bw 17:75 N 27 '44
Parthenon, Athens
Acropolis, Athens photog bw
18:56 Ja 1 '45
Parthenon photogs bw 35:152-
62 O 26 '53; 36:44 Ja 11 '54
Elgin marbles bw 35:152-
62 O 26 '53
Parzinger, Tommi, silversmith
Silver design: salt and pepper,
coffee set, inkwell, library
clock, ashtray bw 7:74-6
N 20 '39
Tommi Parzinger photog bw
7:74 N 20 '39 port.
Pas de deux. Reinhart 16:45 Ja
3 '44
Paasenger pigeons. Audubon 7:
60 N 27 '39
The passing leap. bw Curry 15:
19 N 29 '43
Passing tow. Etnier 23:68-9 Jy
14 '47
The passion of Sacco and Vanzetti. bw Shahn 37:96 O 4
'54
Pastels
Bone. Whitehall-Thorough-
fare of empire 24:60 My
10 '48
Davis, G. R. Noel, the artist's son 14:45 Ap 19 '43

Degas. Ballet girls on stage
11:59 S 8 '41
Pittman. Charleston houses
22:68-72 Ap 14 '47
Pastime bowling alley. Thomas,
B. 10:52 Je 23 '41
Pastoral. Lee, D. 5:25 Ag 22 '38
Pastoral Scenes
Currier and Ives print. The
four seasons of life: child-
hood 9:30 D 30 '40
Watteau. Reunion in the coun-
try 40:110-11 My 7 '56
Boucher. La noble pastorale
bw 4:28 Ja 24 '38 tapestry.
Pastoral staff photog bw 16:77 Ja
24 '44
Pastoral symphony. Giorgione
23:52 Ag 4 '47; 39:170-1 O
24 '55
Pasture at Elk. Brook 10:52 Ja
13 '41
Paterson, William
William Paterson 39:63 Jy 4
'55
Path of investigation. bw Vaughn
27:47 N 14 '49
Patiner, Joachim and Massys,
Quentin
The temptation of St. Anthony
31:62-3 O 1 '51
Patrick, James
Inquisitive model 11:73 O 27
'41
Patriotic still life. Bouche 11:49
Ag 18 '41
Patrix, George
Clown bw 20:64 Je 17 '46
Artist and his work photog bw
20:64 Je 17 '46 port.
Pattison, Abbott
Striding man sculpture bw 32:
78 Ja 7 '52
Patton, George
Lt. Gen. George Patton,
"Time" cover portrait 17:
60 D 11 '44
Paul, Saint
Castellon. Rights of citizens
30:89 Mr 12 '51
Christ between Peter and Paul

mosaic, Early Christian
28:68 Mr 27 '50
Dore. Shipwreck of St. Paul
bw 39:37 D 26 '55
El Greco. St. Paul bw 39:78
Ag 8 '55
Grunewald. St. Paul, the her-
mit 30:80 Mr 26 '51
Story of St. Paul, Codex Paul-
inus 34:88 F 23 '53
Paul III, Pope
Titian. Pope Paul III 27:64 O
24 '49 bw 6:32 F 13 '39
Pauling, Linus C.
Dr. Linus Pauling photog bw
11:43 O 13 '41
Paulus, James
Nude study 25:100 D 6 '48
Artist at work photog bw 25:
103 D 6 '48 port.
Pavloff, Nickolas
Nickolas Pavloff, photog bw
41:80 Ag 13 '56 port.
Pawnee Bill See Lillie, Gordon
Payday at the arsenal, Venice
bw Renaissance 23:59 Ag 4
'47
Payday, "Newfie" workmen. bw
Coale 13:92-3 Jy 13 '42
Paying the exciseman, Revolu-
tionary cartoon, U.S. bw
29:36 Jy 3 '50
Peace and plenty, detail. bw
Inness 19:82 S 10 '45
The peace of Westphalia. van
Nieulandt 24:58 Je 14 '48
The peaceable kingdom. Hicks
17:72 O 16 '44
Peacock, Claude
American toads and frogs 7:
46 Jy 10 '39
Peacock Throne photog bw 20:34
Ap 8 '46
Peacocks
Peacock mobile, Northland
shopping center, Detroit
37:82 Ag 30 '54
Peale, Charles Willson
The exhumation of the masto-
don 6:28 Je 19 '39
George Washington bw 24:22

Peale, Charles Willson (cont₀)
    F 23 '48
    George Washington, head, 1779
        bw 24:22 F 23 '48
    James Peale, the artist's
        brother bw 12:64 Mr 20 '42
    Jefferson as Secretary of
        State 14:63 Ap 12 '43
    John Lewis, c1775 12:66 Mr
        20 '42
    Portrait of a woman* miniature
        bw 6:52 Mr 20 '39
    Self-portrait bw 6:26 Je 19 '39;
        12:64 Mr 20 '42 port₀
    Self-portrait, age 81 38:69 Mr
        28 '55 port₀
Peale, Eleanor
    Peale, Rembrandt₀ The artist's
        daughters, Rosalba and
        Eleanor 12:65 Mr 20 '42
Peale, James
    Fruit in a bowl 12:66 Mr 20 '42
    Peale, C₀W₀ James Peale,
        the artist's brother bw 12:
        64 Mr 20 '42
Peale, Raphaelle
    Melons 12:66 Mr 20 '42
    Raphaelle Peale bw 12:64 Mr
        20 '42 port₀
Peale, Rembrandt
    The artist's daughters, Rosalba
        and Eleanor 12:64 Mr 20 '42
    Dolly Madison 41:158-9 D 24
        '56
    George Washington, head bw
        24:23 F 23 '48
    Mrs₀ Rembrandt Peale bw 12:
        64 Mr 20 '42
    Self-portrait bw 12:65 Mr 30
        '42 port₀
Peale, Mrs₀ Rembrandt
    Martha Washington, after
        Rembrandt Peale 12:66 Mr
        20 '42
    Peale, Rembrandt₀ Mrs₀ Rem-
        brandt Peale bw 12:64 Mr
        20 '42 port₀
Peale, Rosalba
    Peale, Rembrandt₀ The art-
        ist's daughters, Rosalba
        and Eleanor 12:65 Mr 20 '42

Pearl Harbor₀ Gropper 16:78 Je
    12 '44
Pearl Harbor attack₀ Foujita 28:
    67 F 27 '50
Pearl of Asia, gemstone 33:34 D
    29 '52
Pearlstein, Philip
    Merry-go-round 10:57 Je 16
        '41
    Wylie Avenue barber shop 10:
        57 Je 16 '41
Pears, Charles
    Convoy 28:73 F 20 '50
Pearson, Charles D₀
    War correspondents--cartoons
        from "Yank" bw 18:12-4 Ja
        8 '45
Peasant mother and child₀ sculp-
    ture bw Michnick 4:62 Ap
    25 '38
Peasants, Caceres, Spain₀ Bone
    1:43 D 7 '36
Peasants and angel₀ mural Gau-
    gin 28:93 My 1 '50
Peccaries
    Audubon₀ Collared peccary
        30:48 Ja 29 '51
Peel, Robert
    Winterhalten₀ Duke of Welling-
        ton and Sir Robert Peel 25:
        90 N 22 '48
Pehriska-Ruhpa, war chief of
    the Minnetaree tribe, Da-
    kota lithograph 27:41 Jy 4
    '49
Peikov, sculptor
    Artist and his work photogs
        bw 27:51 Ag 1 '49 port₀
Peiping, China
    Architecture, sculpture,
        temples, pagodas photogs
        20:67-77 Ap 29 '46
    Confucian altar of Heaven
        photog bw 38:71 Ap 4 '55
    Guardian image, Chinese
        Buddhist temple 38:65 Ap
        4 '55
    Temples, sculpture, summer
        palace photogs bw 3:54-5
        Ag 23 '37
Peirce, Waldo

After the show 12:74 Ap 20 '42

Alzira, the artist's wife 10:47 F 3 '41

Alzira cuts Mike's hair* 19:83 N 12 '45

Anna digs clams 19:85 N 12 '45

Anna turns painter 19:85 N 12 '45

The baby twins* bw 19:82 N 12 '45

Bill, the artist's son 18:75 My 14 '45

Bill plays an old mandolin 19: 85 N 12 '45

The birches 12:61 Je 15 '42

County fair 3:34 Ag 30 '37; 21: 74 N 25 '46

Europa and the bull 22:95 Ap 21 '47

God Rest You Merry, Gentle-men 23:56 D 22 '47

Maine swimming hole bw 18: 44 Ja 1 '45

Maine trotting race 3:34 Ag 30 '37

Mike, the artist's son 19:86 N 12 '45

Mike fishes in Maine 19:85 N 12 '45

Spring bw 17:29 O 16 '44

The twin's concert 19:84 N 12 '45

Bellows. Waldo Peirce 20:82 Mr 25 '46 port.

Self-portrait--the artist paint-ing his family bw 19:82 N 12 '45

Waldo Peirce; family home photogs bw 3:34 Ag 30 '37

Peirce mansion, Portsmouth, N.H., 1799 15:12 D 6 '43

Pekinese sculpture bw 18:91 F 19 '45

El pelele (The manikin). tapestry cartoon Goya 40:73 My 28 '56

Peleliu Island
Lea. Peleliu invasion, Septem-ber 15, 1944 18:61-7 Je 11 '45

Pelham, Henry

Copley. Boy with squirrel bw 5:28 O 31 '38

Pelleas and Melisande. sculpture bw Laurent 10:67 Je 2 '41

Pelton, O.
Poor Richard steel engraving bw 40:74-5 Ja 9 '56.

Pena, Feliciano
Chapultepec park drawing bw 20:58 Je 3 '46

Pendants See Jewelry--Pend-ants and Necklaces

Penguins
De Bry. Penguin massacre* drawing bw 24:86 Mr 22 '48

Penhurst Place, England, 17th century 19:100 O 29 '45

The penitent Magdalene. El Greco 7:55 O 9 '39 bw 6: 58 Mr 27 '39

Penn, Irving
Alfred Hitchcock photog bw 24: 15 My 10 '48

George Jean Nathan and H.L. Mencken photog bw 24:14 My 10 '48

Penn, John
John Penn bw 15:9 Jy 5 '43

Penn, William
Birch. Penn's tree 38:70-1 Mr 28 '55

Hicks. The grave of William Penn, Jordans, England 17:72 O 16 '44

Hicks. The peaceable kingdom 17:72 O 16 '44

Hicks. Penn treating with the Delawares, 1682 24:71 Je 14 '48; 36:78 Mr 8 '54

Penn in armor, age 22, c1666 17:71 O 16 '44

Penn's arrival in America, 1682 bw 33:96 S 29 '52

West. Penn's treaty with the Indians 6:27 Je 19 '39

William Penn bw 33:95 S 29 '52; 39:44 D 26 '55 statue, tower top, Philadelphia City Hall bw 17:75 O 16 '44

Penniman, John Ritto
Meeting house hill, Roxbury,

Penniman, John Ritto (cont.)
in 1790 13:80 N 23 '42
Pennsylvania, map, in "History
of Pennsylvania, 1698 bw
18:66 My 21 '45
Pennsylvania Academy of Fine
Arts
150 years of painting: C.W.
Peale to Demuth, exhibit 38:
68-75 Mr 28 '55
Sculpture, speed and skill con-
test, annual photogs bw 2:
26-7 Ap 19 '37
Pentagon, Washington, D.C. airview photog bw 14:11 My 24
'43 exterior photog bw 14:
13 My 24 '43
Penthesileia, Queen of the Ama-
zons bw 14:6 Ja 4 '43
Pepi I, King of Egypt sculpture
41:78 O 1 '56
Pepperell, William
Copley. Sir William Pepperell
and his family 41:73 D 10
'56
Percy Family shield of arms 22:
69 My 26 '47
Pereira, Irene Rice
Deep vision 34:73 Ja 26 '53
Melting horizon 34:73 Ja 26 '53
Transflux 34:74-5 Ja 26 '53
Perfume box, Etruscan bronze,
8th century B.C. 40:61 F
13 '56
Perfume shop, Paris.* Davis, F.
19:52 Jy 16 '45
Pergamum Greek theater photog
bw 8:79 Ap 8 '40
Pericles, bust bw 5:46 D 25 '38
Perisphere
Trylon and perisphere, tri-
angular tower and steel
sphere, New York World's
Fair, 1939. photog bw
Dreyfuss 4:11 Ja 31 '38 plan
5:54-7 Ag 1 '38
Perkins, Marion
Moses sculpture bw 21:62 Jy
22 '46
Perkins, Lawrence Bradford,
architect

Perkins and Will. Heathcote
elementary school, Scars-
dale, N.Y. photog bw 37:
73 N 15 '54
Perkins and Will. Junior high
school, plans and sketches
bw 36:74 F 1 '54
Perlin, Bernard
Landscape in the Abruzzi 28:
91 Mr 20 '50
Tokyo street scenes, September 1945, first days of oc-
cupation 19:73-6 N 19 '45
War in Greece--Aegean ac-
tions 18:47-54 F 26 '45
War in Greece--Priest, peas-
ant, and partisan bw 17:35
S 4 '44
Bernard Perlin photog bw 19:
73 N 19 '45; 28:98 Mr 20
'50 port.
Peron, Juan
Boschi. Juan Peron, pinhead
portrait 30:146 Je 11 '51
Peroz I, King of Persia
King Peroz hunting ibexes,
gilded silver dish 20:92 Je
24 '46
Perry, Shaw and Hepburn, archi-
tects
Two-story house, U.S.A.
photog bw 9:84-5 Jy 1 '40
Perry's arrival in Japan, 1853
bw 19:58 S 17 '45
Persephone See Mythological
Themes--Persephone
Persepolis
Architecture, sculptures, 515
B.C. photog bw 35:155-8
N 23 '53
Ruins photog bw 30:108-9 Je
18 '51
Pershing, John
General Pershing photog bw
24:14 Ja 12 '48
Persian girl. lithograph bw Ma-
tisse 31:110 N 26 '51
The persistence of memory. Dali
1:25 D 14 '36; bw 19:64 S
24 '45
Person throwing a stone at a

bird. Miro 25:60 O 11 '48;
bw 19:65 S 24 '45
Personages with a star. Miro 33:
97 O 27 '52
Personification in Art See Allegorical and Symbolical Themes
Perspective
Eakins. Study for sculling painting, perspective drawing bw
16:77 My 15 '44
Escher. Drawing, multiple and
distorted pespective 30:18-
9 My 7 '51
Fasola. Poliepipedi (Three dimensional) glass paintings
41:188-9 N 26 '56
Hogarth. False perspective bw
1:27 D 14 '36
Paintings distorted unless re-
flected in conical or cylin-
drical mirrors, 18th cen-
tury bw 27:18-20 S 12 '49
Pereira. Paintings on glass
layers 34:73-5 Ja 26 '53
Picasso. Figure, multiple
perspective 17:74 N 13 '44
Tchelitchew. Phenomena,
"triple perspective" painting bw 5:57 S 5 '38
Peter, Saint
Christ between Peter and Paul
mosaic, Early Christian
28:68 Mr 27 '50
Dore. Deliverance of St. Peter
bw 39:37 D 26 '55
Hountouaji. St. Peter and the
cock sculpture bw 29:63 S
4 '50
St. Peter 28:74 Je 19 '50
Velazquez. St. Peter 7:55 O 9
'39
Peter I, The Great, Czar of Russia bw 14:94 Mr 29 '43; 24:
120 F 23 '48
Peter in San Patricio. Wyeth, H.
10:74 Ap 14 '41
Peterhoff palace, Russia, 1715
photog bw 14:83 Mr 29 '43
Peters, Fritz
Fritz Peters photog bw 28:35
Ja 30 '50

Peters (Harry Twyford) collec-
tion of Currier and Ives
prints 9:27-34 D 30 '40
Peterson, Roger Tory
American song and marsh
birds 4:26-31 My 23 '38
Bald eagles 21:51-4 Jy 1 '46
Bird courtship 18:69-74 Je 4
'45
Birds 22:84-8 Je 2 '47
Birds of prey: owls, carrion
scavengers, fish scaven-
gers, hawks 7:60-4 S 25
'39
Blue jays 12:43-5 Je 1 '42
Hummingbirds: rubythroat
and others 25:78-80 Jy 26
'48
Mocking birds 20:72-5 Ap 8
'46
Shore birds and marsh birds
11:49-52 Ag 4 '41
State birds 8:58-62 Je 17 '40
Winter birds 18:55-8 Ja 15
'45
Petra, Trans-Jordan
El Khazna, The Treasury,
ruined temple photog 27:67
O 31 '49
Palace and urn tombs photogs
27:68-9 O 31 '49
Roman theater photog 27:69 O
31 '49
Petrarch, Francesco
Francesco Petrarch bw 22:79
Mr 3 '47
Petrouchka, ballet. Davis, G. R.
16:78 Mr 20 '44
Pettus (William B.) collection of
Chinese Christian art 11:
41-8 D 22 '41
Petty, George
Petty girls 6:34-5 Je 26 '39
George Petty photogs bw 6:
36-7 Je 26 '39 port.
Petty, Mary
"New Yorker" cover 21:70 Jy
15 '46
Pevsner, Antoine
The unknown political prisoner
sculpture bw 34:40 Je 1 '53

Pewter room, Webb Museum,
  Shelburne, Vt. 35:51 Jy 6
  '53
The pheasant. Soutine 38:108 My
  23 '55
Pheasants
  Curry. Wisconsin still life bw
    15:20 N 29 '43
  Jacques. The ring-necked
    pheasant 9:58 N 4 '40
Pheasants in New England. Ripley
  29:124-5 D 4 '50
Phelps, William Lyon
  William Lyon Phelps; wife;
    home photogs bw 5:72-81 D
    5 '38
Phenomena. Tchelitchew 5:57 S
  5 '38
Phidias, attributed
  Pallas Athene sculpture bw 5:
    46 D 25 '38
Philadelphia
  Birch. State House engraving
    bw 39:61 Jy 4 '55
  Bouche. Broad Street station,
    Philadelphia 11:49 Ag 18 '41
  Fourth of July, 1876 engraving
    bw 25:49 Jy 5 '48
  Greek revival architecture
    photog 39:64-5 Ag 29 '55
  Krimmel. Fourth of July,
    Centre Square 25:48 Jy 5
    '48; 39:62 Ag 29 '55
  Market (High) Street engraving
    40:77 Ja 9 '56
  Playground equipment 37:118-
    20 S 13 '54
  Sample. The Schuylkill River*
    34:78-9 Ja 5 '53
  Second and High Streets, *
    c1800 39:61 Jy 4 '55
  State House photog bw 11:104
    N 10 '41
Philadelphia Museum of Art
  Collections, patrons 31:66-73
    S 3 '51
  International sculpture exhibit
    bw 9:54-5 Ag 12 '40 bw
    Third sculpture internation-
    al 26:112-4 Je 20 '49
Philip II, King of Spain

Anguissola, King Philip 24:80
  Mr 22 '48; bw 31:60 O 1
  '51
Eworth. Philip and Mary bw
  41:104 O 29 '56
Philip of Macedonia bw 39:90 N
  14 '55
Philipp, Robert
  Brooke Hayward bw 8:62 Ap 8
    '40
  Derelicts 8:64 Ap 8 '40
  Jordy bw 8:62 Ap 8 '40
  Letty 8:63 Ap 8 '40
  Margaret Sullavan bw 8:62 Ap
    8 '40
  My wife and I 8:64 Ap 8 '40
  Nude bw 6:45 My 1 '39
  Rochelle, the artist's wife 10:
    47 F 3 '41
  Robert Philipp photogs bw 8:
    62, 65 Ap 8 '40 port. in
    group photog 29:172-3 O
    16 '50 port.
  Self-portrait--My wife and I
    8:64 Ap 8 '40 port.
Philipp, Rochelle
  Philipp, Robert. My wife and
    I 8:64 Ap 8 '40
  Philipp, Robert. Rochelle,
    the artist's wife 10:47 F 3
    '41
Philipp, Walter
  Clowns 24:160 Mr 15 '48
  Street scene bw 24:160 Mr 15
    '48
  Walter Philipp photogs bw 24:
    159-60 Mr 15 '48 port.
Phillips, Aaron Francis
  General store, New Salem,
    Illinois 36:81 F 15 '54
  Rutledge Mill, New Salem,
    Illinois 36:80-1 F 15 '54
  Sawmill on the Sangamon
    River, New Salem, Illi-
    nois 36:79 F 15 '54
  Tree-trunk portrait of Abra-
    ham Lincoln, New Salem,
    Illinois 36:80-1 F 15 '54
  Two-story cabin, New Salem,
    Illinois, 1835 36:80 F 15
    '54

Self-portrait, age 34 36:79 F
15 '54 port.
Phillips, Duncan
Mr. and Mrs. Duncan Phillips
photog bw 38:106 My 23 '55
Phillips, Marjorie
Mr. and Mrs. Duncan Phillips
photog bw 38:106 My 23 '55
port.
Phillips Gallery, Washington,
D.C.
Phillips (Duncan) collection of
European and American
paintings 38:106-10 My 23
'55
Philosopher with open book. bw
forgery in style of Rem-
brandt 39:142-3 S 26 '55
Phipps, Mrs. Henry
Sargent. Mrs. Phipps and
grandson 25:94 O 18 '48
"Phiz" See Browne, Hablot
Knight
Phoenix See Animals, Imagin-
ary
The photographer. sculpture bw
Rogers 6:8 Mr 6 '39
Photography See also names of
photographers, as Beaton,
C.; Bourke-White, M.;
Brady, M.; Cartier-Bres-
son, H.; Feininger, A.;
Karsh, Y.; Muybridge, E.;
Newman, A.; Pach Brothers;
Steichen, E.; Weston, E.;
Ylla
Autochromes of early 1900--
pioneer colored photographs
28:10-1 Ja 2 '50
Daguerrotypes--earliest,
Daguerre's studio bw 2:4-5
Mr 29 '37

Collections
Conan Doyle collection of
spirit photographs bw 7:8-11
N 13 '39
Merserve collection of photo-
graphs of the 1880's bw 13:
10-3 O 19 '42
U.S. Army Signal Corps--his-

toric photographs, 1850 to
present bw 7:46-55 Ag 28
'39

Exhibits
"The Exact Instant," news
photographs of the past 100
years, Museum of Modern
Art exhibit bw 26:12-4 F
21 '49
"Forgotten Photographs,"
Museum of Modern Art ex-
hibit bw 31:12-4 S 10 '51
"In and Out of Focus," Muse-
um of Modern Art exhibit
24:14-6 My 10 '48
Phyfe, Duncan, Furniture maker
Furniture--chairs, sofa,
tables photogs 39:60-1 Ag
29 '55
Phyfe headquarters, Fulton
Street, New York City 39:
60 Ag 29 '55
Physicians See Medical Themes
Physicians as Artists 23:98-9 N
10 '47
Sunshine. Plastic surgeon
"improves" sculptures of
historic personages bw 12:
12-5 Je 8 '42
Piano Players See Musicians
and Musical Instruments--
Piano
Piatigorsky, Gregor
Adams, W. Gregor Piatigor-
sky 16:75 Ap 24 '44
Halsman. Gregor Piatigorsky
photog bw 16:49 Mr 13 '44
Picabia, Francis
Dance at the spring 28:61 Ja
2 '50
Portrait (montage) bw 34:25
My 25 '53
Gertrude Stein bw 23:15 Ag 18
'47(drawing)
Francis Picabia, 1914 photog
bw 28:61 Ja 2 '50 port.
Picador. sculpture bw Gargallo
24:95 Ap 12 '48

Picasso, Pablo
  The absinthe drinker 40:74 My
    28 '56
  Accordionist bw 26:82 My 2 '49
  Algerian women, variations of
    Delacroix's Algerian women
    38:130 Je 27 '55
  The artist's wife, 1930 bw 16:
    79 Ap 24 '44
  Les demoiselles d'Avignon,
    1907 23:93 O 13 '47
  Design for a monument bw 23:
    95 O 13 '47
  Dora Maar bw 23:100 O 13 '47
  Early paintings 38:125-6 Je 27
    '55
  The family of saltimbanques
    23:93 O 13 '47 bw 5:29 O 10
    '38
  Figure, multiperspective 17:
    74 N 13 '44
  Gertrude Stein bw 23:15 Ag 18
    '47
  Girl* 38:126 Je 27 '55
  Girl before a mirror 23:96 O
    13 '47; 25:58 O 11 '48
  Girl with cock bw 8:59 Mr 4 '40
  Guernica fresco bw 3:64 Jy 26
    '37
  Head, Negro period, c1907 33:
    93 O 27 '52
  The lovers 23:95 O 13 '47
  Ma jolie 25:59 O 11 '48
  Moulin de la Galette 8:57 Mr
    4 '40
  The old Jew bw 40:168 Ap 9
    '56
  Pigeons bw 38:128 Je 27 '55
  Portrait of a woman* 31:71 S
    3 '51
  The red tablecloth 23:95 O 13
    '47
  Spanish girl* 38:125 Je 27 '55
  Sylvette, series of portraits
    bw 37:119 N 8 '54
  The three dancers 8:58 Mr 4
    '40
  The three musicians 4:43 My 2
    '38
  Two acrobats with dog 8:57 Mr
    4 '40 bw 6:83 My 22 '39
  La vie 8:57 Mr 4 '40
  Woman asleep in an armchair
    1:25 D 14 '36
  Woman in white 23:95 O 13 '47
  Woman in yellow 8:58 Mr 4 '40
  Woman with loaves bw 2:51 Ap
    5 '37
  Woman with mandolin 8:58 Mr
    4 '40
  The bathers bw 23:94 O 13 '47
    (drawings)
  Blind beggar bw 38:128 Je 27
    '55 (drawings)
  Centaurs bw 23:97 O 13 '47
    (drawings)
  Flashlight drawings in dark
    photogs by Mili bw 28:10-2
    Ja 30 '50 (drawings)
  Owner of "Chez Camille Re-
    nault" bw 36:110 Ap 26 '54
    (drawings)
  Horses and figures drypoint,
    1905 bw 23:93 O 13 '47
    (engraving)
  Departure 33:84 Jy 14 '52
    (lithograph)
  Confidence 21:84 S 30 '46
    (tapestry)
  Artist and his work photog bw
    23:97 O 13 '47; 38:124 Je
    27 '55 port.
  Artist at work photog bw 17:
    73 N 13 '44; 37:119 N 8 '54
    port.
  Gallatin. Picasso in his studio
    photog bw 4:45 My 2 '38
    port.
  Karsh. Picasso and his work
    photog bw 37:134 O 4 '54
    port.
  Mili. Pablo Picasso, age 68
    photog 27:92 D 12 '49 port.
  Pablo Picasso photog 39:142
    N 14 '55 bw 8:56 Mr 4 '40;
    23:92, 104 O 13 '47 port.
  Picasso and Gertrude Stein
    photog bw 23:14 Ag 18 '47
    port.
Piccadilly Circus, London
  Hacker. Wet night in Picca-
    dilly Circus 23:85 N 17 '47

"Piccoli," illustrations. Julian
35:197-200 D 7 '53
Piccolomini, Aeneas Sylvius See
Pius II, Pope
Pickens, Alton
Carnival 28:88 Mr 20 '50
Pickering, Rebecca (White)
Stuart. Mrs. Timothy Picker-
ing, 1817 bw 9:74 D 9 '40
Picking lemons. Gauguin 21:64 Jy
29 '46
The picnic ground. Sloan 12:73
Ap 20 '42
Picnic in the Catskills. Inman 27:
57 Ag 29 '49
Picnic party near Mount Mans-
field, Vermont. bw Thomp-
son, J. 25:90 O 18 '48
The picnic--or the Fourth of July,
a day to be remembered.
Spencer 25:48 Jy 5 '48
Picture of Dorian Gray. bw Al-
bright brothers 16:70-1 Mr
27 '44; 18:99-105 Mr 19 '45
The piebald giraffe. Priebe 21:79
N 25 '46
Pied Piper of Hamlin stained glass
bw 16:125 My 29 '44
Pierce, Leona
Stilts woodcut 37:89 O 18 '54
Pierce house, Salem, Massachu-
setts
McIntire. Decoration; Chippen-
dale staircase 38:62-3 My
30 '55
Piero della Francesca
The baptism 39:20-1 D 26 '55
Death of Adam fresco detail
20:61 Ap 22 '46
Resurrection 39:30-1 D 26 '55
Saint 3:34 D 27 '37
Solomon receiving the Queen
of Sheba fresco detail 20:63
Ap 22 '46
Story of the true cross fresco,
San Francesco chapel,
Arezzo, Italy c1460 20:60-
8 Ap 22 '46
Visit of the Queen of Sheba to
King Solomon fresco detail
20:62 Ap 22 '46

Piero di Cosimo
Adoration of the Child 7:33 Jy
31 '39
Pieta See Jesus Christ--Pieta
Pietro de Crescenzi
"Treatise on Rural Economy,"
manuscript, Flemish, 15th
century 22:78-80 My 26 '47
Pigeon. glassware bw Waugh 7:
32 S 18 '39
Pigeons
Audubon. Passenger pigeons
7:60 N 27 '39
Hooft. Tumblers and pigeons
30:36-7 Ja 15 '51
Picasso. Pigeons bw 38:128
Je 27 '55
Sloan. Pigeons 7:46 D 11 '39
Piggin, wood, U.S. Colonial
photog 38:119 Ap 18 '55
Pigs
Colombe. Pigs, November
page of "Book of Hours" 24:
49 Ja 5 '48
Curry. Hogs killing a rattle-
snake bw 15:19 N 29 '43
watercolor bw 15:18 N 29
'43
Lalk. They're cute when
they're small 10:78 Mr 31
'41
Mount. Ringing the pig 18:66
Je 25 '45
Shepard. Piglet drawing from
"Winnie-the-Pooh" illus-
trations bw 30:76 F 19 '51
Young. Duck and shoat sculp-
ture bw 10:79 F 17 '41
Pignon, Edouard
Still life* 17:76 N 13 '44
Artist in his studio photog bw
17:74 N 13 '44 port.
Pike, John
Thumbing a ride 29:72 O 9 '50
Pikes, boarding, U.S.S. Consti-
tution photog bw 9:54 O 28
'40
The pilgrim. sculpture bw,
Saint-Gaudens 24:110 Mr
15 '48

Pilgrim meeting house, 1683
   drawing bw 19:54 N 26 '45
Pilgrims
   Brownscombe. The first A-
     merican Thanksgiving 13:77
     N 23 '42
   Church. Quest for freedom bw
     24:70 Je 14 '48
   Moran, E. Embarkation of the
     Pilgrims from Southampton,
     1620 13:75 N 23 '42 bw 24:
     68-9 Je 14 '48
   Moran, P. Signing the Compact
     13:75 N 23 '42
   Myths and facts, locale of pil-
     grims from Willison's book,
     "Saints and Strangers" bw
     19:51 N 26 '45
   Scenes and portraits 13:74-86
     N 23 '42
   Pilgrim's first Thanksgiving*
     bw 19:52 N 26 '45
   Plymouth Rock, Plymouth,
     Mass. photog bw 24:69 Je
     14 '48
   Prayer at sailing of Mayflower*
     bw 25:132 N 29 '48
   Rothermel. Landing of the Pil-
     grims 13:76 N 23 '42 bw 19:
     56 N 26 '45
   Schwartze. The Pilgrim
     fathers in public worship
     13:77 N 23 '42 bw 24:68 Je
     14 '48
   Signing of Mayflower Compact
     bw 25:130 N 29 '48
Pilgrims. Van Eyck brothers 26:
   65, 67 Ap 18 '49
Pilipili
   Birds and bees 34:106 My 4'53
   Funeral procession 34:107 My
     4 '53
   Ilunga and Pilipili. Birds, bugs
     and foliage frieze 34:106-7
     My 4 '53
Pillbox with Benjamin Franklin
   portrait 40:82 Ja 9 '56
Pilsudski, Jozef
   Marshal Pilsudski photog bw 17:
     93 Ag 28 '44
Pimlico Race Track. Glannery 32:

   70-2 My 5 '52
Pinart, Robert
   Artist at work photog bw 37:
     124 O 25 '54 port.
Pinckney, Thomas
   Thomas Pinckney bw 10:26 Mr
     3 '41
Pine, Robert Edge
   The Congress voting independ-
     ence, c1784 (painting fin-
     ished by Savage) 40:78-9 Ja
     9 '56 bw 29:52 Jy 3 '50
   George Washington, 1785 bw
     24:22 F 23 '48
Pines. Chapman 33:92 S 15 '52
Pingree House, Salem, Mass.
   photog bw 15:13 D 6 '43
Pink cow. Dubuffet 33:96 O 27
   '52
Pink house. Whitaker 16:45 Ja
   3 '44
The pink shirt. Davis, G.R. 6:
   30 F 13 '39
Pinkerton, Allan
   Allan Pinkerton photog bw 3:
     83 S 20 '37
Pinkfeet flying at dusk. Scott 1:
   42-3 D 21 '36
Pinkie (Sarah Moulton-Barrett).
   Lawrence, T. 4:25 Ja 24
   '38
Pinkham, Lydia E.
   Lydia E. Pinkham sculptured
     bust bw 27:165-6 S 19 '49
Pinocchio. sculpture bw Castro-
   giovanni 40:128 Je 4 '56
Pinocchio. sculpture bw, Collodi,
   Italy Greco 40:127 Je 4
   '56
Pinocchio. sculpture bw Venturi
   40:128 Je 4 '56
Pins See also Jewelry--
   Brooches and Pins
   Etruscan safety-pin, c600 B.
     C. photog bw 6:52 Mr 20
     '39
Pinson-Berthet, Jean
   Forged paintings of Vlaminck
     and Utrillo bw 30:70 Ap 9
     '51
   Jean Binson-Berthet, art

forger photogs bw 30:70 Ap
9 '51   port.

Pinturicchio, Bernardino Betto
Aeneas Sylvius Piccolomini
(Pius II)--4 scenes from
life, Piccolomini Library,
Siena, c1508 22:73-6 Mr 3
'47

Pinza, Ezio
Halsman. Ezio Pinza photog
bw 16:44 Mr 13 '44

Piombo, Sebastiano del
Adultress brought before Christ
(Painted with Giorgione and
Titian) 39:169 O 24 '55

"Pioneer" (locomotive) Chicago
and Northwestern photog bw
25:12 S 27 '48

Pioneer Themes See Frontier
and Western Themes

Pip and Flip. Marsh 40:80-1 F
6 '56

Pipe dance. bw Blakelock 5:29 O
31 '38

Pippin, Horace
John Brown goes to his hanging
21:64 Jy 22 '46
Newman. Horace Pippin photog
bw 20:12 F 4 '46 port.

Pirogues, Cambodia photogs bw
2:49 Mr 8 '37

Pisa airview photog bw 15:27 Ag
9 '43 leaning tower photog
bw 18:107-8 Je 18 '45

Pisano, Giovanni
Nude sculpture bw 41:102 O 22
'56

Pissarro, Camille Jacob
The Louvre, morning 13:94 N
9 '42
St. Lazare station 33:94 O 27
'52
Cezanne and Pissarro photog
bw 32:92 F 25 '52 port.

Pistols See Weapons

Pitcher, Molly
Molly Pitcher bw 14:7 Ja 4 '43;
29:51 Jy 3 '50

Pitcher and basket of fruit.
Braque 26:83 My 2 '49

Pitchers

Bull headed pitcher, Etruscan,
6th century B.C. 40:61 F
13 '56

Duck-shaped pitcher, Etruscan, c300 B.C. 40:60 F
13 '56

Prehistoric pitcher, neolithic
40:81 Ap 16 '56

Toleware pitcher, U.S. 39:56
Jy 18 '55

Venetian glass pitcher, Renaissance bw 23:50 Ag 4 '47

Wistarberg-type (South Jersey) "Lilypad" pitcher 39:
58 Jy 18 '55

Pitt, William, the elder
Pitt stricken in House of
Lords* 25:107 S 13 '48
William Pitt statue bw 18:96
Je 4 '45
William Pitt, Earl of Chatham
24:70 My 24 '48 bw 4:60
Ap 18 '38; 25:113 S 13 '48

Pitt, William, the younger
William Pitt 24:70 My 24 '48

Pitti palace, Florence photog bw
4:31 Mr 21 '38

Pittman, Hobson
Charleston houses pastels 22:
68-72 Ap 14 '47
An evening in Maine 18:70 F
19 '45
Four a.m. 18:69 F 19 '45
The gossips 18:70 F 19 '45
Miss Pat and Miss Eva Lion
18:69 F 19 '45
Summer evening 18:70 F 19
'45
Hobson Pittman; home photogs
bw 18:68 F 19 '45 port.

Pittsburgh. Emett 37:44 Jy 5 '54

Pittsburgh creamer glassware,
American 39:59 Jy 18 '55

The Pittsburgh horse market.
Blythe 9:76 D 9 '40

Pius II, Pope (Aeneas Sylvius
Piccolomini)
Pinturicchio. Aeneas Sylvius
Piccolomini (Pius II)--4
scenes from life 22:73-6
Mr 3 '47

Pius II, Pope (cont.)
Pope Pius II bw 22:71 Mr 3 '47
Pius X, Saint
Gregarti. Pius X, official
portrait 36:99 My 31 '54
Pizzinato, Armando
Worker bw 29:14 O 30 '50
Place Pas de Loup. Davis, S. 22:
80 F 17 '47
Place du Tertre, Montmartre.
drawing bw Utrillo 28:89 Ja
16 '50
Placentia Bay, Newfoundland.
Lea 28:74 F 20 '50
Placer mining in California.
Chadwick 6:29 Je 19 '39; 27:
48 Jy 4 '49
Plaidy, Jean
Jean Plaidy photog bw 24:22
My 17 '48
Plantation Houses
Greek revival, Steamboat gothic
houses, Louisiana photogs
32:72-83 Je 9 '52
Plates
Audubon bird plates, Steuben
glassware bw 23:19 N 10 '47
Chagall. Four plates 33:100 O
6 '52
Earthenware plates, U.S.,
early 19th century 39:56 Jy
18 '55
Jamnitzer. Silver-gilt basin
with cupid, kings, conti-
nents, Nurnberg, 17th cen-
tury bw 31:20-1 S 24 '51
Landscape plates, gift to Duke
of Wellington 26:71 F 7 '49
Persian gold and enamelled
plate 33:43 D 29 '52
Plate of Khosru II, carved
medallions on gold, Persia,
600   33:42 D 29 '52
Plates painted by artists and
celebrities 27:91 D 19 '49
Portrait plate, Venice, 15th
century 37:55 Ag 2 '54
Slipware plate, U.S., early
19th century 39:57 Jy 18 '55
Staffordshire plate, 15 stars
and federal eagle, U.S.,

1792 17:59 S 4 '44
Staffordshire plates bw 5:47 N
28 '38
Plattner, Karl
Chickens 36:82 My 31 '54
Playground. Cadmus 29:172-3 O
16 '50
Playroom. Sharon 33:75 Jy 21 '52
Plaza Hotel, Mexico City. Pani,
archt. photog bw 22:99 F
24 '47
Plaza Hotel, c1910. mural Shinn
21:88 N 18 '46
Pleissner, Ogden
Aetna Life Insurance Company
Building, Hartford, Conn.
bw 41:78 Ag 13 '56
Airmen in the Aleutians: 10
paintings 16:57-62 My 22
'44
Battlefields of Europe: 9
scenes 20:67-72 My 13 '46
Hunting scenes: 8 watercolors
21:63-8 O 7 '46
Ore boats, Soo Locks, Michi-
gan 25:65 Ag 23 '48
Remagen Bridge 20:70-1 My
13 '46; 35:94 N 16 '53
St. Lo, world war scenes 18:
46-52, Ja 8 '45; 20:68 My
13 '46; 35:86 O 26 '53
Stacking alfalfa 13:47 Ag 31
'42
Trout fishing 25:66-7 Ag 23
'48
Captain Pleissner photog bw
16:56 My 22 '44 port.
Ogden Pleissner. in group
photog 29:172-3 O 16 '50
port.
Plekhanov, George
George Plekhanov photog bw
31:111 O 29 '31
Ploughing the Valley of the Great
Salt Lake. painting, sculp-
ture bw Young, M. 10:76
F 17 '41
Pluto. statue bw, French Lick
Springs, Indiana 17:110 N
20 '44
Plymouth hooker. Hemy 23:84 N

17 '47

Plymouth Rock, Plymouth, Mass.
  photog bw 24:69 Je 14 '48

Pocahontas
  Chappel. Pocahontas saving
    Captain Smith* bw 31:154
    D 3 '51
  Pocahontas, 1616 bw 6:26 Je
    19 '39
  Pocahontas, in Jacobean dress
    bw 31:153 D 3 '51
  Pocahontas received at court*
    bw 31:154 D 3 '51
  Pocahontas' wedding to John
    Rolfe* print bw 31:154 D 3
    '51

Pocock, Nicholas
  Constitution and Java, 1812 9:
    48 O 28 '40

Poe, Edgar Allan
  "The Tell Tale Heart, " illustra-
    tions from animated motion
    picture of his story 35:99.-
    102 S 7 '53

Poetzsch, James
  Paintings 35:67 Ag 31 '53

Pogany, Mademoiselle
  Brancusi. Mlle Pogany sculp-
    ture 39:130 D 5 '55

Pogo. cartoon bw Kelly, W. 37:
  134 N 22 '54

Pogofenokee-land. cartoon Kelly,
  W. 32:12-3 My 12 '52

Pointillism See Seurat, Georges

Poisson, Louverture
  Toilette 23:60 S 1 '47

Poker game bw 35:31 S 14 '53

Pol de Limbourg See Limbourg,
  Pol de

Poland
  Castles, heroes, sculpture
    photogs bw 5:46-56 Ag 29
    '38
  Historical scenes and portraits
    17:86-7 Ag 28 '44
  Nazi emblem: 14-cogged wheel
    bw 8:13 Je 17 '40
  Polish eagles and horseman,
    grille, Cracow bw 17:84 Ag
    28 '44
  White eagles of Poland bw 5:54

Ag 24 '38; 17:96 Ag 28 '44

Poland's murder.* bw 17:87 Ag
  28 '44

Poleo, Hector
  Marketgoers, Venezuela 36:
    79 My 31 '54

Polevitzky, Igor, architect
  Bird-cage house, Miami,
    Florida photog 28:63-5 Je
    5 '50

Polevoy, Serge Alexandrovitch
  Serge Polevoy photog bw 10:
    96 My 5 '41

Poliepipedi (three dimensional)
  paintings. bw Fasola 41:
  188-9 N 26 '56

The Polish rider. Rembrandt 3:
  36 D 27 '37

Politics. sculpture bw Rogers 6:
  7 Mr 6 '39

Polk, Charles
  George Washington, c 1790
    head, bw 24:22 F 23 '48

Polk, James Knox
  James Polk bw 16:46 Ja 31
    '44

Pollaiuolo, Antonio del
  Hercules slaying Antaeus
    sculpture bw 6:32 F 13 '39

Pollock, Jackson
  Cathedral 25:63 O 11 '48
  Number nine 27:42-3 Ag 8 '49
    detail bw 41:58 Ag 27 '56
  Number seventeen 27:43 Ag
    8 '49
  Number twelve 27:42 Ag 8 '49
  Artist and his work photog bw
    41:58 Ag 27 '56 port.
  Jackson Pollock photog 27:42,
    45 Ag 8 '49 bw 30:34 Ja 15
    '51

Polo See Games and Sports--
  Polo

Polonsky, Arthur
  Portrait 25:101 D 6 '48
  Artist at work photog bw 25:
    103 D 6 '48 port.

Polynesian woman. sculpture bw
  Carlton 5:70 D 5 '38

Pomarede, Lee
  St. Louis, 1832 28:74-5 Mr
    6 '50
Pompadour, Jeanne Antoinette,
    Marquise de
  Boucher. Mme de Pompadour
    23:81 S 15 '47 bw 5:39 S 26
    '38
Pompano, Florida. Haberman 24:
    73 Ap 5 '48
"Pont" See Laidler, Graham
The Pont Neuf. Renoir 32:92 My
    19 '52
Pony express. sculpture bw
    Young, M. 10:79 F 17 '41
The pool. Kroll 24:68 Je 28 '48
Poole, Abram
  Olinsky. Abram Poole 10:48
    F 3 '41 port.
Poole, Burnell
  A critical moment 9:50 O 28
    '40
Poor, Henry Varnum
  Custom House workers mural,
    U.S. Justice Dept., Wash-
    ington, D.C. 2:36 Ja 4 '37
  Gold case mural, U.S. Justice
    Dept., Washington, D.C.
    2:36 Ja 4 '37
  March sun 12:61 Je 15 '42
  Surveying new lands mural,
    U.S. Justice Dept., Wash-
    ington, D.C. 2:36 Ja 4 '37
  Tennessee Valley Authority
    mural, U.S. Justice Dept.,
    Washington, D.C. 2:36 Ja
    4 '37
  Artist at work photog bw 2:32
    Ja 4 '37 port.
  Biddle, G. Henry Varnum
    Poor, in Tenement, mural
    2:35 Ja 4 '37
  Self-portrait, in Gold case,
    mural 2:36 Ja 4 '37
Poor Richard. steel engraving bw
    Pelton 40:74-5 Ja 9 '56
"Poor Richard's Almanac," illus-
    trations of Benjamin Frank-
    lin's mottoes. steel engrav-
    ings bw Pelton 40:74-5 Ja
    9 '56

Poor house inmates, 1875. draw-
    ing bw, from "Leslie's"
    16:54 F 14 '44
Poot, Rik
  Wolf sculpture bw 41:84 O 8
    '56
Pope, John
  General John Pope bw 11:102
    N 10 '41
Pope, John Russell
  Pope, Eggers, and Higgins.
    Jefferson memorial, Wash-
    ington, D.C. photog 23:49
    Jy 7 '47 bw 14:Cover Ap
    12 '43
Pope
  Cranach. Christ and the Pope, *
    series of anti-papist wood-
    cuts bw 24:60-1 Je 14 '48
Popes
  Alexander II. in Battle of
    Hastings, French chronicle,
    15th century 40:86 Mr 26
    '56
  Boniface VIII. Sciarra Colon-
    na threatening Pope Boni-
    face VIII bw 27:52 Ag 1 '49
  Innocent III. plaque bw, U.S.
    Congress 30:74 F 5 '51
  John VII. mosaic 28:69 Mr 27
    '50
  Leo X. Raphael. Pope Leo X
    (Giovanni Medici) and two
    cousins bw 4:33 Mr 21 '38
  Martin V. Luti. Apotheosis
    of Pope Martin V bw 18:91
    Mr 5 '45
    Pope Martin V (Otto Colon-
    na) bw 27:52 Ag 1 '49
  Paul III. Titian. Pope Paul III
    27:64 O 24 '49 bw 6:32 F
    13 '39
  Pius II. Pinturicchio. Aeneas
    Sylvius Piccolomini (Pius
    II)--4 scenes from life 22:
    73-6 Mr 3 '47
    Pius II bw 22:71 Mr 3 '47
  Pius X. Gregarti. Pope Pius
    X, official portrait 36:99
    My 31 '54
  Sixtus II. Raphael. Sistine

Madonna 40:113 My 7 '56

Porcelains See Ceramics

Porch of Maidens, Erechtheum,
Athens, 407 B.C. photog
bw 18:58-9 Ja 1 '45

Porringers
Silver porringer, England bw
3:77 D 13 '37
Silver porringer, U.S., colonial. van Inburgh 38:117 Ap
18 '55

Port-au-Prince
Bernedetto. Morning in Port-
au-Prince 8:36 Ja 1 '40

The portentous city. Diego 20:81
Mr 11 '46

Porter, Cole
Cole Porter photogs bw 3:108
N 8 '37; 7:63 D 11 '39

Porter, David G.
Admiral Porter photog bw 14:
76 F 15 '43

Portinari, Candido
St. Francis preaching to birds*
mural, Brazil 27:76 Jy 4
'49
Victims of drought 29:108 D
11 '50

Portland, William John
Sargent. William Cavendish-
Bentinck, Duke of Portland
23:80 N 17 '47

Portland, Winifred
Sargent. Duchess of Portland
23:81 N 17 '47

Portrait.* bw School of Frans
Hals 11:54 N 10 '41

Portrait of a boy. Cox, G. 10:
47 F 3 '41

Portrait of a boy with red hair.
Modigliani 40:72 My 28 '56

Portrait of a child. Renoir 25:77
N 1 '48

Portrait of a farmer. Wyeth, N.C.
16:78 Ap 24 '44

Portrait of a gentleman. Hals 5:
34 Ag 29 '38

Portrait of a knight. El Greco 31:
70 O 1 '51

Portrait of a knight, Van Dyck, A.
27:65 O 24 '49

Portrait of a man. Van Dyck, A.
29:84 N 27 '50

Portrait of a man aged 54. bw
Holbein 39:147 S 26 '55

Portrait of a man in a red cap.
Titian 23:Cover Ag 4 '47

Portrait of a nobleman. bw Titian 6:58 Mr 27 '39

Portrait of a woman. Bonnard
25:54 Jy 26 '48

Portrait of a young man. Botticelli 4:30 Mr 21 '38

Portrait of a young man. bw Hals
31:23 S 3 '51

Portrait of a young man. bw
Raphael 16:66 Ja 10 '44

Portrait of a young merchant.
bw Holbein 39:147 S 26 '55

Portrait of a youth (Girolamo
Casio). bw Boltraffio 24:
67 Ja 26 '48

Portrait of classmate. sculpture
bw Neagle 10:59 Je 16 '41

Portrait of old Parr. Rubens 7:
54 O 9 '39

Portrait of sis. Jones, Amy 10:
47 F 3 '41

Portraits See also Children;
Family Groups; Mother and
Child; names of individuals,
as Washington, George.
See also names of portrait
painters, as Copley; Gains-
borough; Peale; Reynolds;
Sargent; Whistler

Aitken. World's greatest ar-
tists--68 portraits frieze
bw 4:36-7 Ja 3 '38

American primitive portraits
36:95-6 Je 28 '54

American Revolutionary military leaders--American
and British bw 29:52-3 Jy
3 '50

Authors--English and American, at Mark Twain's
birthday banquet, Decem-
ber 5, 1905 photogs bw 16:
96-9 My 8 '44

Brigham Young's wives--20
of 27 wives bw 5:24 Jy 25 '38

Portraits (cont.)
  College graduation portraits of 30 famous American men photogs bw 14:6-9 Ap 26 '43
  Contemporary U.S. portrait painters 10:46-8 F 3 '41; 41:77-8 Ag 13 '56
  English dukes--26 portraits photogs bw 15:100-3 N 15 '43
  English prime ministers 24:69-71 My 24 '48
  English queens--7 reigning queens bw 32:22-4 F 18 '52
  German general staff corps bw 15:93-101 N 22 '43
  Great loves of great artists 29:104-13 S 11 '50
  Guthrie. Great statesmen of World War I 24:29 Ap 19 '48
  Henry VIII's wives bw 41:88 O 29 '56
  Halsman. Master musicians in the United States photogs bw 16:43-50 Mr 13 '44
  Hurd. U.S. airmen, World War II 14:67-73 F 15 '43
  Law givers--Castellon. History of western law bw 30:87-97 Mr 12 '51
  Medieval saints and kings bw 22:70 Ap 7 '47
  Musicians--candid camera shots at rehearsals with Philadelphia orchestra photogs bw 14:45-50 Ja 18 '43
  Pach Brothers. Portraits of great Americans photogs bw 3:16-9 O 25 '37
  Reformation leaders bw 24:60-1 Je 14 '48
  Russian generals--victorious generals of World War II photogs bw 17:31-2 Jy 31 '44
  Russian military leaders, 1939-43 photogs 14:98-9 Mr 29 '43
  Russian scientists photogs bw 17:Cover, 14-6 O 23 '44
  "Time" cover portraits--30 A-merican and European World War II leaders 17:59-66 D 11 '44
  U.S. ambassadors to Britain: 24 paintings and photographs bw 10:26-7 Mr 3 '41
  U.S. Constitution--drafters of preamble, 5 portraits bw 16:47 Ja 17 '44
  U.S. Constitution--framers of the Constitution 39:58-64 Jy 4 '55
  U.S. Declaration of Independence--56 portraits and signatures of signers bw 15:8-10 Jy 5 '43
  U.S. losing candidates for President of the U.S.--19 portraits bw 14:6-7 My 31 '43
  U.S. Presidents--portraits on campaign songs 25:22-4 O 4 '48
  U.S. Secretaries of State--16 portraits 19:84-9 S 24 '45
  U.S. Supreme Court justices, 1790-1940: 80 justices in 150 years bw 8:48-9 F 12 '40; group photog of members upon appointment of new member, 1882-1937 photog bw 3:28-9 N 29 '37; in 1865 photogs bw 14:76 F 15 '43
  U.S. Vice-Presidents, 1789-1940 bw 9:8-11 Ag 5 '40
  Women warriors through history bw 14:6-8 Ja 4 '43
Post, Catalynje
  Catalynje Post, American primitive, 1730 bw 36:96 Je 28 '54
Post, Emily
  Emily Post photogs bw 20:59-60 My 6 '46
  Flagg. Emily Post drawing bw 20:66 My 6 '46
  Fuchs. Emily Post, age 26 20:64 My 6 '46
Post office. Blythe 40:125 Je

4 '56

Postal Service

Emett. Mailbox art cartoon bw
37:47 Jy 5 '54

Marsh. Sorting mail 2:33 Ja
4 '37

Marsh. Transfer of mail from
liner to tugboat 2:33 Ja 4
'37

Van Gogh. Roulin the postman
bw 27:82 O 10 '49

Young, M. Pony express sculpture bw 10:79 F 17 '41

Postage stamps

Winning and losing designs in
competition for postage
stamps for Germany bw 21:
12-5 N 4 '46

Posters

Army recruiting posters, World
War II bw 20:104-5 F 25 '46

"Artists for Victory" posters,
Museum of Modern Art Ex-
hibit 13:54-7 D 21 '42

Bird. "Carless talk costs
lives" bw 26:62-3 Mr 7 '49

British posters for more U.S.
aid to Britain, World War
II bw 9:35 D 9 '40

Cox, P. Advertising poster,
U.S., c1900 28:41 Ja 2 '50

Early American advertising
posters c1900 28:39-42 Ja
2 '50

English and French war
posters, World War II 8:47-
8 Mr 8 '40

Falter. Quality of mercy, Red
Cross poster 26:101 F 21
'49

GOP political poster, 1868 40:
69 Ja 30 '56

Humphrey. A busy day, advertising poster, c1900 28:40
Ja 2 '50

Hungerford. War posters to
prevent sabotage 10:12-4
Mr 24 '41

Latin and North American
posters, World War II,
Museum of Modern Art com-

petition 13:12-5 N 2 '42

Russian posters of World War
II 13:10-3 Ag 24 '42

Toulouse-Lautrec. Billboard
posters: Jane Avril, May
Belfort 28:92-3 My 15 '50

U.S. Socialist Party poster,
with Debs and Hanford bw
24:105 Ja 19 '48

U.S. theater posters, c1890:
tom shows, melodramas
31:112, 115 N 19 '51

Uncle Tom's Cabin 41:60 S 3
'56

The potato eaters. Van Gogh 27:
83 O 10 '49 bw 41:67 O 1
'56

Potemkin, Grigori

Marshal Potemkin bw 14:94
Mr 29 '43

Potiphar's wife. engraving bw
Schnorr 6:55 Ja 30 '39

Potomac River

Blythe. General Doubleday
crossing the Potomac,
1863 6:29 Je 19 '39

Potter, Beatrix

"Tale of Peter Rabbit, "
"Tale of Tom Kitten" illustrations 33:113-4 D 8 '52

Beatrix Potter; home photog
bw 33:113 D 8 '52 port.

Pottery See Ceramics

Poultryman, India. Sheets 20:82
Ja 21 '46

Pounding surf. bw Waugh, F.J.
5:57 N 28 '38

Pousette-Dart Richard

Richard Pousette-Dart photog
bw 30:34 Ja 15 '51

Poussin, Nicolas

Parnassus bw 25:78 O 11 '48

The triumph of Bacchus 7:53
O 9 '39

Powder horn, U.S. colonial
photogs 38:58-60 My 30
'55

Powell, Lewis

Lewis Powell photog bw 4:46
F 14 '38

Powell, William Henry
  De Soto's discovery of the
    Mississippi bw 24:88 Mr
    22 '48
The power of music. Mount 18:
  66 Je 25 '45
Powers, Hiram, sculptor
  Greek slave plaster model bw
    33:97 S 15 '52
    "Greek slave" exhibited,
      New York, 1887 bw 19:8
      S 24 '45; 27:56 Ag 29 '49
    Hiram Powers photog bw 33:97
      S 15 '52
Practice landing. Majors 13:32
  Jy 6 '42
The Prado, Madrid
  Celebrated paintings; galleries;
    building 31:58-72 O 1 '51
Praetor
  Castellon. The Roman praetor,
    Forum, 120 B.C. 30:87 Mr
    12 '51
Prairie fire. Ranney 27:42 Jy 4
  '49
Prairie rose quilt pattern 11:62
  S 22 '41
Praslin, Duke de
  Duke de Praslin bw 9:35 Jy 1
    '40
Pratt, Ann
  Luks. Ann Pratt 41:162 D 24
    '56
Pratt, Davis J., furniture de-
  signer
  Occasional chair photog bw 28:
    99 My 8 '50
Pratt, Matthew
  The American school bw 6:31
    Je 19 '39
Praxitiles, sculptor
  Head bw Greece, 350 B.C. 7:
    37 Jy 31 '39
Praxitiles, follower of Venus
  sculpture bw 34:137-8 Ap 27
    '53
Prayer and Worship
  Binford. The preaching deacon
    bw 13:140 N 16 '42

  Catholic missionaries in Po-
    land* bw 17:86 Ag 28 '44
  Curry. Holy rollers bw 15:18
    N 29 '43
  Fox in America bw 33:97 S 29
    '52
  John Wesley preaching,* Eng-
    land, 18th century 25:103
    S 13 '48
  Night services led by John Mc-
    Millan print bw 39:77 D 26
    '55
  Prayer at sailing of Mayflower*
    bw 25:132 N 29 '48
  Revival meeting, 1800 bw 33:
    107 N 17 '52
  Rogers. Neighboring pews
    sculpture bw 6:6 Mr 6 '39
  Schwartze. The Pilgrim
    fathers in public worship
    13:77 N 23 '42 bw 24:68 Je
    14 '48
  Siqueiros. The Devil in church
    29:106 D 11 '50
Prayer Wheels
  Buddhist prayer wheels photogs
    bw 8:35 Ja 8 '40; 24:80 F
    16 '48
Pre-Columbian Art See Art,
  Pre-Columbian
Preening sparrow. Graves 35:88
  S 28 '53
Pregnant woman. sculpture bw
  Wickey 12:54 F 23 '42
Prelude to battle. Ardizzone 26:
  60 Mr 21 '49
Prendergast, James
  Young American artist 20:79
    F 18 '46
Presentation of Mary. Cima da
  Conegliano 40:107 My 7
  '56
Presentation to the King and
  Queen of England, drawing
  bw Gibson 23:88-9 N 17 '47
Pressed Glass
  Sandwich bowl, U.S. 39:58 Jy
    18 '55
Previtali, Andrea
  Madonna with St. John and St.
    Catherine bw 6:32 F 13 '39

Price, George, cartoonist
"Lancashire Lad," illustra-
tions bw 8:110-1 My 6 '40
"Who's in Charge Here" bw 16:
12-4 F 7 '44
Priebe, Karl John
Carnival interlude 23:71 N 24
'47
The colloquy 23:69 N 24 '47
The lady on the hill 23:70 N
24 '47
The piebald giraffe 21:79 N 25
'46
Return to castle 23:71 N 24 '47
The weasel 23:71 N 24 '47
The zebra 23:70 N 24 '47
Karl Priebe photog bw 23:68 N
24 '47 port.
Priestley, John Boynton
Epstein. J.B. Priestley sculp-
ture bw 3:90 N 15 '37
J. B. Priestley; home photogs
bw 10:80 My 19 '41
Priests
Mayan priest,* Bonampak mur-
al 27:81 N 21 '49
Sumerian high priest marble
sculpture bw 5:Cover Ag 15
'38
Prime minister's lady. Manchu
dynasty, 18th century 15:65
O 11 '43
Primitive figure. sculpture bw
Brancusi 39:135 D 5 '55
Primrose, George
George Primrose photog bw
11:74 Ag 25 '41
Prin, Alice ("Kiki")
Alice Prin, model, portraits,
including photographs bw 34:
12-4 Je 29 '53
A prince of Saxony. Cranach 24:
66 Ja 26 '48
Princess of Saxony. bw Cranach
24:67 Ja 26 '48
Printing See Books and Printing
Prints See also Currier and Ives
Prints; and names of print
techniques, as Engravings;
Etchings; Lithographs
Benjamin Franklin, 1780 40:

80 Ja 9 '56
Benjamin Franklin crowns
Mirabeau 40:80 Ja 9 '56
Boston Tea Party, 1774 bw 22:
99 Mr 24 '47
Cassatt. Afternoon tea party
36:98 My 17 '54
Cassatt. The coiffure 36:98 My
17 '54
Chicago, 1820; 1857 39:89 N
14 '55
Chief Keokuk and son, 1812 bw
21:106 S 30 '46
Christian Drakenberg bw 38:
156 Ap 25 '55
The circuit rider bw 39:78 D
26 '55
Humboldt River, Elko County,
Nevada bw 26:101 Ap 18 '49
Monsieur Blondia, Tight-rope
walker spanning Niagara
Gorge, 1859* 26:80 Je 6 '49
Murder of Marcus Whitman,
1847* bw 39:74-5 D 26 '55
Night services led by John
McMillan bw 39:77 D 26 '55
Picasso. Horses and figures
drypoint bw 23:93 O 13 '47
Pocahontas' wedding to John
Rolfe bw 31:154 D 3 '51
Railroad workers bw 26:101 Ap
18 '49
Riggs. Prints 3:46-7 S 13 '37
Stradanus. Vespucci in South
America, 1552 bw 37:105
O 11 '54
Swearing in of President
Hayes, 1876 bw 40:69 Ja 30
'56
Whaling bw 5:17 D 19 '38
Waldseemuller. Map of New
World, 1507 37:101 O 11
'54
Young, J. Richard Humphreys,
boxer mezzotint bw 6:42
F 6 '39

Japanese
"The 47 Ronin," scenes from,
by Hiroshige, and Hokusai
15:53-6 N 1 '43

Prints - Japanese (cont.)
　Sekiguchi War Prints--Japa-
　　nese conquest of China,
　　Sino-Japanese War, 1894-5
　　3:25-32 D 6 '37
Prisoners as Artists
　Amano. Prison life in Siberia
　　labor camp watercolor 29:
　　65-7 N 6 '50
　Japanese war prisoners. Life
　　in Sugamo prison wood
　　blocks 34:10-1 F 16 '53
　Watton. Germany's prison
　　camps drawings bw 13:138-41
　　N 9 '42
Prisoners from the front. Homer
　5:33 O 31 '38
Prisons and Prison Scenes See
　also Prisoners as Artists
　Millman. Bilibrid prison,
　　Manila 19:67 O 8 '45
　Michel. Devil's Island scenes
　　4:47-8 Ap 4 '38
　Torture of Mayan prisoners,
　　Bonampak mural 27:83 N 21
　　'49
Private Collections See also
　name of collection; Bache;
　　Bloch; Berenson; Booth;
　　Culberg; Dale; Davies;
　　Farouk; Gallatin; Garbisch;
　　Gilcrease; Bulbenkian;
　　Habsburg; Hearts;
　　Kress; Lehman Family;
　　Ludgin; Marx; Newton;
　　Peters; Pettus; Rothschild;
　　Spaulding; Steuer; Tatsuta;
　　Tyson
　Hollywood stars' art collec-
　　tions 24:65-8 Mr 1 '48
　Student's collection (Mason
　　Faulconer Lord) covering
　　every period of Western art
　　30:67-8 Je 4 '51
　Yale alumni collections 40:70-
　　6 My 28 '56
Prize Fights See Games and
　Sports--Boxing
Procession. Martins da Silveira
　36:82-3 My 31 '54
A procession of women, India.

　Sheets 20:83 Ja 21 '46
Procession to Ascot. Munnings
　28:120-1 My 22 '50
Processions See Parades
The prodigal son. bw Curry 15:
　18 N 29 '43
Products of Missouri. mural
　McCreery 10:45 Ja 27 '41
Professor, misericord, wood
　carving bw 37:82 S 27 '54
Professionals at rehearsal.
　Eakins 16:74 My 15 '44
Progress. sculpture bw Noel 11:
　144 O 13 '41
Promenade. bw Burchfield 6:82
　My 22 '39
Prometheus See Mythological
　Themes--Prometheus
Prophets See names of prophets,
　as Jeremiah
　Prophet. sculpture bw James,
　　M. 30:143 My 21 '51
　The prophet. Koerner 24:78
　　My 10 '48
Prophetess. woodcarving bw
　Steig 6:35 Ap 10 '39
Propylaea, Acropolis gateway,
　Athens photog bw 18:56
　Ja 1 '45
Provencal interior. lithograph
　Singier 33:86 Jy 14 '52
Provence in stone--Roman and
　Medieval landmarks.
　photogs Mili 35:76-85 Jy
　13 '53
Proverbs
　Brueghel, P., the elder.
　　Flemish proverbs 24:74-5
　　Mr 22 '48
Protestant Revolution
　Scenes and portraits. paint-
　　ings, prints, sculpture 24:
　　58-78 Je 14 '48
Proudhon, Pierre Joseph
　Pierre Proudhon, 1848 photog
　　bw 25:91 N 22 '48
Prows See Figureheads
Psalters
　Canterbury Psalter 34:80 F
　　23 '53
　Psalter of Ingeborg 34:78, 85

F 23 '53

Psaltery See Musicians and
Musical Instruments--Psaltery

Pseudosphere photog bw 9:61 Jy
15 '40

Pskov cathedral, 1200 bw 14:93
Mr 29 '43

Psyche See Mythological
Themes--Psyche

Psychotics as artists
Bellevue Hospital patients art
5:26-7 O 24 '38

Ptolemy's world map, 150 bw 13:
58 Ag 3 '42

Public Architecture See also
names of public buildings,
as United Nations; United
States Capitol Building
Jefferson. Virginia State Capi-
tol model, photog bw 14:70
Ap 12 '43
National Lottery Building,
Mexico City photog bw 21:98
F 24 '47
New meeting hall, Frankfort,
Germany photog bw 36:150
My 10 '54
Niemeyer. Education and
Health Building, Rio de Ja-
neiro 22:35 My 26 '47
Nowicki and Dietrick. Fair
grounds building, Raleigh,
N.C. photog 36:34-5 Ja 4
'54
Old ship meeting house, Hing-
ham, Mass., 1681 photog
38:128-9 Ap 18 '55
"Public Buildings," photogs
bw, from book 8:61-7 Ap 1
'40

Public sale. Wyeth, A. 24:105
My 17 '48

Public Works Administration See
United States   Works Progress Administration

Public Works of Art Project See
United States   Treasury De-
partment, Section of Fine
Arts

Puck. sculpture bw, Folger
Shakespeare Library, Wash-

ington, D.C. 4:33 Ap 25 '38

Puebla cathedral, Mexico photogs
6:33, 36 Ja 23 '39

Public gardens at Arles. Van
Gogh 38:109 My 23 '55

Pueblos
Adobe pueblo, Taos, N. Mex.
photog 40:47 Ja 16 '56
Cliff House, Flagstaff, Ariz.
photog 40:47 Ja 16 '56
San Ildefonso pueblo, New
Mexico photog 8:71 My 13
'40

Puerto de Andraitx. Cadmus 2:
46 Mr 29 '37

Puget, Pierre
Alexander and his horse, Bucephalas, riding over foes
bw 39:86 N 14 '55

Pulitzer, Joseph
Rodin. Joseph Pulitzer sculpture bw 35:41 D 14 '53

Puma, Fernando
They will not conquer 16:78
Je 12 '44
Fernando Puma 16:76 Je 12
'44 port.

"Punch" cartoons
Emett. Cartoons bw 15:6-8
Ag 2 '43
"Punch and the War," 11:61-3
Ag 25 '41
World War II cartoons bw 7:
6-9 Jy 10 '39

Punch bowl, silver, 1768. Revere
38:56 My 30 '55

Puppets See Dolls and Puppets

Puritans--scenes and portraits
13:74-86 N 23 '42

Puritan church, Groton, Mass.,
1755 photog bw 13:Cover
N 23 '42

Puritan triumph at Naseby* bw
41:200 N 12 '56

Puritan. sculpture bw Saint-
Gaudens 19:56 N 26 '45

Purple cow. illustration bw 31:
37 O 1 '51

Purse of House of Lords, London photog bw 16:86 My 22
'44

Purse seiner. Brandt 11:76 O 27
    '41
Pushing for rail. Pleissner 21:68
    O 7 '46
Pushkin, Aleksandr Sergeevich
    Pushkin bw 14:94 Mr 29 '43
Pussy cat and roses. Benton 6:71
    Ap 24 '39
Pussy willows. Burchfield 1:27
    D 28 '36
Puvis de Chavannes, Pierre
    The sacred grove bw 28:88 Ja
    16 '50
    Summer 15:66 S 20 '43
Puzzle cup, spilling liquid on
    drinker, Italy, 18th century
    25:129 D 6 '48
Pyle, Ernie
    Ernie Pyle; home photogs bw
    15:57-8 N 15 '43
Pyle, Howard
    "The Merry Adventures of
    Robin Hood," illustrations
    bw 20:78 Je 17 '46
Pyle, Lou
    Brown. Lou Pyle sculpture bw
    12:90 My 19 '41
Pym, John
    John Pym, American patriot
    bw 41:184 N 12 '56
Pyramids
    Giza pyramids, Egypt photog
    24:75 Ja 19 '48
    Great pyramid of Khufu, models
    showing steps in construction
    bw 19:75-80 D 3 '45 photog
    24:75 Ja 19 '48
    Temple of Quetzalcoatl, Toltec,
    Teotihuacan, Mexico photog
    bw 4:57 Ap 11 '38; 22:100 F
    24 '47
    Temple of the Warriors, May-
    an, Chichen Itza, Mexico
    photog 22:60 Je 30 '47
Pythagorus sculpture, Ulm cathe-
    dral, Germany 35:31 D 28
    '53

Q

Quail in Georgia. Ripley 29:126
    D 4 '50

Quality of mercy, Red Cross
    poster. Falter 26:101 F 21
    '49
Quakers--leaders, history bw 33:
    95-7 S 29 '52
The quarry. Roualt 34:58-9 F 2
    '53
Quarry on the Cape. Kroll 23:70
    Jy 14 '47
Quastler, Gertrude
    Counterpoint woodcut 37:89 O
    18 '54
Quebec Act, 1774 cartoon bw 27:
    138 S 19 '49
Queen, Ellery See Dannay,
    Frederic; Lee, Manfred B.
"Queen Charlotte" (ship) English,
    1794 in The glorious first
    of June 24:67 My 10 '48
Queen of Africa. Benoit 23:59 S
    1 '47
Queen of the Benin, bronze head,
    Nigeria, c1550 bw 33:123
    S 8 '52
"Queen of the Pirate Isle." illus-
    trations Greenaway 23:88
    D 1 '47
Queen of the West vs. Morning
    Star. Currier and Ives
    print 21:74 S 2 '46
Queens of England, portraits of
    7 reigning queens bw 32:
    22-4 F 18 '52
Queenstown Heights battle, 1812
    bw 12:96 My 25 '42
Quest for freedom. bw Church 24:
    70 Je 14 '48
Quetzalcoatl
    Mosaic mask, c1519 bw 24:84
    Mr 22 '48
    Temple of Quetzalcoatl, Tol-
    tec, Teotihuacan, Mexico
    photog bw 4:57 Ap 11 '38;
    22:100 F 24 '47
Quiberon Bay battle, 1759 24:66
    My 10 '48
Quiet mill pont. Klein 16:46 Ja
    3 '44
Quilting bee, * U.S., 19th cen-
    tury 31:72 Jy 2 '51
Quilts

"Counterpane and Coverlets, " exhibit in New Hampshire pageant 11:61-4 S 22 '41

Quilt room, Webb Museum, Shelburne, Vt. 35:51 Jy 6 '53

Quintain bw 22:68 My 26 '47

Quirt, Walter
Walkowitz bw 16:79 F 21 '44

Quoits See Games and Sports-- Quoits

R

The rabbi. Weber 19:86 Ag 20 '45

Rabbi of Vitebsk. Chagall 22:58 My 5 '47

Rabbis
Weber. Two patriarchs 33:99 O 27 '52

Rabbits
Bufano. Rabbit sculpture bw 17:107 D 4 '44
Dozier. Texas jack rabbits* bw 5:30 O 31 '38
Harnett. Trophy of the hunt 10:74 Ap 14 '41
Potter. Peter rabbit, illustration bw 33:113 D 8 '52
Raeburn. Boy with rabbit bw 14:111 Ja 25 '43
Wright. Brer Rabbit hitting Tar Baby* bw 29:124 Ag 28 '50

Rachmaninoff, Sergei
Sergei Rachmaninoff photogs bw 14:4-7 Ap 12 '43

Racing horse and charioteers, Etruscan terra cotta, c550 40:59 F 13 '56

Raczka, Hubert
The blue bench 28:90 Mr 20 '50
Hubert Raczka photog bw 28:93 Mr 20 '50 port.

Radar. Xceron 24:69 F 2 '48

Radebaugh, Arthur
"Black light" paintings, to be viewed by ultraviolet light 28:93 Mr 6 '50

Radetzky, Johan
Field Marshal Radetzky of Austria bw 15:19 Ag 9 '43

Radio
Addams. House of horrors cartoon on radio horror programs bw 24:14-5 F 16 '48
Webster. The unseen audience cartoon bw 20:129-30 Mr 25 '46

Raeburn, Henry
Boy with rabbit bw 14:111 Ja 25 '43
Master William Blair 4:27 Ja 24 '38
The sisters 9:48 Jy 29 '40

Raemaeker, Louis
European War cartoons 6:48-50 My 1 '39

Raetze, Griswold, architect
Beach cottage, Malibu, Calif. photog bw 26:148 Ap 11 '49

Raffles, Stamford
Sir Stamford Raffles statue bw 10:18 Mr 17 '41

Rafinesque, Constantine Samuel
Fish, described by Audubon drawing bw 30:51 Ja 29 '51

Raffling for a goose. Mount 18:66 Je 25 '45

Raftsmen playing cards. Bingham 7:41 S 11 '39 drawing bw 7:40 S 11 '39

Rahotep, Prince of Egypt statue 41:109 N 26 '56

Railroad crossing. Lutz 11:75 O 27 '41

Railroad workers,* Elko County, Nevada print bw 26:101 Ap 18 '49

Railroads
Becker. First train of Central Pacific in Utah* 36:78 Mr 8 '54
Bouche. Train through the night 11:50 Ag 18 '41
Currier and Ives print. Across the continent: Westward the course of empire takes its way 9:34 D 30 '40
Daugherty. The iron horse mural 3:50 O 25 '37

Railroads (cont.)

Dehn. Tracks along the Hudson 11:41 Ag 11 '41

Dohanos. Casey's famous wreck bw 12:62 Ja 28 '42

English locomotive, 1848 cross-section drawing 25:95 N 22 '48

Feininger, Lyonel. Big wheel locomotive 31:92-3 N 12 '51

Feininger, Lux. Old engine 31:93 N 12 '51

First elevated railroad, New York City, 1867 photog bw 22:92 Ja 13 '47

Fulwider. Dead head 6:30 F 13 '39

Genoa, standard American eight-wheeled locomotive, 1872 photog 39:82-3 N 28 '55

Henry. The 9:45 accommodation, Stratford, Conn., 6:30 Je 19 '39

Hill. Driving the golden spike, May 10, 1869 27:50-1 Jy 4 '49

Linking of East and West rail lines, Utah, 1869* photog bw 25:14 S 27 '48

Liverpool and Manchester line, England, 1830* 25:95 N 22 '48

Model locomotives, constructed to scale photogs 29:34 D 25 '50

Model trains--Lionel Corporation toy trains photogs bw 3:51-2 D 13 '37

Santa Fe railway at war 13:92-4 D 7 '42

Train, U.S., 1840-50 bw 27:58 Ag 29 '49

Turner. Rain, steam and speed 25:96 N 22 '48

U.S. locomotives since 1830 photogs bw 25:12-4 S 27 '48

Westinghouse air brake in action bw 22:80 Ja 13 '47

Railway Stations

Bohrod. Paddington station, London 31:78 O 29 '51

Bouche. Broad Street station, Philadelphia 11:49 Ag 18 '41

Hahn. Central Pacific station, Sacramento, California, 1870 39:83 N 28 '55

Pissarro. St. Lazare station 33:94 O 27 '52

Sloan. Grand Central station 7:46 D 11 '39

A railway terminus. Carr 26:48-9 Mr 7 '49

Rain, steam and speed. Turner 25:96 N 22 '48

Rainbow. Trumbull 26:78 Je 6 '49

Raindrops and dancers. Ernst 32:58 Ja 21 '52

Rainy night. Bohrod 11:93 N 10 '41

The raising of Lazarus. See Lazarus

Raleigh, Walter

Gheeraerts. Sir Walter Raleigh 41:71 D 10 '56

Ralph, Lester

"Circular Staircase," illustrations bw 20:56 F 25 '46

Rameses II, King of Egypt sculptured head 41:116 N 26 '56 statue 24:84 Ja 19 '48 bw 2:5 Mr 29 '37; 40:55-6 Mr 19 '56

Ranches

Emett. Dude ranch cartoon bw 37:50 Jy 5 '54

Hurd. Bar-X ranch, New Mexico* 23:76-7 Ag 18 '47

Metcalfe. A friend's ranch 29:72 Jy 17 '50

Rand, Ellen Emmet

Mrs. Millicent McIntoch 10:48 F 3 '41

Rand, Ted

Seascape with figures 39:114 S 12 '55

"Ranging the Maine Coast," illustrations. Wilson, E.A. 18:57 Ap 23 '45

Rank, J. Arthur

Mason. J. Arthur Rank

caricature bw 22:34 Ja 6 '47

Ranney, William
Emigrant train bw 27:40 Jy 4
'49
Prairie fire 27:42 Jy 4 '49
Retreat 27:42 Jy 4 '49

Rapagnetta, Gaetano See D'Annunzio, Gabriele

The rape of Europa. sculpture
bw Derujinsky 6:36 Mr 13
'39
The rape of Europa. Rembrandt
6:39 My 29 '39
The rape of Europa. bw Titian
26:160 Ap 11 '49

Raphael, Sanzio
Alba Madonna 13:Cover D 28
'42
Battle of Milvian Bridge fresco,
Vatican bw 39:39 D 26 '55
La belle jardiniere bw 19:50
Jy 30 '45
Creation of Eve 27:119 D 12 '49
Giuliano de' Medici 2:42 Je 28
'37
Madonna and Child (Small Cow-
per Madonna, 1505) 4:27
Mr 21 '38
Madonna, Child and two saints
bw 19:24 D 31 '45
Madonna of the chair bw 6:31
F 13 '39
Madonna of the pinks 6:61 My
22 '39
Pope Leo X (Giovanni Medici),
and two cousins bw 4:33 Mr
21 '38
Portrait of a young man bw 16:
66 Ja 10 '44
St. George and the dragon 33:
37 D 29 '52
Sistine Madonna 40:113 My 7
'56
Transfiguration bw 5:46 D 25
'38; 8:26 F 26 '40
Raphael bw 4:26 Mr 21 '38 port.

Raphael, Archangel
Couturier. Angel Raphael
stained glass 28:74 Je 19 '50

Rasputin, Grigoryi
Grigoryi Rasputin photog bw
14:97 Mr 29 '43
Rasputin with ladies of the Rus-
sian court photog bw 31:113
O 29 '51

The rattlesnake. sculpture bw
Remington 13:72 S 14 '42

Rattner, Abraham
Transcendence 27:62 Ag 29
'49
Untitled painting 33:98 O 27
'52

Raven's beak (Bec de corbin) 40:
187 Ap 9 '56

Rawnsley, David
Pottery, oscillogram decora-
tions photog bw 37:109-10
N 22 '54
Artist at work photog bw 37:
109-10 N 22 '54 port.

Rattle and Snap, Greek revival
house, Corinthian, 1845
photog 39:67 Ag 29 '55

Ravana, Hindu festival figure
30:92 F 12 '51

Rawson, Clayton
Clayton Rawson photog bw 22:
21 Mr 10 '47

Ray, Man
Gift art object bw 34:25 My
25 '53
Kiki bw 34:12 Je 19 '53 photog.

Raymond and Rado, architects
Catholic church, Negros Island, Philippines photogs
30:14-5 Ap 30 '51

Razing old New York post office.
bw Fiene 8:69 My 27 '40

The razor fight. bw Binford 13:
140 N 16 '42

Re tomb painting, Egypt 24:82
Ja 19 '48

Rea, Gardner
"New Yorker" cover 21:71
Jy 15 '46

The reach. Freund 39:116 S 12
'55

Read, George
George Read bw 15:9 Jy 5 '43
Read, Mary
Mary Read, pirate, c1719 bw
14:7 Ja 4 '43

Read the slope, swallow the sky.
  Ernst 32:58 Ja 21 '52
Reading the Tribune. Mount 18:
  65 Je 25 '45
Reaping winter wheat, India.
  Sheets 20:81 Ja 21 '46
Recamier, Jean Francoise (Ber-
  nard)
    David. Madame Recamier 35:
    60 Ag 17 '53
    Gerard. Madame Recamier 10:
    74 Ap 28 '41
Recemption of the English ambas-
  sadors by King Mauro.
  Carpaccio 23:57 Ag 4 '47
Reception of the Immortals at the
  court of Hsi Wang Mu 38:
  76-7 Ap 4 '55
Reclining figure. sculpture bw
  Callery 26:114 Je 20 '49
Reclining figure. sculpture bw
  Moore, H. 22:78-9 Ja 20
  '47
Reclining figure. sculpture bw
  Wotruba 38:87 Je 20 '55
Reclining woman of fruit and vege-
  tables* (Summer). Arcim-
  boldo, School of 7:24 Ag 28
  '39
Reclining young woman. Monet
  40:71 My 28 '56
Recollections of an English abbey.
  Finck 39:113 S 12 '55
The reconcilliation (La retour au
  logis) bw Fragonard 16:63
  Ja 10 '44
Recruit's farewell. Repin 14:46
  Mr 29 '43
Red barns. Alger 16:46 Ja 3 '44
Red buildings in sunlight.
  Lucioni 3:48 Jy 19 '37; 21:
  74 N 25 '46
Red burlesque. bw Waugh, C. 5:
  57 N 28 '38
Red fox. Audubon 30:48 Ja 29 '51
Red interior. Matisse 31:116 N
  26 '51
Red is green if gray is blue
  Ernst 32:59 Ja 21 '52
Red Jacket, Seneca chief
  Catlin. Red Jacket 36:72 Mr 8

  '54
  Humphreys. Red Jacket,
  "Jack of Hearts, " playing
  card 38:Cover My 30 '55
Red Jacket's grandson. Le Clear
  36:73 Mr 8 '54
Red studio. Matisse 31:114-5 N
  26 '51
Red table. Hofmann 33:98 O 27
  '52
The red tablecloth. Picasso 23:
  95 O 13 '47
Reder, Bernard
  Wounded woman bw 26:113 Je
  20 '49 (sculpture)
  Medieval lady 37:88 O 18 '54
  (woodcut)
  Bernard Reder. in group
  photog bw 26:112 Je 20 '49
  port.
Reed, John.
  John Reed photog bw 31:115 O
  29 '51
Reeves, Richard
  Armed (race horse) 24:101 Ap
  12 '48
Refinery. Nack 28:86 Mr 20 '50
Reflections of St. Jean. Church-
  ill 20:46 Ja 7 '46
Reflections on a shop window.
  Bohrod 14:44 Mr 8 '43; 21:
  77 N 25 '46
Reformation
  Men of the reformation bw 24:
  60-1 Je 14 '48
  Reformation monument, Gen-
  eva sculpture bw 20:31-2
  Mr 18 '46
Refrigier, Anton
  Oklahoma's development*
  mural 30:78 Mr 5 '51
Regnier
  Ice skater lithograph 6:40 F 6
  '39
Rehearsal. Taubes 4:25 Je 13
  '38
Reich, Jean
  Beauty shop ceramics bw 9:
  130 N 10 '40
Reid, Neel, architect
  Trygveson, Italian baroque

style, Atlanta photog 24:80
Je 7 '48
Reims cathedral photog bw 22:68
Ap 7 '47
Reindeer. sculpture bw Rosen-
thal, B. 34:134 Ap 6 '53
Reindel, Edna
Net menders 3:36 Ag 9 '37
New England harbor 3:36 Ag
9 '37
Storm over Menemsha 3:35
Ag 9 '37
Women war workers 16:75-8
Je 5 '44
Artist at work photog bw 16:
74 Je 5 '44 port.
Edna Reindel photog bw 3:34
Ag 9 '37 port.
Reiner, Fritz
Conductor Reiner photog bw
18:79 Ja 29 '45
Reinhardt, Ad
Ad Reinhardt photog bw 30:34
Ja 15 '51 port.
Reinhardt, Siegfried
Flashy autos 32:90 Mr 24 '52
Mandrill and maidens 32:89
Mr 24 '52
Resurrection 28:84 Mr 20 '50
bw 32:88 Mr 24 '52
Strings and dead bird 32:90 Mr
24 '52
Strongman 32:90 Mr 24 '52
Artist and his work photog bw
32:88 Mr 24 '52 port.
Reinhardt, Stewart
Pas de deux 16:45 Ja 3 '44
Reisman, Philip
"Anna Kerenina," illustrations
8:46-9 F 5 '40
Philip Reisman photog bw 8:46
F 5 '40 port.
Reiss, Wallace
Judgment day bw 32:88 Mr 17
'52
Wallace Reiss photog bw 32:
87 Mr 17 '52 port.
Relief of Vienna, 1683* bw 17:87
Ag 28 '44
Religious Themes See Biblical
and Christian Themes; Gods

and Goddesses; and names
of religions, as Baha'i;
Buddha and Buddhism;
Confucius and Confucian-
ism; Hinduism; Jainism;
Mohammed and Mohammed-
anism
Reliquary, enamelled, France,
13th century bw 6:52 Mr
20 '39
Rembrandt van Rijn
Anatomy lesson of Professor
Tulp 1:30 N 30 '36
Artist's brother, Adriaen van
Rijn bw 28:58 Ja 30 '50
Artist's father, Harmem
Gerritsz van Rijn bw 28:58
Ja 30 '50
The beef bw 7:24 Ag 28 '39
Esther's feast 41:74 D 10 '56
Flora bw 28:58 Ja 30 '50
Jan Six bw 31:65 Jy 16 '51
Lamentation over Christ bw
6:58 Mr 27 '39
Lisbeth, the artist's sister 1:
33 N 30 '36
Man with golden helmet bw
19:24 D 31 '45
A married couple 24:76 Je 14
'48
Meditating philosopher bw 39:
142-3 S 26 '55
The mill 5:33 Ag 29 '38
Night watch bw 21:106 O 28
'46
Old woman cutting her nails
6:56 Mr 20 '39
The painter's study bw 29:
104 S 11 '50
Pallas Athena 29:85 N 27 '50
The Polish rider 3:36 D 27
'37
The rape of Europa 6:39 My
29 '39
St. Bartholomew 25:59 O 11
'48
Samson's feast 40:112 My 7
'56
The standard bearer bw 16:
66 Ja 10 '44

Rembrandt van Rijn (cont.)
  Storm on the Sea of Galilee 1:
    31 N 30 '36
  Supper at Emmaus 11:78 D 1
    '41; 35:61 Ag 17 '53; 39:30
    D 26 '55
  Susanna and the elders 24:79
    Mr 22 '48
  Titus, the artist's son 1:30
    N 30 '36 bw 28:58 Ja 30 '50
  Toilet of Bathsheba 1:33 N 30
    '36 bw 12:44 Mr 9 '42
  A woman bathing 29:105 S 11
    '50
  Young girl at an open half-
    door 11:57 S 8 '41
  Youth with a black cap 7:55 O
    9 '39
  Sacrifice of Isaac bw 6:54 Ja
    30 '39 (etching)
  Self-portrait, age 24 28:59 Ja
    30 '50 port.
  Self-portrait, 1660 1:29 N 30
    '36 port.
  Self-portrait bw 5:30 Ag 29
    '38; 26:160 Ap 11 '49 port.
Rembrandt, attributed work
  Philosopher with open book,
    art forgery bw 39:142-3 S
    26 '55
Remenick, Seymour
  To auction 10:58 Je 16 '41
Remington, Frederic
  Aiding a comrade bw 21:116 O
    21 '46
  Around the campfire 13:75 S
    14 '42
  Attack on the supply wagon 13:
    76 S 14 '42
  Bronco buster 13:73 S 14 '42
  Cavalry charge on the south-
    ern plains 13:76 S 14 '42
  Cowboy bw 5:29 O 31 '38
  The discovery 36:77 Mr 8 '54
  Fight for the water hole 13:75
    S 14 '42
  Fired on 9:77 D 9 '40
  Howl of the weather 13:74-5
    S 14 '42
  Navajos at the water hole 13:
    74 S 14 '42

  The sentinel 13:74 S 14 '42
  Spanish police searching Cuban
    woman* 31:27 Ag 27 '51
    (drawing)
  Bronco buster bw 11:54 N 10
    '41; 13:72 S 14 '42 (sculp-
    ture)
  The Cheyenne bw 13:72 S 14 '42
  The cowboy bw 13:72 S 14 '42
  The outlaw bw 13:72 S 14 '42
  The rattlesnake bw 13:72 S
    14 '42
  The scalp bw 13:72 S 14 '42
  Frederic Remington photog bw
    13:72 S 14 '42 port.
Remus
  Romulus and Remus statue 27:
    45 Ag 1 '49
Renaissance art, Lehman Family
    collection 37:67 Ag 9 '54
Rendova
  Bohrod. Rendova--10 paint-
    ings of landing in New
    Georgia 15:72-7 D 27 '43
Reno, Nevada. cartoon Emett
    37:48 Jy 5 '54
Renoir, (Pierre) Auguste
  Apres le bain 24:66 Mr 1 '48
  Bather 41:109 O 22 '56
  Bathers 7:53 N 20 '39
  Boating party at Chatou (Boat-
    men at Chatou) 3:46 Jy 5
    '37; 32:93 My 19 '52
  By the seashore 3:46 Jy 5 '37
  The city dance bw 28:88 Ja 16
    '50
  The country dance bw 28:88
    Ja 16 '50
  Dance at Bougival (Bal a Bou-
    gival) 3:45 Jy 5 '37
  Farmhouse at Les Collettes
    32:97 My 19 '52
  Gabrielle and Jean 32:91 My
    19 '52
  Gabrielle with roses 32:95 My
    19 '52
  Girl combing her hair 37:66
    Ag 9 '54
  The hunter (Jean Renoir) 32:
    98 My 19 '52
  Jean sewing, the artist's son

32:94 My 19 '52

The judgment of Paris 32:97
My 19 '52

Luncheon of the boating party
32:94 My 19 '52; 38:10 My
23 '55

Mme. Charpentier and her
children 3:47 Jy 5 '37

Mme. Renoir, 1915 32:96 My
19 '52

Mme. Renoir and Pierre 32:
94 My 19 '52

Model on pink chair 37:66 Ag
9 '54

Monet at Argenteuil 32:93 My
19 '52

Nude 9:48 Jy 29 '40 bw 12:44
Mr 9 '42

Paul Cezanne, 1880 32:93 My
19 '52

Paul Durand-Ruel 32:98 My
19 '52

The Pont Neuf 32:92 My 19 '52

Portrait of a child 25:77 N 1
'48

Three bathers with crab 3:47
Jy 5 '37

Two girls in spring meadow*
5:26 O 10 '38

Two little circus girls 11:59
S 8 '41

Claude, the artist's son bw 32:
98 My 19 '52 (sculpture)

Artist at work photog bw 3:44
Jy 5 '37 port.

Auguste Renoir photog bw 3:44
Jy 5 '37; 5:24 O 10 '38 port.

Self-portrait, 1910 32:99 My 19
'52 port.

Renoir, Mme. Auguste
Renoir, A. Luncheon of the
boating party 32:94 My 19
'52; 38:10 My 23 '55

Renoir, A. Mme Renoir, 1915
32:96 My 19 '52

Renoir, A. Mme. Renoir and
Pierre 32:94 My 19 '52

Renoir, Claude
Renoir, A. Claude, the artist's
son sculpture bw 32:98 My
19 '52

Renoir, Jean
Renoir, A. Gabrielle and Jean
32:91 My 19 '52

Renoir, A. The hunter (Jean
Renoir) 32:98 My 19 '52

Renoir, A. Jean sewing, the
artist's son 32:94 My 19
'52

Replin, Ilya Efimovitch
Recruit's farewell 14:46 Mr
29 '43

Repplier, Agnes
Agnes Repplier photog bw 10:
86 Je 9 '41

Reprobatus. Lewicki 39:66 D 19
'55

The residence of David Twining
in 1787. Hicks 9:76 D 9
'40

Resting chimney sweep. Koch 3:
26 D 20 '37

Restoration of Art Objects See
Art Cleaning and Restoration

Resurrection. Reinhardt 28:84
Mr 20 '50 bw 32:88 Mr 24
'52

Resurrection of Christ See Je
Jesus Christ--Resurrection

Resurrection of Lazarus. Duccio
1:46 D 28 '36

Resurrection of Lazarus. Tintoretto 31:38 D 24 '51

Retablo
Espalargus. Life of Christ,
1490 4:29 F 7 '38

Retief, Piet
Moerdyk. Piet Retief memori-
al, bw Pretoria 28:25-6
Ja 16 '50

Le retour au logis. Fragonard
16:63 Ja 10 '44

Retreat. Ranney 27:42 Jy 4 '49

Return from Rouen. Hurd 14:52-
3 Je 21 '43 bw 14:6 Je 28
'43

Return from the hunt. Watteau
23:82-3 S 15 '47

Return of H.M.S. Exeter.
Cundall 10:65 F 24 '41

Return of Miles Standish bw 19:
57 N 26 '45

Return to castle. Priebe 23:71 N 24 '47

Return to the detested city. lithograph Jorn 33:85 Jy 14 '52

Returned volunteer. sculpture bw Rogers 6:6 Mr 6 '39

Returning from work, India. Sheets 20:81 Ja 21 '46

The reunion. sculpture Barlach 41:137 N 5 '56

Reunion in the country. Watteau 40:110-11 My 7 '56

Reuterdahl, Henry
The U.S. fleet in the Straits of Magellan, 1908 9:50 O 28 '40

Revere, Paul
Symbol of American colonies-- nine-segmented snake bw 38:56 My 30 '55 (cartoons)
Symbol of England--griffin bw 38:56 My 30 '55 (cartoons)
Boston Massacre, March 5, 1770 29:39 Jy 3 '50 (engraving)
Punch bowl, 1768 38:56 My 30 '55 (silversmithing)
Copley. Paul Revere 38:57 My 30 '55 port.
Paul Revere, equestrian statue, Boston bw 18:66 Ja 15 '45 port.
Paul Revere's ride sculpture bw 8:114 My 20 '40 port.
Wood, G. The midnight ride of Paul Revere 3:28 D 20 '37; 14:54 Ja 18 '43 port.

Reverie. Thon 20:98 Ap 29 '46

Revolutions and Riots
Delacroix. Liberty leading the people (Revolution of 1828) 25:84 N 22 '48
Duchamp. Rioting at Austerlitz 32:103 Ap 28 '52
Fall of the Bastille, Paris, July 14, 1789 3:32, 35 Jy 5 '37
Hagnauer. Street fights in Paris, 1848 25:88-9 N 22 '48
Homestead riot, 1892 bw 33:32

D 8 '52
Mob storming the Bastille, July 14, 1789* bw 31:78-80 Jy 30 '51
New York draft riots, 1863 bw 12:99 My 25 '42
Social, industrial, scientific changes--Europe and America, 1848 25:85-101 N 22 '48
Surikob. Storming of the Winter Palace 14:58 Mr 29 '43

Rey, Jose Luis, watercolorist
A hero 2:34 F 22 '37
She saw him fall 2:35 F 22 '37
Steel 2:35 F 22 '37
Triumphal march 2:34 F 22 '37
Wrestler 2:35 F 22 '37

Reykjavik
Coale. U.S. ships entering Reykjavik bw 13:90-1 Jy 13 '42

Reynolds, Joshua
Caroline, Fourth Duchess of Marlborough 24:36 Ap 19 '48
James Boswell bw 29:97 D 4 '50
Samuel Johnson 25:108 S 13 '48
Sarah Siddons as the tragic muse 4:24 Ja 24 '38
Sir Joshua Reynolds bw 4:23 Ja 24 '38 port.

Rhine, Joseph
Joseph Rhine photogs bw 8:86-7 Ap 15 '40

Rhode Island
Baker. Economic activities in the days of Naragansett planters mural 10:44 Ja 27 '41
Roger Williams welcomed by Rhode Island Indians bw 16:44 Ja 31 '44

Rhode Island School of Design, Providence, Rhode Island
American cartoonists, exhibit bw 8:71-4 Ap 22 '40

Rhoden, John, sculptor

Artist at work photog bw 33:97
S 15 '52 port.
Riazan cathedral, 17th century
photog bw 14:85 Mr 29 '43
Ribblesdale, Thomas
Sargent. Lord Ribblesdale 23:
81 N 17 '47
Ribera, Jusepe de
Holy family with Saint Cather-
ine 4:42 My 16 '38
St. John The Baptist 41:72 D
10 '56
Ribero's world map, 1529 bw 13:
59 Ag 3 '42
Ricardo, David
David Ricardo bw 22:100 Mr
24 '47
Ricart
Miro. Ricart 33:92 O 27 '52
port.
Rice, Elmer
Elmer Rice and his wife, Betty
Field photog bw 19:38 D 31
'45
Rice, T. D.
T. D. Rice, "Jim Crow"
dancer bw 11:74 Ag 25 '41
Richard I, Coeur de Lion, King
of England
Richard I bw 22:84 My 26 '47
Richard, Coeur de Lion tomb
effigy bw 40:115 Mr 26 '56
Richard II, King of England bw
2:48 Ap 5 '37 Bible 34:80
F 23 '53 Shield of arms 22:
69 My 26 '47
Richard III, King of England bw
40:208 Ap 9 '56
Richards, Ivor Armstrong
I. A. Richards photog bw 15:
57 O 18 '43
Richardson, H. H., architect
Tudor-style Victorian house,
Newport, 1874 40:98 Mr 5
'56
Richmond, Virginia, 1861. bw
Viztelly 13:72 N 16 '42
Riddle, Mrs. Robert
Cassatt. Lady at the tea table
38:74 Mr 28 '55
Riddle, W. D., architect

Contemporary house photog,
plan bw 31:125 S 10 '51
A ride home after a blank day.
print bw Leech 6:38 F 6
'39
Ridin' high. Burden 25:99 D 6
'48
Ridley, John, architect
Contemporary house, Seattle
photog, plan 31:126 S 10 '51
Rigaud, Hyacinthe
Louis XV, King of France,
age 20 23:80 S 15 '47
Riggs, Kate Douglas
Kate Douglas Riggs photog bw
16:96 My 8 '44
Riggs, Robert
Hamilton-Burr duel 23:69 Jy
7 '47
Advertising art bw 3:48 S 13
'37 (drawings)
Center ring bw 3:46 S 13 '37
(prints)
Clown acrobats bw 3:47 S 13
'37 (prints)
Clown alley bw 3:47 S 13 '37
(prints)
On stage four bw 3:46 S 13 '37
(prints)
Tumblers bw 3:47 S 13 '37
(prints)
Robert Riggs photogs bw 3:48
S 13 '37 port.
Right to the jaw. sculpture bw
Young, M. 10:79 F 17 '41
Right uppercut. sculpture bw
Brown, Joseph 12:90 My
19 '41
Rights of citizens. Castellon 30:
87 Mr 12 '51
Rinaldo and Armida. Van Dyck,
A. 4:31 Ap 11 '38
Rinehart, Mary Roberts
Mary Roberts Rinehart photogs
bw 20:55, 62 F 25 '46
Rinehart, William
Latona and her children sculp-
ture bw 19:10 S 24 '45
Ringing the pig. Mount 18:66 Je
25 '45
Rings See Jewelry

Rio de Janeiro
  Harrison and Abramovitz. U.
    S. embassy 34:45 Je 22 '53
  Landowski. Christ the redeem-
    er, Rio harbor statue bw
    10:60 Ja 6 '41
  Niemeyer. Education and
    Health building photog bw
    22:35 My 26 '47
Rioting at Austerlitz. Duchamp
    32:103 Ap 28 '52
Rip van Winkle statue bw 17:63
    O 30 '44
Ripley, Alden Laswell
  Hunting game birds, scenes 29:
    123-7 D 4 '50
Risom, Jens, furniture designer
  Modern furniture--chair, side-
    board, tables photogs bw
    25:118 N 15 '48
  Jens Risom photog bw 25:118 N
    15 '48 port.
Rita. sculpture bw Epstein 3:90 N
    15 '37
Rittenhouse, David
  "Grandfather" clock, Chinese
    Chippendale case, Philadel-
    phia, c1770 photog 39:64 Jy
    18 '55
Rivals. Craig 11:74 O 27 '41
"The Rivals," illustration: Mrs.
    Malaprop bw 25:109 S 13 '48
The river. sculpture bw Laurent
    10:68 Je 2 '41
River Jordan. mural bw Binford
    13:138-9 N 16 '42
River scene: Bathers and cattle.
    Wilson 5:43 S 12 '38
Rivera, Diego
  Cortes conquest of Mexico, 2
    mural details, Palace of
    Cortes, Cuernavaca, Mexi-
    co 6:41 Ja 23 '39
  Enriqueta Davila 29:109 D 11
    '50
  History of Mexico,* mural bw
    Del Prado Hotel, Mexico
    City 23:104-6 N 3 '47
  Man's dependence on water,
    mural Water storage tank,
    Mexico City 31:73 S 17 '51

  Nudes mural bw, Ciro's,
    Hotel Reforma, Mexico
    City 16:78 F 28 '44; 23:106
    N 3 '47
  Pan-American unity* mural,
    San Francisco Junior Col-
    lege 10:52-6 Mr 3 '41
  Sellers waiting watercolor 4:
    29 Mr 14 '38
  Artist at work photog bw 9:49
    Jy 29 '40; 10:52 Mr 3 '41;
    16:80-1 F 28 '44; 23:104-5
    N 3 '47; 31:75 S 17 '51
    port.
  Artist; wife and friends photog
    6:42 Ja 23 '39 bw 4:28 Mr
    14 '38 port.
  Diego Rivera photog bw 6:84
    Mr 27 '39; 9:69 O 14 '40
    port.
  Self-portrait, in Del Prado
    Hotel mural, Mexico City
    bw 23:105 N 3 '47 port.
Rivera, Frieda See also Rivera,
    Diego
  Frieda Rivera photog 6:42 Ja
    23 '39
Rivera, Jose de
  Bust sculpture, polished alum-
    inum bw 5:4 N 7 '38
Riverbank farm.* Hurd 23:78 Ag
    18 '47
Riverside Church, New York City
    photogs bw 3:35-7 D 20 '37;
    19:75 D 24 '45
The Riviera. Bonnard 25:54-5
    Jy 26 '48
Riviere, Marie
  Ingres. Mlle. Riviere 34:87
    My 11 '53
Road and rain. Burchfield 1:26
    D 28 '36
The road from the cove. bw
    Kroll 16:79 Ap 24 '44
Road home. Simkhovitch 11:39
    D 29 '41
Road to Danbury. Varga 10:72
    Ap 14 '41
Road with cypresses. Van Gogh
    2:33 F 15 '37
"The Robe," illustration.

Cornwell 23:91-4 D 8 '47
"Robert E. Lee" (Mississippi
   steam boat)
   Currier and Ives print. Low
      water 21:72 S 2 '46
Roberts, Kenneth
   Kenneth Roberts photogs bw 8:
      52-4 Mr 18 '40
Roberts, Peter
   Isaac Bitton, boxer etching bw
      6:42 F 6 '39
Roberts, Tom
   Bailed up bw 12:79 F 9 '42
   Shearing the rams bw 12:79 F
      9 '42
Robertson, H. O.
   Winter afternoon 6:29 F 13 '39
Robeson, Paul
   Paul Robeson bw 5:58 O 3 '38
   Ryan. Paul Robeson sculptured
      head bw 8:95 Je 24 '40
Robida, Albert
   War of the future, 1975 bw
      1883 12:12-5 Je 15 '42
Robin, Joannes
   Merry Christmas of Rosette
      bw 27:57 D 26 '49
Robin Hood
   Pyle. Illustrations of book bw
      20:78 Je 17 '46
   Wyeth, N. C. Illustrations of
      book 20:81 Je 17 '46
Robin Hood cove, Maine. Hartley
   32:88 Je 16 '52
Robinson, Boardman
   "Judson Stoddard," illustra-
      tion of Edgar Lee Master's
      poem 20:79 F 18 '46
   Artist at Colorado Springs
      Fine Arts Center photog bw
      11:40 Ag 11 '41 port.
   Artist at work photog bw 9:65
      O 7 '40 port.
Robinson, William Heath
   World War British cartoons
      from "Sketch" bw 7:4-6 D
      25 '39
Robinson Crusoe
   Basile. Robinson Crusoe as a
      young man 1:44 N 30 '36
   Crusoe and Friday illustrations

bw 25:109 S 13 '48
Wilson, E. A. Robinson Cru-
   soe illustrations 18:55 Ap
   23 '45
Robsjohn-Gibbings, Terence
   Harold, furniture and in-
   terior designer
   Coffee table photog 35:17 D 14
      '53
   Modern furniture--tables,
      chairs, chest, ottoman,
      desk photogs bw 25:116-7
      N 15 '48
   Modern living room photog 27:
      60-1 O 3 '49
   Walnut armchair photog 29:90
      D 25 '50
   T. H. Robsjohn-Gibbings
      photog bw 25:116 N 15 '48;
      27:55 O 3 '49 port.
Robus, Hugo, sculptor
   Girl washing her hair bw 6:
      83 My 22 '39
   Suppliant figure, lamp design
      bw 21:106 N 18 '46
   Woman combing her hair bw
      14:42 Mr 8 '43
Robusti, Jacopo See Tintoretto
Rocco, Saint
   St. Rocco statue bw 3:71 S 6
      '37
Roche, Martin, architect
   Holabird and Roche. Takoma
      Building, 1887, Chicago
      bw 40:99 Mr 5 '56
The rock. Blume 26:108-9 Ap 11
   '49
Rockefeller, John Davison, I
   Pach Brothers. J. D. Rocke-
      feller photog bw 3:17 O 25
      '37
Rockefeller Center, New York
   City
   Harrison, archt. Views, in-
      terior photogs 12:51-61 Ja
      12 '42 bw 22:34 My 26 '47
   Lawrie. Atlas sculpture 4:52
      Je 27 '38
Rockwell, Norman
   The American way 18:45 Ja
      1 '45

Rockwell, Norman (cont.)
   Boy scout calendar 18:45 Ja
      1 '45
Rodeos
   Martin. July 4th, 5th add 6th
      9:91 N 11 '40 bw 15:13 O
      25 '43
Rodgers, Richard
   Richard Rodgers photogs bw
      15:103 My 15 '50; 16:82 Mr
      6 '44; 33:53 D 29 '52
Rodin, Auguste, sculptor
   Dressing gown of Honore de
      Balzac bw 38:22 My 9 '55
   Eternal springtime bw 6:57 Mr
      20 '39
   Honore de Balzac statue and
      heads bw 38:21 My 9 '55
      statue, copy, Museum of
      Modern Art, New York City
      bw 38:21 My 9 '55
   Honore de Balzac nude bw
      38:22 My 9 '55
   Joseph Pulitzer bw 35:41 D
      14 '53
   The kiss bw 26:7-9 Je 27 '49
   The thinker bw 38:20 My 9 '55
      bronze model bw 6:57 Mr
      20 '39
   Victor Hugo bw 38:20 My 9 '55
   Steichen. Rodin and his work
      photog bw 38:20 My 9 '55
      port.
Rodney, Caesar
   Caesar Rodney bw 15:9 Jy 5
      '43
Roemburg, Cornelius van
   Satan, book jacket 32:96 Ap 14
      '52
Roentgen, William Konrad
   Physicist Roentgen photog bw
      3:43 O 11 '37
Roese, Herbert F.
   Babe cartoons 10:12-5 Ap 21
      '41
Rogers, Bruce
   Conrow. Bruce Rogers 18:75
      My 14 '45
Rogers, John, sculptor
   Challenging the Union vote bw
      6:6 Mr 6 '39

   Football bw 6:8 Mr 6 '39
   A frolic at the old homestead
      bw 6:7 Mr 6 '39
   Neighboring pews bw 6:6 Mr
      6 '39
   The photographer bw 6:8 Mr
      6 '39
   Politics bw 6:7 Mr 6 '39
   Returned volunteer bw 6:6 Mr
      6 '39
   Romeo and Juliet bw 6:7 Mr
      6 '39
   The tap on the window bw 6:6
      Mr 6 '39
   The watch on the "Santa Ma-
      ria" bw 6:8 Mr   '39
   John Rogers photog bw 6:7
      Mr 6 '39 port.
Rogers, Will
   Davidson. Will Rogers statue
      bw 27:79 Jy 18 '49
   Will Rogers; family photogs
      bw 27:78-94 Jy 18 '49
   Will Rogers, equestrian
      statue, Fort Worth bw 28:
      25 Ja 23 '50
The Rokeby Venus
   Velazquez. Venus and cupid
      41:104 O 22 '56
Rokossovsky, Konstantin
   Marshal Konstantin Rokossov-
      sky, "Time" cover por-
      trait 17:64 D 11 '44
Rolick, Esther
   Artist at work photog bw 21:
      111 Jy 15 '46 port.
Rolling his own. sculpture bw
      Young, M. 10:79 F 17 '41
Rolling-star quilt pattern 11:62
      S 22 '41
Romain-Desfosses, Pierre
   Pierre Romain-Desfosses
      photog 34:106 My 4 '53
      port.
Roman calendar, first centuries
      A.D. sculpture bw 18:41
      Ja 1 '45
The Roman praetor, Forum,
      120 B.C. Castellon 30:87
      Mr 12 '51
Romanic Painting, Catalan, Na-

tional Palace, Montjuich,
Barcelona bw 2:41 F 22 '37
Romano, Uberto
Walkowitz bw 16:77 F 21 '44
Romans, Bernard
Bunker Hill engraving 29:41
Jy 3 '50
Romantic Painters
Paintings of the 1840's; Turner,
Corot, Millet 25:96-7 N 22
'48
Romanus, Saint
Zurburan. St. Romanus 33:91
O 27 '52
Rome See also St. Peter's;
Vatican
Arch of Constantine photog bw
5:59 Jy 18 '38
Arch of Titus photog bw 16:13
Je 5 '44; 17:95 S 4 '44
Baths of Caracalla photog bw
25:80 Ag 9 '48
Bierstadt. Arch of Octavius
33:91 S 15 '52
The Colosseum photog 27:44 Ag
1 '49 bw 17:95 S 4 '44
The fall of Rome bw 16:62 Mr
20 '44
Fountain, Forum Mussolini,
Imperial Square photog bw
4:33 My 9 '38
Healy. Arch of Titus 33:89 S
15 '52
Innes. St. Peter's basilica 33:
90 S 15 '52
Palazzo Colonna interiors,
sculpture and paintings, ex-
terior, gardens photogs bw
18:87 Mr 5 '45 art gallery
27:53 Ag 1 '49
Pantheon photog bw 16:12 Je
5 '44
Pillage of the Temple, Jerusa-
lem, 70 A.D. relief 38:99
Je 13 '55
Roman Forum photog bw 17:95
S 4 '44
Rome airview photog bw 15:27
Ag 9 '43
Temple of Vesta photog bw 17:
94 S 4 '44

Temples, arches, aqueducts,
towers photogs bw 16:12-3
Je 5 '44
Rome, Harold
Cosgrave. Harold Rome and
wife bw 24:18 Ja 19 '48
Harold Rome photog bw 24:18
Ja 19 '48
Rommel, Erwin
Field Marshal Rommel,
"Time" cover portrait 17:
66 D 11 '44
Romeo and Juliet. sculpture bw
Rogers 6:7 Mr 6 '39
Romero, Carlos Orozco
Marionette 4:29 Mr 14 '38
Romney, George
The Beckford children 4:27 Ja
24 '38
Emma Hamilton bw 10:41 Ap
7 '41
Lady Hamilton as "Nature"
3:33 D 27 '37
Master Hartley bw 6:58 Mr
27 '39
Miss Constable 29:83 N 27 '50
George Romney bw 4:23 Ja
24 '38 port.
Romulus and Remus statue 27:45
Ag 1 '49
"Ronin"
Hiroshige; Hokusai. Scenes
from "The 47 Ronin" bw 15:
53-6 N 1 '43
Ronin hero prints bw 18:97 Ap
16 '45
The room number five. Cortor
28:85 Mr 20 '50
Roosevelt, Franklin Delano,
architect
Summer cottage, New York
State photogs, plan bw 5:
25 O 17 '38
Chandor. President Franklin
Roosevelt 26:82 Mr 14 '49
port.
Davidson. Franklin Roosevelt
sculpture bw 32:34 Ja 14
'52

Roosevelt, F. D. (cont.)
  Dick. Franklin Delano Roose-
    velt sculpture bw, Grosven-
    or Square, London 24:32-3
    Ap 26 '48 model bw 21:33 D
    2 '46
  Franklin D. Roosevelt carica-
    ture as sphinx bw 11:21 Jy
    14 '41
  Mulk. Mr. Churchill and his
    friends overthrowing Hitler
    and his 35:70 N 9 '53
  Wheelock. Roosevelt sculptured
    head bw 8:115 My 20 '40
Roosevelt, Mrs. F. D.
  Chandor. Eleanor Roosevelt
    30:101 Je 18 '51
Roosevelt, Sara D.
  Sara D. Roosevelt bw 23:121 O
    6 '47
Roosevelt, Theodore
  Ave Theodore political cartoon
    bw 31:19 O 22 '51
  Borglum. Theodore Roosevelt,
    Mt. Rushmore National
    Memorial bw 7:19 Jy 17 '39
  Bull moose in the bullrushes,
    1912 political cartoon 40:72
    Ja 30 '56
  Laning. T. R. in Panama 6:
    44-5 My 15 '39
  Theodore Roosevelt photog bw
    9:9 Ag 5 '40
  Theodore Roosevelt, cartoons
    opposing third term, 1912
    bw 8:13 Ap 22 '40
Roosevelt, Mrs. Theodore
  Koch. Mrs. Theodore Roose-
    velt and family bw 41:78 Ag
    13 '56
Roosters. Chagall 27:89 D 12 '49
Rooster and chick. sculpture bw
    Cherry 22:140 Je 16 '47
Roosters. Jakuchu 31:66 D 31 '51
Root, Elihu
  Elihu Root 19:88 S 24 '45
  Pach Brothers. Elihu Root,
    age 58 photog bw 3:16 O 25
    '37
Roper, J.
  Gold diggers, Ararat, 1854 bw

    12:78 F 9 '42
Roper's gymnasium, Philadel-
    phia, 1840 bw 6:41 F 6 '39
Roque See Games and Sports--
    Roque
Rose and scroll hooked rug pat-
    tern 8:45 Ja 29 '40
Rose Windows
  Connick. Rose window stained
    glass 6:31 Ap 3 '39
Rosecliff, Newport. photogs bw
    White, archt. 11:82-5 Ag
    18 '41
Rosello, Florentino F.
  World map, 1532 18:62-3 My
    21 '45
Rosemary. sculpture bw Epstein
    3:90 N 15 '37
Rosen, Katherine
  Bellows. Miss Katherine
    Rosen 20:82 Mr 25 '46
Rosenthal, Bernard, sculptor
  Fountain of the sea bw 34:134
    Ap 6 '53
  Bernard Rosenthal photog bw
    34:134 Ap 6 '53 port.
Rosenthal, Doris
  At the blackboard 15:66 N 22
    '43
  Between two screens 12:46
    Mr 9
  Boys sleeping 10:73 Ap 14 '41
  By the sea 15:68 N 22 '43
  Corn foliage 22:96 Ap 21 '47
  Girls and bananas 15:68 N 22
    '43
  Nude at table 15:67 N 22 '43
  Tops 15:65 N 22 '43
  Sacred music 15:66 N 22 '43
  The source 15:67 N 22 '43
  Artist at work in Mexico
    photogs bw 15:64 N 22 '43
Rosenthal, Joe, photographer
  Mr. Suribachi flag raising bw
    18:17 Mr 26 '45
Rosoman, Leonard
  House collapsing on two fire-
    men, Shoe Lane 12:40 Mr
    2 '42; 26:49 F 28 '49
Rospigliosi cup. goldsmithing
    bw Cellini 6:53 Mr 20 '39;

31:26 O 15 '51

Ross, Betsy
  Beale. Betsy Ross bw 32:58 F
    18 '52
  Betsy Ross, "Harper's Month-
    ly," 1873 32:58 F 18 '52
  Ferris. Betsy Ross bw 32:58
    F 18 '52
  Mosler. Betsy Ross bw 32:58
    F 18 '52
  Weisgerber. Betsy Ross bw
    32:57 F 18 '52
Ross, Elizabeth
  Elizabeth Ross, part-Cherokee
    Indian 36:73 Mr 8 '54
Ross, George
  George Ross bw 15:9 Jy 5 '43
Ross, Mother
  Mother Ross bw 14:6 Ja 4 '43
Rossi, Lucius
  The Astors of New York, 1870
    25:92-3 O 18 '48
Rossiter, Thomas Prichard
  The founding fathers at the
    Federal Convention, c1850
    39:58-9 Jy 4 '55
Rotator. Duchamp 32:102, 104 Ap
    28 '52
Rotheneufs Family
  Foure. Rotherneufs Family
    history, rock sculpture,
    Brittany coast bw 39:14-5
    Jy 25 '55
Rothermel, Peter Frederick
  Landing of the Pilgrims 13:76
    N 23 '42 bw 19:56 N 26 '45
Rothko, Mark
  Mark Rothko photog bw 30:34
    Ja 15 '51 port.
Rothschild collections of art bw
    16:63 Ja 10 '44
Rothstein, Arthur
  Dust bowl storm* photog bw
    28:53 Ja 2 '50
The rotunda, Ranelagh Gardens
    London, 18th century 25:100
    S 13 '48
Roualt, Georges
  Bouquet 34:61 F 2 '53
  Christian nocturne 34:62 F 2
    '53

Couple in cabaret 34:59 F 2
    '53
The crown of thorns 39:28 D
    26 '55
Figure of woman* 24:67 Mr 1
    '48
Funeral 34:61 F 2 '53
The judges 34:61 F 2 '53
Maria Lani bw 19:15 D 3 '45
Mr. X 34:59 F 2 '53
The quarry 34:58-9 F 2 '53
Three clowns 34:60 F 2 '53
Three judges 25:60 O 11 '48
Madonna and Child, from
    Misere series bw 34:56 F
    2 '53 (etchings)
Christ 28:75 Je 19 '50 (stained
    glass)
Circus dancer, Aubusson 21:
    84 S 30 '46 (tapestry)
Artist and his work photog bw
    25:58 N 22 '48 port.
Georges Rouault photog 34:57
    F 2 '53 port.
Rouchomovski, Israel, gold-
    smith Tiara of Saltapher nes
    bw 39:144 S 26 '55
Rouen. Monet 5:26 O 10 '38
Roulin the postman. bw Van
    Gogh 27:82 O 10 '49
Round ship, England 41:79 O 29
    '56
The round table. Braque 38:109
    My 23 '55
Rousseau, Henry (Le Douanier)
  The dream 29:110-1 S 11 '50
  Exotic landscape 33:95 O 27
    '52
  The waterfall 11:58 S 8 '41
  Self-portrait, age 46 bw 29:
    110 S 11 '50 port.
Rousseau, Jean Jacques
  Jean Jacques Rousseau bw
    23:87 S 15 '47
  Jean Jacques Rousseau, por-
    trait on snuff box 40:82
    Ja 9 '56
Rowan, Andrew Summers,
    bearer of "Message to
    Garcia"

Rowan, A. S. (cont.)
  Captain Rowan photogs bw 4:
    23 Je 13 '38; 22:86 Ja 13
    '47
Rowing See Games and Sports-
  Rowing
Rowland, Henry A.
  Eakins. Henry A. Rowland 12:
    60 Je 15 '42
Rowlandson, Thomas
  Johnson and Boswell, carica-
    ture bw 29:93 D 4 '50
  Quoits caricature 25:102 S 13
    '48
Rowntree, Kenneth
  Coastal defense bw 10:64 F 24
    '41
Rox, Henry
  Joan of Arc sculpture bw 27:
    146 O 17 '49
Roxbury, Massachusetts
  Penniman. Meeting house hill,
    Roxbury, in 1790 13:80 N
    23 '42
Royal Standard of Ur, mosaic
    panels, Sumerian 40:90-1 Je
    4 '56
Roymerswalen, Marinus van
  Tax collection, Flemish, 16th
    century bw 22:98 Mr 24 '47
Rubbings
  Dienes. Tombstones, U.S. bw
    37:133-6 N 15 '54
Rubens, Peter Paul
  Danae receiving the golden
    shower 4:24 Ap 11 '38 bw
    12:44 Mr 9 '42
  Death of Dido bw 16:65 Ja 10
    '44
  Departure of Lot and his fam-
    ily from Sodom 4:24 Ap 11
    '38
  Diana of the hunt 40:112 My 7
    '56
  The feast of Venus 27:66-7 O
    24 '49
  Helene Fourment, the artist's
    wife, c1635 29:84 N 27 '50
  Holy family 6:39 My 29 '39
  Isabella Brant, the artist's
    first wife 24:63 My 3 '48

Joan of Arc 41:74 D 10 '53
Nymphs pursued by satyrs 31:
  64-5 O 1 '51
Three graces 41:107 O 22 '56
Portrait of old Paar 7:54 O
  9 '39
A bear hunt bw 6:58 Mr 27
  '39 (drawing)
Peter Paul Rubens bw 4:20 Ap
  11 '38 port.
Rubens, P. P. The artist
  and his first wife, Isabella
  Brant 7:56 N 20 '39 port.
Rubenstein, Anton
  Anton Rubenstein bw 3:71 N
    15 '37
Rubinstein, Artur
  Halsman. Artur Rubinstein
    photog bw 16:47 Mr 13 '44
Ruby-throated hummingbird.
  Audubon 3:41 Jy 12 '37
Rudolph, Prince of Austro-
  Hungary photogs bw 26:
    127-8 Mr 28 '49
Rudolph, Rella
  Artist and his work photog bw
    35:114 Jy 13 '53 port.
Rudolph of Hapsburg bw 24:28
  Mr 8 '48
Rudy, Charles, sculptor
  Animal figures bw 15:81-2
    D 20 '43
  Artist at work; wife photogs
    bw 15:84 D 20 '43 port.
Ruellan, Andree
  Sixth Avenue bw 9:79 D 9 '40
  Spring in Bleecker Street 10:
    72 Ap 14 '41
Rueter, Georg
  Jan Six VIII bw 31:66 Jy 16
    '51
  Jan Six X, age 2 bw 31:66 Jy
    16 '51
Rugby See Games and Sports--
  Rugby
Rugs See Carpets and Rugs
Ruhtenberg, Jan, furniture de-
  signer
  Swedish modern furniture bw
    5:36-8 D 12 '38
Ruiz, Antonio

The strike 4:30 Mr 14 '38

Rumba dancer. sculpture bw
Maldorelli 22:138 Mr 24 '47

The runaway. bw Lee, D. 3:47
S 20 '37

Runic stone, carving bw 24:128
F 23 '48

Runnels, David B., architect
Contemporary house, Kansas
City, Mo. photog, plan 31:
126 S 10 '51

Running See Games and Sports--
Running

Rural courtship. bw Knight 36:
84 Mr 8 '54

Rurik bw 14:92 Mr 29 '43

Rush, Benjamin
Benjamin Rush 15:9 Jy 5 '43

Rush, Richard
Richard Rush bw 10:26 Mr 3
'41

Rush, William, sculptor
American eagle, woodcarving
bw 1838 5:27 O 31 '38
Nymph and waterbird sculpture in Krimmel. Fourth
of July 39:62 Ag 29 '55
Eakins. William Rush carving
his allegorical figure of
Schuylkill river 16:73 My
15 '44 bw 5:29 O 31 '38

Russell, Bertrand
Bertrand Russell; family;
home photogs bw 8:23-5 Ap
1 '40; 27:17 O 10 '49; 32:
36 My 26 '52
Eisenstadt. Bertrand Russell
photog bw 32:97 Ja 14 '52

Russell, Charles Marion
Gilcrease collection: "Russell
Room" paintings and sculp-
tures 36:76-7 Mr 8 '54
In without knocking 39:86 N 14
'55
Lewis and Clark expedition
mural bw 33:65 N 10 '52
The Navahos 24:65 Mr 1 '48
Charlie Russell, age 62 photog
bw 33:68 N 10 '52 port.

Russell, Lillian
Lillian Russell photog bw 31:

116 N 19 '51

Russell, Mary Anette
Mary Anette Russell photogs
bw 8:106-7 Ap 29 '40

Russia
Coronation of Alexander II,
Czar of Russias, 1856,
series of paintings 38:60-7
Ja 31 '55
Dore. Illustrations for humor-
ous Russian history bw 30:
108-13 Mr 5 '51
Emblem: Double-headed eagle,
adopted 1472, by Ivan III
18:50 Ja 29 '45
Fredenthal. Russian soldiers,
Soviet army in Yugoslavia,
World War drawings bw
18:83-9 F 5 '45
Historical scenes and portraits of 1000 years of history bw 14:92-9 Mr 29 '43
History of Russia, 900-1800,
in pre-Soviet paintings 18:
45-52 Ja 29 '45
Mavrina. Churches of Russia
17:64-8 N 27 '44
Nine statesmen, Stalin's
aides photogs bw 11:18-9
Jy 14 '41
Russian generals--victorious
generals of World War II
photogs bw 17:31-2 Jy 31
'44
Russian military leaders,
1939-43 photogs 14:98-9
Mr 29 '43
Russian scientists photogs bw
17:Cover, 14-6 O 23 '44
Vereshchagin. The 1812 series: Napoleon in Russia
bw 12:61-8 F 2 '42

Russian ball, New York, 1863 bw
19:88 Ag 27 '45

Russian cavalrymen in Paris,
1814 bw 14:95 Mr 29 '43

The Russian fleet visits New
York, 1863 bw 19:88 Ag
27 '45

Rustam
  Persian illuminated manuscript
    20:91 Je 24 '46
The rustic concert. Giorgione 23:
    52 Ag 4 '47; 39:170-1 O 24
    '55
"Rustic-Pointed" Architecture
  Downing. Vassar house photog
    bw 7:63 O 2 '39
Ruth, Babe
  Wheelock. Sultan of swat sculp-
    ture bw 8:116 My 20 '40
Ruth gleaning, historiated letter,
    Richard II's Bible 34:80 F
    23 '53
Rutledge, Edward
  Edward Rutledge bw 15:9 Jy 5
    '43
Rutledge, John
  John Rutledge bw 3:27 Ag 16
    '37
Rutledge mill, New Salem, Illi-
    nois. Phillips, A. 36:80-1
    F 15 '54
Rutuli, illumination, Virgil's
    "Aeneid" 32:86 Ap 14 '52
Ruvolo, Felix
  Alert one bw 22:78 F 17 '47
Ruysdael, Jacob
  View of Haarlem 24:74-5 Je
    14 '48
Ryan, Sally, sculptor
  Arturo Toscanini bw 8:95 Je
    24 '40
  Edna Ferber bw 8:94 Je 24 '40
  Paul Robeson bw 8:95 Je 24 '40
  Thou sayest it statue bw 8:94
    Je 24 '40
  Vero of Ceylon bw 8:95 Je 24
    '40
  Artist at work photog bw 8:93
    Je 24 '40 port.
  Epstein. Sally Ryan, sculpture
    bw 3:90 N 15 '37 port.
Ryder, Albert Pinkham
  Christ appearing to Mary 30:
    88 F 26 '51
  Death on a pale horse 5:36 O
    31 '38; 15:67 S 20 '43
  The forest of Arden 30:90 F
    26 '51

In the stable 30:88 F 26 '51
Night and clouds 13:96 N 9
    '42
Shore scene 30:90 F 26 '51
Siegfried and the Rhine
    maidens 30:87 F 26 '51
Smugglers' cove 30:91 F 26
    '51
The temple of the mind (E. A.
    Poe) 30:91 F 26 '51
Toilers of the sea bw 30:94-
    5 F 26 '51
Under a cloud 30:88-9 F 26
    '51
Albert Pinkham Ryder photog
    bw 30:93 F 26 '51 port.
Hartley. Albert Pinkham Ry-
    der bw 30:101 F 26 '51
    port.
Self-portrait 30:86 F 26 '51
    port.

S

Saarinen, Eero, architect and
    furniture designer
  Gateway to the West, memor-
    ial arch, St. Louis, Mo.
    bw 24:113 Mr 8 '48
  General Motor's Technical
    Center, Warren, Michigan
    photogs 40:102-5 My 21
    '56
  Massachusetts Institute of
    Technology Auditorium
    photog bw 38:79-81 Mr 14
    '55
    Chapel photog 39:114-5 D
    26 '55
  Chairs 34:74 Mr 2 '53 (furni-
    ture design)
  Easy chair bw 35:16 D 14 '53
    (furniture design)
  Fabric-covered plastic shell
    chair bw 25:115 N 15 '48
    (furniture design)
  Ottoman 34:72-3 Mr 2 '53
    (furniture design)
  Eero Saarinen photog bw 25:
    115 N 15 '48; 38:82 Mr 14
    '55 port.
Saarinen, Eliel and Eero, archi-

tects
Christ Evangelical Lutheran
church, Minneapolis photog
bw 30:17 Ap 30 '51
Sabor, Clifford
Bar patrons mural bw 27:16-7
D 5 '49
Sabrina. sculpture bw, Amherst
College mascot 32:110 Je
30 '52
Sacco, Nicola
Borglum. Memorial Sacco-
Vanzetti plaque bw 3:24 S 6
'37
Shahn. The passion of Sacco
and Vanzetti, one painting
from series of 23 bw 37:96
O 4 '54
Sacraments
Extreme unction, tapestry,
Flemish, Middle Ages 22:
79 Ap 7 '47
Marriage, tapestry, Flemish,
Middle Ages 22:79 Ap 7 '47
Sacre-Coeur at Rue Saint-Rust-
ique. Utrillo 28:93 Ja 16
'50
Sacred and profane love. Titian
23:52 Ag 4 '47 bw 16:65
Ja 10 '44
Sacred cod, 1760, State House,
Boston sculpture 38:118 Ap
18 '55
The sacred grove. bw Puvis de
Chavannes 28:88 Ja 16 '50
Sacred music. Rosenthal, D.
15:66 N 22 '43
Sacrifice of Isaac. etching bw
Rembrandt 6:54 Ja 30 '39
Sad sack. cartoon bw Baker, in
"Yank" 15:118-9 N 15 '43;
19:8-10 D 31 '45
Saddles, western--7 types photogs
40:50-1 Ja 16 '56
Safe convoy. bw Davis, F. 14:6
Je 28 '43
Sagamore Lodge, photog 28:89-
92 Ja 2 '50
The sailfish. Lawrence, W. G.
6:29 F 2 '39
Sailors

Cadmus. The fleets' in bw 2:
44 Mr 29 '37
Cadmus. Sailors and floosies
bw 9:68 O 14 '40
Carr. Adoration for heroes
bw 9:59 Ag 12 '40
Davis, F. Sailor and girl* 13:
95 S 21 '42; 21:91 N 25 '46
Greenwood. Sea captains ca-
rousing in Surinam, 1758
26:84-5 F 28 '49
Kennington. Spirit of the
British sailor* (Stoker
Martin) 24:60 My 10 '48
The sailors' barracks. bw Chir-
ico 1:27 D 14 '36
Saint. Piero della Francesco 3:
34 D 27 '37
St. Anne de Beaupre church,
Quebec photog bw 9:107
S 9 '40
Saint Augustine, Florida, first
city map, 18:64 My 21 '45
St. Bartholomew's Day mass-
acre, Paris, August 23,
1572 bw 24:60 Je 14 '48
St. Basil's Cathedral, Moscow
Mavrina. St. Basil cathedral
17:64-5 N 27 '44
St. Basil cathedral in Coro-
nation proclamation of
Alexander II 38:60-1 Ja
31 '55
St. Basil's cathedral photog
bw 2:54 My 3 '37; 14:88-9
Mr 29 '43; 22:118 Mr 10
'47
St. Bavon cathedral, Ghent, Van
Eyck brothers altarpiece
26:58-69 Ap 18 '49
St. Benedict the Moor church
photog bw 34:95-6 Mr 16
'53
St. Edward's crown, England
photog 2:37 Mr 15 '37
St. Edward's staff, England
photog 2:39 Mr 15 '37
St. Francis church, Belo Horizonte, Brazil. Niemeyer,
archt. photog bw 25:76-7
Jy 4 '49

St. Francis Xavier basilica,
   Dyersville, Iowa photogs
   bw 41:95 D 3 '56
Saint-Gaudens, Augustus, sculptor
   Diana bw 4:27 My 30 '38; 24:
   112 Mr 15 '48
   General Sherman, equestrian
   statue with angel of Victory,
   New York City bw 24:109 Mr
   15 '48
   Grief, Washington, D.C. bw
   24:110 Mr 15 '48
   Homer Saint-Gaudens, the
   sculptor's son, age 4 bw
   24:112 Mr 15 '48
   The Pilgrim, Fairmont Park,
   Philadelphia bw 24:110 Mr
   15 '48
   Puritan, Springfield, Missouri
   bw 19:56 N 26 '45
   Artist at work; portraits
   photogs bw 24:109-110 Mr
   15 '48 port.
Saint-Gaudens, Mrs. Augustus
   Sargent. Mrs. Saint-Gaudens
   and son, 1890 25:94 O 18
   '48
Saint-Gaudens, Homer
   Homer Saint-Gaudens photog
   bw 5:72 D 12 '38; 24:112 Mr
   15 '48
   Saint-Gaudens, A. Homer
   Saint-Gaudens, the sculp-
   tor's son, age 4 bw 24:112
   Mr 15 '48
St. Giles church, Edinburgh
   photog bw 22:100 My 5 '47
St. George and the Dragon
   See also George, Saint
   Parade figure, Portugal photog
   bw 23:28 Ag 11 '47
St. Georges d'Elle church, Nor-
   mandy. drawing bw Martin
   17:23 Ag 7 '44
St. George's spurs, English royal
   symbol photog 2:38 Mr 15
   '37
St. Ives, England
   Artists working in Cornwall
   fishing village photogs 29:

44-7 Ag 14 '50
St. John churchyard, Richmond,
   Virginia 6:28 Je 19 '39
   photog bw 11:104 N 10 '41
St. Lazare station. Pissaro 33:
   94 O 27 '52
St. Lo
   Pleissner. World War II
   scenes 18:46-52 Ja 8 '45;
   35:86 O 26 '53
St. Louis cemetery. Herron 20:
   80 F 18 '46
St. Louis' City Art Museum
   Treasures of sculptures and
   painting from collections
   13:92-6 N 9 '42
St. Louis in 1832. Pomarede 28:
   74-5 Mr 6 '50
St. Mark's Cathedral, Venice,
   details of mosaics and
   sculpture photogs 35:28-
   35 D 28 '53
   Bellini. The Corpus Christi
   procession 23:54-5 Ag 4
   '47
   Congden. St. Mark's square
   33:95 S 15 '52
St. Michael (ship) England, 1669,
   90-gunner model 41:84 O
   29 '56
St. Patrick's Cathedral, New
   York City 16:67 Ja 31 '44
   altar photog bw 4:32 Mr
   21 '38
   Feininger, A. St. Pat-
   rick's photog bw 14:75 F 1
   '43
St. Paul's cross preacher* 41:
   190-1 N 12 '56
St. Peter's basilica. Inness 33:
   90 S 15 '52
St. Peter's Cathedral, Rome
   photog bw 20:31-3, 36-7
   Mr 11 '46; 27:49 Ag 1 '49
   Bernini. Altar photog bw
   18:27 Ja 15 '45
   Early Christian and Roman
   mosaics, frescoes, sculptures in Vatican grottoes
   28:65-78 Mr 27 '50
   Michelangelo. St. Peter's

dome photog bw 17:94 S 4
'44
Vidar. Consistory scenes
bw 20:34-5 Mr 11 '46
St. Peter's square, Rome photog
bw 25:49 Ag 1 '49
St. Pierre cathedral, Geneva
photog bw 20:32 Mr 18 '46
Saint-Severin, Church of. Utrillo
28:93 Ja 16 '50
St. Stephan's cathedral, Vienna
photogs bw 21:51 N 11 '46
St. Stephen's crown of Hungary
photog bw 2:14 Mr 22 '37
Saints See names of saints, as
Francis, Saint
Sakamoto, Kanao, architect
Fujimi girls high school,
Tokyo photog bw 38:79-81
Mr 14 '55
Architect and his work photog
bw 38:82 Mr 14 '55 port.
Saladin, Sultan of Egypt and Syria
bw 22:84 My 26 '47
Salamina. ceramic dinner service
Kent 9:78 S 9 '40
Salazar, Tono
Kiki cartoon bw 34:14 Je 29 '53
Saldana, Martin
Paintings 35:163 O 19 '53
Artist and his work photog 35:
163-5 O 19 '53 port.
Salem, Massachusetts
Orne. Washington Street,
Salem, Massachusetts, 1765
13:80 N 23 '42
The Salem martyr. Noble 13:79
N 23 '42
Salemme, Antonio
Head of a little girl sculpture
bw 7:36 Jy 17 '39
Salisbury, Frank O.
Silver jubilee at St. Paul's s,
May 6, 1935 28:68-9 My 29
'50
Salisbury cathedral, England
photog bw 8:84-5 Je 3 '40
Salett, armor photog 40:186 Ap 9
'56
Salmon, Robert W.
Boston harbor--Long and Cen-
tral Wharves 6:29 Je 19
'39
Salome
Martin. Je veux la tete de
Jokanaan sculpture bw 11:
157 D 8 '41
Salon of Fakes, Paris bw 39:141
4 S 26 '55
Salon of the Comtesse de St.
Brisson, Paris, 18th cen-
tury bw 23:78 S 15 '47
Salt of State, England, jewelled
gold work 2:42 Mr 15 '37
Salt-box house. drawing, photog,
plan. Wills, archt. 21:72
Ag 26 '46
Saltcellars
Cellini. Saltcellar, gold,
c1540 31:18-9 S 24 '51
Saltholder, glass, Amelung 39:
59 Jy 18 '55
Saltonstall, Gordon
Gordon Saltonstall, 1700 bw
9:74 D 9 '40
Saltonstall, Richard
Richard Saltonstall bw 13:74
N 23 '42
Salut au monde. sculpture bw
Wheelock 8:114 My 20 '40
Salvage of the U.S.S. Mononga-
hela, 1867 9:49 O 28 '40
Salvation Army meeting bw 29:
72 Jy 31 '50
Salver, silver, U.S. colonial.
Savage 38:116-7 Ap 18 '55
Salzburg marionettes: Grimm
and Anderson fairy story
characters 33:Cover, 68-
73 D 29 '52
Samaria, Palestine, basilica,
ruin, Roman photog bw
20:52-3 Ap 1 '46
Sample, Paul
Band concert 3:44 N 15 '37
Barber shop 3:43 N 15 '37
Cathedral encampment,
Leyte 35: 56 N 2 '53
The fox hunt bw 18:44 Ja 1
'45
The invasion of Leyte 19:66-
7 O 8 '45

Sample, Paul (cont.)
  Janitor's holiday 3:44 N 15
    '37; 21:74 N 25 '46
  Matthew 6:19 or "Lay not up
    for yourselves treasures
    upon earth" 8:66 My 27 '40
  Naval aviation World War--
    planes, portraits, scenes
    14:36-41 Ja 4 '43
  Norris Dam bw 3:42 N 15 '37
  PBM hauled to rest bw 14:6
    Je 28 '43
  Roque 3:43 N 15 '37
  Shell factory 11:63 Jy 7 '41 bw
    14:7 Je 28 '43
  Submarine warfare 15:54-9 D
    27 '43
  Ward room bw 3:42 N 15 '37
  World War--South Pacific 16:
    57-62 Je 26 '44
  Indian, drawn at age 9 bw 3:
    42 N 15 '37 (drawing)
  Artist and his wife photog bw
    3:42 N 15 '37 port.
  Paul Sample photog bw 11:60
    Jy 7 '41; 15:84 D 27 '43
    in uniform 14:8 Je 28 '43
    port.
Sampson, Deborah
  Deborah Sampson bw 14:7 Ja
    4 '43; 22:88 Ja 13 '47
Samson and Delilah. ceramics bw
    Schreckengost 9:129 N 11
    '40
Samson's feast. Rembrandt 40:
    112 My 7 '56
San Clemente church, Venice.
    Zerbe 33:96 S 15 '52
San Estaban Rey church, Acoma,
    New Mexico photog 8:74 My
    13 '40; 40:48 Ja 16 '56
    stairway photog 40:48 Ja 16
    '56
San Francesco chapel, Arezzo
  Piero della Francesca. Story
    of the true cross fresco 20:
    60-8 Ap 22 '46
San Francesco church, Assisi
  Giotto. Story of St. Francis of
    Assisi fresco 16:65-71 Ap
    10 '44

San Francisco, California
  "Bay Region Modern" archi-
    tecture photogs 27:44-53 S
    5 '49
  Emett. San Francisco car-
    toon 37:52 Jy 5 '54
  Miller, B. San Francisco
    harbor in war 15:73-4 Jy
    12 '43
San Francisco, 1816 litho-
    graph 40:49 Ja 16 '56
San Francisco public build-
    ings, monuments photogs
    15:70-83 Jy 12 '43
San Francisco, 1849, steam-
    boat gothic plantation
    house, Louisiana photog
    32:80-1 Je 9 '52
San Ildefonso pueblo, New Mexi-
    co photog 8:71 My 13 '40
San Jose mission, Laguna, New
    Mexico Holy Trinity, san-
    tero altarpiece 40:48-9 Ja
    16 '56
"San Josef" (ship) Spanish, 1797
    in Battle of Cape St. Vin-
    cent 24:67 My 10 '48
San Juan Capistrano mission,
    garden photog 40:46 Ja 16
    '56
San Pietro di Castello, Venice.
    Guardi 29:87 N 27 '50
San Rocco, School of
  Tintoretto. Life of Christ 31:
    30-49 D 24 '51
San Simeon, Hearst estate,
    California photogs bw 31:
    28-9 Ag 27 '51
San Xavier del Bac, Arizona
    mission photog 26:74 Mr
    14 '49
Sanakht, Pharoah of Egypt
    drawing 36:24 Je 14 '54
Sanctuary. Bohrod 35:67 N 2 '53
Sanctuary. Curry 1:30 N 23 '36
    bw 15:19 N 29 '43
Sand, George See Dupin, Aurore
The sand team. Bellows 20:81
    Mr 25 '46
Sandburg, Carl
  Carl Sandburg photogs bw

4:42-3 F 21 '38; 13:109 N 9
'42; 18:57, 60 Je 18 '45
Hoffman. Carl Sandburg photog
bw 4:Cover F 21 '38
Sanders, Morris, furniture de-
signer
Module furniture--interchange-
able units photogs bw 21:128-
9 S 23 '46
Sanderson, Robert, silversmith
Hull and Sanderson. Communi-
on cup 38:116 Ap 18 '55
Hull and Sanderson. Dram cup
38:117 Ap 18 '55
Sandgate, Vermont. Schwarz 16:
46 Ja 3 '44
Sandwich pressed glass bowl,
U.S. 39:58 Jy 18 '55
Sanford, Marian
Diana sculpture bw 10:120 Ap
21 '41
Sanger, Margaret
Margaret Sanger photog bw 28:
66 Ja 2 '50
Sangre de Cristo, Santo wood
carving bw 24:58 My 17 '48
Sans-Gene, Madame
Mme. Sans-Gene attacking
Austrians* bw 14:7 Ja 4 '43
Sansone, Leonard
The wolf, cartoons of U.S.
army life, World War II bw
17:6-8 Jy 31 '44
Sant' Angelo castle, Rome photog
bw 17:94 S 4 '44
Sant' Angelo in Formis frescoes,
11th century 17:62 Jy 24 '44
Santa Chiara, Naples frescoes,
14th and 18th centuries 17:
60-2 Jy 24 '44
Santa Fe, New Mexico, 1849 litho-
graph 40:49 Ja 16 '56
"Santa Maria" (ship)
Davis, G.H. Columbus' Santa
Maria 31:98-9 O 15 '51
Rogers. The watch on the
"Santa Maria" sculpture bw
6:8 Mr 6 '39
Santa Maria, full-size replica
photog bw 31:100 O 15 '51
Santa Maria della Salute. Guardi

35:152-3 N 16 '53
Santa Sophia, Istanbul, architec-
ture, dome, mosaics 29:
54-61 D 25 '50
Santa Sophia Greek Orthodox
cathedral, Los Angeles
photogs 33:54-5 N 3 '52
Santero Painting
Holy Trinity, altarpiece,
Mission San Jose, Laguna,
New Mexico photog 40:48-
9 Ja 16 '56
Santiano, Cesar
Man and his passions sculp-
ture bw, Buenos Aires 11:
147 O 13 '41
Santo Tomas church, Chichicas-
tenango, Guatemala photog
22:67 Je 30 '47
Santo Tomas University, Manila.
Millman 19:66 O 8 '45
Santos, wood carvings
Death bw 24:57 My 17 '48
Our Lady of Sorrows bw 24:
60 My 17 '48
Saint Acacius bw 24:58 My 17
'48
Sangre de Cristo bw 24:58 My
17 '48
Sanu-San-gen-do Temple, Kyoto
Kwannon statues bw 20:52-3
Je 17 '46
Sapajou
March of Time cartoon bw 28:
65 F 27 '50
Sarasvati, Hindu goddess statue
bw 24:29 Ap 5 '48
Saratoga Springs, New York
Grand Union Hotel: Lobby,
porches, ballroom bw 33:
43-4 S 29 '52
Sarcophagi
Egyptian sarcophagus 37:34
Ag 2 '54 bw 36:24-5 Je 21
'54
Sarcophagus--statue of
Merenptah, Egypt bw 24:
85 Ja 19 '48
Sardis, ruins photog bw 8:79 Ap
8 '40

Sargent, Epes
  Copley. Epes Sargent, 1762 bw
    9:74 D 9 '40
Sargent, John Singer
  Daughters of Edward Boit
    (Boit children) 36:96-7 My
    17 '54
  Duchess of Portland 23:81 N
    17 '47
  Duke of Portland (William
    Cavendish-Bentinck) 23:80
    N 17 '47
  Egyptian girl 36:97 My 17 '54
  Joseph Jefferson bw 6:31 Je
    19 '39
  Lady Sassoon (Aline de Roth-
    schild) 23:80 N 17 '47
  Lord Ribblesdale 23:81 N 17
    '47
  Madame X (Madame Gautreau)
    36:96 My 17 '54 bw 6:54 Mr
    20 '39
  Mrs. Henry White 27:59 Ag 29
    '49
  Mrs. Jack Gardner 41:161 D
    24 '56
  Mrs. Phipps and grandson 25:
    94 O 18 '48
  Mrs. Saint-Gaudens and son,
    1890 25:94 O 18 '48
  Princess Demidoff 7:36 Jy 31
    '39
  Robert Louis Stevenson 36:96
    My 17 '54
  Sir Ian Hamilton 23:80 N 17 '47
  Sir Thomas Devitt 23:81 N 17
    '47
  The Sitwell family bw 25:172
    D 6 '48
  The Wyndham sisters (The
    three graces) 5:37 O 31 '38;
    23:79 N 17 '47
  Self-portrait bw 36:92 My 17
    '54 port.
Sargon, Ruler of Akkad bronze
    head, 24th century B.C. 40:
    95 Je 4 '56
Saroyan, William
  William Saroyan, photog bw 9:
    96 N 18 '40; 31:34 Jy 16 '51
Sarto, Andrea del

  Lucrezia del Fede 29:109 S 11
    '50
  The Virgin and Child with St.
    John 41:72 D 10 '56
  Self-portrait, age 25 c1511
    bw 29:109 S 11 '50 port.
Sartre, Jean-Paul
  Jean-Paul Sartre photog bw
    20:59, 66 Je 17 '46
Sassetti, Francesco
  Ghirlandaio. Francesco Sas-
    setti and his son Teodoro
    2:43 Je 28 '37
Sassoon, Aline de Rothschild
  Sargent. Lady Sassoon 23:80
    N 17 '47
Satan See Devil
Satan, in The last judgment.
    fresco bw Michelangelo 24:
    78 F 2 '48
Satan, bookjacket. van Roemburg
    32:96 Ap 14 '52
Satan brooding, illustration for
    "Paradise Lost." bw Dore
    24:76 F 2 '48
Satire See Caricature and
    Satire
Saturday night. sculpture bw
    Wickey 12:53 F 23 '42
Saturday night in Harlem. cer-
    amics bw Wolford 9:129
    N 11 '40
Satyrs See Mythological
    Themes--Satyrs
Savage, Augusta, sculptor
  Artist and her work photog
    bw 5:55 O 3 '38 port.
Savage, Edward
  The Congress voting inde-
    pendence, c1784 (painting
    begun by Pine) 40:78-9 Ja
    9 '56 bw 29:52 Jy 3 '50
  George Washington head bw
    24:23 F 23 '48
  The Washington family 6:27
    Je 19 '39
Savage, Thomas, silversmith
  Salver, U.S. colonial 38:116-
    7 Ap 18 '55
Savannah. Dodd 27:64 S 26 '49
Savery, Roelandt

Dodo, sketch from life, 1599
bw 29:171 D 11 '50

Savitzki, K. A.
Army recruits, copy 14:45 Mr
29 '43

Savonarola, Girolamo
Savonarola bw 23:61 Ag 4 '47

Sawin and Dyer, clock makers
Lyre clock, Boston, 1815
photog 17:58 S 4 '44

Sawmill on the Sangamon river,
New Salem, Illinois.
Phillips, A. 36:79 F 15 '54

Sawyers, Martha
Indian Lascars -12 portraits
drawings 16:63-4 Ja 24 '44

Saxon, Lyle
Lyle Saxon photog bw 14:92-4
My 10 '43

The scalp. sculpture bw Reming-
gon 13:72 S 14 '42

Scarab bracelet, Egypt 24:81 Ja
19 '48

Scaravaglione, Concetta
Mother and child; father and
child lamp design bw 21:
104 N 18 '46

Scare Crow, illustrations from
"The Wonderful Wizard of
Oz." Denslow 35:53-9 D 28
'53

Scarseth, Lloyd
Milking time 10:78 Mr 31 '41
Artist at work photog bw 10:
76 Mr 31 '41 port.

Scene in a tavern. bw Hogarth
35:31 S 14 '53

Scene in Canne harbor. Churchill
20:46 Ja 7 '46

Scene in the Catskills. Church 19:
84 S 10 '45

Scenic grandeur of the west.
Miller, A. J. 27:46-7 Jy 4
'49

Sceptre, royal, England photog
2:39 Mr 15 '37

Scharl, Josef
Gethsemane bw 27:149 O 17 '49

Scharnhorst, Gerhard Johann
David von
von Scharnhorst bw 15:96 N 22
'43

Schary, Saul
Walkowitz bw 16:79 F 21 '44

Schenley mansion. Kane 2:46 My
17 '37

Schmidt-Rottluff, Karl
Artist and his work photog
36:145 My 10 '54 port.

Schmitt, Max
Eakins. Max Schmitt in a
single scull bw 5:33 O 31
'38; 16:72 My 15 '44

Schnakenberg, Henry
Marta 10:48 F 3 '41
Walkowitz bw 16:79 F 21 '44
Works of man 10:73 Ap 14 '41
Henry Schnakenberg. in
group photog 29:172-3 O
16 '50 port.

Schneider iron works, Le Cre-
usot, France, c1848* 25:
95 N 22 '48

Schneklud--Cellist. Gauguin 21:
62 Jy 29 '46

Schnier, Jacques
India sculpture bw 5:70 D 5
'38

Schnorr, Julius
Biblical characters and
scenes engravings bw 6:
55 Ja 30 '39; 6:53 F 20 '39

Schoeffer, Peter
Peter Schoeffer print bw 36:
85 Mr 1 '54

"Scholastic" sponsored 14th annual show of high school
painting and sculpture 10:
56-9 Je 16 '41

Schonbrunn palace, Vienna
photog bw 26:133 Mr 28 '49

School Architecture See Archi-
tecture--School

"School for Scandal," scene,
c1810. Dunlap 31:110-1 N
19 '51

A school in Moscow, 17th century 18:51 Ja 29 '45

School of San Rocco, Venice
Tintoretto. Life of Christ
31:30-49 D 24 '51

Schoolgirl. woodcarving bw Steig 6:35 Ap 10 '39
Schoolhouse quilt pattern 11:61 S 22 '41
Schools and School Rooms
 Homer. New England country school 6:30 Je 19 '39
 North-Taylor. Harrow School speech room, October, 1940 12:39 Mr 2 '42
 Puritan schoolroom, New England photog bw 13:85 N 23 '42
 Rosenthal, D. At the blackboard 15:66 N 22 '43
 Teachers discipline, U.S., 19th century* 31:71 Jy 2 '51
 University of Paris, schoolroom, Middle Ages bw 22:76 Ap 7 '47
 Winter school, Chine* woodcut bw 18:60 Ap 9 '45
 Wood, G. Arbor day 14:56 Ja 18 '43
Schreckengost, Viktor
 Samson and Delilah ceramics bw 9:129 N 11 '40
Schroeder, Leon, architect
 Whitewashed brick house photog bw 3:15 D 13 '37
Schurz, Carl
 Carl Schurz photog bw 25:100 N 22 '48
Schuster, Max Lincoln
 Max Lincoln Schuster photog bw 7:50 N 20 '39
Schuyler, Betsy
 Betsy Schuyler bw 23:66 Jy 7 '47
Schuyler, Philip
 Colonel Philip Schuyler bw 23:67 Jy 7 '47
Schuyler house photog bw 7:63 O 2 '39
Schwartz, Lester
 Aerial fantasy 32:70 Ja 14 '52
Schwartze, George Johann
 The Pilgrim fathers in public worship 13:77 N 23 '42 bw 24:68 Je 14 '48
Schwarz, Frank Henry
 On the Oregon trail mural bw 7:45 Ag 14 '39
Schwarz, William Tefft
 Sandgate, Vermont 16:46 Ja 3 '44
Schweiker, Paul, architect
 Schweiker and Elting. U.S. suburban house plan, photogs 22:78-81 Ap 28 '47
Schweitzer, Albert
 Albert Schweitzer photogs bw 27:74 Jy 25 '49
Schwerzmann, Wilhelm, ice sculptor
 Human and animal figures-- bear with nude, Buddha, fox, the three knaves bw 6:6 Ja 16 '39
Scientific Themes
 Buffano, R. Puppets showing advance of science bw 6:6-8 My 1 '39
 Calculating, Middle Ages bw 22:82 My 26 '47
 Dudley. Awaiting the reply (Atlantic cable) 6:30 Je 19 '39
 Kent. End of world theories bw 3:55-6 N 1 '37
 Palomar telescope 3:52 N 8 '37
 Peale, C.W. The exhumation of the mastodon 6:28 Je 19 '39
 Russian scientists photogs bw 17:Cover, 14-6 O 23 '44
 Stephens. Milky way; eclipse of sun 3:49-51 N 8 '37
 West. Benjamin Franklin and the lightning 40:81 Ja 9 '56 bw 6:26 Je 19 '39
Scone, Stone of See Stone of Scone
Scopes, John
 John Scopes, age 48 photog 28:54 Ja 2 '50
Scotland
 Clan tartans 22:103 My 5 '47
 The honors of Scotland: crown, sword, other photog bw 3:67 Jy 19 '37

Scotland's River Tay.* Thomas
31:80 O 29 '51; 17:61 O 9
'44

Scott, Harold Winfield, illustrator
Western magazine covers and
illustrations bw 12:67-8 Je
29 '42
Artist at work photog bw 12:
67 Je 29 '42 port.

Scott, Peter
Game birds 7:53-4 N 13 '39
Wild ducks 1:41-3 D 21 '36
Lighthouse bw 7:52 N 13 '39
(drawing)
Peter Scott photog bw 7:52, 55
N 13 '39 port.
Self-portrait bw 1:41 D 21 '36
port.

Scott, Winfield
General Winfield Scott bw 22:
110 Je 9 '47 photog bw 11:
99 N 10 '41; 14:6 My 31 '43
"Scottish Chiefs," illustrations.
Wyeth, N.C. 20:81 Je 17
'46
The Scottish highlands. Dore 7:
33 Jy 31 '39

Scottsboro Boys photogs bw 3:30-
1 Jy 19 '37

Screens See Furniture--Screens

The Scribe Hotel barroom. Davis,
F. 19:50-1 Jy 16 '45

Scrimshaw, whalebone carving,
U.S., 1860: corset-stay,
bodkin, pie crimpers, cane,
clothespin 39:109 O 17 '55

Scriptoria
Medieval manuscripts.* mural
panel Laning 9:65 S 30 '40
St. Jerome translating the
Scriptures, France, 15th
century 4:30 F 7 '38
Scriptorium, illumination 34:
83 F 23 '53

Scrolls
Isaiah scroll, manuscript bw
34:83 F 23 '53

Chinese
Buddha's journey through Hell,

prayer scroll, Nashi King-
dom, bw 8:30 Ja 8 '40
Chinese scrolls 31:72 S 3 '51
Lu Hung Nien. Flight into
Egypt; Joseph at inn gate*
bw 11:49 D 22 '41
Spring festival on the Yellow
River, Ch'ing Ming scroll,
c1500 31:44-9 D 31 '51

Japanese
Battle scroll, Japan 9:51 Jy
22 '40
Gukei. In and around Kyoto
31:66-7 D 31 '51
Jakuchu. Roosters 31:66 D
31 '51

Hebrew
Dead Sea scrolls photogs bw
34:95-6 Je 15 '53; 41:41 Jy
23 '56
Torah scrolls photog 29:160
S 11 '50

Scrubwoman. sculpture bw
Decker 5:5 N 28 '38
Scrubwoman. sculpture bw Ep-
ping 7:37 Jy 17 '39

Sculling See Games and Sports
--Rowing

Sculpture See also Bronzes;
Carving; Equestrians;
Memorials and Monuments;
Mobiles; Terra Cottas.
Also names of sculptures,
as Statue of Liberty; and
names of sculptors, as
Bertoia, A.; Brancusi, C.;
Calder; Davidson, J.; Ep-
stein, J.; Greenough, H.;
Gross, C.; Lachaise, G.;
Maillol, A.; Mestrovic,
I.; Michelangelo; Milles,
C.; Moore, H.; Rodin, A.;
Rogers, J.; Saint-Gaudens,
A.; Zorach, W.
African sculpture--masks,
fetishes, utensils bw 33:
116-25 S 8 '52
Balinese relief sculpture bw
3:51 S 27 '37

Sculpture (cont.)

Buenos Aires nude statues
censored bw 11:144-7 O
13 '41

Christ story, frieze, Notre
Dame, Paris bw 22:83 Ap
7 '47

Etruscan sculpture--terra
cottas, bronzes 40:58-65
F 13 '56

Jericho heads, oldest portraits
bw 34:119 My 11 '53

Kineglyph: sculpture for the
blind. bw Amendola 21:102
N 11 '46

Historical persons appear
"improved" by plastic surgeon. bw Sunshine 12:12-
3 Je 8 '42

Techniques of plaster sculpture. bw Zorach 24:75-9
My 31 '48

Exhibits

Metropolitan Museum of Art
sculpture exhibit, from
collection bw 6:52-3 Mr 20
'39

Philadelphia Museum of Art.
International sculpture exhibit bw 9:54-5 Ag 12 '40

Third international sculpture exhibit bw 26:112-4 Je
20 '49

Sculptors Guild, Brooklyn
Museum bw 5:4-7 N 7 '38

Sculpture, Battersea Park,
London: Fifty years of European sculpture 25:100-3 S
27 '48

Sculpture at the crossroads,
Art Museum, Worcester,
Mass. 24:95 Ap 12 '48

Sculpture, American

American Gothic garden figures cast iron 12:11 My 11
'42

California sculptors bw 9:79-
82 O 21 '40

"Duplicate Originals" of U.S.
sculpture bw 7:36-7 Jy 17

'39

Golden Gate International Ex-
position--Court of Pacific
sculpture bw 5:70-1 D 5
'38

Sacred cod, State House,
Boston, 1760 38:118 Ap 18
'55

Soldiers as artists--clay sculpture bw 14:56-8 Mr 1 '43

Speed and skill sculpture contest, Pennsylvania Aca-
demy of Fine Arts bw 2:
26-7 Ap 19 '37

"Yankee Stone Cutters,"
works of Powers, Green-
ough, others bw 19:8-10
S 24 '45

Sculpture, Chinese

Compassionate Buddha of the
future bw 9:50 Jy 22 '40

Crane, Peiping 20:74 Ap 29
'46

Dragon screen, Peiping 20:
74-5 Ap 29 '46

Guardian figures: warriors,
horses, camels, Ming
dynasty bw 3:57 Ag 23 '37

Lion of Peiping bronze bw 3:
55 Ag 23 '37

Lions, stone, Peiping 20:75
Ap 29 '46

Peiping sculpture: Buddha,
statues, architectural 20:
67-77 Ap 29 '46

Sculpture, Egyptian

Amen, gold statue 41:115 N
26 '56

Amenemhet III head bw 29:
107 N 27 '50

Horus, the hawk god, basalt
bw c350 B.C. 6:53 Mr 20
'39

Khufu, Pharoah of Egypt bw
36:22 Je 14 '54

Khafre, King of Egypt 41:108
N 26 '56

Mycernus and his queen bw
9:50 Jy 22 '40

Nofret, Princess of Egypt
c2500 B.C. 24:76 Ja19 '48

Osokon II, King of Egypt, kneeling statue bw 39:155 N 14 '55

Queen Hatshepsut black granite bw 9:93 D 9 '40

Rameses II, Pharoah of Egypt c1200 B.C. 40:55-6 Mr 19 '56

Statues and reliefs 24:74-85 Ja 19 '48; 41:78, 81 O 1 '56

Thut-Mose, Pharoah of Egypt 41:111 N 26 '56

Trial of tax delinquents, tomb relief 41:81 O 1 '56

Tutankhamen--annointing the king, relief 41:112-3 N 26 '56 portrait statues bw 24: 76 Ja 19 '48

Ubasti, cat goddess, 6th century B.C. bw 6:16 Ag 29 '38; 13:92 N 9 '42

Sculpture, Greek
Apollo Belvedere, 4th century B.C. bw 5:46 D 25 '38

Calf bearer, c450 B.C. bw 23: 22 Jy 7 '47

Demeter, Elgin marbles bw 35:137 O 26 '53

Elgin marbles bw 35:152-62 O 26 '53

Figure, copy after Praxitiles bw 41:102 O 22 '56

Heads, male bw 23:21 Jy 7 '47

Horse, c800 B.C. bw 6:52 Mr 20 '39

Horse, 5th century B.C. bw 6:52 Mr 20 '39

Laocoon bw 5:46 D 25 '38

Parthenon, frieze, inner wall bw 36:44 Ja 11 '54

Venus de Milo bw 19:48 Jy 30 '45; 35:51 Ag 17 '53

Victory of Samothrace, c306 B.C. bw 19:49 Jy 30 '45

Water carrier, 442 B.C. bw 23:22 Jy 7 '47

Zeus, bust bw 5:46 D 25 '38

Sculpture, Ice
Dartmough College, U.S. carnival sculptures bw 6:8 Ja 16 '39

Russian ice sculpture, Sokolini Park, Moscow bw 6:7-8 Ja 16 '39

Schwerzmann. Human and animal figures bw 6:6 Ja 16 '39

Sherbloom. Human and animal figures bw 22:96 My 12 '47

Sculpture, Indian (East Indian) See also Buddha and Buddhism

Indian sculpture bw 9:69-73 N 25 '40

Jain temple, Calcutta photog bw 12:86 Mr 16 '42

Shwe Dagon Pagoda, Rangoon photogs bw 26:64 My 9 '49; 38:88-9 Mr 7 '55

Shiva, aspects of the god, Elphanta Caves, Bombay photog 38:62 F 7 '55

Siva temple, South India photog bw 16:62 Ja 24 '44

Sri Sri Iswari Bhuba Neswari Thak Urani, Indian idol bw 2:57 My 10 '37

Sculpture, Japan See also Buddha and Buddhism

Goblin, 1215 34:95 Ap 20 '53

Hachiman, god of war, masked bw 17:28 N 27 '44

Japanese sculpture 31:58-69 D 31 '51

Japanese sculpture from 14 centuries 34:94-101 Ap 20 '53

Oyamakui-No-Mikoto, Japanese war god with bow and arrow bw 18:95 F 19 '45

National Museum, Tokyo, sculpture collection: tomb and guardian figures, masks, religious figures; monkey 30:70-4 My 28 '51

Yakushi, 8th century 34:95 Ap 20 '53

Sculpture, Mesoptoamian
Abu, Sumerian God, "Lord of Vegetation," and wife statue 40:89 Je 4 '56

Sculpture, Mesopotamian (cont.)
  Ashurnasirpal II, King of As-
    syria bas-relief bw Nimrud,
    Iraq 32:151 Ap 21 '52
  Ashurnasirpal winged lion,
    Mesopotamia, c850 B.C.
    bw 6:53 Mr 20 '39
  Assyrian bas-reliefs bw 32:
    151 Ap 21 '52
  Assyrian taxpayers frieze bw
    22:98 Mr 24 '47
  Dudu, the scribe, Sumerian,
    c2500 B.C. 40:88 Je 4 '56
  Head, female, limestone,
    c2600 B.C. 40:91 Je 4 '56
  High priest, Sumerian,
    marble bw 5:Cover Ag 15
    '38
  Hittite sphinx, Ankara bw 8:
    81 Ap 8 '40
  Lion hunt, Assyrian bas-re-
    lief bw 32:154 Ap 14 '52
  Sumerian sculpture--figures,
    vase bw 5:59 Ag 15 '38
Sculpture, Mountain See Mount
  Rushmore National Memorial
Sculpture, Pre-Columbian
  Idols, Tula, Mexico bw 22:
    101 F 24 '47
  Quetzalcoatl, feathered ser-
    pent, Toltec bw 28:62 Ja
    9 '50
  Mayan head, Palenque, Mexi-
    co, c650 bw 34:71 Ap 27 '53
  Mayan sculpture 22:51-67 Je
    30 '47
  Olmec head, Mexico, c50 B.C.,
    plaster cast bw 28:89 My
    29 '50
  Tlaloc bw 28:62 Ja 9 '50
Sculpture, Rock
  Aspects of the God Shiva,
    Elphanta Caves, Bombay
    38:62 F 7 '55
  Buddha, Inner Mongolia bw 7:
    50-1 Jy 10 '39
  Cave of Buddhas, Petchburi
    31:32-3 D 31 '51
  Darius the Great, cliff carv-
    ings bw 26:149 My 23 '49
  Foure. Rotheneufs family his-

    tory, Brittany coast bw 39:
    14-5 Jy 25 '55
  Reclining Buddha, Ajanta
    Caves, India 38:80 Mr 7 '55
  Vagis. Rock sculptures bw 40:
    123 Je 11 '56
Sculpture, Roman
  Mithras, head, 2nd century
    37:53 O 11 '54
  Pillage of the temple, Jerusa-
    lem, 70 A.D. relief bw
    38:99 Je 13 '55
  Roman emperors statues bw
    31:58 O 1 '51
  Rome's publicans bas-relief
    bw 22:98 Mr 24 '47
  Satyr holding Bacchus, c3rd
    century 28:76 Mr 27 '50
Sculpture, South Seas
  Balinese sculpture 3:51 S 27
    '37
  Easter Island stone heads bw
    21:80 N 4 '46; 24:126 F
    23 '48
  Religious figure 38:74 Ja 24
    '55
  South Seas art 21:76-83 N 4
    '46
Sculpture, Tibet
  Buddha statues, Hall of Gods,
    Kumbum bw 24:79 F 16
    '48
  The Golden Buddha, Gyàntze
    temple 6:26 Je 12 '39
Sea captains carousing in Suri-
  nam 1758. Greenwood 26:
  84-5 F 28 '49
Sea God, bronze relief, Etrus-
  can, c500 B.C. 40:59 F
  13 '56
Sea Gulls
  Hartley. Give us this day 32:
    87 Je 16 '52
  Thon. Sea gulls 16:78 Ap 24
    '44
Seabury, Samuel
  Blessing of Bishop Seabury, *
    1784 bw 3:34 O 18 '37
Seahorses See Animals,
  Imaginary--Sea Horses
Seal. sculpture bw Lauda 41:84

O 8 '56

Seals

Seal of Edward the Confessor
  bw 40:107 Mr 19 '56

Sumerian cylinder seal, lapis
  lazuli 40:85 Je 4 '56

The search. Callahan 35:86 S 28
  '53

Searle, Ronald

Big four meeting, Palais des
  Nations, Geneva drawing
  39:40-2 N 7 '55

Churchill in Commons drawing
  38:29 Ap 4 '55

Sears, William

Wing-e-es, toys based on
  Leonardo da Vinci design
  39:63 O 3 '55

Sears children, sculpture bw
  Greenough 37:41 O 25 '54

Seascape with figures. Rand 39:
  114 S 12 '55

Seascapes See also Harbors;
  Ships

Agnew. A day in port 23:98
  N 10 '47

Basile. Robinson Crusoe as a
  young man 1:44 N 30 '36

Binford. New York harbor 17:
  55-60 N 20 '44

Bouche. Long Island sound 8:
  68 My 27 '40

Brandt. Purse seiner 11:76 O
  27 '41

Brown, G. L. Castello Dell
  'Ovo 33:91 S 15 '52

Chamberlain. Golden Gate
  bridge 23:98 N10 '47

Churchill. Seascape* 20:50 Ja
  7 '46

Copley. Watson and the shark
  9:76 D 9 '40

De Martini. Lighthouse point
  23:69 Jy 14 '47

Delacroix. The storm on Galilee 39:23 D 26 '55

Etnier. Passing tow 23:68-9
  Jy 14 '47

Eurich. Invasion of North Africa* 29:90-1 N 6 '50

Eurich. Survivors from a

torpedoed ship 26:54-5 Mr
  21 '49

Feininger, Lux. The emerald
  coast 31:94-5 N 12 '51

Feininger, Lyonel. Glorious
  victory of the sloop, Maria 26:87 F 21 '49

Fischer. The North Atlantic
  14:75-6 F 8 '43

Grant. Kennebunkport, Maine,
  1825 mural bw 18:34 Ap 2
  '45

Gropper. Pearl Harbor 16:78
  Je 12 '44

Guardi. San Pietro de Castello, Venice 29:87 N 27
  '50

Harsanyi. Manana Island 29:
  73 Ag 21 '50

Hartley. Give us this day 32:
  87 Je 16 '52

Hartley. The wave 32:88 Je
  16 '52

Hecht. Summer sea 16:45 Ja
  3 '44

Hemy. Plymouth Hooker 23:
  84 N 17 '47

Homer. Driftwood 2:27 Ja 11
  '37

Homer. Eight bells 12:60 Je
  15 '42

Homer. The gulf stream 2:
  26 Ja 11 '37; 5:36 O 31 '38

Homer. Kissing the moon bw
  6:82-3 My 22 '39

Homer. Watching the breakers
  bw 6:58 Mr 27 '39

Hopper. Ground swell 8:66
  My 27 '40; 28:104-5 Ap 17
  '50

Jamieson. Embarkation port
  14:70-2 My 3 '43

Jamieson. Seascape 38:83 F
  28 '55

Kent. Below Black Head 29:
  71 Ag 21 '50

Lea. Placentia Bay, New-
  foundland 28:74 F 20 '50

Lea. Sinking of U.S.S. Wasp
  14:48-9 Ap 5 '43

Seascapes (cont.)

Lee, D. The overseas highway 22:72 My 12 '47

MacIver. Floating palaces 33: 94-5 S 15 '52

McIntyre. Disabled landing craft* 28:57 F 6 '50

Marin. Boat and sea 29:63 Jy 10 '50

"Marin-Marie." Battle at Oran* 26:50 Mr 7 '49

"Marin-Marie." British bombardment of Dakar* 26:50 Mr 7 '49

Martin, F. Home from the sea 9:91 N 11 '40

Mattson. Night and the sea 6: 44 My 1 '39

Mattson. 1942 16:78 Ap 24 '44

Nakamura. Off Malaya* 28:68-9 F 27 '50

O'Keefe. Cross by the sea 4: 30 F 14 '38

Peirce. God Rest You Merry, Gentlemen 23:56 D 22 '47

Poole. A critical moment 9: 50 O 28 '40

Renoir. Boating party at Chatou (Boatmen at Chatou) 3:46 Jy 5 '37; 32:93 My 19 '52

Ripley. Coots on the open sea 29:127 D 4 '50

Ryder. Night and clouds 13:96 N 9 '42

Ryder. Toilers of the sea bw 30:94-5 F 26 '51

Ryder. Under a cloud 30:88-9 F 26 '51

Sho Kler. Net menders 16:45 Ja 3 '44

Sloan. Wake of the ferry 7:45 D 11 '39

Spanish armada 41:80-1 O 29 '56

Storck. Four days fight in the Channel 41:82-3 O 29 '56

Stuempfig. White boat 25:100 S 20 '48

Thon. Convoy 20:97 Ap 29 '46

Thon. The outpost 20:97 Ap 29 '46

Thon. Sea gulls 16:78 Ap 24 '44

Turner. Cologne: The arrival of a packet boat 3:36 D 27 '37

Van Rosen. Rescue of the Maria Carlota bw 23:46 N 24 '47

Volpe. Embarkation of Henry VIII, Dover, 1520 41:78-9 O 29 '56

Waugh, F.J. Ante meridian bw 2:57 Je 14 '37; 3:24 D 20 '37

Waugh, F.J. The big water 2:57 Je 14 '37 bw 3:24 D 20 '37

Waugh, F.J. Meridian bw 3: 24 D 20 '37

Waugh, F.J. Pounding surf bw 5:57 N 28 '38

Waugh, F.J. Tropic seas bw 2:56 Je 14 '37; 3:24 D 20 '37

Whistler. Southampton waters 36:94-5 My 17 '54

Whitcombe. Siege of Gibralter 24:67 My 10 '48

Wilkinson. British convoy under German attack* 26:53 Mr 7 '49

Wilkinson. Graf Spee defeat 24:68 My 10 '48

Seasons See also names of seasons: Autumn; Spring; Summer; Winter

"Book of Hours" of the Duc de Berry, calendar pages 24: 38-50 Ja 5 '48

Corcos. Artist's home, summertime 37:91 Jy 12 '54

Corcos. Artist's home, wintertime 37:90 Jy 12 '54

Judson. Winter; Spring; Summer; Autumn sculpture bw 10:118-9 Ap 21 '41

Seated figure. Davis, G.R. 14: 46 Ap 19 '43; 21:75 N 25 '46

Seated figure. bw Eilshemius

7:51 N 6 '39

Seated Kuan Yin, Yuan dynasty,
13th century 15:65 O 11 '43

Seated man.* collage Marca-Relli
39:112 S 12 '55

Seated nude. Kroll 24:68 Je 28 '48

Seated nude. bw Shimada 28:104
Ja 23 '50

Seated woman. Bores 17:76 N 13
'44

Seated woman. woodcarving bw
Steig 6:35 Ap 10 '39

Sebastian, Saint
Antonello da Messina. Saint
Sebastian bw 40:104 F 20
'56
Botticelli. Saint Sebastian bw
19:24 D 31 '45
Grunewald. St. Sebastian 30:
77 Mr 26 '51

Second and High Streets, Philadelphia, c1800* 39:61 Jy 4
'55

Secord, Laura
Laura Secord, warns the
British, 1813 bw 9:114 S 9
'40

Secota, Indian village. watercolor, c1585 White, J. 22:
83 Mr 10 '47

Secretariat Building, United Nations See United Nations

Secretaries See Furniture--
Secretaries

Sedlacek, Franz
Coming home at night bw 2:58
Ap 26 '37
End of the world* bw 2:57 Ap
26 '37
Ghost over the trees bw 2:57
Ap 26 '37
Song at twilight bw 2:58 Ap 26
'37
The wax figures cabinet bw 2:
58 Ap 26 '37
Franz Sedlacek photog bw 2:57
Ap 26 '37 port.

Sedwick, Margaret, interior designer
Southwest style house 38:114-
5 F 21 '55

The seed of Areois. Gaugin 21:
63 Jy 29 '46

Seeking work. Weber 19:85 Ag
20 '45

Segy, Ladislas
Walkowitz bw 16:77 F 21 '44

Sekiguchi War Prints
Japanese conquest of China,
Sino-Japanese War, 1894-
5 3:25-32 D 6 '37

Self-Portraits
Albright, I. bw 16:64 Mr 27
'44
Albright, M. bw 16:64 Mr 27
'44
Andre. drawing bw 29:54 Jy
3 '50
Audubon. 9:115 O 21 '40 bw
30:46 Ja 29 '51
Beerbohm. caricature bw 33:
125 S 22 '52
Bingham. bw 7:40 S 11 '39
Blake. bw 36:66 Ap 19 '54
Bohrod. bw 15:12 O 25 '43
Bosch. bw 27:75 N 14 '49
Buffet. bw 38:80 Mr 21 '55
Cadmus. bw 15:13 O 25 '43
Caniff. cartoon bw 15:14 O
25 '43
Cassatt. 41:162 D 24 '56 bw
36:92 My 17 '54; 1878 12:
54 Ja 19 '42
Cezanne. bw 32:77 F 25 '52
Portrait of the artist be-
fore his easel, c1885 2:45
Ap 12 '37
Chagall. Double portrait (The
artist and his wife) 22:59
My 5 '47
Chardin. bw 5:34 S 26 '38
Clear. Group of myselves,
self-portrait at six differ-
ent ages lithograph bw 24:
79-82 Ja 26 '48
Colette. drawing bw 37:83 Ag
16 '54
Cosgrave. bw 24:20 Ja 19 '48
Courbet. Self-portraits (3)
in 3 paintings bw 26:60 My
30 '49 in The studio 26:62-
3 My 30 '49

Cox. 25:86 Jy 12 '48

Curry. bw 15:12 O 25 '43

Davidson. sculpture bw 32:34
Ja 14 '52

Delacroix. in Liberty leading
the people 25:84 N 22 '48

Durer. age 26 31:68 O 1 '51

Eichenberg. wood engraving
bw 15:4 D 20 '43

El Greco, attributed. age 68,
bw 28:86 Ap 24 '50

Escher. drawing bw 30:19 My
7 '51

Evergood. bw 15:13 O 25 '43

Feininger, Lyonel. bw 15:12
O 25 '43

Fulton. 39:67 Jy 18 '55

Gauguin. age 43, 13:51 S 14
'42; age 45 bw 29:112 S 11
'50

Giorgione. copy, 39:165 O 24
'55

Goya. age 69, 1815 bw 29:106
S 11 '50

Grunewald. drawing bw 30:74
Mr 26 '51 as St. Paul, in
Eisenheimer altarpiece 30:
80 Mr 26 '51

Guareschi. cartoon 36:59 Je
14 '54

Hals. bw 5:30 Ag 29 '38

Healy. in Arch of Titus 33:89
S 15 '52

Hickson. in Song in the night
30:36 Ja 15 '51

Hogarth. Artist at work bw 21:
77 D 16 '46 in Calais Gate
21:81 D 16 '46

Hogue. bw 2:61 Je 21 '37

Holbein. 1542 5:40 Jy 11 '38

Ingres. bw 34:86 My 11 '53;
age 85 bw 10:72 Ap 28 '41

James, A. bw 30:149 My 21
'51

James, William. 1867 bw 30:
149 My 21 '51

Kane. 2:45 My 17 '37

Ket. 38:40 Ja 10 '55

Kraus. bw 16:12 Ja 31 '44

Kroll. 24:67 Je 28 '48

Leighton, F. bw 35:162 O 26

'53

Lippi, Fra Filippo. age 35,
1441 bw 29:109 S 11 '50

McCrady. 3:40 O 18 '37

Marsh. 40:81 F 6 '56

Martin, F. bw 15:12 O 25 '43

Mason. caricature bw 22:34
Ja 6 '47

Matisse. age 37 31:115 N 26
'51

Mattson. 1923 bw 15:13 O 25
'43

Mendes-France, Lily. 37:85
Jy 19 '54

Modigliani. age 35, 1919 bw
29:112 S 11 '50

Morse, S.F.B. age 23 12:59
Je 15 '42

Peale, C.W. age 81 38:69 Mr
28 '55 bw 6:26 Je 19 '39;
12:64 Mr 20 '42

Peale, Rembrandt. bw 12:64
Mr 30 '42

Peirce. The artist painting
his family bw 19:82 N 12
'45

Philipp, R. My wife and I 8:
64 Ap 8 '40

Phillips, A. age 34 36:79 F
15 '54

Pittman. Summer evening 18:
70 F 19 '45

Poor. in Gold case mural 2:
36 Ja 4 '37

Pratt. The American school
bw 6:31 Je 19 '39

Rembrandt. age 24 28:59 Ja
30 '50; 1660 1:29 N 30 '36
bw 5:30 Ag 29 '38; 26:160
Ap 11 '49

Renoir. 1910 32:99 My 19 '52

Rivera. in History of Mexi-
co mural bw, Del Prado
Hotel, Mexico City 23:105
N 3 '47

Rousseau, H. age 46, 1890
bw 29:110 S 11 '50

Rubens. The artist and his
first wife, Isabella Brant
7:56 N 20 '39

Ryder. 30:86 F 26 '51

Sargent. bw 36:92 My 17 '54

Sarto. age 25, c1511 bw 29: 109 S 11 '50

Scott, P. bw 1:41 D 21 '36

Seurat. bw 31:64 Jy 23 '51

Shahn. as a child, in German band 37:97 O 4 '54 in Bronx church 37:97 O 4 '54

Smith, T. 1680 bw 6:26 Je 19 '39

Soyer, R. 33:99 O 27 '52

Steen. bw 5:30 Ag 29 '38 in Worship of the golden calf 41:74 D 10 '53

Steichen. photog bw 6:27 Ja 9 '39 age 19, photog bw 28: 117 My 15 '50

Steinberg. drawing bw 31:50 Ag 27 '51

Taylor, R. cartoon bw 15:14 O 25 '43

Thurber. cartoon bw 15:14 O 25 '43

Toulouse-Lautrec. drawing bw 28:96 My 15 '50

Turner, B. bw 29:12-4 Jy 10 '50

Valadon. in Family portrait, 1912 28:91 Ja 16 '50

Van Eyck brothers. in Last judgment bw 26:58 Ap 18 '49

Van Gogh. 33:94 O 27 '52 bw 2:32 F 15 '37; 27:26 D 19 '49 Study by candlelight bw 27: 27 D 19 '49; 29:17 O 9 '50

Velazquez. in The maids of honor 31:61 O 1 '51

Vermeer. The artist in his studio 27:71 O 24 '49 bw 5: 30 Ag 29 '38; 16:63 Ja 10 '44

Vigeland. sculpture bw 25:21 O 25 '48

Vuillard. 37:74 N 1 '54

Whistler. bw 36:92 My 17 '54 Whistler in his studio 36: 93 My 17 '54

Williams, G. cartoon bw 15: 14 O 25 '43

Wyeth, A. 35:83 Jy 27 '53

Zoffany. in The Tribuna 25: 104-5 S 13 '48

Self-portraits of contemporary painters, illustrators, cartoonists, de Young Museum, San Francisco 15:12-4 O 25 '43 (exhibit)

Sellers waiting. Rivera 4:29 Mr 14 '38

Sellitti, Tony Afternoon shift 10:58 Je 16 '41

The Senate. Gropper 2:24 F 1 '37

Senate Rooms, U.S. Capitol Brumidi. Ceiling and corridor paintings 31:56 Jy 2 '51 Senate chamber, lounges, offices photogs 31:54-5 Jy 2 '51 bw 2:22 Je 14 '37

Seneca, Lucius Annaeus Seneca sculpture, Ulm cathedral, Germany 35:30 D 28 '53

Sen-Mut, architect Temple of Queen Hat-Shepsut photog 41:110-1 N 26 '56

Sentimental ideas. bw Brook 8:69 My 27 '40

Sentimental letter. ceramics bw Boru 9:130 N 11 '40

Sentimental moment. Guston 20: 91 My 27 '46

The sentinel. Remington 13:74 S 14 '42

Seong Moy Girl juggling woodcut 37:88 O 18 '54

Sepeshy, Zoltan End of day 20:80 F 18 '46 New England siesta 8:66 My 27 '40

September morn. bw Chabas 2: 53 My 24 '37; 21:90 D 23 '46; 29:96 N 27 '50

Septre, Royal, England 2:39 Mr 15 '37

"Serapis" (ship) Bonhomme Richard and Serapis 29:55 Jy 3 '50

Serfs traded for hounds bw 14: 95 Mr 29 '43

Sergei, Patriarch
  Patriarch Sergei, "Time"
    cover portrait 17:64 D 11
    '44
Serkin, Rudolf
  Halsman. Rudolf Serkin pho-
    tog bw 16:49 Mr 13 '44
Serra, Junipero
  Father Junipero Serra statue
    bw, Golden Gate Park, San
    Francisco 15:71 Jy 12 '43
  Father Serra statue bw 3:28
    S 20 '37
Service club, World War. Martin,
  F 11:62 Jy 7 '41
Sessions, Roger
  Roger Sessions, composer
    photog bw 40:145 My 21 '56
Seton, Mother
  Mother Seton bw 27:150 S 19
    '49
Setting the table. Taubes 6:29 F
  13 '39
Seurat, Georges
  Jeune femme se poudrant
    (Madeleine Knobloch) bw 31:
    64 Jy 23 '51
  A Sunday afternoon on the Is-
    land of La Grande-Jatte 31:
    60-2 Jy 23 '51
  Georges Seurat photog bw 31:
    63 Jy 23 '51 port
  Self-portrait bw 31:64 Jy 23
    '51 port.
Seven A. M. Hopper 28:101 Ap
  17 '50
Seven bishops imprisoned by
  James II England* bw 41:
  180 N 19 '56
The seven lively arts. bw Dali
  18:4-6 Ja 1 '45
Seventh and Canal. Hattorf 10:
  68 My 26 '41
Severin, Kurt
  Kurt Severin photog bw 22:21
    Mr 10 '47
Sevres Porcelain
  Ice bucket, 18th century photog
    bw 5:39 S 26 '38
Seward, Anna
  Anna Seward engraving bw 35:

91 S 28 '53
Seward, William Henry
  William Henry Seward 19:87 S
    24 '45 photog bw 9:115 S 9
    '40; 14:75 F 15 '43
Sewell, Samuel
  Samuel Sewell bw 13:74 N 23
    '42
Seymour, Jane
  Jane Seymour bw 41:88 O 29
    '56
Seymour, Thomas, furniture de-
  signer
  Elliptical commode, Boston,
    c1880 photog 38:66-7 My
    30 '55
  Tambour secretary, "Amer-
    ican Hepplewhite," Bos-
    ton, 18th century 38:67 My
    30 '55
Sforza, Francesco
  Francesco Sforza bw 26:160
    Ap 11 '49
Sgraffito jug, U.S., 1781 photog
  39:57 Jy 18 '55
Shad fishing at Gloucester, New
  Jersey. Eakins 16:73 My
  15 '44
The shady grove. Fragonard 5:
  35 S 26 '38
Shahn, Ben
  Acrobats 37:100 O 4 '54
  Bronx church, including self-
    portrait 37:97 O 4 '54
  Facade, patchwork of colors,
    1953 37:99 O 4 '54
  German Band 37:97 O 4 '54
  Handball 37:98-9 O 4 '54
  Landscape, Ohio, 1945 37:
    98 O 4 '54
  The passion of Sacco and
    Vanzetti, one painting
    from series of 23 bw 37:96
    O 4 '54
  Spring idyl 37:99 O 4 '54
  Artist and his work photog
    bw 37:96 O 4 '54 port.
  Ben Shahn. in group photog
    29:172-3 O 16 '50 bw 32:
    87 Mr 17 '52 port.
  Self-portrait, in Bronx

church 37:97 O 4 '54 as a
child, in German band 37:
97 O 4 '54

Shaker buildings. Sheeler 5:43 Ag
8 '38

Shaker ceremony, New York,
1873 bw 26:143 Mr 21 '49

Shaker furniture 39:102 O 17 '55

Shakespeare, William
William Shakespeare, portrait
from First Folio, 1623 bw
40:63 Ja 16 '56

Shakespearean Themes See Literary Themes

Shanksville, Crist 16:45 Ja 3 '44

"Shannon" (ship) English, 1812
Shannon capturing the Chesapeake 24:67 My 10 '48

Shanties, Rio de Janeiro. Maeck
36:84 My 31 '54

Shapero, Harold
Harold Shapero photog bw 40:
147 My 21 '56

Sharks
Copley. Watson and the shark
9:76 D 9 '40

Sharon, Mary Bruce
Afternoon refreshments 33:76
Jy 21 '52
Family reunion 33:76 Jy 21
'52
May-day party 33:75 Jy 21 '52
Playroom 33:75 Jy 21 '52
Artist at work photog bw 33:
74 Jy 21 '52 port.

Sharp, John
Spring night 16:45 Ja 3 '44

Sharples, James
George Washington bw 24:22
F 23 '48

Sharrer, Honore
Man at fountain 28:88 Mr 20
'50
Tribute to the working man
31:12 D 17 '51
Artist at work photog bw 31:
12 D 17 '51 port.

Shaw, George Bernard
"Bernard Shaw's Rhyming Pic-
ture Guide to Ayot Saint
Lawrence," photogs bw 30:

20-1 My 14 '51

Beerbohm. Shaw as the Devil
caricature bw 23:89 N 17
'47 port.

Elwell. Shaw as St. Peter, in
I dreamt St. Peter sat for
his portrait bw 22:40 My
19 '47 port.

Flagg. G. B. Shaw drawing
bw 41:104B Ag 6 '56 port.

George Bernard Shaw photog
bw 33:65 O 6 '52; age 82,
5:30 D 12 '38; age 90, 21:
41 Jy 29 '46 port.

George Bernard Shaw--por-
traits, family, associates
from "Bernard Shaw
Through the Camera" 25:
71-2 N 15 '48 port.

Karsh. George Bernard Shaw
bw 16:Cover F 7 '44; 22:
40 My 19 '47; 41:104A Ag
6 '56 port.

Maurice Evans and Shaw dis-
cuss "Superman" photog
bw 23:115 O 27 '47 port.

Shaw before gift statue of St.
Joan photog bw 23:41 Ag
4 '47 port.

Shaw with Helen Keller photog
bw 4:20 F 28 '38 port.

Shor. Shaw sculptured head
bw 41:104B Ag 6 '56

Steichen. G.B.Shaw, 1907
photog bw 28:119 My 15
'50

Troubetskoy. G.B.Shaw
sculptured head bw 41:104B
Ag 6 '56

Shaw, Ruth Faison
Rabbit and carrots, finger-
painting bw 11:41 Jy 28 '41
Mexican scene, fingerpaint-
ing bw 11:39 Jy 28 '41
Artist at work photogs bw 11:
39-41 Jy 28 '41 port.

Shaw, Naess & Murphy, architects
Three-bedroom house photog,
plan bw 9:89-90 Jy 1 '40

"She," illustrations bw 15:8 D 27
'43
She saw him fall. Rey 2:35 F 22
'37
Shearing the rams. bw Roberts
12:79 F 9 '42
Sheba, Queen of
Piero della Francesca. Solo-
mon receiving the Queen of
Sheba fresco detail 20:63
Ap 22 '46
Piero della Francesca. Story
of the true cross fresco
20:60-8 Ap 22 '46
Piero della Francesca. Visit
of the Queen of Sheba to
Solomon fresco detail 20:
62 Ap 22 '46
The Virgil Master. Journey of
the Queen of Sheba 35:150-
1 N 16 '53
Sheehan, John, furniture designer
Windsor chair photog bw 35:18
D 14 '53
Sheeler, Charles
City interior 5:43 Ag 8 '38
Kitchen, Williamsburg 5:44 Ag
8 '38
Shaker buildings 5:43 Ag 8 '38
Staircase, Doylestown 5:44 Ag
8 '38
Upper deck 5:44 Ag 8 '38
Meta-mold aluminum portraits
bw 34:154 My 18 '53 (sculp-
ture)
Artist at work photogs bw 5:
42 Ag 8 '38 port.
Charles Sheeler. in group
photog 32:87 Mr 17 '52 port.
Sheep
El Greco. The Virgin with
Santa Ines and Santa Tecla
7:26 D 25 '39
Ford. St. Germaine 17:37 D
25 '44
Lu Hung Nien. An angel sum-
mons the shepherds 11:43 D
22 '41
Roberts. Shearing the rams bw
12:79 F 9 '42
Sheets, Millard

Famine scenes, India 18:60-
1 Ap 30 '45
Hindu woman bw 20:80 Ja 21
'46
Poultryman, India 20:82 Jy 21
'46
A procession of women, India
20:83 Ja 21 '46
Reaping winter wheat, India
20:81 Ja 21 '46
Returning from work, India
20:81 Ja 21 '46
Village carpenter, India 20:
82 Ja 21 '46
Water carrier, India 20:82 Ja
21 '46
Water for irrigation, India*
bw 20:80 Ja 21 '46
Sheldon, Mrs. J.B.
Mrs. J.B. Sheldon, American
primitive, 1825 bw 36:95
Je 28 '54
Shell factory. Sample 11:63 Jy 7
'41 bw 14:7 Je 28 '43
Shells, fruit and insects. bw
Van der Ast 7:24 Ag 28 '39
Shelter for the homeless, 1873,
from "Harper's Weekly"
bw 16:54 F 14 '44
Shepard, Ernest Howard
Blessings of peace cartoon bw
24:60 Ap 26 '48
"Wind in the Willows," illus-
trations. drawings bw 27:
69 N 21 '49
"Winnie-the-Pooh," and other
Milne books, illustrations
bw 30:75-6 F 19 '51; 40:
117-22 F 27 '56
Shepheard's Hotel, Cairo
photogs bw 13:118-22 D 14
'42
Shepherd's Kalendar, London,
1631 bw 18:43 Ja 1 '45
Shepler, Dwight
World War in Guadalcanal
15:50-3 D 27 '43
Dwight Shepler photog bw 15:
84 D 27 '43 port.
Sheraton, Thomas, furniture
maker

Chairs, desk, sideboard,
   table photog bw 23:78 Ag
   25 '47
Sherbloom, Tom, ice sculptor
   Human and animal figures bw
   22:96 My 12 '47
   Artist at work photog bw 22:
   94-5 My 12 '47 port.
Sheridan, Philip Henry
   General Sheridan photog bw
   14:76 F 15 '43
Sheridan and Mack, dancers,
   1865 photog bw 11:74 Ag
   25 '41
The Sheridan Theater. Hopper
   2:46 My 3 '37
Sherman, James S.
   James S. Sherman photog bw
   9:9 Ag 5 '40
Sherman, Roger
   Earl. Roger Sherman 38:64
   My 30 '55
   Roger Sherman 39:63 Jy 4 '55
   bw 6:31 Je 19 '39; 15:9 Jy
   5 '43
Sherman, William Tecumseh
   Saint-Gaudens. General Sher-
   man, equestrian statue,
   with angel of Victory, New
   York City bw 24:109 Mr 15
   '48
   William Tecumseh Sherman
   photog bw 14:76 F 14 '43
Sherwood, Robert Emmet
   Robert E. Sherwood photog bw
   9:98 O 7 '40; 13:39 Jy 27
   '42
Shields See Armor
Shields, Emma Gordon
   Morse. Miss Emma Gordon
   Shields 17:60 D 18 '44
Shields of Arms See Heraldry
Shilow, Palestine photog 20:56
   Ap 1 '46
Shimada, Haruo
   Seated nude bw 28:104 Ja 23
   '50
   Artist at work photog bw 28:
   104 Ja 23 '50 port.
Shinn, Everett
   Plaza Hotel, c1910 mural 21:

88 N 18 '46
Shintoism
   Empress, 10th century sculpture 30:72 My 28 '51
   Sacred foxes sculpture bw 31:
   58 D 31 '51
Ship Burial
   Sutton Hoo treasure: arms
   and armor, jewelry, drinking horn, 7th century 31:
   82-5 Jy 16 '51
Ships See also Seascapes; U.S.
   Navy; and names of specific ships and naval en-
   gagements, as "Constitution," Spanish Armada De-
   feat
   "American Turtle," first
   U.S. submarine drawing
   bw 22:82 Ja 13 '47
   Buddhist boat for the Gods
   38:Cover, 66 Ap 4 '55
   Cambodian pirogues photogs
   bw 2:49 Mr 8 '37
   Fiene. Hudson River navigation boat 12:76 Ap 20 '42
   Hemy. Plymouth hooker 23:
   84 N 17 '47
   Houseboat, Kashmir Lake
   photog bw 10:90 My 12 '41
   Junk, Chinese photog bw 24:
   102 Je 21 '48
   Keelboat, U.S. frontier
   photog 39:80 N 28 '55
   Kingman. Junk sailing under
   Brooklyn bridge* bw 30:
   100 My 14 '51
   Lee, D. Hudson River excur-
   sion 3:46 S 20 '37
   Memling. Shrine of St. Ur-
   sala, details 34:82-5 Ap
   6 '53
   Perry's flagship, 1853, Japa-
   nese artist bw 19:56 S 17
   '45
   Philadelphia East Indiaman,
   Delaware, c1790* 38:68
   My 30 '55
   Pleissner. Ore boats, Soo
   Locks, Michigan 25:65
   Ag 23 '48

Ships (cont.)
  Portuguese sardine bark
    photog 26:66-8 Je 13 '49
  Rembrandt. Storm on the Sea
    of Galilee 1:31 N 30 '36
  Royal bergan of navigator
    kings of Portugal, c1500
    photog bw 23:26-7 Ag 11 '47
  The Russian fleet visits New
    York, 1863 bw 19:88 Ag 27
    '45
  Ryder. Under a cloud 30:88-9
    F 26 '51
  Solar funary bark of Pharoah
    Khufu, Egypt, c2600 B.C.
    photog 36:20-2 Je 14 '54
  Sterne. Warship 31:54 Ag 27
    '51
  Stuempfig. White boat 25:100
    S 20 '48
  Turner. Cologne: The arrival
    of a packet boat 3:36 D 27
    '37
  Viking boat in Russian paint-
    ing 18:45 Ja 29 '45
  Viking ship photog bw 40:94
    Mr 19 '56
  Volpe. Embarkation of Henry
    VIII, Dover, 1520* 41:78-9
    O 29 '56

      Canoes
Bingham. Fur traders descending the Missouri 28:76-7 Mr
  6 '50
Covarrubias. Balinese fishermen 3:48 S 27 '37
Micronesian canoe wood carving bw 21:79 N 4 '46
Outrigger canoe, Carolines
  photog 26:103 Ap 25 '49
White, J. Indians fishing*
  watercolor, c1585 22:81 Mr
  10 '47

      Ferry Boats
Bouche. Ten cents a ride 14:
  45 Mr 8 '43
Sloan. Wake of the ferry 7:45
  D 11 '39

      Flatboats
Currier and Ives print. Low
  water on the Mississippi
  9:33 D 30 '40
Phillips, A. Flatboat, in
  Rutledge mill 36:80-1 F
  15 '54

      Sailboats
Feininger, Lyonel. Yachts
  31:95 N 12 '51
Hopper. Ground swell 28:104-
  5 Ap 17 '50
Sailboat, model, Neolithic
  pottery 40:81 Ap 16 '50
Sailboats, tomb painting,
  Egypt, c2500 B.C. 24:77
  Ja 19 '48

      Steamboats
Bouche. The Eads Bridge
  over the Mississippi 11:50
  Ag 18 '41
Bunn. Mississippi steam-
  boats 9:71-2 O 14 '40
Clermont, Robert Fulton's
  steamboat 39:67 Jy 18 '55
Currier and Ives print.
  Loading cotton by moon-
  light 21:71 S 2 '46
Currier and Ives print. Low
  water on the Mississippi
  9:33 D 30 '40
Currier and Ives print. A
  night on the Hudson:
  Through at daylight 9:34
  D 30 '40
Daugherty. Steamboat around
  the bend mural 3:50 O 25
  '37
"Mississippi," river steam-
  boat, 1882 photog 39:80
  N 28 '55
Mississippi steamboat photog
  bw 16:95 My 8 '44
Steamboat rounding Indian
  mounds near Natchez, *
  1850 39:81 N 28 '55
Ships of the plains. Colman 39:
  74 N 28 '55
The shipwreck. Zorthian 8:46

F 12 '40
Shipwreck of St. Paul. bw Dore
    39:37 D 26 '55
Shiva
    Aspects of the god Shiva,
        Elphanta Caves, Bombay
        sculpture 38:62 F 7 '55
    Temple of Shiva, South India
        38:65-6 F 7 '55
    Tower, with statues of Siva,
        Madras 27:98-9 S 12 '49
Shivaree, 1872 32:115 Ap 7 '52
Shmarinov, Dimenti
    Nazi war atrocities in Russia
        drawings bw 14:57-62 Je
        14 '43
Shmoo. cartoon bw Capp 25:46
    S 20 '48
Shofar photog bw 3:32 S 20 '37
Shokler, Harry
    Net menders 16:45 Ja 3 '44
Shooting See Games and Sports--
    Shooting; Hunters and Hunting
The shooting gallery. Miller, B.
    .5:30 O 31 '38
The shooting of Huey Long. Mc-
    Crady 6:49 Je 26 '39 bw
    21:121 D 9 '46
Shopping Center
    Gruen and Associates. North-
        land, Detroit, Michigan
        photogs 37:81-3 Ag 30 '54
Shops and Markets
    Bellotto. Dresden market 40:
        104 My 7 '56
    Blythe. The Pittsburgh horse
        market 9:76 D 9 '40
    Bohrod. Reflections on a shop
        window 14:44 Mr 8 '43
    Brughel, P., the elder. Al-
        chemist's shop drawing bw
        22:84 Ap 7 '47
    Hopper. Drug store 28:103 Ap
        17 '50
    Lasker. El candy store 28:84
        Mr 20 '50
    Lee, D. Market in Tunis 33:
        112 N 10 '52
    Lee, D. Thieves market, Mex-
        ico City 22:77 My 12 '47
    Lockwood. Corner grocery,

    Taos 6:30 F 13 '39
    Mrs. McCormick's general
        store, Catskill, New York
        6:28 Je 19 '39
    Old Feather store, Boston,
        1820-5 13:81 N 23 '42
    Pearlstein. Wylie Avenue
        barber shop 10:57 Je 16
        '41
    Phillips, A. General store,
        New Salem, Illinois 36:81
        F 15 '54
    Rosenthal, D. By the sea 15:
        68 N 22 '43
    Sample. Barber shop 3:43 N
        15 '37
    Sloan. Hairdresser's window
        27:61 Ag 29 '49
    Wood, T. New England coun-
        try store 6:30 Je 19 '39
Shor, Hal, sculptor
    George Bernard Shaw head
        bw 41:104B Ag 6 '56
    Har Shor photog bw 41:104B
        Ag 6 '56 port.
Shore scene. Ryder 30:90 F 26
    '51
Shostakovich, Dmitri
    Dmitri Shostakovich; home;
        family photogs bw 15:43-
        6 N 22 '43
    Dmitri Shostakovich, "Time"
        cover portrait 17:65 D 11
        '44
Show boat. Lee, D. 7:48-9 N 27
    '39
Shreve, Lamb, and Harmon,
    architects
    Modern conservative house
        plan, photog bw 9:88-9 Jy
        1 '40
The shrimp girl. Hogarth 21:79
    D 16 '46
Shrine of St. Ursala. Memling
    34:81-6 Ap 6 '53
Shrines See also Temples
    The golden tower, Buddhist
        shrine, Tibet photog 6:
        26 Je 12 '39
    Home shrine, Goering home,
        Germany photog bw 11:28

Shrines (cont.)
N 10 '41
Roadside shrine, Quebec
photog bw 9:106 S 9 '40
Street shrine, Leningrad
photog bw 2:54 My 3 '37
Shulman, Julius, photographer
Photographs of houses to show
architecture, site bw 26:
146-8 Ap 11 '49
Shwe Dagon pagoda, Rangoon
photog 26:64-5 My 9 '49;
38:88-9 Mr 7 '55
Sibelius, Jean
Jean Sibelius photog bw 7:75
O 30 '39
Karsh. Jean Sibelius, age 84
photog bw 29:78 Ag 7 '50
Sibyls
Michelangelo. The Delphic
sybil fresco detail 21:65
Jy 1 '46
Sicily
Jamieson. Sicily invasion--
World War 15:78-9 D 27
'43
Sickles, Noel
"The Bridges of Toko-Ri," il-
lustrations 35:58 Jy 6 '53
Siddons, Sarah
Reynolds. Sarah Siddons as
the tragic muse 4:24 Ja 24
'38
Sideboard with candelholder,
Sheraton furniture photog
23:78 Ag 25 '47
Sidney, Sylvia
Martin, F. Sylvia Sidney 19:
61 S 10 '45
Sidney in 1809. bw Eyre 12:78 F
9 '42
Siege of Gibralter. Whitcombe
24:67 My 10 '48
Siegel, Arthur, photographer
Modern art in color photo-
graphs 29:78-84 N 20 '50
Arthur Siegel photog bw 29:
78 N 20 '50 port.
Siegfried, Andre
Karsh. Andre Siegfried photog
bw 37:130 O 4 '54

Siegfried and the Rhine maidens.
Ryder 30:87 F 26 '51
Siena cathedral, Italy photog bw
22:82-3 Mr 3 '47
Sienkiewicz, Henryk
Henryk Sienkiewicz bw 17:90
Ag 28 '44
Sierra peaks. bw Waldo 22:40
Je 16 '47
Sigismonda. bw Hogarth 7:61 S
18 '39
Sigismund II, King of Poland bw
5:55 Ag 29 '38
Coat of arms 35:92 D 14 '53
Tapestry commissioned 35:
92-9 D 14 '53
Union of Poland and Lithu-
ania* bw 17:87 Ag 28 '44
The signing of the Constitution.
bw Christy 8:26 Je 10 '40
Signing the Compact. Moran, P.
13:75 N 23 '42
Signorelli, Luca
Madonna and Child with
saints 35:154 N 16 '53
Signs
Bull's head sign, Bissell's
Tavern, East Windsor,
Connecticut, c1760 38:118
Ap 18 '55
Signs of the zodiac. Fornasetti
34:61 Je 22 '53
Silent Night, Holy Night. Brein-
in 23:50-1 D 22 '47
Silenus head, Theater of Diony-
sus, Athens bw 18:55 Ja
1 '45
Silly fish. sculpture bw Cherry
22:138-9 Je 16 '47
Silhouettes
Jan Six V bw 31:66 Jy 16 '51
Silk
Chang Hsuan. Ladies pre-
paring newly woven silk,
copy by Hui Tsung 15:66-
7 O 11 '43
Silver jubilee at St. Paul's,
May 6, 1935. Salisbury
28:68-9 My 29 '50
Silvers, Herbert Ferber (Her-
bert Ferber, pseudonym)

sculptor
Figure bw 29:147 S 18 '50
Portrait of David Hare bw 29:
146 S 18 '50
Artist at work photog bw 29:
147 S 18 '50 port.
Silversmithing See also Jewelry
American colonial silverwork
38:116-7 Ap 18 '55
Andirons, England, George I
bw 3:77 D 13 '37
Candlesticks, James I bw 3:
77 D 13 '37
Chalice, jewelled, gift of
Czarina Alexandra to Ras-
putin bw 25:129 D 6 '48
Coconut cups, Elizabethan bw
3:77 D 13 '37
Concha belt, Indians, South-
west, 40:54 Ja 16 '56
Coney. Communion cup 38:116
Ap 18 '55
Coney. Inkstand, Boston,
c1700 bw 6:52 Mr 20 '39
Coney. Tobacco box 38:116 Ap
18 '55
Cups, two-handled, with
covers, James II, England
bw 3:77 D 13 '37
Elizabethan covered cup bw 3:
77 D 13 '37
Gilded silver dish--King Peroz
I hunting ibexes, Sasanian
dynasty 20:92 Jy 24 '46
Hull and Sanderson. Communion cup; dram cup 38:116 Ap
18 '55
Inburgh. Porringer, U.S. colonial 38:117 Ap 18 '55
Indian, American, Southwest
40:54-5 Ja 16 '56
Le Roux. Sugar caster, U.S.
colonial 38:117 Ap 18 '55
Mugs, Oxford College, 1690's
and Chinese bw 3:77 D 13
'37
Mumtaz Mahal's marriage cup,
enamelled, France, 17th
century 25:129 D 6 '48
Parzinger. Silverwork: salt
and pepper; coffee set; ink-

well; library clock; ash
tray; cigarette urn bw 7:
74-6 N 20 '39
Porringer, England bw 3:77 D
13 '37
Revere. Punch bowl, 1768,
U.S. colonial 38:56 My 30
'55
Savage, T. Salver, U.S. col-
onial 38:116-7 Ap 18 '55
Silver inkstand, U.S., 1770's
41:67 Jy 2 '56
Sweden--modern designs by
Fleming; Angman bw 7:59
Jy 3 '39
Table center piece, silver
and gilt 26:71 F 7 '49
Tableservice, silver and
gilt, Duke of Wellington
33:44 D 29 '52
Torah cases bw 4:47 Ap 18
'38
Van Dyck, P. Mustard pot,
U.S. colonial 38:117 Ap
18 '55
Van Dyck, P. Teapot, U.S.
colonial 38:116 Ap 18 '55
Wax jack, taper reel,
Charles II bw 3:77 D 13
'37
Western saddles, silver de-
coration 40:50-1 Ja 16 '56
Winslow. Chocolate pot, U.
S., colonial, 1700 bw 6:
53 Mr 20 '39
Winslow. Two-handled cup,
U.S., colonial 38:117 Ap
18 '55
Simkhovitch, Simka
Back country: 11:40 D 29 '41
Child* 18:75 My 14 '45
Jennifer 10:47 F 3 '41
Road home 11:39 D 29 '41
Sleet storm, 1940 11:39 D
29 '41
Winter in Connecticut 11:40
D 29 '41
Artist at work photogs bw
11:38 D 29 '41 port.

Simon, Richard L.
Richard Simon photog bw 7:
50 N 20 '39
Simon, Saint
El Greco. St. Simon bw 39:77
Ag 8 '55
Simon de Montfort bw 22:84 My
26 '47
Simons, Henry C.
Henry C. Simons photog bw
22:100 Mr 24 '47
Simpson, Wallace Warfield
Biddle. Mrs. Simpson, in
Society freed through jus-
tice mural 2:34 Ja 4 '37
Singapore
Public buildings, Singapore
island estate photogs bw
11:61-73 Jy 21 '41
Singers See Musicians and
Musical Instruments--Singers
Singier, Gustave
Provencal interior lithograph
33:86 Jy 14 '52
Sinking of Wasp. Lea 14:48-9 Ap
5 '43
Sintenis, Renee, sculptor
Artist and her work photog
36:145 My 10 '45
Siphon. Leger 33:96 O 27 '52
Siporin, Mitchell
Boy with tops bw 27:56 D 26
'49
St. Louis Post Office histori-
cal mural, painted with
Millman 13:71-4 O 12 '42
A Sioux on the warpath. Miller,
A. J. 36:78-9 Mr 8 '54
Siqueiros, David Alfaro
The Devil in church 29:106
D 11 '50
Sunrise of Mexico 20:60 Je 3
'46
Siren See Mythological Themes
--Sirens
Siren and fishes. sculpture bw
Milles 2:32 F 22 '37
The sisters. Austin 19:81 O 1 '45
The sisters. Raeburn 9:48 Jy 29
'40
Sistine Chapel, Rome photog bw

27:25 D 16 '49
Michelangelo. Sistine chapel
frescoes 21:62-9 Jy 1 '46;
27:25-49 D 26 '49
Sistine Madonna. Raphael 40:113
My 7 '56
Sittich, Marcus
Archbishop Sittich bw 29:105
S 18 '50
Sitting Bull photog bw 22:69 Ap
28 '47 Sitting Bull and
Buffalo Bill photog bw 16:
110 Ap 10 '44
Sitwell, Edith
Edith Sitwell photogs bw 25:
164-6 D 6 '48
Tchelitchew. Edith Sitwell
sculptured head bw 25:170
D 6 '48
Sitwell, Osbert
Osbert Sitwell photogs bw 25:
164-6 D 6 '48
The Sitwell family. bw Sargent
25:172 D 6 '48
Siva See Hinduism
Six, Jan I
Rembrandt. Jan Six bw 31:65
Jy 16 '51
Six, Jan II
Booner. Jan Six II bw 31:66
Jy 16 '51
Six, Jan III
Booner. Jan Six III bw 31:66
Jy 16 '51
Six, Jan IV
De Jonge. Jan Six IV bw 31:
66 Jy 16 '51
Six, Jan V
Jan Six V, silhouette bw 31:
66 Jy 16 '51
Six, Jan VII
Allebe. Jan Six VII bw 31:66
Jy 16 '51
Six, Jan VIII
Rueter. Jan Six VIII bw 31:
66 Jy 16 '51
Six, Jan IX
Jan Six IX drawing bw 31:66
Jy 16 '51
Six, Jan X

Rueter. Jan Six X, age 2 bw
31:66 Jy 16 '51
Six house, Amsterdam, 17th
century bw 31:68 Jy 16 '51
Six o'clock. Burchfield 1:26 D
28 '36
Sixth avenue. bw Ruellan 9:79 D
9 '40
Sixtus, Saint
Raphael. Sistine Madonna 40:
113 My 7 '56
Skating See Games and Sports--
Skating
Skeezix
King, F. O. Gasoline Alley
cartoon bw 12:62 F 16 '42
Skeletons
Baskin. The anatomist wood-
cuts 37:79 O 18 '54
Skeletons in the sky, 17th century
bw 23:16 Jy 21 '47
Skidmore, Owings and Merrill,
architects
Central Lutheran church,
Eugene, Oregon photog 39:
112 D 26 '55
H. J. Heinz Vinegar Factory,
Pittsburgh photog 36:35 Ja
4 '54
Lever house, New York City
photogs 32:44-5 Je 2 '52
Manufacturers Trust Company,
Fifth Avenue Office, New
York City photog 37:62 O 25
'54
Skiing See Games and Sports--
Skiing
Skin-diving, Florida. cartoon
Emett 37:46 Jy 5 '54
Skinner, Otis
Otis Skinner photogs bw 25:
8-10 Ag 30 '48
Otis Skinner and May Irwin,
1884 photog bw 26:76 Je 6
'49
Skittles See Games and Sports--
Bowling
Skulls
Plastered, ornamented human
skulls, Jericho, 5000 B.C.
34:119 My 11 '53

Skunk cabbage. bw Burchfield
1:24 D 28 '36
Skyscrapers See also Archi-
tecture; Office Buildings
Feininger, Lyonel. City at
night 31:91 N 12 '51
Marin. Manhattan No. 2   29:
65 Jy 10 '50
Philipp, W. Street scene bw
24:160 Mr 15 '48
Sterne. New York skyscraper
31:51 Ag 27 '51
Slap that bass. sculpture bw
Halle 10:59 Je 16 '41
Slaughter, Frank G.
Frank G. Slaughter photog
bw 24:22 My 17 '48
The slaughter wall. Montenegro
4:29 Mr 14 '38
Slaves and Slavery
Ingre. Slave drawing 34:86
My 11 '53
Michelangelo. Bound slave
sculpture bw 27:99 D 5 '49
Power. Greek slave, plaster
model bw 33:97 S 15 '52
Serfs traded for hounds bw
14:95 Mr 29 '43
Uncle Tom's Cabin, theater
poster 41:60 S 3 '56
Underground railroad, U.S.
bw 33:97 S 29 '52
Slaveship, English, c1790 plan
bw 5:50-1 O 3 '38
Sleep. Dali 6:44 Ap 17 '39
Sleeping. bw Carroll 8:120 My
13 '40
Sleeping. sculpture bw Borgatta
37:102 D 6 '54
Sleeping Venus. Giorgione 41:
104-5 O 22 '56 bw 40:103
F 20 '56
Sleeping woman. wood carving
bw Steig 6:36 Ap 10 '39
Sleet storm, 1940. Simkhovitch
11:39 D 29 '41
Sleighs
Albany Cutter, U.S., 1860
photog 39:104-5 O 17 '55

Sleighs (cont.)

Leighton. Mr. Morgan and
Mr. Vanderbilt in a sleigh,
1885 bw 6:31 Je 19 '39

One-horse open sleigh, U.S.,
1860 photog 39:105-6 O 17
'55

Sleigh of Peter the Great,
Czar of Russia photog bw
14:94 Mr 29 '43

Slim deer. Zao Wou-Ki 36:104 F
22 '54

Slipware plate, U.S., early 19th
century 39:57 Jy 18 '55

Sloan, John

Backyards, Greenwich Village
bw 5:29 O 31 '38

The City from Greenwich Village 7:46 D 11 '39

Grand Central station 7:46 D
11 '39

Hairdresser's window 27:61
Ag 29 '49

Lafayette hotel 7:46 D 11 '39

McSorley's bar 7:46 D 11 '39;
26:85 F 21 '49

Night life 38:72-3 Mr 28 '55

Nude and chief blanket 7:45
D 11 '39

The picnic ground 12:73 Ap
20 '42

Pigeons 7:46 D 11 '39

Sunday, women drying their
hair 2:33 F 1 '37

Susanna in Santa Fe bw 7:44 D
11 '39

Wake of the ferry 7:45 D 11
'39

The white way 7:46 D 11 '39

Artist at work photog bw 5:29
O 31 '38; 7:44 D 11 '39 port.

John Sloan photog bw 2:32 F
1 '37 port.

Sloan, Samuel

Pach Brothers. Samuel Sloan
photog bw 3:19 O 25 '37

Sloan, Mrs. Samuel

Pach Brothers. Mrs. Samuel
Sloan photog bw 3:19 O 25
'37

Sloth, detail from Seven deadly

sins bw 28:24 Ja 23 '50

Slowly toward the north. Tanguy
25:64 O 11 '48

Small Cowper Madonna. Raphael
4:27 Mr 21 '38

Small fry. cartoon bw Steig 6:35
Ap 10 '39; 20:8-10 F 18
'49

Small town fire. McCrady 3:41
O 18 '37

Smelt Brook falls. Hartley 13:
96 N 9 '42

Smibert, John

John Turner, c1730 bw 9:74
D 9 '40

Smith, Adam, economist

Adam Smith bw 15:104 S 13
'43; 22:100 Mr 24 '47

Smith, Alfred Emanuel

Al Smith photog bw 14:7 My
31 '43

Smith, Betty

Betty Smith photogs bw 26:5
Je 6 '49

Smith, Caleb

Caleb Smith photog bw 14:75
F 14 '43

Smith, David D., sculptor

Banquet bw 33:76 S 22 '52

Billiard player bw 33:78 S
22 '52

Four soldiers bw 33:78 S 22
'52

Hudson River landscape bw
33:78 S 22 '52

Artist at work photog bw 33:
75-6 S 22 '52 port.

Smith, Earl W., contractor

Contemporary house, El Cer-
rito, California photog,
plan bw 31:125 S 10 '51

Smith, Ed

Artist and his work photog bw
35:115 Jy 13 '53 port.

Smith, H. Allen

H. Allen Smith photog bw 2:
84 Je 28 '37

Smith, Jack

Artist and his work photog
bw 40:163-4 Ap 23 '56
port.

Smith, Jacob Getlar
The hypochondriac 12:45 Mr
9 '42
Smith, James
James Smith bw 15:9 Jy 5 '43
Smith, Jessie Willcox
Mother and child, "Good House-
keeping" covers bw 12:57
Ja 19 '42
Smith, John
Captain John Smith's Adven-
tures--illustrations bw 18:
67 My 21 '45
Smith, Thomas
Captain Thomas Smith, self-
portrait, 1680 bw 6:26 Je
19 '39
Smith, Tracy
Still life, fish and fruit 25:
100 D 6 '48
Artist at work photog bw 25:
103 D 6 '48 port.
Smoking and Smokers
Lubin. Smokers* 29:105 D 11
'50
Mary Frith, smoking pipe,
17th century 24:82 Mr 22
'48
Opium smokers, San Fran-
cisco, 1892. photog bw
Taber 31:13 S 10 '51
Teniers. Interior of a public
house 4:22 Ap 11 '38
Smoky black (Lili). Dubuffet
25:23 D 20 '48
Smuggler's cove. Lie 4:26 Je 13
'38
Smugglers' cove. Ryder 30:91
F 26 '51
Smuts, Jan Christian
Field Marshal Smuts 24:53
Ap 26 '48
Jan Christian Smuts; wife;
home photogs bw 15:Cover,
104-7 N 8 '43 "Time"
cover portrait 17:63 D 11
'44
The snail. architectural model
bw Terry 1:24 D 14 '36
Snake charmer. Lee, D. 33:109
N 10 '52

Snakes See also Animals,
Imaginary--Snakes
Bevans. American snakes--
most common species 28:
49-52 My 29 '50
Cobra, emblem of Lower
Egypt, 4th dynasty photog
bw 41:94 O 1 '56
Curry. Hogs killing a rattlesnake bw 15:19 N 29 '43
watercolor bw 15:18 N 29
'43
Dore. The brazen serpent bw
4:48 Ap 18 '38; 23:45 S 22
'47
Remington. The rattlesnake
sculpture bw 13:72 S 14
'42
Revere. Nine-segmented
snake, symbol of Ameri-
can colonies bw 38:56 My
30 '55
Snell, Hannah
Hannah Snell, c1745 bw 14:
6 Ja 4 '43
Sneyd, Honora
Honora Sneyd engraving bw
35:91 S 28 '53
Snow Scenes See also Winter
Hartley. Waxenstein peaks
32:86 Je 16 '52
Zhaba. Skiers (copy by Mira-
nova) 14:46 Mr 29 '43
Snuffboxes
Benjamin Franklin portrait
on snuffbox cover 40:82
Ja 9 '56
Enamelled gold, diamond-
studded snuffbox, France
photog bw 6:53 Mr 20 '39
Jean Jacques Rousseau por-
trait on snuffbox cover 40:
82 Ja 9 '56
Snuffboxes, gold, gifts to
Duke of Wellington pho-
togs 26:72 F 7 '49
Snyder, Emelia
Oil 10:77 Mr 31 '41
Artist at work photog bw 10:
76 Mr 31 '41 port.

Soap bubbles. Chardin 5:37 S 26
'38

Sobieski, John, King of Poland
John III, King of Poland bw
17:86 Ag 28 '44

Sobrat, I.
Witch play, Bali* bw 3:51 S
27 '37

Social Comment See also Taxes;
War Themes; Work and
Workers

Benton. Communists and
Fascists in Michigan drawings bw 3:22-5 Jy 26 '37

Biddle. Society freed through
justice mural 2:34 Ja 4 '37

Biddle. Tenement mural 2:35
Ja 4 '37

Blume. The eternal city bw
3:20 D 6 '37

Borglum. Sacco-Vanzetti memorial plaque bw 3:24 S 6
'37

Brook. Georgia jungle 10:52
Ja 13 '41; 21:74 N 25 '46
bw 16:79 Ap 24 '44

Daumier. Three lawyers 38:
108 My 23 '55

Delacroix. Liberty leading
the people 25:84 N 22 '48

Delacroix. Massacre at Scio
25:86 N 22 '48

Diego. Blueprint of the future
20:81 Mr 11 '46

Dore. London slum, c1850
bw 4:52 My 23 '38

Gomez. The unknown political
prisoner sculpture bw 34:
42 Je 1 '53

Goya. Maria Luisa, Queen
of Spain 31:63 O 1 '51

Gropper. Civilization bw 8:71
My 27 '40

Gropper. The Senate 2:24 F
1 '37

Grosz. I was always present
16:77 Je 12 '44

Hogarth. Drawings and paintings of eighteenth century
London 21:77-83 D 16 '46

Hogarth. Gin lane bw 20:66

My 27 '46; 21:83 D 16 '46

Hogarth. Marriage-a-la-
mode, six scenes 21:80 D
16 '46

Hogue. Drouth-stricken area
2:60 Je 21 '37

Hogue. Drouth survivors bw
2:61 Je 21 '37

Hogue. Dust bowl 2:60 Je 21
'37

Kallem. Country tenement 24:
103 Je 28 '48

Marsh. Twenty cent movie
21:77 N 25 '46

Martin, F. Tomorrow and
tomorrow 9:92 N 11 '40

Martin, F. Trouble in Frisco 9:92 N 11 '40 bw 5:30
O 31 '38

Millet, J. F. The man with a
hoe 9:46-7 Jy 29 '40

Picasso. Guernica fresco
bw 3:64 Jy 26 '37

Poor. Gold case mural 2:36
Ja 4 '37

Poorhouse inmates, 1875
drawing from "Leslie's"
bw 16:54 F 14 '44

Portinari. Victims of drought
29:108 D 11 '50

Reinhardt. Strings and dead
bird 32:90 Mr 24 '32

Rivera. Cortes conquest of
Mexico, 2 mural details,
Palace of Cortes, Cuer-
navaca, Mexico 6:41 Ja
23 '39

Rouault. Three judges 25:60
O 11 '48

Shahn. Handball 37:98-9 O 4
'54

Shahn. The passion of Sacco
and Vanzetti bw 37:96 O
4 '54

Shelter for the homeless,
1873, from "Harper's
Weekly" bw 16:54 F 14 '44

Siqueiros. The Devil in
church 29:106 D 11 '50

Van Gogh. The potato eaters
27:83 O 10 '49

Vaughn. Path of investigation
bw 27:47 N 14 '49

Weber. Seeking work 19:85 Ag
20 '45

Wood, G. Daughters of revolution 14:53 Ja 18 '43; 21:
73 N 25 '46

Young, A. The enemy of socialism cartoon bw 24:108
Ja 19 '48

Social consciousness. sculpture
bw Epstein 33:65 N 3 '52

The social push. drawing bw
Gibson 28:17 Ja 2 '50

Society freed through justice.
mural Biddle 2:34 Ja 4 '37

Sofas See Furniture--Sofas

Sokole, Miron
Sunday fishing 23:68 Jy 14 '47

Socrates sculptured head bw 12:
13 Je 8 '42

Soestdijk palace, Netherlands
photog bw 5:29 S 5 '38

Soft construction with boiled
beans: Premonition of civil
war--1936. Dali 3:27 D 20
'37 bw 19:64-5 S 24 '45

Softball See Games and Sports--
Baseball

Softball game in Hyde Park,
London.* Davis, F. 16:66-
7 Ap 3 '44; 31:79 O 29 '51

Soglow, Otto, cartoonist
Otto Soglow. in group photog
29:172-3 O 16 '50 port.

Sokolov See Kukrynisky

Solana, Marquesa de la
Goya. Marquesa de la Solana
16:65 Ja 10 '44

Solarium. Mergenthaler 10:57
Je 16 '41

Soldiers See also War Themes
The attack forms up, Japanese pilots, World War II
39:53 Ag 15 '55

Avilov. Communication troops
14:47 Mr 29 '43

Berry. Artillerymen in desert
26:59 Mr 21 '49

Brueghel. Massacre of the
innocents, details 37:36-7

D 27 '54

Craig. Veterans from battle
lines drawings bw 17:97 O
2 '44

Edward VII, England, reviewing troops, * 1903 23:82-3
N 17 '47

European soldier, c1619 bw
40:39 Ja 9 '56

Evzone ("well girdled"),
Greek soldier photog bw
9:Cover D 16 '40

Fighting Maya spearmen,
Bonampak mural 27:84 N
21 '49

Fredenthal. Russian soldiers,
Soviet army in Yugoslavia,
World War drawings bw
18:83-9 F 5 '45

Frederick the Great and staff,
Battle of Zorndorf, 1758
bw 15:95 N 22 '43

Gericault. Officer of the imperial guard 35:62 Ag 17
'53

German army reviw by
Frederick the Great, 1779
bw 15:96 N 22 '43

Grunewald. Soldiers, in
Resurrection panel, Isen-
heimer altarpiece 30:83-
5 Mr 26 '51

Hoplite and charioteer, detail, bronze urn, Greek,
6th century 37:87 S 13 '54

Jordan. Cossack division
soldiers, World War* 28:
67 F 20 '50

Kennington. British home
guard volunteer* 26:48 F
21 '49

Kennington. RAF fighter
pilots of World War II 26:
45 F 28 '49

Lea. Bruce Bieber, Top
Sergeant 11:64 Jy 7 '41

Lea. Soldiers at work 12:44
Ap 27 '42

Memling. Soldiers, in
Shrine of St. Ursala, de-
tails 34:84-5 Ap 6 '53.

Soldiers (cont.)

Miller. Soldiers of the U.S. army bw 31:85-6 D 10 '51

Ninos heroes, Battle of Chapultepec, 1847 bw 22:47 Mr 17 '47

Paoli massacre of continental soldiers print bw 35:92 S 28 '53

Persian soldiers, illuminated manuscript, 14th and 15th centuries 20:91 Je 24 '46

Rembrandt. Night watch bw 21:106 O 28 '46

Remington. Cavalry charge on the southern plains 13:76 S 14 '42

Rey. A hero 2:34 F 22 '37

Rey. Steel 2:35 F 22 '37

Rockwell. The American way 18:45 Ja 1 '45

Rogers. Returned volunteer sculpture bw 6:6 Mr 6 '39

Russian generals--victorious generals of World War II photogs bw 17:31-2 Jy 31 '44

Russian military leaders, 1939-43 photogs 14:98-9 Mr 29 '43

Smith, D. Four soldiers bw 33:78 S 22 '52

U.S. Civil War--Confederate, Union cavalry bw 39:165 S 12 '55

U.S. officer, c1853, Japanese artist bw 19:55 S 17 '45

Van Dyck. Commander in armor, 1641 40:107 My 7 '56

Vereshchagin. The 1812 series: Napoleon in Russia bw 12:61-8 F 2 '42

Veronese. Christ and the centurion 7:53 O 9 '39

Virgil's "Aeneid," manuscript 32:86 Ap 14 '52

Warrior, bronze, Etruscan, 450 B.C. 40:62-3 F 13 '56

Warrior's head, terra cotta, Etruscan, 5th century B.C. 40:58 F 13 '56

West. Death of General Wolfe 5:31 O 31 '38; 25:106-7 S 13 '48 bw 7:70 S 25 '39; 9:112 S 9 '40

Wilhelm, Crown Prince of Germany, 1917; and German soldiers, European War 8:56-7 Mr 25 '40

Willard. Spirit of '76 bw 9:55 Ag 5 '40

Woman as warriors through history bw 14:6-8 Ja 4 '43

Soldiers as Artists

Clay sculpture: animals, figures, caricatures bw 14:56-8 Mr 1 '43

LIFE's art competition for men in the armed services 13:31-6 Jy 6 '42 paintings as Christmas cards bw 13:138-9, 141 O 19 '42

"Our Life in the Service," art contest 12:64-6 F 9 '42

Prize-winning cartoonists among enlisted men bw 12:8-10 Mr 23 '42

Le soleil rouge. Chagall 39:140 N 14 '55

Solid comfort. lithograph 27:49 Jy 4 '49

Solman, Joseph

Sunlit windows bw 36:90 Ja 25 '54

Artist and his work photog bw 36:90 Ja 25 '54 port.

Solomon

Piero della Francesca. Solomon receiving the Queen of Sheba 20:63 Ap 22 '46

Piero della Francesca. Visit of the Queen of Sheba to King Solomon 20:62 Ap 22 '46

Solomon's temple, model photogs bw 6:50-2 My 15 '39

Solon, sculptured plaque, U.S. Congress bw 30:74

F 5 '51

Solvey the brigand, ice sculpture
bw 6:7 Ja 16 '39

Song at twilight. bw Sedlacek 2:
58 Ap 26 '37

Song in the night. Hickson 30:36
Ja 15 '51

Song of David. Chagall 33:99 O
6 '52

Song of David. sculpture bw
Vodicka 41:76 S 10 '56

"Songs of Innocence," illustrations, title page. bw Blake
36:66 Ap 19 '54

Sopris peak. Dehn 11:43 Ag 11 '41

Sorcerer. White, J. 22:82 Mr 10
'47

Soriano, Juan
Mulátto from Alvarado 20:60
Je 3 '46

Sorrell, Alan
Stoa of King Attalus, Athens,
c140 B.C. drawing bw 41:
165 S 17 '56

"The Sorrows of Young Werther,"
illustrations bw 27:22 Jy
25 '49

Sorting mail. mural Marsh 2:33
Ja 4 '37

Sothern, Ann
Clemens. Ann Sothern 24:65
Mr 1 '48

Sounding the terrain of New Belgrade. Ilic 29:105 D 11 '50

Sounds in the rock. Stamos 25:
63 O 11 '48

The source. Rosenthal, D. 15:
67 N 22 '43

Source of power. mural Gould,
A. 10:45 Ja 27 '41

A South American woman grinding corn. sculpture bw
Graham 4:14 F 21 '38; 5:
70 D 5 '38

South Dakota. Dehn 11:42 Ag 11
'41

South Jersey glassware See
Wistarberg glassware

South of Scranton. bw Blume 16:
79 Ap 24 '44

South Pacific Islands picture map.

Covarrubias 26:96 Ap 25
'49

South wind. Clemens 8:67 My 27
'40; 21:75 N 25 '46

Southern gate. Cortor 21:63 Jy
22 '46

Southampton waters, a "Nocturne." Whistler 36:94-5
My 17 '54

Soutine, Chaim
Hotel valet bw 9:67 O 14 '40
Man in a green coat 33:93 O
27 '52
The pheasant 38:108 My 23
'55

"Soverign of the Seas" (ship)
English, 1637 24:66 My 10
'48

Sovereign of the Seas and
builder, Peter Pett 41:84
O 29 '56

Sowald, Edward
George Washington 39:60 Jy
4 '55

Sowers, Robert
Stained glass window, St.
George's Episcopal church
Durham, N.H. 38:64 Ap
11 '55

Sowing and plowing, Bishop
Hill, Illinois, c1850 31:72
Jy 2 '51

Soyer, Isaac
Nude* 12:45 Mr 9 '42

Soyer, Raphael
Doctor's office 4:27 Je 13 '38
Walkowitz bw 16:77 F 21 '44
Self-portrait 33:99 O 27 '52
port.

Spaatz, Carl
Lt. Gen. Spaatz, "Time"
cover portrait 17:60 D 11
'44

The spaghetti eaters. bw
Greaves 40:166 Ap 23 '56

Spain. Dali 25:64 O 11 '48

Spain
Falangist emblem, 5 yoked
arrows photog bw 3:101
N 1 '37; 31:63 Ag 27 '51

Spain (cont.)

Civil War, 1936-1939
Picasso. Guernica fresco bw
3:63 Jy 26 '37
Rey. Civil war--scenes and
portraits watercolors 2:
34-5 F 22 '37
Weber. Fighters for freedom
16:78 Je 12 '44
The Spanish Armada defeat, 1588
24:80 Mr 22 '48; 24:66 My
10 '48; 41:80-1 O 29 '56
bw 7:70 S 25 '39; 32:22 F
18 '52
Spanish girl. Matisse 37:66 Ag
9 '54
Spanning the continent. sculpture,
model, bw Laurent 10:68
Je 2 '41
Spaulding (John) collection of
modern French paintings
25:76-80 N 1 '48
Spears and Spear Throwers See
Weapons
Spectral fish. Zao Wou-Ki 36:104
F 22 '54
Speicher, Eugene
Alicia bw 8:70 My 27 '40
The blue necklace 3:27 D 20
'37
Georgia O'Keefe, 1908 bw 25:
63 D 6 '48
Jean in blue 11:77 O 6 '41
Katharine Cornell as "Can-
dida" 8:47 Ap 29 '40 bw
10:70 Ap 14 '41
Portrait of Jean Bellows 11:
78 O 6 '41
Woodstock cowboy 5:26 Ag 29
'38
Eugene Speicher photog bw 5:
72 D 12 '38 in group pho-
tog 29:172-3 O 16 '50 port.
Spence, Basil, architect
Church, Coventry, England
photogs bw 34:63-4 Mr 23 '53
Basil Spence photog bw 34:64
Mr 23 '53 port.
Spencer, Herbert
Herbert Spencer photog bw 15:

104 S 13 '43
Spencer, Lillie Martin
The picnic--or the Fourth of
July, a day to be re-
membered 25:48 Jy 5 '48
Spengler, Oswald
Oswald Spengler photog bw
16:58 Mr 20 '44
Sphinx
Great sphinx, Giza photog
41:107 N 26 '56 bw 13:
Cover, 14 O 19 '42
Hittite sphinx, Ankara sculp-
ture bw 8:81 Ap 8 '40
Winged sphinx, Schonbrunn,
Vienna sculpture bw 2:13
Mr 22 '37
Spiegel, Jacobus van der, gold-
smith
Pap spoon, with bells, U.S.
colonial 38:116 Ap 18 '55
The spielers. Luks 12:61 Je
15 '42
Spillane, Frank Morrison
(Mickey)
Mickey Spillane photogs bw
32:79 Je 23 '52
Spindletop, Texas oil gusher.
Hogue 10:40 F 10 '41
Spinets See Musicians and
Musical Instruments--Spinet
Spinning Wheels
Mahatma Gandhi's spinning
wheel photog bw 24:27 F
9 '48
Spirit of '76. bw Willard, A.M.
9:55 Ag 5 '40
Spirit of the dance. sculpture
bw Zorach 8:92 Ap 1 '40
Spring. bw Peirce, W. 17:29
O 16 '44
Spring. sculpture Wheeler 25:
101 S 27 '48
Spittoons
"Spit box," molded maple,
U.S. Shakers, 1850 pho-
tog 39:103 O 17 '55
Sporting Prints
Prints from "Four Centuries
of Sporting Prints" exhib-
it 19th century 6:38-42 F

6 '39

Spring festival, Ming dynasty, 17th century 15:64 O 11 '43

Spring festival on the Yellow River, Ch'ing Ming scroll, c1500 31:44-9 D 31 '51

The spring house. Wyeth, N.C. 20:79 Je 17 '46

Spring idyl. Shahn 37:99 O 4 '54

Spring in Bleecker Street. Ruellan 10:72 Ap 14 '41

Spring in the country. Wood, G. 14:56 Ja 18 '43

Spring in town. Wood, G. 14:56 Ja 18 '43

Spring night. Sharp 16:45 Ja 3 '44

Spring on the highway, Mexico. Lee, D. 22:78 My 12 '47

Spring turning. Wood, G. 2:34-5 F 8 '37

Spurs, St. George's, England, royal symbol photog 2:38 Mr 15 '37

Squirrels
    Audubon. Black squirrel 30: 47 Ja 29 '51
    Audubon. Flying squirrels 9: 115 O 21 '40
    Copley. Boy with squirrel (Henry Pelham) bw 5:28 O 31 '38

Stabiles See Calder, Alexander

Stacking alfalfa. Pleissner 13:47 Ag 21 '42

Stackpole, Ralph, sculptor
    Kneeling woman bw 9:79-80 O 21 '40
    Pacifica bw 5:71 D 5 '38
    Artist at work photog bw 9:79- 80 O 21 '40 port.

Stafford, Jean
    Jean Stafford photog bw 22:76 Je 2 '47

Staffordshire Ware
    Plate, 15 stars and eagle, U.S., 1792 17:59 S 4 '44
    Plates bw 5:47 N 28 '38

Stag at Sharkey's. Bellows 5:38 O 31 '38; 26:85 F 21 '49

Stage Coaches See also Carriages

American stage coach, c1820 photog 39:62 Jy 18 '55

Stained Glass See Glass, Staining

Stair Rail, wrought iron, Home Moravian church, Winston Salem, N.C., 1800 photog bw 37:168 O 25 '54

Staircase, Doylestown. Sheeler 5:44 Ag 8 '38

Stairway at Auvers. Van Gogh 13:95 N 9 '42

Stairways
    Chippendale stairway, Pierce house, Salem, Mass. photog 38:62 My 30 '55
    Eighteenth century staircase, Wachovia Museum, New Salem, N.C. photog bw 37:168 O 25 '54
    Gothic stairway, Morlaix, France, 16th century photog bw 13:92 N 9 '42
    Greek revival circular stairway, The Hermitage, Tennessee photog 13:65 Jy 6 '42; 18:52-3 My 7 '45
    Hentrich. Glass encased stairway, Office building, Dusseldorf, Germany photog bw 36:150 My 10 '54
    Jackson. Spoke-shaped spiral stairway, contemporary U.S. photog bw 39:99 D 12 '55
    Marble staircase, Egyptian royal palace, Ras el Tin photog 33:90 N 24 '52
    Mayan hieroglyphic stairway, Copan, Honduras photog 22:56-7 Je 30 '47
    Pittman. Flying staircase, Ashley Hall, Charleston pastel 22:72 Ap 14 '47
    Roman steps, Palazzo Colonna, c50 B.C. photog bw 18:94 Mr 5 '45
    Saarinen, Eero. Staircase, Administration building, General Motors Techni-

Stairways (cont.)
    cal Center, Warren, Mich.
    photog 40:102-5 My 21 '56
  Sakamoto. Spiral staircase,
    Fujimi girls high school,
    Tokyo photog bw 38:80-1 Mr
    14 '55
  San Esteban Rey mission, A-
    coma, New Mexico photog
    40:48 Ja 16 '56
  Snail-shaped stairs, Afton Vil-
    la, Louisiana photog bw 32:
    85 Je 9 '52
  Spiral staircase, Charles
    Eames' home photog bw 29:
    150 S 11 '50
  Spiral staircase, heart-shaped
    well, Houmas House,
    Louisiana photog bw 32:85
    9 '52
  U.S. Supreme Court building
    eliptical stairway, self-sup-
    porting, white Alabama
    marble with bronze railing
    photog 8:52 F 12 '40
  Victorian oak stairway,
    Chateau-sur-Mer, Newport,
    R.I. photog 40:87 Mr 5 '56
  White. Stair, Rosecliff, New-
    port, R.I. photog bw 11:82
    Ag 18 '41
Stalin, Josef
  Joseph Stalin; history; associ-
    ates photogs bw 31:109-17
    O 29 '51 "Time" cover por-
    trait 17:83 D 11 '44
  Joseph Stalin statue bw, Mos-
    cow 18:62 Ja 1 '45
  Lenin and Stalin sculpture bw
    6:17 Ja 30 '39
  Merkurov. Stalin sculpture,
    copy 14:90 Mr 29 '43
  Mulk. Mr. Churchill and his
    friends overthrowing Hitler
    and his 35:70 N 9 '53
  Wolverton. Stalin caricature
    bw 22:16 My 5 '47
Stamos, Theodore
  The bier 28:87 Mr 20 '50
  Sounds in the rock 25:63 O 11
    '48

Theodore Stamos photog bw
    30:34 Ja 15 '51 port.
Stamp Act repeal, 1766 cartoon
    bw 22:99 Mr 24 '47
The standard bearer. bw Rem-
    brandt 16:66 Ja 10 '44
Standard Oil Company of Indi-
    ana, Whiting, Indiana
    photog 36:35 Ja 4 '54
Standing nude. Picasso 8:58 Mr
    4 '40
Standing nude. sculpture bw
    Cash 9:55 Ag 12 '40
Standing youth. sculpture Lehm-
    bruck 25:47 Ag 16 '48
Standish, Miles
  Return of Miles Standish bw
    19:57 N 26 '45
Stangl ceramics photogs 9:76-
    Je 9 '52
Stanley, George, sculptor
  Muse of music bw 9:82 O 21
    '40
  Artist at work photog bw 9:
    82 O 21 '40 port.
Stanley, Henry
  Henry Stanley caricature
    from "Vanity Fair" bw 7:
    60 Ag 14 '39
  Stanley and Kalulu 2 drawings
    bw 7:60 Ag 14 '39
  Stanley meeting Livingstone*
    bw 7:60 Ag 14 '39
  Stanley's search for Living-
    stone, 1872 bw 13:76 N 16
    '42
Stanton, Edwin McMasters
  Secretary Stanton photog bw
    11:100 N 10 '41; 14:75 F
    15 '43
The star of Bethlehem. Ford
    7:25 D 25 '39
Star of David, emblem, Judaism
    38:57 F 7 '55
Star of India, emblem, India bw
    16:62 Ja 24 '44
Star of the East, gemstone, dia-
    mond 32:67-8 Mr 17 '52
Stark, Margaret
  Hark! The Herald Angels
    Sing 23:55 D 22 '47

Stars above the town. bw Feininger, Lyonel 31:89 N 12 '51

Stars and Sky
Kent. End of world theories bw 3:55-6 N 1 '37
Stephens, D.O. Milky Way; eclipse of sun; sky in South America 3:49-51 N 8 '37

The State apartments, Chatsworth. bw Halliday 9:59 Ag 12 '40

State birds, U.S. Peterson 8: 58-62 Je 17 '40

State executive mansions, 48 States bw 10:22-3 Ja 20 '41

State flags, U.S. 15:77-82 D 6 '43

State House, Philadelphia photog bw 11:104 N 10 '41
Birch. State House, Philadelphia engraving 39:61 Jy 4 '55

Statuary Hall, U.S. Capitol, Washington, D.C. photog 31:50-1 Jy 2 '51

Statue of Liberty. sculpture
Bartholdi photog 8:Cover, Je 3 '40; 16:Cover Je 26 '44; 23:48 Je 7 '47 bw 6: Cover Je 5 '39; 10:94-7 Je 2 '41
Torch, Philadelphia Centennial Exposition, 1876 bw 6: 35 Je 5 '39
Liberty enlightening the world, Luxembourg Garden, Paris, preliminary model photog 17:93 O 2 '44 bw 10:6 Je 23 '41

Statues. cartoons bw Molnar 37: 2-3 Ag 30 '54

Stea, Cesare
Man with book sculpture bw 4: 62 Ap 25 '38

Steamboat around the bend. mural Daughtery 3:50 O 25 '37

Steamboat Gothic
San Francisco, plantation house, Louisiana, 1849 photog 32: 80-1 Je 9 '52

Stedman, Kathryn Imlay, landscape architect
Palo Alto, California, house 37:120-2 N 15 '54

Steel. Rey 2:35 F 22 '37

Steele, Frederick Dorr
Sherlock Holmes bw 16:77 My 1 '44

Steen, Jan
Baptismal party 24:77 Je 14 '48
The dancing couple 5:32 Ag 29 '38
The gallant offering 24:78 Je 14 '48
The worship of the golden calf 41:74 D 10 '53
The world upside down 27:70 O 24 '49
Self-portrait bw 5:30 Ag 29 '38 port.
Self-portrait, in Worship of the golden calf 41:74 D 10 '53 port.

The steeplechase. Marsh 40:83 F 6 '56

The Stehlis of Zurich, 1874. Horne 25:91 O 18 '48

Steichen, Edward, photographer
Auguste Rodin and his sculptures 38:20-2 My 9 '55
"Family of Man," exhibition bw 38:132-43 F 14 '55
Greta Garbo, 1928 bw 38: Cover Ja 10 '55
Portfolio of photographs--50 years work bw 28:117-23 My 15 '50
Edward Steichen photog bw 28:117 My 15 '50 port.
Self-portrait, age 19 photog bw 28:117 My 15 '50 port.

Steig, William, cartoonist
"About People" cartoons from his book bw 8:52-3 Ja 8 '40
Cartoons bw 17:77 N 27 '44
"Persisten Faces" bw 20:8-10 F 18 '46
"Small Fry" bw 6:35 Ap 10 '39; 20:8-10 F 18 '46

Steig, William (cont.)
  Ten figures bw 6:35-6 Ap 10
    '39 (wood carvings)
  William Steig photog bw 6:36
    Ap 10 '39; 20:10 F 18 '46
    port.
Stein, Gertrude
  Beaton. Gertrude Stein and
    Alice Toklas photog bw 4:
    49 Ja 3 '38
  Davidson. Gertrude Stein
    statue bw 23:15 Ag 18 '47
  Gertrude Stein photogs bw 23:
    14-5 Ag 18 '47
  Gertrude Stein with Alice
    Toklas, Culoz, France
    photogs 17:83-4 O 2 '44
  Picabia. Gertrude Stein draw-
    ing bw 23:15 Ag 18 '47
  Picasso. Gertrude Stein bw
    23:15 Ag 18 '47
  Vallatoon. Gertrude Stein bw
    23:15 Ag 18 '47
Steinbeck, John
  John Steinbeck caricature bw
    23:83 S 1 '47
  John Steinbeck photogs bw 4:
    32 My 2 '38; 6:67 Je 5 '39;
    17:14 Ag 14 '44
Steinberg, Saul, cartoonist
  "All in Line" cartoons from
    his book bw 19:8-10 Ag 13
    '45
  American parade 31:52-3 Ag
    27 '51
  Baseball--scenes, players
    39:56-66 Jy 11 '55
  Cartoons 31:50 Ag 27 '51
  "Guitavir Line," inventions
    to assist war effort bw 8:
    14-7 My 27 '40
  Saul Steinberg photog bw 31:
    52 Ag 27 '51 port.
  Self-portrait cartoon bw 31:
    50 Ag 27 '51 port.
Stele, Mayan, Copan, Honduras
    photog 22:56-7 Je 30 '47
Stella bw 6:47 Mr 13 '39
Stephen Batory, King of Poland
    bw 5:55 Ag 29 '38
Stephanie, Consort of Rudolph,

Prince of Austro-Hungary
    photog bw 26:127 Mr 28
    '49
Stephens, D. Owen
  Milky Way; eclipse of sun;
    sky in South America 3:49-
    51 N 8 '37
Stephens, Thomas E.
  General Douglas MacArthur,
    age 70 29:Cover Ag 28
    '50
  General of the Army Dwight
    D. Eisenhower 29:92 N
    6 '50
Steppat, Leo
  Tepexpan man sculptured
    head bw 23:95 N 3 '47
Stern, Marie (Masha, pseudo-
    nym)
  "A Child's Book of Prayers,"
    illustrations 11:85 D 15
    '41
Sternberg, Eugene D., archi-
    tect
  Contemporary house, Den-
    ver, Colo. photog, plan
    bw 31:124 S 10 '51
Sternberg, Harry
  Walkowitz bw 16:80 F 21 '44
  Harry Sternberg. in group
    photog 29:172-3 O 16 '50
    port.
Stern, Hedda
  Airport 31:51 Ag 27 '51
  City at night 31:51 Ag 27 '51
  Construction 31:54 Ag 27 '51
  Flivver 31:54 Ag 27 '51
  Mechanical inventions 31:51
    Ag 27 '51
  Moonlight 28:82 Mr 20 '50
  New York skyscraper 31:51
    Ag 27 '51
  Structures of First Avenue
    31:51 Ag 27 '51
  Warship 31:54 Ag 27 '51
  Hedda Sterne photog bw 30:
    34 Ja 15 '51; 31:51 Ag
    27 '51 port.
Sterner, Albert
  Walkowitz bw 16:79 F 21 '44
Steuben, Frederick William,

Baron von
General Steuben bw 29:52 Jy
3 '50
Steuben Glassware
Audubon bird plates bw 23:18-
9 N 10 '47
Steubenville Ceramics photogs
29:89 D 25 '50
Steuer (Max D.) collection of
painting and sculpture bw
erroneous report 11:61-2
O 27 '41   corrected re-
port 11:54 N 10 '41
Stevens, Edward, Jr.
The Chinese swan 28:87 Mr
20 '50
Stevens, Thaddeus
Abolitionist Stevens photog
bw 16:62 F 21 '44; 23:57
N 3 '47
Stevenson, Adlai E.
Vice-president Stevenson
photog bw 9:9 Ag 5 '40
Stevenson, Robert Louis
Sargent. Robert Louis Steven-
son 36:96 My 17 '54
Stewart, Donald Ogden
Donald Ogden Stewart photog
bw 21:50 O 7 '46
Stewart, Walter W.
Eisenstadt. Walter W. Stew-
art photog bw 24:15 My 10
'48
Stiegel, William Henry, glass
maker
"Daisy-diamond" blown flask
39:58-9 Jy 18 '55
Sugarbowl 39:58 Jy 18 '55
Tumbler, enameled 39:58 Jy
18 '55
Stieglitz, Alfred, photographer
Colored photographs, "Auto-
chromes," 1907 28:10 Ja
2 '50
Famous photographs, 1887-
1931 14:6-9 Ap 5 '43
The terminal bw 14:6 Ap 5 '43
Alfred Stieglitz photog bw 4:
31 F 14 '38 age 79, 14:6
Ap 5 '43 port.
The stigmatization of St. Francis.

Veneziano 1:48 D 28 '36
Still, Clifford E.
Clifford E. Still photog bw
30:34 Ja 15 '51 port.
Still, William Grant
William Grant Still photog
bw 5:58 O 3 '38
Still Life Paintings See also
subjects, as Flowers;
Fruit
Albright, I. Ah, God--her-
rings, buoys, the glitter-
ing sea 16:78 Ap 24 '44
Albright, I. Wherefore now
ariseth the illusion of the
third dimension 16:66-7
Mr 27 '44
Albright, M. Victoria 16:65
Mr 27 '44
Anderson, R.L. Still life bw
38:83 F 28 '55
Arcimboldo, School of. Sum-
mer (Reclining woman of
fruit and vegetables) bw
7:24 Ag 28 '39
Bohrod. Reflections on a
shop window 21:77 N 25
'46
Bonnard. Fish 17:75 N 13 '44
Bonnard. Golden hair 25:54
Jy 26 '48
Bouche. Patriotic still life,
club-car mural 11:49 Ag
18 '41
Brackman. Still life with
mask 8:60 F 5 '40
Braque. Compote dish, bottle
and mandolin 26:85 My 2
'49
Braque. Pitcher and basket
of fruit 26:83 My 2 '49
Braque. The round table 38:
109 My 23 '55
Braque, Still life, 1908 bw
26:82 My 2 '49
Braque. Still life: Le Jour
26:84 My 2 '49 ·
Braque. Still life with grapes
39:109 My 23 '55
Braque. Still life with pink
background 26:84 My 2 '49

Still Life Paintings (cont.)

Braque. Sugar bowl with fruit 26:83 My 2 '49

Braque. The waltz 4:44 My 2 '38

Bratby. Jean and still life in front of window bw 40:168 Ap 23 '56

Buffet. Still life bw 38:78, 80 Mr 21 '55

Burchfield. Pussy willows 1: 27 D 28 '36

Cezanne. Still life with apples 2:46 Ap 12 '37

Chardin. Still life 38:125 My 2 '55

Chardin. Still life 40:72-3 My 28 '56

Churchill. Still life 20:49 Ja 7 '46

Claesz. Lunch table bw 7:24 Ag 28 '39

Cress. Interior shadows 39: 115 S 12 '55

Curry. Wisconsin still life bw 15:20 N 29 '43

D'Arista. Table with bottles and cheese 39:136-7 N 21 '55

Davis, S. Eggbeater no. 5 22: 79 F 17 '47

Feuerherm. Meat market 30: 36 Ja 15 '51

Fiene. Kitchen table 7:25 Ag 28 '39

Gischia. Egg plants 17:76 N 13 '44

Grosz. The blue chair 7:26 Ag 28 '39

Guston. Lemonade and dough-nuts 20:92 My 27 '46

Harnett. Emblems of peace 7:25 Ag 28 '39

Harnett. Old models 27:60 Ag 29 '49

Harnett. Trophy of the hunt 10:74 Ap 14 '41

Hickson. Song in the night 30: 36 Ja 15 '51

Kuniyoshi. Boquet and stove 26:86 F 21 '49

Kuniyoshi. Objects on a sofa. 6:28 F 13 '39

Lane. Autumn still life 16:45 Ja 3 '44

Matisse. Black table 31:115 N 26 '51

Matisse. Goldfish and sculp-ture 25:60 O 11 '48

Modern artists and Dutch masters still life paintings 7:24-6 Ag 28 '39

Monet. Still life 29:90 N 27 '50

O'Keefe. Horses head with pink rose 4:29 F 14 '38

Pignon. Still life* 17:76 N 13 '44

Picasso. The red tablecloth 23:95 O 13 '47

Rembrandt. Beef carcass bw 7:24 Ag 28 '39

Sepeshy. End of day 20:80 F 18 '46

Smith, T. Still life (fish and fruit) 25:100 D 6 '48

Soutine. The pheasant 38: 108 My 23 '55

Van der Ast. Shells, fruit and insects bw 7:24 Ag 28 '39

Vasilieff. Still life 24:103 Je 28 '48

Weber. Still life with two tables 19:86 Ag 20 '45

Wyeth, A. Interior 35:80 Jy 27 '53

Zao Wou-Ki. Red still life* 36:104 F 22 '54

Stillwell, Alison
Chinese-style paintings: Buddha, trees, bamboo, flowers bw 17:124 O 2 '44

Stilts. woodcut Pierce 37:89 O 18 '54

Stimson, Henry L.
Henry L. Stimson bw 19:89 S 24 '45 "Time" cover portrait 17:61 D 11 '44

Stoa of King Attalus, Athens, c150 B.C. photogs bw 41:165-72 S 17 '56

Stock Exchanges
  Black Friday, 1869 cartoon
     bw 30:71 Je 11 '51
  Degas. Cotton market in New
     Orleans 10:74 Ap 28 '41
  Laning. New York stock ex-
     change, October 24, 1929
     bw 8:78 F 26 '40
Stockman, Frank
  Collages bw 15:10-2 S 6 '43
Stockton, Richard
  Richard Stockton bw 15:9 Jy
     5 '43
Stoddard, Judson
  Robinson. Judson Stoddard
     20:79 F 18 '46
Stoddert, Benjamin
  Benjamin Stoddert, First
     Secretary of the Navy,
     U.S. 10:56 Mr 10 '41
Stoffels, Henrickje
  Rembrandt. Flora bw 28:58
     Ja 30 '50
  Rembrandt. The painter's
     study bw 29:104 S 11 '50
  Rembrandt. A woman bathing
     29:105 S 11 '50
  Rembrandt. Young girl at
     open half-door 11:57 S 8
     '41
Stokes, F. W.
  Artist in his studio photog 29:
     70 Ag 14 '50 port.
Stokowski, Leopold
  Leopold Stokowski photog bw
     18:79 Ja 29 '45
Stone, Edward D., architect
  El Panama Hotel, Panama
     City photogs 32:50-7 Ja 7
     '52
  U.S. country house photogs,
     plan 22:88-91 Ap 28 '47
Stone, Thomas
  Thomas Stone bw 15:10 Jy 5
     '43
Stone City, Iowa. Wood, G. 14:
     54 Ja 18 '43 bw 21:104 S
     30 '46
Stone of Scone photog bw 30:20-
     1 Ja 8 '51; 30:50 Ap 23 '51;
     30:153 My 14 '51

Stonehenge, Salisbury Plain,
  Wiltshire, England photog
     40:78 Mr 19 '56 bw 14:80
     Je 14 '43 night view 8:43
     Je 3 '40
  reconstruction drawing bw
     18:41 Ja 1 '45
Stonorov, Oskar, architect
  House for family living,
     model 29:40-3 Jy 10 '50
  Oskar Stonorov photog bw
     29:41 Jy 10 '50 port.
Stools
  African carved stool, crouch-
     ing woman holding platter,
     Baluba photog bw 33:121
     S 8 '52
  Noguchi. Rocking stool bw
     40:122, 125 F 6 '56
  South Seas saddle-shaped
     stool, with arm for grat-
     ing coconuts photog bw
     21:79 N 4 '46
  Windsor stools photog 38:64-
     5 My 30 '55
Storage Walls, contemporary
     architecture photogs, dia-
     grams 18:64-71 Ja 22 '45
Storck, Abraham
  Four days fight in the Chan-
     nel 41:82-3 O 29 '56
Storm clouds. Hartley 32:85 Je
     16 '52
The storm is coming. woodcut
     Frasconi 37:85 O 18 '54
Storm on the Sea of Galilee.
     Rembrandt 1:31 N 30 '36
Storm over Menemsha. Reindel
     3:3 5 Ag 9 '37
Storming of Chapultepec castle,
     September 13, 1817 4:52
     Ap 11 '38; 22:122 Je 9' 47
Storming of the Winter Palace.
     Surikov 14:58 Mr 29 '43
Storms
  Bierstadt. Thunderstorm in
     the Rockies 19:86 S 10
     '45
  Curry. Line storm 1:30 N
     23 '36 bw 15:19 N 29 '43

Storms (cont.)

Curry. The tornado bw 15:19 N 29 '43

Curry. Tornado over Kansas 1:29 N 23 '36; 21:73 N 25 '46

Delacroix. Christ on the Sea of Galilee 39:23 D 26 '55

Giorgione. The tempest 39: 166-7 O 24 '55

Grosz. Approaching storm 12:76 Ap 20 '42

Hurd. Cloudburst 23:77 Ag 18 '47

Inness. The coming storm 12:59 Je 15 '42

Jesus stills the tempest, China 11:48 D 22 '41

Jones, Joe. Dust storm 8:66 My 27 '40

Leith-Ross. Summer showers 16:46 Ja 3 '44

McCrady. Oil refinery, Baton Rouge* 34:80 Ja 5 '53

Quiberon Bay battle, 1759 24: 66 My 10 '48

Remington. Howl of the weather 13:74-5 S 14 '42

Simkovitch. Sleet storm, 1944 11:39 D 29 '41

Storrs, Constant

Jennys. Mrs. Constant Storrs, 1802 bw 9:74 D 9 '40

Story, W. W.

Cleopatra, sculpture bw 19: 10 S 24 '45

Stoss, Veit

Sculptured figures, altarpiece, Church of Our Lady, Cracow 1489 bw 23:149 S 22 '47

Stoughton, William

William Stoughton, Judge, 1692 bw 27:76 S 26 '49

Stout, Rex

Rex Stout photog bw 16:82 My 1 '44

Stoves See also Furniture-- Stoves

Kuniyoshi. Boquet and stove 26:86 F 21 '49

Lee, D. Thanksgiving bw 3: 44 S 20 '37

Wyeth, A. Interior 35:81 Jy 27 '53

Stradanus

Vespucci in South America, 1552 print bw 37:105 O 11 '54

Strafford, Earl of

Thomas Wentworth, Earl of Strafford bw 41:182 N 12 '56

Stratford Hall, Lee's home, Virginia photog bw 13:57 Jy 6 '42; 21:66-8 Ag 19 '46

Strauss, Johann, the younger

Johan Strauss bw 2:51 Mr 8 '37 grave photog bw 2:51 Mr 8 '37 statue, Stadtpark Vienna bw 2:50 Mr 8 '37

Strauss, Richard

Richard Strauss photogs bw 27:127 S 19 '49

Steichen. Richard Strauss, 1906 photog bw 28:118 My 15 '50

Strauss Memorial, Vienna sculpture bw 20:92 Mr 4 '46

Strawberry Hill, home of Horace Walpole, needlepoint bw 17:118 O 23 '44

Street fights in Paris. Hagnauer 25:88-9 N 22 '48

Street of the Fishing Cat, Paris, Davis, G. R. 19:54 Jy 16 '55

Street Scenes

Banks. Old Richmond 10:68 My 26 '41

Bohrod. Evening in Roscomon 11:94 N 10 '41

Bohrod. Rainy night 11:93 N 10 '41

Bohrod. Taverns at night 11: 93 N 10 '41

Burchfield. Promenade bw 6:82 My 22 '39

Cadmus. Main street mural 2:45 Mr 29 '37

Cloar. Lull bw 32:88 Mr 17 '52

Hattorf. Seventh and Canal 10:68 My 26 '41

Hopper. Manhattan Bridge loop 28:102-3 Ap 17 '50

Hopper. Seven A.M. 28:101 Ap 17 '50

Kingman. New York's Chinatown* 30:102 My 14 '51

McCrady. Town square 3:41 O 18 '37

Orne. Washington Stree, Salem, Massachusetts, 1765 13:80 N 23 '42

Philipp, W. Street scene bw 24:160 Mr 15 '48

Ruellan. Sixth Avenue bw 9: 79 D 9 '40

Ruellan. Spring in Bleeker Street 10:72 Ap 14 '41

Sloan. La Fayette hotel 7:46 D 11 '39

Street scene, Washington, D.C., 1853, Japanese illustration bw 25:6-7 Ag 2 '48

Utrillo. Place du Tertre, Montmartre drawing bw 28: 89 Ja 16 '50

Stretcher party drawing bw, unknown Marine Corps artist 15:81 D 27 '43

Striding figure. sculpture bw Wotruba 38:88 Je 20 '55

Striding man. sculpture bw Pattison 32:78 Ja 7 '52

The strike. Ruiz 4:30 Mr 14 '38

Strikes and Demonstrations
Demonstrating women factory workers, Lynn, Massachusetts, 1860 bw 33:32 D 8 '52

Dispersal of striking workers, St. Petersburg, 1905 14: 45 Mr 29 '43

"Great Strike" of 1877, Pittsburgh bw 33:32 D 8 '52

Homestead Riot, 1892 bw 33: 32 D 8 '52

Homestead Steel Strike, 1892,

memorial photog bw 20:21 F 4 '46

Martin, F. Trouble in Frisco 9:92 N 11 '40 bw 5:30 O 31 '38

String composition. Fuller 27: 77 O 31 '49

String quartette. Levine 14:43 Mr 8 '43; 26:86 F 21 '49

Strings and dead bird. Reinhardt 32:90 Mr 24 '52

Strong man. Reinhardt 32:90 Mr 24 '52

Structures of First Avenue. Sterne 31:51 Ag 27 '51

The struggle of two natures in man. sculpture bw Barnard 6:57 Mr 20 '39

Stuart, Gilbert
Albert Gallatin bw 4:42 My 2 '38

George Washington bw 5:28 O '31 '38; 30:111 F 19 '51 1796, 24:23 F 23 '48 head on 3¢ stamp bw 24: 23 F 23 '48

James Monroe bw 6:31 Je 19 '39

Jefferson as President, 1805 14:64 Ap 12 '43

Mrs. John Thomson Matson bw 6:58 Mr 27 '39

Mrs. Timothy Pickering, 1817 bw 9:74 D 9 '40

Sir Isaac Hull, 1807 23:69 O 27 '47

Stuart, James Elwell Brown (Jeb) French. Cavalrymen crossing a river mural 10:44 Ja 27 '41

Stubbs, George
The Wedgwood family 25:98 S 13 '48

The student. mural lunette Laning 9:66 S 30 '40

Studio, Quai St. Michel. Matisse 38:109 My 23 '55

Studios See also Artists at Work
Braque. Studio* 33:93 O 27 '52

Studios (cont.)
   Courbet. The studio 26:62-3
      My 30 '49
   Cranach. Cardinal Albrecht
      as Saint Hieronymous 5:39
      Jy 11 '38
   Matisse. Red studio 31:114-5
      N 26 '51
   Mommer. Studio interior bw
      36:92 Ja 25 '54
   Rembrandt. The painter's
      study bw 29:104 S 11 '50
   Taubes. Studio interior 8:39
      Ja 15 '40
   Toulouse-Lautrec. Woman in
      a studio 25:79 N 1 '48
Study by candlelight. self-por-
   trait Van Gogh 27:27 D 19
      '49; 29:17 O 9 '50
Stuempfig, Walter
   Industrial town* 25:99 S 20 '48
   Manayunk 25:64 O 11 '48
   Sturgeon 25:101 S 20 '48
   Two houses 25:100 S 20 '48
   White boat 25:100 S 20 '48
Stump speaking. Bingham 7:42
   S 11 '39 drawing bw 7:43
   S 11 '39
Stupas
   Buddhist stupa, Swat Valley,
      India photog bw 10:87 My
      12 '41
   Metal stupa, Ceylon photog
      38:87 Mr 7 '55
   Stone stupa, Pagan, Burma
      photog 38:86-7 Mr 7 '55
Sturgeon. Stuempfig 25:101 S 20
   '48
Sturgis, S. D.
   General S. D. Sturgis photog
      bw 11:102 N 10 '41
Sturtevant, Edgar H.
   Edgar Sturtevant photog bw
      11:42 O 13 '41
Stuyvesant, Peter
   Whitney. Peter Stuyvesant
      sculpture bw 7:45 S 11 '39
Su See Animals, Imaginary
Submarines
   Sample. Submarine warfare
      15:54-9 D 27 '43

Suburbia, 1939. bw Nevinson
   9:59 Ag 12 '40
Succareth (Su) See Animals,
   Imaginary
The suckling. sculpture bw
   Baizerman 25:157 O 4 '48
Sudden panic. sculpture Barlach
   41:138-9 N 5 '56
Suffolk
   Gainsborough. View in Suf-
      folk 13:94 N 9 '42
Sugamo Prison, Tokyo
   Japanese prisoners. Life in
      Sugamo Prison wood-
      blocks 34:10-1 F 16 '53
Sugar bowl with fruit. Braque
   26:83 My 2 '49
Sugars and Creamers
   Le Roux. Silver sugar caster,
      U.S. colonial 38:117 Ap
      18 '55
   Pittsburgh creamer. Ameri-
      can glass 39:59 Jy 18 '55
   Stiegel. Sugar bowl, glass,
      U.S. 39:58 Jy 18 '55
   Waugh. Glass sugar and
      creamer bw 7:32 S 18 '39
   Wistarberg, South Jersey
      sugar bowl 39:58-9 Jy 18 '55
Sugaring-off. bw Moses 25:77
   O 25 '48
Sugden, Earl
   Wisconsin scene 10:77 Mr
      31 '41
   Earl Sugden 10:76 Mr 31 '41
      port.
Suggia, Guilhermina
   John. Madame Suggia bw 16:
      79 Ap 24 '44
Sullavan, Margaret
   Philipp, R. Margaret Sulla-
      van bw 8:62 Ap 8 '40
Sullivan, Louis, architect
   Louis Sullivan photog bw 40:
      102 Mr 5 '56
Sullivan, Mark
   Mark Sullivan photogs bw 2:
      61 Mr 22 '37; 5:60-2 D
      5 '38
Sullivan and Adler, architects
   Guaranty Building, Buffalo,

1895 photog 40:102 Mr 5
'56

Sully, Thomas
George Washington bw 24:22
F 23 '48
Nicholas Biddle 39:59 Ag 29
'55
Rebecca Gratz 41:158 D 24
'56
Thomas Biddle, Major, 1818
38:71 Mr 28 '55
Washington at Trenton 29:
Cover Jy 3 '50

Sultan of swat. sculpture bw
Wheelock 8:116 My 20 '40

Sumerian See Art, Mesopotamian

Sumerian high priest marble
sculpture bw 5:Cover Ag
15 '38

Summer. Puvis de Chavannes
15:66 S 20 '43

Summer. Thomas 10:53 Je 23
'41

Summer (Reclining woman of
fruit and vegetables). bw
Arcimboldo, School of 7:
24 Ag 28 '39

Summer. tapestry Dufy 21:84 S
30 '46

Summer evening. Pittman 18:70
F 19 '45

Summer evening. Taubes 8:39
Ja 15 '40

Summer fragrance. bw Watkins,
F.J. 6:45 My 1 '39

Summer night. Wyeth, N.C. 20:
80 Je 17 '46

Summer pleasures. Palmer, W.
C. 4:26 Je 13 '38

Summer sea. Hecht 16:45 Ja 3
'44

Summer showers. Leith-Ross 16:
46 Ja 3 '44

Summer wind. Brook 10:51 Ja
13 '41

Summers, Mrs. James
Forest fire, after Demishoff-
Uralsky 10:77 Mr 31 '41

Summer's day. bw Morisot 40:
148 Ap 23 '56

Sumner, William Graham
William Graham Sumner
photog bw 15:104 S 13 '43

Sumter, Thomas
Thomas Sumter 29:52 Jy 3
'50

Sun
Lippold. Variations within a
sphere, No. 10: The sun
sculpture 41:90 Jy 30 '56

Sun Clock, Laja, Bolivia photog
25:54 Ag 2 '48

Sun Yat-sen. sculpture bw
Bufano 3:62 N 29 '37

A Sunday afternoon on the Island of La Grande-Jatte.
Seurat 31:60-2 Jy 23 '51

Sunday at Xochimilco. Lee, D.
22:76 My 12 '47

Sunday fishing. Sokole 23:68 Jy
14 '47

Sunday at Central Park, bw
Waugh, C. 5:56 N 28 '38

Sunday morning. cartoon bw
Emett 37:45 Jy 5 '54

Sunday morning in the mines.
Nahl 27:49 Jy 4 '49

Sunday, women drying their
hair. Sloan 2:33 F 1 '37

Sundials
Manship. Sundial: three fates
under tree of life bw 4:14
Ja 31 '38
Mather sun dial, Princeton
University photog 21:87
S 23 '46
Sun clock, Laja, Bolivia
photog 25:54 Ag 2 '48
Sundials, 57 faces to tell
time in 57 cities, Mill
Road photog bw 11:65 N 3
'41

Sunflowers. Braque 26:86 My
2 '49

Sunflowers. bw Van Gogh 27:82
O 10 '49

Sung ceramic vase photog 33:
101 O 27 '52

Sunnyside, home of Washington
Irving photogs bw 17:64-
5 O 30 '44

Sunrise--Fulton Fishmarket.
  woodcut Frasconi 37:86-7
  O 18 '54
Sunrise of Mexico. Siqueiros 20:
  60 Je 3 '46
Sunset after rain. Dehn 11:44 Ag
  11 '41
Sunshine, Louis, sculpture
  Plastic surgeon "improves"
    sculptures of historic per-
    sonages bw 12:12-5 Je 8
    '42
  Louis Sunshine photog bw 12:
    15 Je 8 '42 port.
Sun Valley scene. Eisenhower 28:
  151 Ap 17 '50
Supper at Emmaus. Rembrandt
  11:78 D 1 '41; 35:61 Ag 17
  '53; 39:30 D 26 '55
La suppliante. sculpture bw
  Barberini 19:50 Jy 30 '45
Supreme Commander of the Ger-
  man Army (Hitler). bw
  Hommel 9:97 S 23 '40
Supreme Court justices, 1790-
  1940: 80 justices in 150
  years bw 8:48-9 F 12 '40
  group photog of members
  upon appointment of new
  member, 1882-1937 photog
  bw 3:28-9 N 29 '37. in 1865
  photogs bw 14:76 F 15 '43
Supreme Court Building, Wash-
  ington, D.C. photog bw 18:
  76-7 Ja 22 '45
Surgeons See Medical Themes
Surikov, V.
  Storming of the Winter Palace
    14:58 Mr 29 '43
Surratt, Mary
  Mrs. Mary Surratt photog bw
    4:46 F 14 '38
Surrealism 1:24-7 D 14 '36
  McBean. Surrealist portraits
    of English actresses photogs
    bw 4:4-7 My 16 '38
  Surrealist furniture, Galerie
    des Beaux Arts exhibit,
    Paris bw 4:57 F 7 '38
  Terry. The snail, surrealist
    house 1:24 D 14 '56

Surrealistic ear. Hayden 23:98
  N 10 '47
Surrender of Captain Dacres to
  Captain Hill aboard "Old
  Ironsides, " 1812* bw 23:
  71 O 27 '47
The surrender of Lord Corn-
  wallis. Trumbull 5:31 O
  31 '38
Surrender of the Bastille, 1789*
  print bw 3:32 Jy 5 '37
Surveying new lands. mural
  Poor 2:36 Ja 4 '37
Survivors from a torpedoed ship
  Eurich 26:54-5 Mr 21 '49
Susanna and elders. Hogfeldt
  17:57 Jy 3 '44
Susanna and the elders. Benton
  5:30 O 31 '38; 6:40 F 20
  '39; 6:70 Ap 24 '39
Susanna and the elders. Rem-
  brandt 24:79 Mr 22 '48
Susanna and the elders. Tinto-
  retto 27:69 O 24 '49
Susanna in Santa Fe. bw Sloan
  7:44 D 11 '39
Sutherland, Graham
  Sir Winston Churchill 37:30
    D 13 '54
Sutter, John
  John Sutter photog bw 24:44
    F 2 '48
Sutton Hoo Treasure
  Arms and armor, gold jewel-
    ry, drinking horn Anglian
    ship burial, 7th century
    photogs 31:82-5 Jy 16 '51
Svanberg, Max
  The vigilant heart litho-
    graph 33:86 Jy 14 '52
Swainey, George, architect
  Oak Alley, Greek revival
    plantation house, Louisi-
    ana, 1836 photog 32:76-7
    Je 9 '52
Swallow, W. W.
  As the earth sings sculpture
    bw 14:42 Mr 8 '43
"Swamp Fox" Marion's raid 29:
  57 Jy 3 '50
Swans

Corregio. Leda and the swan bw 19:25 D 31 '45

Dali. Leda atomica bw 25:5 Ag 9 '48

Gauguin. Swan lithograph 33: 85 Jy 14 '52

Laurent. Le cygne sculpture bw 10:64 Je 2 '41

Scott. Bewick's swans on a pond 7:54 N 13 '39

Stevens, E. The Chinese swan 28:87 Mr 20 '50

Wright. Leda and the swan sculpture bw 29:122 Ag 28 '50

Swanson, Neil
Neil Swanson photog bw 24:22 My 17 '48

Swanson, Pipsan Saarinen, interior designer
Nordic modern house, Midwest, U.S. photogs 38:118-9 F 21 '55

Swastika
Artzybasheff. Versions of Nazi swastika 13:11 S 14 '42

Nazi German emblem, Reichstag, Berlin, 1939 photog bw 9:68 Ag 19 '40

Swedenborg, Emanuel
Milles. Swedenborg sculpture, model bw 2:32 F 22 '37

Swedish Modern Furniture
Malmsten. Swedish Modern photogs bw 7:45 Jy 31 '39

Ruhtenberg. Swedish-Modern furniture photogs bw 5:36-8 D 12 '38

Swedish Glass
National Museum, Stockholm, exhibit: vases, bowls, decanters, graal-decorated ware bw 17:65-8 Ag 7 '44

Swimming See Games and Sports--Swimming

The swineherd, Brittany. Gauguin 21:62 Jy 29 '46

The swing. Fragonard 23:79 S 15 '47

Swing Low, Sweet Chariot. Mc-Crady 3:39 O 18 '37

"The Swiss Family Robinson," illustrations. Wyss, Johann Emanuel 37:50-61 D 27 '54

Swope, Mrs. John Clemens. Dorothy McGuire (Mrs. John Swope) 21:57 S 2 '46

Swords See Jewelry; Weapons

Sylvette, portrait series. bw Picasso 37:119 N 8 '54

Symbolical Themes See Allegorical and Symbolical Themes; Biblical and Christian Themes

Symphony in brown and silver. Whistler 36:94-5 My 17 '54

Symphony in red. Vuillard 37: 76 N 1 '54

Syon House, England. Adam, R. designer 23:72-3 Ag 25 '47

Syracuse Museum of Fine Arts
Ceramic exhibit, 8th annual photogs bw 9:129-31 N 11 '40

Szigetti, Joseph
Halsman. Joseph Szigetti photog bw 16:49 Mr 13 '44

T

T. P. and Jake. Benton 6:71 Ap 24 '39 bw 10:70 Ap 14 '41

T. R. in Panama. Laning 6:44-5 My 15 '39

Taber, I. W.
Opium smokers, San Francisco, 1892 photog bw 31: 13 S 10 '51

Tabernacle, gold-jewelled and enamelled, 1409 33:32 D 29 '52

Table with bottles and cheese. D'Arista 39:136-7 N 21 '55

Tables See Furniture--Tables

Tables for ladies. Hopper 2:45 My 3 '37

Tableware

American tableware: Lenox;
Vernon; Stangl; and others
photog 9:76-9 S 9 '40

"America's Best" designed
tableware photog 29:89 D
25 '50

Kent. Dinner service 9:76, 78
S 9 '40

Tacchi, Sergio, furniture maker

Antique furniture reproductions photog 37:91, 92 O
25 '54

Ta-Cheng-Tien Confucian temple
photog bw 4:17 My 16 '38

Tagore, Rabindranath

Rabindranath Tagore photog
bw 5:5 Ag 1 '38

Tagore with Helen Keller
photog bw 4:21 F 28 '38

Tahiti See also Gauguin, P.
Religious figure sculpture
38:74 Ja 24 '55

Tahitian landscape. Gauguin 21:
63 Jy 29 '46

Tahitian woman with red mango
blooms. Gauguin 21:61 Jy
29 '46

Tait, Agnes

Cottonwood trees 16:46 Ja 3
'44

Taj Mahal, Agra aerial photog
bw 16:94 Je 5 '44

Take-off from carrier. Arai 28:
67 F 27 '50

Takis, Nicholas

Composition with figures 16:
45 Ja 3 '44

Talbot, Henry Fox

Outdoor group* calotype bw
2:4 Mr 29 '37

Moffat. Henry Fox Talbot,
1860 photog bw 2:5 Mr 29
'37 port.

Talbot, Mary Ann

Mary Ann Talbot bw 14:7 Ja
4 '43

Taliesin West, Arizona. photogs
bw Wright, archt. 21:84
Ag 12 '46

Tall cow. sculpture bw Hardy

37:123 O 11 '54

Tally-O, Ben See Alken, Henry
Thomas

Tam O'Shanter ceramics bw 26:
83 Ja 3 '49

Tamayo, Rufino

Animals howling for food 34:
101 Mr 16 '53

Cow swishing 34:102 Mr 16
'53

Dancers 36:78 My 31 '54

The flute player 20:59 Je 3
'40

The glutton 34:102 Mr 16 '53

Indian woman with baskets of
flowers* mural 34:103 Mr
16 '53

Musicians 34:101 Mr 16 '53

Olga Tamayo, the artist's
wife 34:98 Mr 16 '53

Pretty little girl 34:99 Mr
16 '53

Woman reaching for the moon
34:100 Mr 16 '53

Rufino Tamayo; wife; home
photog bw 34:98, 103-5
Mr 16 '53 port.

Tanchu, Dalai Lama 10:72 Mr
24 '41

Taney, Roger Brooke

Chief Justice Taney 23:57 N
3 '47 bw 18:82 Ja 22 '45

T'ang Ceramics

Warrior; horse photogs 33:
101 O 27 '52

Tanguy, Ives

Mama, papa is wounded bw
19:65 S 24 '55

Slowly toward the north 25:
64 O 11 '48

Tanks through minefield.*
Ingraham 26:59 Mr 21 '49

Taoism

Reception of the Immortals
at the court of Hsi Wang
Mu 38:76-7 Ap 4 '55

Taos, New Mexico

Adobe pueblo, c1700 photog
40:47 Ja 16 '56

The tap on the window. sculpture bw Rogers 6:6 Mr

6 '39

Tapaderos (foot coverings) parade saddle photog 40:51 Ja
16 '56

Tapestry

Blumenfeld. Tapestry, detail,
France, 15th century bw 7:
4 Jy 3 '39

Boucher. La noble pastorale,
Beauvais bw 4:28 Ja 24 '38

Dufy. Summer 21:84 S 30 '46

Goya. El pelele (The manikin),
cartoon 40:73 My 28 '56

King Sigismund August II,
Poland, tapestry commis-
sioned 35:92-5 D 14 '53

Lurcat. Assy church tapestry,
France 28:76 Je 19 '50

Lurcat. Nazi warfare satire
21:81 S 30 '46

Picasso. Confidence 21:84 S
30 '46

Roualt. Circus dancer, Aubusson 21:84 S 30 '46

Tons. Fighting beasts 35:98-9
D 14 '53

Van Coxie. Cain and Abel 35:
95 D 14 '53

Van Coxie. God and Adam 35:
94 D 14 '53

Werner. Tapestry design 36:
145 My 10 '45

Flemish

Alexander the Great visits
Diogenes, Brussels, 17th
century bw 11:52 N 17 '41

Battle of Blenheim, Brussels
24:34-5 Ap 19 '48

Ecco Homo, 15th century bw
5:48 N 28 '38

The giraffe parade, c1525 24:
76-7 Mr 22 '48

Sacraments: marriage; ex-
treme unction, Middle Ages
22:79 Ap 7 '47

France

Bayeux tapestry photog bw 16:
8-10 Je 26 '44   etching of
40:88-9 Mr 26 '56

Don Quixote, Gobelin, c1714,
2 of 28 tapestries 21:82-3
S 30 '46   bw 6:17 Je 19 '39

Gobelin tapestry wall coverings Osterly Park, Eng-
land 23:71 Ag 25 '47

Rosecliff, Newport bw 11:
83 Ag 18 '41

Louis XIV wins the Battle of
Dole, Gobelin, 1674 bw
5:15 S 5 '38

King Arthur, Paris, 14th
century 22:80-1 Ap 7 '47

St. Anthony tapestry, France
1450 21:81 S 30 '46

Unicorn hunt, France, 16th
century 22:70-2 My 26 '47

Tarkington, Booth

Booth Tarkington; family;
home photogs bw 7:54-8 S
4 '39

MacDonald. Booth Tarking-
ton, 1919 photog bw 14:
13 Ja 11 '43

Tarleton, Banastre

Banastre Tarleton bw 29:53
Jy 3 '50

Tarquin See Mythological
Themes--Tarquin

Tarring nets. Levi, J. 20:78
F 18 '46

Tartans, clan, of Scotland 22:
103 My 5 '47

Tasq

Leander and Hero sculpture
bw 11:146 O 13 '41

Tate Gallery, London

Exhibit of Jacob Epstein's
sculptures 33:65-70 N 3
'52

The Tatsuta (Hoshu) collection
of microscopic writing
bw 34:102 F 23 '53

"Tattooed Sailor," book of cartoons. bw Francois 35:109
S 21 '53

Taubes, Frederic

Alexander Lazuk 10:47 F 3
'41

Taubes, Frederic (cont.)
"The Birth of a Nation" is
filmed by Griffith 8:40-1
Ja 15 '40
Figures at the shore 12:46
Mr 9 '42
Rehearsal 4:25 Je 13 '38
Setting the table 6:29 F 13 '39
Studio interior 8:39 Ja 15 '40
Summer evening 8:39 Ja 15
'40
Artist at work photogs bw 8:
38 Ja 15 '40 port.

Taverns See Barrooms, Inns
and Taverns

Tawney, Richard H.
Richard Tawney photog bw 11:
43 O 13 '41

Tax collector. woodcarving bw,
Balinese 15:116 O 25 '43

Taxes
Assyrian taxpayers frieze bw,
8th century B.C. 22:98 Mr
24 '47
Bridge tolls, painted glass,
Belgium, 15th century bw
22:98 Mr 24 '47
First U.S. income tax, 1862
bw 22:99 Mr 24 '47
French peasant paying taxes,
18th century* bw 22:99 Mr
24 '47
Egyptian taxpayers, tomb
painting, 1445 B.C. bw 22:
98 Mr 24 '47
Paying the exciseman cartoon
bw 29:36 Jy 3 '50
Persian taxpayers, bas-relief, 4th century B.C. bw
22:98 Mr 24 '47
Rome's publicans, bas-relief
bw 22:98 Mr 24 '47
Roymerswaler, Tax collec-
tor, Flemish, 16th century
22:98 Mr 24 '47
Wat Tyler rebelling against
English poll tax, England,
1381 bw 22:100 Mr 24 '47
Window tax repeal, England,
19th century* bw 22:100 Mr
24 '47

Taylor, George
George Taylor bw 15:10 Jy 5
'43

Taylor, Laurette
Beaton. Laurette Taylor in
"The Glass Menagerie"
drawing 21:7 Jy 22 '46

Taylor, Richard, cartoonist
Cartoons bw 17:78-9 N 27 '44
"Fractured French," cartoon
book bw 29:126-7 O 9 '50
Richard Taylor photog bw 15:
14 O 25 '43 port.
Self-portrait cartoon bw 15:
14 O 25 '43 port.

Taylor, Tom
Tom Taylor bw 6:11 F 13 '39

Taylor, Wynne Byard
Madonna woodcarving bw 9:
55 Ag 12 '40

Taylor, Zachary
General Zachary Taylor bw
22:116 Je 9 '47 cartoon
bw 31:18 O 22 '51; 37:14
Jy 5 '54

Tchiakovsky, Petr Ilich
Tchiakovsky photog bw 14:96
Mr 29 '43

Tchelitchew, Pavel
Phenomena bw 5:57 S 5 '38

Drawings
Head* bw 30:12 Ja 29 '51
Head in a state of rhythm 30:
11 Ja 29 '51
Interior landscape with
muscles 30:10 Ja 29 '51
Interior landscape with trachea 30:10 Ja 29 '51
Edith Sitwell, wire and wax
head bw 25:170 D 6 '48
(sculpture)
Pavel Tchelitchew photog bw
5:57 S 5 '38; 30:10 Ja 29
'51 port.

Tea
Tea plant* and a Chinese
man bw 24:83 Mr 22 '48

Tea Caddies
China tea caddy, white with
Federal eagle, 18th cen-

tury 17:59 S 4 '44
Hepplewhite. Ornamented tea
     caddies bw 23:77 Ag 25
     '47
Teapots
     China teapot, white with A-
          merican emblems and mot-
          to, 18th century 17:58 S 4
          '44
     Toleware teapot, U.S. 39:57
          Jy 18 '55
     Van Dyck. Silver teapot, U.S.
          colonial 38:116 Ap 18 '55
Tecla, Saint
     El Greco. The Virgin with
          Santa Ines and Santa Tecla
          7:26 D 25 '39
Tecno, furniture designer
     Sofa, adjustable photog bw
          38:84 Je 27 '55
Tedder, Marshal
     Marshal Tedder, "Time"
          cover portrait 17:63 D 11
          '44
Tekakwitha, Catherine
     Catherine Tekakwitha bw 27:
          150 S 19 '49
Tel Aviv
     Modern row houses, apart-
          ments, suburban house
          photogs bw 3:57 Jy 5 '37
Telegraphy
     First telegraph instrument
          photog bw 17:63 D 18 '44
Telkes, Maria, architect
     Sun-heated house, Dover,
          Massachusetts photogs bw
          26:90 My 2 '49
Teel, Henry
     Wyeth, A. Henry Teel tempera
          24:105 My 17 '48
Tehuantepec woman. Lee, D.
     22:77 My 12 '47
Television backstage. drawings
     bw Marsh 37:47 Jy 26 '54
Tell, William
     Vodicka. William Tell sculp-
          ture 41:75 S 10 '56
"The Tell Tale Heart," animated
     motion picture, United Pro-
     ductions of America 35:99-

102 S 7 '53
Temperence poster. lithograph
     Ackermann 39:72-3 D 26
     '55
The tempest. Giorgione 39:166-
     7 O 24 '55
Temple in the clouds. bw Chiang
     Kai-Shek 33:6 O 13 '52
The temple of the mind. Ryder
     30:91 F 26 '51
Temples See also Churches;
     Missions; Mosques
     El Khazna, the Treasury,
          ruined temple, Trans-
          Jordan photog 27:67 O 31
          '49
     Solomon's temple, model;
          photogs bw 6:50-4 My 15
          '39
     Temple of 500 gods, Buddha
          photog bw 3:55 Ag 23 '37

          Cambodia
Angkor-Wat temple photog
     bw 5:37 Ag 1 '38
Bayon Temple, Angkor-Wat
     photog bw 5:38 Ag 1 '38

          China
Arch of Heaven, Peiping
     photogs 20:71 Ap 29 '46
     bw 38:71, 76 Ap 4 '55
Confucian temple photog 38:
     76 Ap 4 '53
Lama temple, Peiping photogs
     20:69 Ap 29 '46
Temple of Heaven, Peiping
     photog bw 3:55 Ag 23 '37
Temples, Peiping photogs
     20:67-77 Ap 29 '46 bw 3:
     54-5 Ag 23 '37
The Yellow temple, Peiping
     photog bw 3:55 Ag 23 '37

          Egypt
Hatshepsut's temple, Delrel-
     Bahri photog bw 24:78-9
     Ja 19 '48 Thebes photog
     41:110-1 N 26 '56

Temples (cont.)

Egypt
Temple of Amen, Karnak
  photog bw 24:79 Ja 19 '48
  Luxor photog bw 24:79 Ja
  19 '48 Thebes photog 41:
  116 N 26 '56.

Greece
Athena Victorious, Athens
  photog bw 18:56 Ja 1 '45
Didymion, ruin, Turkey
  photog bw 8:81 Ap 8 '40
Erechtheum, Athens photog
  bw 18:57-9 Ja 1 '45
Parthenon 35:152-62 O 26 '53
  bw 36:44 Ja 11 '54
Temple of Neptune, Greek,
  doric photog bw 16:12 Je 5
  '44
Temple of Olympian Zeus,
  Athens photog bw 18:58-9
  Ja 1 '45

India
Buddhist temple, of Boddhnath,
  Katmandu, Nepal photog
  bw 38:43 Mr 28 '55
Jain temple, Calcutta photog
  bw 12:86 Mr 16 '42
Temple of Jagannath photog
  bw 3:61 Ag 16 '37
Temple of Sanu-San-Gen-Do,
  Kyoto photog bw 20:52-3
  Je 17 '46
Temple of Siva, South India
  photog 38:65-6 F 7 '55

Mexico
Monte Alban photog bw 22:100
  F 24 '47
Temple of Quetzalcoatl, Teo-
  tihuacan, Toltec photog bw
  4:57 Ap 11 '38; 22:100 F
  24 '47
Temple of the Inscriptions,
  Mayan, Palenque photog bw
  34:70-1 Ap 27 '53
Temple of the sun, Mayan,
  Palenque photog 22:55 Je
  30 '47

Temple of the Warriors, Mayan, Chichen Itza photog
  22:60 Je 30 '47

Rome
Pantheon photog bw 16:12 Je
  5 '44
Roman temples photog bw 16:
  12-3 Je 5 '44
Temple of Vesta photog bw
  17:94 S 4 '44

Thailand
Temple of Dawn, Bangkok
  photog 31:33 D 31 '51
Temple of Marble, Bangkok
  photogs 31:35 D 31 '51
Temple of the Emerald Bud-
  dha photog 31:32 D 31 '51
Temple of Wat Po, Bangkok
  photog 31:34 D 31 '51
Wat Bovornives, Monastery,
  Bangkok photog 38:80 Mr
  7 '55

Tibet
Buddhist temple, Kumbum
  photog bw 24:80 F 16 '48
Gyantze temple photog 6:26
  Ja 12 '39
The temptation and the expul-
  sion. fresco bw Michel-
  angelo 21:64 Jy 1 '46
The temptation in the wilder-
  ness. Tintoretto 31:36 D
  24 '51; 39:20 D 26 '55
Temptation of Christ. bw Duc-
  cio 4:28 F 7 '38
The temptation of St. Anthony.
  Patiner and Massys 31:
  62-3 O 1 '51
Ten cents a ride. Bouche 14:45
  Mr 8 '43
"Ten Nights in a Barroom," il-
  lustrations and title page
  bw 32:63-4 Mr 17 '52
Tender mother. sculpture bw
  Borgatta 37:102 D 6 '54
Tenement. mural Biddle 2:35
  Ja 4 '37
Teniers, David, the younger

Archduke Leopold in his gal-
lery 27:62-3 O 24 '49
Interior of a public house 4:
22 Ap 11 '38
David Teniers bw 4:20 Ap 11
'38 port.
Tennessee Valley Authority.
mural Poor 2:36 Ja 4 '37
Tenniel, John
Anti-Lincoln cartoons; Lin-
coln caricatures; death
tribute bw 6:8-11 F 13 '39
Illustrations of "Alice in
Wonderland" bw 29:22 N 6
'50; 30:85-7 Je 18 '51
John Tenniel 6:8 F 13 '39
port.
Tennis See Games and Sports--
Tennis
Tennyson, Alfred
Alfred Tennyson photog bw
25:99 N 22 '48
Teotihuacan, Toltec city, Mexico
Temple of Quetzalcoatle photog
bw 4:57 Ap 11 '38; 22:100 F
24 '47
Tepees
Miller, A.J. Fort Laramie,
Wyoming, 1837 39:75 N 28
'55
Tepexpan man. sculptured head
bw Steppart 23:95 N 3 '47
Terborch, Gerard
The concert 24:80 Mr 22 '48
Teresa, Saint
St. Teresa bw 31:58 Ag 27 '51
The terminal. photog bw Stieg-
litz 14:6 Ap 5 '43
Terra Cottas
Benjamin Franklin statue bw,
France 6:52 Mr 20 '39
Gregory. Electron children
bw 6:36-7 Mr 13 '39
Holy family group, Italy,
c1400 bw 6:53 Mr 20 '39
Racing horses and charioteers,
Etruscan, c550 40:59 F 13
'56
Satyr abducting a maiden,
Etruscan c480 B.C. 40:60
F 13 '56

Verrocchio. Lorenzo de'
Medici 38:95 F 21 '55
Warrior's head, Etruscan,
5th century B.C. 40:58 F
13 '56
Terry, Ellen
Ellen Terry photog bw 33:82
O 6 '52
Terry, Emilio
The snail, surrealist house,
model bw 1:24 D 14 '36
"Terry and the Pirates." car-
toon bw Caniff 14:10-1 Mr
1 '43
Tesuque church, New Mexico
photog 8:74 My 13 '40
Texas
Historical scenes and por-
traits bw 6:72-3 Ap 10 '39
Zorach. Female figure,
symbol of Texas sculpture
bw 41:93 Jy 23 '56
Textiles See also Carpets and
Rugs; Embroidery; Tapes-
try
American Pre-Victorian
chintz, c 1830 17:60 S 4
'44
Buddha as Messiah, Kigu
banner, Tibet 6:25 Je 12
'39
Cotton, printed, with Washington and Franklin por-
traits, England, 1782 40:
82 Ja 9 '56
Handblocked prints, Folly
Cove designers Yankee
prints, Cape Anne, Mass-
achusetts 19:80-3 N 26
'45
Inca pouch, c1550 bw 36:26
Ap 5 '54
Jewelled bed-spread with
18,000 stones, India 33:
67 D 1 '52
Liebes woven fabrics 23:94-
5 N 24 '47
Navaho Indian blankets 40:
54 Ja 16 '56
Tapa cloth, South Seas bw
21:79 N 4 '46

Textiles (cont.)
  Textile designs from contem-
    porary paintings 22:94-7 Ap
    21 '47; 38:140-4 N 14 '55
  Titcomb. Adam and Eve,
    Crewel embroidery on lin-
    en, 1760 38:120 Ap 18 '55
Thailand
  Golden Meru, cremation altar
    photog bw 28:132, 138-41
    Ap 17 '50
  Royal family bw 28:142 Ap 17
    '50
  Seven-tiered silk umbrellas
    photogs bw 28:133 Ap 17 '50
  Temples of Bangkok photogs
    31:32-5 D 31 '51
Thanksgiving
  Brownscombe. The first A-
    merican Thanksgiving 13:
    77 N 23 '42
  Lee, D. Thanksgiving bw 3:44
    S 20 '37
  Pilgrim's first Thanksgiving*
    bw 19:52 N 26 '45
That which I should have done I
    did not do. Albright, I. 16:
    68 Mr 27 '44 bw 14:47 Mr
    8 '43
Thayendenega (Joseph Brant)
  Humphreys. "Jack of Clubs,"
    playing card 38:Cover Mr
    30 '55
Theater and Theaters See also
    names of plays and musi-
    cals, as "Oklahoma;" names
    of actors, as Adams, Maude
  Backstage, "The Black Crook,"
    1866 engraving bw 31:114 N
    19 '51
  "Carmen," world premier,
    Paris, March 3, 1857 draw-
    ing bw 16:70 My 8 '44
  Cassatt. In the box 36:98 My
    17 '54
  Central Theater of Red Army,
    Moscow photog bw 14:85
    Mr 29 '43
  The Colosseum, Rome photog
    27:44 Ag 1 '49 bw 17:95
    S 4 '44

Degas. Ballet girls on stage
    11:59 S 8 '41
Degas. The operatic star bw
    6:7 Ap 17 '39
Dock Street Theater, Charles-
    ton, first U.S. theater re-
    stored photogs bw 3:49-50
    D 20 '37
Gala performance, 1856, Im-
    perial Theatre, Moscow
    38:64 Ja 31 '55
Greek theater, Pergamum
    photog bw 8:79 Ap 8 '40
Hopper. The Sheridan The-
    atre 2:46 My 3 '37
Hopper. Two on the aisle
    28:103 Ap 17 '50
Marsh. Monday night at Met
    40:82 F 6 '56
Marsh. Television backstage
    drawings bw 37:47 Jy 26
    '54
Marsh. Twenty cent movie
    12:75 Ap 20 '42; 21:77 N
    25 '46
Opera House, Paris, 1862.
    Garnier, archt. photog
    8:62 Je 3 '40
Opera House, Vienna photog
    39:156-60 N 14 '55 Re-
    building 38:157, 160 Je
    13 '55
Roman theater, Petra,
    Trans-Jordan photog 27:
    69 O 31 '49
The Rotunda, Ranelagh
    Gardens, London, 18th
    century 25:100 S 13 '48
Sobrat. Witch play, Bali*
    bw 3:51 S 27 '37
Theater in America--posters,
    engravings, paintings of
    200yrs. 31:110-20 N 19 '51
Theater of Dionysis, Athens,
    340 B.C--seats; details
    of carvings photogs bw
    18:55 Ja 1 '45
Wilson. Laminated wood
    motion picture theater,
    Los Angeles, California
    photog bw 27:67-8 O 10 '49

Theater Design
  Calder. Mobiles and stabiles
    for "Nuclea," Paris 33:86
    Ag 25 '52
  Du Bois, R. Aquacade set 8:
    63 Ap 29 '40
  Du Bois, R. "Ghost Town"
    ballet costumes 8:63 Ap
    29 '40
  Dufy. "Ring Around the
    Moon" theater curtains 30:
    67 Ja 22 '51
  Jenkins. "I Remember Mama"
    set 17:104-5 N 20 '44
  Jones, R. E. "Lute Song" set
    and costume designs 20:
    54-5 Mr 4 '46
  Noguchi. "King Lear," Lon-
    don--costumes and proper-
    ties photogs bw 39:64 Ag
    8 '55
  Vertes. Circus costumes 40:
    82-5 Ap 23 '56
Thecla, Julia
  Painting 33:98 O 27 '52
Theotocopuli, Domenico See
  El Greco
Thermae of Caracalla, Rome bw
  25:80 Ag 9 '48
They're cute when they're small.
  Lalk 10:78 Mr 31 '41
They will not conquer. Puma 16:
  78 Je 12 '44
Thiacourt War memorial, St.
  Mihiel Offensive, 1914-18
  photog bw 3:22 Ag 30 '37
"Thidwick the Big-Hearted
  Moose," written and illus-
  trated by Geisel (Dr. Seuss)
  bw 25:26-7 N 22 '48
Thiemann, Hans
  Artist and his work photog 36:
  145 My 10 '54 port.
Thiers, Adolphe
  Adolphe Thiers photog bw 4:
  14 Mr 28 '38
Thieves Market, Mexico City.
  Lee, D. 22:77 My 12 '47
The thinker. sculpture bw Clews
  31:119 O 15 '51
The thinker. sculpture bw Rodin

38:20 My 9 '55 bronze
  model bw 6:57 Mr 20 '39
Thirst. Fredenthal 21:80 N 25
  '46
This is the place. sculpture bw
  Young, M. 10:79 F 17 '41
Thomas, Byron
  BBC's nine o'clock news* 17:
    64-5 O 9 '44
  Brook willow 10:51 Je 23 '41
  Butterflies 21:65-8 Ag 12
    '46
  Deserted house 10:52 Je 23
    '41
  Florence McGee, the artist's
    wife 10:47 F 3 '41
  GI's landing at Scottish port*
    31:77 O 29 '51; 17:63 O
    9 '44
  Hotel bw 10:53 Je 23 '41
  The minors--the York White
    Roses vs. the Trenton
    Packers 10:51 Je 23 '41
  Moonlight 14:46 Mr 8 '43
  New Castle bw 10:53 Je 23
    '41
  O Little Town of Bethlehem
    23:46 D 22 '47
  Ohio landscape, Lancaster,
    Ohio 22:62-3 Je 16 '47
  Pastime bowling alley 10:
    52 Je 23 '41
  Scotland's River Tay* 17:61
    O 9 '44; 31:80 O 29 '51
  Summer bw 10:53 Je 23 '41
  Two willows in moonlight 23:
    67 Jy 14 '47
  Wartime England drawings
    and paintings 17:57-66 O
    9 '44
  Christmas tree bw 19:8 D
    24 '45 (drawing)
  Byron Thomas and wife; work
    photog bw 10:50 Je 23 '41
    port.
Thomas, Doubting
  Doubting Thomas illumina-
    tion 18:61 Ap 2 '45
Thomas, Norman M.
  Greenland at war 15:77-8
    S 6 '43

Thomas, Norman M. (cont.)
  Seaman Ben Wolf bw 15:76 S
    6 '43 (drawing)
  Wolf. Coxswain Norman
    Thomas drawing bw 15:76
    S 6 '43
Thomas, Saint, Apostle
  Murillo. St. Thomas of Villa-
    nueva dividing his clothing
    among beggar boys 4:42
    My 16 '38
Thomas Aquinas, Saint
  St. Thomas Aquinas bw 22:70
    Ap 7 '47
Thomasita, Sister Mary, sculp-
    tor
  Eighth station of the cross
    bw 35:157 O 12 '53
  Good shepherd bw 35:157 O 12
    '53
  Artist at work photog bw 35:
    157 O 12 '53 port.
Thompson, Dorothy
  Dorothy Thompson photog bw
    2:60 Mr 22 '37
Thompson, Homer A.
  Homer Thompson photog bw
    41:172 S 17 '56
Thompson, Jerome
  Picnic party near Mount Mans-
    field, Vermont bw 25:90
    O 18 '48
Thompson, John W.
  House* 24:72 Ap 5 '48
Thomson, Giles
  Bishop Giles Thomson sculp-
    ture 41:190 N 12 '56
Thon, William
  Convoy 20:97 Ap 29 '46
  The outpost 20:97 Ap 29 '46
  Owl's head 20:98 Ap 29 '46
  Reverie 20:98 Ap 29 '46
  Sea gulls 16:78 Ap 24 '44
  Venetian church 33:94 S 15
    '52
  Artist at work photog bw 20:
    96 Ap 29 '46 port.
Thorak, Josef
  Dancer sculpture bw 9:96 S
    23 '40
Thoreau, Henry David

Walden Pond literary locale
  of Thoreau photog bw 9:
  95 O 14 '40
Thorne miniature rooms, peri-
  od furniture and interiors,
  Chicago Art Institute 3:
  38-42 N 29 '37
Thorndike, Edward Lee
  E. L. Thorndike photog bw
    30:129 F 12 '51
Thorndike, Sybil
  Sybil Thorndike photog bw
    33:82 O 6 '52
Thornton, Matthew
  Matthew Thornton bw 15:10
    Jy 5 '43
Thou sayest it. sculpture bw
  Ryan 8:94 Je 24 '40
Three apostles, stained glass,
  Bourges cathedral 22:72-
  3 Ap 7 '47
Three babes in the Wisconsin
  woods. Glasier 25:58 N
  29 '48
Three bathers with crab. Ren-
  oir 3:47 Jy 5 '37
Three clowns. Roualt 34:60 F
  2 '53
The three dancers. Picasso 8:
  58 Mr 4 '40
Three fates under tree of life,
  sundial. bw Manship 4:
  14 Ja 31 '38
Three Graces
  Boucher. Cupid and three
    graces bw 29:81 N 27 '50
  Ceschiatti. Three graces
    sculpture 36:82 My 31 '54
  Maillol. The three graces
    sculpture 25:101 S 27 '48
  Marini. Three graces sculp-
    ture bw 22:99 My 22 '50
  Rubens. Three graces 41:
    107 O 22 '56
  Sargent. The Wyndham sis-
    ters (The three graces)
    5:37 O 31 '38; 23:79 N 17
    '47
Three judges. Roualt 25:60 O
  11 '48
Three kings. bw Lewandowski

27:56 D 29 '49

The three knaves. ice sculpture
bw Schwerzmann 6:6 Ja 16
'39

Three lawyers (Les trois avocats). Daumier 38:108 My
23 '55

Three miracles of St. Zenobias.
bw Botticelli 21:104 O 28 '46

Three-mold Glassware
Ohio decanter photog 39:59
Jy 18 '55

The three musicians. Picasso
4:43 My 2 '38

Three philosophers. Giorgione
39:170 O 24 '55

The three red houses. Dehn 11:
41 Ag 11 '41

Three standing figures. sculpture Moore, H. 25:100 S
27 '48

Three strikes and...political
cartoon of W.J. Bryan,
1908 40:72 Ja 30 '56

Three Wise Men
Breinen. Silent Night, Holy
Night 23:50-1 D 22 '47
Davis, G.R. We Three Kings
of Orient Are 23:52 D 22
'47
Ford. Epiphany at Bethlehem,
Connecticut 17:38-9 D 25
'44
Giorgione. The three wisemen
(Three philosophers; Evan-
der showing Aeneas the site
of Rome) 39:170 O 24 '55

Threshing in Minnesota. Dehn
11:42 Ag 11 '41

Thrones
Dragon throne, Hall of Su-
preme Harmony, Forbidden
City, Peiping photog 20:69
Ap 29 '46 bw 3:58 Ag 23
'37
Dutch throne, Riddenzaal, The
Hague photogs bw 3:100-1
O 18 '37
Egyptian throne, contempo-
rary photog bw 3:18 Ag 23
'37; 16:88 Ap 10 '44; 33:88

N 24 '52

The golden throne, New Delhi, India photog bw 10:81
Ja 27 '41

Peacock throne, jewelled
photog bw 20:34 Ap 8 '46

Poland's throne, Zamek,
Warsaw photog bw 17:85
Ag 28 '44

Pope's throne, Vatican
photog 20:52 My 13 '46

Royal thrones, Pre-War
House of Lords, England
photog bw 16:88 My 22
'44

Throne of St. Peter, photog
bw 5:41 D 25 '38

Throne of the Nizam of Hyderabad, India photog bw
2:56 Mr 22 '37

Viceroy's Palace thrones,
India photog bw 20:101 My
27 '46

Westminster Abbey throne
photog bw 2:Cover Mr 15
'37

Through the bayou by torch-
light. Currier and Ives
print 21:74 S 2 '46

Thumbing a ride. Pike 29:72
O 9 '50

Thunderstorm in the Rockies.
Bierstadt 19:86 S 10 '45

Thunderbolt crest, Dalai Lama,
Tibet photog bw 36:83 F
22 '54

Thurber, James
Animals bw 20:55 Ja 21 '46
(drawings)
Drawings bw 18:12-3 F 19
'45
"Fables for Our Time,"
book of drawings bw 24:
80 Ap 19 '48
"The Last Flower," book of
drawings bw 7:10-1 N 27
'39
James Thurber photogs bw
18:12-4 F 19 '45 port.
Self-portrait cartoon bw 15:
14 O 25 '43 port.

Thurston, Gerald, furniture de-
   signer
   Hanging lamp photog bw 35:18
      D 14 '53
Thut-Mose, Pharoah of Egypt
   sculpture 41:111 N 26 '56
Tiaras See Jewelry--Tiaras
Tibet
   Dalai Lama
      Tanchu 10:72 Mr 24 '41
      Thunderbolt crest photog bw
         36:83 F 22 '54
   Kigu banner of Buddha 6:25 Je
      12 '49
   Temples
      Buddhist temple, Kumbum
         photog bw 24:80 F 16 '48
      Gyantze temple photog 6:26
         Ja 12 '39
T'ien-T'ai trinity, T'ang dynasty,
   9th century 15:64 O 11 '43
Tiepolo, Giovanni Battista
   The building of the Trojan
      horse 9:48 Jy 29 '40
   Moses spurns the crown of
      Pharoah 35:153 N 16 '53
Tierney, Gene
   Art students portraits. Gene
      Tierney, age 3 28:129-31
      Ap 17 '50
Ties, old school, 32 schools 8:
   73-4 Je 3 '40
Tiffany, Louis Comfort, glass
   maker
   Lamps, shades, vases,
      dishes photogs 40:92-3 Mr
      5 '56
Tiger-man, Inca, painted mantle,
   c930 36:100 Ap 12 '54
Tigers
   Austin. Beast enchanted 19:82
      O 1 '45
   Hardy. Fat running tiger sculp-
      ture bw 37:124 O 11 '54
   Shepard. Tigger drawing bw
      30:76 F 19 '51
Tight rope walker spanning Niaga-
   ra Falls, 1859 print 26:80
   Je 6 '49
Tilden, Samuel Jones
   Samuel Tilden photog bw 14:7

My 31 '43
Tiles See also Mosaics
   Janeway. Decorative tiles and
      plates 19:12-4 Jy 23 '45
   Tile wall, Poland, 17th cen-
      tury bw 17:85 Ag 28 '44
Tilley, Edward
   Coat of arms bw 19:56 N 26
      '45
Tilley, Eustace
   Eustace Tilley, "New Yorker"
      magazine trade mark. Ir-
      vin 21:68 Jy 15 '46
"Time" cover portraits--30
   paintings 17:59-66 D 11 '44
Times square. Dufy 30:65 Ja 22
   '51
Timmie. Christy 20:94 Ap 22 '46
Timoshenko, Semyon
   Marshal Timoshenko, "Time"
      cover portrait 17:64 D 11
      '44
Tin can skipper. Lea 12:55 My
   25 '42
Tin Woodman. Denslow 35:53-9
   D 28 '53
Tinsmithing
   Tin chandelier, 24-candle,
      U.S. colonial photog 38:
      118 Ap 18 '55
Tintagel castle, Cornwall, Eng-
   land photog 40:90-1 Mr 19
   '56 bw 14:76 Je 14 '43
Tintoretto (Jacopo Robusti)
   Abduction of the body of St.
      Mark 23:51 Ag 4 '47
   Adoration of the kings 31:33
      D 24 '51
   The allegory of vigilance 35:
      149 N 16 '53
   Annunciation 31:30-1 D 24
      '51
   Ascension of Christ 31:49 D
      24 '51
   Bacchus and Ariadne bw 12:
      44 Mr 9 '42
   Baptism of Christ 31:36 D 24
      '51
   Christ before Pilate 31:42 D
      24 '51
   Crucifixion 31:44-6 D 24 '51

Flight into Egypt 31:33 D 24 '51

Gethsemane 31:41 D 24 '51

Holy family, detail from Nativity 31:Cover D 24 '51

The last supper, 31:40 D 24 '51; 39:26-7 D 26 '55

Life of Christ mural, School of San Rocco, Venice 31: Cover, 30-49 D 24 '51

Lucretia and Tarquinius 28:73 Je 5 '50

Madonna and Child bw 24:68 Ja 26 '48

Massacre of the innocents 31: 34-5 D 24 '51

Miracle of the loaves and fishes 31:39 D 24 '51

Nativity 31:Cover, 32 D 24 '51

Procession to calvary 31:43 D 24 '51

Resurrection of Christ 31:47-8 D 24 '51

Resurrection of Lazarus 31:38 D 24 '51

Susanna and the elders 27:69 O 24 '49

The temptation in the wilderness 31:36 D 24 '51; 39:20 D 26 '55

"Titanic" (ship)
Sinking of the Titanic, survivor's sketch bw 13:78 N 16 '42

Titcomb, Mary Sarah, textile maker
Adam and Eve, Crewel embroidery on linen, 1760 38: 120 Ap 18 '55

Titian (Tiziano Vecelli)
Adoration of the Magi 1:45 D 28 '36

Adultress brought befor Christ, (painted with Giorgione and Piombo) 39:169 O 24 '55

Antoine Perrenot de Granvella 7:55 O 9 '39

Charles V, King of Spain bw 31:60 O 1 '51

The concert (The musicians) (painted with Giorgione) 39:

168-9 O 24 '55

Danae 27:69 O 24 '49 bw 17: 80 Jy 31 '44

Diana and Actaeon 41:106-7 O 22 '56

Entombment of Christ bw 11: 81 D 1 '41

Jupiter and Antiope bw 12:44 Mr 9 '42

Lavinia with a fan, artist's daughter 40:107 My 7 '56

Man with glove bw 11:83 D 1 '41

Pope Paul III 27:64 O 24 '49 bw 6:32 F 13 '39

Portrait of a man in a red cap 23:Cover Ag 4 '47

Portrait of a nobleman bw 6: 58 Mr 27 '39

The rape of Europa bw 26:160 Ap 11 '49

Sacred and profane love 23: 52 Ag 4 '47 bw 16:65 Ja 10 '44

Tarquin and Lucretia 27:68 O 24 '49

Venus and Adonis 4:29 Mr 21 '38

Venus with organ player 24: 76 Mr 22 '48

Titian bw 4:26 Mr 21 '38 port.

Tito, Marshal
Davidson. Marshal Tito sculpture bw 32:34 Ja 14 '52

Titus, the artist's son. Rembrandt 1:30 N 30 '36 bw 28:58 Ja 30 '50

Tlaloc, ancient rain god sculpture bw 28:62 Ja 9 '50

Tlingit Indians, Alaska
Carved cedar screen, c1825 photog 41:53 Jy 16 '56

To auction. Remenick 10:58 Je 16 '41

To be looked at with one eye, close to, for almost an hour. bw Duchamp 34:26 My 25 '53

To be stared at closely for al-
    most an hour. Duchamp 32:
    103 Ap 28 '52
To the morrow. sculpture bw
    Whitney 7:45 S 11 '39
Toads
    Peacock. American toads 7:46
    Jy 10 '39
Toast of the town. Armstrong 18:
    46 Ja 1 '45
Tobacco Box. silver, U.S. col-
    onial Coney 38:116 Ap 18 '55
Tobey, Alton
    Flood survivors 8:46 F 12 '40
Tobey, Mark
    Electric night 35:85 S 28 '53
    Mark Tobey photog 35:84 S 28
    '53 port.
Todd, Anne Ophelia
    Flowering shrubs 38:95-101 Ap
    11 '55
Toilers of the sea. bw Ryder 30:
    94-5 F 26 '51
The toilet. Cassatt 12:55 Ja 19 '42
Toilet of Bathsheba after the bath.
    Rembrandt 1:33 N 30 '36
    bw 12:44 Mr 9 '42
The toilét of Venus. Boucher 23:
    85 S 15 '47 bw 16:68 Ja 10
    '44; 33:2 D 29 '52
Toilette. Poisson. 23:60 S 1 '47
Toklas, Alice B.
    Alice B. Toklas photog bw 23:
    14 Ag 18 '47
    Beaton. Gertrude Stein and
    Alice Toklas photog bw 4:49
    Ja 3 '38
Tokyo
    Perlin. Tokyo street scenes,
    September 1945--first days
    of occupation 19:73-6 N 19
    '45
Toledo (Ohio) Art Museum--col-
    lection; building; galleries
    7:32-7 Jy 31 '39
Toledo, Spain
    El Greco. View and plan of
    Toledo 28:88-9 Ap 24 '50
    El Greco. View of Toledo 4:
    41 My 16 '38
Toleware

Box, U.S. 39:56 Jy 18 '55
    "Coffin" tray, U.S. 39:57 Jy
    18 '55
    Pitcher, U.S. 39:56 Jy 18 '55
    Teapot, U.S. 39:57 Jy 18 '55
Tolman, John
    Double crucifix woodcarving,
    Church of the Blessed
    Sacrament, Holyoke,
    Mass. bw 35:93 Jy 6 '53
Tolstoy, Leo
    Count Leo Tolstoy photog bw
    8:46 F 5 '40; 14:96 Mr 29
    '43; 41:62 Ag 20 '56
Tolstoy, Sophia
    Mme. Leo Tolstoy photog bw
    41:69 Ag 20 '56
Toltec Art See Art, Pre-Colum-
    bian
"Tom Jones," illustration: Tom
    comes to London bw 25:109
    S 13 '48
Tom Thumb, General, photog
    bw 11:91 S 8 '41
"Tom Thumb" (locomotive) Bal-
    timore and Ohio, 1830
    photog bw 25:13 S 27 '48
Tomahawks, American Indian
    photog 39:76 N 28 '55
Tombs See also Pyramids;
    Sarcophagi
    Abraham Lincoln cenotaph
    and obelisk, Springfield,
    Illinois photogs bw 32:112-
    3 Je 23 '52
    Edward the Confessor tomb,
    Westminster, England
    photog bw 40:108 My 19 '56
    Etruscan tomb painting-dwarf,
    2nd century B.C. 40:64
    F 13 '56
    Fox. Memorial, Westminster
    Abbey bw 24:30 Ja 12 '48
    George V, King of England,
    stone sarcophagus bw 6:
    22 Ap 3 '39
    Haydn, Joseph, crypt photog
    bw 36:54 Je 28 '54
    Heloise and Abelard tomb,
    Paris photog bw 22:77 Ap
    7 '47

Husain tomb, replica photog
    38:87 My 9 '55
Mary, Consort of George V,
    King of England tomb ef-
    figy. Dick bw 36:44 F 8 '54
Mayan tomb, Temple of the
    Inscriptions, Palenque
    photog bw 34:70-1 Ap 27 '53
Mourning figures, tomb, Bur-
    gundy, 15th century bw 15:
    64 S 20 '43
Napoleon's tomb, Paris photog
    bw 9:15 Ag 5 '40
Ptah-Iruk, guardian statues
    and wall paintings, Egypt,
    2500 B.C. 24:77 Ja 19 '48
Ramesis VI tomb, Egypt,
    c1100 B.C. photog 24:83 Ja
    19 '48
Sutton Hoo, Anglian ship burial,
    7th century photogs 31:82-5
    Jy 16 '51
Taj Mahal, Agra, aerial photog
    bw 16:94 Je 5 '44
Tutankhamen tomb treasures
    41:112-3 N 26 '56
Urn tombs, Petra, Trans-
    Jordan photogs 27:68-9 O
    31 '49
Vatican Caetenii tomb, Rome,
    c3rd century 28:72-3 Mr
    27 '50
White. Indian chief's tomb 22:
    82 Mr 10 '47
Tombstone rubbings, U.S. bw
    Dienes 37:133-6 N 15 '54
Tomlin, Bradley Walker
    Bradley Walker Tomlin photog
    bw 30:34 Ja 15 '51 port.
Tomorrow and tomorrow. Martin,
    F. 9:92 N 11 '40
Tompkins, Daniel
    Daniel Tompkins bw 9:8 Ag 5
    '40
Tonka, Kigu banner of Buddha,
    Tibet 6:25 Je 12 '49
Tons, William
    Fighting beasts, tapestry de-
    sign 35:98-9 D 14 '53
Tools, Agricultural
    Deere. Steel "singing plow,"

1837 photog 39:78 N 28 '55
McCormick's reaper, 1831
    model photog 39:78 N 28
    '55
Rake, mechanized photog 39:
    78 N 28 '55
Rake, sulky--with iron teeth
    photog 39:78 N 28 '55
Sickle, neolithic pottery 40:81
    Ap 16 '56
Toonerville Trolley, final car-
    toon. bw Fox 38:92 F 21
    '55
Top of a town. bw Baum 36:90
    Ja 25 '54
Topiary Garden
    Mill Road, Lake Forest, Ill.
    photogs bw 11:62-6 N 3
    '41
Toplady, Augustus
    Toplady's "Rock of Ages"
    locale photog bw 14:83 Je
    14 '43
Topolski, Feliks
    War around the world draw-
    ings 18:51-4 Mr 19 '45
Tops. Rosenthal, D. 15:65 N
    22 '43
Torah cases, silver photogs bw
    4:47 Ap 18 '38
Torah scrolls photog 29:160 S 11
    '50 bw 36:75 My 24 '54
Torii photog 29:85 Ag 28 '50
The tornado. bw Curry 15:19 N
    29 '43
Tornado over Kansas. Curry 1:
    29 N 23 '36; 21:73 N 25 '46
Torso. sculpture bw Cashwan
    24:95 Ap 12 '48
Torso. sculpture bw Davidson
    10:108 Mr 17 '41
Torso. sculpture Mestrovic 25:
    101 S 27 '48
Torso, male, 1930. sculpture
    bw Wotruba 38:88 Je 20
    '55
Torso of a girl. sculpture bw
    Maillol 8:109 Ap 15 '40
Torso of a young woman. sculp-
    ture bw Maillol 8:107 Ap
    15 '40

Tortoises See Turtles

Torture chamber. Davis, F. 19:
53 Jy 16 '55

Toscanini, Arturo
Arturo Toscanini photog bw 6:
8 Mr 27 '39; 18:78 Ja 29 '45
conducting New York Phil-
harmonic photog bw 3:55 D
27 '37   conducting; family;
colleagues photog bw 16:76-
87 Ja 17 '44   with grand-
daughter photogs bw 7:63-7
N 27 '39
Ryan. Arturo Toscanini sculptured head bw 8:95 Je 24
'40

Tossing the cans. Lea 12:55 My
25 '42 bw 14:6 Je 28 '43

Toulouse-Lautrec, Henri de
At la mie 28:99 My 15 '50
At the cafe 15:68 S 20 '43
At the Moulin Rouge 28:98-9
My 15 '50
Billboard posters: Jane Avril;
May Belfort 28:92-3 My 15
'50
The black countess 28:97 My
15 '50
The dance at Moulin Rouge 28:
99 My 15 '50
In the circus--Fernando the
ringmaster 11:59 S 8 '41
In the salon: Rue des Moulins,
detail 28:100 My 15 '50
Oscar Wilde, caricature 28:97
My 15 '50
Painting* watercolor 31:68 S
3 '51
Suzanne Valadon, age 20 bw
28:88 Ja 16 '50
Woman in a studio 25:79 N 1
'48
Woman with black boa 28:97
My 15 '50

Drawings
Couple dancing at Moulin Rouge
bw 28:96 My 15 '50
Dancing clown bw 28:96 My 15
'50
Horses* bw 36:110 Ap 26 '54

The jockey bw 28:96 My 15 '50
Henri de Toulouse-Lautrec;
family; at work photogs bw
28:93-5 My 15 '50 portrait
33:51 S 29 '52 port.
Self-portrait bw 28:96 My 15
'50 port.

Towers See also religious
structures, as Cathedrals;
Churches; Missions; Pa-
godas
Eiffel tower, Paris photog 8:
63 Je 3 '40
Giotto's tower, Florence
photog bw 25:57 D 27 '48
The golden tower, Buddhist
shrine, Tibet photog 6:26
Je 12 '39
Leaning tower of Pisa photog
bw 18:107-8 Je 18 '45
Siva Hindu tower, Madras
photogs 27:98-9 S 12 '49
Trylon, triangular tower, New
York World's Fair, 1939.
photog bw Dreyfuss, de-
signer 4:11 Ja 31 '38 plan
5:54-7 Ag 1 '38
Wooden towers, Golden Gate
International Exposition
bw 5:71 D 5 '38

Town hall, Auvers. Van Gogh
33:95 O 27 '52

Town square. McCrady 3:41 O
18 '37

Toynbee, Arnold J.
Historian Toynbee photog bw
24:119 F 23 '48

Toys See also kinds of toys, as
Dolls and Puppets
Alexander Graham Bell tetra-
hedral kite photog bw 10:
79 My 12 '41
Building toys 35:125-8 S 14
'53
Chinese-American kites
photogs bw 10:79-82 My
12 '41
Christmas toys photogs 7:64-
6 D 18 '39; 25:49-52 N 29
'48 bw 3:110-1 N 15 '37;
9:97-105 D 9 '40

Eames. Cardboard construction toy photog bw 29:151
S 11 '50

Eames. Punch-out color cards
39:121 O 17 '55

Fiddlestraws, children's construction kit 40:71-2 Je 25
'56

Gilbert, A. Toys--erector
sets; American flyer trains
photogs bw 21:67 N 18 '46

Hughes, T. Plastic carnival
toys 29:32-3 D 25 '50

Lionel corporation toy trains
photogs bw 3:51-2 D 13 '37

Model locomotives photogs 29:
34 D 25 '50

Playground equipment, Philadelphia photogs 37:118-20
S 13 '54

Sears. Wing-e-es, after Leonardo da Vinci design 39:63
O 3 '55

Toy soldiers, Lord Greenway's
collection photogs bw 16:8-
10 My 1 '44

Wheeled horse, Cyprus, c1000
BC photog bw 6:53 Mr 20
'39

"Z-man" photogs bw 41:161 N
12 '56

Exhibits

Houston Art Museum exhibit of
toy design 40:147-150 Mr 19
'56

Museum of Modern Art exhibit
of Hughes' plastic toys 29:
32-3 D 25 '50

Tracks along the Hudson. Dehn
11:41 Ag 11 '41

Tracy, Elizabeth
Bathers* mural bw 18:34 Ap 2
'45

Tracy, William
Jonah and the whale ceramics
bw 9:129 N 11 '40

Trade Marks
"New Yorker" magazine: Irvin.
Eustace Tilley 21:68 Jy 15 '46
Victor Company: Barraud.
His master's voice bw 33:

92 N 17 '52
White Rock trademark drawings
Psyche bw 22:14 Je 30 '47

Trafalgar. Turner 24:67 My 10
'48

The tragic Lincoln. sculpture bw
Wheelock 8:117 My 20 '40

Trains See Railroads

Tranquillity. Weber 19:85 Ag 20
'45; 21:78 N 25 '46

Transcendence. Rattner 27:62
Ag 29 '49

Transfer of mail from liner to
tugboat. mural Marsh 2:33
Ja 4 '37

Transfiguration See Jesus
Christ--Transfiguration

The transfixed hour. Day 10:68
My 26 '41

Transflux. Pereira 34:74-5 Ja
26 '53

Trapper. Chambers 26:78 Je 6
'49

Trapper, 1837. bw Miller 27:40
Jy 4 '49

The trappers' return. Bingham
28:76-7 Mr 6 '50

Traubel, Helen
Helen Traubel photog bw 16:
45 Mr 13 '44

The travellers. Ming dynasty,
16th century, after Kuo Hsi
15:68 O 11 '43

The travellers' halt. Cuyp 41:72-
3 D 10 '56

Trays
Neolithic pottery tray 40:78
Ap 16 '56
Toleware "coffin" tray, U.S.
39:57 Jy 18 '55

Tres Riches Heures du Duc de
Berry. illuminations Lim-
bourg brothers 24:38-50
Ja 5 '48

Treanor and Fatio, architects
Country house, Scarsdale,
New York photogs, plan
bw 9:76, 86-7 Jy 1 '40

"Treasure Island, " illustrations. Wilson, E.A. 18:
56 Ap 23 '45

Treat, Lawrence
  Lawrence Treat photog bw 22:
    20 Mr 10 '47
"Treatise on Rural Economy."
  Flemish manuscript, 15th
  century 22:78-80 My 26 '47
Treaty of Ghent. Forestier 41:72-
  3 Jy 2 '56
Tredwell House, New York City,
  1830--bedroom photog 18:
  58 My 7 '45
Tree in landscape. Lucioni 3:47
  Jy 19 '37
Tree of Jesse illumination 34:85
  F 23 '53
The tree of life. sculpture bw 2:
  72 Je 14 '37
Tree of Life
  Manship. Sundial: Three fates
    under tree of life sculpture
    bw 4:14 Ja 31 '38
Tree planting. lithograph bw
  Wood, G. 14:57 Ja 18 '43
Tree-trunk portrait of Abraham
  Lincoln, New Salem, Ill.
  Phillips, A.F. 36:80-1 F
  15 '54
Trees See also names of trees,
  as Cypresses; Landscapes
  Birch. Penn's tree, c1800 38:
    70-1 Mr 28 '55
  Brownell. The charter oak,
    Hartford, Connecticut 13:
    82 N 23 '42
  Cezanne. House in the trees
    37:66 Ag 9 '54
  Churchill. Olive grove at La
    Dragoniere 20:47 Ja 7 '46
  Dodd. Lumpkin Street 27:63
    S 26 '49
  Ford. Guardian angel 10:71 Ap
    14 '41
  Lucioni. Lake through the lo-
    custs 3:49 Jy 19 '37
  Lutherbaum engraving, c1800
    35:154 S 21 '53
  Peirce. The birches 12:61 Je
    15 '42
  The sacred oak of Guernica,
    Spain photog bw 2:61 My 10
    '37

Tait. Cottonwood trees 16:46
  Ja 3 '44
Thomas, B. Brook willow 10:
  51 Je 23 '41
Thomas, B. Two willows in
  moonlight 23:67 Jy 14 '47
Tung Yuan. Clear weather in
  the valley 15:66-7 O 11 '43
Wood, G. Parson Weems'
  fable 8:32-3 F 19 '40 bw
  14:58 Ja 18 '43
Trellis. Drumlevitch 39:116-7 S
  12 '55
Tremaine, F. Orlin
  F. Orlin Tremaine photog bw
    22:21 Mr 10 '47
Trencher, wood, U.S. colonial
  photog 38:119 Ap 18 '55
Trevelyan, George M.
  George M. Trevelyan photog
    bw 15:102 S 20 '43
Trial by combat, Middle Ages
  bw 40:112 Mr 26 '56
Trial by jury, English court bw
  40:111 Mr 26 '56
Triangular bust. sculpture bw
  Gazzini 32:66 Mr 10 '52
The tribuna. Zoffany 25:104-5
  S 13 '48
The tribute money. fresco Ma-
  saccio 39:22-3 D 26 '55
Tribute to the working man.
  Sharrer 31:12 D 17 '51
Trinidad
  Turnbull. Trinidad, World
    War scenes 18:66-7 Ap 30
    '45
The trinity. El Greco 31:72 O 1
  '51
The trinity, Santero painting 40:
  48-9 Ja 16 '56
Trinity church, New York City
  photogs bw 15:126-9 N 15
  '43
Trinity college chapel, Hartford,
  Connecticut
  Misericords woodcarving bw
    37:82 S 27 '54
Tripoli
  Corne. Bombardment of Tri-
    poli, 1804 9:47 O 28 '40

Triptych See also Altars and
   Altarpieces
   Bosch. The garden of delights,
      with details 27:75-82 N 14
      '52
Tritons See Mythological
   Themes--Tritons
The triumph of Bacchus. Poussin
   7:53 O 9 '39
The triumph of Death. Brueghel,
   P., the elder 31:66-7 O 1
   '51
The triumph of Death. Uccello,
   School of 4:28 F 7 '38
Triumph of justice. mural Kroll
   4:38 Ap 25 '38
Triumph of the egg. sculpture bw
   Flannagan 6:82 My 22 '39
Triumphal Arches See Arches
Triumphal Columns See Columns
Les trois avocats. Daumier 38:
   108 My 23 '55
Trojan Horse
   Tiepolo. The building of the
      Trojan horse 9:48 Jy 29 '40
Triumphal march. Rey 2:34 F 22
   '37
Trompe L'Oeil See also Harnett,
   William
   Cabinet work, Study of the
      Duke of Urbino, 15th century
      photogs bw 18:12-4 My 21 '45
   Veronese. Frescoes, The
      Villa Maser 29:58-65 Jy 24
      '50
Troop movements. Burns 13:31
   Jy 6 '42
Troops landing near Veracruz,
   Mexican War, 1847 bw 22:
   112 Je 9 '47
Trophy of the hunt. Harnett 10:74
   Ap 14 '41
Tropic of Cancer. Cereno 36:80
   My 31 '54
Tropic seas. bw Waugh, F.J. 2:
   56 Je 14 '37; 3:24 D 20 '37
Tropical forest. Mwenze 34:106
   My 4 '53
Troubetskoy, Paul
   George Bernard Shaw sculp-
      tured head bw 41:104B Ag

6 '56
Trotsky, Leon
   Leon Trotsky photog bw 31:
      116 O 29 '51
   Leon Trotsky and wife in Mex-
      ico photog bw 2:67 Ap 26
      '37
   Trotsky; wife; death photogs
      bw 9:17-21 S 2 '40
Trouble in Frisco. Martin, F. 9:
   92 N 11 '40 bw 5:30 O 31
   '38
The trough. Chagall 22:58 My 5
   '47
Trout fishing. Pleissner 25:66-7
   Ag 23 '48
The truant gamblers. Mount 18:
   66 Je 25 '45
Truman, Harry
   Jacobs. Harry Truman 19:59
      N 24 '45
   Kempton. Harry Truman, as
      Masonic Grand Master 26:
      54 Mr 28 '49; 39:105 O 24
      '55
   Lambert. Harry Truman,
      caricature sculpture bw
      21:32 O 7 '46
   Wolverton. Harry Truman,
      caricature bw 22:16 My 5
      '47
Trumbull, John
   Alexander Hamilton, 1805 23:
      64 Jy 7 '47
   Death of General Montgomery
      29:42-3 Jy 3 '50
   Declaration of Independence
      14:64 Ap 12 '43
   Harriet Chew 41:158 D 24 '56
   Rainbow 26:78 Je 6 '49
   The surrender of Lord Corn-
      wallis 5:31 O 31 '38
   Washington resigning his
      commission 16:47 Ja 24 '44
      18:Cover Je 18 '45
   John Trumbull bw 11:91 S 8
      '41 port.
Trumpets See Musicians and
   Musical Instruments--
   Trumpets

Trylon and Perisphere, triangular
    tower and steel sphere,
    New York World's Fair,
    1939. Dreyfuss, designer
    photog bw 4:11 Ja 31 '38
    plan 5:54-7 Ag 1 '38
Tschacbasov, Nahum
    Walkowitz bw 16:79 F 21 '44
Tsong-Kha-Pa, founder of the
    Yellow Hat Order, Tibet 8:
    34 Ja 8 '40
Tube shelter perspective, 1941.
    Moore, H. 26:56 Mr 21 '49
Tudor Architecture
    English country houses photogs
    41:154-61 N 5 '56 bw 19:97,
    102-3 O 29 '45
Tufted drakes diving. Scott 1:42
    D 21 '36
Tuleries gardens, Paris photog
    8:57 Je 3 '40
Tula, Mexico, Toltec idols
    sculpture bw 22:101 F 24
    '47
Tumblers. print bw Riggs 3:47 S
    13 '37
Tumblers (drinking glass) See
    Goblets and Glasses
Tumblers and pigeons. Hooft 30:
    36-7 Ja 15 '51
Tulip farm. De Martelly 25:68 Ag
    23 '48
Tung Yuan
    Clear weather in the valley 15:
    66-7 O 11 '43
Turin airview photog bw 15:26-7
    Ag 9 '43
Turkey-track quilt pattern bw 11:
    64 S 22 '41
Turkeys
    Audubon. Wild turkey bw 5:28
    O 31 '38
    Cowles. Big turkey 24:77 F 9
    '48
    Jacques. The wild turkey 9:58
    N 4 '40
Turkish bath. Ingres 10:73 Ap 28
    '41; 41:107 O 22 '56
The turn in the road (Bend in the
    road). Cezanne 25:78-9 N 1
    '48; 40:76 My 28 '56

Turnbull, James
    Guerilla hero* 39:54 Ag 15 '55
    Lingayen Gulf invasion* 39:57
    Ag 15 '55
    Trinidad, World War scenes
    18:66-7 Ap 30 '45
Turner, Beatrice
    Daddy in death bw 29:12 Jy 10
    '50
    Self-portraits bw 29:12-4 Jy
    10 '50
Turner, John
    Smibert. John Turner, c1730
    bw 9:74 D 9 '40
Turner, John B.
    Wood, G. John B. Turner,
    pioneer 14:53 Ja 18 '43
Turner, Joseph Mallord William
    Cologne: The arrival of a
    packet boat 3:36 D 27 '37
    The Grand Canal, Venice:
    Shylock 5:44 S 12 '38
    Rain, steam and speed 25:96
    N 22 '48
    Trafalgar 24:67 My 10 '48
    Joseph Turner bw 5:42 S 12
    '38 port.
Turning the stake boat. Eakins
    15:68 S 20 '43
Turnstall, J.H.
    J. H. Turnstall photog bw 11:
    68 Ag 4 '41
Turpin, E. A.
    Getting to work 12:40 Mr 2
    '42
Turtles
    Tortoise, Northland shopping
    center, Detroit sculpture
    37:83 Ag 30 '54
    Turtle sculpture bw, Prehis-
    toric Northwest U.S. 32:
    100 My 5 '52
    White, J. Box tortoise 22:84
    Mr 10 '47
    White, J. Terrapin 22:84 Mr
    10 '47
Turtle Creek Valley. Kane, J.
    2:46 My 17 '37
Tutankhamen, King of Egypt
    Tomb treasures--masks,
    sculpture, relief, wall

paintings 41:112-3 N 26 '56

Tutankhamen mummy mask;
portrait statues 24:80-1 Ja
19 '48

Twenty cent movie. Marsh 12:75
Ap 20 '42; 21:77 N 25 '46

Twice a year he laughs. Ernst
32:59 Ja 21 '52

Twilight in Castile. Palencia 29:
102 D 11 '50

Twilight ride, Monterey, Mexico.
Lee, D. 22:78 My 12 '47

Twining, David
Hicks. The residence of David
Twining in 1787 9:76 D 9 '40

The twins concert. Peirce, W.
19:84 N 12 '45

Two acrobats with dog. Picasso
8:57 Mr 4 '40 bw 6:83 My
22 '39

Two dancers. Milles sculpture
bw 2:32 F 22 '37

Two dieties. fresco bw, Chinese,
12th century 35:152, 155 O
5 '53

Two houses. Stuempfig 25:100 S
20 '48

Two little circus girls. Renoir
11:59 S 8 '41

The two lovers, German, 15th
century 4:30 F 7 '38

Two men. sculpture bw Harkavy
32:78 Ja 7 '52

Two musicians. Weber 19:86 Ag
20 '45

291, Studio-salon of Stieglitz.
photog bw Stieglitz 14:7 Ap
5 '43

Two on the aisle. Hopper 28:103
Ap 17 '50

Two patriarchs. Weber 33:99 O
27 '52

Two rowers. Cremonini 38:72-3
Ja 17 '55

Two sisters, American primitive
36:95 Je 28 '54

Two story cabin, New Salem,
Illinois, 1835. Phillips, A.
F. 36:80 F 15 '54

Two willows in moonlight.
Thomas, B. 23:67 Jy 14 '47

Two women. Bellows 20:82 Mr
25 '46

"Two Years Before the Mast,"
illustrations. Wilson, E.
A. 18:60 Ap 23 '45

The two young giants (Russia and
U.S.A.), 1873 cartoon bw
19:94 Ag 27 '45

Tyler, John
John Tyler bw 9:8 Ag 5 '40

Tyler, Wat
Wat Tyler rebelling against
English poll tax, England,
1381* bw 22:100 Mr 24 '47

Tyndale, William
William Tyndale bw 34:84 F
23 '53

Tynys, Arvi
Mother and Child sculpture
bw 28:98 Mr 13 '50

Typewriter Paintings
Escardivol. Pictures with
typewriter designs 35:10-2
Jy 20 '53

Tyson collection of oriental art
33:100 O 27 '52

Tzu Hsi, Empress Dowager of
China photogs bw 24:8-10
Ap 5 '48

U

Ubasti, cat goddess, 6th century
B.C. bw 5:16 Ag 29 '38;
13:92 N 9 '42

Uccello, Paolo, School of
The triumph of Death bw 4:28
F 7 '38

Uhlmann, Hans, sculptor
Artist and his work photog 36:
144 My 10 '54   port.

Ukraine, official seal bw 21:121
O 28 '46

Ulm cathedral, Germany, details of architecture and
sculpture photogs 35:28-31
D 28 '53

Ulysses and the sirens. Draper
23:85 N 17 '47

Uma
  Headless statue sculpture bw
    31:37 D 17 '51
Umberto I, King of Italy
  Assassination of Umberto I bw
    20:28 Je 24 '46
  King Umberto I photog bw 20:
    28 Je 24 '46
Umbrellas, seven-tiered silk,
    Thailand photogs bw 28:133
    Ap 17 '50
Umlauf, Charles
  St. Francis sculptured head bw
    27:145 O 17 '49
"Uncle Pogo's So-So Stories."
    cartoon book bw Kelly, W.
    34:20-1 My 11 '53
Uncle Sam, Symbol of U.S.A.
  Evolution of Uncle Sam car-
    toons bw 41:22-4 Jy 2 '56
"Uncle Tom's Cabin," posters
  Death of Little Eva; Simon
    Legree and Uncle Tom* 41:
    60 S 3 '56
Under a cloud. Ryder 30:88-9 F
    26 '51
Under the pandanus. Gauguin 21:
    63 Jy 29 '46
Underground railroad bw 33:97 S
    29 '52
Underseas ballet. bas-relief bw
    Kane, M. 7:36-7 Jy 17 '39
Undset, Sigrid
  Sigrid Undset photog bw 8:90
    Je 10 '40
Unequal combat. bw Morris 26:
    84 F 21 '49
UNESCO
  "What is Race," illustrations.
    Kleiman 34:101-2 My 18 '53
Unexpected encounter. Diego 20:
    82 Mr 11 '46
Unicorn See Animals, Imagin-
    ary--Unicorns
Union of Poland and Lithuania,
    1569* bw 17:87 Ag 28 '44
Unistrut Building, pre-fabricated
    bolted steel photog bw 38:
    69-70 My 9 '55
United Biscuit Company, Melrose
    Park, Illinois photog 36:34

  Ja 4 '54
United Nations
  Emblem bw 33:115 N 3 '52
United Nations Headquarters,
    New York City
  Architects: Wallace K. Har-
    rison, Sven Markelius, Le
    Corbusier, Oscar Niemey-
    er photogs bw 22:34-5 My
    26 '47
  Leydenfrost. U.N. Head-
    quarters plan drawing bw
    22:32-3 My 26 '47
  U.N. General Assembly
    Building photogs bw 33:34
    O 27 '52; 33:Cover, 113-9
    N 3 '52
  Krohg. Peace and freedom*
    mural bw, Security
    Council 33:114 N 3 '52
  U.N. Secretariat Building
    photogs 30:62-3 Mr 26 '51
United States
  Emett. An answer to Yorktown
    --series of cartoons 37:42-
    53 Jy 5 '54
  "Krokodil," Russian humor
    magazine cartoons of U.S.
    A. 27:145-6 D 12 '49
  U.S. ambassadors to Britain:
    24 paintings and photo-
    graphs bw 10:26-7 Mr 3
    '41
  U.S. losing candidates for
    President of the U.S.--19
    portraits bw 14:6-7 My 31
    '43
  U.S. map, London, 1783 6:
    43 Je 5 '39
  U.S. Presidents--portraits
    on campaign songs 25:22-4
    O 4 '48
  U.S. Secretaries of State--
    16 portraits 19:84-9 S 24
    '45
  U.S. Vice-Presidents, 1789-
    1940 bw 9:8-11 Ag 5 '40
  Yvon. The genius of America
    bw 33:44 S 29 '52
United States--History See also
    War Themes; and names of

historical personages, as
Washington, George; and
events, as Whiskey Rebellion
First U.S. income tax, 1862
bw 22:99 Mr 24 '47
Historical photographs bw 6:
31-9 Je 5 '39
Humphreys. Historical playing
cards 38:Cover My 30 '55
"Meriken Shinshi," 1853, Japanese illustrated history of
U.S. bw 25:6-8 Ag 2 '48
Meserve collection of photographs of the 1880's bw 13:
10-3 O 19 '42
U.S. Army Signal Corps--his-
toric photographs, 1850 to
present bw 7:46-55 Ag 28 '39
U.S. military tradition--Revo-
lutionary to World War bw
12:90 My 25 '42
U.S. shown in 16th century
watercolors and engravings
22:80-5 Mr 10 '47
United States--History--Revolu-
tion
American Revolution--paintings,
cartoons 29:36-59 Jy 3 '50
Blarenberghe. British surrender,
Yorktown, October 19, 1781
29:58-9 Jy 3 '50
Boston Tea Party, 1773 print
bw 22:99 Mr 24 '47
Cornwallis' surrender, 1781*
bw 7:70 S 25 '39
Davies. Capture of Fort Lee
29:45 Jy 3 '50
Davies. Capture of Fort Washington 29:45 Jy 3 '50
Doolittle. On Lexington green
engraving 29:40 Jy 3 '50
Doolittle. Marching in to Concord engraving 29:40 Jy 3
'50
Jasper's rescue of American
civilians from the British,
1779* engraving 13:58 Jy 6
'42
Paoli massacre of continental
soldiers print bw 35:92 S 28

'53
Paying the exciseman cartoon
bw 29:36 Jy 3 '50
Revere. Boston massacre 29:
39 Jy 3 '50
Revolution scenes in the South,
prints and paintings 13:59
Jy 6 '42
Romans. Bunker Hill engrav-
ing 29:41 Jy 3 '50
Stamp Act repeal, 1766 car-
toon bw 22:99 Mr 24 '47
"Swamp Fox" Marion's raid
29:57 Jy 3 '50
Trumbull. Death of General
Montgomery 29:42-3 Jy 3
'50
Trumbull. The surrender of
Cornwallis 5:31 O 31 '38
Willard, A.M. Spirit of '76
bw 9:55 Ag 5 '40
United States--History--War of
1812 See also "Constitution"
Birch. Constitution and
Guerriere 9:47 O 28 '40
Garneray. Battle of Lake Erie
9:48 O 28 '40
The General Armstrong sur-
rounded, 1814. Leutze 9:
48 O 28 '40
Pocock. Constitution and Java
9:48 O 28 '48
United States--History--War with
Mexico, 1845-1848 See
also Chapultepec
Battle of Buena Vista, near
Monterey bw 22:110-1 Je 9
'47
Currier and Ives print. Amer-
ican soldiers return from
Mexican War, 1847* bw
22:125 Je 9 '47
General Scott's triumphal pa-
rade, Mexico City* bw 22:
122 Je 9 '47
Meyers. California naval war,
1847: Scenes of the U.S.
Navy in the Pacific 7:43-4
Ag 28 '39
Troops landing near Veracruz
bw 22:112 Je 9 '47

U.S. History (cont.)
    Woodville. War news from
        Mexico 9:77 D 9 '40; 27:58
        Ag 29 '49
United States--History--Civil
    War See also Balloons
    Andersonville drawing bw,
        1864 39:166 S 12 '55
    Antietam Creek, Maryland,
        1862 13:62 Jy 6 '42
    Bingham. Order No. 11 7:41
        S 11 '39
    Blythe. General Doubleday
        crossing the Potomac, 1863
        6:29 Je 19 '39
    Currier and Ives print. Bom-
        bardment of Island No. 10
        21:72 S 2 '46
    Currier and Ives print. Farra-
        gut's victory at New Orleans
        21:73 S 2 '46
    Davidson. Monitor and Merri-
        mac, 1862 9:49 O 28 '40
    French. Cavalrymen crossing
        a river mural 10:44 Ja 27
        '41
    Gettysburg 13:62 Jy 6 '42
    Homer. Prisoners from the
        front 5:33 O 31 '38
    Nast. Confederate cavalry raid-
        ing Kentucky* drawing bw 6:
        3 Ja 2 '39
    U.S. Civil War--Confederate,
        Union cavalry bw 39:165 S
        12 '55
United States--History--Spanish
    American War, 1898
    Chapman. U.S.S. Maine 9:49
        O 28 '40
    Hereford. "The yellow peril,"
        William R. Hearst cartoon
        bw 31:27 Ag 27 '51
    Remington. Spanish police
        searching Cuban woman* bw
        31:27 Ag 27 '51
    "Yellow Kid," caricature of
        W. R. Hearst, 1898 bw 31:27
        Ag 27 '51
United States Capitol Building,
    Washington, D.C.
    Architectural development of

    the Capitol--5 designs bw
        31:59 Jy 2 '51
    British burn Capitol, 1814 bw
        12:97 My 25 '42
    U.S. Capitol, architecture,
        sculpture, paintings 31:48-
        57 Jy 2 '51
    Dome. Walter, T., archi-
        tect photog 16:56 Mr 20 '44;
        31:49, 52-3 Jy 2 '51 bw 3:
        Cover N 29 '37; 14:70 Ap
        12 '43; 18:71 Je 18 '45
        under construction, 1861
        photog 5:28 O 31 '38 bw 11:
        93 N 10 '41
    Brumidi. Dome murals 31:
        52-3 Jy 2 '51
    Crawford. Armed freedom,
        cast, Dome statue bw 19:9
        S 24 '45
    Dome, rotunda, halls
        photogs 18:Cover, 71 Je 18
        '45
    Hall of Fame photog bw 2:
        23 Je 14 '37
    House of Representatives
        Chamber 30:75 F 5 '51
    lobby, rooms, offices
        photogs 31:50-1 Jy 2 '51
    Sculpture--plaques of great
        law makers, House of
        Representatives Chamber
        bw 30:74 F 5 '51
    Statuary Hall-Car of His-
        tory 31:50 Jy 2 '51
United States Coins
    Samples from Louis Elias-
        berg collection, only com-
        plete collection 34:114-5
        Ap 27 '53
United States Congress
    Gropper. The Senate 2:24 F
        1 '37
    Rossiter. The founding fathers
        at the Federal Convention,
        c1850 39:58-9 Jy 4 '55
United States Constitution
    Christy. The signing of the
        Constitution bw 8:26 Je
        10 '40
    Drafters of preamble, 5 por-

traits bw 16:47 Ja 17 '44
Framers of the Constitution
39:58-64 Jy 4 '55
Ratification of the Constitution
bw 14:62 Ap 12 '43
United States Declaration of Inde-
pendence
American Independence, 1776
print bw 16:46 Ja 17 '44
Congress voting Independence
bw 29:52 Jy 3 '50
Pine and Savage. The Congress
voting Independence 40:78-9
Ja 9 '56
Signers of the Declaration of
Independence--56 portraits
and signatures bw 15:8-10
Jy 5 '43
Trumbull. The signing of the
Declaration of Independence
14:64 Ap 12 '43
United States Embassies
Harrison and Abramovitz.
U.S. embassy, Rio de Ja-
neiro photog 34:45 Je 22 '53
Kerrigan and King. U.S. em-
bassy, Brussels photog bw
34:47 Ap 20 '53
United States Emblems See
Emblems and Decorations--
United States
United States Marine Corps
Flag raising, Mt. Suribachi,
Iwo Jima
De Welden. sculpture,
Washington, D.C. bw 37:
128-33 S 20 '54
Rosenthal. photog bw 18:17
Mr 26 '45
United States Navy
Historic paintings and prints 9:
47-50 O 28 '40
McCoy. Airplanes of the U.S.
Navy 9:71-4 O 28 '40
Meyers. California naval war,
1847: Scenes of the U.S.
Navy in the Pacific 7:43-4
Ag 28 '39
U.S. fleet, 1881 bw 12:99 My
25 '42
United States Presidents

Birthplaces bw 6:6-8 F 20 '39
Losing candidates for President of the U.S.--19 por-
traits bw 14:6-7 My 31 '43
Presidents--portraits on campaign songs 25:22-4 O 4
'48
United States Supreme Court
Court Buildings: 7 court
houses, 1790-1935 bw 8:50
F 12 '40
Justices, 1790-1940: 80 justices in 150 years bw 8:48-
9 F 12 '40
group photog of members
upon appointment of new
member, 1882-1937 photog
bw 3:28-9 N 29 '37
in 1865 photogs bw 14:76
F 15 '43
United States Treasury Department, Section of Fine Arts
Hansen. Young Lincoln sculpture award bw 9:130 S 9
'40
Mural prizewinners: 10 commissions for public buildings 10:42-6 Ja 27 '43
United States Vice-Presidents,
1789-1940 bw 9:8-11 Ag
5 '40
United States War Art See also
Soldiers as Artists; War
Themes
Purchase award paintings,
Office of Emergency Man-
agement Contest 12:58-60
Ap 6 '42
United States Works Project Ad-
ministration
Children's art 1:44 N 30 '36
Federal art project paintings
sold in New York City junk
shop bw 16:85 Ap 17 '44
Los Angeles unit paintings of
General MacArthur bw 13:
51 Ag 17 '42
Public buildings from book,
"Public Buildings" photogs
bw 8:61-7 Ap 1 '40

The U.S. fleet in the Straits of
    Magellan, 1908. Reuterdahl
    9:50 O 28 '40
U.S. ships entering Reykjavik.
    bw Coale 13:90-1 Jy 13 '42
U.S.S. Columbus and Vincennes
    in Japan, 1846 9:48 O 28 '40
U.S.S. Constellation, 1797 9:49
    O28 '40 photogs bw 9:52-4
    O 28 '40
U.S.S. Maine. Chapman 9:49 O
    28 '40
U.S.S. North Carolina. Billings 11:
    60 Jy 7 '41 bw 14:7 Je 28 '43
U.S.S. Washington 13:60-1 N 2
    '42
University See also listings under
    such headings as, Virginia,
    University of
    University of Paris school-
    room, Middle Ages bw 22:
    76 Ap 7 '47
The unknown political prisoner.
    monument competition bw
    34:39-42 Je 1 '53
Unto one of the least of these.
    Hegh 8:44 F 12 '40
Unton, Henry
    Sir Henry Unton, portrait and
    biographical scenes, Eng-
    land, c1550 41:146-7 N 5
    '56
Up front. cartoons bw Mauldin
    18:49-53 F 5 '45
Upper deck. Sheeler 5:44 Ag 8 '38
Uptton, Clive
    U.X.B. (unexploded bomb)
    squad at work bw 26:52 F 28
    '49
Ur of the Chaldees, Sumer,
    Babylonia
    Abu, Sumerian God, "Lord of
    Vegetation," and wife
    statue 40:89 Je 4 '56
    Royal standard, mosaic panels
    40:90-1 Je 4 '56
    Sumerian art: mosaics, gold-
    work, sculpture 40:80-93 Je
    4 '56
    Wrestler vase, Sumerian bw
    5:59 Ag 15 '38

Ur-Nammu, Sumerian King bas-
    relief, third dynasty,
    c2125 B.C. bw 40:95 Je 4
    '56
Urbino, Duke of
    Trompe l'oeil cabinet work,
    Study, Ducal palace, 15th
    century photogs bw 18:12-
    4 My 21 '45
Urns
    Etruscan urns, 1st and 7th
    centuries B.C. 40:60-1 F
    13 '56
    Greek bronze urn, 6th century
    37:86-8 S 13 '54
    Hepplewhite. Carved wooden
    urn bw 23:75 Ag 25 '47
    Mayan urn 22:56 Je 30 '47
    Roman urn. Mausoleum of
    Aelii, c3rd century 28:75
    Mr 27 '50
Ursala, Saint
    Carpaccio. St. Ursala legend
    23:56-7 Ag 4 '47
    Shrine of St. Ursala. Mem-
    ling 34:81-6 Ap 6 '53
Utopia, c1516 bw 24:83 Mr 22
    '48
Utrillo, Maurice
    Artist's arrest bw 28:90 Ja 16
    '50
    The church of Saint-Severin
    28:93 Ja 16 '50
    Hotel du Tertre 28:92-3 Ja
    16 '50
    Moulin de la Galette 28:94 Ja
    16 '50
    Sacre-Coeur et Rue Saint-
    Rustique 28:93 Ja 16 '50
    Street scene* 24:67 Mr 1 '48
    Place du Tertre, Montmartre
    bw 28:89 Ja 16 '50 (draw-
    ing)
    Maurice Utrillo photog bw 2:
    48 Je 21 '37; 28:86-9 Ja
    16 '50 port.
    Self-portrait--Artist's arrest
    bw 28:90 Ja 16 '50 port.
    Valadon. Artist's son, age 11
    drawing bw 28:88 Ja 16
    '50 port.

Valadon. Family portrait, 1912 28:91 Ja 16 '50

U.X.B. (unexploded bomb) squad at work. Uptton 26:52 F 28 '49

Uxmal, Yucatan, Mayan architecture photogs 22:51, 58-9 Je 30 '47

V

"V" for victory photography contest bw 11:10-3 N 24 '41

Vagis, Polygnotos, sculptor
Fish bw 40:123 Je 11 '56
Head of woman bw 40:123 Je 11 '56
Moon bw 40:123 Je 11 '56

Vagnetti, Gianni
Artist at work* bw 29:16 O 30 '50

Vail, Laurence
Collages bw 15:10-2 S 6 '43
Laurence Vail photog bw 15:10 S 6 '43 port.

Valadon, Suzanne
Family portrait, 1912 28:91 Ja 16 '50
Artist's son, Maurice Utrillo, age 11 bw 28:88 Ja 16 '50 (drawings)
Self-portrait in Family portrait 28:91 Ja 16 '50 port.
Suzanne Valadon photogs bw 28:87, 89 Ja 16 '50 port.
Toulouse-Lautrec. Suzanne Valadon, age 20 bw 28:88 Ja 16 '50 port.

Valamo monastery, Finland airview photog bw 7:72 O 30 '39

Valentine Gallery, New York City
Mexican art, exhibit 4:28-30 Mr 14 '38

Valkyrie bw 14:6 Ja 4 '43

Valpincon, Hortense
Degas. Mlle. Hortense Valpincon 25:77 Ag 2 '48

Vallatoon, Felix Edouard
Gertrude Stein bw 23:15 Ag 18 '47

Valtin, Jan
Jan Valtin photog bw 10:82 F 24 '41

Van Bergen, Marten
Marten Van Bergen Farmhouse, Leeds, New York* 39:55 Jy 18 '55

Vanbrugh, John, architect
Blenheim palace, England photog 24:32 Ap 19 '48
Vanbrugh bridge, Blenheim, England photog 24:32 Ap 19 '48

Van Buren, Martin
Martin Van Buren bw 9:8 Ag 5 '40

Van Coxie, Michiel, tapestry designer
Cain and Abel 35:94-5 D 14 '53
God and Adam 35:94-5 D 14 '53

Van der Ast, Balthaser
Shells, fruit and insects bw 7:24 Ag 28 '39

Vanderbilt, Cornelius
Cornelius Vanderbilt bw 31:46 Jy 23 '51 photog bw 30:68 Je 11 '51
Leighton, S. Mr. Morgan and Mr. Vanderbilt in a sleigh 6:31 Je 19 '39

Vanderbilt Gallery, New York bw 27:56 Ag 29 '49

Vanderbilt mansion, New York City photogs bw 11:49-52 N 17 '41

Van der Goes, Hugo
The nativity 39:18-9 D 26 '55

Vanderlyn, John
Death of Jane McCrea 29:49 Jy 3 '50
Mrs. Ann Hivlyn, 1796 bw 9:74 D 9 '40

Van der Venne, Adriaen
Fishers for souls 24:64-5 Je 14 '48

Van Dine, S. S.
S.S. Van Dine photog bw 6:9 Ap 24 '39

Van Dongen, Kees
  Kees van Dongen photog bw 5:
    72 D 12 '38 port.
Van Doren, Mark
  Cosgrave. Mark van Doren bw
    24:18 Ja 19 '48
  Mark van Doren photog bw 24:
    18 Ja 19 '48
Van Duzer, Clarence
  Growth of Tulsa, Oklahoma*
    mural 30:78 Mr 5 '51
Van Dyck, Anthony
  Charles I, King of England,
    accompanied by Duke of
    Epernon bw 41:189 N 12 '56
  Commander in armor, 1641
    40:107 My 7 '56
  Paola Adorno 3:33 D 27 '37
  Portrait of a knight 27:65 O 24
    '49
  Portrait of a man, c1628 29:84
    N 27 '50
  Prince Charles and Prince
    Rupert, newphews of Charles
    I of England 41:73 D 10 '53
  Rinaldo and Armida 4:21 Ap 11
    '38
  Sir Thomas Hanmer 15:66 S 20
    '43
  Sir Anthony van Dyck bw 4:20
    Ap 11 '38 port.
Van Dyck, Pieter, silversmith
  Mustard pot, U.S. colonial 38:
    116 Ap 18 '55
  Teapot, U.S. Colonial 38:117
    Ap 18 '55
Van Eyck, Hubert See Van Eyck
  Brothers
Van Eyck, Jan
  The annunciation bw 13:42 D
    28 '42
  Christ on the cross, the
    Blessed Virgin and St. John
    24:69 Mr 22 '48
  Giovanni Arnolfini and his wife
    33:36 D 29 '52
  Madonna and child with St.
    Catherine and Archangel Mi-
    chael, altarpiece, c1435
    40:108-9 My 7 '56
  Man with pink bw 19:25 D 31 '45

St. Francis receiving the stig-
    mata 4:30 F 7 '38
Van Eyck Brothers (Jan and Hu-
    bert)
  Adoration of the lamb, Ghent
    altarpiece 26:64-5 Ap 18
    '49 bw 16:68 Ja 10 '44
  Adam and Eve 26:64-5 Ap 18
    '49
  Altarpiece, Cathedral of St.
    Bavon, Ghent 26:58-69 Ap
    18 '49
  Crown of the King of Kings,
    detail 26:68 Ap 18 '49
  Knights of Christ. 26:62 Ap 18
    '49
  Lamb of God 26:59 Ap 18 '49
  The Lord 26:64-5, 69 Ap 18
    '49
  Musicians 26:65 Ap 18 '49
  Pilgrims 26:65, 67 Ap 18 '49
  St. Christopher 26:65, 67 Ap
    18 '49
  St. John the Baptist 26:65 Ap
    18 '49
  The virgin martyrs 26:60-1
    Ap 18 '49
  Virgin Mary 26:64 Ap 18 '49
  Self-portraits in Last judg-
    ment bw 26:58 Ap 18 '49
    port.
Van Gogh, Vincent
  L'Arlesienne bw 27:82 O 10
    '49
  Boats of Saintes-Maries bw
    27:82 O 10 '49
  Bridge at Arles 2:34 F 15 '37
  Cypress and flowering trees
    40:72-3 My 28 '56
  The cypresses 27:86 O 10 '49
  Houses at Auvers 7:35 Jy 31
    '39; 25:80 N 1 '48
  Mother and child* 24:67 Mr
    1 '48
  Night cafe 2:34 F 15 '37; 27:
    85 O 10 '49
  The potato eaters 27:83 O 10
    '49 bw 41:67 O 1 '56
  Public gardens at Arles 38:
    109 My 23 '55
  Pond with cypresses 2:33 F

15 '37
Roulin the postman bw 27:82 O
10 '49
Stairway at Auvers 13:95 N 9
'42
Sunflowers bw 27:82 O 10 '49
Town hall, Auvers 33:95 O 27
'52
Vegetable gardens, Arles 27:
83 O 10 '49
Woman with tambourines 27:
84 O 10 '49
Self-portrait 33:94 O 27 '52
bw 2:32 F 15 '37; 27:26 D
19 '49 port.
Self-portrait: Study by candle-
light bw 27:27 D 19 '49; 29:
17 O 9 '50
Van Inburgh, Peter, silversmith
Porringer, U.S. colonial 38:
117 Ap 18 '55
Van-Keppel Green
Tubular steel chaise photog
29:90 D 25 '50
Van Loo, Jean Baptiste
Louis XV bw 5:39 S 26 '38
Van Loon, Hendrik
Klinghoffer. Hendrik van Loon
10:47 F 3 '41
Van Meergeren, Hans, art forger
Christ and the adulterous
woman bw 23:148 N 17 '47
Christ at Emmaus bw, forged
Jan Vermeer 23:148 N 17
'47
Christ in the temple bw 23:146
N 17 '47
Isaac baptizing Jacob bw,
forged Jan Vermeer 23:145
N 17 '47
Hans Van Meergeren photogs
bw 23:145 N 17 '47 port.
Van Nieulandt, Adriaen
The peace of Westphalia 24:58
Je 14 '48
Van Rosen, Gunnar
Rescue of Maria Carlota bw 23:
46 N 24 '47
Van Voorhout, Claes
Hals. Claes Duyst van Voorhout
2:43 Je 28 '37

Van Winkle, Rip
Rip Van Winkle statue bw 17:
63 O 30 '44
Vanity Fair. Koerner 24:78-9
My 10 '48
Vanzetti, Bartolomeo
Borglum. Memorial Sacco-
Vanzetti plaque bw 3:24 S
6 '37
Shahn. The passion of Sacco
and Vanzetti, one painting
from series of 23 bw 37:96
O 4 '54
Vargit, Margit
Road to Danbury 10:72 Ap 14
'41
Variations within a sphere, No.
10: The sun. sculpture
Lippold 41:90 Jy 30 '56
Varnum, James
General James Varnum bw 16:
48 Ja 24 '44
Vas, Ignacia
Last supper bw 29:66 S 4 '50
Vases
Chinese Sung vase ceramic
33:101 O 27 '52
Etruscan vase- Hercules
slaying henchman of King
Busiris, detail, c530 B.C.
40:64 F 13 '56
Greek vase, 6th century 37:
86-8 S 13 '54
Greek revival vase, U.S.,
1830 39:59 Ag 29 '55
Malachite vase, Vanderbilt
mansion, New York City
bw 11:52 N 17 '41
Mayan painted vase, Old Em-
pire, c987 22:57 Je 30 '47
Sumerian vase- Two
wrestlers bw 5:59 Ag 15
'38
Swedish glass vase bw 17:66
7 Ag 7 '44
Tiffany glass vase 40:92-3
Mr 5 '56
Venetian glass vase, modern
37:56 Ag 2 '54
Victorian glass vases, U.S.
40:90-1 Mr 5 '56

Vasilieff, Nicholas
Still life 24:103 Je 28 '48
Vassilevsky, Alexander
Marshal Vassilevsky, "Time"
cover portrait 17:65 D 11
'44
Vatican, Rome See also Sistine
Chapel
Raphael. Battle of Milvian
Bridge fresco bw 39:39 D
26 '55
Vatican--rooms, chapels,
halls, library photogs bw 5:
37-47 D 25 '38
Vatican City airview photog bw
15:26 Ag 9 '43   plan bw 5:
38-9 D 25 '38
Vatican holy year exhibit of
Christian art from the Ori-
ent bw 29:63, 66 S 4 '50
Vatican library photog bw 17:
94 S 4 '44
Vatican treasures--religious
ornaments, jewels, manu-
scripts 32:82-7 Ap 14 '52
"Vatican Vergil;" "Aeneid,"
illuminated manuscript, 5th
century 32:86 Ap 14 '52
Vaughn, Henry
Path of investigation bw 27:47
N 14 '49
Veblen, Oswald
Eisenstadt. Oswald Veblen
photog bw 24:15 My 10 '48
Oswald Veblen photog bw 11:43
O 13 '41
Vecelli, Tiziano See Titian
Vegetable gardens, Arles. Van
Gogh 27:83 O 10 '49
Vegetable symmetry. Arp 33:96
O 27 '52
Velasquez, Loretta
Loretta Velasquez bw 14:8 Je
4 '43
Velazquez, Diego
Don Baltasar Carlos, Prince
of Spain 31:71 O 1 '51
Don Baltasar Carlos and his
dwarf 4:43 My 16 '38
Infanta Margarita Theresa 27:
72 O 24 '49

Job (Seneca) 11:57 S 8 '41
The maids of honor 7:57 N 20
39; 31:61 O 1 '51
Man with a wine glass 7:34 Jy
31 '39
St. Peter 7:55 O 9 '39
Venus with Cupid (Venus at
the mirror) 41:104 O 22
'56
Diego Velazquez bw 4:40 My
16 '38 port.
Self-portrait in The maids
of honor 31:61 O 1 '51 port.
Vence, France, Dominican
chapel. Matisse, design
and decoration photogs 31:
108 N 26 '51
Vendome Column, Paris photog
8:62 Je 3 '40 bw 31:75 Jy
30 '51
Venetian church. Thon 33:94 S
15 '52
Venetian glass See Glassware,
Venetian
Venetian palace. Congdon 30:
108 Ap 30 '51
Venezuela
Map of Castillo del Oro, 1529
bw 33:32 D 29 '52
Venice, Italy See also St.
Mark's Cathedral
Bellini. The Corpus Christi
procession 23:54-5 Ag 4
'47
Carpaccio. St. Ursala legend
23:56-7 Ag 4 '47
Congdon. Florian's Cafe 30:
108 Ap 30 '51
Doge's Palace, Senate cham-
ber photog bw 23:50 Ag 4
'47
Guardi. San Pietro di Cas-
tello 29:87 N 27 '50
Guardi. Santa Maria della
Salute 35:152-3 N 16 '53
Lady gondoliers' race, Re-
naissance bw 23:59 Ag 4
'47
MacIver. Floating palaces
33:94-5 S 15 '52
Mock war, Venice, Renais-

sance bw 23:59 Ag 4 '47

Payday at the arsenal, Renaissance* bw 23:59 Ag 4 '47

Renaissance art of Venice 23:
46-62 Ag 4 '47

Tintoretto. Life of Christ,
School of San Rocco 31:30-
49 D 24 '51

Turner, J.M.W. The Grand
Canal, Venice: Shylock 5:
44 S 12 '38

Venice airview photog bw 15:
26 Ag 9 '43

Wedding of Doge and the sea, *
Renaissance bw 23:59 Ag 4
'47

Zao Wou-Ki. Golden city 36:
102-3 F 22 '54

Venice, 1500 bw 23:48-9 Ag 4
'47 (map)

Venice Biennial Exposition of
Contemporary Art

Highlights of exhibit of other-
than-American art 29:101-9
D 11 '50

Venturi, Venturio
Pinocchio sculpture bw 40:128
Je 4 '56

Venus See Mythological Themes
--Venus

Venus de Milo sculpture bw,
Greek 19:48 Jy 30 '45; 35:
51 Ag 17 '53

Verde. Ernst 32:58 Ja 21 '52

Verdict of the people. Bingham
5:32 O 31 '38; 16:54 Mr 13
'44; 31:96 N 5 '51

Vereshchagin, Vasilyevich
The 1812 series: Napoleon in
Russia bw 12:61-8 F 2 '42
V. Vereshchagin bw 12:61 F
2 '42 port.

Vermeer, Jan
The lacemakers 35:55 Ag 17
'53
Mistress and maid 3:33 D 27
'37
Woman weighing gold 5:31 Ag
29 '38; 24:73 Je 14 '48
Young lady with a pearl necklace 24:77 Mr 22 '48 bw 19:

25 D 31 '45
Self-portrait: The artist in his
studio 27:71 O 24 '49 bw 5:
30 Ap 29 '38; 16:63 Ja 10
'44   port.

Vermeer forgeries. Van Meergeren 23:145 N 17 '47

Vernont
Durand. View of Rutland,
Vermont 19:85 S 10 '45
Lucioni. Paintings of Vermont
3:46-9 Jy 19 '37
Schwarz. Sandgate, Vermont
16:46 Ja 3 '44
Thompson, J. Picnic party
near Mount Mansfield,
Vermont 25:90 O 18 '48

Vermont classic. Lucioni 3:49
Jy 19 '37

Vernon ceramics, U.S. photogs
9:76-9 S 9 '40

Vero of Ceylon sculpture bw 8:
95 Je 24 '40

Veronese, Paolo
Allegory of virtue and vice
(The choice of Hercules)
3:38 D 27 '37
Baptism of Christ 16:70 Ap
10 '44
Battle of Lepanto, 1571 23:58
Ag 4 '47
Christ and the centurion 7:53
O 9 '39
The finding of Moses bw 40:
104 F 20 '56
Frescoes, The Villa Maser
29:58-65 Jy 24 '50

Veronica's veil. lithograph
Dix, O. 33:84 Jy 14 '52

Verrocchio, Andrea del
Child* sculpture bw 26:105
Mr 21 '49
David sculpture bw 6:32 F 13
'39
Lorenzo de' Medici terra cot-
ta 38:95 F 21 '55

Versaille Palace, Paris airview
photogs 8:64 Je 3 '40 bw
5:39 S 26 '38
Royal chapel photog 23:86 S
15 '47

Vertes, Marcel
  Costumes for circus photogs
    40:82-5 Ap 23 '56
"Very well alone." cartoon bw
    Low 26:63 F 21 '49
Vespucci, Amerigo
  Amerigo Vespucci bw 37:106 O
    11 '54 woodcut bw, 16th
    century 40:46 Ja 9 '56
  Botticelli. Amerigo Vespucci
    37:106 O 11 '54
  George Washington calling on
    Vespucci, Japanese illus-
    tration, 1853 bw 25:7 Ag 2
    '48
  Ghirlandaio. Amerigo Vespuc-
    ci bw 37:106 O 11 '54
  Maurin. Amerigo Vespucci bw
    37:106 O 11 '54
  Stradanus. Vespucci in South
    America bw 37:105 O 11 '54
  Vespucci in Brazil drawing bw,
    17th century 37:110 O 11 '54
  Waldseemuller. Amerigo Ves-
    pucci, in Map of New
    World, 1507 print 37:101 O
    11 '54
Vesta, Temple of, Rome photog
    bw 17:94 S 4 '44
Vestal virgin. sculpture bw
    Mestrovic 22:132 Je 2 '47
Vetsera, Mary
  Mary Vetsera photog bw 26:127
    Mr 28 '49
Victims of drought. Portinari 29:
    108 D 11 '50
Victor Emmanuel II, King of Italy
  Garibaldi and Victor Emmanuel
    II bw 15:21 Ag 9 '43; 20:28
    Je 24 '46
  Victor Emmanuel II photog bw
    15:18 Ag 9 '43; 15:104 Ag
    23 '43; 20:28 Je 24 '46
    coronation bw 15:22 Ag 9
    '43
Victoria. Albright, M. 16:65 Mr
    27 '44
Victoria, Queen of England
  Beerbohm. The rare and rather
    awful visits of Albert Ed-
    ward...to Windsor cartoon

  bw 23:75 N 17 '47
  Knighting of Disraeli, 1878 bw
    13:76 N 16 '42
  Opening of Parliament by
    Queen Victoria, January 24,
    1846 bw 13:76 N 16 '42
  Queen Victoria bw 23:72 O 20
    '47; 23:116 D 8 '47 statue
    bw, Bombay 10:85 My 12
    '41
  Victoria and Albert, with their
    children bw 23:76 O 20 '47
  Victoria and Wilhelmina,
    Queen of the Netherlands,
    1895 photog bw 25:80 Ag 16
    '48
  Victoria in bridal gown* bw
    32:23 F 18 '52
  Von Angeli. Queen Victoria
    35:82 N 23 '53
Victoria, wife of Louis Alexander
    Mountbatten photog bw 23:
    72 O 20 '47
Victoria Alice, Consort of An-
    drew of Greece photog bw
    23:72 O 20 '47
Victorian Architecture and Deco-
    ration
  Belter. Victorian parlor 39:
    102 O 17 '55
  Gould mansion, New York City
    1859 photogs bw 13:140-1
    D 7 '42
  U.S. pre-Civil War furniture
    39:102 O 17 '55
  Victorian age of gilded opu-
    lence, U.S.: desks, chairs,
    lamps, bedroom 40:86-91
    Mr 5 '56
  Victorian Christmas cards,
    U.S., late 19th century 5:
    6-7 D 12 '38
  Victorian quilted rocking
    chair, iron flower pot draw-
    ing bw 27:59 Ag 29 '49
  Victorian sculpture bw 10:121
    Ap 21 '41
Victorian mansion. Kingman
    30:101 My 14 '51
Victoria's diamond jubilee,
    1897, bw 13:76 N 16 '42

Victoria's golden jubilee bw 32:22
F 18 '52
"Victory" (ship) English, 1805
Turner, J. M. W. Trafalgar
24:67 My 10 '48
Victory monument, Gettysburg bw
4:36 Je 27 '38
Victory of Samothrace (Nike of
Samothrace) sculpture bw,
Greece 19:49 Jy 30 '45
Vidal, Gore
Gore Vidal photog bw 22:82 Je
2 '47
Vidar, Frede
Dead Jap 19:70 O 8 '45
"Don Giovanni," illustrations
of Mozart's opera 22:58-65
F 3 '47
Leyte* 39:56 Ag 15 '55
Return to Manila* 39:57 Ag 15
'55
St. Peter's, Rome--consistory
scenes bw 20:34-5 Mr 11 '46
La vie. Picasso 8:57 Mr 4 '40
Vienna
St. Stephan's cathedral photog
bw 21:51 N 11 '46
State Opera House photog 39:
156-7 N 14 '55   Rebuilding
38:157, 160 Je 13 '55
Vienna, 1880 bw 4:13 Mr 28
'38
View and plan of Toledo. El Greco
28:88-9 Ap 24 '50
View in Suffolk. Gainsborough 13:
94 N 9 '42
View of Athens. Dodd 27:64-5 S
26 '49
View of Catskill House. Cropsey
19:84 S 10 '45
View of Haarlem. Ruysdael 24:
74-5 Je 14 '48
View of Kingston. Klitgaard 5:25
Ag 22 '38
View of Naples. Corot 25:96 N 22
'48
View of Old Boston, 1730-40 13:
81 N 23 '42
View of Rutland, Vermont. Durand
19:85 S 10 '45
View of Sing Sing. Havell 19:85 S

10 '45
View of Toledo. El Greco 4:41 My
16 '38
View on the Stour near Dedham.
Constable 5:44 S 12 '38
Vigeland, Gustav, sculptor
Statues and monoliths, Frog-
ner Park, Oslo bw 25:20-
2 O 25 '48
Self-portrait sculpture bw 25:
21 O 25 '48 port.
Vigenere Table, aid in cryptog-
raphy 19:70 N 26 '45
Vigil. Gottlieb 25:63 O 11 '48
The vigilant heart. lithograph
Svanberg 33:86 Jy 14 '52
La Vigornia. Galvan 4:30 Mr 14
'38
Viking ornament photog bw 40:
97 Mr 19 '56
Viking ship photog bw 40:94 Mr
19 '56
Villa, Pancho (Doroteo Arango)
Pancho Villa photogs bw 4:54
Ap 11 '38; 24:14 Ja 12 '48
Villa Borghese, Rome photog bw
17:98 S 4 '44
Villa d'Este, gardens and foun-
tains photogs 28:78-9 My
8 '50
Villa Hugel, Werden, Germany
photogs bw 19:80-1 Ap 27
'45
Villa La Pietra, Italy, garden
photog 28:73 My 8 '50
Villa-Lobos, Heitor
Heitor Villa-Lobos 25:108 O
25 '48
The Villa Maser, Italy. Palladio,
architect; Veronese, frescoes, 16th century 29:58-
65 Jy 24 '50
Villa on the Nivelle. Churchill
20:47 Ja 7 '46
Villa Torrigiani, Italy, garden
28:75 My 8 '50
The village. bw Marsh 5:30 O
31 '38
The village blacksmith. Currier
and Ives print 9:28 D 30
'40

"The Village Blacksmith," illus-
    trations. Wilson, E.A. 18:
    59 Ap 23 '45
Village carpenter, India. Sheets
    20:82 Ja 21 '46
The village church. Ganso 2:34
    F 1 '37
"Ville de Paris" (ship) French
    Battle of the saints 24:66 My
    10 '48
Villet, Grey, photographer
    Photographs by Villet bw 40:
    26-7 Ap 9 '56
    Grey Villet photog bw 40:26
    Ap 9 '56 port.
Villiers, Barbara
    Barbara Villiers 41:167 N 19
    '56
Villiers, George, Duke of Buck-
    ingham
    George Villiers bw 41:182 N
    12 '56
Villon, Jacques
    Marcel Duchamp 32:101 Ap 28
    '52
"Vincennes" (ship)
    U.S.S. Columbus and Vincen-
    nes in Japan, 1846 9:48 O
    28 '40
Vinci See Leonardo da Vinci
Vinck, Franz
    Lady Godiva bw 25:164 N 15
    '48
Viola da Gamba See Musicians
    and Musical Instruments--
    Viola da Gamba
Viola d'Amour See Musicians
    and Musical Instruments--
    Viola d'Amour
Violin Players See Musicians
    and Musical Instruments--
    Violin
Virgil's "Aeneid," illuminated
    manuscript, 5th century,
    Vatican 32:86 Ap 14 '52
The Virgil Master
    Journey of the Queen of Sheba
    35:150-1 N 16 '53
Virgin and Child See Mary,
    Virgin--Madonna and Child
The virgin martyrs. Van Eyck

brothers 26:60-1 Ap 18 '49
Virginia
    Patrick Henry before the
    Virginia Assembly, 1775
    bw 25:110 S 13 '48
    State Capitol building. Jeffer-
    son, archt. model, photog
    bw 14:70 Ap 12 '43
    Westover, 18th century
    country house photog bw
    25:110-1 S 13 '48
    Map of Virginia, in Capt.
    John Smith's Adventures
    18:67 My 21 '45 (map)
Virginia, University of. Jeffer-
    son, archt.
    Library and dormitories
    photog 2:48-9 Je 7 '37
    University photog bw 14:71 Ap
    12 '43
Virginia Museum of Fine Arts,
    Richmond
    Exhibit of Virginia artists,
    8th 10:66-8 My 26 '41
Vishnu float, parade of Jagan-
    nath, Puri, India photogs
    bw 3:60-1 Ag 16 '37
The vision at dusk. Ford 17:44
    D 25 '44
Vision of La Salette. Ford 17:
    43 D 25 '44
The visit. Chalabi 29:104 D 11
    '50
"Visit from St. Nicholas," illus-
    trations. Ogden 31:96-100
    D 10 '51
Visit of the Queen of Sheba to
    Solomon. Piero della Fran-
    cesca 20:62 Ap 22 '46
Vitti, Timoteo
    Christ on the Mount of Olives
    1:46 D 28 '36
Vittoria, Alessandro
    Negro, bronze, Venice, c1600
    bw 6:53 Mr 20 '39
Viztelly, Frank
    Richmond.Virginia, 1861 bw
    13:72 N 16 '42
Vladimir, Saint
    St. Vladimir bw 14:92 Mr 29
    '43

Vlaminck, Maurice de
  Houses at Chatou 33:97 O 27
    '52
  Village scene* bw 30:69 Ap 9
    '51
  Mili. Maurice Vlaminck, age
    73 photog 27:90 D 12 '49
    port.
Vodicka, Ruth, sculptor
  Outcry bw 41:76 S 10 '56
  Song of David bw 41:76 S 10
    '56
  Artist at work photog bw 41:
    75-6 S 10 '56 port.
Vogelein, Nick
  Mist over the marshes bw 18:
    44 Ja 1 '45
Vogelsdorf castle, Silesia photog
  bw 15:94 N 22 '43
Volga titan ice sculpture bw 6:7
  Ja 16 '39
Volk, Douglas
  Accused of witchcraft 13:78 N
    23 '42
Vollard, Ambroise
  Ambroise Vollard photog bw
    2:44 Ap 12 '37
  Cezanne. Ambroise Vollard
    32:81 F 25 '52
Voilles, Jean
  Czarina of Russia, and chil-
    dren miniature painting 33:
    35 D 29 '52
Volpe, Vincent, Attributed to
  Embarkation of Henry VIII,
    Dover, 1520* 41:78-9 O 29
    '56
Volpi, Alfredo
  Houses 36:82 My 31 '54
Voltaire, Francois
  Houdon. Voltaire, copy sculp-
    ture bw 12:15 Je 8 '42
  Voltaire bw 23:88 S 15 '47 por-
    trait on snuffbox cover 40:
    82 Ja 9 '56 sculpture bw 31:
    78 Jy 30 '51
Volterra, Daniele da
  Michelangelo, bronze head
    from death mask bw 27:49 D
    26 '48
Von Angeli, Heinrich

Queen Victoria 35:82 N 23 '53
Von Arnim Family, Germany--4
    portraits, Thirty Years
    War to 1943 bw 15:94 N 22
    '43
Von Blucher, Gebhard
  Von Blucher at Waterloo bw
    8:25 Ap 22 '40
Von Hindenberg, Paul
  Field Marshal and Frau von
    Hindenberg photogs bw 28:
    65 Mr 6 '50
Von Ludendorff, Eric
  General von Ludendorff photog
    bw 31:114 O 29 '51
Von Moltke, Helmuth
  General von Moltke bw 15:96
    N 22 '43
  Von Moltke at Battle of Sedan,
    1870 15:97 N 22 '43
  Von Moltke, the elder photog
    bw 8:24 Ap 22 '40
Von Physter, George
  Destiny lithograph bw 5:55
    Ag 8 '38
  Jam session lithograph bw
    5:55 Ag 8 '38
Von Rundstedt, Karl
  Field Marshal von Rundstedt,
    "Time" cover portrait 17:
    66 D 11 '44
Von Schlieffen, Alfred
  General von Schlieffen bw 15:
    96 N 22 '43
Von Soest, Conrad
  Coronation of the Virgin 1:48
    D 28 '36
Von Steuben, Frederick
  Baron von Steuben bw 8:24
    Ap 22 '40
Von Troppau, Johannes, Gospel
    book of 34:86 F 23 '53
Voodooism
  Benedetto. Calling the loa 8:
    35 Ja 1 '40
  Bigaud. A voodoo rite 28:101
    Mr 13 '50
  Voodoo altar, sacred objects
    and food, Port-au-Prince
    photog bw 3:28 D 13 '37

Voronov, Nikolai
  Marshal Voronov, "Time"
    cover portrait 17:65 D 11
    '44
Vorse, Mary Heaton
  Mary Vorse photog bw 9:73 Jy
    15 '40
Vos, Marius
  The birth of a nation sculpture
    bw 3:71 Ag 9 '37
Vuillard, Edouard
  Bench in a park 37:76-7 N 1
    '54
  Gardens 37:75 N 1 '54
  House of Mallarme 37:77 N 1
    '54
  The kitchen 40:71 My 28 '56
  The meal 37:76 N 1 '54
  Painter's family 37:75 N 1 '54
  Symphony in red 37:76 N 1 '54
  Thadee Natanson and his wife
    37:78 N 1 '54
  Self-portrait 37:74 N 1 '54 port.
Vulcan See Mythological Themes
  --Vulcan
Vulture, emblem of Upper Egypt,
  4th dynasty photog bw 41:
  94 O 1 '56
Vytlacil, Vaclav
  Vaclav Vytlacil. in group photog
    29:172-3 O 16 '50 port.

W

W.P.A. (Works Progress Admin-
  istration) See United States
  Works Project Administration
Wacker, Hal
  Portraits drawings bw 37:63-4
    Ag 16 '54
Wadsworth house, Cambridge,
    Massachusetts photog 15:
    13 D 6 '43
Wagner, Adolf
  Adolf Wagner photog bw 22:100
    Mr 24 '47
Wagner, Richard
  Richard Wagner photog bw 25:
    99 N 22 '48 sculptured bust
    bw 12:12 Je 8 '42
Wagoner, Harold, architect

Presbyterian church, Vero
  Beach, Florida 39:116 D
  26 '55
Wagons and Carts See also
  Carriages
American pleasure wagon,
  1860 photog 39:104-5 O 17
  '55
Curry. Oklahoma land rush
  7:36 D 25 '39
Circus bandwagon, "Five
  Graces" photog 20:51 F 4
  '46
Nottingham. Landscape with
  goat cart 10:68 My 26 '41
Skeleton trotting wagon, U.
  S., 1860 photog 39:105-6
  O 17 '55
Wyeth, A. Blue dump 24:104
  My 17 '48
Zebra cart, Kapurthala, In-
  dia photog bw 9:69 N 25
  '40

            Covered Wagons
Church. Scene in the Cats-
  kills 19:84 S 10 '45
Colman. Emigrant train 6:29
  Je 19 '39
Colman. Ships of the plains
  39:74 N 28 '55
Mili. Conestoga wagon photog
  39:74-5 N 28 '55
Ranney. Emigrant train bw
  27:40 Jy 4 '49
Remington. Attack on the sup-
  ply wagon 13:76 S 14 '42
Remington. The sentinel 13:
  74 S 14 '42
Wimar. Attack on an emi-
  grant train 27:43 Jy 4 '49
Wailing wall, Jerusalem photog
  bw 6:54 My 15 '39
Waiting. bw Degas 6:7 Ap 17 '39
Waiting. drawing bw Gibson 23:
  94 N 17 '47
Waiting for the curtain. Davis,
  G.R. 16:79 Mr 20 '44
Waiting for the departure.
  Archer 10:68 My 26 '41
Waiting for the train. Lopez 25:

66 Ag 23 '48
Wake of the ferry. Sloan 7:45 D
    11 '39
Walcott, Joe
    Mili. Louis knockdown by Joe
        Walcott photog bw 24:16 My
        10 '48
Walden Pond, Thoreau's literary
    locale photog bw 9:95 O 14
    '40
Waldenstein peaks. Hartley 32:86
    Je 16 '52
Waldo, Edith
    Sierra peaks bw 22:40 Je 16
        '47
    Edith Waldo photog bw 22:40
        Je 16 '47 port.
Waldo, Samuel Lovett
    Andrew Jackson bw 6:31 Je 19
        '39
Waldseemuller, Martin, cartog-
    rapher
    Map of Atlantic Ocean, 1513
        bw 18:61 My 21 '45
    Map of New World, 1507, with
        portrait of Amerigo Vespuc-
        ci print 37:101 O 11 '54
    World map, 1507 bw 13:58-9
        Ag 3 '42
Walewska, Marie
    Countess Walewska of Poland
        bw 3:41 N 8 '37
Walker, James
    Chapultepec 13:60-1 Jy 6 '42
Walker, Mary
    Dr. Mary Walker photog bw
        22:88 Ja 13 '47
Walker, Robert
    Oliver Cromwell, c1655 41:
        160 N 19 '56
Walking man. bronze sculpture
    bw Wotruba 38:88 Je 20 '55
Walking up on quail. Pleissner
    21:66-7 O 7 '46
Walkowitz, Abraham
    Abraham Walkowitz, photog
        and 25 portraits by famous
        artists bw 16:77-80 F 21 '44
        port.
Wall, William Guy
    Hudson River from West Point

19:83 S 10 '45
Wall Decoration See Mural Paint-
    ing and Decoration; Tapes-
    try
Wall Paper
    Revolutionary wallpaper, U.S.
        17:60 S 4 '44
Wallace, Henry A.
    Henry A. Wallace photog bw
        9:9 Ag 5 '40
Walled Cities
    Avila, Spain photogs bw 33:
        50-1 Ag 18 '52
    Carcassone, France photogs
        bw 22:66-7 My 26 '47
    Walmer castle, England photog
        26:53 F 21 '49
Walpole, Horace
    Horace Walpole bw 25:112 S
        13 '48 age 37 17:118 O 23
        '44
    Strawberry Hill, Walpole's
        home needlepoint bw 17:
        118 O 23 '44
Walpole, Robert
    Sir Robert Walpole 24:69 My
        24 '48 bw 25:12 S 13 '48
Walrus, Eskimo stone carving
    bw 36:70 My 24 '54
Walter, Mary
    Mary Walter 41:166 N 19 '56
Walter, Thomas, architect
    Dome, U.S. Capitol, Washing-
        ton, D.C. photog 16:56 Mr
        20 '44; 31:49, 52-3 Jy 2
        '51 bw 3:Cover N 29 '37;
        14:70 Ap 12 '43; 18:71 Je
        18 '45 under construction
        1861 photogs 5:28 O 31 '38
        bw 11:93 N 10 '41 Dome,
        rotunda, halls photogs 18:
        Cover, 71 Je 18 '45
Walton, George
    George Walton bw 15:10 Jy 5
        '43
Walton, Marion
    Woman sculpture bw 4:62 Ap
        25 '38
The waltz. Braque 4:44 My 2
    '38

Wanamaker House. Du Bois, Y.
8:62 Ap 29 '40
Wanderlust. Bacon, P. 20:80 F
18 '46
Wang Tse-Mei
Chinese cartoonists' group
caricature bw 4:50 Ja 17
'38
The Wansted Assembly (The
dance). Hogarth 21:81 D 16
'46; 25:99 S 13 '48
War bride. sculpture Gross, C.
30:63 Ja 8 '51
War hammer photog 40:187 Ap 9
'56
"War is No Damned Good," cartoon book. Osborn 22:14-6
Ja 27 '47
War landscape* bw 38:77 Mr 21
'55
War news from Mexico. Wood-
ville 9:77 D 9 '40; 27:58 Ag
29 '49
War of 1812 See United States--
History--War of 1812
War Themes See also names of
battles; names of countries,
as United States--History;
names of soldiers. Also,
Memorials and Monuments;
Cartoons; Posters
Besieged castle, Middle Ages
bw 22:66 My 26 '47
British Empire victories,
1588-1915 bw 6:70-1 S 25
'39
Corne. Bombardment of Tripoli
1804 9:47 O 28 '40
Cortes capturing Mexico City,
August 13, 1521 bw 4:52
Ap 11 '38; 21:46 D 16 '46
Delacroix. Massacre at Scio
25:86 N 22 '48
Evacuation from Corunna,
Spain, Peninsular War,
1809* print 26:43 F 14 '49
Greek phalanx opposing Persian
hordes* bw 13:108 O 5 '42
Hegh. Unto one of the least of
these 8:44 F 12 '40
"Illustrated London News,"

illustrations from first
century of publication,
1842-1942 13:71-8 N 16 '42
Johnson, T.L. Twenty great
battles of the world mural
bw, West Point mess hall
11:4 N 24 '41
Lu Hsun Academy. China war
scenes and portraits, Chi-
nese-Japanese War, 1937
18:57-60 Ap 9 '45
Miller, A.J. A Sioux on the
warpath 36:78-9 My 8 '54
Picasso. Guernica fresco bw
3:64 Jy 26 '37
Relief of Vienna, 1683* bw
17:87 Ag 28 '44
Rey. War in Spain, 1936 2:
34-5 F 22 '37
Robida. War of the future,
1975. drawings bw, 1883
12:12-5 Je 15 '42
Sino-Japanese war, 1894-5,
Sekiguchi war prints, Ja-
pan 3:25-32 D 6 '37
Turner. Trafalgar 24:67 My
10 '48
Vereshchagin. The 1812 series: Napoleon's Russian
Campaign bw 12:61-8 F 2
'42
Village raid, Middle Ages bw
22:67 My 26 '47
Weber. Fighters for freedom,
Spain, 1936 16:78 Je 12
'44

European War, 1914-1918
Big Four at Versailles: Orlando, Lloyd George,
Clemenceau, Wilson, 1919
photog bw 15:22 Ag 9 '43;
33:41 D 22 '52
Canadians at Ypres* bw 9:
116 S 9 '40
French artists (128). Pantheon of war, 402 foot
canvas 35:55-6 Ag 10 '53
Guthrie. Great statesmen of
World War I* 24:29 Ap
19 '48

Hitler. World War I scenes 1: 42-3 N 30 '36

World War II, 1939-1945 See also names of artists, as Bohrod; Coale; Cole; Craig; Davis, F.; Eurich; Fredenthal; Jamieson; Lea; Marsh; Martin; Miller, B.; Pleissner; Sample; Sheets; Thomas, B.; Turnbull; Wilkinson

Ardizzone. British army officers in the Middle East caricatures bw 15:55-6 N 29 '43

Ardizzone. Prelude to battle 26:60 Mr 21 '49

Artzybasheff. War machines as human beings 11:10-3 N 3 '41

Beddoes. Burnt out Italian tanks 26:60 Mr 21 '49

Berry. Artillerymen in desert 26:59 Mr 21 '49

Biddle. Italian front; 1944 bw 16:13-7 Ja 3 '44

Bone. Life lines drawing bw 10:64 F 24 '41

Bone. The miracle of Dunkerque--arrival at Dover bw 10:64 F 24 '41

Brenet. Refugees* 9:58 Ag 12 '40

British and French war paintings 9:57-9 Ag 12 '40

British war art 10:64-6 F 24 '41

Brooks, J. Sinking of the Bismark 11:34-5 Ag 11 '41

Cundall. Return of H.M.S. Exeter 10:65 F 24 '41

Davis, M. Army life, World War drawings bw 12:68-9 Ap 13 '42

De Grineau. British troops in France: trench life drawing bw 8:66-7 Ja 22 '40

Dessau. Incendiaries* 26:50 F 28 '49

De Weldon, Felix. Flag raising, Mt. Suribachi, Iwo Jima sculpture bw 37:128-33 S 20 '54

Ezaki. Japanese capturing Guam* 28:68 F 27 '50

Fischer. "George N. Campbell," Coast Guard Cutter in the Atlantic 15:59-69 Jy 5 '43

Fischer. The North Atlantic 14:75-6 F 8 '43

Foujita. Pearl Harbor attack 28:67 F 27 '50

German army destruction in Belgium bw 24:66-7 My 24 '48

German war artists. Portraits of Cossack Division 28:67 F 20 '50

Gifted childrens' impressions of War drawings bw 9:45-6 Jy 15 '40

Gropper. Pearl Harbor 16:78 Je 12 '44

Gross, A. Medical orderlies 26:60 Mr 21 '49

Grosz. I was always present 16:77 Je 12 '44

Groth. Barrage 16:78 Je 12 '44

Halliday. The State apartments, Chatsworth bw 9: 59 Ag 12 '40

Harding. Jungle 19:63 O 8 '45

Ingraham. Tanks through minefield* 26:59 Mr 21 '49

Japanese artist. The attack forms up* 39:53 Ag 15 '55

Japanese artist. Raid on Clark Field, Philippines* 39:52-3 Ag 15 '55

Japanese artist. Surrender meeting, Bataan* 39:53 Ag 15 '55

Japanese war artists. Pacific victories, 1941 28: 65-70 F 27 '50

Kennington. Night flyer at readiness 26:44 F 28 '49

Laning. Italy's war damage 19:69-72 S 17 '45

World War II (cont.)
  LIFE (magazine)
    Art competition for men in
    the armed services 13:31-
    6 Jy 6 '42 paintings as
    Christmas cards bw 13:138-
    9, 141 O 19 '42
    Defense paintings by 7 ma-
    jor American artists 11:60-
    4 Jy 7 '41
    War art of World War II by
    major American artists 11:
    60-4 Jy 7 '41; 15:49-84 D
    27 '43; 18:42-67 Ap 30 '45;
    19:58-70 O 8 '45
    London bombing fires 12:38-40
    Mr 2 '42
    Lurcat. Nazi warfare satire
    tapestry 21:81 S 30 '46
    McIntyre. Disabled landing
    craft* 28:57 F 6 '50
    "Marin-Marie" Battle of Oran*
    36:50 Mr 7 '49
    "Marin-Marie" British bom-
    bardment of Dakar* 26:50
    Mr 7 '49
    Menkes. Martyrdom of War-
    saw 35:55 N 2 '53
    Millman. Bilibrid Prison, Ma-
    nila 19:67 O 8 '45
    Millman. Santa Tomas Univer-
    sity, Manila 19:66 O 8 '45
    Mills. London Blitz, Septem-
    ber 7, 1940 26:50 F 28 '49
    Mitchell, B. Iran in World War
    II 18:58-9 Ap 30 '45
    Miwa. Cavite navy yard attack,
    December 10, 1941 28:68 F
    27 '50
    Miyamoto. Japanese para-
    troops at Palembourg 28:69
    F 27 '50
    Moore, H. Tube shelter per-
    spective, 1941 25:56 Mr 21
    '49
    Mullen. Daily occurrence in
    the Channel 26:53 Mr 7 '49
    Nakamura. Off Malaya* 28:68-
    9 F 27 '50
    Nash. Dead Sea 26:46 F 28 '49
    Nevinson. Suburbia, 1939 bw

    9:59 Ag 12 '40
    Norris. Army planes in Ha-
    waii 13:51 N 9 '42
    "Our Life in the Service,"
    servicemen art contest 12:
    64-6 F 9 '42
    The Pacific War 19:58-70 O
    8 '45
    Pears. Convoy 28:73 F 20 '50
    Perlin. Aegean actions; war
    in Greek Sea 18:47-54 F
    26 '45
    Prize-winning cartoonists a-
    mong enlisted men bw 12:
    8-10 Mr 23 '42
    Puma. They will not conquer
    16:78 Je 12 '44
    Reindel. Women war workers
    16:75-8 Je 5 '44
    Rosenthal, B. Mt. Suri-
    bachi flag raising photog
    bw 18:17 Mr 26 '45
    Rosoman. House collapsing
    on two firemen 12:40 Mr
    2 '42; 26:49 F 28 '49
    Rowntree. Coastal defense
    bw 10:64 F 24 '41
    Shepler, War in Guadalcanal
    15:50-3 D 27 '43
    Shmarinov. Nazi war atroci-
    ties in Russia drawings
    bw 14:57-62 Je 14 '43
    Storck. Four days fight in the
    Channel 41:82-3 O 29 '56
    Stretcher party, unknown
    Marine Corps artist draw-
    ing bw 15:81 D 27 '43
    Thomas, N. M. Greenland at
    war 15:77-8 S 6 '43
    Topolski. War around the
    world drawings 18:51-4
    Mr 19 '45
    U.S. Government war art:
    Purchase award paintings
    in Office of Emergency
    Management contest 12:
    58-60 Ap 6 '42
    Uptton. U.X.B. (unexploded
    bomb) squad at work bw
    26:52 F 28 '49
    Vidar. Leyte* 39:56 Ag 15

'55
Vidar. Return to Manila* 39:
57 A 15 '55
Wartime paintings of GI's in
Britain before D-day 31:77-
80 O 29 '51
Wolf. Greenland at war draw-
ings bw 15:76 S 6 '43
Wootton. End of a retreat,
Falaise 35:87 O 26 '53
Wright, M. London bombing*
26:50 F 28 '49
Yamaguchi. General attack on
Hong Kong 28:60 F 27 '50
Warburg, Mrs. E. M.
Baskerville. Mrs. E. M. War-
burg 10:48 F 3 '41
Ward. Birds of Paradise 31:103-
5 Jy 16 '51
Ward room. bw Sample 3:42 N 15
'37
Warnecke, Heinz
The last supper sculpture bw
39:119 S 19 '55
Warren, Robert Penn
Robert Penn Warren photog bw
23:84 S 1 '47
Warrior bronze, Etruscan, 450
B.C. 40:62-3 F 13 '56
Warrior ceramic, T'ang 33:101
O 27 '52
Warriors
Guardian figures, Ming dy-
nasty, China bw 3:57 Ag 23
'37
Warrior's head terra cotta,
Etruscan, 5th century B.C.
40:58 F 13 '56
Warsaw Uprising
Merkes. Martyrdom of War-
saw, August, 1944 35:55 N
2 '53
Warshaw, Howard
Wrecked automobiles 28:84 Mr
20 '50
Warship. Sterne 31:54 Ag 27 '51
"Warspite" (ship) English, 1940
Wilkinson. The battleship
Warspite 24:66 My 17 '48
Wartik, Patricia
Mountain landscape 39:136-7

N 21 '55
"Washington" (ship)
U.S.S. Washington 13:60-1
N 2 '42
Washington, Booker Taliaferro
Booker T. Washington bw 5:
51 O 3 '38
Washington, George
Baker. George Washington in
Masonic dress sculpture
bw 26:56 Mr 28 '49
Battle of Saratoga, Japanese
illustration, 1853 bw 25:7
Ag 2 '48
Battle of Trenton, 1776 print
29:47 Jy 3 '50
Borglum. George Washing-
ton, Mt. Rushmore Na-
tional Memorial sculpture
4:26 Je 27 '38 bw 3:104 O
4 '37; 7:19 Jy 17 '39; 11:
103 O 6 '41
Cadena. George Washington
9:67 S 2 '40
Columbia placing victory
wreath on bust of Washington 31:69 Jy 2 '51
General Washington's arrival
in New York harbor for in-
auguration, * c1800 31:68
Jy 2 '51
George Washington bw 13:105
O 5 '42; 16:44 Ja 24 '44
caricature 24:24 F 23 '48
George Washington, playing
card, "King of Hearts."
Humphreys 38:Cover My
30 '55
George Washington and Benjamin Franklin printed
cotton textile, England,
1782 40:82 Ja 9 '56
George Washington clock,
Paris, 1780-1819 17:58 S
4 '44
Greenough. George Washington, statue, nude to waist
bw 5:5 N 7 '38; 19:9 S 24
'45
Hicks. Washington at the Delaware 29:46 Jy 10'50

Washington, George (cont.)
Leutze. Washington cross-
ing the Delaware bw 5:28 O
31 '38; 6:54 Mr 20 '39; 18:
17 Mr 26 '45; 22:118 F 17
'47
Peale, Rembrandt. George
Washington bw 24:23 F 23
'48
Peale, C.W. George Washington bw 24:22 F 23 '48 1779
bw 24:22 F 23 '48
Pine. George Washington,
1785 bw 24:22 F 23 '48
Polk. George Washington,
c1790 bw 24:22 F 23 '48
President and Lady Washington's levee* bw 14:62 Ap
12 '43
Savage. George Washington bw
24:23 F 23 '48
Savage. The Washington family
6:27 Je 19 '39
Sharples. George Washington
bw 24:22 F 23 '48
Soward. George Washington 39:
60 Jy 4 '55
Stuart. George Washington bw
5:28 O 31 '38; 30:111 F 19
'51 1796, 24:23 F 23 '48
head on 3¢ stamp bw 24:23
F 23 '48
Sully. George Washington bw
24:22 F 23 '48
Sully. Washington at Trenton
29:Cover Jy 3 '50
Trumbull. Washington resigning his commission bw 16:
47 Ja 24 '44; 18:Cover Je
18 '45
Washington and Lee at Battle
of Monmouth bw 29:51 Jy 3
'50
Washington at Valley Forge
sculpture bw 8:114 My 20
'40
Washington calling on Amerigo
Vespucci, Japanese illus-
tration, 1853 bw 25:7 Ag
2 '48
Washington on his white horse

woodcarving, U.S., mid-
19th century 31:69 Jy 2 '51
Washington presides over the
Federal Convention, 1787
bw 16:45 Ja 24 '44
Washington's farewell to his
officers, December 4,
1783 bw 16:46 Ja 24 '44
Wheelock. Washington head
sculpture bw 8:115 My 20
'40
Wood, G. Parson Weems'
fable 8:32-3 F 19 '40 bw
14:58 Ja 18 '43
Wright, J. George Washing-
ton 31:98 N 5 '51 bw 24:
23 F 23 '48
Washington arms (Book
plate?) bw 30:107 F 19 '51
(coat of arms)
Washington's flag: 13 white
stars on blue ground 17:
57 S 4 '44 (flag)
Washington, Martha
Peale, Mrs. Rembrandt.
Martha Washington, after
Rembrandt Peale 12:66 Mr
20 '42
Washington, Samuel
Samuel Washington bw 30:110
F 19 '51
Washington Arch, New York
City photog bw 16:13 Je 5
'44; 29:71 Ag 14 '50
Washington, D.C. See also
Memorials and Monuments;
United States Capitol;
White House
Street scene in Washington,
Japanese illustration,
1853 bw 25:6-7 Ag 2 '48
Washington, D.C. airview,
showing public buildings,
monuments bw 11:112-3
N 10 '41
Washington in 1861 airview
bw 11:92-3 N 10 '41
Williams. Washington in
wartime cartoon bw 13:
98-9 D 7 '42
Washington Street, Salem,

Massachusetts, 1765. Orne
13:80 N 23 '42

Wat Arun (Temple of Dawn),
Bangkok photog 31:33 D 31
'51

Wat Benjamabopit (Temple of
Marble), Bangkok photogs
31:35 D 31 '51

Wat Bovornives monastery--
Golden Buddha, Bangkok
38:80 Mr 7 '55

Wat Po, Bangkok photog 31:34 D
31 '51

The watch on the "Santa Maria."
sculpture bw Rogers, J. 6:
8 Mr 6 '39

Watches See Clocks and Watches

Watching the breakers. bw Homer
6:58 Mr 27 '39

Water
Hurd. Paintings showing sig-
nificance of water in Southwest, U.S. 23:74-8 Ag 18
'47
Rivera. Man's dependence on
water, mural, water storage
tank, Mexico City 31:73 S
17 '51

Water carrier, India. Sheets 20:
82 Ja 21 '46

Water carrier. sculpture bw,
Greek, 442 B.C. 23:22 Jy
7 '47

Water for irrigation, India. bw
Sheets 20:80 Ja 21 '46

Water organ--fountain, Villa
D'Este, Italy photog 28:79
My 8 '50

Waterfalls
Bornet. Niagara Falls lithograph bw 26:77 Je 6 '49
Boy drowning in falls, Niagara Falls, 1873 bw 26:76
Je 6 '49
Brown, J. F. Sacrifice of Indian maiden, Niagara Falls
26:80 Je 6 '49
Chambers. Trapper 26:78 Je
6 '49
Church. Horseshoe Falls 26:
78-9 Je 6 '49

DeGrailly Maid of mist 26:
79 Je 6 '49
De Martelly. Niagara Falls*
26:79 Je 6 '49
Emett. Niagara Falls cartoon
37:45 Jy 5 '54
Hartley. Smelt Brook falls
13:96 N 9 '42
Monsieur Blondin, tightrope
walker, spanning Niagara
Gorge, 1859* print 26:80
Je 6 '49
Rousseau, H. The waterfall
11:58 S 8 '41
Trumbull. Rainbow 26:78 Je
6 '49

Watermelons
Peale, Raphaelle. Melons 12:
66 Mr 20 '42
Rosenthal, D. By the sea 15:
68 N 22 '43
Tamayo. The glutton 34:102
Mr 16 '53

Waterval, A. K. N., architect
Cinder-block house photog 3:
15 D 13 '37

Watkinson, Franklin Chenault
Fire eater 26:86 F 21 '49
Sturgis Ingersoll, 1938 38:
71 Mr 28 '55

Watkins, Francis J.
Summer fragrance bw 6:45
My 1 '39

Watrous, James
Paul Bunyan and his blue ox,
Babe 25:58 N 29 '48

Watson and the shark. Copley
9:76 D 9 '40

Watteau, Jean Antoine
Artist's dream 5:37 S 26 '38
The elysian fields 23:84 S
15 '47
Embarkation for Cytherea
23:84 S 15 '47 bw 19:50
Jy 30 '45
Return from the hunt 23:82-
3 S 15 '47
Reunion in the country 40:
110-1 My 7 '56
Antoine Watteau bw 5:34 S
26 '38 port.

Watton, John Fessenden
  Germany's prison can.ps bw
    13:138-41 N 9 '42
Waugh, Carleton
  Burial of burlesque bw 5:56 N
    28 '38
  Red burlesque 5:57 N 28 '38
  Sunday in Central Park bw 5:
    56 N 28 '38
  Dickie Dare bw 5:57 N 28 '38
    (cartoons)
  Carleton Waugh photog bw 5:57
    N 28 '38 port.
Waugh, Evelyn
  "Decline and Fall," author's
    sketch of characters in his
    book bw 20:58 Ap 8 '46
  Evelyn Waugh photog bw 20:53
    Ap 8 '46 and family photogs
    bw 27:134, 155 S 19 '49
Waugh, Frederick Judd
  Ante meridian 3:24 D 20 '37 bw
    2:57 Je 14 '37
  The big water 2:57 Je 14 '37
    bw 3:24 D 20 '37
  Meridian bw 3:24 D 20 '37
  Pounding surf bw 5:57 N 28 '38
  Tropic seas bw 2:56 Je 14 '37;
    3:24 D 20 '37
  Frederick Judd Waugh photog
    bw 2:57 Je 14 '37; 5:57 N 28
    '38 port.
Waugh, Sidney, glass designer
  Glassware: Zodiac bowl; com-
    pass bowl; pigeon; fish;
    figures; sugar and creamer
    photog bw 7:32 S 18 '39
  Merry-go-round bowl, Steuben
    glass photog bw 23:18 N 10
    '47
  Artist at work photog bw 7:32
    S 18 '39 port.
The wave. Harley 32:88 Je 16 '52
Wave architecture, Barcelona
  photog bw 2:40 F 22 '37
Wavell, Archibald Percival
  General Wavell bw 26:55 Mr 7
    '49
Wavel castle, Poland photog bw
  5:52 Ag 29 '38
The wax figures cabinet. bw Sed-

lacek 2:58 Ap 26 '37
Wax jack, taper reel, silver,
  Charles II bw 3:77 D 13 '37
Wayne, Anthony
  "Mad" Anthony Wayne bw 29:
    52 Jy 3 '50
Wdowiszewski, Czeslaw
  The burial 3:25 D 20 '37
We Three Kings of Orient Are.
  Davis, G.R. 23:52 D 22
    '47
Weaning the calf. Homer 41:72-
  3 D 10 '53
Weapons
         Artillery
  Breach-loading swivel guns,
    late 15th century print bw
    40:42 Ja 9 '56
  Cannon, Middle Ages in Be-
    seiged castle bw 22:66 My
    26 '47

         Battle Axes
  Battle axe photog 40:187 Ap 9
    '56
  Bec de corbin (Raven's beak)
    photog 40:187 Ap 9 '56

           Bows
  Cross bow in Beseiged castle
    Middle Ages bw 22:66 My
    26 '47
  Crossbow bold photog 40:186
    Ap 9 '56
  Longbows in Battle of Agin-
    court 40:188 Ap 9 '56

          Daggers
  Gold dagger, Egypt, c1375
    B.C. photog 24:81 Ja 19
    '48
  Gold jewelled dagger, Persian
    19th century photog 33:43
    D 29 '52

          Firearms
  Colt .44 dragoon six shooter,
    U.S. frontier, 1847 pho-
    tog 39:75 N 28 '55
  Colt .44 frontier model pho-
    tog 39:75 N 28 '55

Weapons--Firearms (cont.)
  Colt 1861 Navy revolver
    photog 39:75 N 28 '55
  Gatling gun photog 39:111 O
    17 '55
  Hawken-type "plains rifle,"
    U.S. frontier photog 39:75
    N 28 '55
  Pennsylvania rifle; American
    long guns, Revolutionary
    War photog 38:58-60 My 30
    '55
  Philadelphia derringer, single-
    shot, "gambler's pistol,"
    U.S. frontier photog 39:75
    N 28 '55
  Pistol, flintlock, U.S. coloni-
    al photog 38:60 My 30 '55
  Pistol of Emperor Charles V,
    1540 bw 6:52 Mr 20 '39
  Pistol-sword, Italian, 16th
    century 35:96 D 14 '53
  Sharps' carbine, single-shot,
    U.S. frontier and Civil War
    photog 39:75 N 28 '55
  Spencer carbine, seven-shot
    photog 39:75 N 28 '55
  Springfield carbine, Indian
    fighting, 1870 photog 39:75
    N 28 '55
  Winchester 66 carbine, U.S.
    frontier photog 39:75 N 28
    '55
  Winchester 73 rifle, U.S.
    frontier photog 39:75 N 28
    '55

Halberd
Halberd photog 40:187 Ap 9 '56
Halberd, U.S. colonial photog
  38:60 My 30 '55

Hammers
War hammer photog 40:187 Ap
  9 '56

Mace
Mace 40:186 Ap 9 '56

Pike
Boarding pikes, U.S.S. Constellation photog bw 9:54 O
  28 '40

Spears and Spear Throwers
Boar spear photog 40:186 Ap
  9 '56
Spear thrower, gold, Inca
  photog 36:102 Ap 12 '54
Spear thrower, paleolithic
  photog 39:79 D 12 '55

Stone Throwers
Bombards (stone throwers)
  in Battle at Barbary,
  1390 40:188 Ap 9 '56

Swords
Cavalry sword, Polish, 17th
  century photog 35:96 D 14
  '53
English sword photog 40:186
  Ap 9 '56
German sword, 15th century
  photog 40:185 Ap 9 '56
Italian sword photog 40:186
  Ap 9 '56
Jewelled sword of state, Eng-
  land photog 2:39 Mr 15 '37
King's sword, Anglian, 7th
  century photog 31:84-5 Jy
  16 '51
Swords used in the United
  States photog bw 40:171
  My 14 '56
Toothed swords of South Seas
  photog 21:79 N 4 '46
U.S. Revolutionary War
  swords--officers and en-
  listed photog 38:58-60 My
  30 '55

Tomahawks
Tomahawks photog 39:76 N
  28 '55
The weasel. Priebe 23:71 N 24
  '47
Weathervanes
Drowne. Indian, copper 38:
  121 Ap 18 '55
Eagle, American symbol,
  c1784 bw 17:56 S 4 '44

Weathervanes (cont.)
  Pennsylvania weathervanes,
    1670 38:121 Ap 18 '55
  Weathervanes, Webb Museum,
    Shelburne, Vermont 35:48-
    9 Jy 6 '53
Weavers
  At the loom, c1795, American
    primitive 24:68 Mr 1 '48
  Campigli. Weavers 29:108 D
    11 '50
Weaving See Tapestry; Textiles
Webb, Beatrice
  Beatrice Webb photog bw 24:
    100 Ja 19 '48
Webb, Sidney
  Sidney Webb photog bw 24:100
    Ja 19 '48
Webb Museum of American Arts
    and Crafts, Shelburne, Vt.
  Treasures of collection; room
    35:46-53 Jy 6 '53
Weber, Aloysia
  Aloysia Weber bw 40:121 Ap
    23 '56
Weber, Constanze bw 40:121 Ap
    23 '56
Weber, Max
  Fighters for freedom, War in
    Spain, 1936 16:78 Je 12 '44
  The Rabbi 19:86 Ag 20 '45
  Seeking work 19:85 Ag 20 '45
  Still life with two tables 19:86
    Ag 20 '45
  Tranquillity 19:85 Ag 20 '45;
    21:78 N 25 '46
  Two musicians 19:86 Ag 20 '45
  Two patriarchs 33:99 O 27 '52
  Figure bw 19:84 Ag 20 '45
    (sculpture)
  Gilded mask bw 19:84 Ag 20
    '45 (sculpture)
  Artist at work; family photogs
    bw 19:87 Ag 20 '45 port.
  Max Weber and his work photog
    bw 16:76 Je 12 '44 port.
Weber, Warren, architect
  Church, Cedar Hills, Oregon
    photog 39:112-3 D 26 '55
Webster, Daniel
  Daniel Webster 19:86 S 24 '45

bw 6:31 Je 19 '39 photog
bw 23:55 N 3 '47
  Healy. Webster replying to
    Hayne, January 26-7, 1830
    16:54 F 21 '44
Webster, H. T., cartoonist
  "Life's Darkest Moment,"
    and other cartoons bw 33:
    51 O 6 '52
  "The Unseen Audience" bw
    20:129-30 Mr 25 '46
  Flagg. Webby bw 33:51 O 6
    '52 port.
  H. T. Webster photog bw 20:
    129 Mr 25 '46 port.
Webster, Noah
  Noah Webster bw 30:126 F 12
    '51
The wedding dance. Brueghel,
    P., the elder 4:22 Ap 11
    '38 bw 35:31 S 14 '53
Wedding of Doge and the sea,
    Venice, Renaissance* bw
    23:59 Ag 4 '47
The wedding of the Mississippi
    and the Missouri, foun-
    tain, St. Louis. sculpture
    bw Milles 2:Cover, 26 F
    22 '37 copy bw 8:110-2 Je
    10 '40
Wedding scene, England, c1550*
    41:146 N 5 '56
Weddings
  Brueghel, the younger. The
    groom 7:56 O 9 '39
  Lee. Country wedding 14:45
    Mr 8 '43
  Pocahontas' wedding to John
    Rolfe print bw 31:154 D
    3 '51
  Shivaree, 1872 32:115 Ap 7
    '52
  Van Eyck, J. Giovanni Ar-
    nolfini and his wife 33:36
    D 29 '52
The Wedgwood family. Stubbs
    25:98 S 13 '48
Weed, Robert Law and Marion
    I. Manley, architects
  University of Miami, Florida
    photogs bw 25:72-3 D 27 '48

Weeden, Eleanor
  Johnie 10:47 F 3 '41
Weems, Mason Locke
  Wood, G. Parson Weems'
    fable 8:32-3 F 19 '40 bw
    14:58 Ja 18 '43
Weeping Virgin wood carving,
    German 15th century bw 15:
    64 S 20 '43
Weights, scale photog bw 40:46
    Ja 9 '56
Weimar, Duke of
  Duke of Weimar returns from
    the hunt bw 27:22 Jy 25 '49
Weinstock, Carol
  East River Drive 16:45 Ja 3
    '44
Weisgerber, Charles H.
  Betsy Ross bw 32:57 F 18 '52
Weld, Francis
  Brackman. Francis Weld 8:
    60 F 5 '40
Welles, Gideon
  Gideon Welles photog bw 11:
    100 N 10 '41; 14:75 F 15
    '43
Wellington, Arthur Wellesley,
    1st Duke of
  Duke of Wellington 24:70 My
    24 '48 bw 4:60 Ap 4 '38
  Wellington at Waterloo* bw 7:
    71 S 25 '39
  Winterhalter. Duke of Welling-
    ton and Sir Robert Peel 25:
    90 N 22 '48
Wells, Herbert George
  Beerbohm. H. G. Wells cari-
    cature bw 23:88 N 17 '47
  Karsh. H.G. Wells photog bw
    16:94 F 7 '44
Wells Fargo overland stage--
    concord coach photog 39:82
    N 28 '55
Wenceslas, King of Bohemia
  King Wenceslas bw 24:28 Mr
    8 '48
  Lee, D. Good King Wenceslas
    23:45 D 22 '47
Wendell, Raymond J.
  Dream world 25:101 D 6 '48
  Artist and his work photog bw

25:98 D 6 '48 port.
Wentworth, Thomas
  Thomas Wentworth, Earl of
    Strafford bw 41:182 N 12
    '56
Werden Crucifix, 11th century
    39:Cover D 26 '55
Werner, Betsy and Hans
  Artists at work, Santa Fe,
    New Mexico photog bw 25:
    133 S 27 '48 port.
Werner, Theodore
  Artist and his work photog
    30:145 My 10 '54 port.
Werner, Woty, tapestry de-
    signer
  Artist and her work photog
    36:145 My 10 '54 port.
Werther, illustration for "The
    Sorrows of Young Wer-
    ther" bw 27:22 Jy 25 '49
Wesley, Charles
  Charles Wesley bw 23:114
    N 10 '47
Wesley, Frank
  Mary Magdalene bw 29:63 S
    4 '50
Wesley, John
  John Wesley--portraits, bio-
    graphical scenes bw 23:
    114 N 10 '47
  John Wesley preaching, Eng-
    land, 18th century* 25:
    103 S 13 '48
West, Benjamin
  Benjamin Franklin and the
    lightning 40:81 Ja 9 '56 bw
    6:26 Je 19 '39.
  Death of General Wolfe 5:31
    O 31 '38; 25:106-7 S 13
    '48 bw 7:70 S 25 '39; 9:112
    S 9 '40
  Mrs. Benjamin West 12:59 Je
    15 '42
  Penn's treaty with the Indians
    6:27 Je 19 '39
West, Elizabeth Shewell
  West, B. Mrs. Benjamin
    West 12:59 Je 15 '42

West, Mae
  Bush. Mae West sculpture 1:
    33 D 7 '36
Westermann, William L.
  William L. Westermann
    photog bw 11:43 O 13 '41
Western landscape. Moran, T.
    19:86 S 10 '45
Westin, Fredrik
  King Charles XIV of Sweden
    and his family* bw 33:92
    D 1 '52
Westinghouse air brake in action
    bw 22:80 Ja 13 '47
Westminster Abbey
  Battle of Britain window,
    stained glass memorial to
    RAF heroes, World War II
    26:58 F 7 '49
  Coronation of Charles II, King
    of England, 1661 bw 41:164
    N 19 '56
  Westminster Abbey photogs
    bw 2:39 My 10 '37
Weston, Edward, photographer
  "Cats of Wild Cat Hill," book
    of photographs bw 25:10-2
    S 6 '48
  Documents of the West 3:4-6
    D 27 '37
  Photographs 2:76, 78 Ap 12
    '37
  Edward Weston photog bw 2:
    76 Ap 12 '37; 3:5 D 27 '37
    port.
Westover, country house, Vir-
    ginia, 18th century photog
    bw 25:110-1 S 13 '48
"Westward the course of empire."
    Leutze 36:76 Mr 8 '54
Westward the course of empire
    takes its way. Currier and
    Ives print 9:34 D 30 '40
Wet night in Piccadilly Circus.
    Hacker 23:85 N 17 '47
Weyhe, Erhard
  Newman. Erhard Weyhe photog
    bw 35:18-9 D 7 '53
Whalebone Carving
  Scrimshaw: corset stay; bod-
    kin, pie crimpers, cane,

clothespin, U.S. 1860 39:
    109 O 17 '55
Whales See Jonah and the Whale
Whaling* print bw 5:17 D 19 '38
"What is Race," UNESCO book-
    let, illustrations Kleiman
    34:101-2 My 18 '53
Whatnot, spool turned, Victori-
    an, U.S. photog 40:90-1
    Mr 5 '56
Wheat. Cox, J. R. 25:86-7 Jy 12
    '48
Wheatley, Phillis
  Phillis Wheatley bw 5:51 O
    3 '38
Whedon, Harriet
  Decoys 16:46 Je 3 '44
The wheel of life, China 8:32-
    3 Ja 8 '40
Wheel of the law, Buddhist em
    blem 38:57 F 7 '55; 38:61
    Mr 7 '55
Wheel shop, Hangtown, Cali-
    fornia, c1850 31:74 Jy 2
    '51; 39:104 O 17 '55
Wheeler, Charles
  Spring sculpture 25:101 S 27
    '48
Wheeler, William A.
  William A. Wheeler photog
    bw 9:8 Ag 5 '40
Wheelock, Warren, sculptor
  Black dancer bw 8:116 My 20
    '40
  Mayor La Guardia bw 7:36
    Jy 17 '39
  Paul Revere's ride bw 8:114
    My 20 '40
  Roosevelt head bw 8:115 My
    20 '40
  Salut au monde bw 8:114 My
    20 '40
  Sultan of swat bw 8:116 My
    20 '40
  The tragic Lincoln bw 8:117
    My 20 '40
  Washington at Valley Forge
    bw 8:114 My 20 '40
  Washington head bw 8:115
    My 20 '40
  Young girl bw 8:115 My 20

'40
Artist at work photog bw 8:114
My 20 '40 port.
Wheels See also kinds of wheels,
as Prayer Wheels; Spinning
wheels
Carved stone wheel, Black pagoda, Kanarak, Orissa
photog bw 12:90 Mr 16 '42
Wherefore now ariseth the illusion of the third dimension.
Albright, I. 16:66-7 Mr 27
'44
Whipple, William
William Whipple bw 15:10 Jy
5 '43
Whipple house, Ipswich, Massachusetts, 1683- main bed
room photog 18:58 My 7 '45
Whiskey Rebellion, 1794 bw 22:
99 Mr 24 '47
Whistler, James Abbott McNeill
Arrangement in black and
white (Whistler's model,
Maud Franklin) 36:94 My
17 '54
Arrangement in flesh color and
black (Theodore Duret) 36:
95 My 17 '54 bw 6:54 Mr 20
'39
Arrangement in grey and black,
no. 1 (Mother) bw 5:29 O 31
'38
Old Battersea bridge 12:62 Je
15 '42
Old Battersea bridge (Sym-
phony in Brown and Silver)
36:94-5 My 17 '54
Southampton waters 36:94-5
My 17 '54
The white girl 27:59 Ag 29 '49
Chase. James McNeill Whist-
ler bw 5:29 O 31 '38; 6:54
Mr 20 '39 port.
Self-portrait bw 36:92 My 17
'54 port.
Self-portrait: Whistler in his
studio 36:93 My 17 '54 port.
Whistler, Rex
Faces, reversible, depending
upon Gestalt drawing bw

22:22-3 Mr 31 '47
Whistler's father bw 2:102 Je 28
'37
Whitaker, Frederic
Pink house 16:45 Ja 3 '44
Whitcombe, Thomas
Siege of Gibralter 24:67 My
10 '48
White, Mrs. Henry
Sargent. Mrs. Henry White
27:59 Ag 29 '49
White, John Blake, watercolor-
ist
Chief's wife, c1585 22:82 Mr
10 '47
Indian chief's tomb, c1585 22:
82 Mr 10 '47
Indian meal,* c1585 22:82 Mr
10 '47
Indians fishing,* c1585 22:81
Mr 10 '47
Indians of Virginia, illustra-
tions for De Bry's "Voy-
ages" bw 18:60 My 21 '45
Secota, Indian village, c1585
22:83 Mr 10 '47
Sorcerer, c1585 22:82 Mr 10
'47
White, Stanford, architect and
decorator See also Mc-
Kim, Mead and White,
architects
Hyde Park, New York 28:89-
92 Ja 2 '50
Rosecliff, Newport photogs
bw 11:82-5 Ag 18 '41
White barn. O'Keefe 4:30 F 14
'38
White boat. Stuempfig 25:100 S
20 '48
White castels on the upper Mis-
souri. Bodmer 15:87 Ag
30 '43
White cloud. Cox, J.B. 16:78
Ap 24 '44
White footed mouse. Grossen-
heider 21:86-8 O 28 '46
The white girl. Whistler 27:59
Ag 29 '49
The white horse. Bellows 20:
81 Mr 25 '46

The White House, Washington,
    D.C.
    The White House, c1861 pho-
        tog bw 11:95 N 10 '41
    The White House--halls;
        studies; rooms; exterior
        photogs 9:66-70 S 2 '40
    The White House--historic
        and present photogs, plans
        bw 21:59 O 14 '46
    The White House--renovation
        of interior photogs 31:56
        N 5 '51
        interior after third major
        renovation and redecora-
        tion photogs 33:46-53 Jy 7
        '52
White lace. Carroll 7:36 Jy 31
    '39; 21:75 N 25 '46
The white marlin. Lawrence, W.
    G. 6:29 F 2 '39
White Sands Proving Ground, New
    Mexico. cartoon Emett 37:
    51 Jy 5 '54
The white way. Sloan 7:46 D 11
    '39
Whitefield, George
    George Whitefield bw 23:114
        N 10 '47
Whitehall, London 41:168 N 19
    '56
Whitehall, thoroughfare of em-
    pire. Bone 24:60 My 10 '48
Whitehead, Alfred North
    Alfred North Whitehead photog
        bw 10:96 My 5 '41
Whitman, Marcus
    Marcus Whitman--statue; wife;
        mission; massacre; memori-
        al; map of ride bw 15:95-7
        S 17 '43
    Murder of Marcus Whitman, *
        1847 print bw 39:74-5 D 26
        '55
    Norling. Marcus Whitman bw
        15:100 S 27 '43
Whitman, Walt
    Davidson. Walt Whitman sculp-
        ture bw 26:12 Je 20 '49
    Eakins. Walt Whitman, 1887
        9:45 Jy 29 '40 bw 6:31 Je

19 '39
    Locale of Whitman poems
        photogs bw 38:113-21 Je
        20 '55
    Walt Whitman photog bw 31:
        111 N 5 '51 72 years of age
        38:120 Je 20 '55
    Walt Whitman, age 36, front-
        ispiece, "Leaves of
        Grass," first edition en-
        graving bw 38:113 Je 20
        '55
Wheelock. Salut au monde
    sculpture bw 8:114 My 20
    '40
Whitney, Eli
    Morse. Eli Whitney 39:66 Ag
        29 '55 bw 6:31 Je 19 '39
Whitney, Gertrude Vanderbilt,
    sculptor
    Christopher Columbus, me-
        morial statue, Palos,
        Spain 39:118 O 10 '55
    The kiss bw 7:45 S 11 '39
    Pieter Stuyvesant bw 7:45 S
        11 '39
    To the morrow bw 7:45 S 11
        '39
    Artist at work photog bw 7:
        44 S 11 '39 port.
Whitney Museum of American
    Art
    Outstanding paintings from
        collection 12:73-5 Ap 20
        '42
Whittemore, Thomas
    Thomas Whittemore photog bw
        29:61 D 25 '50
Whittier, John Greenleaf
    John Greenleaf Whittier
        photog bw 33:97 S 29 '52
    Whittier's "Snowbound" farm
        house photog bw 9:100 O
        14 '40
Who'll turn the grindstone.
    Mount 12:73 Ap 20 '42;
    18:65 Je 25 '45
Why not sneeze (Lumps of
    marble in a cage). Du-
    champ 32:103 Ap 28 '52

Wickey, Harry, sculptor
  Eleventh Avenue flapper bw 12:
    54 F 23 '42
  Garbage man eating his lunch
    bw 12:54 F 23 '42
  Kids wrestling bw 12:53 F 23
    '42
  Little brother and sister bw
    12:54 F 23 '42
  Little girls bw 12:53 F 23 '42
  Pregnant woman bw 12:54 F
    23 '42
  Saturday night bw 12:53 F 23
    '42
  Harry Wickey in his studio
    photog bw 12:53 F 23 '42
    port.
Widener collection, Philadelphia
  Dutch paintings; gallery 6:30-
    5 Ag 29 '38
Widmann, Oscar O., interior de-
    signer
  Trade Secrets house decora-
    tion photog 34:8-10 Ja 5 '55
The widow. Lee, D. 8:66 My 27
    '40
Widow's Walk
  Falmouth, Massachusetts,
    mansion photog bw 9:71 Jy
    15 '40
  New England houses photog bw
    15:12-3, 15 D 6 '43
  Three-story house, Nantucket
    photog bw 3:40 Ag 9 '37
"Wien" (ship)
  Hitler. Battleship Wien 7:53
    O 30 '39
Wife of the artist. Davis, G. P.
    10:48 F 3 '41
Wiggins, Frank
  Frank Wiggins bw 15:106 N
    22 '43
Wild cat. Audubon 30:49 Ja 29
    '51
Wild flowers. lithograph Wood,
    G. 7:25 Ag 28 '39
Wild flowers of Michigan. Lee,
    D. 25:68 Ag 23 '48
Wild turkey. bw Audubon 5:28
    O 31 '38
Wilde, Oscar

Beerbohm. Oscar Wilde lec-
    turing in U.S. bw 5:43 D
    5 '38; 33:126 S 22 '52
  Oscar Wilde photog bw 5:43 D
    5 '38
  Toulouse-Lautrec. Oscar
    Wilde caricature 28:97 My
    15 '50
Wilde, Percival
  Percival Wilde photog bw 22:
    21 Mr 10 '47
Wilder, Thornton
  Gertrude Stein and Thornton
    Wilder photog bw 23:14 Ag
    18 '47
Wilhelm, Crown Prince of Ger-
    many
  German soldiers, European
    War, 1914-1918 drawings
    8:56-7 Mr 25 '40
Wilhelm II, Emperor of Germany
  Emperor Wilhelm II photog bw
    4:13 Mr 28 '38 portraits;
    family 10:36 Je 16 '41
  The yellow peril cartoon bw
    6:11 Ja 2 '39
Wilhelmina, Queen of the Ne-
    therlands
  Queen Wilhelmina photogs bw
    18:49 Ap 16 '45 portraits;
    family; homes; associ-
    ates 5:26-9 S 5 '38; 25:79-
    83 Ag 16 '48
Wilkie, David
  Preaching of John Knox 24:66
    Je 14 '48
Wilkie, Wendell L.
  Wendell Wilkie photog bw 14:
    7 My 31 '43
Wilkinson, Norman
  The battleship Warspite 24:
    66 My 17 '48
  British convoy under German
    air attacks* 26:53 Mr 7
    '49
  Graf Spee defeat 24:68 My 10
    '48
  The Jervis Bay 24:68 My 10
    '48
  The Navy's here* 24:66 My
    17 '48

Wilkinson, Norman (cont.)
  Raid at Nazaire* 29:92 O 30
    '50
Willard, Aaron, clockmaker
  Banjo clock, U.S. photog 39:
    64 Jy 18 '55 bw 6:52 Mr 20
    '39
  Shelf clock, U.S., c1800 pho-
    tog 39:64 Jy 18 '55
Willard, Archibald M.
  Spirit of '76 (Yankee Doodle)
    bw 9:55 Ag 5 '40
Willard, Emma
  Emma Willard bw 23:90 O 27
    '47
Willard, Simon, clockmaker
  Wall clock, with carved eagle,
    U.S., c1810 photog 17:58
    S 4 '44
Willet, Henry Lee
  Stained glass window, West-
    wood community church,
    Los Angeles photog 38:66-
    7 Ap 11 '55
Willi, Anton
  Fastnacht masks of spirits
    and furies photog 22:8-10
    Ja 13 '47
  Artist and his work photog bw
    22:8, 10 Ja 13 '47 port.
William I, The Conqueror, King
    of England
  William the Conqueror bw 22:
    84 My 26 '47
  William the Conqueror in
    Battle of Hastings, French
    chronicle, 15th century 40:
    86 Mr 26 '56
William I, The Silent, Prince of
    Orange-Nassau bw 4:11 F
    21 '38
William and Mary College. Wren,
    archt. photog bw 14:66 Ap
    12 '43
William of Normandy 40:86 Mr
    26 '56
Williams, Garth
  "Little Fur Family" illustra-
    tions 21:59-61 D 2 '46
Williams, George
  George Williams, founder of
    the YMCA bw 31:82 Jy 23 '51
Williams, Gluyas, cartoonist
  "The Americans, A Study in
    Character" illustrations
    bw 23:94 Ag 18 '47
  "Chips off the Old Benchley"
    illustrations bw 27:24-9
    O 10 '49
  Washington in wartime bw 13:
    98-9 D 7 '42
  Self-portrait cartoon bw 15:
    14 O 25 '43 port.
Williams, Mrs. Harrison
  Dali. Mrs. Harrison Willi-
    ams bw 19:66 S 24 '45
Williams, Mary Adeline
  Eakins. "Addie" 41:160 D 24
    '56
Williams, Paul, architect
  Music Corporation of Ameri-
    ca, office, Beverly Hills,
    Calif. photog bw 5:54 O
    3 '38
  Paul Williams photog bw 5:
    58 O 3 '38 port.
Williams, Roger
  Roger Williams statue bw 39:
    44 D 26 '55
  Roger Williams welcomed by
    Rhode Island Indians bw
    16:44 Ja 31 '44
Williams, Tennessee
  Tennessee Williams photog
    bw 23:101 D 15 '47
  Tennessee Williams and his
    family photogs 24:113 F
    16 '48
Williams, Wheeler, sculptor
  Pan gilded bronze bw 10:118-
    9 Ap 21 '41
  Venus and Manhattan bw 27:
    100 D 19 '49
Williams, William
  William Williams, signer of
    the Declaration of Inde-
    pendence bw 15:10 Jy 5 '43
Willingham, Calder
  Calder Willingham photog bw
    22:78 Je 2 '47
Wills, Royal Barry, architect
  Portfolio of houses sketches,

plans, photogs 21:68-74 Ag
  26 '46
Royal Barry Wills photog bw
  21:67 Ag 26 '46 port.
Wilmington, North Carolina
  Holloway. Oil storage tanks*
  34:79 Ja 5 '53
Wilson, Edward A., illustrator
  "Anthony Adverse" 18:57 Ap
  23 '45
  "Iron Men and Wooden Ships"
  18:55 Ap 23 '45
  "The Last of the Mohicans"
  18:58 Ap 23 '45
  "The Man Without a Country"
  18:58 Ap 23 '45
  "Ranging the Maine Coast" 18:
  57 Ap 23 '45
  "Robinson Crusoe" 18:55 Ap
  23 '45
  "Two Years Before the Mast"
  18:60 Ap 23 '45
  "Treasure Island" 18:56 Ap 23
  '45
  "The Village Blacksmith" 18:
  59 Ap 23 '45
Wilson, Harry Leon
  Harry Leon Wilson photog bw
  7:58 S 4 '39
Wilson, Henry
  Henry Wilson photog bw 9:8 Ag
  5 '40
Wilson, James
  James Wilson, signer of the
  Declaration of Independence
  bw 15:10 Jy 5 '43; 39:63 Jy
  4 '55
Wilson, John
  Mother and child 21:65 Jy 22
  '46
Wilson, Lewis Eugene, archt.
  Laminated wood motion pic-
  ture theater, Los Angeles,
  Calif. photog bw 27:67-8 O
  10 '49
  Lewis Eugene Wilson photog
  bw 27:68 O 10 '49 port.
Wilson, Richard
  River scene: Bathers and
  cattle 5:43 S 12 '38
  Richard Wilson bw 5:42 S 12

'38 port.
Wilson, Woodrow
  Davidson. Woodrow Wilson
  sculpture bw 32:34 Ja 14
  52; 41:103 D 17 '56
  Orpen. Woodrow Wilson 16:
  49 F 28 '44
  Woodrow Wilson photog bw 28:
  81 Ja 2 '50 in Big Four at
  Versailles photog bw 15:22
  Ag 9 '43; 33:41 D 22 '52
Wimar, Charles
  Attack on an emigrant train
  27:43 Jy 4 '49
  Indians pursued by American
  dragoons 27:43 Jy 4 '49
The wind. Hofer 5:73 D 12 '38
Wind from the sea. Wyeth, A.
  35:82 Jy 27 '53
Wind god, Japanese, 17th cen-
  tury 34:100-1 Ap 20 '53
"The Wind in the Willows," illus-
  trations. drawing bw
  Shepard 27:69 N 21 '49
Winding up. Mount 18:68 Je 25
  '45
Windmills
  Courbet. Landscape with
  windmill near Ornans 26:
  64 My 30 '49
  Hogue. Drouth-stricken area
  2:60 Je 21 '37
  Hurd. Desert windmill water
  tank* 23:75 Ag 18 '47
  Hurd. The windmill crew 14:
  46 Mr 8 '43
  Phillips, A. Rutledge mill,
  New Salem, Illinois 36:
  80-1 F 15 '54
  Phillips, A. Sawmill on the
  Sangamon River, New
  Salem, Ill. 36:79 F 15 '54
  Rembrandt. The mill 5:33 Ag
  29 '38
  Wright. Windmill, Wisconsin
  photog of mill designed by
  the architect bw 21:88 Ag
  12 '46
Windsor, Duchess of
  Brockhurst. Duchess of
  Windsor 28:110 Je 12 '50

Windsor, Duke of
  Duke of Windsor photogs bw
    23:116 D 8 '47
  Munnings. Duke of Windsor,
    Fox hunter, 1921 28:122
    My 22 '50
  Orpen. Duke of Windsor, 1922
    28:114 My 22 '50
Windsor castle photogs 28:119 My
    22 '50; 40:88 Mr 19 '56
  Royal suite photogs 21:84-8
    21 '46; White, crimson,
    and green rooms photogs 21:
    85-8 O 21 '46
Wine-making, Egypt bas-relief
    41:89 O 1 '56
Winebreiner, Henry Fielding
  Myrna Loy sculpture bw 3:46
    O 11 '37
"Winesburg, Ohio," portraits
    and scenes depicted in po-
    ems. Fredenthal 20:74-9
    Je 10 '46
Winged victory sculpture bw,
    Greece 19:49 Jy 30 '45
"Winnie-the-Pooh," and other
    Milne books, illustrations,
    drawings bw Shepard 30:75-
    6 F 19 '51; 40:117-22 F 27
    '56
Winslow, Edward, silversmith
  Cup, two-handled, U.S. coloni-
    al photog 38:117 Ap 18 '55
  Silver chocolate pot, U.S.,
    1700 photog bw 6:53 Mr 20
    '39
Winsor, Kathleen
  Kathleen Winsor bw 17:41-4
    O 30 '44 photog 23:86 S 1
    '47
Winston-Salem, North Carolina
  Moravian architecture of Old-
    Salem photog bw 37:166-7
    O 25 '54
Winter, Fritz
  Artist and his work photog 36:
    146 My 10 '54 port.
Winter
  Avilov. Communication troops
    14:47 Mr 29 '43
  Becker. First train of Central

Pacific in Utah* 36:78 Mr
    8 '54
  Bellows. Floating ice 12:75
    Ap 20 '42
  Bohrod. Blackhawk Street,
    Chicago 8:68 My 27 '40
  Brueghel, P., the elder.
    Adoration of the Magi 37:
    38-9 D 27 '54
  Brueghel, P., the elder. Ar-
    rival of Joseph and Mary
    at Bethlehem 37:30 D 27
    '54 detail 37:Cover, 31-3
    D 27 '54
  Brueghel, P., the elder.
    Massacre of the innocents
    37:36-7 D 27 '54
  Brueghel, P., the younger.
    Massacre of the innocents,
    copy 24:65 Je 14 '48
  Burchfield. Wire fence in
    snow 1:27 D 28 '36
  Chiang. Enjoying snow scene
    bw 33:8 O 13 '52
  Churchill. Terrace at Chart-
    well* 20:48 Ja 7 '46
  Cowles. High water in winter
    24:76 F 9 '48
  Currier and Ives print. A-
    merican winter scene:
    Evening 9:27 D 30 '40
  Dehn. The three red houses
    11:41 Ag 11 '41
  Dehn. Winter over the Hud-
    son 11:41 Ag 11 '41
  Ford. Epiphany at Bethlehem,
    Connecticut 17:38-9 D 25
    '44
  Ford. No room in the inn 5:
    27 Jy 4 '38
  Ford. The star of Bethlehem
    7:25 D 25 '39
  Ford. Vision at dusk 17:44 D
    25 '44
  Homer. Skating in Central
    Park, 1860 32:118 Ap 7
    '52
  Lee, D. Good King Wences-
    las 23:45 D 22 '47
  Lee, D. Winter in the Cats-
    kills bw 3:47 S 20 '37

Limbourg, Pol de. February
  24:40 Ja 5 '48
Lu Hung Nien. An angel sum-
  mons the shepherds 11:43
  D 22 '41
Moses. Sugaring-off bw 25:77
  O 25 '48
Moses. Winter is here bw 25:
  77 O 25 '48
Nichols. Home for Christmas
  bw 5:9 D 12 '38
Sample. The fox hunt bw 18:
  44 Ja 1 '45
Simkhovitch. Road home 11:39
  D 29 '41
Simkhovitch. Sleet storm 1940
  11:39 D 29 '41
Simkhovitch. Winter in Con-
  necticut 11:40 D 29 '41
Sloan. Backyards, Greenwich
  Village bw 5:29 O 31 '38
Sloan. The white way 7:46 D
  11 '39
Thomas, B. Little Town of
  Bethlehem 23:46 D 22 '47
Thon. Owl's Head 20:98 Ap 29
  '46
Wood, G. January bw 14:57
  Ja 18 '43
Winter afternoon. Robertson 6:
  29 F 13 '39
Winter in Connecticut. Simkho-
  vitch 11:40 D 29 '41
Winter in the Catskills. bw Lee,
  D 3:47 S 20 '37
Winter is here. bw Moses 25:77
  O 25 '48
Winter over the Hudson. Dehn
  11:41 Ag 11 '41
Winter pines. bw Chiang Kai-
  Shek 33:7 O 13 '52
Winter reflections. Hendrickson
  32:70 Ja 14 '52
Winterhalter, Franz Xavier
  Duke of Wellington and Sir
    Robert Peel 25:90 N 22 '48
Winthrop, John
  Governor Winthrop bw 13:74
    N 23 '42
The wire. Kingman 11:76 O 27
  '41

Wire fence in snow. Burchfield
  1:27 D 28 '36
Wirz, Henry bw 39:166 S 12 '55
Wisconsin
  Curry. Wisconsin landscape
    8:65 My 27 '40
  Curry. Wisconsin still life
    bw 15:20 N 29 '43
  Grotenrath. My Wisconsin 25:
    58 N 29 '48
  Sugden. Wisconsin scene 10:
    77 Mr 31 '41
  Wisconsin "airscapes," paint-
    ings from aerial perspec-
    tive 32:68-70 Ja 14 '52
  Wisconsin life and history 25:
    58-9 N 29 '48
  Wisconsin rural painters 10:
    76-8 Mr 31 '41
The wise and foolish virgins. bw
  Blake 10:94 Je 9 '41
Wistarberg Glassware. Wistar,
  Casper
  Candlestick photog 39:58-9
    Jy 18 '55
  Pitcher, "Lily pad" photog
    39:58 Jy 18 '55
  Sugar bowl photog 39:58-9 Jy
    18 '55
Witches and Witchcraft
  Denslow. Wicked witch began
    to shrink 35:57 D 28 '53
  Goya. The witches' Sabbath
    mural 31:64-5 O 1 '51
  Hals. The witch of Haarlem
    (Hille Bobbe) 24:71 Mr 22
    '48
  Harrison. The trial of George
    Jacobs 13:78 N 23 '42
  Ilunga. Witch doctors 34:107
    My 4 '53
  Noble. Witch hill (The Salem
    martyr) 13:79 N 23 '42
  Sobrat. Witch play, Bali* bw
    3:51 S 27 '37
  Volk. Accused of witchcraft
    13:78 N 23 '42
Withdrawal from Dunkirk.
    Eurich 10:65 F 24 '41; 26:
    44-5 F 14 '49

Withers, Edward
  Carol bw 22:40 Je 16 '47
  Edward Withers photog bw 22:
    40 Je 16 '47 port.
Witherspoon, John
  John Witherspoon bw 15:10 Jy
    5 '43
Wittenberg, Germany
  Church doors where Luther's
    95 theses posted photog bw
    24:62 Je 14 '48
Wodwylle Family coat of arms
    40:187 Ap 9 '56
Wolcott, Oliver
  Oliver Wolcott bw 15:10 Jy 5
    '43
Wolf, Ben
  Coxswain Norman Thomas
    drawing bw 15:76 S 6 '43
  Greenland at war drawing bw
    15:76 S 6 '43
  Thomas, N. M. Seaman Ben
    Wolf drawing bw 15:76 S 6
    '43 port.
The wolf, cartoons of army life,
    World War II. bw Sansone
    17:6-8 Jy 31 '44
Wolf. sculpture bw Poot 41:84
    O 8 '56
Wolf by the lake. Krause 10:78
    Mr 31 '41
Wolfe, James
  West. The death of General
    Wolfe 5:31 O 31 '38; 25:106-
    7 S 13 '48 bw 7:70 S 25 '39;
    9:112 S 9 '40
Wolfe, Thomas
  Gorsline. Thomas Wolfe 10:
    47 F 3 '41
  Thomas Wolfe photog bw 17:
    14 Ag 14 '44 caricature bw
    23:83 S 1 '47
  Thomas Wolfe--portraits;
    family; locale of novels
    photogs bw 19:59-61 D 24
    '45; 41:178 S 17 '56; 41:168-
    9 S 24 '56
Wolfkill, Grant
    327 Wellar 10:58 Je 16 '41
Wolford, Richard
  Saturday night in Harlem cer-

amics bw 9:129 N 11 '40
Wollaton hall, English country
    house, Italian style, 16th
    century 19:100 O 29 '45
Wolverine. Audubon 30:49 Ja 29
    '51
Wolverton, Basil, cartoonist
  Cartoons bw 40:69-73 Ap 16
    '56
  Harry Truman caricature bw
    22:16 My 5 '47
  John L. Lewis caricature bw
    22:14-5 My 5 '47
  Stalin caricature bw 22:16 My
    5 '47
  Thomas Dewey caricature bw
    22:16 My 5 '47
Wolves
  Romulus and Remus sculp-
    ture 27:45 Ag 1 '49
Woman. Albright, I. 16:65 Mr
    27 '44; 21:78 N 25 '46
Woman. sculpture bw Walton 4:
    62 Ap 25 '38
Woman VI. De Kooning 39:134-
    5 N 21 '55
Woman asleep in an armchair.
    Picasso 1:25 D 14 '36
Woman at table. Gwathmey 38:
    74 Mr 28 '55
Woman bathers, Mexico, Lee,
    D. 22:76 My 12 '47
A woman bathing. Rembrandt
    29:105 S 11 '50
Woman combing her hair.
    sculpture bw Robus 14:42
    Mr 8 '43
Woman in a studio. Toulouse-
    Lautrec 25:79 N 1 '48
Woman in white. Picasso 23:95
    O 13 '47
Woman in yellow. Picasso 8:58
    Mr 4 '40
Woman mounting a horse. Mc
    Crady 3:42 O 18 '37
Woman, old man and flower.
    bw Ernst 19:64 S 24 '45
Woman weighing gold. Ver-
    meer 5:31 Ag 29 '38; 24:
    73 Je 14 '48
Woman with a dog. Cassatt 40:

67 Ja 23 '56
Woman with basket of fruit.
Braque 26:84 My 2 '49
Woman with a black boa. Tou-
louse Lautrec 28:97 My
15 '50
Woman with loaves. bw Picasso
2:51 Ap 5 '37
Woman with mandolin. Braque
25:75 O 11 '48
Woman with mandolin. Picasso
8:58 Mr 4 '40
Woman with parrot. Courbet 6:
56 Mr 20 '39
Woman with tambourines. Van
Gogh 27:84 O 10 '49
Wombat drawing bw 30:131 F
12 '51
Women reaching for the moon.
Tamayo 34:100 Mr 16 '53
Women voting in New Jersey,
c1800 print bw 16:45 Ja 31
'44
Women warriors through history
bw 14:6-8 Ja 4 '43
"Wonderful Wizard of Oz," illus-
trations. Denslow 35:52-9
D 28 '53
Wood, Ella Miriam
Artist at work photog bw 41:
83 Ag 13 '56 port.
Wood, Grant
Adolescence bw 14:58 Ja 18
'43
American gothic 14:52-3 Ja 18
'43 bw 5:30 O 31 '38; 6:58
Mr 27 '39
Arbor Day 14:56 Ja 18 '43
Birthplace of Herbert Hoover
14:55 Ja 18 '43
Daughters of Revolution 14:53
Ja 18 '43; 21:73 N 25 '46
Death on Ridge Road 14:55 Ja
18 '43
Dinner for threshers 13:46-7
Ag 31 '42; 21:77 N 25 '46
Fall plowing bw 14:57 Ja 18
'43
January bw 14:57 Ja 18 '43
John B. Turner, pioneer 14:
53 Ja 18 '43

The midnight ride of Paul Re-
vere 3:28 D 20 '37; 14:54
Ja 18 '43
Paris observatory fountain
bw 14:57 Ja 18 '43
Parson Weems' fable 8:32-3
F 19 '40 bw 14:58 Ja 18
'43
Spring in the country 14:56 Ja
18 '43
Spring in town 14:56 Ja 18 '43
Spring turning 2:34-5 F 8 '37
Stone City, Iowa 14:54 Ja 18
'43 bw 21:104 S 30 '46
Young corn bw 14:57 Ja 18
'43
Tree planting bw 14:57 Ja 18
'43 (lithographs)
Wild flowers 7:25 Ag 28 '39
(lithographs)
Artist at work photog bw 14:
52 Ja 18 '43 port.
Grant Wood photog bw 5:30
O 31 '38 teaching 6:54-5
Je 5 '39 port.
Wood, John Musgrave (Emm-
wood, pseudonym)
Britons as birds caricatures
bw 24:16-8 Ap 12 '48
Wood, Thomas
New England country store 6:
30 Je 19 '39
Wood Carving See Carving--
Wood
Wood Engraving
Brussel-Smith. Hunting inci-
dents 39:190-2 N 14 '55
Eichenberg. Self-portrait bw
15:4 D 20 '43
Eichenberg. "Wuthering
Heights" bw 15:102-3 N 29
'43
Maillol. "Daphnis and Chloe"
bw 8:108 Ap 15 '40
Maillol. Virgil's "Georgics"
bw 8:109 Ap 15 '40
Mueller. Technique and
finished engravings 7:71-
2 D 4 '39
Woodcock in Canada. Ripley 29:
127 D 4 '50

Woodcuts
  Amerigo Vespucci bw, 16th
    century 40:46 Ja 9 '56
  Baskin. Anatomist 37:89 O 18
    '54
  Chinese war prints, 1937-45
    18:57-60 Ap 9 '45
  Cranach. Christ and the pope*
    24:60-1 Je 14 '48
  Crusaders disembark at Da-
    mietta bw 16:67 Ap 10 '44
  Frasconi. The storm is com-
    ing 37:85 O 18 '54
  Frasconi. Sunrise--Fulton
    Fishmarket 37:86-7 O 18
    '54
  Foster. Richard Mather, first
    American woodcut 38:121
    Ap 18 '55
  "Gleason's Pictorial Drawing-
    Room Companion," first
    illustrated weekly in Amer-
    ica, 1851-59 31:14-5 Ag 6
    '51
  Hiroshige. Enkyo bridge 31:
    67 D 31 '51
  Japanese war prisoners. Life
    in Sugamo Prison 34:10-1
    F 16 '53
  Kent, R. Angel bw 5:9 D 12
    '38
  Ku Yuan. Yenan art academy
    bw 18:60 Ap 9 '45
  Liu. Moonlight march bw 18:
    59 Ap 9 '45
  Lu Hsun Academy. China war
    scenes and portraits 18:
    57-60 Ap 9 '45
  O'Hara. Bullfight 37:88 O 18
    '54
  Peirce. Stilts 37:89 O 18 '54
  Quastler. Counterpoint 37:89
    O 18 '54
  Reder. Medieval lady 37:88 O
    18 '54
  Seong. Girl juggling 37:88 O
    18 '54
  Woodcuts of contemporary art-
    ists 37:84-9 O 18 '54
Wooden head, Dada art object bw
  34:24 My 25 '53

Wooding up, on the Mississippi
  print, after Momberger
  28:73 Mr 6 '50
Woodstock cowboy. Speicher 5:
  26 Ag 29 '38
Woodville, Elizabeth, Consort
  of Edward IV, King of
  England bw 40:199 Ap 9
  '56
Woodville, Richard
  War news from Mexico 9:77
  D 9 '40; 27:58 Ag 29 '49
Woolman, John
  John Woolman bw 33:96 S 29
  '52
Woosung, Chang
  Christian martyrs bw 29:63
  S 4 '50
Wootton, Frank
  End of retreat, Falaise 35:
  87 O 26 '53
Wootton, John
  The great race meeting, Eng-
  land, 18th century 25:102-
  3 S 13 '48
Worcester cathedral, England,
  misericord woodcarvings
  bw 37:80 S 27 '54
Wordsworth, William
  William Wordsworth, age 48
  bw 29:83 Jy 17 '50
Work and Workers See also
  Strikes and Demonstrations
  Coale. Pay day, "Newfie"
  workmen bw 13:92-3 Jy 13
  '42
  Hine. Child worker in a cot-
  ton mill, 1908 photog bw
  28:82 Ja 2 '50
  Ilic. Sounding the terrain of
  New Belgrade 29:105 D 11
  '50
  Labor union history--strikes,
  parades, leaders of U.S.
  labor prints and photogs
  bw 33:32-3 D 8 '52
  Millet. The man with a hoe
  9:46-7 Jy 29 '40
  "The Molly Maguires," 1870
  bw 33:33 D 8 '52
  Payday at the arsenal, Ven-

ice, Renaissance* bw 23:
59 Ag 4 '47

Pizzinato. Worker bw 29:14
O 30 '50

Railroad workers print bw 26:
101 Ap 18 '49

Reindel. Women war workers
16:75-8 Je 5 '44

Sellitti. Afternoon shift 10:58
Je 16 '41

Sharrer. Tribute to the working man 31:12 D 17 '51

Weber. Seeking work 19:85
Ag 20 '45

Woman mine worker, England,
1842 bw 25:94 N 22 '48

Works of man. Schnakenberg 10:
73 Ap 14 '41

World Maps See Maps--World

World of Tomorrow See Fairs--
New York World's Fair

The world upside down. Steen 27:
70 O 24 '49

World War I See War Themes--
European War, 1914-1918

World War II See War Themes--
World War, 1939-1945

World's Fair, 1938 See Fairs

Wormley, Edward, furniture designer
Furniture--cabinet, chairs,
desk, sofa, tables photog bw
25:116-7 N 15 '48
Morris chair bw 35:17 D 14
'53
Edward Wormley photog bw
25:116 N 15 '48 port.

The worship of the golden calf.
Steen 41:74 D 10 '53

Wortman, Denys, cartoonist
Shopgirls and bums cartoons
bw 6:60-1 F 27 '39
Denys Wortman photog bw 6:
61 F 27 '39 port.

Wotruba, Fritz, sculptor
Female figure* 38:90 Je 20 '55
Reclining figure bronze bw 38:
87 Je 20 '55
Striding figure bw 38:88 Je 20
'55
Torso male, 1930 bw 38:88 Je

20 '55
Walking man bronze bw 38:88
Je 20 '55
Fritz Wotruba photog bw 38:
87 Je 20 '55 port.

Wounded woman. sculpture bw
Reder 26:113 Je 20 '49

The wreck. Homer 2:26 Ja 11
'37

Wrecked automobiles. Warshaw
28:84 Mr 20 '50

Wren, Christopher, architect
Chatsworth house, Devonshire
England--bedroom photog
bw 15:106-7 N 15 '43
College of William and Mary,
Virginia photog bw 14:66
Ap 12 '43

Wrestler. Rey 2:35 F 22 '37

Wrestling See Games and
Sports--Wrestling

Wright, Frank Lloyd, architect
Fallingwater, house, Bear
Run, Pennsylvania photog
bw 21:94 Ag 12 '46
Guggenheim Gallery, New
York City, spiral design
for modern art gallery
photog bw 19:12-5 O 8 '45
Horizontal style house,
Springfield, Ill. 1903
photog 40:98 Mr 5 '56
Imperial Hotel, Tokyo photog
bw 21:93 Ag 12 '46
S.C. Johnson and Son Ad-
ministration Building, Ra-
cine, Wisc. photogs bw
6:15 My 8 '39; Research
laboratory, "Heliolab,"
Racine, Wisc. photogs 29:
8-10 D 11 '50
Taliesin West, Arizona pho-
tog bw 21:84 Ag 12 '46
Unitarian Church, Madison,
Wis. photog bw 30:16-7
Ap 30 '51
Windmill, Wisconsin photog
bw 21:88 Ag 12 '46
Frank Lloyd Wright photog
bw 13:109 N 9 '42; 19:12
O 8 '45 age 77 21:85 Ag

Frank Lloyd Wright (cont.)
12 '46 port.
Wright, Harold Bell
Harold Bell Wright photog bw
10:68 Ap 21 '41
Wright, Henry architect
Architect's house photog bw
26:84 Ja 31 '49
Henry Wright photog bw 26:
84 Ja 31 '49 port.
Wright, Joseph
George Washington 31:98 N 5
'51; bw 24:23 F 23 '48
Wright, Matvyn
London bombing* 26:50 F 28
'49
Wright, Paul, sculptor
Androcles and the lion bw 29:
124 Ag 28 '50
Brer Rabbit hitting Tar-Baby*
bw 29:124 Ag 28 '50
Golden egg bw 29:124 Ag 28
'50
"How the Elephant Got Its
Trunk" bw 29:122 Ag 28 '50
Leda and the swan bw 29:122
Ag 28 '50
Wright, Russell
Ceramics photogs 29:89 D 25
'50
Wright-Molyneux, Edward
World map, mercator projec-
tion, 1600 bw 18:65 My 21
'45
Writing
Cunieform clay tablets,
Babylon, c2050 B.C. 24:
147-8 Mr 15 '48
Hieroglyphic writing, hieratic
script bw 41:97 O 1 '56
Sumerian clay tablets, c3000
B.C. 40:87 Je 4 '56
Tatsuta Hoshu. Microscopic
writing, Japanese 34:102
F 23 '53
Wrought Iron See Iron Work
Wuolijoki, Hella
Hella Wuolijoki photog bw 3:
76 Jy 26 '37
"Wuthering Heights," illustra-
tion. wood engravings

Eichenberg 15:102-3 N 29
'43
Wycliffe, John
John Wycliffe bw 24:60 Je 14
'48; 34:84 F 23 '53
Wyeth, Andrew
Afternoon 24:106 My 17 '48
Arthur Cleveland 24:103 My
17 '48
Blue dump 24:104 My 17 '48
Deserted house 35:80-1 Jy 27
'53
Dr. Margaret Handy 41:162-3
D 24 '56
Henry Teel 24:105 My 17 '48
Hoffman's slough 24:104 My
17 '48
Public sale 24:105 My 17 '48
Wind from the sea 35:82 Jy
27 '53
Artist at work photog bw 35:
80, 82 Jy 27 '53 port.
Artist in his studio photog bw
24:102 My 17 '48 port.
Andrew Wyeth photog bw 38:
83 F 28 '55 port.
Self-portrait 35:83 Jy 27 '53
port.
Wyeth, Henriette
Peter Hurd, the artist's hus-
band 10:48 F 3 '41
Peter in San Patricio 10:74
Ap 14 '41
Wyeth, Newell Convers
"Drums," illustrations 20:81
Je 17 '46
Mrs. Cushman's house 20:
79 Je 17 '46
Nightfall 20:80 Je 17 '46
Portrait of a farmer 16:78
Ap 24 '44
"Robin Hood," illustration
20:81 Je 17 '46
"Scottish Chiefs," illustra-
tion 20:81 Je 17 '46
The spring house 20:79 Je
17 '46
Summer night 20:80 Je 17
'46
"The Yearling," illustrations
20:81 Je 17 '46

Artist at work photog bw 20:
78 Je 17 '46; 24:102 My 17
'48 port.
Wylie Avenue barber shop.
Pearlstein 10:57 Je 16 '41
The Wyndham sisters (The three
graces). Sargent 5:37 O 31
'38; 23:79 N 17 '47
Wyoming, evening on the range.
cartoon Emett 37:49 Jy 5
'54
Wyss, Johann Emanuel
"The Swiss Family Robinson,"
illustrations of the artist's
father's book 37:50-61 D 27
'54
Johann Emanuel Wyss bw 37:
63 D 27 '54 port.
Wythe, George
George Wythe bw 15:10 Jy 5
'43

X

Xavior, Saint Francis
St. Francis Xavier bw 24:61
Je 14 '48 statue bw 26:49
Je 27 '49
Xceron, Jean
Radar 24:69 F 2 '48
Xochimilco, Mexico
Lee, D. Sunday at Xochimilco
22:76 My 12 '47

Y

Y. M. C. A. locker room. Cadmus
2:46-7 Mr 29 '37
Yachts. Feining, Lyonel 31:95 N
12 '51
Ya-'el See Animals, Imaginary
--Yales
Yak drawing bw 30:131 F 12 '51
Yakushi sculpture Japanese, 8th
century 34:95 Ap 20 '53
Yale School of Fine Arts
Students at work; paintings of
students and alumni 8:44-6
F 12 '40
Yales See Animals, Imaginary--
Yales

Yamaguchi, Hoshum
General attack on Hong Kong
28:70 F 27 '50
Yang and Yin, emblem, Chinese
cosmic forces 38:57 F 7
'55; 38:69 Ap 4 '55 bw 24:
131 F 23 '48
"Yank," U.S. army weekly hu-
mor magazine cartoons bw
15:118-21 N 15 '43; 18:
12 3 My 7 '45
Yankee Doodle (Spirit of '76).
bw Willard, A. M. 9:55 Ag
5 '40
Yankee peddler. Ehninger 6:29
Je 19 '39
Yankee pedlar, U.S. 31:74 Jy
2 '51
Yaroslav bw 14:92 Mr 29 '43
Yazdekhast photog bw 6:42-3
My 29 '39
"The Yearling," illustrations.
Wyeth, N.C. 20:81 Je 17
'46
Yeats, William Butler
Beerbohm. Mr. W. B. Yeats
presenting Mr. George
Moore to the Queen of the
Fairies caricature bw
23:89 N 17 '47
The yellow cage. Michel 20:60
Je 3 '46
The yellow cloth. bw Braque 3:
24 D 20 '37
"Yellow Kid," 1898 caricature
of W. R. Hearst bw 31:27
Ag 27 '51
Yellow moon. Miro 33:96 O 27
'52
"The Yellow Peril," cartoon bw
(W. R. Hearst). Herford
31:27 Ag 27 '51
The yellow peril. cartoon bw
Wilhelm II, Kaiser of Ger-
many 6:11 Ja 2 '39
Yellow sky. Hultberg 39:114-5
S 12 '55
The yellow temple, Peiping
photog bw 3:55 Ag 23 '37

Yen Han
  Medical cooperative bw 18:
    60 Ap 9 '45
Yenan art academy. woodcut bw
    Ku Yuan 18:60 Ap 9 '45
Ylla (pseudonym of Camilla
    Koeffler), photographer
  Animal portraits bw 38:16-7
    Ap 25 '55
  Dog portraits bw 23:Cover,
    18-9 N 17 '47
  Ylla photog bw 38:17 Ap 25
    '55 port.
Yoga exercises and postures
    photogs bw 2:8-11 Ap 19
    '37; 10:10-2 F 24 '41
Yorke, Henry (Henry Green,
    pseudonym)
  Henry Yorke photog bw 33:83
    Ag 4 '52
Yosemite. Dehn 11:44 Ag 11 '41
Young, Art
  Beast and man cartoon bw 25:
    23 N 29 '48
  The enemy of socialism car-
    toon bw 24:108 Ja 19 '48
Young, Brigham
  Brigham Young photog bw 5:
    24 Jy 25 '38
  Wives of Brigham Young--
    portraits of 20 of 27 wives
    bw 5:24 Jy 25 '38
Young, Chic, cartoonist
  Blondie bw 13:8-11 Ag 17 '42
Young, John
  Richard Humphreys, boxer
    mezzotint bw 6:42 F 6 '39
Young, Mahonri, sculptor
  Alkmena bw 10:79 F 17 '41
  Buffo and foal bw 10:79 F 17
    '41
  Duck and shoat bw 10:79 F 17
    '41
  The knock down bw 10:79 F
    17 '41
  Ploughing in the Valley of the
    Great Salt Lake painting,
    sculpture in round, relief
    bw 10:76 F 17 '41
  Pony express bw 10:79 F 17
    '41

Right to the jaw bw 10:79 F
    17 '41
  Rolling his own bw 10:79 F
    17 '41
  This is the place bw 10:79
    F 17 '41
  Artist at work photo bw 10:
    76 F 17 '41 port.
Young, Rodger Wilton
  Rodger Wilton Young drawing
    bw 18:111 Mr 5 '45
Young American artist. Pren-
    dergast 20:79 F 18 '46
Young corn. bw Wood, G. 14:
    57 Ja 18 '43
Young girl. Kidd 29:71 O 9 '50
Young girl. sculpture bw
    Wheelock 8:115 My 20 '40
Young girl at an open half door.
    Rembrandt 11:57 S 8 '41
Young girl holding a bird. sculp-
    ture bw Zadkine 24:95 Ap
    12 '48
Young girl with arms raised.
    sculpture bw Haller 26:
    114 Je 20 '49
Young girl with grapes. bw
    Constant 9:67 O 14 '40
Young girl with horse. bw Car-
    reno 10:107 Mr 17 '41
Young lady with a pearl neck-
    lace. Vermeer 24:77 Mr
    22 '48 bw 19:25 D 31 '45
Young Lincoln. sculpture bw
    Hansen 9:130 S 9 '40
Young man from ballet. Davis,
    G. R. 16:78 Mr 20 '44
Young mother sewing. Cassatt
    12:56 Ja 19 '42
A young New Yorker. bw Bacon,
    P. 6:57 My 8 '39
Young woman with a bag. Es-
    teve 17:76 N 13 '44
Yoshimura, J.
  Japanese 16th century house,
    exhibited at Museum of
    Modern Art, New York
    City photogs bw 37:71-4
    Ag 23 '54
Youssoupoff, Prince
  Prince Youssoupoff photog

bw 29:99 N 27 '50

Youth. sculpture bw Zorach 8:
90-1 Ap 1 '40; 9:54 Ag 12
'40

Youth with a black cap. Rembrandt 7:55 O 9 '39

Yrurtia, Rogelio
Boxeadores sculpture bw 8:
17 Ja 29 '40

Yugoslavia
Fredenthal. Yugoslavia after
World War--scenes and
portraits 20:50-62 Ja 28
'46
Fredenthal. Russian soldiers;
partisans--in Yugoslavia
drawings bw 18:83-9 F 5
'45

Yvon, Adolphe
The genius of America bw 33:
44 S 29 '52

Z

"Z-Man" toys photogs bw 41:161
N 12 '56

Zadkine, Ossip, sculptor
Young girl holding a bird bw
24:95 Ap 12 '48
Mili. Ossip Zadkine, age 59
photog 27:90 D 12 '49 port.

Zamoyski, August, sculptor
Frederic Chopin bw 26:98 F
14 '49
Human figures bw 26:97 F 14
'49
Artist and his work photog
bw 26:98 F 14 '49 port.

Zoa Wou-Ki
Crimson city 36:102 F 22 '54
Golden city, Venice, Italy
36:102-3 F 22 '54
Green landscape* 36:104 F 22
'54
Red still life* 36:104 F 22 '54
Slim deer 36:104 F 22 '54
Spectral fish 36:104 F 22 '54
Birds and rocks 33:87 Jy 14
'52 (lithograph)
Artist and wife in studio pho-
tog bw 36:102 F 22 '54 port.

The zebra. Priebe 23:70 N 24
'47

Zebra cart, Kapurthala, India
photog bw 9:69 N 25 '40

Zebras
Jonas. Mother and baby zebra
sculpture bw 12:90 Mr 23
'42·

Zemayas. De Castro 41:71 D 10
'56

Zenger, John Peter
Castellon. Freedom of the
press 30:95 Mr 12 '51

Zenobia, Queen of Palmyra bw
14:6 Ja 4 '43

Zenobias, Saint
Botticelli. Three miracles
of St. Zenobias bw 21:104
O 28 '46

Zerbe, Karl
San Clemente church, Venice
33:96 S 15 '52

Zeus See also Mythological
Themes--Jupiter
Temple of Zeus, Athens
photog bw 18:58-9 Ja 1 '45

Zhaba
Skiers, copy by Mironova
14:46 Mr 29 '43

Zhukov, Georgi
Marshall Zhukov, "Time"
cover portrait 17:64 D 11
'44

Ziegler, Laura
St. Stephan's Episcopal
church, Columbus, Ohio
--plexiglass cross 39:116
D 26 '55

Ziolkowski, Korczak
Crazy Horse, model of proposed monument photog bw
25:53 Jy 12 '48
Korczak Ziolkowski photog
bw 25:53 Jy 12 '48 port.

Zodiac
Fornasetti. Signs of the
zodiac 34:61 Je 22 '53
Maldarelli. Gemini sculpture
bw 22:139 Mr 24 '47
Roman calendar, first centuries A.D. sculpture bw

Zodiac (cont.)
    18:41 Ja 1 '45
    Signs of the zodiac, "Book of
        Hours" of the Duke de
        Berry 24:39-50 Ja 5 '48
    Waugh, S. Zodiac bowl, en-
        graved glass photog bw 7:32
        S 18 '39
Zoffany, John
    A colonial family 25:99 S 13
        '48
    The tribuna 25:104-5 S 13 '48
    Self-portrait in The tribuna
        25:104-5 S 13 '48 port.
Zola, Emil
    Cezanne. Emile Zola bw 32:
        88 F 22 '52
    Cezanne. House of Emil Zola
        At Medan 2:47 Ap 12 '37
Zoopraxiscope Photographs See
    Muybridge
Zorach, William, sculptor
    Benjamin Franklin statue bw
        8:93 Ap 1 '40
    Conflict bw 8:92-3 Ap 1 '40
    Female figure, symbol of
        Texas bw 41:93 Jy 23 '56
    Linesman bw 8:92 Ap 1 '40
    Mother and child bw 7:37 Jy
        17 '39; 8:92-3 Ap 1 '40;
        32:77 Ja 7 '52
    Spirit of the dance bw 8:92 Ap
        1 '40
    Youth bw 8:90-1 Ap 1 '40; 9:
        54 Ag 12 '40
    Artist at work photog bw 8:91
        Ap 1 '40; 24:75-9 My 31
        '48 port.
    Newman. William Zorach
        photog bw 20:12 F 4 '46
    William Zorach. in group
        photog 29:172-3 O 16 '50
    William Zorach photog bw 32:
        87 Mr 17 '52 teaching in
        Art Students' League 5:27
        O 31 '38
Zoroaster bw 20:34 Ap 8 '46; 29:
    160 D 11 '50
Zorthian, Jirayr Hamparzoon
    The shipwreck 8:46 F 12 '40

Zsissly See Albright, Malvin
    Mar
Zucker, Jacques
    Walkowitz bw 16:79 F 21 '44
Zurburan, Francisco de
    Flight into Egypt 4:42 My 16
        '38
    St. Romanus 33:91 O 27 '52
Zwingli, Huldreich
    Zwingli in Cranach. Luther
        and his friends 24:63 Je
        14 '48